The
All England
Law Reports
Annual Review
1983

ENGLAND: Butterworth & Co (Publishers) Ltd
88 Kingsway, **London** WC2B 6AB

AUSTRALIA: Butterworths Pty Ltd, **Sydney, Melbourne,
Brisbane, Adelaide** and **Perth**

CANADA: Butterworth & Co (Canada) Ltd, **Toronto**
Butterworth & Co (Western Canada) Ltd, **Vancouver**

NEW ZEALAND: Butterworths of New Zealand Ltd, **Wellington**

SINGAPORE: Butterworth & Co (Asia) Pte Ltd, **Singapore**

SOUTH AFRICA: Butterworth Publishers (Pty) Ltd, **Durban**

USA: Mason Publishing Company, **St Paul,** Minnesota

Butterworth (Legal Publishers) Inc, **Seattle,** Washington;
Boston, Massachusetts; and **Austin,** Texas

D & S Publishers, **Clearwater,** Florida

©
BUTTERWORTH AND CO (PUBLISHERS) LTD
1984

General Editor
JANE ALLEN, JP, MA

ISBN 0 406 87960 5

Printed in Great Britain by Thomson Litho Ltd, East Kilbride, Scotland

THE
ALL ENGLAND
LAW REPORTS
ANNUAL REVIEW
1983

London
BUTTERWORTHS
1984

Contributors

Administrative Law
Keith Davies, MA, LLM
Barrister, Reader in Law,
University of Reading

Arbitration
J E Adams, LLB, FCIArb
Solicitor, Professor of Law,
Queen Mary College,
University of London

Commercial Law
N E Palmer, BCL, MA
Barrister, Professor of Law,
University of Reading

Company Law
D D Prentice, MA, LLB, JD
Barrister, Fellow of Pembroke College,
Oxford

Conflict of Laws
J G Collier, MA, LLB
Barrister, Fellow of Trinity Hall,
Cambridge

Consumer Law and *Contempt of Court*
C J Miller, BA, LLM
Barrister, Professor of Law,
University of Warwick

Contract
Michael P Furmston, TD, BCL, MA, LLM
Barrister, Professor of Law,
University of Bristol

Criminal Law and Sentencing
G J Bennett, MA
Barrister, Lecturer in Law and
Brian Hogan, LLB
Barrister, Professor of Law,
University of Leeds

Criminal Procedure and *Police*
Graham Zellick, JP, MA, PHD
Professor of Public Law,
Queen Mary College,
University of London

Damages
J R Spencer, MA, LLB
Fellow of Selwyn College,
Cambridge

Employment Law
Patrick Elias, LLB, MA, PHD
Barrister, Fellow of Pembroke College,
Cambridge

European Community Law
C J Greenwood, MA, LLB
Fellow of Magdalene College,
Cambridge

Evidence and *Practice and Procedure*
Adrian A S Zuckerman, LLM, MA
Fellow of University College,
Oxford

Family Law
Ruth L Deech, MA
Barrister, Fellow of St Anne's College,
Oxford

Land Law and *Trusts*
P J Clarke, BCL, MA
Barrister, Fellow of Jesus College,
Oxford

Landlord and Tenant
Philip H Pettit, MA
Barrister, Professor of Equity,
University of Buckingham

Shipping
Robert P Grime, BA, BCL
Senior Lecturer in Law,
University of Southampton

Solicitors
Brian Harvey, MA, LLM
Solicitor, Dean of the Faculty of Law,
University of Birmingham

Succession
C H Sherrin, LLM, PHD
Barrister, Senior Lecturer in Law,
University of Bristol

Taxation
John Tiley, MA, BCL
Barrister, Fellow of Queen's College,
Cambridge

Tort
B A Hepple, MA, LLB
Barrister, Professor of English Law,
University College,
University of London

Town and Country Planning
Paul B Fairest, MA, LLB
Professor of Law,
University of Hull

Publishers' Note

This is the second All England Law Reports Annual Review. The Annual Review is designed as a companion to the All England Law Reports. Each year a volume is published containing articles evaluating the decisions of the courts reported in that series in the preceding year.

The authors of the articles are leading academic lawyers and their aim is to review the reported decisions systematically and critically and to place them in the context of their particular subject area. The enthusiastic reception given to the first Annual Review shows that it has indeed lived up to its aim, expressed by Sir Roger Ormrod in the Foreword, of establishing contact between academic lawyers and a large body of practitioners so as to 'enlarge the horizon of practitioners and enable them to see...judgments in perspective'.

Not all of the cases, of course, fall neatly into one or other of the categories of conventional legal classification. The authors have tried to avoid duplication in their discussion of cases and there are a number of cross-references to be found in the articles. Some cases, however, are examined in more than one article because different aspects are of importance in different contexts.

It is inevitable that the reported decisions in any one year do not cover all aspects of the law. They merely reflect those areas which were the subject of litigation and which caught the attention of the law reporters and editors. The question of which cases are reported and which are not is discussed by Mr Zuckerman in the article on Practice and Procedure where he examines (at pp 277–279) the issues raised by the comments of members of the House of Lords in *Roberts Petroleum Ltd v Bernard Kenny Ltd* on the growing practice of citing unreported cases.

This 1983 Annual Review contains articles on arbitration, conflict of laws, European Community law and town and country planning, topics which did not appear last year. There are not, however, separate articles on extradition, prisons and sentencing. In addition to new articles, the 1983 Annual Review covers a new specialist series of reports. Dr Prentice, contributor of the article on company law, is the editor of Butterworths Company Law Cases. His article this year (and the article on trusts) discusses cases reported in the 1983 volume of BCLC as well as those in the All England Law Reports. As before, the article on taxation covers cases reported in Simon's Tax Cases.

Cases from the 1983 All England Law Reports, Simon's Tax Cases and Butterworths Company Law Cases are printed in bold type in the Table of Cases. A bold page number indicates where discussion of the case is to be found.

This volume should be cited as All ER Rev 1983.

BUTTERWORTH LAW PUBLISHERS LTD

Contents

Table of Cases

A

M

N

O

P

R

S

Abbreviations

BCLC	Butterworths Company Law Cases
BYIL	British Yearbook of International Law
CLJ	Cambridge Law Journal
CLR	Commonwealth Law Reports
CMLR	Common Market Law Reports
Conv	Conveyancer
Cr App R	Criminal Appeal Reports
Cr LR	Criminal Law Review
DLR	Dominion Law Reports
ECR	European Court Reports
EG	Estate Gazette
EHRR	European Human Rights Reports
EIPR	European Intellectual Property Review
EL Rev	European Law Review
Fam Law	Family Law
FSR	Fleet Street Reports
ICLQ	International and Comparative Law Quarterly
ICR	Industrial Cases Reports
IR	Irish Reports
JBL	Journal of Business Law
JP	Justice of the Peace Reports
JPN	Justice of the Peace Newspaper
JSPTL	Journal of the Society of Public Teachers of Law
LPA	Law of Property Act 1925
LQR	Law Quarterly Review
LRA	Land Registration Act 1925
LS Gaz	Law Society Gazette
Med Sci & Law	Medicine, Science and the Law
MLR	Modern Law Review
NLJ	New Law Journal
NZLR	New Zealand Law Reports
P & CR	Property and Compensation Reports
PL	Public Law
RPC	Reports of Patent, Design and Trade Mark Cases
SC	Session Cases
SCR	Supreme Court Reports
Sh Ct Rep	Sheriff Court Reports (Scottish Law Review)
SJ	Solicitors' Journal
SLT	Scots Law Times
STC	Simon's Tax Cases
VLR	Victorian Law Reports
WWR	Western Weekly Reports

Administrative Law

KEITH DAVIES, MA, LLM
Barrister, Reader in Law, University of Reading

Public and private law

In 1982 the House of Lords in *O'Reilly v Mackman* [1982] 3 All ER 1124 and *Cocks v Thanet DC* [1982] 3 All ER 1135 stressed the separate nature, and marked out the extent, of actions in public law as against private law. In 1983 the House of Lords provided a counterpoint to this by showing the limitations of the concept of public law when giving judgment in *Davy v Spelthorne BC* [1983] 3 All ER 278. This was to the effect that an action would lie in private and not public law even if it arose in relation to the exercise by a public body of one of the specific public functions cast on it by statute.

The salient facts of *Davy v Spelthorne BC* were that the authority, in the exercise of their planning functions, served an enforcement notice on the respondent landowner in order to make him undo some unauthorised development at his premises in Nutty Lane, Shepperton. Discussions followed between him and them which resulted in an agreement that if he refrained from challenging the enforcement notice, they in return would not make him comply with it until three years had elapsed—ie by a compromise he could enjoy his unauthorised development for that limited period. After a time he tumbled to the fact that s 88(2)(d) of the Town and Country Planning Act 1971 (as amended by the Local Government and Planning (Amendment) Act 1981) might well have enabled him to appeal with success to the Secretary of State for the Environment against the enforcement notice, but that s 88 required any such appeal to be made within a specified period before the enforcement notice had taken effect (now long past) and at no later time, and s 243 (as similarly amended) prohibited an appeal to the courts on the grounds specified in s 88(2)(d). The long and short of this was that the making of the agreement had effectively edged the landowner out of a right of appeal previously enjoyed by him. He did not allege fraud, but he did allege negligence on the part of the authority. Whether a claim by him in tort on this basis would succeed was not in issue at the interlocutory stage. There the authority sought to have his action struck out on the basis that the cause lay in public law, and not in private law as a claim in tort, or that it should be transferred to the Crown Office list in the Queen's Bench Division, in accordance with *O'Reilly v Mackman*.

The Court of Appeal held that certain items of claim should indeed be struck out on this ground; but these were not germane to the claim in tort, and the landowner dropped them. The negligence claim was upheld as a proper matter to be initiated by a writ of summons and statement of claim, ie as an action in private law. The House of Lords upheld that decision. This means that a fundamental distinction of substantive law has to be drawn between *O'Reilly v Mackman* and *Cocks v Thanet DC*, on the one hand, and *Davy v Spelthorne BC*, on the other hand, despite the fact that all three cases arose from the exercise by public bodies of their official functions. This distinction of substance is reinforced by the corresponding distinction of procedure. The very existence of the substantive distinction is contested in some quarters, let alone its application in particular cases, so the analysis conducted by the House of Lords is central to the whole question.

In *Davy v Spelthorne BC*, Lord Fraser said (at 283):

> 'The present proceedings may be contrasted with *Cocks v Thanet DC* . . . In that case the plaintiff had to impugn a decision of the housing authority, to the effect that he was intentionally homeless, as a condition precedent to establishing the existence of a private law right to be provided with accommodation.'

It should be pointed out here that this 'private law right' is of the kind recognised in the law of tort as the 'statutory duty' owed to a plaintiff who sues for 'breach of statutory duty'. One aspect of this is that the existence of a statutory duty may seem to be connected with the ultra vires doctrine and therefore with public law rather than private law. But this is in fact not so, because many statutes impose duties, on natural and artificial persons alike, in tort and other branches of private law (eg the Occupiers' Liability Act 1957). In *Anns v Merton London Borough* [1977] 2 All ER 492 at 504–5, Lord Wilberforce said: '. . . since it is the duty of the builder . . . to comply with [building regulations made under the Public Health Act 1961] I would be of opinion that an action could be brought against him, in effect, for breach of statutory duty by any person for whose benefit or protection the [regulations were] made', if he should fail in that duty.

Lord Fraser continued:

> 'It is quite clear from the speech of Lord Bridge, with which all the other members of the House agreed, that the plaintiff was asserting a present right to impugn or overturn the decision [of Thanet District Council that they were under no duty to give him housing accommodation] . . . In the present case, on the other hand, the respondent does not impugn or wish to overturn the enforcement order. His whole case on negligence depends on the fact that he has lost his chance to impugn it. In my opinion therefore the general rule in *O'Reilly* is inapplicable.'

Lord Wilberforce, giving judgment to the same effect, said:

> 'There is no doubt that, side by side with their statutory duties, local authorities may in certain limited circumstances become liable for negligence at common law in the performance of their duties . . . In what circumstances then can it be said to be an abuse of process to sue then for negligence in the common law courts?'

Presumably these circumstances are 'limited' in as much as they arise in regard to the carrying out of statutory functions, such as building inspection, which are official duties not conferred on ordinary people. Apart from such matters the circumstances in which public bodies are liable in contract, tort and analogous cases are, in principle, no more 'limited' for them than for anyone else.

Lord Wilberforce went on to deal with the terms 'public law' and 'private law', which 'have recently been imported into the law of England from abroad. (The terminology may be new but the principles are not.)

> 'In this country they must be used with caution, for, typically, English law fastens not on principles but on remedies. The principle remains intact that

public authorities and public servants are, unless clearly exempted, answerable in the ordinary courts for wrongs done to individuals.'

There must not be 'a dual system of law with the rigidity and procedural hardship for plaintiffs which it was the purpose of [the reform of RSC Ord 53 in 1977, and the enactment of s 31 of the Supreme Court Act 1981] to remove.' Yet 'public law' and 'private law' are fundamental and opposed concepts. 'Public law' is now being, and must continue to be, given clarity of definition to make it suitable for modern use, 'by an extension of remedies and a flexible procedure . . .' Yet, as Lord Scarman said in *IRC v National Federation of Self-Employed and Small Businesses Ltd* [1981] 2 All ER 93 at 109, the reform of RSC Ord 53 'is a procedural innovation of great consequence but it neither extends nor diminishes the substantive law'. This statement brings us down to earth. The main principles of private law are substantially unchanged; and if on analysis it appears that the plaintiff's cause of action truly lies in contract or tort or an analogous case then he is as entitled to bring proceedings by writ or originating summons as if the defendants were not a public body. There is no question, therefore, of his having to obtain the leave of the High Court by showing 'sufficient interest'; and if he proves his case at common law he is entitled to judgment and damages as of right and is not at the mercy of the court's prerogative, statutory or equitable discretion whether or not to grant him a remedy at all.

This is the case here. Lord Wilberforce concluded by saying:

> 'The only "public law" element involved in the present claim is that which may require the court, after it has decided the issue of duty of care and of negligence, in assessing damages to estimate, as best it can, the value of the chance which the [plaintiff] lost of resisting enforcement of the [authority's] notice. The presence of this element is . . . quite insufficient to justify the court [preventing the plaintiff from proceeding by writ in the manner appropriate to a civil action in private law]. If he had been suing his solicitor for negligent advice, exactly the same problem in assessing damages would have arisen . . . I cannot see that it makes any difference that the [defendants are] a public authority; the claim remains one the essence of which is a claim at common law; and the "public law" element is peripheral.'

The decision in *Davy v Spelthorne BC*, though welcome, will not dispel all uncertainty in this area because it was focussed on the question of procedure even though the determining factor was the substantive law. In *substantive* terms the plaintiff's claim was held to be 'private' and not 'public'. This conceptual distinction was expressly held to ante-date the reform of RSC Ord 53 in 1977 and to be unaltered by that reform. What lawyers' minds have *not* been directed to is any authority which clearly spells out what 'private' and 'public' law actually comprise, in substantive terms. We know, or have been confirmed in the knowledge, that an action in negligence is 'private' in nature even against a public body. We can say with some confidence that 'private' law includes contract, tort and certain analogous matters (eg quasi-contract, and other aspects of common law and equity). But we do not know authoritatively where the boundary of 'private' law is precisely drawn, because we do not know where the boundary of 'public' law is drawn; though ex hypothesi these two terms must be mutually exclusive, and, taken together, they must be comprehensive of all English law. This matter needs to be clarified further by Parliament or the courts, or both, to complete the work the House of Lords has undertaken so far.

Local authority finance

An impressive number of other leading cases reported in 1983 can be seen to involve local authorities, particularly over finance. The London fares case, *Bromley London BC v Greater London Council*, [1982] 1 All ER 129, in which the 'fares fair' policy for London Transport in its original form was struck down as being ultra vires, was followed by *R v London Transport Executive, ex p Greater London Council* [1983] 2 All ER 262, in which this same policy in its revised form was found to be intra vires and upheld in consequence by the Queen's Bench Divisional Court (Kerr LJ and Glidewell and Nolan JJ). The revised policy was worked out by the GLC; but the LTE rejected it on legal advice as being contrary to the principles authoritatively stated by the House of Lords in the *Bromley* decision. The GLC sought and obtained leave to apply for judicial review under RSC Ord 53 in the form of declarations that the revised policy was valid. The judgment of the Divisional Court, granting in substance (though not in every detail) the declarations sought, is technical and intricate, but is worth study for many reasons, legal and non-legal. The reason which matters most to lawyers is that the learned judges, who were handling one of the hotter specimens of hot potato cooked by the political process, and obviously conscious that all eyes were on them to see whether they would handle it with sufficient skill, devoted the utmost care to applying the ultra vires doctrine in this area. They did so in order to show as convincingly as possible how a fares policy can be adjudged to be either within or 'outwith' the boundary of legal validity. Unlike the *Spelthorne* case, this is of course a 'public' question par excellence.

The gist of the decision is as follows. The 'fares fair' policy in its original or *Bromley* phase had been concocted 'almost within a matter of days, without consultation and apparently without legal advice', as Kerr LJ expressed it (at 268), so that fares were reduced without any regard to the powers of the GLC under the 1969 Act and worked out arbitrarily, 'without any regard to the interests of ratepayers but solely in the interest of passengers'. The statute referred to is the Transport (London) Act 1969. The same policy in its revised form was then successfully purged of these errors. There was 'full consultation' between the GLC and the LTE, resulting in a 'balanced plan', which in the words of Kerr LJ (at 269) 'is a totally different exercise from the arbitrary decision in 1981 . . . [and] derives from a "draft medium-term plan" which was carefully researched and subjected to full consultation, as required by s 2(2) of the 1969 Act.' The 'balanced plan' aimed at reducing fares in 1983 to the levels obtaining before the 'fares fair' policy of 1981 was applied (instead of further reducing them, as that policy had proposed); though the intervening increases in costs meant that there would have to be a subsidy for this purpose which would be *nearer* the high level of the 'fares fair' subsidy than the lower level of the subsidy prevailing before that.

The 'full consultation' and the 'balanced plan' which was its outcome went a long way to justify the revised policy devised by the GLC, but not all the way. The essence of the judgment concerns the interpretation of the statutory provisions authorising the GLC and LTE to act at all. These of course are also contained in the Act of 1969. The effect of s 5(1) was to give the LTE the function of providing public transport in Greater London, subject to the guidance of the GLC in regard to main lines of policy, with the general requirement of aiming at 'efficiency, economy and safety of operation'. The effect of s 7(6) was to empower the GLC to 'take such action' as should be necessary to enable the LTE to balance its books. The effect of s 3(1) was to empower the GLC to make grants to the LTE 'for any purpose'. In the *Bromley* case the original 'fares fair' scheme had been held to fall outside the scope of these provisions because it had not been devised in a manner consistent with business principles. More specificially, s 7(3) required that any deficit incurred by the LTE must be made up in a subsequent accounting period 'so far as practicable'. In effect everything turned on this last phrase. It was interpreted in such a way that the decision of what is 'practicable' lies within the GLC's discretion—ie its freedom to make policy decisions as all public authorities must do within the proper sphere for which they have been set up. This discretion must be exercised within the general limits of well-established principles governing such exercise by public bodies, ie 'not effectively, or at any rate substantially, narrower than is inherent in the obligation to comply with the principles laid down in *Wednesbury* and, in particular, *Prescott* in the present context' (per Kerr LJ at 274).

So lawyers find themselves back at the familiar basic concept: the *Wednesbury* principle. A public authority's chosen policy is not to be upset by the courts unless matters have been taken into account which should not have been taken into account, or have not been taken into account which should have been taken into account or (more fundamental still) the policy decision is *objectively* 'unreasonable', ie *no* reasonable authority could have arrived at it. The locus classicus for this is found in the judgment of Lord Greene MR in *Associated Picture Houses Ltd v Wednesbury Corpn* [1947] 2 All ER 680 at 682. *Prescott v Birmingham Corpn* [1954] 3 All ER 698 is 'an important illustration of this principle' because a local authority's policy will not be objectively 'reasonable' if it affects the ratepayers without their interests having been considered in arriving at it, and also if it relates to a trading undertaking yet 'ordinary business principles' (per Jenkins LJ in [1954] 3 All ER at 706–7) are disregarded by the authority. Applying this to the vexed question of whether fares can lawfully be subsidised—ie set at a level that will result in loss or 'shortfall' which a grant is intended to cover—Nolan J (in [1983] 2 All ER at 288) quoted the words of Lord Scarman in the *Bromley* case (see [1982] 1 All ER at 177), as follows:

> 'Though the LTE may be compelled by circumstances to budget for a loss which will have to be made good by grant, the [1969 Act] requires it to avoid it, if it can. Its principal weapon is fares income. The [1969 Act], though it envisages budgeting for a deficit, permits it not as an object of social or transport policy, but as a course of action which it may not be practicable or possible to avoid. Loss may be unavoidable: but it does not thereby become an acceptable object of policy'.

A closely similar case where the Queen's Bench Divisional Court applied the *Wednesbury* principle is *Pickwell v Camden London BC* [1983] 1 All ER 602, in which the metropolitan district auditor applied for a declaration against the defendant council, to the effect that certain wage increases paid to manual workers employed by the council were contrary to law. The application was made under the Local Government Act 1972, s 161; but this procedure is in effect merely a special variant of judicial review made available to local government auditors.

The application failed, despite the fact that the increases paid were higher than those paid nationally. Unusually high expenditure is not of itself illegal, though it is evidence from which illegality of decision-making may be inferred. The court held that the council's decision was not ultra vires, in accordance with the *Wednesbury* test. It was not arbitrary, nor made for any ulterior motive. The fact that it was made in an emergency, under threat of a breakdown in the provision of essential services, told in its favour. A close comparison and an instructive contrast can be drawn with the decison of the House of Lords in *Roberts v Hopwood*, [1925] All ER Rep 24, another case in which wage increases allowed by a local authority were unusually high. Forbes J in the *Pickwell* case distinguished *Roberts v Hopwood*, in which the House of Lords declared the high wages paid by the council to be ultra vires, on the ground that those wages were 'agreed to be paid without any regard to any commercial consideration and solely on some extraneous principle . . . [ie] philanthropy . . .' In *Pickwell*, 'comercial consideration' was (to some extent at least) present and 'extraneous principle' was not.

The most weighty disputes involving local authorities, however, have arisen over income, not expenditure. Income from property and services has to some extent featured in the above cases; but what must now be considered are forms of income which are special: grants and rates.

Grants came in for judical consideration by the Queen's Bench Divisional Court in a monumental case, *R v Secretary of State for the Environment, ex p Brent London BC* [1983] 3 All ER 321. The sole judgment in the case was delivered by Ackner LJ (sitting with Phillips J). It is long and full of technicalities relating to the 'rate support grant'. The difficulties in comprehending it are fully accounted for by the arcane nature of the subject matter. The only reservation is that the judgment reads in some places as if government advocacy is the same thing as objective truth.

The biggest single source of revenue for local authorities in modern times is the payment to them of taxpayers' money by the central government in the form of grants. As Ackner LJ explained:

'After taking account of income from fees and charges for services provided, about 60% of local goverment revenue expenditure has in recent years been met by government grants, the most important being the rate support grant. The remainder is met by rates' (at 325).

The system in accordance with which central government grants are paid to local authorities is complex, and is frequently altered (usually on a change of government). A constant factor in the complexity is the distinction between specific grants for particular services, such as the provision of local authority housing, and general grants for expenditure as a whole. The *Brent* case arose from the introduction of a new scheme for paying general grants. The changeover was enacted in the Local Government, Planning and Land Act 1980, Part VI, and comprises permanent provisions for the proposed new system and transitional provisions for the financial year 1980–81. Before the legislation received the Royal Assent the Secretary of State for the

Environment instructed local authorities to make certain reductions in proposed expenditure. After the submission of budgets, and in some cases revised budgets, he decided that certain authorities had not sufficently reduced their budgets and should have their general grant, ie the rate support grant, reduced in consequence when the Act came into force. The transitional provisions took effect immediately at the date of the Royal Assent (13 November 1980), namely ss 48–50. But before the Secretary of State could reduce the grant he had first to make a 'multipliers order' for the purposes of calculating the reductions in detail, and to obtain the approval of the House of Commons. In a surprising display of partisanship the headnote (at 321), without quotation marks, speaks of local authorities which 'blatantly disregarded' expenditure targets.

The Rate Support (Principles for Multipliers) Order 1980 was laid before the House of Commons on 16 December 1980. The local authorities thought to be most likely to incur the grant reductions were told that the deadline for being allowed to escape the penalty would be the date when the Order was approved, which it was expected would be 15 January 1981. On 19 December 1980 the Association of Metropolitan Authorities, through its chairman, wrote asking the Secretary of State to meet a delegation before making up his mind to penalise those authorities. On 9 January 1981, he replied refusing to do so and recommending that the authorities should meet his officials to discuss how to reduce their expenditure sufficiently to escape being penalised on 15 January. In the result, on 26 January they were duly penalised by a decision to reduce their rate support grant under the transitional provisions. Of the eight authorities affected—all London boroughs: Brent, Camden, Hackney, Hounslow, Tower Hamlets, Waltham Forest, Lambeth and Lewisham—the first six promptly sought leave, which was granted, to apply for judicial review by way of certiorari (to quash the decision of 26 January) and declarations relating to the validity of the 'multipliers order' and to the rights of the applicants and the respondent Secretary of State.

At the end of his judgment, Ackner LJ commented on the complexity and technicality of the case and thanked counsel for their efforts. He said:

> 'Having learned a few weeks before the hearing that the affidavits and exhibits numbered close on 1,000 pages we had a pre-hearing review. At our request we were most helpfully provided with a useful glossary of terms, a reading guide, a chronological statement of events and an outline of the submissions to be made. This enabled us to save much hearing time by some useful advance reading.'

The judgment was delivered on 21 October 1981, after 11 days of the hearing in July. The report was not published in the All England Law Reports for another two years (4 November 1983).

The applicants succeeded in having the Secretary of State's decision (26 January 1981) to reduce their rate support grants quashed; and orders of certiorari were duly granted. Their other submissions were rejected. Ackner LJ said, in regard to the result of the case:

> 'It will of course be open to the Secretary of State after considering the applicants' representations, now fully documented, to reach any decision he considers right, and which is within the terms of the 1980 Act and the multipliers order.'

This comment admirably pinpoints the realities of these administrative law cases, ie as a whole and not merely disputes relating to local authorities' grants. As with innumerable disputes relating to planning and other matters, the real *quarrel* is over issues of policy but the only effective *challenge* (and that not more than rarely) is over issues of law. The Secretary of State (or other authority) has his decision invalidated on legal grounds; but in a general way there is no reason why the policy underlying that decision should not be immediately reapplied, in a new decision to the same effect save only that the legal flaw affecting the first decision is cured or avoided.

This very point was made by counsel for the respondent Secretary of State, as a ground for urging that the applicants should not be granted the relief claimed even if they succeeded in showing as a matter of substantive law that their challenge was justified. Ackner LJ took the point but countered it by observing that although the respondent was at liberty to adhere to his previous policy in toto he could equally well change it. There were factors that might cause him to do so. After all, three members of the watch committee in *Ridge v Baldwin* did so—see [1963] 2 All ER 66 at 80: 'The importance of the principles to which we have referred above far transcend the significance of this case. If our decision is inconvenient, it cannot be helped.'

The reason for the applicants' success, as far as it went, was that the respondent's decision to reduce grants payable to them was arrived at without giving them a hearing in regard to that decision. The fact that the policies underlying that decision had been publicised and debated does not alter this. Lord Reid's well-known statement in *British Oxygen Co Ltd v Minister of Technology* [1970] 3 All ER 165 at 170, was quoted: 'The general rule is that anyone who has to exercise a statutory discretion must not "shut [his] ears to an application . . ." ' Lord Denning MR quoted this in *Sagnata Investments Ltd v Norwich Corpn* [1971] 2 All ER 1441 at 1448, and added:

> 'The applicant is entitled to put forward reasons urging that the policy should be changed, or saying that in any case it should not be applied to him. But so long as the administrative body is ready to hear him and consider what he has to say, it is entitled to apply its general policy to him as to others.'

The respondent was thus entitled to apply his policy to the applicants, within the statutory limits laid down. But what he did wrong was to 'shut his ears' to the applicants before making the specific decision embodied in the letters of 26 January 1981. The sequence was that his statutory discretion was not exercised in the way that the law requires, which is as much as to say in legal terms that it was not 'exercised' at all. Therefore his official decision was 'invalid' or 'vitiated', to use wording recommended by Lord Wilberforce in *Calvin v Carr*, [1979] 2 All ER 440 at 445–446 (speaking of decisions 'made contrary to natural justice', though not necessarily to the exclusion of other illegalities in the field of public law). In the broadest sense, which embraces procedural as well as substantive issues, the decision in question was ultra vires.

There was a sequel to this decision: *R v Secretary of State for the Environment, ex p Hackney London BC* [1983] 3 All ER 358. Hackney and Camden Councils sought judicial review by way of challenge to the Secretary of State's consequent decision not to pay an increased rate support grant until he had considered what policy to follow in the light of the decision in the *Brent* case.

One ground of challenge was that, on a proper interpretation of the relevant statutory wording, it was by this time (ie the beginning of 1982, after the decision in the *Brent* case, which was not appealed against) too late to reduce the amount of the relevant grant (which related to the financial year 1980–81). The other ground of challenge rested on the ground of 'issue estoppel', namely that the decision in the *Brent* case prevented the Secretary of State from arguing in the instant case that the payment of grant was anything other than an accrued legal right because that very issue had already been decided by 'a court of competent jurisdiction' and decided against him.

The claim failed, and it is of some interest in the field of public law to see why. One ground is that the 'issue' itself was misstated. In the *Brent* case Ackner LJ had spoken of entitlement to grant as an 'existing right'. But that was in point only because deprivation of such a right established a clear case of natural justice, so that a fair hearing must be given to the entitled party before a discretion is exercised to deprive him of that right. It does *not* make that 'existing right' unalterable. Another ground is that 'issue estoppel' is in any case inappropriate in judicial review, because it is derived from the deeper 'rule of public policy that there shall be finality in litigation', as May LJ put it, and that rule requires to be given effect by 'issue estoppel' only in private civil actions. In public law it is given effect in a different way: in criminal law by the 'rule against double jeopardy', and in administrative law by the principle that relief in judicial review and related procedures is not available 'as of right' but lies within the court's discretion. Further to this, 'there are no formal pleadings' in judicial review 'and it will frequently be difficult if not impossible to identify a particular issue which the [previous] application will have decided'. There is 'lack of mutuality' in these public law cases, since there exists no 'true lis' between the Crown and the respondent, or between the ex parte applicant and the respondent; whereas in private civil actions there is 'mutuality' between plaintiff and defendant.

This decision strongly reinforces the principle laid down the year before with such emphasis by the House of Lords in *O'Reilly v Mackman*, and *Cocks v Thanet DC*, that a fundamental difference exists between proceedings in public law and private law respectively. The controversy over estoppel focusses this argument. Time and again in recent years claimants have attempted to upset public authorities' policy decisions by making use of the concept of estoppel, ie by saying that even if such a decision may be unimpeachable on other grounds (in any given case) it may still be invalidated because the public authority is 'estopped' from relying on it. This may be common law estoppel, ie that the authority have relied to their own advantage on an assertion of facts and cannot subsequently deny that assertion even if the facts are contrary to what was previously stated. But more probably it is equitable estoppel, ie the authority have given an express or implied promise, on the faith of which the claimant has committed himself so that it would be unconscionable to break the promise even though no consideration is supplied for it such as would make it enforceable at common law, on a contractual basis. Estoppel has its true place in private law—and public authorities as *persons* have their rights and duties in private law, as natural persons have—but its appearance in public law is an intrusion which the courts are resisting with great determination. Nevertheless it has considerable appeal to litigants as a last resource when other legal argument fail; and the temptation then to put it forward will not easily be resisted.

From the rate support grant to the rate itself is a short step. Leading cases on rates and rating reported in 1983, however, have arisen on comparatively narrow and technical points. The only one to reach the House of Lords is *K Shoe Shops Ltd v Hardy (Valuation Officer)* [1983] 3 All ER 609, in which the dispute arose over the appropriate day in relation to which hereditaments should be valued. It is common knowledge that the last general rating revaluation came into effect throughout the country on 1 April 1973, subsequent revaluations being postponed for the sake of economy and in consequence of political controversy over local government finance. The appellants' premises were valued by the local valuation officer as at 1 April 1973; but the information on which this was based was sought as part of inquiries pursued generally in the area late in 1970, the answers to which were received in 1971; while the valuations were worked out in 1972. The appellants said that the ultimate figures were reasonable for 1973; but they should have been kept down to 1970 levels since that was the date at which information was being sought. The House of Lords rejected the appeal and upheld the decision of the Court of Appeal in the valuation officer's favour. This was because the scheme of the relevant statute—the General Rate Act 1967—was held to require a common valuation date throughout the country, and no date other than 1 April 1973 was expressly or impliedly indicated by the Act. It was thus reasonable and necessary that values should be taken as at the date the valuation lists were to come into force, and on no other date. Lord Templeman said that

'it does not seem to me that the . . . valuation officer or any other trained valuer would have any great difficulty in estimating the rents obtainable on 1 April 1973 . . . The appellants asserted, by reference to a graph which their surveyor dignified by the name of a tonogram and by deductions from that graph by a process which their surveyor exalted to the science or art of "tonometry", that [various other premises had been valued at 1970 levels].'

This 'jargon' was rejected by their Lordships, together with the conclusions drawn from its use.

In *Broxtowe BC v Birch*, [1983] 1 All ER 641, the question to be decided was whether premises occupied by a religious sect known as the Exclusive Brethren were exempt from rating altogether, as 'places of public religious worship' within the meaning of the General Rate Act 1967, s 39(2)(a). The Court of Appeal upheld the decision of the Lands Tribunal that the premises (two meeting halls) were not exempt. On the authorities the exemption could only be validly claimed if the public were 'invited to worship there by some outward and visible indication', or if 'there was evidence that the public at large in fact attended the premises to worship'. Neither of these requirements was met. The premises did not look like places of worship and were not advertised as such by notice boards. The sect, in fact, lived up to its name.

In *Verrall v Hackney London BC* [1983] 1 All ER 277, the question concerned 'occupation' of premises giving rise to a liability to pay rates thereon. The appellant, a member of the National Front (an unincorporated association, among other things) arranged the holding of meetings at a converted warehouse owned by a company, National Front Properties Ltd. Rates not having been paid on the premises despite the fact that they were a rateable hereditament, the rating authority applied for a distress warrant against the appellant, which was issued. His appeal by way of case stated was dismissed by Woolf J, but granted on appeal to the Court of Appeal, which held that the appellant was not the 'occupier'. On the facts he was merely a member of an unincorporated association which was itself not capable of being an 'occupier'. Nor was he, on the facts, a 'paramount occupier' by virtue of having actual and exclusive occupation, despite the organising rôle he performed in regard to the use of the premises by the National Front. It may be that the owning company was the 'occupier' after all.

Another case in which a distress warrant was issued is *R v Poole Justices, ex p Fleet* [1983] 2 All ER 897. Insufficient goods were found on the premises in question, and the rating authority applied for a warrant of commitment to prison. The magistrates duly inquired first into the defendant's means, under the General Rate Act 1967, ss 102–3. The defendant offered to pay off his rate arrears at £50 a week, whereupon the magistrates postponed the issue of the warrant of commitment to prison, although they also fixed the term of the imprisonment. On failure by the defendant to continue making the weekly payments the rating authority were entitled to renew their application for committing him to prison and did so. The magistrates issued the warrant without further inquiry into his means. He applied for judicial review by way of certiorari to quash the warrant and mandamus to direct the magistrates to make further inquiry into his means before issuing a new warrant. Forbes J granted the application. He pointed out that although there is power under the Magistrates' Courts Act 1980, s 77(2), to activate a decision to commit an offender to prison in default of payment without a further hearing, that relates to cases where payment is due to the court itself. It is different if payment is due to a body other than the magistrates' court, eg the rating authority, because the circumstances do not lie within the court's knowledge. Therefore a hearing must be allowed in such a case before the delinquent is committed to prison; and he can then furnish further details as to his means which may convince the court that it would not be right to imprison him.

It is difficult, however, to see why a hearing should not also be given even where payment is due to the court itself, since it is equally possible that there are good reasons in such a case for the failure to pay. The *ratio* stated for not allowing a hearing is that the issue of a warrant for commitment to prison, after conditions subject to which its issue was postponed have been broken, is 'not a judicial order but a mere judicial act' (*R v Chichester Justices, ex p Collins* [1982] 1 All ER 1000). It is difficult to see the justice of this distinction. If a delinquent is genuinely unable to pay, as distinct from displaying 'wilful refusal or ... culpable negligence' (1967 Act, s 103(1)), surely he should be given the chance to establish this, whether the sum is owed to a separate body or to the court itself.

Local authority procedure

In *R v City of Birmingham DC, ex p O* [1983] 1 All ER 497, the House of Lords gave judgment in a matter involving two fundamental principles of public authority law which were in conflict. One is that the public interest requires council members as a whole to be fully notified of all council business so as to be as well informed as possible for the purpose of carrying out their duties: the disclosure principle, as it might be called. The other is that the public interest requires files relating to sensitive issues to be kept as confidential as possible: this is the converse non-disclosure principle. Both principles are inherently justifiable.

The facts were that the council's social services committee had to consider whether the foster-parents of a child placed in the care of the local authority ought to adopt the child. A councillor who was not a member of that committee but was for other official reasons familiar with the circumstances of the foster-parents asked to be shown confidential files relating to them. The social services department was concerned about this, but the local authority's solicitor advised that the files should be shown to the councillor. The foster-parents thereupon sought judicial review for a prerogative order of prohibition to prevent disclosure. The Divisional Court refused this application; the Court of Appeal (by a majority) reversed their decision and granted the application; the House of Lords reversed this decision in turn and restored the Divisional Court's decision. Thus the disclosure principle ultimately prevailed. But this does not invalidate the non-disclosure principle. By what overriding principle therefore is a conflict between them to be resolved?

Lord Brightman, delivering the House's decision in his speech, expressed this overriding principle in the phrase 'a need to know'. A member or officer of a public authority has a right to see confidential documents if this need can be demonstrated. It involves a 'screening process', which in 'an area as delicate and confidential as that of child care and adoption' must 'be administered with great strictness'. The decision is 'ultimately one to be taken by the councillors themselves sitting in council' though it can be delegated, probably to particular committees, or members, or chief officers and their deputies, subject to that ultimate control.

> 'If the adoption had taken place and come to grief, the . . . councillors could not have washed their hands of a disaster . . . In the case of a councillor with a bona fide and reasonably based concern . . . who is not a busybody, . . . the bias, if any, should be in favour of allowing access to information rather than concealing information.'

(Judges these days are fond of pointing to 'busybodies' as the persons who must not receive consideration in issues of public law, the implication being that anyone *not* appearing to be a 'busybody' is at least prima facie deserving of attention.) Over and above all these propositions rises the *Wednesbury* principle itself, which is that an exercise of discretion is in general terms valid, and thus intra vires, so long as it is *not* one which *no* reasonable council or other official body would make.

This is an admirable formulation of principle, and in terms enables lawyers to reconcile other decisions in this area, equally satisfactory though with different results on their own facts. One example is *R v Lancashire County Police Authority, ex p Hook* [1980] 2 All ER 353, in which the details of a report on police corruption were withheld from a councillor; the Court of Appeal refused judicial review for mandamus to compel disclosure. But in *Campbell v Tameside Metropolitan BC* [1982] 2 All ER 791, a teacher suing the council for negligence as a result of being injured by a violent pupil succeeded in an application for 'preliminary discovery' of confidential documents containing relevant official reports. In the earlier case a 'need to know' was not established, and the confidentiality principle prevailed over the disclosure principle. In the later case the 'need to know' was established, and the disclosure principle prevailed over the confidentiality principle.

Another decision of the House of Lords with considerable significance for the workings of local authorities is *Shah v Barnet London BC* [1983] 1 All ER 226. Three local education authorities (Barnet and Brent London Borough Councils and Shropshire County Council) had refused applications by five students from abroad to be awarded grants for further education. The Court of Appeal upheld the authorities' decisions in respect of four of the five students. Appeals by the four disappointed students to the House of Lords were allowed, and the relevant local authority's cross-appeal in regard to the fifth student was dismissed. Education authorities (central and local), and various institutions of higher education as well, were not pleased by this 'change' in the law to their disadvantage. But of course it is educational administrative practice, not law, which has changed, the law in its true form having at last been brought to their attention in this authoritative manner by the House of Lords.

Although the decision is fundamental and far reaching in its practical consequences, it does not turn on a broad principle like that of objective reasonableness—ie the *Wednesbury* principle—but on statutory interpretation of particular wording, namely the phrase 'ordinarily resident'. The Local Education Authority Awards Regulations 1979 (SI 1979/889, now re-enacted in the Education (Mandatory Awards) Regulation 1981, SI 1981/943), states in reg 13:

'An authority shall not be under a duty to bestow an award . . . upon a person who has not been ordinarily resident, throughout the three years preceding the first year of the course in question, in the United Kingdom . . .'

This delegated legislation had been duly made under the Education Act 1962, s 1 (now the Education Act 1980, s 19 and Sch 5). The double negative in the rule establishes an exception to the mandatory requirement, but an exception which was not meant to extend to persons 'ordinarily resident' for the relevant period. The central and local authorities took the view that the applicants had indeed been 'resident', but *not* 'ordinarily' resident.

The House of Lords, reversing the Court of Appeal, held that the words 'ordinarily resident' must be construed in accordance with their natural and ordinary meaning in English. The Act and the Regulations did not introduce any qualification of meaning in terms of place of origin, domicile or nationality. Courts have no justification for imposing their own views as to policy except insofar as the relevant statute as a whole conveys an expression of Parliament's policy. Lord Scarman, expressing in his speech the unanimous judgment of the House, pointed out that although 'the meaning of ordinary words is, as Lord Reid observed in *Brutus v Cozens* [1972] 2 All ER 1297 at 1299, a question of fact, the meaning to be attributed to enacted words is a question of law, being a matter of statutory interpretation'. It is true that this 'arises only at a preliminary stage in the process of determing a question of fact, namely whether the ... applicant has established the fact of ordinary residence for the prescribed period ... If a local education authority gets the law right, and, as lawyers would put it, directs itself correctly in law, the question of fact, ie has the student established the prescribed residence?, is for the authority, not the court, to decide.'

Lord Scarman went on to show that the local authorities had not, however, 'got their law right' in regard to this crucial question of statutory interpretation. The words 'ordinarily resident' were construed by the House of Lords in two tax cases, *Levene v IRC* [1928] All ER Rep 746 at 750 and 753–754, and *IRC v Lysaght* [1928] All ER Rep 575 at 580, per Viscount Cave LC and Lord Warrington (in *Levene's* case) and Viscount Sumner (in *Lysaght's* case). They signify 'residence ... with some degree of continuity, and apart from accidental or temporary absences' (Viscount Cave). 'Ordinarily' is the converse of 'extraordinarily', and 'that part of the regular order of a man's life adopted voluntarily and for settled purposes is not "extraordinary"' (Viscount Sumner). The words 'resident' and 'ordinarily resident' have 'no technical or special meaning for the purposes of the Income Tax Act' (Lord Warrington). Therefore, as Lord Scarman insisted, those words must be given 'their natural and ordinary meaning as words of common usage in the English language' (short of a clear indication to a contrary effect in any statute—which is not the case with the Education Acts). The applicant students were, by this test, 'ordinarily resident' in the United Kingdom after all. Their residence was voluntary and had no peculiar or illegal features. It had 'a degree of settled purpose', which involves 'a sufficient degree of continuity' but does not require intention to stay 'indefinitely' and so 'may be for a limited period'. Moreover this purpose can be a specific one. 'Education in adolescence or early adulthood can be as settled a purpose as a profession or business in later years'. This must distinguish 'ordinary residence' from 'domicile'; for it is true that 'the notion that lies at the root of the concept of domicile is that of permanent home' (*Dicey and Morris on the Conflict of Laws*, (8th edn, 1967) ch 8, p 78, as quoted by Lord Scarman).

> 'The choice of ordinary residence for determining the test of eligibility for a mandatory award suggests to my mind a legislative intention not to impose on local education authorities who are entrusted with the duty of making mandatory awards the infinitely difficult, if not impossible, task of determining whether a student has established a permanent home in the United Kingdom.'

Thus Lord Scarman and his colleagues were laudably engaged in saving local authorities from a stubborn resolve which could have lumbered them with the burden of having to interpret 'domicile'—for that is what the concept of a 'permanent home' or 'real home' for student applicants would imply.

The House of Lords also held that a local education authority which refuses (lawfully) to grant a mandatory award has a duty to go on to consider granting a discretionary award. The House expressly related its decision to *Associated Provincial Picture Houses Ltd v Wednesbury Corpn* and to its recent decision in *O'Reilly v Mackman*. The decision is therefore clearly placed in context, which is the mainstream of authority in regard to public law, more particularly judicial review. Relief, if granted at all in such a case, is discretionary. Lord Scarman had no doubt that it must be granted because in principle the applicant 'has a right to receive, and the local authority a duty to bestow, an award', a right and duty which otherwise will be frustrated. But the appropriate remedies in the case were prerogative orders of certiorari to quash the ultra vires refusals to make awards and of mandamus to require the authorities to reconsider the various applications. Declarations 'are appropriate to declare an entitlement or a right, or a duty. But this is exactly what the courts cannot, and must not, do in these cases . . . The function of the courts is to ensure due observance of the law; that is all.' The authorities, provided that they comply with the law, must still determine, *according to the facts*, what, if anything, is due by way of a particular award to each applicant.

Immigration

The case just discussed makes it appropriate to go on to consider immigration cases, in that the applicants for awards were immigrants even though no challenge to the lawfulness of their presence in this country had been raised. During 1983 several more leading cases on immigration control have found their way into the reports, raising a variety of issues of law, both broad and narrow.

Particularly broad is the ground on which Glidewell J quashed a decision of the Home Secretary in *R v Immigration Appeal Tribunal, ex p Bastiampillai* [1983] 2 All ER 844. This was no less than the *Wednesbury* principle itself. The judge granted an order of certiorari quashing a decision to refuse to grant the applicants indefinite leave to remain in this country as dependants of their daughters who were married and settled here. The applicants came over from Sri Lanka. A previous application to remain, after a period of temporary residence had been granted and had expired, was rejected, and the Home Secretary's decision had been upheld on an appeal to an official adjudicator. That appeal decision was upheld on a further appeal to the Immigration Appeal Tribunal. These decisions were upheld by the judge on an interpretation of the Immigration Act 1971, s 14, and of the statement of Changes in Immigration Rules (HC Paper (1979–80) no 394), para 48. The original application had been made out of time, and there was no 'emotional dependence' of the applicants on their children, over and above ordinary family affection, which would justify an exception in their favour. The appeals had, however, been adjourned so as to enable an application to be made to the Home Secretary to reconsider his original decision, which he refused; and it was this decision that the judge quashed. He did so on the ground, which is part of the *Wednesbury* principle, that the Home Secretary failed to take into account a matter which he ought to have taken into account because of its relevance to the decision which he had to reach. This was a change of circumstances brought about by the applicant's retirement from work (he was 69), which affected the question whether he and his wife were 'wholly or mainly dependent' on a particular daughter and son-in-law. The failure meant that the Home Secretary's discretion was not properly exercised; and the case was remitted for him to reconsider it in the light of that finding.

With this case may be compared the decision of the House of Lords in *Khawaja v Secretary of State for the Home Dept* [1983] 1 All ER 765. Two immigrants were detained, pending deportation for being illegal entrants under the Immigration Act 1971, s 33(1). In both cases the immigration officer had been unaware that the applicant was married, which would affect his status. The House of Lords held that a statement by an immigration officer that he had 'reasonable grounds' for deciding that anyone was an illegal entrant did not prevent the court from examining the evidence considered by that officer. The relevant evidence, when thus examined, showed that the first applicant had deceived the immigration authorities as to his marriage; and they would have refused him leave to enter originally had they known the truth. His appeal was therefore dismissed. The second applicant, however, could not be said on the evidence to have deceived the authorities and so his appeal was allowed. The House held that 'the civil standard of proof to a high degree of probability' was required for a court to be satisfied of the existence of facts justifying the official decision taken, and that this applies to applications for habeas corpus and judicial review alike. Immigration cases previously decided to a contrary effect were overruled. But it was emphasised that RSC Ord 53, while giving a discretion to allow cross-examination of deponents to affidavits in judicial review, must be regarded as restricting this to cases when justice so demands; and cases when it is justifiable for a deponent from overseas to be required to come to the United Kingdom for this purpose will be rare indeed.

Another general principle was expressed in *R v Immigration Appeal Tribunal, ex p Weerasuriya* [1983] 1 All ER 195, in which Webster J held that an appeal from a decision of the Home Secretary, to an immigration adjudicator under the Immigration Act 1971, s 19(1), is a process for reviewing the Home Secretary's decision and is not an extension of his administrative functions. Evidence of facts occurring after the Home Secretary's decision being reviewed is therefore inadmissible before the adjudicator. The Court of Appeal later endorsed this ruling, in *R v Immigration Appeal Tribunal, ex p Kotecha* [1983] 2 All ER 289. The Immigration Act 1971, s 19(2) and the Immigration Appeals (Procedure) Rules 1972, rr 18(1) and 29(1), are to be interpreted in accordance with these decisions.

Taking these three foregoing cases together, their combined principles were applied by the Court of Appeal in *R v Immigration Appeal Tribunal, ex p Khan (Mahmud)* [1983] 2 All ER 420. The applicant had married a prostitute in Bradford. The Home Secretary thereupon subjected him to a deportation order on the ground that it was a 'marriage of convenience'. The Court of Appeal thought that the tribunal, which dismissed the applicant's appeal against the Home Secretary's order, had not required the necessary *intention* of the applicant, to treat his marriage as one of convenience only, to be proved by evidence; rather it was regarded (wrongly) as self evident. The reasons for the decision were thus insufficiently stated; and moreover the tribunal's findings on the evidence were not clearly indicated. The decision was quashed and the matter remitted for hearing by a differently constituted tribunal.

A more limited point came up for consideration in *R v Immigration Appeal Tribunal, ex p Coomasaru* [1983] 1 All ER 208, when the Court of Appeal had to deal with the applicant's claim that he was 'settled in the United Kingdom' at a time when he returned here, after having served previously for three years in the Sri Lanka High Commission and then been sent abroad for a short period. On his return he was admitted only conditionally and for 12 months. It was held that he was not 'settled' here because his original entry was clearly shown, from wording in his passport, to have been restricted to admission solely for the purposes of serving as a member of a diplomatic mission, in the employment of the High Commission, and not unconditionally.

Finally there is the decision of the House of Lords, in *Amin v Entry Clearance Officer, Bombay* [1983] 2 All ER 864, relating to a narrow point on 'special vouchers'. These vouchers are, in point of fact, non-statutory, and are issued only as a concession to heads of households who are being subjected to pressure to leave the country where they reside. The appellant's father had been granted such a voucher, covering himself, his wife and unmarried children; but the appellant herself, being married and living with her husband, had not been included. It was held that the refusal to issue her with a 'special voucher' was purely a matter of administrative favour, not an exercise of a statutory function subject to procedures for appeal or challenge under the Immigration Act 1971, s 13(2), under the Sex Discrimination Act 1975 ss 1 and 29(1). A 'special voucher' is not 'an entry clearance' under the 1971 Act, s 33(1). Lords Scarman and Brandon of Oakbrook would have allowed her appeal under the Act of 1975 as raising a legal issue on discrimination; but the majority of the House did not take this view.

Postscript

The observations on cross-examination in judicial review made by the House of Lords in the *Khawaja* case, as referred to above (p 15) and in the article on Evidence, below, were taken up by McNeill J in the Queen's Bench Division on 15 March 1984 in *R v Secretary of State for the Home Department, ex p Manuel* (Times, 21 March). An application to call and cross-examine the applicant seeking judicial review was granted, but only because his counsel had already offered to submit him for cross-examination. The judge 'had a reservation whether an applicant could so tender himself, but that difficulty had been resolved by the Secretary of State's application'—ie both sides were in agreement. (The substantive application for judicial review succeeded and on the following day an order of certiorari was granted.)

Arbitration

J E ADAMS, LLB, FCIArb
Solicitor, Professor of Law, Queen Mary College, University of London

The twelve cases on arbitration reported in the All England Reports in 1983 fall into four convenient groupings. Two are the continuation of familiar and relatively contentious themes, namely the treatment of appeals under the 1979 Act and the problems of delay and alleged frustration. There were two cases with foreign elements and five on miscellaneous topics. Several of the cases in the third and fourth groups are of considerable individual importance. Efforts continue to be made to preserve and enhance the position of London as an arbitration centre, and the efforts of professional arbitrators, especially in the Chartered Institute of Arbitrators, have concentrated on the issue of conciliation and the continued progress towards the agreement of UNCITRAL (United Nations Committee on International Trade Law) proposals for a Model Law. If such agreement were to be reached, a serious decision would face British arbitrators, namely whether to accept the rules, at least for disputes involving foreign nationals or companies, or to continue with established practices possibly in increasing isolation from the main competitors in the provision of arbitration facilities. That is, however, a matter for the future.

Appeals

To turn to the 1983 decisions, *Moran v Lloyd's* [1983] 2 All ER 200 was unusual both in involving an appeal against expulsion from Lloyd's rather than a shipping or commodity dispute and in involving applications to set aside or remit the award, founded on allegations of misconduct in the conduct of the arbitration by an umpire, as well as application for leave to appeal. A preliminary point had to be settled on whether the appeal to the Court of Appeal from the decision below of (coincidentally) Lloyd J required leave. The point was new, in the sense that the Master of the Rolls referred to 'the usual practice' of seeking leave to appeal in case it should be necessary, which avoided the need to decide whether or not leave was necessary. No problem rose over the proper test in the circumstances, for the issue turned on whether the appeal below had led to a final or to an interlocutory order. Two tests had been applied in earlier cases. One test was to consider the nature of the application to the court, ie what the party had sought and the other was to examine the judgment or order made, ie what the party obtained. The latter was adopted as the test, in reliance largely on *Re Croadsdell and Cammel Laird & Co Ltd* [1906] 2 KB 269, where an order setting aside an award was held to be interlocutory, and the same ruling was made in the present case in relation to the order to remit the award. This aspect of the case may well affect the issue over a wider field than arbitration cases, but while close analysis of the wording shows a preference for the 'order made' test it does so without expressing outright rejection of the 'nature of the application' test, so the question may arise again in the future.

Having ruled that leave was necessary, the court considered whether to grant it, first bemoaning the fact that the concept of 'misconduct' had not been given a less pejorative label, as suggested by the Commercial Court Committee in its 1978 Report on Arbitration. No suggestion of impropriety was made against the umpire, but his alleged failure had to be called misconduct. The court stressed that neither s 22 (power to remit) nor s 23 (power to set aside) was to be used to side-step the new restrictions on appeal contained in the 1979 Act. Mistakes of fact or law are not per se misconduct; inconsistency between two parts of an award, as alleged here, would probably never suffice, despite a contrary indication in Halsbury's Laws of England. A distinction must also be drawn between inconsistency in the award and inconsistency in the reasoning: the former might justify remission under s 22 without misconduct but not the latter. No such inconsistency could be found. The second allegation was that two complaints had been upheld on a basis not argued for by Lloyd's, so depriving the applicant of the opportunity to defend himself properly. Such a state of affairs could constitute misconduct or other sufficient ground to remit under s 22, but was not here made out. So leave to appeal was refused.

The judgment of Sir John Donaldson MR, with his background of the Commercial Court and strong interest and involvement in arbitration matters, usefully clarifies and restates various principles and the relationship between the different methods for attacking an arbitral award.

The judge in *Finelvet AG v Vinava Shipping Co Ltd, The Chrysalis* [1983] 2 All ER 658 was Mr Justice Mustill, co-author of a new text book on The Law and Practice of Commercial Arbitration in England (Mustill and Boyd *Commercial Arbitration* (1982) Butterworths) which has been well received. It is routinely cited in the judgments and referred to as 'the' or 'one of' the leading textbooks. The case involved one more dispute arising from the outbreak of Irani-Iraqi hostilities in 1980, trapping the Chrysalis, and some 60 other ships, in the Persian Gulf The arbitrator had ruled that the charterparty had been frustrated not by the formal declaration of war on September 22 but only on November 24 when it was clear that safe departure was to be delayed for an uncertain period. His decision was upheld, and his choice of frustration date would not be upset, as it was within the range of permissible dates.

Appeal had been agreed on before the award, under s 1(3)(a) of the 1979 Act, but the judge still considered the guidelines laid down in *The Nema* (*Pioneer Shipping Ltd v BTP Tioxide Ltd* [1981] 2 All ER 1030) as subsequently refined in other cases including *The Evia* (*Kodros Shipping Corp v Empresa Cubana de Fletes* [1982] 3 All ER 350, also in the House of Lords). He stressed that the approach to application for leave to appeal differs from the approach to the appeal itself. The interests of finality predominate over the legal accuracy of the award in the former situation, although the stronger the argument that the arbitrator was wrong the more compelling an argument that was in support of the grant of leave, which still remain discretionary. On an appeal, discretion disappears and the court must rule whether the decision of the arbitrator was right or wrong. To decide that question, the judge continued, the award is to be broken into three components:

(1) the facts ascertained
(2) the law ascertained
(3) the decision reached.

Stage (2) is the proper subject of an appeal, but the judge found it unnecessary to decide if (3) could ever be, because of *The Nema* and *The Evia* laid down that in commercial frustration the power of intervention ends once the award is shown to be within the range of possible correct answers. He rejected an argument that an agreement to appeal, under s 1(3)(a), made a difference.

In upholding the arbitration award, Mustill J examined cases and statements in textbooks dealing with the effect on contracts of the outbreak of war and reached the conclusion, stated above, that one looks to the acts of war (in the absence of supervening illegality, eg trading with the enemy) rather than the declaration of war. He rejected various other complaints and dismissed the appeal, but gave leave to appeal against his own judgment.

What the cases stress is that agreement on an appeal avoids what some may see as the obstacle of *The Nema* guidelines, but does not guarantee an authoritative ruling from the court when the case does not justify upsetting the award. There thus remains a substantial chance that the judge will not over-rule the arbitrator. One more aspect of the effect of the 1979 reforms has been illuminated, nevertheless.

Leave to appeal was directly in issue in *Antaios Cia Naviera SA v Salen Rederierna AB, The Antaios* [1983] 3 All ER 777. Arbitrators found that the issue of inaccurate bills of lading by a charterer was not a breach within the meaning of a clause in a standard New York Produce Exchange time charter permitting the owners to withdraw the vessel, not being a repudiatory breach. Alternatively, any right of withdrawal had been lost by failure to exercise it in a reasonable time, held to be 48 hours. On seeking leave to appeal, the charterers argued that there was a conflict of judicial opinion on the meaning of the relevant clause (as indeed there is) which substantially affected their rights. That ground prima facie fell within the guidelines in *The Nema*. Secondly, they argued that the notice given on discovery of the alleged default and stated to be without prejudice to their right to withdraw showed they had neither waived nor lost that right. Staughton J refused leave, on the basis that the first issue on construction was immaterial as the arbitrators were prima facie right on the withdrawal issue. He gave leave to appeal against his decision refusing leave to appeal from the award.

The Court of Appeal first dealt with the issue of whether that leave should have been given. The judge had accepted a threefold classification. In cases where the judge was himself pronouncing general guidelines, glossing or expanding on those already laid down, leave should be granted. In decisions in the exercise of discretion it should not. In the third case, where a substantial and arguable point of law arose, but the judge's view is that the arbitrators probably got it right what should he do? The judge felt he should refuse leave, in furtherance of the policy of finality embodied in the 1979 Act. However, that was to apply a general principle on which the Court of Appeal should be allowed to pronounce under the first head, so he gave leave. His decision to do so was approved by the Master of the Rolls. Arguments that such leave should normally be given where issues of general importance were raised, where the decision was of particular importance to the parties or where there was a conflict of judicial opinion were firmly rejected by the Master of the Rolls. Ackner LJ is less firm. Accepting the philosophy of the Act as favouring finality, he still would not confine leave to appeal, against refusal of leave to appeal from the award, to cases involving guidelines.

Judicial conflict on an important point of principle was an example of a situation which he thought should justify leave under s 1(6A). Fox LJ agrees with him. 'I would not . . . tie the granting of leave to appeal wholly to cases where the judge requires guidance as to principles relating to leave to appeal, though . . . that would be the normal case' is his conclusion (at 789 c).

On the substantive question of leave to appeal from the award, that should be refused if the judge thought the award correct, whatever the basis on which it was reached, and he should ignore the fact that the Court of Appeal might differ, because, in effect, 'appeal courts are like that'. Where a conflict of judicial opinion existed and the parties' rights would be substantially affected, leave should be given. These tests are common to all three judgments.

Applying these tests, the Master of the Rolls and Fox LJ concluded that on the timely withdrawal issue the arbitrators were probably correct, whatever was the true basis of the doctrine, so leave had been properly refused. Ackner LJ dissented on this. Three tests (1) determination of the point of law would substantially affect the rights of a party (2) it concerned a standard clause in a standard form and (3) the issue was not finally settled on the authorities had been advanced as reasons to give leave, all were common ground between the parties, and he added the fourth (4) the arbitrator was prima facie wrong on the point. On his analysis, leave should have been granted by reference to these tests.

There is a substantial body of opinion, acknowledging the desire of the House of Lords to give a firm lead and to ensure that everyone got quickly into a proper frame of mind vis-à-vis the 1979 Act, to the effect that the statement of guide-lines in *The Nema* is being shown by experience to have been a little hasty and over-sweeping. The difference of emphasis between the judgment in *The Antaios* manifests this slight unease, and Ackner LJ once more quotes Lord Denning in *The Rio Sun* (*Italmare Shipping Co v Ocean Tanker Co Inc* [1982] 1 All ER 517 at 521): 'Useful as guidelines often are, nevertheless it must be remembered they are only guidelines. They are not barriers'. Particular disquiet is felt amongst landlord and tenant practitioners, for there was no contribution from that area to the 1978 Report and the debates on the Bill, and the harshness of the promulgated criteria in their application to arbitrations on rent or value is keenly felt and somewhat resented. In any event, one can safely predict that the process of refining, if not redefining, the guidelines will continue, as it has in these 1983 cases, and as practitioners learn to fit their applications into the emerging pattern of pigeon-holes. It was predictable that there would need to be a familiarisation and settling in process following the 1979 Act. The pity is that a 'rush to judgment' by the House of Lords may have pre-empted the more usual progress through a series of Court of Appeal decisions then followed by a synthesis of opinions and firm pronouncement at the highest level.

Excessive delay

The problems of delay in the pursuit of arbitrations were not directly touched on by the 1979 reforms and still trouble the courts. Dilatoriness of the highest order is still apparent in the reported cases.

In *The Hannah Blumental (Paul Wilson & Co A/S v Partenreederei Hannah Blumenthal* [1983] 1 All ER 34) a ship was sold in September 1969, complaints were raised about it in 1972, and two arbitrators appointed in that year, although the third never was, and points of claim and defence were delivered in 1974. Desultory progress was made over discovery, and when the buyers proposed, in July 1980, that a hearing date be fixed, the sellers issued a writ for a declaration that the arbitration agreement had been discharged by repudiation, frustration or abandonment. The Commercial Court gave judgment in July 1981, the Court of Appeal upheld its judgment in favour of the sellers in March 1982 but the House of Lords found for the buyers in December 1982.

On the abandonment issue, Staughton J found no evidence to support the claim, the Court of Appeal upheld him on that point and so did the House of Lords, dismissing the sellers' cross-appeal. No contract to abandon could be found, whether by implied agreement or because the buyers' conduct led the sellers to a reasonable belief that the buyers had given up following which they had significantly altered their position. The inter-solicitor correspondence, though scanty, and intermittent, and evidence of other steps taken, prevented such a finding. Abandonment had been established in *The Splendid Sun (Andre & Cie SA v Marine Transocean Ltd* [1981] 2 All ER 993), but it was not shown here. Despite these rulings, abandonment will continue to be pleaded, as indeed it was in the next case to be discussed.

The issue of repudiation led to an examination of the Lords' own decision in *Bremer Vulkan Schiffbau und Maschinenfabrik v South India Shipping Corp* ([1981] 1 All ER 289). That case laid down principles which the trial judge and Court of Appeal in *The Hannah Blumenthal* clearly regretted, viz, that the parties must be treated as under a mutual obligation to keep the arbitration moving, and a party in breach of that obligation may not treat the other's failure as repudiatory. Lord Denning MR, in the Court of Appeal, had found that part of the *Bremer Vulkan* decision either obiter or wrong, Kerr LJ had found it part of the ratio, and Griffiths LJ, unhappy at the Lord's decision, had dissented from the result reached in the Court of Appeal but had agreed with Kerr LJ on this point. Lord Brandon (with whose speech Lord Keith of Kinkel concurred), Lord Roskill and Lord Brightman all declined to depart from the earlier decision although invited to do so, as did Lord Diplock whose speech in the earlier case had contained the formulation of the principle. It was said that it had been much criticised and had caused concern at home and abroad. The House nevertheless unanimously and firmly declined to reverse what it had decided two years before. Stress is laid on the fact that the mutual obligations extend beyond co-operation to maintain progress and involve several obligations to apply to the arbitrator if necessary to achieve movement. Nothing, it would seem, short of legislation will change this principle, although the unconverted lower judiciary may continue to try to distinguish it out of their way.

Frustration was the third issue raised. Staughton J and the majority of the Court of Appeal had found that a fair trial had become impossible, so bringing about frustration. Unanimously the House of Lords reversed them on this. It was not denied that a satisfactory and fair trial might no longer be possible. However, no independent act or event (not provided for in the contract) had rendered performance impossible or radically different from that contemplated when the contract was made, nor was there absence of fault of either party. Those two essential pre-requisites for frustration to be invoked not being established, the doctrine could not be applied. The formulation of mutual obligations in *Bremer Vulkan* showed that lack of fault could not be shown and on the facts there was neither an outside event nor extraneous change of circumstance, Lord Diplock acknowledges (at 51 (b) & (c)) the contrast with litigation where striking out under the court's inherent powers is a remedy for inordinate delay but is unmoved by it; Lord Roskill draws attention (at 54 h) to the 'drastic powers' in s 5 of the 1979 Act 'which can and no doubt will from time to time be properly used by arbitrators and umpires to avoid delay and to dispose of stale arbitrations'.

Perhaps this last hing shows a partial way forward, other than frontal assault by Parliament on the principles established in the *Bremer Vulkan* case and reaffirmed in *The Hannah Blumenthal*. Those who deplore the result will doubtless continued to lobby for such a change, to bring arbitration closer to litigation in its machinery for preventing the manifest injustice of stale litigation. Others will see in the process of invoking s 5 a means to terminate an unedifying saga of inaction or slumber; if neither party does so, however, this latest decision leaves them, arguably as they deserve, to face up to the severe consequences of their own quiescence or, regrettably perhaps, belatedly to turn on their lawyers for letting it happen!

Abandonment by inaction was raised in *The Leonidas D (Allied Marine Transport Ltd v Vale do Rio Doce Navegacao SA The Leonidas D* [1983] 3 All ER 737, Mustill J) where 5½ years elapsed between the appointment of arbitrators and delivery of the points of claim. The judge held that, once the arbitrator had been appointed, the statutory limitation period became irrelevant to the issue of abandonment. Abandonment by accord and satisfaction could come about, the mutual ending of the respective rights providing sufficient consideration for the contract. A party might only abandon a reference to particular arbitrators whilst preserving the right to pursue the claim before another tribunal, but that state of affairs must be shown to exist. On the facts, the claimant charterers had tacitly represented that they would pursue neither reference nor claim and the owners had accepted that tacit offer by their conduct. Furthermore, the owner's reaction to the charterer's silence in not preparing their case was a detriment sufficient to raise an estoppel against the charterers. The case contains a useful tabulation of the principles of abandonment (at 741) (including those derived from *The Hannah Blumenthal*) and a further plea (at 747) for legislative intervention to give judge, or arbitrator, discretionary powers to discuss a claim in an arbitration for want of prosecution because the 'jurisdiction at common law . . . is cumbersome, and in all but the clearest cases unpredictable and s 5 of the Arbitration Act is far from providing a complete solution'. The present writer, whilst not jibbing at the result, is a little worried at a contract brought about by tacit, ie uncommunicated offer and acceptance. Whatever happened to *Felthouse v Bindley* (1862) 11 CB (NS) 869?

Arbitration with a foreign element

Kuwait Minister of Public Works v Sir Frederick Snow & Partners (a firm) [1983] 2 All ER 754 held that an arbitration award in a foreign state which is a party to the New York Convention on the Recognition and Enforcement of Foreign

Arbitral Awards could be enforced in the United Kingdom. It was a 'Convention award' under s 3 of the 1975 Act, whether the award pre-dated or post-dated the foreign state's accession. Lengthy argument and much citation of English and foreign material preceded the Court of Appeal's judgment and both Kerr LJ (at 760 a and b) and Stephenson LJ (at 762 f and g) pointed out how readily and easily Parliament could have covered the point, as had been done in comparable statutes, including the Arbitration Act 1950. So, in March 1983, the enforceability of an award of £3½m, under a contract made in 1958, terminated in 1964 and referred to arbitration in 1966, which award was given in 1973 by an arbitrator appointed in 1972 was upheld, thanks to the UK having become party to the 1958 Convention in 1975 and Kuwait in 1978. As Kerr LJ remarks, 'The time-scale... is... not a good advertisement for the legal process of international arbitrations'. A short point, but an important one, has finally been authoritatively determined. In the context of economic activity in the Middle East it may have profound effect.

Reference has been made above to London's role as an arbitration forum for international disputes. A Greek company agreed with an Iranian Bank regarding land development in Iran, the contract to be governed by Iranian law. Neither party carried on business in England, nor had any other connection here. Yet they agreed to refer disputes to London arbitration under the ICC rules (the Rules on Conciliation and Arbitration of the International Chamber of Commerce in Paris). At issue in the litigation— *Bank Mellat v Hellinki Techniki SA* [1983] 3 All ER 428—was whether security for costs might be ordered. Substantial deposits had been paid to the ICC, under its Rules, to cover its expenses, and the Bank sought an order for security for costs, on the basis that the Greek company was not resident in England and would not be able to meet the Bank's costs if the Bank succeeded. Bingham J declined to order security and so, in the outcome, did the Court of Appeal.

Section 12(6) of the Arbitration Act 1950 gave the court the discretionary power to order security, and this was to be taken to be part of the applicable procedural law. The absence of connection of the parties with England, and the choice of arbitration rules, were identified as factors relevant to the discretion, and the exceptional nature of the court's powers, in the international legal context, was noted. The principle to be applied was that an order for costs in circumstances such as the present would be unusual. Something more than the fact of the arbitration taking place in London was called for, and scrutiny of the ICC Rules showed that such orders were not envisaged. That the party in question was a non-resident or of doubtful solvency (as some of the evidence suggested) were not good reasons to order security.

Those who are concerned, for very proper reasons, to maintain London as a flourishing centre for international arbitration will welcome this decision. The unique risk that orders for security of costs, a hazard unknown in other jurisdictions, could have come to rank with the previous allegedly too ready availability of appeal (which led to the 1979 Act, whatever its deficiencies may be, to counter a consequential loss of business), is not fanciful, so its avoidance will give satisfaction. An award of costs may still be enforceable under the New York Convention, moreover, where the relevant states were part to it. If the loser hasn't the money, no system will produce it, hence the popularity of security where it can be ordered.

The remaining five cases in the year under review cover separate aspects. *Rocco Guiseppe & Figli v Tradax Export SA* [1983] 3 All ER 598 dealt with an issue of increasing concern, namely the ability of arbitrators to award interest. Recently attention has been focussed on interest as an element in the award (see, for example, *Tehno-Impex v Gebr van Weelde Scheepvaartkantoor BV* [1981] 2 All ER 669) but the question raised in this case was interest on the sum awarded. Under s 20 of the Arbitration Act 1950, the award carries interest at that applicable to judgments. On the date of the award, that rate was 10% per annum. Later statutory instruments, under the Administration of Justice Act 1970, s 44, increased it after 20 months to 12½% and 7 months later to 15%. Such an increase is obviously material. Parker J was bound by the House of Lords' judgment (albeit by a majority) in *Timber Shipping Co SA v London and Overseas Freighters Ltd* [1971] 2 All ER 599 to the propositions that arbitrators can award no higher rate, although they may award that no interest shall be payable. That was not in issue. The wording of the successive orders was that each would apply to judgments entered after the coming into operation of the order, and that, the judge ruled, indicated that a fluctuating rate was not intended to attach to each judgment. Moreover, no order repealed the earlier order, so they operated in parallel, as it were, attaching irrevocably by reference to the date of each judgment. The same interpretation was to be afforded to arbitration awards. Alternative arguments based on the exact wording of s 20 and on an alleged inherent power also failed.

The injustice of the result is manifest, for it may give a substantial financial incentive to delay satisfaction of an award. This becomes even more marked in the commercial context which is a feature of most arbitration awards. It is, however, unlikely to be altered for arbitration awards alone, and there are different considerations once any proposed change is applied to judgments generally. The tasks of sheriffs and bailiffs would be more complicated for one thing. Wider issues of policy are involved. Nevertheless, where courts award interest on pre-judgment sums, fluctuating rates are often applied, and there is little logic in sticking to the present rigid rules for post-judgment sums. Whether Parliament will act remains to be seen, but no great pressure for change has manifest itself so far. Perhaps an easier solution would be to free arbitrators from the present constraints on what they may award.

Power to order inspections

A useful elucidation of the powers of the court, and of arbitrators, emerged in *The Vasso, Vasso (owners) v Vasso (cargo owners)* [1983] 3 All ER 211. The arbitrator had made an order for inspection of a ship at the instance of the cargo owners, in a salvage arbitration. Lloyd J held that this was a power exercisable by the arbitrator under s 12(1) of the 1950 Act, falling within the general words of the sub-section, and was not amongst those only exercisable by a High Court judge under s 12(6). There was, however, a measure of overlap between the two sets of powers. The objection that the cargo owners and ship owner may be treated as on one side with the salvor on the other did not impress the judge, and he pointed out that the owners of ship and cargo may also be in dispute. He queried whether he should even have entertained the application under s 2 of the 1979 Act for, whilst one party might desire a ruling and the arbitrator might consent, neither of the two conditions in the section were fulfilled. No saving of costs could be predicated, and the test of whether leave to appeal would have been granted under s 1(3)(b) was difficult because the particular issues would hardly have arisen in an appeal from an award. His rulings on the two issues were given despite these expressed misgivings.

Parties to arbitrations will derive considerable assistance from this decision. In rent-reviews, for example, refusal to permit inspections of the subject premises could be overcome by use of the powers, and the same will be true of many other types of arbitration far removed from salvage disputes.

Other decision

The relationship between arbitration and court proceedings arose both in *Westfal-Larsen & Co A/S v Ikerigi Compania Naviera SA, The Messiniaki Bergen* [1983] 1 All ER 382 and *Lloyd v Wright; Dawson v Wright* [1983] 2 All ER 969, but neither call for extended treatment. In *The Messiniaki Bergen* an election to arbitrate was sufficient to constitute an agreement to arbitrate, without the need for further agreement; the election was held to be in time on the constuction of the contract, although a similar ruling in the New York District Court did not, in the particular circumstances, give rise to a valid plea of res judicatea. Concurrent arbitration and court proceedings features in *Lloyd v Wright*. The former were held to have survived the commencement of the latter. An order for directions by the arbitrator was within his powers, and was to be complied with, notwithstanding that he could not make an effective award whilst the court was seised of the matter. Both judgments in the Court of Appeal restate this principle.

Extension of time limit for taking a step to common arbitration proceedings is possible under s 27 of the Arbitration Act 1950, to avoid undue hardship. Was a written claim such a step? 'Yes' said the Court of Appeal in *Jedranska Slobodna Plovidba v Oleagine SA, The Luka Botic* [1983] 3 All ER 602 at least if the parties had so agreed. The Centrocon arbitration claim in the charterparty had that effect, because of the way it linked the claim and the appointment of the arbitrator. In reaching this decision the court distinguished *The Oltenia, (Babanaft International Co SA v Avant Petroleum Inc* [1982] 3 All ER 244) which had dealt with a difference clause in a different form and in which the Court of Appeal had ruled the s 27 power inapplicable.

Conclusions

Arbitration flourishes: the oft-lauded expertise of English arbitrators, counsel, solicitors and commercial judges enables London to continue to compete with rival arbitration centres abroad. The protagonists of the 1979 reforms continue to assert that it has reversed any feared decline and has ended the abuse of appeal merely to delay payment (which was not wholly the case anyway—see *The Furness Bridge* [1979] 3 All ER 186). The process of elucidating the Act continues. There is no method of determining how freely the power to contract out of the new rights of appeal in most non-domestic contracts has been exercised, first because it is too early for that pattern to have emerged and secondly because collecting negative statistics is always a matter of uncertainty. There is no reason to challenge the strong arguments of the Commercial Court Committees 1978 Report that it was the denial of such freedom which most irked foreign 'consumers' of arbitration facilities, so that the unlitigated s 3 may be more significant in fact that the much rehearsed ss 1 and 2. Everyone is looking to Parliament to remedy the scandal of excessive delay, as the judicial road to reform is surely blocked. Not a vintage year, then 1983, but a busy one all the same.

Commercial Law

N E PALMER, BCL, MA
Barrister, Professor of Law, University of Reading

The past year has been a prolific one and 18 cases are summarised in the ensuing survey. Banking law has produced some interesting decisions, while the activities of bailees, both common law and statutory, errant and insolvent, have been well in evidence. One of the biggest events of 1983— Whitford J's decision in *Re American Greetings Corp's Application* and its endorsement by the Court of Appeal—has since been overtaken by the dismissal of the appeal to the House of Lords in January 1984, with ominous implications for the practice of 'character merchandising' in this country. We provide only a very brief account of the Court of Appeal's decision, reserving fuller analysis for the discussion of the House of Lords' reasoning in our 1984 issue.

1 Banking

(a) Letters of credit

Documentary credits continue to provide material for litigation. Quite apart from the specific questions which it raised, *Banque de l'Indochine et de Suez SA v J H Rayner (Mincing Lane) Ltd* [1983] 1 All ER 1137 suggests two aspects of contemporary practice which may give rise to difficulty. The first arises when a condition in the letter of credit breaks the cardinal rule (now embodied in art 8(a) of the Uniform Customs and Practice) that the parties should deal in documents, not in facts or goods. Such a breach occurred in this case, where the letter of credit required the vessel on which the goods were shipped to belong to a company which belonged to an International Shipping Conference: in other words, it required the existence of a particular state of fact. As Donaldson MR said, the better course would have been for the letter of credit to call for a specific document which was acceptable to the buyer and his bank, evidencing the fact that the vessel was owned by a conference member. In the event, this point caused little difficulty because Donaldson MR agreed with the trial judge (Parker J) that the alleged defect had been cured; but without this escape the evidential and other problems could have been substantial. A second possible source of contention is the use of phrases which are insufficiently defined and understood. The expression at issue in this case was 'payment under reserve', as used by a confirming bank which alleged that the documents presented were defective. Of course, such a payment will not normally be made unless, inter alia, the confirming bank is satisfied as to the creditworthiness of the party drawing on the letter of credit and as to the likely concurrence of the issuing bank and its customer. But even when made, its legal effect can be unclear. Does it render the money repayable on demand once the issuing bank refuses to ratify the payment on grounds which correspond (at least in part) with those which prompted the confirming bank to impose the 'reserve' condition? Or does it entitle the confirming bank to demand repayment only when there is additionally some proof by way of judgement (or some clear acceptance by the payee) that the appropriate defects were present?

In *Banque de l'Indochine*, the Court of Appeal opted squarely for the first solution. Donaldson MR interpreted the agreement to pay under reserve as requiring the seller to reimburse the confirming bank if the issuing bank refuses to reimburse the confirming bank for 'the same reasons' as those for which the confirming bank had declined to pay the seller unconditionally. He pointed out that if (as Parker J had accepted: see [1983] 1 All ER 468) the confirming bank were unable in a case of continued disagreement about the adequacy of the documents to demand repayment other than on the substantiation of the alleged defects in the documents by a suit brought against the beneficiary, a payment 'under reserve' would have no greater legal significance than simply eliminating the beneficiary's ability to claim that the money was irrecoverable as money paid under a mistake of law. Donaldson MR thought it improbable that a commodity merchant and a commercial bank would have had this abstruse and limited meaning in mind as the exclusive effect of their agreeing a payment under reserve.

Kerr LJ agreed broadly with Donaldson MR. It was unrealistic to regard the confirming bank as having agreed to become engaged in legal proceedings once the issuing bank rejected the documents, whether these might arise as proceedings against the beneficiary (to prove the validity of the confirming bank's objection to the documents) or as proceedings against the issuing bank (to prove the invalidity of the issuing bank's objection to the documents). The true construction of the agreement for payment under reserve, in this case at least, was that the beneficiary was bound to repay the confirming bank on demand once the issuing bank rejected the documents, whether the issuing bank did so of its own initiative or on the instructions of the buyer. However, Kerr LJ also thought (albeit without considering it necessary to decide the point) that a restriction on the right to demand repayment should be implied, limiting it to cases where the issuing bank's grounds of rejection included at least one ground on which the confirming bank had relied. The lack of a clear-cut definition on the degree of overlap, if any, which is necessary between the two sets of reasons for rejection is perhaps unfortunate. The *Banque de l'Indochine* case leaves it undecided whether there needs to be a complete correspondence between the grounds adopted by the confirming and issuing banks, or a partial correspondence or none at all. Donaldson MR appeared to favour the first view, Kerr LJ the second and Sir Sebag Shaw agreed with both.

Finally, the Court of Appeal held that the confirming bank had, in fact, been entitled to reject the seller's documents. There were two discrepancies justifying the rejection, viz the clausing of the bill of lading 'not portmarked, vessel not responsible for incorrect delivery. Any extra expense incurred in consequence to be borne by consignee' and, secondly, the fact that certain certificates relating to weight, quality and packing, and certificates relating to origin and three EUR/I certificates, could not be related to the remaining documents or to the letter of credit itself. Donaldson MR's judgment contains an extremely interesting analysis of the latter problem in particular. He accepted that the effect of the earlier decisions in *Rheincold v Hanslow* (1896) 12 TLR 422 and *Bank Melli Iran v Barclay's Bank (Dominion Colonial and*

Overseas) [1952] 2 Lloyd's Rep 367 was to require, not merely a relevant certificate which was 'not inconsistent' with the other documents, but one which is 'consistent *and only* consistent' with them in order to satisfy the letter of credit, but he held that this principle applied in its unqualified version only to cases where art 7 of the Uniform Customs and Practice (1974 revision) did not apply. Nevertheless the more permissive tenor of the UCP did not entitle the merchants to succeed in this case. Article 32(c), while permitting latitude in the 'description' of the relevant goods, did not permit an equivalent latitude in their identification. Here the identification was not, on the facts of the case, 'unequivocal'. The certificates *could* be taken to refer to the goods but did not necessarily do so; and that was not enough.

An ambiguity on the face of the letter of credit itself fell to be considered in the next case. *European Asian Bank AG v Punjab and Sind Bank* [1983] 2 All ER 508 arose as an appeal from a decision of Staughton J that the facts disclosed a triable issue which the defendants should be given unconditional leave to defend. The decision of the Court of Appeal, allowing the appeal and ordering judgment to be entered for the appellants (the plaintiffs in the proceedings), contains useful amplification of the functions of the judge in proceedings under RSC Ord 14, r 3(1), and of the nature of an appeal from such proceedings. This aspect of the case is discussed within the title Practice and Procedure p 276, below.

The facts are elaborate and most of the judgment of the Court of Appeal was concerned with the construction of voluminous correspondence passing between the appellant and respondent banks. In a nutshell, the appellants claimed to be negotiating bankers under a letter of credit issued by the respondents. As such, they argued that they were entitled to payment of some US$2,250,000, representing the price of goods bought by clients of the respondent bank and paid by the appellants (as a result of the letter of credit and other correspondence) to the sellers. The dispute arose because the buyers, an Indian company referred to as 'Jain', had claimed against their insurers when the goods were allegedly lost at sea *en route* from the sellers. The insurers repudiated liability on the ground of fraud; in their assertion the goods had never been shipped at all. The appellants accepted that there was prima facie evidence of fraud on the part of the sellers but no allegation of fraud, or complicity in fraud, was made against the appellants themselves. Jain obtained an injunction in the Indian courts restraining the respondent bank from paying under the letter of credit. Having failed to obtain payment from a third bank, ABN (who had been named in para 9 of the letter of credit as the party to whom negotiations under the credit were restricted), the appellants now sued for the amount they had paid to the sellers.

The case resolved itself into three broad areas of contention. First, the appellants contended that the letter of credit authorised negotiation by the appellants. If correct, this created, in their assertion, direct privity of contract between them and the respondent bank and entitled them to recover contractually the price which they had credited to the sellers' account. The appellants conceded that the credit was not unambiguous on this point, in so far as para 9 appeared to confine the authority to negotiate to ABN. But they pointed by way of counter-argument to para 6 of the same document, which stated that the credit should be 'divisionable (sic) and unrestricted for negotiation'. Thus, argued the appellants, we adopted a reasonable interpretation of an ambiguously-worded document as conferring permission to negotiate on us and were entitled to act on this interpretation. Reliance was placed upon *Ireland v Livingstone* [1861–1873] All ER Rep 585 and *Midland Bank Ltd v Seymour* [1955] 2 Lloyd's Rep 147. Goff LJ (delivering the judgment of the court) rejected this argument. In his view, some limitation must be placed on the principle that an offeree who relies on an objectively reasonable interpretation of the contractual document is entitled to enforce the contract as if it had been expressly concluded on the terms as he understood them. That limitation requires that the offeree should have acted reasonably in all the circumstances in relying on his interpretation of the document. When an ambiguity in his instructions is patent he may well be bound (given the facility of modern communications) to inquire further before proceeding. *Ireland v Livingstone* may itself have been distinguishable on the ground that it involved an agent, because an agent may understandably expect to be entitled to act on his instructions without more; whereas in no sense 'can a negotiating bank be regarded as an agent of an issuing bank'. But even if this distinction were without substance, the apparent conflict on the credit made it proper for the plaintiffs to inquire of the defendants, before acting on the credit, whether negotiation was restricted or unrestricted.

This aspect of the case is important to an understanding of the practical significance of the 'objective theory' of contract and thus to contract law in general. It suggests that the reasonableness of a particular interpretation of an ambiguous document is not sufficient by itself to create a contract on the interpreted terms if it was unreasonable for the interpreting party to 'go it alone' in conducting the interpretation exercise in the first place: cf *Centrovincial Estates Ltd v MIA Ltd* (1983) Times 8 March.

In the event, Goff LJ also held para 6 of the credit could be reconciled with para 9 without detracting from the restriction on negotiation contained in para 9. Paragraph 6, the kernel of the appellants' case, related only to the entitlement of the beneficiary's pre-sellers to draw on the credit and not to negotiation with the beneficiary (ie the seller in this case) himself.

Secondly, the respondents argued that the appellants were not negotiating bankers at all but merely agents for collection on behalf of the sellers and thus affected by the sellers' fraud in making the sale. Goff LJ held that this defence was insupportable on the facts of the case. In correspondence between the parties, almost everything which the appellants did 'was consistent only with their being in the process of negotiating the letter of credit or having negotiated it'. Even if, as the facts might suggest, they had originally been appointed agents for collection by the sellers, by the crucial and relevant time that payment fell due, and was claimed and refused, the appellants had negotiated the relevant documents in good faith.

Finally, the appellants succeeded on the issue of estoppel. Goff LJ agreed that the correspondence amounted to an unequivocal representation by the respondents to the appellants that the documents were in order and that the appellants were entitled to act as negotiating bankers under the credit. This representation carried an implied acknowledgement by the respondents that they were liable on the due date to pay the plaintiffs the sum due under the credit.

In upholding the estoppel, Goff LJ held that Staughton J had been wrong in attaching decisive importance to the 'misrepresentation' of the appellants, that they had already in fact negotiated the documents, as a ground for negativing this aspect of the claim. There was no conceivable way in which the respondents could have acted on this alleged misrepresentation because it was of no significance to them whether the negotiation had actually taken place or was in process. Further, Goff LJ rejected the assertion that there was a triable issue as to whether the respondent bank's communications had indicated only that the buyers ('Jain') had accepted the draft.

One last point of interest concerns the appellant's reliance, as part of their plea of estoppel, on art 8 of the UCP to show that the issuing bank must determine without delay on receipt of the documents whether it will sanction payment and must return them or hold them at the disposal of the remitting bank if payment is not to be made. This reinforced, in their view, the contention that an issuing bank which does not take the aforementioned steps is impliedly accepting responsibility for the payment. The point seems a persuasive one, but in the event Goff LJ offered no specific comment on it.

(b) Joint accounts and joinder of parties

The history behind the decision in *Catlin v Cyprus Finance Corp (London) Ltd* [1983] 1 All ER 809 was full of human interest, but the essential facts were straightforward. Mr and Mrs Catlin deposited funds in a joint deposit account with the defendant bank. They gave an express mandate that all orders for payment or transfer from the account were to be signed by both of them. The mandate was on a single form of application; it had both of their names at the top and they both signed it. Subsequently the Catlins separated and Mr Catlin instructed the bank to make certain transfers from the account. These instructions came in a series of letters signed by Mr Catlin, which had the names of his wife and himself at the top. Mrs Catlin did not know of these transfers and was found to have given her husband no actual authority to make them. She discovered the transactions later, by which time the amount on deposit had dwindled from some £21,000 to £897. She sued for a declaration that the debiting of the account was in breach of the bank's mandate, and claimed damages and interest.

Bingham J held that this was a clear and negligent breach of the bank's mandate and awarded Mrs Catlin £12,497 damages. In so doing, he rejected a defence based on *Brewer v Westminster Bank Ltd* [1952] 2 All ER 650 and declined to follow that decision. *Brewer* involved a non-negligent breach of mandate, but Bingham J conceded that, if correct, its ratio clearly governed the present case. He preferred, however, the solution adopted by Park J in *Jackson v White and Midland Bank Ltd* [1967] 2 Lloyd's Rep 68 and by Martin J in the Victorian case of *Arden v Bank of New South Wales* [1956] VLR 569, which had been advocated by Sir Arthur Goodhart in (1953) 68 LQR 446.

In *Brewer*, McNair J had held that the bank's undertaking not to pay or transfer funds without the signature of both account-holders was a single, joint obligation. It could not therefore be enforced by one of them unless the other (ie the account-holder who had wrongfully authorised release of the funds) were joined as a party to the action: either as a co-plaintiff or, if unwilling to join in the action, as a co-defendant. But in either event the claim fell to be determined as if both account-holders were plaintiffs; and it failed because the wrong-doer could not sue in respect of his own wrong.

In *Catlin*, Bingham J held that in order to make any sense at all of the bank's obligation not to honour instructions without the joint signature of the account-holders, that obligation must be construed as being owed severally to the account-holders, and thus as capable of enforcement by either of them whenever the bank wrongfully released funds to the other. He emphasised that the only purpose of requiring two signatures was to safeguard against one account-holder's acting detrimentally to the other, and that that safeguard would be worse than worthless if the rule for which the bank contended were upheld; for the innocent party could easily be misled into a false sense of security and thus refrain from taking more active steps to check the account.

It followed from this analysis that Mrs Catlin had been justified in omitting to join her husband as a defendant. The bank, however, had served a third-party notice on him, and judgment was entered for them in the third party proceedings. Bingham J held that Mr Catlin had practised a deceit on the bank and that this had been a significant, if not the sole, cause of their conduct.

The decision has the merit of fairness and should contribute significantly to the eradication of what was regarded as a regrettable aspect of our modern law of banking. An equivalent principle should presumably now apply in comparable cases such as those of joint bailment.

(c) Undue influence

In *National Westminster Bank plc v Morgan* [1983] 3 All ER 85, the Court of Appeal set aside a charge over the appellant's property in favour of the respondent bank on the ground that the bank had failed to rebut the presumption that the execution of the charge was procured by undue influence. The appellant's husband (who had since died) was in continual financial difficulties over the relevant period and had wished to re-finance the first mortgage over their house. The appellant signed the charge which enabled this to be done only after receiving the bank manager's assurance that it was solely 'to cover the house mortgage' and not to cover any business liability of her husband's. She signed the document at her home, having been visited there by the bank manager at her husband's request. Her husband was present but took no part in the discussion, being at the other end of the room, which was 'L-shaped'. Unfortunately the manager's assurance, although given in good faith, was incorrect. When the husband died shortly afterwards, the wife sought to have the charge set aside.

Dunn and Slade LJJ rejected the bank's contention that the doctrine of undue influence did not apply unless the transaction were 'manifestly disadvantageous' to the party alleged to have been influenced. In this case, the husband in fact owed no business debts at all to the bank when he died; his sole liability to them was under the new mortgage, so that the inaccurate assurance about the extent of the mortgage was, in one sense, immaterial. But the court, following *Lloyd's Bank Ltd v Bundy* [1974] 3 All ER 757 (in particular the judgement of Sachs LJ) and certain observations of Cotton LJ in *Allcard v Skinner* (1887) 36 ChD. 145, held that a relationship of confidence might be abused whether or not the consequence was financially disadvantageous to the victim. The principle was founded on public policy and existed (per Slade LJ) to mitigate the *risk* of an abuse of confidence rather than merely to avoid disadvantageous transactions. It followed that, if the present relationship were one which gave rise to a fiduciary duty on the bank, the bank could not resist the normal consequences of a breach of that duty simply by demonstrating that, in a narrow financial sense, the transaction was 'truly for the benefit of the wife'.

Further, the court held that the necessary relationship existed in this case and that the bank had failed to discharge its duty. The wife was treating the manager as a confidant and clearly relying on him to advise her whether to sign the charge. She was worried and vulnerable and had not personally invited the manager to visit her; but when he came, she made it plain that she did not want her husband to be involved in the discussion. Moreover, the arrangement to which she eventually agreed was undoubtedly considered beneficial to the bank. Accordingly, it would have been prudent and proper for the manager to advise her to seek independent legal advice. That was what other representatives of the bank had recommended when mortgages had been discussed on previous occasions.

The decision turned on its own, relatively special facts and both members of the Court of Appeal acknowledged that a presumption of undue influence does not arise merely from the relationship of banker and customer per se. But, as Slade LJ pointed out, when a bank assumes the mantle of adviser and should be aware that its customer is looking to it for protection, it can very easily come about that there is a conflict between duty and interest. Then the presumption of undue influence may, almost imperceptibly, arise. The judgment of Slade LJ also confirms in passing that there may be other ways of rebutting the presumption of undue influence than by recommending independent advice (see the statement of Lord Hailsham LC in *Inche Noriah v Shaik Alli Bin Omar* [1928] All ER Rep. 189, PC). But in this case, such a recommendation should have been given.

2 Bankruptcy

The sole case reported under this rubric in 1983, *Re a debtor (No 75N of 1982, Warrington), ex p the debtor v National Westminster Bank plc* [1983] 3 All ER 545, is of such general importance that any adviser concerned in bankruptcy proceedings should peruse the full report thoroughly. What follows is no more than a summary of the main propositions enunciated in the judgments of Sir Robert Megarry V-C and Warner J in the Chancery Division.

1. A debtor on whom a bankruptcy notice has been served and who chooses the third option given to him on the statutory form must, on a literal construction of the form, satisfy the court within ten days that he has a counterclaim, set-off or cross-demand which equals or exceeds the debt and which he could not have set up in the action in which the judgment was obtained. But if, within the 7 days there specified, the debtor files an appropriate affidavit under rr 137 and 138 of the Bankruptcy Rules 1952, the registrar must by r 139(2) extend the 10 day period of the notice if the application cannot (as is usually the case) be heard within that period; and no act of bankruptcy can be deemed to be committed under the notice till the application is determined.

2. It may be assumed that a debtor who, in response to a bankruptcy notice, makes an offer to secure or compound for the debt, is likewise entitled to have it decided by the court whether or not the creditor should accept the offer. Although, literally construed, the statutory form of bankruptcy notice requires an actual securing or compounding of the debt within the ten-day period to the satisfaction of the creditor (or his agent) or the court, a similar measure of respite to that under 1. above should be capable of being extended to the debtor via s 109(4) of the Bankruptcy Act 1914, although apparently only where the debtor invokes that provision within the ten day period of the notice: *Re a debtor (No 6864 of 1980, High Court), the debtor v Slater Walker Ltd* [1981] 2 All ER 987.

3. This right in the debtor to have the period extended cannot, however, deprive the creditor of the power to withdraw the bankruptcy notice without the debtor's consent. The creditor remains free to withdraw the notice if he chooses, thereby causing whatever right the debtor had to an adjudiciation of the merits of his offer by the court to lapse.

4. In seeking an order ex parte for substituted service of a bankruptcy notice, the applicant must be candid with the court, but this obligation of candour is limited to the disclosure of those facts within his knowledge which might tell in the debtor's favour. He is under no obligation to place before the court every fact which might reinforce his own case.

5. An application for substituted service can be made ex parte, so long as the application is made by motion and so long as any party affected by the resultant order could apply to set it aside. A motion can be made ex parte and the application ex parte in this case was one which the creditor was entitled to make. Rules 141 and 154 of the Bankruptcy Rules 1952 prevail in this respect over the provisions of rr 31 and 32 to the extent of any further incompatibility.

6. A debtor who wishes to invoke the third option in the bankruptcy notice in order to file an affidavit under rr 137 and 138 of the 1952 Rules must provide affirmative proof (a) that the cross-demand is genuine, is put forward in good faith and raises a triable issue or has a reasonable probability of success (the necessary degree of proof depends on the circumstances of the case); (b) that the cross-demand could not have been set up in the action in which the creditor's judgment was obtained; (c) that the cross-demand equals or exceeds the judgment debt.

7. Although, for this purpose, the cross-demand need be neither for a liquidated sum nor indeed for a monetary claim at all, it must be capable of quantification in monetary terms and must be quantified by the affidavit.

8. Section 1(1)(g) of the 1914 Act entitles a judgment creditor who is confronted with a cross-demand by the debtor to set up in opposition to it another claim of his own against the debtor which 'when added to the judgment debt, overtops the debtor's cross-demand'. The wording of the section cannot be construed, in its reference to a counterclaim, set off or cross-demand of the debtor, as meaning one which, if set up in an independent action, would itself be defeated by a counterclaim by the creditor. It must mean a cross-demand which has 'at least some chance of success'.

9. The language of the statutory bankruptcy forms is calculated to puzzle, perplex or mislead debtors and should be revised to bring those forms to the same standard as that which courts demand from those who complete them.

3 Carriers

(a) Carriage of goods by road and air

Two decisions reported in 1983 clarify significant aspects of the liability of the international carrier of goods by air. *Data Card Corp v Air Express International Corp* [1983] 2 All ER 639 involved a contract of carriage between the USA and England, governed by the unamended Warsaw Convention. A package weighing 659 kg and belonging to the first or second plaintiffs was damaged en route. It was one of a total consignment of 8 packages. Lloyd J in chambers ordered judgment against the first defendants for £6,623 plus interest, based on a sterling equivalent rate of £10.05p per kilogramme, under art 22(2) of the Convention. The judge ordered that the balance of damages be assessed by a judge of the Commercial Court. Before Bingham J, the defendants argued that the foregoing figure represented their total liability under art 22(2). The plaintiffs contended that the provision justified a higher award and they advanced two alternative constructions: either that the stated figure of limited damages per kilogramme (250 francs) applied to the weight of the whole consignment covered by the air waybill ('entire weight') or that that figure applied to the weight of the whole of those packages within the consignment covered by the waybill which had had their value affected by the damage to the particular package ('affected weight'). The defendants contended that only the weight of the actually damaged package should determine the damages payable. Article 22(2) itself does not state a concrete multiplier: it merely says that the carrier's liability is limited to 250 francs 'per kilogramme'. The question for Bingham J, therefore, was 'per kilogramme of what'?

The bulk of the plaintiffs' argument was directed to the first of their suggested alternatives ('entire weight'). They relied principally on various travaux préparatoires in the form of minutes of conferences up to and including the Warsaw Conference in 1929, and on other provisions in the Convention which, in their contention, could be explained only by reference to the fact that art 22(2) applied to the whole weight of the cargo. Bingham J, invoking the speech of Lord Wilberforce in *Fothergill v Monarch Airlines Ltd* [1980] 2 All ER 696, 703 rejected the invitation to rely on the travaux préparatoires because they did not afford a clear and indisputable indication as to what the legislative intention was on this question and, indeed, did not begin to offer a solution. The learned judge was likewise unconvinced by the plaintiffs' reliance upon arts 8(1) and 7 of the Convention: on art 8(1) because it suggested that cargo-weight was the only weight with which the Convention was concerned, and on art 7 because it would not have allowed a carrier to protect himself by insisting on separate waybills for each package unless it were assumed that this reduced his units of liability. He preferred the argument of the defendants, which in their contention had the appeal of commercial convenience, appeared to make better semantic sense of the wording of art 22(2) itself, and accorded more with common sense: why, for example, should the carrier's limit escalate in proportion to the number of undamaged packages in regard to which, so long as *they* arrived safely, the carrier owed no liability anyway? The defendants also argued that there were several reasons apart from that proposed by the plaintiffs why a carrier might wish to issue separate air waybills. Bingham J conceded that it was odd that the carrier's limit should be calculated by reference to the weight of a package which need not be specified in the waybill, but thought that this would normally be calculated by subtraction. He considered it unlikely that the authors of the Convention had intended that a carrier should be able to limit his damages by reference to package-weight only by the costly and time-consuming procedure of separate waybills. Bingham J was not persuaded to the contrary view, moreover, by certain dicta in the Superior Court of the District of Columbia, Small Claims Branch, in *Norwood v American Airlines Inc* 1980 US Av R 1854.

So far as concerned the 'affected weight' argument, Bingham J concluded that this was without authority and 'quite unarguable'. It was, admittedly, the solution adopted in the Hague Amendment, but that had no significance whatever in the present case. He accordingly held that the 'package weight' measure was the full sum of the defendants' liability under art 22(2) and that no further damages were payable by them.

In *American Express Corp v British Airways Board* [1983] 1 All ER 557 the defendant airline were sub-bailees for reward of a package of travellers cheques which the plaintiff had despatched by post. One of their loaders stole the package and its contents were never recovered. The defendants claimed an immunity from liability by virtue of s 29(1) and (3) of the Post Office Act 1969. The plaintiffs argued that this immunity was ineffective in the present proceedings, since their claim was (i) for breach of bailment and (ii) to enforce a statutory liability created by art 18 of the amended Warsaw Convention. The relevant provisions of the Post Office Act 1969 safeguarded the defend-ants only against proceedings 'in tort', and each of the foregoing heads of claim was, in the plaintiffs' submission, an independent cause of action unaffected by any such immunity.

Lloyd J rejected both contentions, holding that the 1969 Act applied both to liability in bailment and to liability under the amended Convention. So far as concerned the bailment claim, he appeared to accept that bailments are transactions sui generis and can generate a cause of action which is juridically distinct from contract or tort. He nevertheless concluded that to permit the avoidance of the 1969 Act by the simple expedient of suing in bailment would create an absurdity which Parliament could not conceivably have intended. It would mean that s 29(1) failed to protect the Post Office and its delegates against a more severe form of liability (viz, that in bailment, because the bailee carries the burden of proof) while safeguarding it against a less severe form of liability (viz, that in conversion or negligence, where the burden of proof is on the claimant). The result for which the plaintiffs contended would also suggest an absurdity in relation to s 30 of the 1969 Act which replaces the statutory immunity by a limited liability in the case of inland registered packets. It would be curious if this were complemented by a total liability in the case of all other postal packets. (Indeed, the plaintiffs' argument may have meant that even this limited liability could be disregarded by a plaintiff who sued in bailment.) In rejecting this argument, Lloyd J relied on a dictum of Geoffrey Lane LJ in *Harold Stephen & Co Ltd v Post Office* [1978] 1 All ER 939, 944 and the decision in *Triefus & Co Ltd v Post Office* [1957] 2 All ER 387.

Lloyd J's arguments derived from presumed Parliamentary intention and legislative common sense are challenging and persuasive, but they do not, with respect, appear to constitute a conclusive answer to the argument on this point. It may perhaps be acceptable to apply the Act when bailment liability corresponds exactly with an acknowledged liability in tort. But in this case the source of the claim (a theft by the bailees' employee) could arguably be characterised as peculiar to bailment and without complement in the general law of tort. To accept that the Act is inapplicable to liabilities which can arise only from the fact of the bailment relation could therefore leave the Act a considerable area of wrongdoing on which to bite, without disfiguring its phraseology or blurring the independent quality of different juridical relations. It is worth noting the comment of Samuel on this case in (1983) 99 LQR 524. Samuel suggests, inter alia, that if 'restitution' is not covered by 'tort' in a statute (as follows from *Universe Tankships Inc of Monrovia v ITF* [1982] 2 All ER 67, see also *Basildon UDC v Lesser* (1984) Times 15 February) 'then neither should bailment'.

Lloyd J's reasons for rejecting the plaintiffs' second argument were broadly similar. He observed that breach of statutory duty is generally equated with tort, and that this assimilation applies whether or not the breach itself can be equated with any particular tort (cf the preceding paragraph). In his view, the phrase 'proceedings in tort' was used in the 1969 Act in the more general sense of including a breach of statutory duty if the remedy for the breach could legitimately be described as 'tortious in character'.

(b) International carriage of goods by road: the CMR

Worldwide Carriers Ltd v Ardtran International Ltd [1983] 1 All ER 692 is an important case on the commencement of limitation periods under art 32 of the Geneva Convention on the International Road Carriage of Goods, the Schedule to the Carriage of Goods by Road Act 1965. Brass-plated steelcord was consigned by road from Lens in France to Wrexham. The first defendant carriers sub-contracted the Lens-Zeebrugge section of the journey to the third defendant carriers, who in turn sub-sub-contracted it to the second defendant carriers. While the steelcord was in the second defendants' possession, an accident occurred which resulted in its exposure to the elements and ultimate deterioration. The Belgian surveyor's report confirmed the consignment as a total loss with no value other than as scrap.

The relevant contracts of carriage were formed, and the misadventure occurred, in June 1979, but the consignors' writ against all three carriers was not issued until March 1981. In the interim, in July 1979, the consignors had submitted a written claim against the first defendants, which had been referred by them in a telex to the third defendants, and in a letter enclosing a copy of the telex from the third defendants to the second defendants. It therefore came about that, within a week of the consignors' written claim to the first defendants, the second defendants were aware of that claim, but not as the result of any direct notification to them by the consignors. There were also, about 11 months later, some inconclusive negotiations between the consignor and the first defendants for an extension of the statutory limitation period, of which the second defendants became similarly aware.

Parker J, on a summons heard in chambers, held that the action against the second defendants was in these circumstances statute-barred. In his view, art 32(1)(b) applied to this claim since it was to be regarded as a claim for 'total loss'. The learned judge was assisted in this conclusion by art 20(1), which provides that where goods have not been delivered within 30 days of the agreed time limit or (failing an agreed time limit) within 60 days from the time when the carrier took over the goods, the fact of non-delivery shall be 'conclusive evidence of the loss of the goods' and shall entitle a claimant to 'thereupon treat them as lost'. Accordingly, the general limitation period of one year prescribed by art 32 began to run from 'the thirtieth day after the expiry of the agreed time limit [here there appeared to be none] or from the sixtieth day from the date on which the roads were taken over by the carrier': art 32(1)(b). On this computation, the plaintiffs were too late in commencing their action, since the limitation period would have begun to run at around early to mid-September 1979. Alternatively, Parker J held that, if art 32(1)(b) were inapplicable, this was a claim falling within the phrase 'in all other cases' as employed in art 32(1)(c), which dictated a commencement of the limitation period 'on the expiry of a period of three months after the making of the contract of carriage'. On this analysis, equally, the plaintiffs' action was out of time. Parker J derived support from a decision of the Paris Tribunal de Commerce on the combined effect of art 20(1) and 32(1)(b) and noted the omission of any consideration of art 20(1) from Mocatta J's judgment in *Moto Vespa v MAT (Britania Express) Ltd* [1979] 1 Lloyd's Rep 175. With regard to art 32(1)(c), he observed that the opening words of Article 32 'plainly show that [*Article 32*] was intended to be comprehensive and to cover all claims arising under CMR'.

These conclusions were accompanied by a rejection of an argument constructed by the plaintiffs on art 32(1)(a). Broadly, the plaintiffs contended that the facts disclosed a case of 'damage', thereby bringing their claim prima facie within art 32(1)(a). Accordingly, the commencement date specified in that article was the only possible appropriate one. If, for some other reason, that date were inapplicable, there could therefore be no commencement of the period and hence no effective period of limitation. But there was, in the plaintiffs argument, some other reason why art 32(1)(a) could not apply to their claim. That reason was the stipulation in art 32(1)(a) of the time of 'delivery' as the commencement date; and here there was no delivery. A case like this, where there was damage but no delivery, therefore fell in the plaintiffs' argument through the net of art 32 altogether, for on this construction the only possible applicable alternative provision was art 32(1)(c), and this was ruled out by the fact that it applied only in 'all other cases', ie in cases outside art 32(1)(a) and (b).

This analysis was principally refuted by Parker J's conclusion that the claim related to 'total loss' and not to 'damage'. But the learned judge went on to suggest (without deciding the point) that even in certain cases which did fall prima facie within art 32(1)(a) as instances of 'damage', an effective limitation period might be defined by reference to art 12(1) and (2) and 13(c). Broadly, these constructed a notional 'delivery' in cases where the consignor required the goods to be returned to him. If, therefore, a consignor, on hearing of the damage to his goods, required a return of the goods to him, he would be effectively changing the identity of the consignee and the place of delivery; and the occurrence of such substituted 'delivery' would provide a starting point for the operation of art 32(1)(a). As Parker J tentatively observed, there was some evidence from the documents that this may have been the position in the present case.

The plaintiffs in *Worldwide Carriers* advanced a further argument against the defence that the limitation period had expired. They contended that, even if art 32(1) applied so as to set the clock ticking, that had been arrested by the issue of a 'written claim' against the second defendants within the meaning of art 32(2). That provision operates to suspend the period of limitation until the rejection of the claim by the carrier against whom the claim is issued and the return of the documents by him. Such suspension had taken effect, according to the plaintiffs, by the issue of a written claim by them to the defendant carriers or, alternatively, by the second defendants' admitted knowledge of that claim, via the first and third defendants who notified them of it. Both aspects of the argument were firmly rejected by Parker J. He outlined some of the absurdities of permitting the delivery of a written claim against one of a succession of carriers to deprive other carriers from the benefit of the limitation period when those others had no knowledge whatever of the claim in the first place, and where the carrier against whom the claim was issued may have failed to reject for a number of reasons wholly unassociated with the position of any other carrier (for example, for the reason that he was obviously liable). In Parker J's view there was 'no basis' for such a construction of art 32(2): there must be a written claim by the consignor or other 'goods interest' directly against the relevant carrier in order to suspend the limitation period. Likewise, the mere indirect knowledge by one carrier of a written claim against an adjoining carrier will not suffice. Whereas art 32(2) 'does not require any particular formality', it 'does require a written claim of some sort'. This written claim cannot be synthesised from a claim by one carrier against another, or from the particular defendant carrier's knowledge of a claim by the goods owner against another carrier: 'it must be clear that the claim is a claim by the goods owners'.

Parker J's conclusions appear, with respect, to be entirely appropriate. The discovery of loopholes in art 32(1), the dilution of the identity of a written claim in art 32(2), and the temptation to aggregate succeeding carriers for purposes related to a goods-owners' claim, are to be resisted in so far as this is justifiable within the text of the Convention; and in this case there was ample justification. Among more general features of interest in the judgement are the citation and endorsement of three continental authorities and some useful guidance from Parker J as to the circumstances in which a case such as the present can properly be disposed of without the necessity for a trial.

(c) *Air carriers and personal injury*

The litigation in *Goldman v Thai Airways International Ltd* [1983] 3 All ER 693, which attracted much public attention when it was commenced, has now been before the Court of Appeal. The airline's appeal against full liability for the plaintiff's injury was allowed, the court holding that the plaintiff had failed to displace the limitation of liability imposed by art 22(1) of the amended Warsaw Convention. The decision centred partially on the meaning of the word 'recklessly' in art 25, a provision which forfeits the air carrier's general limitation of liability in certain narrow circumstances indicating a high degree of culpability. The Court held that a plaintiff invoking art 25 must affirmatively establish three things: first that the damage which he suffered resulted from an act or omission of the carrier; secondly, that the carrier either intended by the act or omission to cause damage or was aware that damage would probably result, but had nevertheless acted or abstained from action regardless of that probability; and thirdly, that the damage of which the plaintiff complains is of a kind which was known to be a probable result of the act or omission. The test of recklessness was subjective insofar as the wrongdoer's responsibility could not be increased by treating him as having knowledge which he ought objectively to have possessed but did not in fact possess. Likewise, the nature of the risk involved was relevant. In the case, a pilot who failed to illuminate the 'fasten seat belts' sign when entering an area for which moderate clear air turbulence had been forecast was held not to have acted recklessly, despite the fact that the airline's operations manual contained instructions for the sign to be lit whenever turbulence was being experienced or was expected. Such instructions would not necessarily be interpreted as requiring the pilot to activate the sign when entering clear air turbulence and there was nothing to show that the pilot knew that damage would probably result from failing to do so. It followed that the plaintiff, who had suffered serious injury to the lumbar region of his spine when severe clear air turbulence was encountered, was held entitled to recover only the limited quantum of £11,799 under art 22(1) of the amended Convention and not the full quantum of c £42,000 which he had claimed as damages at large.

4 Conversion

Last year's Review (All ER Rev 1983, pp 106–107) contained an interesting discussion of the forms of damages which might be awarded against a bailee who had wrongfully detained goods, the deprivation of which did not cause any identifiable pecuniary loss to the bailor. In the result, the amount awarded in *Brandeis Goldschmidt & Co Ltd v Western Transport Ltd* [1982] 1 All ER 28 was purely nominal. *Hillesden Securities Ltd v Ryjack Ltd* [1983] 2 All ER 184 involved a somewhat different form of damages, namely the amount which it would have cost a converter of goods to hire equivalent goods over the period of his detention. This species of compensation had been acknowledged as legitimate by the Court of Appeal in an action for detinue in *Strand Electric and Engineering Co Ltd v Brisford Entertainments Ltd* [1952] 1 All ER 796, although not without some divergence between Denning LJ and the other members of the court as to the precise limits of the principle. In the *Hillesden Securities* case there was no assault on the validity of the *Strand Electric* level of damages, but considerable dispute as to the legitimacy and manner of its application to the instant facts.

The lessee of a Rolls-Royce sold it without authority in September 1980. The purchaser was either the second defendant Edwards or the first defendants Ryjack (a company of which Edwards was a director and shareholder). Eventually Edwards admitted liability for conversion and contested only the issue of damages, so the exact identity of the original converter was for this purpose immaterial. The owner traced the vehicle and his solicitors made verbal demands for its redelivery but without success, and in July 1981 he assigned his rights to the plaintiff finance company. They immediately made a demand for the car's return and, when this proved unavailing, commenced an action for conversion in August 1981. In March 1982

Edwards sold his shares in Ryjack and ceased his connection with it. Ryjack retained the car until December 1982 when it was returned to the finance company. Only Edwards appeared in the present proceedings.

In response to the plaintiff's claim for the amount which it would have cost Edwards to hire an equivalent car from September 1980 to December 1982 (viz £13,282) Edwards argued that since the abolition of detinue such a measure was recoverable only under s 3 of the Torts (Interference with Goods) Act 1977, and s 3 was inapplicable. That section, by confining itself to 'proceedings for wrongful interference against a person who is in possession or in control of the goods' could not govern a defendant who (like Edwards) had ceased to be in possession or control at some time before judgment. Therefore, Edwards argued, his liability was limited to the common law level of damages for conversion, which was the value of the car at the date of conversion and interest thereafter. It was agreed that the value of the car in September 1980 was £7,500; so the difference was substantial. Parker J rejected this defence and awarded damages against both defendants for £13,282 with interest.

In the learned judge's view, the notion that a converter could avoid the assessment of his damages under s 3 (and thus the payment of 'hire charges') by disposing of the goods before judgment was wholly misconceived. It would enable the converter, who had enjoyed the use of the goods over a long period, to avoid damages quantified under the *Strand Electric* principle completely, merely by the expedient of returning the goods to the owner shortly before judgment, or indeed by disposing of them to a third party. Parker J pointed to the word 'proceedings' in s 3(1) and concluded that the section applied to any defendant who was in possession or control of the goods 'when the proceedings were launched'. It made no difference that, in a case such as this, an order for delivery up could not be made, for s 3(1) provides that the relief there specified may be given 'so far as appropriate'.

Nor was Parker J persuaded by Edwards' conservative definition of the damages payable by a converter of goods at common law. He held that the *Strand Electric* principle was not limited to cases of detinue but applied equally to conversion, and he pointed out that consequential damages are always recoverable in an action against a converter if not too remote: even at common law the plaintiff is not restricted to recovering the full value of the goods alone.

It followed in this case that Edwards was liable for the putative cost of hiring the Rolls-Royce for the whole of the period during which the car was in his or Ryjack's control. He could not reduce this amount by relying on his abdication of control over the car in March 1982 because that simply involved his putting it out of his power to return the car—an insufficient defence. In any event, he might alternatively have been liable to pay damages for conversion based on the value of the car at that time.

The decision clarifies an important point on the interpretation of the 1977 Act and contains a useful modern restatement of the principle adopted by the majority in *Strand Electric*. One further point of interest is Parker J's apparent acceptance of the plaintiffs' argument that, although the Act abolishes detinue, s 3 'preserves the remedies for what previously would have constituted detinue'. This appears to support the dictum of Sir Robert Megarry V-C in *Howard Perry Ltd v British Railways Board* [1980] 2 All ER 579 that every case of detinue is now a case of conversion. But, even if this is so, does it necessarily mean that, where a disparity would formerly have existed between the measure of damages recoverable in detinue and those in conversion, the former measure can continue to apply: and if so, when?

The issue of damages for conversion under the 1977 Act also received a brief passing reference from Bush LJ in the second case on conversion, *Chubb Cash Ltd v John Crilley & Son* [1983] 2 All ER 294. The learned Lord Justice observed that the Act, while abolishing detinue, 'did not interfere with the common law rules relating to damages for conversion'.

The principal significance of this case lies in the gloss which it recognises on the decisions in *Wickham Holdings Ltd v Brook House Motors Ltd* [1967] 1 All ER 117 and *Belvoir Finance Co Ltd v Stapleton* [1970] 3 All ER 664. Manufacturers of cash registers leased one on hire purchase to a firm, repayment to be made over 60 months. Shortly afterwards, the manufacturers assigned the instalments to Barclay Masterloan on terms that, if the purchaser defaulted on payment of an instalment, the manufacturers should pay to Barclay Masterloan the difference between the amount paid to the manufacturers in consideration for the assignment and the amount of any instalments already paid by the lessee to the assignees. The manufacturers retained property in the machine.

The defendants were bailiffs who took possession of the register pursuant to a distraint warrant, relying on an assurance by the lessee that it was his. It was sold at public auction for £178.25. In the manufacturers' action for conversion, it was claimed that the proper measure of damages was (a) the amount outstanding under the hire purchase agreement or (b) the amount which the manufacturers were obliged to repay to Barclay Masterloan under the assignment. These amounts were c £1,200 and c £952 respectively. The trial judge awarded damages for the latter amount, rejecting the bailiffs' contention that the proper measure of damages was the market value of the goods, ie £178.25. The bailiffs appealed and the Court of Appeal upheld them, substituting the sale price of the goods for the plaintiffs' indebtedness under the assignment as the true measure of damages.

The Court of Appeal appeared to discern no injustice in this result. Bush LJ cited the words of Greer LJ in *JE Hall Ltd v Barclay* [1937] 3 All ER 620 that 'Where you are dealing with goods which can be readily bought in the market, a man whose rights have been interfered with is never entitled to more than what he would have to pay to buy a similar article in the market'. He then took the proposition a stage further and, in answer to the plaintiffs' assertion that without the conversion they would have exercised their right to repossess the machine, renewed the case and sold it for c £900, he remarked that the plaintiffs 'could have mitigated their damage by purchasing a secondhand register and done the same with that, purchasing it, that is to say, in the market'.

The central issue of the case lies in the Court of Appeal's rejection of two arguments relied on by the plaintiffs. First, they maintained that the decisions in *Wickham Holdings Ltd v Brooke House Motors Ltd* and *Belvoir Finance Co Ltd v Stapleton* entitled them to the amount due under the hire-purchase agreement; or, putting it more controversially, to the value of their 'interest' in the goods. These decisions were summarily distinguished on the ground that the amounts outstanding under the agreements there were less than the value of the goods. In the words of Fox LJ:

'The cases are not authorities for the proposition that the hire-purchase company can recover the value of the chattel at the date of conversion or the outstanding instalments, whichever is the greater. ...I see no reason for displacing [*the ordinary measure of damages based on the value of the chattel*] here... (T)he public auction... is prima facie good evidence of the value of the chattel on 11 September 1979 and there is nothing to indicate that its condition on 11 September was any different from its condition on 30 July.'

Nor, added Fox LJ, was there any evidence that the market itself had varied between these two dates. A similar view was taken by Bush LJ.

The second argument asserted that the plaintiffs should be entitled to recover the lesser amount outstanding under the agreement with Barclay Masterloan, or indeed the unsatisfied hire-purchase debt, as consequential loss flowing from the conversion. The Court of Appeal found this argument equally objectionable. Whether asserted in relation to the hire-purchase debt or in relation to the Barclay Masterloan agreement, it would make the defendants (who were 'inadvertent' converters) guarantors of the relevant debt to the plaintiffs. Such damage, in Bush LJ's words, 'does not... flow from the conversion, but flows from the failure of the debtor to perform his obligations under the agreement'; cf *Millar v Candy* (1981) 58 FLR 145 (Fed Ct of Aus). It is tempting to conjecture whether a different result might follow where the conversion is 'deliberate' and the converter can be shown to have foreseen the owner's resultant loss. Arguably if the question is one of pure causation, the defendant's state of mind is irrelevant.

The limitation placed on the *Wickham Holdings* formula (no recognition of which appears explicitly in *Wickham Holdings* itself or in *Belvoir Finance*) will, it is suggested, cause further debate. At first sight it appears asymmetrical, if not illogical, to allow the quantum of the hire-purchase debt to count as the lessor's damages only when this amount is lower than the market value of the goods. But if the court in *Wickham Holdings* was, in effect, sanctioning an assessment of the lessor's damages according to his surviving property interest (or, correspondingly, was recognising a complementary and deductible property interest in the lessee), it could be argued that no contract which increases the profitability of the goods purely to the lessor, and in a manner not related to their market value as 'property', should be relevant to the valuation of his interest in them. Such losses fall to be awarded, if at all, only as consequential loss. Thus far, the market value of the goods and not the expected benefit of any associated contract (even the hire purchase contract) might appear the preferable measure in a case like *Chubb*. However, the lessor's proprietary interest does not appear, by inference from *Wickham Holdings*, to equate with the whole value of the goods themselves but merely with the unpaid proportion of the hire purchase debt. Should not the market value which he recovers from the converter therefore be diminished pro rata, according to the proportion which the whole of the original hire-purchase debt bears to the amount left outstanding at the time of the conversion? Further, if (as in *Chubb*) the full market value is awarded, what should the lessee recover in later proceedings against the same converter? Presumably this may be a proper case for the application of ss 7 and 8 of the Torts (Interference with Goods) Act 1977.

These are merely questions and are undoubtedly open to challenge. But if they have substance, it might then be regarded as irrational to decline to apply a similar proportional exercise in cases where the market value actually exceeds the outstanding debt.

5 Insurance

(a) The position of sub-contractors under a contractors' all risks policy

Petrofina (UK) Ltd v Magnaload Ltd [1983] 3 All ER 35, is a case where one of the principles of the law of bailment (viz the bailee's ability to recover the full value of the bailed goods on an appropriately-termed insurance policy) was applied by analogy to the position of a subsidiary contractor under a building contract, thereby entitling the subsidiary contractor to insure the entire contract works and not merely those parts of the works in which he had a proprietary interest or in respect of which he might be liable. Lloyd J considered that the position of a sub-contractor in relation to contract works as a whole is sufficiently similar to that of a bailee in relation to goods bailed to justify the conclusion, by analogy, that the sub-contractor is entitled to insure the entire contract works, and in the event of a loss to recover the full value of those works in his own name.

Lloyd J justified this conclusion partly by examining the traditional reasons for the parent principle in cases of bailment and considering whether these reasons justified an equivalent rule in favour of the sub-contractor. One reason was historical: the bailee could traditionally sue in trover and the right to recover insurance moneys was, for present purposes, sufficiently comparable to the right of action acknowledged by cases like *The Winkfield* [1902] P 42. Another reason was the existence in the bailee of a 'general responsibility' for the goods; this went beyond mere liability to the bailor but was sufficient to entitle him to insure. Neither of these justifications was, in Lloyd J's opinion, sufficient to sustain a corresponding privilege in the non-possessing sub-contractor. But a third reason, that of commercial convenience, did justify the analogy. In this regard, Lloyd J drew attention to the speech of Lord Pearce in *Hepburn v A Tomlinson (Hauliers) Ltd* [1966] 1 All ER 418 at 431, which had recognised the right of insurance as applying to bailees, mortgagees 'or others in analogous positions' and had remarked that any contrary principle would be both commercially inconvenient and offensive to common sense. *Hepburn* was a case of bailment by way of carriage, and Lloyd J observed that the Form J insurance policy involved in that case was indistinguishable on its wording from the present contractors' all risks policy, the whole of the wording of s 1 of which was appropriate to property and not merely to liability. In the learned judge's view, the arguments adopted in *Hepburn* apply with equal force to 'a building or engineering contract where numerous different contractors may be engaged'. The policy should therefore cover every contractor in respect of loss or damage to the whole of the contract works, and should not be limited to each contractor's own property or to his own liability for the property of others. Lloyd J felt that such a principle also accorded with the convenience of insurers. It was supported by a decision of the Supreme Court of Canada, *Commonwealth Construction Co Ltd v Imperial Oil Co Ltd* (1976) 69 DLR (3d) 558.

The result in this case was to debar the insurers of the contract works from exercising a right of subrogation against the first and second defendants, who were sub-sub-contractors and sub-sub-sub-contractors respectively, and who were assumed for the purposes of the case to have been liable for certain damage to the contract works. The first and second defendants were within the expression 'sub-contractors' in the policy; that policy entitled them to recover as insurers for damage in respect of the entire contract works; they had a legitimate insurable interest in respect of those entire works (which was not, incidentally, rendered illegal by s 3 of the Life Assurance Act 1774); and the doctrine in *Simpson & Co v Thompson, Burrell* (1877) 3 App Cas 279 accordingly applied. Lloyd J acknowleged, of course, that any insurance monies recovered by the sub-contractor in excess of his own property interest or personal liability would be held by him on trust for the other interested parties.

Two final points should be made. First, the Canadian case (cited earlier) had held that *Simpson & Co v Thompson, Burrell* was applicable not only where there is a true case of joint insurance (where the interests of the various insureds are inseparably connected) but also where the insurance is 'several', provided that the different interests were 'pervasive' and each 'relates to the entire property, albeit from different angles'. Lloyd J expressed agreement with this view, notwithstanding earlier reservations which he had expressed about the application of *Simpson & Co v Thompson Burrell* to a case where bailor and bailee are co-insured and the bailee's insurance is in respect of goods rather than in respect of his mere liability for them: see *The Yasin* [1979] 2 Lloyd's Rep 45.

Secondly, it should be recalled that s 8 of the Torts (Interference with Goods) Act 1977 has effectively abolished the bailee's right to sue for extra-compensatory damages in tort under the principle of *The Winkfield*. Does the existence of and necessity for such legislation weaken Lloyd J's analogy, or suggest a comparable need in the case of the bailee's or sub-contractor's right to recover extra-compensatory insurance monies? It is submitted not, because commercial convenience favours that very right, as Lloyd J remarked. But it seems strange that, if this view is correct, similar considerations of expediency were not considered to operate with comparable force in favour of the preservation of *The Winkfield* principle itself.

(b) Permitted users and the Motor Insurers' Bureau

Section 143(1) of the Road Traffic Act 1972 provides that it is not lawful for a person to use, or cause or permit another to use, a motor vehicle on a road unless a policy of insurance is in force in relation to such use which complies with that Part of the Act. *Cooper v Motor Insurers' Bureau* [1983] 1 All ER 253, a decision of Barry Chedlow QC sitting as a Deputy Judge of the High Court, has decided that this provision does not require insurance against the policy holder's liability to a permitted driver for injuries sustained by that permitted driver in the course of using the vehicle. Accordingly, the Motor Insurers' Bureau were not required by virtue of the Motor Insurers' Bureau (Compensation of Victims and Uninsured Drivers) Agreement 1972, to satisfy the permitted driver's judgment against the owner who had permitted him to use it.

(c) Insurance and the conflict of laws

See Conflict of Laws, p 86 below.

6 Mareva injunctions

See Company Law, p 78 and Practice and Procedure, p 262, below.

7 Monopolies and mergers

R v Secretary of State for Trade, ex p Anderson Strathclyde [1983] 2 All ER 233 concerned the extent of the Secretary of State's powers under Part V of the Fair Trading Act 1973 to decide whether a takeover bid should be approved. Dunn LJ and McCullough J, sitting in the Queen's Bench Division, held that the wording of ss 73(2) and 73(3) of the Act conferred on the minster 'a complete discretion whether to make any order [*under Sched 8 to the Act*] or whether to make no order at all'. Dunn LJ considered that the argument to the contrary, whereby the applicants had contended that the minister was bound to follow a majority decision of the Monopolies and Mergers Commission which concluded that a merger may be expected to operate against the public interest and which specified the expected adverse effects, was inconsistent with other provisions in the Act: with s 82(3), which provided that a dissent might be included in the Commission's report (thereby implying that the minister could take account of it); with s 86(1), which required the minister to take account of the advice of the Director General of Fair Trading; and with s 91(2), which imposed a duty upon him to consider representations made after notice and before making his order. The applicants' view would give the exlusive power to decide whether a proposed merger was inimical to the public interest to the Commission, and disable the minister from taking appropriate action in the event of a change of circumstances following publication of the Commission's report. Dunn LJ concluded that the Act, read as a whole, showed that the minister:

> '. . . is not bound by the conclusions of the majority of the Commission, . . . has a wide discretion in deciding whether to make any order at all, and in exercising that discretion he is entitled to take into account all the relevant circumstances, and to consider the opinion of the minority of the Commission, and also representations and advice from persons other than members of the Commission.'

McCullough J agreed with this interpretation, placing particular emphasis on the possibility that the minister might receive a copy of any dissent from any conclusion (not, significantly, 'any recommendation') contained in the report. In his view, the options given to the minister under s 73(2) and recognised by s 73(3) 'are expressed in the most unfettered terms'. Even if s 73(2) could be regarded as ambiguous (and McCullough J did not think it could) since ambiguity should be resolved 'in the way least calculated to lead to ministerial interference with the rights of private citizens, individual or corporate, to contract as they please'. McCullough J stressed, in common with Dunn LJ, the fact that the court's decision itself was not a decision as to whether the projected merger would in fact adversely affect the public interest.

The court further held, on the facts of the case, that it had not been established that the minister took into account irrelevant considerations in reaching his decision and that there was no proper evidence to show either that the minister had improperly abdicated the power to reach a decision to his minister of state or that, if he retained responsibility for the decision, he had allowed his proprietorship of a small shareholding in the take-over company to influence his decision. *Associated Provincial Picture Houses v Wednesbury Corp* [1947] 2 All ER 680 was cited and applied on this issue.

One final point of interest is the court's refusal, founded on art 9 of the Bill of Rights (1688), to take account of certain reports in Hansard which had been proffered in support of the factual basis of the applicants' submission. In the view of Dunn LJ, 'there is no distinction between using a report in Hansard for the purpose of supporting a cause of action arising out of something which occurred in the House [*see Church of Scientology of California v Johnson-Smith* [1972] 1 All ER 378] and using a report for the purpose of supporting a ground for relief in proceedings for judicial review in respect of something which occurred outside the House'.

8 Receivers

Occasions still arise when a court is requested to appoint a receiver of property, although in commercial cases such appointments are rare because the relevant agreement will normally make the necessary provision. One recent case where the court exercised its power to appoint under s 37(1) of the Supreme Court Act 1981 in novel circumstances is *Hart v Emelkirk Ltd* [1983] 3 All ER 15. There, Goulding J made the appointment on the motion of certain tenants in a block of flats. The defendant company, the reversioner under the leases, had neither attempted to collect rent and maintenance contributions for a long period nor performed the covenants as to repair and insurance. The property was now deteriorating seriously and the tenants approached the court to obtain the appointment of a named chartered surveyor as receiver, without security, to receive the rents and profits, give a good receipt for certain other moneys, and manage the property. The motions arose in two actions for a mandatory injunction against the reversioner. Goulding J, citing *Riches v Owen* (1868) LR 3 Ch App 820, held that it clearly appeared to him to be just to appoint a receiver in this case because the appointment would be to support the enforcement by the court of covenants affecting property. Such an appointment was also convenient because the state of the properties demanded urgent action. He did not, however, discern any reason for dispensing with security in this case.

9 Sale of goods

(a) Reservation of title

The search continues for a satisfactory technique of reserving title to goods which are to be rendered into manufactured products. *Re Peachdart Ltd* [1983] 3 All ER 204, [1983] BCLC 225, is the latest reported illustration of the supplier's difficulties (for an even more recent, but unreported, decision see *Hendy Lennox (Industrial Engines) Ltd v Grahame Puttick Ltd* 16 September 1983, Staughton J, post). If correctly decided, it suggests that the exercise of title retention is normally futile in a case of mixed, compounded or even altered goods, and that nothing short of a duly-registered charge will suffice.

The goods to which the supply contracts related were a quantity of leather, sold and delivered to Peachdart by a supplier called Freudenbergs. The contracts provided, inter alia, that Freudenbergs were to retain ownership of the leather until payment, and that payment became immediately due on delivery. Peachdart became insolvent and a receiver was appointed by a debenture-holder, Barclay's Bank. Debts then outstanding to Freudenbergs comprised £16,200. Assets held by the receiver included c£1,400 worth of unused stocks of Freudenbergs leather still in the possession of Peachdart, c£1,500 worth of fully or partially completed handbags manufactured from leather supplied by Freudenbergs and remaining in Peachdart's possession, and trade debts of some £27,300 owing to Peachdart by third parties in respect of sales of manufactured handbags.

The facts therefore bore resemblances to both *Aluminium Industrie Vaassen BV v Romalpa Aluminium Ltd* [1976] 2 All ER 552 and *Borden (UK) Ltd v Scottish Timber Products Ltd* [1979] 3 All ER 961. On the one hand, the supplier's conditions not only (as in *Romalpa*) declared a clear reservation of 'ownership' to the supplier in respect of goods originally supplied but also (unlike the terms in *Borden*) contained explicit provision for the consequences of any rendering of those goods into manufactured items. In that event, 'the property' in the whole of the resultant products was to remain with the supplier until payment, and all the supplier's rights in the original goods were to extend to those products. Further, the buyer's position was expressly defined as 'fiduciary' for the period between supply and payment and the conditions explicitly purported to confer a right on the supplier to 'trace' the proceeds of any onward sale of raw or made-up goods. But the litigation in *Romalpa* had related, of course, only to raw aluminium and the proceeds of its sale; no question arose as to mixed or made-up aluminium and the only relevance of cl 13(2) of Aluminium Industrie's terms (which specifically addressed this issue) lay in the guidance which it afforded to the meaning of cl 13(1), the 'raw aluminium' provision. That was where the crucial difference lay between *Romalpa* and the present case, for in *Peachdart* the preponderate part of the supplier's claim concerned made-up artefacts and the proceeds (or claims for proceeds) of their sale. It was thus that certain observations by the Court of Appeal in *Borden,* about the difficulty of establishing the surviving identity of the supplied goods throughout the process of their manufacture into artefacts, began to appear ominously relevant to the supplier's claim.

Factually, there was still a considerable difference between this case and *Borden.* There, the resin had become totally absorbed and transformed in the process of manufacture into chip-board. Other ingredients had been added which were at least as significant a constituent as the resin. Here, however, part of the leather had been merely cut and shaped, while even that position which had been worked into completed handbags remained the dominant constituent: the sole additions were hasps, handles and thread, all of minor relative value. Nevertheless, Vinelott J held that the title retention clause was, except in relation to the small quantity of unmarked leather, ineffective. Once the process of manufacture had started 'so that in the course of manufacture work and materials provided by [Peachdart] would result in the leather being converted into (that is incorporated in or used as material for) other goods of a distinctive character', Freudenbergs had property in those other goods only as security for the unpaid portion of the price of the relevant consignment of leather. In short, the suppliers had merely a charge, and that (by the concession of their counsel) was void for non-registration under s 95 of the Companies Act 1948.

Vinelott J reached this conclusion on a construction of Freudenbergs' terms. Despite the presence of the word 'remain' in the clause relating to Freudenbergs' title to worked or made-up leather—'the property in the whole of such other goods shall be and remain with the seller'—he held that it was impossible to construe the contract as constituting Peachdart a bailee of every piece of leather, throughout the process of manufacture, until it was paid for or sold, and as conferring on Freudenbergs in the event of a sale before payment a right against Peachdart, as their agents and fiduciaries, to satisfaction of the debt from the proceeds. In Vinelott J's view (at 210):

> '... the parties must have intended that at least after a piece of leather had been appropriated to be manufactured into a handbag and work had started on it (when the leather would cease to have any significant value as raw material) the leather would cease to be the exclusive property of Freudenbergs (whether as bailor or as unpaid vendor) and that Freudenbergs would thereafter have a charge on handbags in the course of manufacture and on the distinctive products which would come into existence at the end of the process of manufacture (the value of which would be derived for the most part from [*the reputation and skill in design of Peachdart's workforce*). The charge would in due cause shift to the proceeds of sale.'

Two particular factors seem to have persuaded the learned judge in favour of this construction. The first, and strongest, was the absence of anything in the relevant contract which obliged Peachdart to keep records identifying those handbags which were made up and sold with Freudenbergs' leather, and thus as agents and bailees of Freudenbergs. On this point, the case was distinguishable from *Romalpa*, where the acquirers specifically undertook to store the suppliers' aluminium separately so that it remained identifiable as the suppliers' property. Even if the rendered leather could be identified, particular sets of proceeds (or claims for proceeds) could not, and it would have been impossible for Freudenbergs to prove that handbags sold by Peachdart and not paid for by the time of the receiver's appointment were in fact made from Freudenbergs' leather. The second, more allusive, reason seems to have been the sheer improbability that the parties intended (as the contract indicated) that Freudenbergs should be entitled to enter Peachdart's premises at any time before payment for the purpose of identifying and removing its leather, or that Peachdart should be obliged to isolate the relevant proceeds from its normal working funds and to keep those proceeds in a separate interest-bearing account. On the latter point, the decision can be contrasted with *Romalpa*, where the argument that the fiduciary responsibilities of the buyers made a nonsense of their entitlement to 75 days' credit did not persuade the Court of Appeal that those responsibilities were therefore inappropriate. In *Peachdart*, no credit was stipulated because the price became payable on delivery. On a more general level, it is interesting that the one respect in which Freudenbergs' terms were notably stronger than those in *Romalpa* (viz their right to enter Peachdart's premises and regain their leather) should have counted for so little in favour of Peachdart's tenure of the leather in the capacity of bailees throughout manufacture.

It can be seen from a comparison of *Borden* and *Peachdart* that industrial commodities may fail to qualify as the subject of a reservation of title for two (often interrelated) reasons: first (as in *Borden* or *Re Bond Worth* [1979] 3 All ER 919 or *Clough Mills Ltd v Martin* [1984] 1 All ER 721) because they have, irrespective of the parties' intentions, lost their original identity and disappeared; or secondly because the terms of the contract themselves negate any intention to project the retention of title into the period within which they are altered, developed, processed or consumed. The decision in *Peachdart* seems to rely more on the latter approach than on the former, and it may be that, but for the absence of any contractual term requiring the keeping of records about the destination of Freudenbergs' leather, a different result would have been justified. But the general tenor of Vinelott J's judgment seems consistent with a highly pronounced judicial tendency to confine *Romalpa* to cases where the condition of the disputed commodities remains, in all but the most insignificant respects, unchanged from that in which they were supplied. This attitude seems complemented by the more recent, unreported decision of Staughton J in *Hendy Lennox (Industrial Engines) Ltd v Grahame Puttick Ltd* where, even though certain engines which had been reversibly incorporated by the acquirers into generators might be held to be supplied to the acquirers, and held by them, as bailees, the suppliers were held to have no right to claim against the acquirers as fiduciaries for the proceeds of their sub-sales. At least it can be said that one of Professor Goode's early misgivings (see (1977) Times, 17 May) about *Romalpa*—that it might fall to be applied in a case where materials supplied by two different manufacturers under title retention clauses are commingled in a finished product—now seems less alarming than it did seven years ago.

(b) Exclusion clauses and the reasonableness test

See Consumer Law, p 103 and Contract, p 112, below.

10 Trade marks

In *Re American Greetings Corp's Application* [1983] 2 All ER 609 the proprietors of a trade mark consisting of the drawing of 'Holly Hobbie', a fictional small girl, sought to have the trade mark registered under s 17 of the Trade Marks Act 1938. The applicants were an Ohio company which had successfully used the character on greeting cards and related products of their own manufacture and had licensed its use by other trading enterprises on a much wider range of merchandise in America. They now wished to extend their licensing operations to England and, in this respect also, the proposed range of goods was much wider than those which the applicants manufactured personally: it included slippers, toys, table-mats, toilet products and sleeping bags. To this end they concluded licensing agreements with various companies for the use of the mark in the UK. These agreements included provision for the approval by the applicants of the specifications for the goods manufactured by the licensees and for their packaging and advertising.

The Court of Appeal, upholding Whitford J, held that the grant of the applications would tend to facilitate trafficking in the trade mark within the meaning of s 28(6) of the 1938 Act and would tend to deceive and confuse the public with regard to the origin of goods marketed under the mark. The applications had accordingly been properly refused. Dillon LJ stressed the necessity for a trade connection between the proprietor of the mark and the goods of the licensee on which the mark is to be used, in order to avoid the stigma of trafficking. The mere presence of quality control provisions in the licensing agreement did not, in his view, automatically provide the necessary trade connection in a case where there would otherwise have been none. He adopted Earl Loreburn's definition of trafficking (in *Bowden Wire Ltd v Bowden Brake Co Ltd* (1914) 31 RPC 385 at 392) as disposing of the mark or the reputation in the name, as itself a marketable commodity. Sir Denys Buckley attempted a definition of his own (at [1983] 2 All ER 623) and in the applicants' subsequent, unsuccessful appeal to the House of Lords, Lord Brightman has since said that he has no quarrel with that definition: [1984] 1 All ER 426 at 433. But Lord Brightman went on to offer his own version, the essence of which was 'the notion of dealing with a trade mark primarily as a commodity in its own right and not primarily for the purpose of identifying or promoting merchandise in which the proprietor of the mark is interested'. The precise impact of the Holly Hobbie case will take some time to be absorbed, but there can be little doubt that the initial sensation is one of severe setback to the practitioners of character merchandising: a practice which, in Lord Bridge of Harwich's view, deceives nobody. A scintilla of comfort may, however, be derived from Lord Bridge's assertion in the final appeal that s 28(6) of the 1938 Act 'has become a complete anachronism and . . . the sooner it is repealed the better' ([1984] 1 All ER at 428).

Company Law

D D PRENTICE, MA, LLB, JD
Barrister, Fellow of Pembroke College, Oxford

Introduction

This was something of a bumper year for the reporting of company law cases due to what appears to be the increased work load of the Companies Court ((1984) 134 NLJ 97). In addition, a new series of specialists reports, Butterworths Company Law Cases (BCLC), was launched and it is proposed to deal with the cases reported in that series in this survey. As usual, the bulk of reported cases deal with winding up and in the current year two important cases in this field, one dealing with the rights of judgment creditors (at p 61) and the other with the rights of tort claimants (at p 60), were reported. Not commented on in this part of the survey, but dealt with in the article on Trusts, p 352 post, but of relevance to company lawyers, is the very important decision of Peter Gibson J in *Baden Delvaux and Lecuit v Société General pour Favouriser le Developpement du Commerce d'Industrie du France* [1983] BCLC 325 which deals with the issue of the application of constructive trust doctrines to the operation of bank accounts by persons in a fiduciary status, something of obvious relevance to the operation of company accounts.

Book debts: failure to register: Companies Act 1948, s 95(2)(e)

Section 95(2)(e) of the Companies Act 1948 requires the registration of charges created by a company over its book debts, otherwise the normal consequences of invalidity will follow. The Companies Act 1948 does not define book debts and the cases merely produce the somewhat indeterminate test that a debt which would in the ordinary course of business be entered in well-kept accounts as a debt is a book debt for the purpose of the sub-section (*Paul and Frank Ltd v Discount Bank (Overseas) Ltd* [1966] 2 All ER 922). In *Re Brush Aggregates Ltd* [1983] BCLC 320, a company assigned to its creditors part of the sum of £100,000 which was due to it under a contract with a third party. The company, having gone into liquidation, the question arose as to whether this assignment should have been registered as a charge on its book debts. The mere fact that the debt in question had an element of futurity to it did not, of course, dispose of the matter as it is clear that charges on future book debts are registerable (*Independent Automatic Sales Ltd v Knowles and Foster* [1962] 3 All ER 27). It was argued in *Re Brush Aggregates Ltd* that the transaction was merely an assignment of contingent contractual rights and as such not registerable. The court rejected this argument. It did so primarily on the construction of the language of the assignment which directed its terms to the money due to the company under the contract and was not easily interpreted as an assignment of a contingent contractual claim. Also, the court considered it of importance that there were a number of assignments of part of a total sum due rather than one block assignment. This may be of some probative value, but its weight is limited as there is no objection to the assignment of part of a debt, although it does give rise to its own special problems (Chitty, *Contracts* (25th edn) para 1276). How *Re Brush Aggregates Ltd* is to be distinguished from *Paul and Frank Ltd v Discount Bank (Overseas) Ltd* is far from clear (cf *Durham Bros v Robertson* [1898] 1 QB 765). In the former case the charge related to a definite amount from a definite sum, whereas the latter case involved an undefined amount from an unquantified fund ((1980) LS Gaz 2421). But this legally is not dispositive of the issue as the first type of interest is as capable of assignment (perhaps more so) as the latter. At the end of the day, perhaps all one can say is that the matter is one of construction and the moral of *Re Brush Aggregates Ltd* is the usual one when dealing with s 95, when in doubt register.

Directors: disqualification order

Although the Companies Act 1976, s 28, has been replaced by a modified s 188 of the Companies Act 1948 (Companies Act 1981, s 93), the decision of Nourse J in *Re Civica Investments Ltd* [1983] BCLC 456, on the sentencing policy to be followed in making a disqualification order under the Companies Act 1976, s 28, remains of relevance to the current provisions on disqualification. Nourse J, citing a number of unreported judgments, considered that it was no longer necessary in an application for a disqualification order for the court to be taken through the facts of the previous cases, as the courts had now acquired sufficient experience in dealing with such applications as not to require this. In imposing an order of disqualification, the maximum period of disqualification was not to be imposed irrespective of the degree of blame, leaving it to the disqualified director to seek at some time in the future a modification of the order:

> 'the longer periods of disqualification are to be reserved for cases where the defaults and the conduct of the person in question have been of a serious nature, for example, where defaults have been made for some dishonest purpose, or wilfully and deliberately, or where they have been numerous and have not been substantially alleviated by remedial action and convincing assurances that they will not recur in the future' (at 458d).

In the instant case, although there had been persistent default on numerous occasions, the court imposed a 'lenient' sentence of disqualification for one year as there had been a substantial effort made to remedy the defects.

Winding up: relationship between voluntary and compulsory winding up: role of voluntary liquidator

In *Re Medisco Equipment Ltd* [1983] BCLC 305 a petition was presented by a creditor for the compulsory winding up of a company which was already subject to a creditors' voluntary winding up. The first issue before the court, and one of some practical importance, was the role, if any, of the liquidator in a voluntary winding up in proceedings brought for the compulsory winding up of a company. Harman J considered it proper for him to be represented by counsel and, he 'perhaps should', for the assistance of the court, give evidence of what he has found. He should not, however, adopt a partisan attitude, his role was to assist the court and not press for a view one way or the other (at 307 i–308 a). Failure to adopt this posture of neutrality could, of course, have serious consequences when it comes to the awarding of costs.

In *Re Medisco Equipment Ltd,* Harman J, following the principles in *Re JD Swain Ltd* [1965] 2 All ER 761 at 765, refused to grant the winding-up order as there was no evidence to suggest that the interests of the petitioning creditor, who held a majority in value, but not a majority in number, of the debts owed by the company, would not be adequately protected in a creditors' voluntary winding up.

There was one other point touched on by Harman J in *Re Medisco Equipment Ltd* and that related to the significance to be attached to the views of creditors who were also members of the company and who, as in this case, opposed the petition. Harman J considered that the fact that a creditor was also a member should be a factor in determining the weight to be attached to the views of such a creditor but that it would be improper to ignore his views completely. No doubt, where there are well-founded suspicions that a member-creditor is opposing a petition for ulterior reasons then perhaps the weight to be attached to his views should be discounted to close to zero.

Company accounts: shareholder standing to complain

It is a characteristic of English company law that a shareholder has only limited access to the courts to remedy personal grievances or to vindicate the company's rights, a principle which was very firmly endorsed by the Court of Appeal in *Prudential Assurance Co Ltd v Newman Industries Ltd (No 2)* [1982] 1 All ER 354 (All ER Rev 1982, pp 47–48). *Devlin v Slough Estates Ltd* [1983] BCLC 497 is another illustration of this principle. The plaintiff, a shareholder in the defendant company, commenced an action, either personal as an individual shareholder, or derivative on behalf of the company, complaining that the defendant company's accounts had not been prepared in accordance with the provisions of the Companies Acts and the company's articles and seeking appropriate redress. The company's accounts had contained for a number of years a note on a 'contingent liability' in connection with litigation in France in which the company and one of its subsidiaries were defendants but which was omitted without explanation from its 1979 accounts. As regards the plaintiff's personal action, the court held that the provisions in the company's articles obliging the directors to prepare accounts in compliance with the Companies Acts and deliver them to the shareholders did not confer on a shareholder the right to bring a personal action in connection with their method of preparation; the directors' duty to prepare accounts was a duty owed to the company. Dillon J was fearful of the threat of multiplicity of actions were a shareholder accorded standing to complain of the way in which the accounts were prepared. This is unquestionably a legitimate concern, but it is surely one that could be dealt with by appropriate amendments to the Rules of Court so as to oblige all interested parties to be joined in any action by a shareholder against his company where it would be appropriate for the action to be representative in form. Dillon J's ruling is another limitation of a shareholder's right to enforce the contract constituted by s 20 of the Companies Act 1948 and, as is so often the case in this area, no explanation was forthcoming as to why some parts of the articles are enforceable by an individual shareholder whereas other parts are not. Also, given the importance of accounts to shareholders, a point recognised by Dillon J (at 502 b–c), it is a little surprising that a shareholder should not be accorded standing to insist on compliance with the provisions of the articles relating to the preparation of accounts (cf Companies Act 1967, s 14).

Dillon J also thought that this was not the type of situation where a derivative action would lie. The dispute (the appropriate treatment of a contingent liability in the accounts) involved matters of business judgment and normally the court would not interfere in disputes of this kind. In such a situation, an aggrieved shareholder could either attempt to requisition a shareholders' meeting or, where appropriate, seek the assistance of the Department of Trade. There were, however, certain limited circumstances where it would be appropriate for a shareholder to be accorded standing to bring a derivative action in connection with the preparation of a company's accounts; for example, where it is alleged that the accounts showed profits out of which a dividend could be payed whereas this was not in fact the case (*Drown v Gaumont British Picture Corpn Ltd* [1951] 2 All ER 994). The dispute in *Devlin v Slough Estates Ltd* was not of this nature and therefore the plaintiff shareholder had no standing to complain by way of derivative action.

Meetings: Companies Act 1948, s 132

The Jenkins Committee (Cmnd 1749, para 458), in commenting on the Companies Act 1948, s 132, considered that the whole purpose of the section could be evaded if it merely required directors to summon a meeting within 21 days of the deposit of the necessary requisition, but did not oblige them to set the date on which the meeting was to be held within this period. In *Re Windward Islands (Enterprises) Ltd* [1983] BCLC 293, Nourse J had to deal with this question of whether the directors had not only to convene, but also to hold, a meeting summoned under s 132 within 21 days from being requested to do so. He held that they did not. He recognised that this would go a long way to defeating the whole purpose of the section, but felt that the wording was not capable of any other interpretation. The Jenkins Committee recommended that s 132 should be amended to require directors to convene a meeting within 28 days of the notice convening the meeting (para 458), and on their failure to so convene the meeting, s 132(3) should be made applicable. The decision in *Re Windward Islands (Enterprises) Ltd* clearly indicates that such a reform is much needed.

Director's guarantee of company's debt

It is a commonplace observation that for many companies the principle of limited liability is illusory as the principal shareholders and directors are often obliged to personally guarantee the company's liabilities. *First National Finance Corpn v Goodman* [1983] BCLC 203 involved the question of the continued enforceability of such a guarantee entered into by a director where there had been a change in the identity of the company's creditor and the director had ceased to play an active part in the company's affairs. In that case the defendant director had entered into a guarantee with C with respect to all advances made by C to the company of which he was a director. C was amalgamated with the plaintiff company and the question arose as to whether or not advances made by the plaintiff subsequent to the amalgamation were covered by the guarantee, the director having ceased, at the time the advances were made, to take an active part in the company's affairs. The normal rule is that 'a change in the identity of the creditor or debtor, whether those persons are firms, companies or individuals', operates to revoke 'the guarantee unless there is agreement to the contrary expressed or implied' (at 209 h–i). The underlying rationale for this being that a 'guarantor's knowledge of both creditor and debtor may be material to [the] . . . guaranteeing [of] the debts' (at 209 i). In *First National Finance Corpn v Goodman* the court found that the guarantee by its terms was intended to operate even where there had been a change in the creditor's identity as it was specifically worded to cover to advances made by C's assigns or any company with which it might amalgamate. Accordingly, the director remained liable on the guarantee.

Mortgagee: duty in exercising power of sale

In the last issue of the Review comment was made (All ER Rev 1982, pp 39, 40) on the significance of *Standard Chartered Bank Ltd v Walker* [1982] 3 All ER 938 on the nature of the proprietary interest acquired by a mortgagee. The opinion of the Privy Council in *Tse Kwong Lam v Won Chit Sen and others* [1983] BCLC 88, [1983] 3 All ER 54, also has a direct bearing on this issue. The facts, somewhat simplified, were that the respondent mortgagee exercised his power of sale and put the mortgaged property up for auction without taking any expert advice on how best to dispose of the property so as to obtain the best possible price. At the auction, the successful and only bidder was a company in which the mortgagee and his family held all the shares. The mortgagor challenged the validity of the sale and sought to have it set aside either on the grounds of impropriety or because it had been made at an undervalue: he was unsuccessful on the first point, but succeeded on the second.

As to the first point, Lord Brightman, giving the opinion of the Privy Council, considered that there was 'no hard and fast rule that a mortgagee may not sell to a company in which he is interested' (at 93 i, at 59 b). This principle was applicable even on the facts of *Tse Kwong Lam* where the mortgagee's interest in the acquiring company was virtually absolute. No argument was made that the court should pierce the corporate veil, although this appears to be the type of case where the facts would at least prima facie support a departure from the corporate entity doctrine. If a vendor of property cannot successfully defeat the purchaser's equitable interest under a contract of sale by selling the property to a company which he controls (*Jones v Lipman* [1962] 1 All ER 442), then it is equally arguable that the corporate form should not be usable so as to jeopardise the value of a mortgagor's equity of redemption.

However, although the sale was not impeachable on the grounds of impropriety, it was impeachable on the grounds that it had not been made in a way which would obtain the best price reasonably obtainable at the time of sale. There were a number of points the court made on this: (a) Where there is a close relationship between the mortgagee and the purchasing company, then the sale will be scrutinised and will only be upheld if the mortgagee proves that he took 'reasonable precautions to obtain the best price reasonably obtainable at the time of sale' (at 60 g, at 96 a). (b) The mortgagee should consult experts as the best method of sale, for example, whether the property should be sold by auction or by private treaty. At the very least, the mortgagee should take expert advice on the reserve price where the sale is to be by auction. (c) The mere fact that the sale is by auction is not conclusive evidence that the price obtained was the best reasonably obtainable; the mortgagee must go further and show that, in the circumstances of the case, sale by auction, and the conduct of the auction (particularly the setting of the reserve price), were likely to produce the best price reasonably obtainable. (d) The mortgagee is not obliged to postpone the sale or adopt a method of piecemeal sale for the purpose of enhancing the best price obtainable (at 59 b, at 94 a). This affirms the important principle that the timing of the exercise of a right of sale by a mortgagee is within his unfettered discretion, and is further authority against Lord Denning's heterodox views to the contrary (*Standard Chartered Bank Ltd v Walker* ([1982] 3 All ER at 942f, All ER Rev 1982, p 40).

As stated earlier, the Privy Council found that the mortgagee had failed to do all that was reasonable to obtain the best possible price by, in particular, failing to obtain expert advice on a sale of the magnitude of that involved *Tse Kwong Lam* and by not taking expert advice on the reserve price which the mortgagee obviously had an interest in setting as low as possible. Where a mortgagee exercises his power of sale in circumstances like those in *Tse Kwong Lam,* the court would normally set the sale aside (at 63c, at 99 b). However, in the circumstances of the case, the mortgagor had unreasonably delayed in seeking relief and therefore it would be inequitable to allow him to upset the sale. The court, therefore, confined the mortgagor to his remedy of damages which would be the difference between the price paid and the best price reasonably obtainable at the time of sale.

Given previous case law, the outcome in *Tse Kwong Lam* comes as no surprise. However, it does forcefully bring home the constraints on a mortgagee's power of sale. Although it concerned a case where the sale gave rise to a conflict between the interests of the mortgagee and those of the mortgagor, much of what was said on the mortgagee's obligation to obtain the best price reasonably obtainable has general application whatever the circumstances in which the power of sale is exercised.

Winding up: disputed ownership of shares

It is firmly established that winding up is not to be used to resolve disputes as to the ownership of shares (*Re JN2 Ltd* [1977] 3 All ER 1104 at 1109 b). *Re Garage Door Associates Ltd* ([1983] BCLC 164) involves an interesting qualification of this principle. There the petitioner, who was the registered holder of one share and was therefore undoubtedly a member, sought a winding-up order and relief under s 75 of the Companies Act 1980. The petitioner complained that there had been a falling out between himself and the other members of a 'joint venture' company and that there had been an improper allotment of shares to the other members. Although there was obviously a dispute about the ownership of shares, Mervyn Davies J refused to dismiss the petition, as the petitioner did not merely seek a winding up but also sought relief under s 75 of the 1980 Act. He reasoned that s 75 proceedings would be an appropriate means of resolving the ownership dispute and once resolved the winding-up petition could, if necessary, be proceeded with. It is important to note that the petitioner in *Re Garage Door Associates Ltd* was clearly a member and, had there been any dispute as to his status as a member, his right to present a petition under s 75 would have been cast in doubt as the section is only available to members. Thus the principle in *Re Garage Door Associates Ltd* probably only applies where there is no doubt as to the petitioner's status as a member. The solution adopted by Mervyn Davies J in *Re Garage Door Associates Ltd* has the undoubted advantage that all the matters in dispute between the parties will be settled in one proceeding rather than compelling a separate action to determine the ownership of the shares (cf *Re Bambi Restaurants Ltd* [1965] 2 All ER 79 at 91). Any prejudice caused to the company by the presentation of the winding-up petition can quite easily be dealt with by a favourable exercise of the court's discretion under s 227 of the Companies Act 1948, as was done in *Re Garage Door Associates Ltd*.

Corporate entity: duty of solicitor to principal shareholder of company which he advises

In *R P Howard Ltd & Richard Alan Mitchell v Woodman Matthews* [1983] BCLC 117 a company and its principal shareholder brought an action against the solicitor who advised the company in which they alleged negligence against the solicitor for failing to advise the company with respect to the exercise of its rights under the Landlord and Tenant Act 1954. The court found that the solicitor owed both the company and the principal shareholder a contractual duty of care (at 121b), although where the consideration for the contract between the principal shareholder and the solicitor came from is unclear as the solicitor's bill for the allegedly negligent advice, although addressed to the shareholder, was paid by the company (at 120 f). No doubt one could speculate on the right of a joint promisee to a contract to rely on the consideration provided by the other promisee, but such speculation would be out of place as it in no way entered the reasoning of the court. The factors giving rise to the contract, reliance and the importance to the principal shareholder of the company's commercial health, were factors, one would have thought, more appropriate for a finding of a duty in tort. Staughton J would have been willing to find that such a duty is owed in the circumstances of *R P Howard Ltd & Richard Allen Mitchell v Woodman Matthews* as it could be foreseen that negligent advice could cause foreseeable harm to the principal shareholder (at 121 c, citing *Anns v Merton London Borough Council* [1978] AC 728 at 751), but having found a duty in contract there was no need to pursue the point.

The court found that the solicitor had been negligent and awarded damages to both the company and its principal shareholder. The defendant argued that the court could not grant damages to the principal shareholder as his damages were merely a reflection of the damages suffered by the company and as such only recoverable in an action by the company (*Prudential Assurance Co Ltd v Newman Industries Ltd (No 2)* [1982] Ch 204 at 222). Staughton J rejected this reasoning, as on the facts the principal shareholder had suffered a loss which was independent of that suffered by the company:

because of the defendant's negligence he had been obliged to enter into a covenant constraining his right to sell his shares and this limitation on the saleability of his shares reduced their market value (at 123i).

Interregotaries served on a company

Stanfield Properties Ltd v National Westminster Bank plc (London and County Securities Ltd, third party) ([1983] 2 All ER 249, [1983] BCLC 197) raises that perennial but elusive problem in company law, how does a company know? The case involved an appeal against a Master's refusal to make an order under RSC Ord 26, r 5, requiring the plaintiffs and the third party, both companies and both in liquidation, to make further answers to interregotaries. The answers to the initial interregotaries, given by the liquidators of the respective companies, were alleged to be inadequate primarily because the liquidators failed to make inquiries of existing and past officers of the companies, confining their answers to what was obtainable from various written records and accounts. Megarry V-C held that a company answering interregotaries must 'procure the making of proper inquiries from the company's officers, servants and agents' (at 250 h, at 199 a) and this extended to persons who had left the company's service. However, in the case of the latter, the company, as is the general requirement, was only obliged to make reasonable inquiries, and therefore 'if the departure or retirement was a long while ago, it might well be unreasonable to expect inquiries to be made' (at 251 a, at 199 c). The overriding test was one of reasonableness. It is also important to note, as Megarry V-C pointed out, that when interregotaries are addressed to a company, their purpose is to discover what is known to the collective mind of the company. It is not sufficient for the person to whom the interregotaries are addressed to answer only from his own personal knowledge; he must go farther and 'make all reasonable inquiries which are likely to reveal, or may reveal, what is known to the company' (at 251 c, at 199 f). And where a company which is interrogated (at 253 a, at 201 h),

> 'gives answers which give no indication whether there has been any attempt to tap obvious sources of information [it] must be prepared, on inquiry made, to give explanations of reasonable amplitude and, if required, verify them by affidavit.'

On the facts of the instant case Megarry V-C considered that it would be pointless to order that further answers be given as the parties who could provide the relevant information were not available.

Winding up: tort claims

The Cork Committee (Cmnd 8858, pp 299–300) considered it unacceptable that tort claims should not be provable in bankruptcy and voiced approval of the judgment of Vinelott J in *Re Berkeley Securities (Property) Ltd* [1980] 3 All ER 513 that such damages were recoverable in a winding up provided they were liquidated by judgment before the claim was to be proved. However, in *Re Islington Metal and Plating Works Ltd* [1983] 3 All ER 218, [1983] BCLC 215, Harman J refused to follow this 'undoubtedly surprising' decision. He reasoned that it was a basic principle of winding up that 'the liquidation and the distribution are to be treated as notionally simultaneous' (at 221 e, at 218 g) and, as a result, damages in tort which were not liquidated before the commencement of the winding up were not provable. No doubt this produces a convenient result, but scarcely a principled one, and the logic of the argument would exclude other claims of an uncertain and contingent nature which are presently provable. The proof and quantification of unliquidated damages is no more complex than the proof of other uncertain claims provable in a winding up and given the freedom which a plaintiff now possesses to bring a case in either contract or tort (cf *Re Great Orme Tramways Co* [1934] 50 TLR 450) it is 'anomalous' (*Re Berkeley Securities (Property) Ltd* at 513 f–g) that the right to prove for a debt should turn on the technical classification of the cause of action (see *Re Southern Cross Coaches Ltd* [1932] 49 WN (NSW) 230, cited in McPherson *The Law of Company Liquidation* (2nd edn) p 335).

Harman J had also to deal with a second point in *Re Islington Metal and Plating Works Ltd* and his decision on this to some extent compensates the tort creditors for his refusal to follow the *Berkeley* case. The point was simple: what happens where a company which is insolvent at the commencement of the winding up becomes solvent during the process, but if the tort claimants are admitted the company will once again become insolvent. This was somewhat akin to what Vinelott J aptly referred to as 'a paradox worthy of Epimenides' (*Re Berkeley Securities (Property) Ltd* at 528 g–h):

> 'If the company is treated as an insolvent company to which s 317 applies the [tort] claim is excluded, and if the claim is excluded the company is solvent. If the company is treated as a solvent company to which s 316 applies, the admission of the claim makes the company insolvent.'

Harman J resolved this 'eternal state of oscillation' by holding that once a company moved from being insolvent to solvent (ie from s 317 to s 316) then s 316 applied and the section remained applicable even though the claims of the tort claimants exceeded the surplus available for distribution to them after the claims of the other creditors have been satisfied. That a company can move from insolvent to solvent status during the winding up, is clearly recognised in the cases (*Re Fine Industrial Commodities Ltd* [1955] 3 All ER 707) and although it has not always been to the advantage of all classes of creditors (*Re Rolls-Royce Ltd* [1974] 3 All ER 646) it was obviously to the advantage of the tort claimants in *Re Islington Metal and Plating Works Ltd*. As a result of this aspect of the judgment in *Re Islington Metal and Plating Works Ltd*, the principle that liquidation and distribution are notionally simultaneous events has to be slightly qualified, but this is a small price to pay for what is an obviously correct decision on principle. But, it makes even more anomalous the continued exclusion of tort claims in an insolvent winding up.

Winding up: rights of judgment creditors

Roberts Petroleum Ltd v Bernard Kenny Ltd ([1983] 1 All ER 564, [1983] BCLC 28) involved a question of considerable importance on the right of a judgment creditor to enforce his judgment against an insolvent company and it shows the vulnerability of the rights of such 'procedural' security holders (Goode, *Commercial Law*, p 732) unless they have perfected their security.

The case arose under s 35 of the Administration of Justice Act 1956, now replaced by the Charging Orders Act 1979, but it still has relevance to the exercise of the court's discretion under the latter act. The facts were straightforward. The plaintiff signed judgment and obtained a charging order nisi on 23 March 1979 against the defendant company's land, the order providing that it would be made final on 4 April unless the company showed sufficient cause to the contrary why this should not be done. On 16 March, Roberts Petroleum Ltd was informed of a meeting of the company's creditors which was to be held, and which was held, on 26 March. On 2 April, the company was placed in voluntary liquidation as part of a plan to deprive Roberts Petroleum Ltd of any advantage it may have acquired by the charging order nisi of 23 March in its favour. The charging order nisi was made absolute on 4 April and the issue before the House of Lords was quite simple: should a charging order nisi be made absolute where a company has resolved to be wound up voluntarily between the time when the order was made and an order absolute is sought. As Lord Brightman pointed out, the case involved a conflict between two well-established principles. On the one hand, there was the principle that a judgment creditor was entitled to enforce a money judgment by any of the means of execution prescribed for this purpose. While on the other, there was the principle that where a judgment debtor was insolvent all its unsecured creditors should be treated equally (at 571–572, at 36 e–f). The House of Lords opted for the latter principle: where a winding up is commenced it brings into operation a statutory scheme for the distribution of a company's assets and, assets subject to a charging order nisi, were prima facie subject to this scheme as an order only created a defeasible right which the court should not make permanent. The imposition of this statutory scheme on the assets of an insolvent company was 'a "sufficient cause" for not converting the order nisi into an order absolute' (at 576 g, at 42 b).

The justification for the refusal to make the order absolute in *Roberts Petroleum* was to ensure parity of treatment of unsecured creditors in the winding up of an insolvent company. It also prevents an unseemly scramble, as Lord Brightman pointed out, of creditors seeking to obtain some advantage over their fellow creditors. More importantly, it provides a very clear rule to guide the parties and avoids the uncertainties of the type of enquiry made necessary by the judgment of the Court of Appeal (eg had an arrangement at the time of the application been set on foot which had a reasonable prospect of success). This arguably is the most important justification for the *Roberts Petroleum* decision. It does, however, mean that the creditors of companies will have less of an incentive to take legal proceedings to enforce their debts where there is a possibility that the company is insolvent, with the consequence that companies may continue to trade in circumstances where it would be in the interests of all that they should be wound up. However, the inability to obtain an advantage by breaking ranks may induce creditors to consider collectively some plan of rescue and to the extent that this is a consequence of the *Roberts Petroleum* decision then its effects will be beneficial.

Voluntary winding up: failure to give notice to creditors

The purpose of the modifications of the Companies Act 1948, s 293, effected by the Companies Act 1981, s 106, would appear to be the proscription of the practice of 'centrebinding' (*Re Centrebind Ltd* [1966] 3 All ER 889), whereby shareholders would waive the normal notice requirements for the passing of an extraordinary resolution to wind up the company (Companies Act 1948, s 133) and then proceed to the appointment of a liquidator without any prior notice to the creditors. The decision of his Honour Judge Finlay QC in *E V Saxton & Sons Ltd v R Miles (Confectioners) Ltd* ([1983] 2 All ER 1025, [1983] BCLC 70) shows that, if this was the object of the reform, it has failed to achieve its purpose. In that case the plaintiff sought to enforce a judgment debt against the defendant company but before the defendant's goods had been sold by the sheriff's officers the defendant company passed a resolution that the company be wound up. The normal notice for an extraordinary resolution was waived and no notice of the meeting was given to the creditors. The plaintiff argued that the failure to comply with the seven days' notice requirement in the new Companies Act 1948, s 293(1) resulted in the resolution being invalid because of the effect of the new sub (7) of s 293 and, accordingly, the creditors could proceed to enforce their judgment, the Companies Act 1948, s 325, being inapplicable as the company was not being wound up.

The validity of the plaintiff's argument turned on the construction of the Companies Act 1948, s 293(7), which provides:

'Failure to give notice of the meeting of the company mentioned in subsection (1) above as required shall not affect the validity of any resolution passed or other thing done at the meeting which would be valid apart from the subsection.'

Two different interpretations were canvassed before the court as the meaning of this subsection, the relevant part of which was the concluding phrase 'which would be valid apart from that subsection' (ie s 293(1) laying down the seven day notice requirement). The first, the 'substantive construction', which would have invalidated the resolution, was that the words meant 'which would be valid apart from that subsection'. The second, the 'procedural construction', which would have validated the resolution, was the words meant 'in the absence of that subsection' or 'if subsection (1) had not been enacted'. It was argued that the background of the 1981 amendments to s 293 favoured the substantive construction, coupled with the fact that there is little sense in prescribing a minimum period of notice if the only sanction is criminal. The court, however, opted for the procedural construction. This was partly because s 293(7) was not necessary to achieve the invalidity of a resolution which contravened s 293(1): if sub-s (7) had been omitted, a failure to give seven days' notice as required by sub-s (1) would prima facie have rendered the resolution invalid. Accordingly, sub-s (7) must have been inserted for another purpose. Secondly, to achieve invalidity, the subsection could have been more forcefully worded (cf Companies Act 1948, s 142, 'the resolution shall not be effective unless notice . . .'). Thirdly, Judge Finlay felt that it was not the legislature's intention to introduce a new and different sanction to deal with breach of s 293, that is, to introduce the sanction of invalidity in addition to criminal sanctions.

Given the background of the 1981 alterations to s 293, the decision in *E V Saxton & Sons Ltd v R Miles (Confectioners) Ltd* comes as something of a surprise. However, it can be supported and, more importantly, it is more compatible with the broad principles of insolvency law than the alternative interpretation. To have that breach of s 293(1) invalidated a winding–up resolution would have allowed the plaintiff to complete execution and to this extent the principle of parity of treatment of creditors in an insolvency would have been departed from. One can also imagine somewhat similar problems arising with respect to the treatment of dispositions of property made after a company has gone into a creditors' voluntary winding–up were it to be held that breach of s 293(1) invalidated a winding–up resolution. The preferable solution to this problem would be the adoption of the proposals of the Cork Committee that 'notice to the creditors of the company's insolvency should follow and not . . . precede the commencement of the liquidation and the appointment of a provisional liquidator' (Cmnd 8558, para 669).

Winding up: incorporation of bankruptcy rules

The way which bankruptcy rules are made to apply in company liquidation does not produce a very coherent regime for dealing with corporate insolvencies. The Companies Act 1948, s 317, does not make all of the bankruptcy rules applicable to the winding–up of insolvement companies and the Act has its own provisions dealing with certain aspects of corporate insolvency (see eg s 227 and s 319). *Re Jessel Securities Ltd* [1983] BCLC 1), a decision of the Court of Appeal decided in 1978, is a case of some importance on the application of bankruptcy rules in the winding up of insolvent companies. The case involved three important issues.

(1) The first question before the court was whether s 317 of the 1948 Act made s 66(1) of the Bankruptcy Act 1914 applicable to the winding up of an insolvent company. The court, on the basis of authority, in particular *Re Whitaker* [1901] 1 Ch 9, and legislative history, had no doubt that it did. This has always been considered to be the case since *Re Theo Garvin* [1967] 3 All ER 497, but it is good to have a Court of Appeal decision affirming the position. The Court also held that s 66(1) applied even where the issue involved the proof of claims of creditors with similar rights as to security and not merely where there was a conflict between secured and unsecured creditors or between creditors with different security entitlements.

(2) The proving creditors in *Re Jessel Securities Ltd* were entitled to interest on their loan and the question arose as to how the limitation in s 66(1) that interest 'be calculated at a rate not exceeding five per cent annum' was to be applied. The problem arose in *Re Jessel Securities Ltd* because the amount of interest paid to the creditors, holders of 9¾% unsecured loan stock, exceeded interest 'calculated at 5% per annum on the amounts of stock from time to time outstanding from the respective dates of issue averaged out over the whole period from the date of issue . . . to the commencement of the winding up' (at 59 a–b). However, no interest had been paid for approximately an 18-month period preceding the date of the company's winding up. Goff LJ allowed interest at the statutory rate for this period: he reasoned that the five per cent ceiling related only to the claims 'included in the proof' (at 22 d) and 'nothing received by the creditor before the commencement of that period is relevant' (at 22 e). This interpretation mitigates to some extent the harshness of s 66(1) which operates to limit the interest claims of creditors to an

unrealistically, and arguably unfairly, low level. The court also found that s 66(2)(b) of the Bankruptcy Act 1914 did not apply to the facts in *Re Jessel Securities Ltd*. Although the actual scope of this provision is not clear, it is to be doubted if it could at all extend to payments which in normal accountancy practice would be treated as payments of interest (at 23).

(3) The third point in *Re Jessel Securities Ltd* related to that part of s 66(1) which restricts any pecuniary consideration payable to a creditor in lieu of interest also to the 5% limit. The problem arose because one tranche of the loan stock issued by the company had been issued at a discount and the question was whether the premium payable by the company on the loan stock's repayment was consideration in lieu of interest. The court held that it was not, although its reasoning on this is far from clear. Expert evidence in the case indicated that it was normal to treat any discount at which fixed interest stock was issued as being in lieu of additional interest (at 10 d–e). But the court declined to accept this position in *Re Jessel Securities Ltd*. This was partly a matter of 'impression'; to treat the discount as an alternative to higher interest was a much too sophisticated analysis and that it would be more appropriately treated as an inducement to purchase the stock (at 26 d). Also Goff LJ felt that the flat yield on the stock (ie the yield on the price paid for the stock) was achieved by the company agreeing to calculate the interest on the redemption price of the stock, and therefore the premium on redemption was not in lieu of anything. However, the premium would obviously affect the redemption yield (which takes into consideration the premium payable on redemption in calculating the yield) but this increase was not, in Goff LJ's opinion, interest. But this, with respect, is not the point under s 66(1). The question is whether the consideration is 'in lieu of interest' and in *Re Jessel Securities Ltd* it is difficult to avoid the conclusion that it was. The decision in *Re Jessel Securities Ltd* on this point may be in need of further examination, but as Goff LJ saw this aspect of the case as being principally one of construing the terms of the loan stock, a subsequent court is no doubt free to adopt its own interpretation.

Directors: fiduciary duties

Although the status of Bell and Snelling as directors (chairman and vice-chairman respectively) was not completely ignored by *Bell v Lever Bros Ltd* [1932] AC 161, [1931] All ER Ref 1, they were viewed primarily as employees and consequently their fiduciary obligations of good faith as directors was not given the prominence it undoubtedly deserved. Coupled with this, the severance payments appear to have been made by the principal shareholder in Niger (Lever Bros Ltd) and not the employing company itself and Lord Atkin at least was unwilling to find any fiduciary nexus between the errant directors and the company's principal shareholder ([1932] AC 161, at 228). Two recent cases of considerable importance illustrate that by emphasising fiduciary status rather than contractual nexus, a director will be treated as being under a duty to disclose to some extent his past misdeeds and, failure to do so, will enable a company to avoid, on the grounds of unilateral mistake, a contract between itself and a director who fails to make such a disclosure.

The first case, *Sybron Corpn v Rochem Ltd* ([1983] 2 All ER 707, [1983] BCLC 43), involved wrongdoing by the senior manager of the plaintiff company's European operation who, in conjunction with subordinate employees, conspired to carry on secretly a business which competed with that of the plaintiff company. The manager had retired and the company sought to set aside the severance arrangements it had entered into with him. In particular, it sought to recover a lump sum it had paid to the employee and also sought a declaration that certain annuities which had been bought to provide the employee with a pension were free of any trust the employee's in favour of the employee. The action was also brought against the employee's wife, but it was agreed that as a volunteer she was in no better position than her husband. The Court of Appeal upheld Walton J's decision in favour of the company (the lump sum was recoverable and the pension was not subject to a trust in favour of the employee and his wife) and in so doing it not only agitated the waters around *Bell v Lever Bros Ltd*, but it opened the door for the creation of a positive duty on directors to disclose breaches of their fiduciary duty.

Stephenson LJ, who gave the principal judgment, saw the decision of the House of Lords in *Bell* as laying down the principle, which the court was bound to accept, that 'a contract of employment, though often described as creating a relationship of trust between master and servant, is not a contract uberrimae fidei so as to require disclosure by the servant of his own misconduct' (at 714 g, 52 r). He was also at pains to emphasise that Bell and Snelling in the *Bell* case were innocent of any fraud, a factor which could be invoked to restrict the scope of the decision. However, Stephenson LJ was able to distinguish the problem in *Bell* from that facing the court in *Sybron: Bell* was concerned with the duty to confess, whereas *Sybron* involved the duty of a senior employee to inform on wrongdoing subordinates even where fulfilment of this duty would disclose the informant's own wrongdoing. Stephenson LJ held that there was such a duty to inform, citing *Swain v West (Butchers) Ltd* ([1936] 1 All ER 224, [1936] 3 All ER 261). It was not, however, a general duty (for example, one based on an implied term in all contracts of employment) but was dependent on the:

> 'terms of employment of the particular servant. He may be so placed in the hierarchy as to have a duty to report either the misconduct of his superior, as in *Swain's* case, or the misconduct of his inferiors, as in this case' (at 717 g, at 56 a).

The senior manager in the instant case was at the apex of the company's European operations and had a specific obligation to report on matters within the European zone, an obligation which required disclosure of the repeated malpractices of his subordinates. Having breached his duty, the company was entitled to recover the severance payment and relieve itself of its pension obligations as they had been made under a mistake of fact, for had the company known of the breach of duty it was agreed that it would have exercised its contractual right not to make the payments in question and would have dismissed the employee for misconduct.

It is clear from *Sybron* that the duty to disclose will be a function of the status of the employee and the implication of this for directors is self-evident. Although the management responsibilities of a director are to a large extent determined by the articles, where a company's articles are in the form of Article 80 of Table A, a director would possess the necessary status. And it may be that irrespective of the articles, a director will always have such a duty, a duty which could quite easily be extended to 'shadow directors' (cf Companies Act 1980, s 63(1)). Whether *Sybron* would oblige a director to disclose the wrongdoings of a fellow director of equal status is unclear in that there is no hierarchical relationship. Arguably *Bell* gives a negative answer to this. However, although Snelling and Bell were vice-chairman and chairman respectively, they appear to have been treated as virtually of equal status, and anyhow great significance should not be attached to the position of chairman when determining managerial status. It would be, however, anomolous to hold that a director had a duty to disclose the wrongdoing of subordinates but not that of his peers, particularly in light of *Swain v West (Butchers) Ltd* which recognises a duty on the part of a subordinate in an appropriate situation to disclose the wrongdoing of superiors. Once, however, a director is obliged to disclose the wrongdoing of his equals, superiors, or subordinates, then the rule that he is not obliged to confess his own wrongdoing looks distinctly odd.

One way out of this problem, which seems a direct consequence of *Bell*, is provided by the judgment of Glidewell J in *Horcal Ltd v Gatland* [1983] BCLC 60 who considered that the post-*Bell* developments of the principles pertaining to a director's fiduciary duty, particularly *Regal (Hastings) Ltd v Gulliver* [1942] 1 All ER 378, obliged a director to disclose his own wrongdoing when entering into a contract involving the payment of compensation for severance of his employment contract (at 68 a). Failure to make such disclosure would render any ensuing severance agreement void on the grounds of unilateral mistake. However, on the facts in *Horcal Ltd v Gatland*, Glidewell J did not invoke the principle as he found that the agreement between the plaintiff company and the defendant director was entered into at a time when the defendant was not in breach of duty.

If the reasoning of Glidewell J is too heady, an alternative approach to containing *Bell* is suggested in *Sybron*, particularly in the judgment of Kerr LJ. For Kerr LJ, it was important that in *Bell* the employees' concealment was not fraudulent, and he 'was far from convinced' that *Bell* applied where 'the concealment was fraudulent' (at 720 c, at 59 d). This interpretation of *Bell* provides a neat solution for the situation where an otherwise faultless director merely fails to report the wrongdoings of others which he has a duty to report. Neither *Swain* or *Sybron* are in point on this issue, as in both cases the employees were personally guilty of wrongdoing. It would be anomalous to exempt a wrongdoing director from a duty to confess, but to impose a duty to inform on an otherwise innocent director. This anomaly would be eliminated if *Bell* were confined to cases where the employee was not fraudulent in concealing his own wrongdoing. The alternative, to adopt the approach of Glidewell J in *Horcal Ltd v Gatland*, would also eliminate this anomaly: directors would then have a duty to confess and inform, a solution, it is submitted, in keeping with their fiduciary duty.

There are other aspects of the *Sybron* and *Horcal* decisions which give rise to vexed issues of principle. Is the perception of a pension as deferred remuneration accurate? If so, is it then necessary to develop a doctrine of public policy, akin to that relating to penalty clauses in contract, to deal with what is in reality the forfeiture of a pension? (Cf in another context, *Bull v Pitney Bowers Ltd* [1966] 3 All ER 384). Was Glidewell J correct in holding that a salary already paid should be forfeited because the director had failed to disclose his breach of duty at the time of payment? The former question (on the forfeiture of pension rights) raises issues outside the scope of this note, but on the latter point the judgment of Glidewell J must be read in light of *Healey v Société Anonyme Français Rubastic* ([1917] 1 KB 946).

Sybron is also discussed in the articles on Contract, p 115 and Employment, p 176 below.

Share valuation: challenging expert's valuation

In *Burgess v Purchase & Sons (Farms) Ltd* [1983] 2 All ER 4, [1983] BCLC 176 shares in a family company were sold by the plaintiffs, the price being set according to a provision in the company's articles requiring a sale of shares to be at a 'fair value', this figure to be set by the company's auditors whose decision was made 'final, binding and conclusive'. The auditors explained the basis on which they arrived at their figure and it was therefore a 'speaking' (as opposed to 'non-speaking') valuation. The plaintiffs challenged the accuracy of the valuation on the grounds that it was carried out on a fundamentally erroneous basis and the issue before the court was whether the plaintiff's statement of claim disclosed a reasonable cause of action. Nourse J held that it did.

In reaching his conclusion the learned judge felt bound by previous authority (*Johnston v Chestergate Hat Manufacturing Co Ltd* [1915] 2 Ch 338; *Dean v Prince* [1954] 1 All ER 749 (Harman J at first instance); *Frank H Wright (Constructions) Ltd v Frodoor Ltd* [1967] 1 All ER 433, to distinguish between a non-speaking and a speaking valuation. The former cannot be impugned provided it is made in good faith, on the right property, and by the right person. However, in the case of an uncompleted transaction equitable relief may be refused where a non-speaking valuation was made on an apparently erroneous basis and the party who sought to sustain the valuation left to his remedy in damages (at 11 a, at 183 b, cf *Baber v Kenwood Manufacturing Co Ltd* [1978] 1 Lloyd's Rep 175). Although Nourse J was hesitant on this point, it would be consistent with the principles on which courts of equity have exercised their discretion in granting equitable relief for breach of contract (see, eg Chitty, *Contracts* (25th edn) pp 197–198). Where a valuation is of the speaking variety, as was the case in *Burgess v Purchase & Sons (Farms) Ltd*, Nourse J held that it could be challenged on the grounds that it was made on a fundamentally erroneous basis. The justification for distinguishing speaking from non-speaking valuations in this way is far from clear. Nourse J was not particularly happy with this 'anomaly' but felt obliged to follow it on the grounds of authority (at 11 d–f, at 183 h). He did suggest that it may be that the rule with respect to speaking valuations 'can be justified on the footing that a valuation made on a fundamentally erroneous basis is no more that for which the parties have contracted than one made of the wrong property or by the wrong man or in bad faith' (at 11 d, at 183 f). But this is true for both speaking and non-speaking valuations. A slightly different, but arguably more plausible way of framing a 'contract explanation' for the difference, is that the parties by agreeing to a non-speaking valuation must have both equally assumed the risk of the valuation being conducted on an erroneous basis. The finality that this produces, particularly in a world 'peopled by the indeterminate spirits of fictitious or unborn sales' (per Danckwerts J, *Re Holt*

[1953] 1 WLR 1488 at 1492) is something of obvious value to both parties to a transaction. But finality is also of importance to the parties to a speaking valuation and, more importantly, it would appear that a non-speaking valuation can be turned into a speaking one, not by the acts of the parties, but by the valuer deciding to give reasons for his opinion even though not obliged to do so (*Dean v Prince*). It may be that the distinction between speaking and non-speaking valuations simply cannot be justified and, in the interests of finality, the non-speaking rule should prevail. An aggrieved party would not necessarily be without a remedy and may have an action in negligence against the valuer (*Arenson v Arenson* [1975] 3 All ER 901). This, however, would not apply to all situations where a valuation is made on a fundamentally erroneous basis. As Nourse J pointed out, the alleged error may not consitute negligence; for example, 'the valuer who proceeds on a fundamentally erroneous construction of the agreement which it is not within his professional competence to detect' (at 11 h, at 184 b). More importantly, the valuer will often exclude liability for negligence (cf Supply of Goods and Services Act 1982, s 16).

Winding up: restraining advertisement of petition as an abuse of the process of the court

Re a company ([1983] BCLC 492) involved the exercise of the court's discretion to restrain the advertisement of a winding-up petition and to have it dismissed as an abuse of the process of the court. A peculiarity of the case was that the petition was presented on the grounds of non-payment of a debt, the debt being costs which had been neither taxed nor agreed, awarded in favour of the petitioner on the morning of the day on which the petition was presented. Another peculiarity of the case was that the plaintiff, unlike any other of the company's creditors, was entitled to take up a lease of land of which the company was the lessee if the company were wound up. Harman J dismissed the petition. As Harman J pointed out, as he has done on other occasions, a winding up is not a true *lis* between the parties. The petitioner is invoking a class right and the 'only proper purpose for which a petition can be presented is for the proper administration of the company's assets for the benefit of all in the relevant class' (at 495 f). Improper motive, however, did not make 'unlawful that which is otherwise lawful' (at 495 e-f), but there was a difference between improper motive and the requirement that the petitioner's 'class stand together and will benefit or suffer rateably' (at 495 h–j). In *Re a company* this requirement of parity of treatment was absent as the petitioner obtained a special benefit (the lease) from the winding up and, accordingly, the petition should be dismissed.

Harman J also considered it an improper use of the Companies Court to present a petition for the non-payment of a debt which had never been demanded, or with respect to which no opportunity to pay had been given to the company or a third party (at 496 a–c). Coupled with this, he considered it arguable that until costs had been taxed or agreed, the debt was a disputed one (at 496 c–e).

Fraudulent trading: Companies Act 1948, s 332

Section 332 of the Companies Act 1948 has been a very ineffectual weapon in dealing with the fraudulent trading. Over 20 years ago, its shortcomings were pointed out by the Jenkins Committee (Cmnd 1749, para 503), and more recently it was criticised by the Cork Committee (Cmnd 8558, Ch 44). The recent decision in *R v Cox and Hedges* [1983] BCLC 169 amply justifies these criticisms and demonstrates, if such be needed, that the section is very much in need of an overhaul. The case emphasises, what probably was clearly the law beforehand (*Re Patrick and Lyon Ltd* [1933] Ch 786), that the requirement of intent to defraud under s 332 'contains the ingredient of dishonesty' (at 175 a) which applies equally to the civil and the criminal aspects of the section. This requirement of subjective wrongdoing means that the section will only operate within a very narrow compass and will fail to pick up unreasonable or reckless behaviour provided the person responsible can persuade the court that he acted in good faith. Given the protection afforded by limited liability, it is inevitable that those who control companies on the brink of insolvency will be afflicted by unrealistic optimism about the company's prospects and therefore the burden of showing dishonesty will be extremely difficult to satisfy. *Cox and Hedges* highlights the need to reform s 332 along the lines recommended by the Cork Committee so that a director will be liable under the section where a company incurs liabilities and he knows, or ought to have known, that there was no reasonable prospect of the company meeting them.

Examination of the persons having relevant information: Companies Act 1948, s 268

Re Highgrade Traders Ltd [1983] BCLC 137 is a case of some importance on the application of s 268 of the Companies Act 1948. Section 268 confers 'an extraordinary power . . . of an inquisitorial kind' (*Re North Australian Territory Company* (1890) 45 Ch D 87 at 92) and the courts, although recognising that it must not be used for an oppressive or vexatious purpose, have been reluctant to fetter the exercise of their discretion by confining or categorising the circumstances in which it may be invoked. In *Re Highgrade Traders Ltd* a company's premises had been destroyed by fire and the insurance company which insured the premises had a number of reports prepared on the circumstances of the fire. These reports, by a firm of specialists in fire investigations, accountants, and insurance assessors respectively, were prepared because the insurance company suspected arson and they were submitted to the insurance company's solicitors with a view to determining whether the insurance company should honour any claim under the policies. The insurance company, on the basis of the reports, refused to honour the policies on the grounds that the fire was caused by arson. Eventually the company was wound up and the liquidator sought an order (against the officer of the insurance company responsible for handling the claim but as a matter of substance against the insurance company) under s 268 for the production of the reports. The insurance company resisted the application on two grounds: (a) the reports came into existence subsequent to the cessation of the company's business and were made by a person who was not involved in the company's affairs and (b) were subject to the legal professional privilege. Mervyn Davies J decided against the insurance company on both counts.

As regards legal professional privilege, the learned judge reasoned that the reports were communications between a client and a third party and for such communications to be covered by legal professional privilege they must have been prepared for the purpose of litigation. In this case the reports had been prepared for a twin purpose: (a) to enable the insurance company, if necessary, to resist an unfounded claim and (b) to provide the insurance company's solicitors with information relevant to potential litigation. As the first purpose was the dominant one, Mervyn Davies J ruled that the reports were not privileged. This, of course, is the application of accepted legal principles to the facts and the trial judge has the undoubted advantage to canvass fully the whole of the evidence. But given that even purpose (a) for which the report was prepared has implicated in it the obvious possibility of litigation, it is surprising that the court did not find that the reports were brought into being because of the very real chance of litigation.

On the second question, the scope of s 268, the judgment in *Re Highgrade Traders Ltd* will probably prove more durable. Mervyn Davies J held that both as regards jurisdiction, and the exercise of discretion, this was an appropriate case for ordering an examination of the responsible officer of the insurance company. As regards jurisdiction, an order may be made against 'any person whom the court deems capable of giving information' concerning the affairs of a company (s 268(1)) and there is no requirement that the person to be examined has been in some way formally connected with the management or the affairs of the company. Nor is there any requirement for the information sought to have been in existence before the company ceased to carry on business. As regards the exercise of the court's discretion, no hard and fast rules could be formulated. In the present case the liquidator had stated that the information would enable him to form a concluded view whether or not to sue and this was a proper and sufficient justification for an order under s 268 and was not an oppressive use of the section by the liquidator to obtain some advantage beyond what would normally be available to a litigant (see *Re Castle New Homes Ltd* [1979] 2 All ER 775 at 789 a–b). Accordingly, Mervyn Davies J considered it proper to exercise his discretion and confirm the order obtained by the liquidator.

(The judgment of Mervyn Davies J was reversed by the Court of Appeal on the grounds that the reports were privileged and, in light of this, the court should not have exercised its discretion to order the examination of the officer of the insurance company. The Court of Appeal judgment will be dealt with in the next issue of the survey.)

Vinelott J had also to consider the scope of s 268 in *Re Norton Warburg Holdings Ltd and Norton Warburg Investment Management Ltd* [1983] BCLC 235, in which a liquidator sought to have a s 268 examination ordered under s 307 of the Companies Act 1948 in a creditors' voluntary winding up. In *Norton Warburg* the liquidator sought an examination of the auditor of a company and of its subsidiary in circumstances where there was no allegation of wrongdoing on the part of the auditor or that he was attempting to conceal relevant information. The auditor applied to have an examination ordered by the Registrar set aside until the liquidator had submitted to him questions in writing and he had a reasonable opportunity to answer them. Vinelott J considered that there was no absolute requirement for an examination under s 268 to be preceded by written submissions, it all depended on the circumstances of the case (see *Re Rolls Razor Ltd (No 2)* [1969] 3 All ER 1386). The court had to balance the views of the liquidator, which were entitled to great weight, as to how the liquidation could best be carried out, against the requirement that parties should not be treated unfairly or oppressively by having to submit to an examination under s 268. It was also of importance that in the present case the persons against whom the order was sought were not personally accused of any wrongdoing nor was there any danger that they would destroy relevant evidence. On the facts, Vinelott J considered that the oral examination should be preceded by written questions and only then could the oral examination be proceeded with. In addition, the liquidator should specify the matters on which he sought clarification and invite comments which would further sharpen and narrow the focus of any oral examination.

The procedure proposed by Vinelott J in *Norton Warburg* has much to commend it. It will undoubtedly make an oral examination more productive and expeditious than one conducted at large. Also, by merely being a rule of guidance rather than an inflexible principle, it leaves the court's discretion unfettered for those cases where the delay inevitable in such a procedure would provide an opportunity for relevant evidence to be destroyed, or where it is otherwise undesirable that prospective witnesses should be forewarned as to the line of enquiry to be pursued at the examination. Surprise, where appropriate, thus still remains available under s 268.

Agents: liability of company for acts of its agents

British Bank of the Middle East v Sun Life Assurance Co of Canada (UK) Ltd [1983] BCLC 78 involved a straightforward application of agency principles to a situation where it was alleged that the defendant insurance company was bound by guarantees made on its behalf to the plaintiff bank by one of its employees. On the facts, the court found that the agent in question had neither the actual or apparent authority to enter into the transaction. Nor was it possible to find that the representations of a branch manager employed by the defendant, that the agent had authority to enter into the contract, estopped the defendant as the mere title of branch manager did not import that the holder had authority to make such representations. As is often the question in problems concerning the liability of a company for the acts of its agents, the issue turns on the application of agreed principles to the facts, but given the unanimity of the lower courts, it is surprising that this case was seen to have the necessary stamina to reach the House of Lords.

Ultra vires: political contributions

Simmonds v Heffer ([1983] BCLC 298) deals with a topic of some importance and current interest and on which curiously there is little modern authority, namely, the capacity of a company to make gifts to political parties or for political purposes. In *Simmonds v Heffer* the League Against the Cruel Sports Ltd, which as its name indicates has as its objects the prevention of cruelty to animals, made two separate gifts to the Labour Party to finance its campaign in the 1979 general election. The first of £30,000 was made specifically to advertise the Labour Party's commitment to the abolition of certain cruel sports, and the other of £50,000 was made for the general purposes of the Labour Party without any restriction as to its use. Mervyn Davies J held that the first payment to be intra vires and the second to be ultra vires. He reasoned that, as the first payment could only be used by the Labour Party for purposes which were similar to the League's objects, the payment was obviously valid. But the failure to so restrict the second payment was fatal to its validity as it could be devoted to purposes wholly unconnected with the League's objects. As regards the second gift, it was argued that a provision in the company's objects empowering it to 'do all such other lawful things as are incidental or conducive to the attainment' of its objects, coupled with the reasoning in *Evans v Brunner, Mond & Co Ltd* ([1921] 1 Ch 359), saved the gift. Mervyn Davies J rejected this. The provision was a power, an 'incidental' or 'conducive' power, (at 304 c) which could only 'be used in the pursuit of, or to extend, an express authorised object' (at 304 c). *Evans v Brunner, Mond & Co Ltd* could be explained on the grounds that the gifts for educational purposes in that case were justified as being connected with the company's business as a chemical manufacturer. However, such an argument was not possible in *Simmonds v Heffer* as there was no necessary connection between the League's objects and the general political programme of the Labour Party.

The question has been raised of the implications of *Simmonds v Heffer* for the broader issue of the validity of contributions made by companies to political parties ([1983] JBL 485). While the decision undoubtedly has some implications for this issue, its impact will probably be minimal. It will merely act as a warning, and paradoxically provide guidelines as to how a gift should be made so as not to be open to an ultra vires challenge. Corporate donors will merely have to ensure that the terms of the gift link it to the welfare of the donor, something which should not constitute a very taxing hurdle.

Floating charge: Companies Act 1948, s 322

Re GT Whyte & Co Ltd [1983] BCLC 311 involved the application of s 322 on the Companies Act 1948 to a somewhat complex arrangement whereby Lloyds Bank provided financial support to a secondary bank during the banking crisis in the early 1970s. A wholly-owned subsidiary of Lloyds Bank provided Whyte with, among other things, a credit line of £27m and, as part of the transaction, Lloyds entered into an indemnity agreement with its subsidiary. For various reasons it was not possible to secure the loan as had been originally agreed. As a result it was agreed that the subsidiary of Lloyds would call in its loan, and Lloyds would itself enter into a new loan agreement with Whyte which would enable Whyte to pay off the subsidiary's loan, then standing at £12.75m. The new agreement with Lloyds was secured by a floating charge over Whyte's undertaking. Whyte was wound up within a year of the creation of the floating charge and, on the assumption that Whyte was insolvent when the charge was created, the question arose as to the validity of the charge under s 322. This raised the issue of whether the money provided by Lloyds to repay its subsidiary was 'cash paid to the company' at the time of the creation of the charge. Nourse J held that it was not. The substance of the transaction was that Lloyds and its subsidiary were principal and agent and that when the original advances were made they were made as a matter of substance by Lloyds (at 317 f–g). Accordingly, when Lloyds provided the money to enable Whyte to repay the loan to its subsidiary and took the floating charge, the old facility in substance remained in force and all that had changed was the term dealing with the loan's security. However, this was the type of transaction caught by s 322, as it was merely an attempt to improve Lloyds' security without extending any new cash to Whyte. Nourse J also rejected the suggestion that there had to be some type of underhand conduct for a transaction to be caught by s 322: the section operated whether or not there was an intention to prefer improperly the interests of a particular creditor (at 317 b–d).

Winding up: alternative remedy: Companies Act 1948, s 225(2)

Re a company [1983] 2 All ER 854, [1983] BCLC 151 raised important issues on the application of the Companies Act 1948, s 225(2), which confers a discretion on the court to refuse a winding up where it is of the opinion that 'some other remedy is available to the petitioners and that they are acting unreasonably in seeking to have the company wound up instead of pursuing that other remedy'. In *Re a company* two directors of a company, after disagreement with the third and only other director, excluded him from participation in the management of the company. The excluded director was not paid a salary, but was provided with management accounts and offered access to the company's books and accounts. After negotiations, the two directors offered to purchase the excluded director's shares at a fair market value to be fixed by an independent expert. The offer was not accepted and the excluded director brought an action for the compulsory winding up of the company. It was generally agreed that the excluded director had a legitimate expectation to participate in the company's management and that his exclusion prima facie entitled him to a winding-up order under the principle in *Ebrahimi v Westbourne Galleries Ltd* [1972] 2 All ER 492. Vinelott J, however, exercising his discretion under s 225(2) of the Companies Act 1948, declined to grant the remedy on the grounds that the petitioner had acted unreasonably in refusing the offer for his shares, and, in the course of his judgment, he laid down a number of important points on the operation of the subsection.

(a) In determining whether s 225(2) applies, it is not necessary for the respondent to show that the petitioner has some alternative 'legal' remedy available to him (eg under s 75 of the Companies Act 1980). The subsection would apply where some alternative step is available to the petitioner to alleviate his plight (eg the offer in the present case to purchase his shares) and the question would then revolve around the reasonableness of his conduct in not adopting it.

(b) The court's jurisdiction under s 225 is discretionary and it would be entitled to refuse a winding-up order where it would be unfair to the other shareholders to grant the order in light of any offer they had made to purchase the petitioner's shares. Vinelott J made the important point that in making this evaluation it was the position at the time of the application which was of importance and the court was not confined to circumstances existing at the date of the presentation of the petition (at 860f, at 158h–i). This will obviously provide the parties with an opportunity to seek an agreed solution right up to hearing of the petition.

(c) In exercising its discretion under s 225, there was no rule entitling a member of an 'incorporated partnership' to have the company wound up and the assets sold in the market in the same way as a partner could require this on the dissolution of a partnership. To give the member of an 'incorporated partnership' such a right would be to ignore the fact that the affairs of the company were to be conducted according to the articles and that the assets of the company were vested in the company and not the members. This is obviously an important limitation on the application of the partnership analogy to companies and illustrates that the fact of incorporation and its consequences cannot be wholly ignored (cf *Re Expanded Plugs Ltd* [1966] 1 All ER 877).

(d) Vinelott J had also to deal with the question of the fairness of the offer made by the majority for the minority shareholder's shares and, in particular, whether the price should be determined as of the date the expert fixed the price (which would obviously be after the judgment), or at the date the petitioner was excluded from the company's affairs. Vinelott J held that there was no hard and fast rule requiring the valuation to be current or retrospective. On the facts in *Re a company,* he thought a valuation on the current value of the shares would be fair and just. This was partly what the petitioner sought by his petition to have the company wound up, and also the petitioner had been responsible for the sale not going through at an earlier date because of his unreasonable refusal to accept the offer for his shares. This valuation point, and in particular the court's discretion to require a current or retrospective valuation, has obvious important implications for s 75 of the Companies Act 1980 which is silent on the principles of valuation to be adopted for the purposes of that section (at 862 i, at 162 d; see also *SCWS v Meyer* [1958] 3 All ER 66).

Re a company clearly illustrates that a bona fide offer by majority shareholders to purchase the shares of a minority shareholder, where there is discord, will greatly lessen the latter's chance of obtaining a winding-up order. It is of importance, however, to note that the case should not be seen as exposing a minority shareholder in an incorporated partnership 'to the hazard that the majority will be able to exclude him from participation in the affairs of the company and then compulsorily acquire his shares, notwithstanding the absence of any power in the articles to do so' (at 862 a–b, at 161 c). Vinelott J considered it of some importance that the minority shareholder had expressed a willingness to sell his shares; had the petitioner insisted all along that he would not sell, then the outcome would not necessarily have been the same.

Take-over bids: duty of directors of offeree company

It is curious that the take-over bid, which has been for some considerable time a dominant feature of English commercial life, has produced no reported cases of substance dealing with the legal principles applicable to this type of acquisition of control of a company. *Heron International Ltd v Lord Grade, Associated Communications Corpn plc* [1983] BCLC 244 is therefore to be welcomed as one of the first cases dealing with the duties of an offeree board in the face of a contested bid. The voting structure of the target company, Associated Communications Corpn (ACC), was somewhat peculiar: it had approximately 54 million non-voting shares which were listed on the Stock Exchange and 150,000 voting shares, which were unlisted, and which were held by the directors of ACC. ACC was in financial difficulties and Mr Holmes a' Court, an Australian, who held through one of his companies 51% of the ACC non-voting shares and who was a director of ACC, agreed to help provided he acquired control of ACC. He made a bid for ACC through another of his companies (Bell) and this was accepted by the directors who, of course, held the voting shares. Heron International Ltd (Heron) also made a bid for ACC which placed a higher value on the ACC shares than the Bell bid. This bid, which was conditional on the offeror obtaining control of ACC, could not succeed in light of the ACC's directors acceptance of the Bell offer for their voting shares. In addition, the Heron bid was also conditional on acquiring the non-voting shares in ACC and Mr Holmes a' Court made it clear that the shares held by his companies were not for sale. Eventually Heron, suing as a representative of the shareholders of the defendant company, sought an injunction to prevent the transfer of the ACC shares to Bell. The plaintiff's case turned to a large extent on the argument that the transfer of the ACC voting shares by the directors was in breach of ACC's articles of association which provided that a voting share could not be transferred at a price exceeding four times the market value of a non-voting share. The Court of Appeal held that the article had been breached and therefore the transfer could not legally be effected as Bell had notice of this fact. This was enough to dispose of the case, but the court went on to deal with other matters involved in the litigation.

The first issue of interest was the bearing of the rule in *Foss v Harbottle* (1843) 2 Hare 461 to the plaintiff's standing to bring the action. For an understanding of this point, one other fact in *Heron International* is of crucial importance. ACC controlled a programme company called Central and the Independent Broadcasting Authority had insisted (as it had a right to do) that, as a condition to Bell taking over ACC and Central being allowed to retain its licence, ACC should agree that it would not exercise control over the affairs of Central. The court, for the purpose of the *Foss v Harbottle* point, assumed that this would depreciate the assets of ACC to the extent that its holding in Central would be less valuable. Thus if the Bell bid were to go ahead it would cause loss in two ways: (a) the loss to ACC because of depreciation in value of its Central's shares and (b) the 'loss to the pockets of the [ACC] shareholders because they are deprived of the opportunity to realising their shares to greater advantage' (at 262 b–c), which is measured by the 'difference between the takeover value per share which they are constrained to accept and the higher takeover value which they lost the chance of accepting' (at 262 h). It is clear that loss (a) could not give rise to a personal action by a shareholder as it was suffered by the company and an individual shareholder is precluded from translating corporate harm into personal wrong (*Prudential Assurance Co Ltd v Newman Industries Ltd (No 2)* [1982] 1 All ER 354 at 366). As regards a derivative action, loss (a) will only give rise to such an action if it is unratifiable. In *Heron International* there was no discussion of this issue as the court refused to grant an injunction on this ground because the quantum of ACC's loss was purely speculative and the derivative action was only a device to enable the plaintiffs to complain of a wrong which they had suffered personally. One can therefore only speculate on the question of ratifiability, but given that there was no allegation of bad faith, this seems to be the type of wrong which is ratifiable (cf *Pavlides v Jensen* [1956] 2 All ER 518).

Having decided that no action could be brought on behalf of the company, the court considered whether the directors owed a duty to the shareholders in ACC. It is important to note that the observations on this point in *Heron International* were made in the context of the exercise by the directors of the power to conferred on them by ACC's articles (art 29) to register the transfer of their voting shares. On this point Lawton LJ stated (at 265 e–h):

> 'Where directors have decided that it is in the interests of a company that the company should be taken over, and where there are two or more bidders, the only duty of the directors, who have powers such as those contained in art 29, is to obtain the best price. The directors should not commit themselves to transfer their own voting shares to a bidder unless they are satisfied that he is offering the best price reasonably obtainable. Where the directors must only decide between rival bidders, the interests of the company must be the interests of the current shareholders. The future of the company will lie with the successful bidder. The directors owe no duty to the successful bidder or to the company after it has passed under the control of the successful bidder. The successful bidder can look after himself, and the shareholders who reject the bid and remain as shareholders do so with their eyes open, having rejected that price which the directors consider to be the best price reasonably obtainable. Thus as a result of art 29, the directors owed a duty to the general body of shareholders who were shareholders on 13 January 1982 to obtain for the shareholders the opportunity to accept or reject the best bid reasonably obtainable.'

This process of defining interests of the company to mean interests of the shareholders when dealing with the constraints on the exercise of discretionary powers by directors, is one that has been pointed out by others (Finn, *Fiduciary Obligations,* pp 66–67) and, in particular, its effect of imposing willy nilly fiduciary obligations on directors towards shareholders despite conventional wisdom to the contrary (*Percival v Wright* [1902] 2 Ch 421, cf Companies Act 1948, s 193(3)). However, there is no suggestion in the cases that the duty can be enforced directly by the shareholders, they still have to enforce the duty by bringing the action in the name of the company to whom the directors nominally owe their duty. Although this aspect of *Heron International* is far from clear, and Lawton LJ does speak in terms of the 'former shareholders in ACC' seeking to sue the 'directors in order to recover for the benefit of their own individual pockets' (at 262 h, see also 263 b), it is to be doubted if he intended to take the radical step of conferring a right on shareholders to enforce such duties directly. On the facts in *Heron International,* the court found that the directors had not acted improperly as they had formed the opinion, reasonable in the circumstances, that the bid of Heron was effectively blocked and therefore the only realistic suitor was Bell.

Charges: reservation of title

Re Peachdart Ltd ([1983] 3 All ER 204, [1983] BCLC 225) illustrates, if further illustration be needed, that reservation of title clauses taken by suppliers of goods which are subsequently incorporated into the products of the purchaser, will operate (if at all) as charges and will not be effective to reserve a proprietary interest in the supplier. Accordingly, failure to register the reservation of title clause as a charge under the Companies Act 1948, s 95, will have the usual consequences of invalidity, a fate which befell the reservation of title clause in *Re Peachdart Ltd*. See, for further discussion, the article on Commercial Law, p 48, above.

Winding-up: practice

Re Pleatfine Ltd [1983] BCLC 102 and *Re Shushella Ltd* [1983] BCLC 505 are both cases involving small but important points on winding-up practice. The first involved the practice which appears to have grown up of District Registries, without the necessary jurisdiction, hearing winding-up petitions. Harman J considered this an improper and undesirable practice as such courts simply lacked the manpower and skills available in the Companies Court to deal with winding-up petitions expeditiously, an obvious necessity in light of s 227 of the Companies Act 1948. For example, in the present case there had been a span of over 11 weeks from presentation of petition to hearing. The petition before Harman J in *Re Pleatfine Ltd* was for a validation order under s 227 of the Companies Act 1948 and, although the winding-up petition had started life in the Birmingham District Registry, which lacked the necessary jurisdiction, it was nevertheless valid because of s 218(7) of the Companies Act 1948 and, on the facts, Harman J considered it proper to exercise his discretion under s 219(1) of the Act to clothe the Birmingham District Registry with the necessary jurisdiction to complete the proceedings (see now Companies (Winding-up) (Amendment No 2) Rules 1983 SI 1983 (No 1645) conferring winding-up jurisdiction on the District Registries of Birm-ing-ham, Bristol and Cardiff).

Re Shusella Ltd involved the important question of costs. Nourse J made it clear that the modern practice of dismissing a petition and awarding costs where the petitioner had been paid his debt, but no provision made for costs, only applied where there had been proper compliance with all the provisions of the Companies (Winding-up) Rules 1949. Where a petition is struck out for failure to comply with the rules, no order for costs could be made. And, in particular, the court would not be willing to dispense with the advertisement of a petition, although it has power to do so (Companies (Winding-up) Rules 1949, r 28). To exercise its discretion in this way would weaken the incentive on petitioners to get their petitions in order and encourage them to use the Companies Court as a debt collecting agency merely to put pressure on corporate debtors.

Director's duties: the Mareva injunction

The Mareva injunction appears to be sailing into the waters of company law as is illustrated by *PCW (Underwriting Agencies) Ltd v Dixon* [1983] 2 All ER 158, [1983] BCLC 105. Once the injunction was made available against resident defendants (*Barclay-Johnson v Yuill* [1980] 3 All ER 190) then its use to try to obtain not merely a freezing of the defendant's assets, but also some type of security, was inevitable, particularly as *Lister v Stubbs* (1890) 45 Ch D 1 was not seen as standing in the way of the granting of the injunction. The courts, however, have been at pains to prevent the injunction from being used to accord a plaintiff priority for his debts, or to give the plaintiff an advantage denied him by the normal principles of insolvency (*The Angel Bell* [1980] 1 All ER 480 at 486 d–e). Although the Mareva injunction should not be viewed as involving a pre-trial attachment of the injuncted funds (Harpum and Jones (1983) 3 OJLS 136, 142), it is inevitable that plaintiffs will attempt to use it for this purpose. *PCW (Underwriting Agencies) Ltd v Dixon* illustrates a line of argument as to how this could be done.

There the plaintiff company had commenced an action against the defendant, a former director of the plaintiff, for the recovery of secret profits which it was alleged the defendant had improperly made when acting as a director of the company. The company had been successful in obtaining a Mareva injunction with respect to the ex-director's assets and in the present proceedings he sought to have it varied to provide a more generous allowance for living expenses and legal costs. In resisting the application for the variation, counsel for the company put forward the argument that the injunction in this case was not merely designed to preserve assets out of which a judgment might be satisfied, but it also was designed to restrain the defendant from using other people's money: the Mareva injunction was being invoked as an adjunct to the company's right to trace property in equity (see *A v C (No 1)* [1980] 2 All ER 347). Where an injunction is sought on this latter basis, its purpose, of course, is 'to secure the trust fund' (at 164 e, at 121 h), and to protect the plaintiffs proprietary interest. The logic of this claim, however, is that a defendant, as is normal with Mareva injunctions, should be allowed nothing for living expenses out of the injuncted funds as these funds would simply not belong to the defendant (at 163 e, at 111 e).

On the facts, Lloyd J doubted whether the circumstances justified the Mareva claim on this broader ground as it was not at all clear how 'the whole of man's assets' (against which the injunction had been issued in *Dixon*) could be regarded as constituting a trust fund (at 164 g, at 113 a). Also, as the variation of the order in *Dixon* was to enable the plaintiff to meet living expenses (school fees, rent etc) and pay his legal costs, Lloyd J considered that he should exercise his discretion to vary the injunction irrespective of the company's proprietary claim. He considered the latter point, that the plaintiff should have the wherewithal to defend himself, particularly compelling. Thus, although Lloyd J varied the order in *Dixon*, the case illustrates how the Mareva injunction may be usable to give a plaintiff security by protecting funds in which the plaintiff claims a proprietary interest. To have any chance of success a plaintiff will have to identify clearly the allegedly trust assets and the effect of the order sought must not be to deprive the defendant of the means of conducting his case.

Minority oppression: Companies Act 1980, s 75

The effectiveness of s 75 of the Companies Act 1980 in protecting the interests of minority shareholders will obviously depend on the interpretation placed by the courts on the somewhat open-textured language of the section. 'Unfairly prejudicial' is self-evidently a phrase that gives considerable latitude for judicial creativity. The first reported cases on s 75 indicate, however, that the courts may be reluctant to use to the full the freedom which the section offers them to chart the remedy in ways which radically depart from the unsatisfactory position under the Companies Act 1948, s 210.

In *Re a company* ([1983] 2 All ER 36, [1983] BCLC 126, noted (1983) 46 MLR 1 Rev 643, (1983) 3 OJLS 417), Lord Granchester QC (sitting as Deputy Judge of the High Court) was not disposed to seize the opportunity to depart from the type of reasoning reminiscent of cases under the old s 210 of the 1948 Act, but it must be admitted that the petitioners in the case were seeking to use the section in a very bold way indeed. In *Re a company*, executors who represented infant beneficiaries, sought an order under s 75 on the grounds that the company had acted in an unfairly prejudicial manner by failing to use its liquid resources to purchase their shares either under ss 46 and 47 of the Companies Act 1981, or by means of a scheme of reconstruction under s 287 of the Companies Act 1948. The executors also complained that a proposal before the directors that the company diversify into a new line of business was also 'unfairly prejudicial'. Not surprisingly, Lord Granchester found that the executors were not entitled to a remedy under s 75. There was no obligation on the part of an incorporated partnership to provide a market for the shares of a locked-in minority, particularly in view of on the fact that in *Re a company* the company had declared a dividend (a most uncommon occurrence in the case of 'incorporated partnerships') and the principal shareholder had waived her rights to dividend (an even more uncommon occurrence). There was thus no question of the petitioners being excluded from any participation at all in the income stream of the company. Also, the executors could scarcely complain of their exclusion from corporate management as they had no legitimate expectation that they would be allowed to participate, and on this point were not unlike the petitioner in *Re Fildes Bros Ltd* [1970] 1 All ER 923. The complaint about the director's flirtation with a proposal for a new line of business was premature, they had decided nothing concrete, and it fell within the director's duty 'to manage the business of the company, and to put its assets to the best use, or realise them for the best advantage for the benefit of the company as a whole' (at 45 f–g, at 136 e–f). However, Lord Granchester did recognise that decisions by the directors (or a failure to make decisions) could constitute grounds for relief under s 75, but they would have to have reached a stage of ripeness which they simply had not done in *Re a company*.

It was not so much the outcome of *Re a company* that is of concern, but the somewhat narrow approach adopted to the interpretation of s 75. In particular, Lord Granchester considered that the reasoning in *Ebrahimi v Westbourne Galleries Ltd* had no application to s 75: interests in s 75 were to be confined to 'interests of the petitioner as a member' (at 44 f, at 135 c–d). Lord Granchester appears to have been persuaded to adopt this definition by the argument of counsel that a more expansive concept of the interests protected by s 75 might have given a remedy to 'a shareholder who objected to his company carrying out some operation on land adjoining his dwelling-house, which resulted in that house falling in value' (at 44 e, at 135 b–c). But surely this is something of a red herring. A shareholder's interests as defined in *Ebrahimi* for the purposes of s 222(f) of the Companies Act 1948 are much more restricted, and are confined within manageable and reasonably ascertainable bounds to cover the right to participate in the management of a company (with of course the remuneration that this entails) where the company is formed on the basis of an expectation that the members will have such a right of management participation. There is no reason why this concept of a member's rights (interests) should not be adopted when determining the scope of the interests protected by s 75. The courts' failure to so interpret s 210 of the Companies Act 1948 constituted one of the major limitations on the effectiveness of that section (*Re Lundie Bros Ltd* [1965] 2 All ER 692). There are some indications, however, that not all judges will adopt the narrow perception of 'interests' as reflected in the judgment of Lord Granchester. Vinelott J in another case named *Re a company* (see p 74) obviously considered that s 75 was intended to be more far-reaching than s 210 and considered it 'unlikely that the legislature could have intended to exclude from the scope of s 75 of the 1980 Act a shareholder in the position of Mr Ebrahimi' in the *Westbourne Galleries* case (at 859 b, at 158 d). This was partly because the new section substituted the words 'unfairly prejudicial' for 'oppressive', and partly because it refers to 'the *interests* of some of the members' whereas s 210 referred to '*some part* of the members'. These linguistic differences (the latter of which is scarcely compelling) could obviously be invoked to distance s 75 from s 210 and to make sure that the former section does not suffer the stultifying fate of the latter.

An unresolved conundrum is the relationship between s 75 and s 222(f) of the Companies Act 1948. As a matter of principle, it would be preferable for s 75 to be given the dominant role in protecting minority shareholders as it confers on the court a more flexible remedial jurisdiction, and s 222(f) should be reserved for those rare cases where the break-up value of a company exceeds its going concern value, or where the only way in which a minority shareholder could be compensated is by winding up the company and selling its assets. Nourse J had to consider the relationship between these provisions in *Re A Noble & Sons (Clothing) Ltd* [1983] BCLC 273 in which he refused to make an order under s 75 but ordered that the company should be wound up under s 222(f), a result which at first glance appears anomalous. This, of course, was the result reached in a number of cases involving s 210, but this was because that section was restricted to conduct which affected a petitioner qua member and thus, unlike s 222(f), it could not be invoked by a petitioner oppressed in some capacity other than that of member. But this was not the reasoning adopted in *Re A Noble & Sons (Clothing) Ltd* where the petitioner's grievance was his exclusion from management. Rather, Nourse J found that the exclusion was conduct justifying an order under s 222(f) but nevertheless was not 'unfairly prejudicial' so as to justify an order under s 75. He did not take the easy way out (which was apparently not argued) and dismiss the plaintiff's s 75 claim on the grounds that it did not relate to the petitioner's rights as a member.

The facts in *Re A Noble & Sons (Clothing) Ltd* were that two businessmen set up a small retail clothing business, it being expected that, although the day-to-day affairs of the company would be run by one of them, the other would be consulted on major commercial decisions affecting the company. Relationships between the parties deteriorated so that the member of the company who was to be responsible for the management of the company's day-to-day affairs took over complete responsibility for running the company and did not consult the other member on any important decisions affecting the management of the company's affairs. The excluded member sought relief under s 75, or alternatively under s 222(f). As regards s 75, Nourse J cited with approval the general observations of Slade J in the unreported decision, *Re Bovey Hotel Ventures Ltd* (31 July 1981), that 'unfairly prejudicial' in the section did not import a subjective test in the sense that a petitioner had to show that 'the persons who have had de facto control of the company have acted as they did in the conscious knowledge that this was unfair to the petitioner or that they were acting in bad faith' (at 290 g–i). The test was objective, and a petitioner could bring himself within the section by showing that the value of his 'shareholding in the company has been seriously diminished or at least seriously jeopardised' (at 290 g–h) by the unfair conduct of the other members who control the company. In *Re A Noble & Sons (Clothing) Ltd*, Nourse J refused to grant an order under s 75 partly becaue the petitioner had shown a lack of interest in the company's affairs and also because the controlling shareholder had not acted in an underhand way. Therefore there was nothing unfair with respect to the manner of the petitioner's exclusion from the affairs of the company and he was accordingly not entitled to a remedy under s 75. As regards s 222(f), the court found that the company had been formed on the basis of mutual confidence and that there was an 'implied agreement' that the excluded member would participate in all major decisions relating to the company. The exclusion of the petitioner had irreparably destroyed that confidence and the petitioner was therefore entitled to an order under s 222(f). The court was willing to make this order even though the petitioner had to some extent been responsible for the situation by his lack of interest, as the substantial cause for the breakdown of confidence had been the conduct of the other shareholder. This is an important point as it shows that a petitioner can succeed under s 222(f) even though not blameless. The overall outcome of *Re A Noble & Sons (Clothing) Ltd* is, however, to say the least, anomalous and the last word has probably not been heard on the relationship of s 75 to s 222(f).

Directors: breach of duty: adoption, ratification, release by all shareholders

An order will not be granted under RSC Ord 11, s 1(j) for service out of the jurisdiction where the person against whom it is sought has a good defence. In *Multinational Gas and Petrochemical Co v Multinational Gas and Petrochemical Services Ltd* [1983] 2 All ER 563, [1983] BCLC 461, noted (1984) 47 MLR 87, a majority of the Court of Appeal held that the requirement was satisfied by the foreign defendant and refused to make an order. In so doing, it had to deal with some of the most difficult, and as yet unresolved, problems of company law. In that case, the plaintiff company, incorporated in Liberia, had been set up by three multinational oil companies who were the sole shareholders and who also appointed the directors of the plaintiff. The multinational oil companies also set up the first defendant to act as the plaintiff's agent and advisor. The plaintiff company was wound up insolvent (under s 399 of the Companies Act 1948) and it brought an action against the first defendant alleging negligence and also sought an order under, inter alia, RSC Ord 11, s 1(j), against the multinational oil companies and the former directors on the grounds that they were a necessary and proper party to the action against the defendant. The plaintiff's application to serve its writ out of the jurisdiction was unsuccessful. A majority of the Court of Appeal (May LJ dissenting) reasoned that the plaintiff company had no cause of action against its directors for negligence as the allegedly negligent acts were the acts of the shareholders and therefore the plaintiff could not complain of acts which were its own acts. The acts were the acts of the company because all the shareholders of the plaintiff company (ie the multinational oil companies) knew and approved of what the plaintiff company was doing and this was sufficient to make the acts those of the company. Lawton LJ in discussing the relationship of the multinational oil companies (the sole shareholders in the plaintiff) with the acts of the directors of the plaintiff whom they appointed, stated (at 469 e–f, 411 f–g):

> 'When approving whatever their nominee directors had done, the oil companies were not, as the plaintiff submitted, relinquishing any causes of action which the plaintiff may have had against its directors. When the oil companies as shareholders, approved what the plaintiff's directors had done there was no cause of action because at that time there was no damage. What the oil companies were doing was adopting the directors' acts as shareholders, in agreement with each other, making those acts the plaintiff's acts.'

A similar point was made by Dillon LJ (at 586 d–f, 488 e–g) who also stressed that it was irrelevant that the meetings which were taken to have constituted the adoption of the acts by the shareholders were called board meetings, as the consents of all the shareholders, even though expressed informally, constituted valid shareholder acts (see eg *Re Duomatic Ltd* [1969] 1 All ER 161). This is further recognition of the fact that special constitutional status is accorded to the acts of all the shareholders (cf *Cane v Jones* [1981] 1 All ER 533). The significance of this type of reasoning with respect actions alleging breach of duty by directors where all the shareholders (who may of course be the directors) are aware of what the directors have done is of considerable importance. This would be particularly so if the courts were to blur the distinction (if one really exists) between acquiescence and approval as is suggested in a case such as *Re Bailey Hay & Co Ltd* [1972] 3 All ER 693. A number of points need to be stressed with respect to *Multinational Gas*.

First, the alleged wrongful acts were acts of negligence and there was no allegation that the acts were ultra vires or in some way fraudulent or illegal. Where the acts are illegal or ultra vires then the conceptual device of 'adoption' used by the majority in *Multinational Gas* would not be available because the acts would simply be acts which a company could not enter into (cf *Re Exchange Banking Co, Flitcroft's Case* (1882) 21 Ch D 519). It would nevertheless be possible for the courts to adopt the 'ratification' device; that is, the shareholders by their acts have ratified the breach of duty provided, of course, it is ratifiable (eg the directors enter into a contract ultra vires the company and the shareholders ratify the breach of duty that this involves). A variant on this would be to find that the shareholders had 'released' a cause of action. It is unclear in company law to what extent the concept of ratification of wrongs, and that of release of a cause of action, are merely mirror images, at least as concerns the shareholders. The relationship between adoption, ratification, and release of a cause of action is a complex one (cf *Bamford v Bamford* [1970] Ch 212) and one which has not been fully worked out (see (1977) 40 MLR 587), but it is obviously in the interests of directors, whenever possible, to argue for the adoption solution. (The effect of Table A, art 80, also needs to be elucidated. There was no mention of this in *Multinational Gas*).

Second, Dillon LJ stressed that the company was solvent when it entered into the allegedly negligent transactions. The bearing of this is not clear. By itself, it could scarcely affect the validity of any adoption by the shareholders of the directors' acts. It could, however, have some bearing for an action under s 332 of the Companies Act 1948 where the adoption type of reasoning would actually be to the disadvantage of the shareholders because they would be held to have participated in the company's management. It may be that Dillon LJ's observations were directed towards some awkward dicta in *Re Horsley & Weight Ltd* [1982] 3 All ER 1045 at 1055–1056. This will be dealt with later.

Third, although the shareholders had no grounds for complaint, the creditors were obviously singing a different tune. But the creditors had no cause of action as the shareholders 'owed no duty to those with whom the plaintiff did business', (at 511 c–d, at 469 b), nor does a company owe a 'duty of care to future creditors' (at 585 f–g, at 487 d). Nor was it possible to get at the shareholders indirectly by holding that they owe their company a duty of care; shareholders, unlike directors, owe no duty of care to a company (at 585 h, at 487 f). Probably the most protean concept in company law is 'interest of the company'. But only the heroic would claim that it includes the interests of creditors. This is a blot on the system and cannot be completely justified on the grounds that creditors can protect themselves, if for no more compelling a reason that creditors will often be involuntary (ie tort claimants). The failure to make adequate provision for creditors gives even greater urgency to the need that the Cork Committee's proposals on 'wrongful trading' be implemented. Although whether this would deal with the real grievance in *Multinational Gas*, the ease with which parent companies in a group can abandon without liability an insolvent subsidiary, is open to doubt.

May LJ dissented in *Multinational Gas* and rejected the 'adoption' principle favoured by Lawton and Dillon LJ. For him, approval by the shareholders of the directors' acts validates any transaction into which a company may enter in the sense that the company would be 'bound by the legal results' of the transaction (at 579 e–f, at 479 g–h). However,

> 'That a shareholder knows that a director has been negligent and yet does nothing about it, or that an act is done by a director with his approval which is later shown to have been negligent, does not preclude the company from suing in respect of it provided that properly authorised and constituted proceedings can be stated in respect of it' (at 580 b, at 480 e).

There is much to be said for distinguishing the issue of the validity of a transaction from that relating to a breach of duty in entering into it when dealing with the effect of shareholder knowledge, acquiescence, or approval as allegedly manifested by the informal acts of the shareholders. The former deals with the protection of third party rights, which raises different issues from those involved in the ratification, implicit or otherwise, of a director's breach of duty, a distinction recognised with respect to the ratification of the unauthorised acts of an agent at least where the principal is forced to ratify (Reynolds (1982) JBL 38). These issues should be clearly demarcated as there is no reason in principle why shareholders may not want to affirm a transaction yet nevertheless reserve the right of any action that the company may have against the directors for entering into the transaction. *Multinational Gas* goes a considerable way to denying shareholders this option. What is interesting about May LJ's reasoning is the route by which he arrived at his conclusion. For him the cause of action was an asset which could not be 'gratuitously released' in the absence of a substantive object authorising this, or the satisfaction of Eve J's tests in *Re Lee Behrens & Co Ltd* ([1932] All ER Rep 889) that the release was incidental to the carrying on of the company's business and made bona fide in the interests of the company. The perception of the cause of action as an asset is not one recognised in company law, Vinelott J was attracted by it in the *Prudential* litigation ([1981] Ch 257 at 307 d) but it did not find favour in the Court of Appeal except in the exceptional case where what is involved in the right of the wrongdoing controllers to prevent the enforcement of 'a judgment in a derivative action which has been permitted to proceed' ([1982] Ch 204 at 217 g–h). Also, to apply the *Lee Behrens* reasoning to the release of such right of action, which in *Multinational Gas* was the act of the shareholders and not the directors, is to impose duties on shareholders which the law has not hitherto recognised. As the majority point out, all the shareholders may with impunity act foolishly. These comments on this aspect of May LJ's judgment obviously appear somewhat negative. It is not, however, because the perception of a cause of action as a corporate asset is an inherently unacceptable idea, but simply because it is not one that as yet has taken root in English company law. Lastly May LJ's judgment is arguably incompatible with the line of principle culminating in *Cane v Jones*. But this needs to be demonstrated. In this area the courts appear to indulge in what is a form of conceptual lucky-dip: the judicial hand plucks out the concept of 'adoption', 'ratification', or 'release' in a somewhat random way. May LJ's judgment is an attempt to disentangle them and his judgment on this can scarcely be held incompatible with those in the past where no such attempt was made.

In the course of his judgment in *Re Horsley and Weight Ltd* ([1982] 3 All ER at 1056; see also Cumming-Bruce LJ at 1055) Templeman LJ expressed the opinion that he would be 'sorry to find the scope of s 333 [of the Companies Act 1948] so restricted' as not to provide a remedy had the directors in that case been guilty of misfeasance by reducing the fund available to creditors by the amount of the sum (or a substantial proportion of it) used to establish the pension for the director. Templeman LJ was 'not satisfied' that directors could excuse themselves of their own 'gross negligence' by arguing that they held all the shares and must therefore be taken to have approved as shareholders of what was done. As was stated earlier, Dillon LJ in *Multinational Gas* emphasised the fact that when the allegedly negligent acts were entered into the company was solvent and this may have been to accommodate Templeman LJ's observations. Dillon LJ did refer to Templeman LJ's dicta but considered that it only applied to 'gross negligence' which he defined as 'conduct nearly approaching fraud' (at 587 g, at 490 a), something which was not alleged in *Multinational Gas*. Lawton LJ dismissed the views of Templeman LJ as being inconsistent with a 'long line' of authority (see *Re B Johnson & Co (Builders) Ltd* [1955] 2 All ER 775 at 781) and on this the learned lord justice appears to be correct (see *Buckley* (14th edn) p 775). Although where the 'misfeasance' takes the form of a taking of property then this would be the type of hallmark which indicated 'fraud' and would be within s 333. It may have been this to which Templeman LJ was referring.

Conflict of Laws

J G COLLIER, MA, LLB
Barrister, Fellow of Trinity Hall, Cambridge

Contract

The determination of the proper law of a contract in the absence of an express stipulation is a question which continues to give rise to litigation, often in the context of applications for leave to serve the writ outside the jurisdiction under RSC Ord 11. Three cases were reported, the most important being an Order 11 case. This was *Amin Rasheed Shipping Corpn v Kuwait Insurance Co* [1983] 2 All ER 884, which must rank as a leading case upon the two questions involved: (1) the ascertainment of the proper law; and (2) the principles governing the exercise of the discretion to allow service on an absent defendant. A Liberian company resident in Dubai insured a vessel with insurers in Kuwait on a standard Lloyd's policy as set out in Sched 1 to the Marine Insurance Act 1906, which was issued in Kuwait. It provided for payment of claims in Kuwait in sterling. In 1980 Saudi Arabian authorities seized the vessel. The insurers rejected the owners' claim whereupon the latter sued in England and sought to leave to serve the insurer in Kuwait.

To obtain leave, they had to show that the contract was 'by its terms or implication governed by English law' (RSC Ord 11, r 1(i)(f)(iii) (the jurisdiction point)) and then, if it was, they must persuade the court to exercise its discretion to permit service (the discretion point). The latter will be dealt with below (see p 89).

This produced confusion. Bingham J held that the proper law was that of Kuwait; but if it was English he would still refuse leave. The Court of Appeal [1983] 1 All ER 873) divided on both points. On the jurisdiction point Sir John Donaldson MR and May LJ held that English law was the proper law, Robert Goff LJ that this was Kuwait law. On the discretion point, the Master of Rolls would allow service out of the jurisdiction, but May LJ would not. On this, Robert Goff LJ was, naturally, silent. Thus there was no ratio decidendi.

The House of Lords was, however, unanimous on both points; it held that English law was the proper law, but refused to allow leave set out of the jurisdiction. With respect to the former, there being no express choice of law, the question was whether English law governed the contract by implication. Lord Diplock, who delivered the leading judgment, pointed out that when Lord Simonds in *Bonython v Commonwealth of Australia* [1951] AC 201 defined the governing law in the absence of express stipulation as 'the system of law by reference to which the contract was made or that with which it has its most real connection', he used the disjunctive 'or'. Thus, the implied choice of law means two things. First, the law which is inferred from the terms of the contract and the surrounding circumstances; second, that system which, in the absence of any inferred choice, is the system of law with which the contract has its closest and most real connection.

In this case, Lords Diplock, Roskill, Brandon and Brightman were able to infer that English law was intended to be the proper law. Lord Wilberforce, in agreement with the lower courts, could not infer any such intention; he concluded that English law was the proper law as being the system with which the contract had its closest and most real connection, since he could find no reason for inferring any mutual intention of the parties to select either English law or that of Kuwait. With this, one has much sympathy; it seems artificial and unnecessary to infer any intention when the parties have refrained from stating it expressly.

The case also shows the great disadvantage of the choice of law doctrine; that it may take a visit to the House of Lords to determine what it is, a process which was deprecated by Lord Wilberforce himself in *Cie Tunisienne de Navigation SA v Cie d'Armement Maritime SA* [1970] 3 All ER 71 and opinions of very learned commercial judges differed in the present case. But it must be admitted that the decision in favour of English law is correct. At the time the contract was made (when the policy was issued), although there was a commercial court in Kuwait, there was no law of marine insurance; this had to wait another three years. Moreover, it was impossible to construe the policy or determine the parties' rights and obligations thereunder without reference to the Marine Insurance Act 1906 and judicial decisions thereon.

These factors clearly outweighed the connections with and pointers to Kuwait law; ie that the insurers were Kuwaiti, the policy was issued there, and provision for payment of claims there (this was in practice disregarded anyway). However, other factors which pointed to English law were regarded as of little significance, including the use of English brokers and payment of premiums here. The use of the English language and sterling were given little consideration, since they are also used worldwide. This accounted for the House of Lords emphatically rejecting the indicator that the contract was in English form, since this was in worldwide use. It was over-reaction against this notion that every time an English form of contract led to the inference of English law which made Bingham J and Goff LJ hold that Kuwait law was the proper law.

Some other points are made clear or reaffirmed. *Renvoi* plays no part in contract: see *Re United Railways of Havana and Regla Warehouses* [1959] 1 All ER 214, CA. The search is for the system of law, not the country, with which the contract is most closely connected; compare the discussion of this matter in *Whitworth Street Estates (Manchester) Ltd v James Miller & Partners Ltd* [1970] 1 All ER 796 HL. Lord Wilberforce reiterated the views expressed in that case that subsequent conduct cannot be used to determine the proper law.

Two other cases involved the determination of the proper law. In *Coupland v Arabian Gulf Petroleum Co* [1983] 2 All ER 434 Hodgson J held that Libyan law was the proper law of a contract of employment concluded between the Scotsman and a Libyan State Oil company. It was argued that English law was the proper law since, inter alia, the job was advertised in an English paper, negotiation and conclusion of the contract took place here, it was in English, the salary was payable in sterling in England, and the plaintiff was a UK taxpayer and treated in Libya as an expatriate.

But the place of performance was Libya, and as in *Sayers v International Drilling Co NV* [1971] 3 All ER 163, CA, the defendant Libyan company employed persons of different nationalities on the same terms; it was inconceivable that the proper law should be other than the one which was common to all, that is, Libyan law. This seems right. The Court of Appeal in *Coupland* ([1983] 3 All ER 226) was content to accept Hodgson J's finding, but thought the matter irrelevant in deciding the case for reasons which will be discussed below.

The determination of the proper law of a banking contract was one point in *XAG v A bank* [1983] 2 All ER 464. The plaintiff had accounts with the London branch of an American bank, and used that account for a major part of their banking operations. It was held that English law was the proper law since the relationship of banker and customer was centred in London, which was also where the relationship began and where the contract was made. There is nothing surprising in this.

Tort

The state of uncertainty, not to say confusion, engendered by the bewildering variety of speeches of the House of Lords in *Boys v Chaplin* [1969] 2 All ER 1085, HL has by now been dispelled by decisions of lower courts, which have in effect adopted the speech of Lord Wilberforce as expressing the ratio decidendi of that case. That is to say, that the choice of law rule governing tort liability is that the conduct must be actionable in tort under the lex fori, but that if it is not civilly actionable under the lex loci, the defendant will not be liable here. If the relevant rule of the lex loci is the same as the English rule, then the case will be decided by English law. This is all subject to the proviso, that as respects the particular issue between the particular parties, the general rule will be displaced and the case governed by that law with which it is most closely connected. (This is the only way in which *Boys v Chaplin* itself can be explained.)

Hodgson J decided this and applied the general rule, after lengthy citation of Lord Wilberforce and by reference to the decision of the Court of Appeal in *Church of Scientology of California v Commissioner of Police* (1976) 120 SJ 690, a case which, as he said, deserved to be more widely reported. The Court of Appeal, through Robert Goff LJ [1983] 3 All ER 226, agreed with Hodgson J and dismissed the defendants' appeal from his decision that English law applied.

In *Coupland*, the Scottish plaintiff suffered an accident while employed in Libya by the defendant Libyan company under a contract of service. The defendants' conduct was prima facie actionable by English law; but it was agreed that Libyan law applied. The courts could find no distinction between English and Libyan law on the question of liablility, held that the 'double actionability' test derived from the House of Lords' restatement of the rule in *Phillips v Eyre* (1870) LR 6 QB 1 was satisfied, and that English law was applicable.

The defendants successfully argued before Hodgson J that Libyan law was the proper law of the contract (see above). The Court of Appeal did not disagree, but pointed out (a) that the plaintiff could sue either in contract or tort as suited him best, and (b) that the contract had no relevance to the tort claim, since, unlike the contract in *Sayers v International Drilling Co NV* it contained no term exempting the defendants from liability. It was therefore unecessary to go further into the difficult questions which may arise with respect to the inter-relation of tort and contract which exemption clauses may produce, and which were not well answered in *Sayers*.

Service out of the jurisdiction

Three cases reported in 1983 concerned applications for leave to serve a writ out of the jurisdiction: *Amin Rasheed Shipping Corpn v Kuwait Insurance Co* [1983] 1 All ER 873, CA, [1983] 2 All ER 884 HL; *Official Solicitor v Stype Investments (Jersey) Ltd* [1983] 1 All ER 629 and *Multinational Gas and Petrochemical Co v Multinational Gas and Petrochemical Services Ltd* [1983] 2 All ER 563. The last two would, if they were to have fallen for decision after the coming into force (which has not yet been effected) of the revised RSC Ord 11 (Rules of the Supreme Court (Amendment No 2) 1983, SI 1983/1181) be affected by it; they do not raise any point of general principle with regard to the exercise by the court of its discretion to permit service.

Such a point was raised by the *Amin Rasheed* case, where leave was sought to serve the writ outside the jurisdiction on the ground that the contract was governed by English law (RSC Ord 11, r 1(1)(f)(iii) and see SI 1983/1181, r 1(1)(d)(iii)). The 'jurisdiction' or 'proper law' point is discussed elsewhere (at p 86 above). The House of Lords held unanimously that English law did govern the contract, but also held unanimously that the discretion should be exercised against the allowing service on the defendants in Kuwait.

The judgment on this point is of the utmost importance; it does not repeat the principles as set out in, for example, *The Hagen* [1908] P 189, but its effect is the same. In any event, if there is an alternative court where the case can be properly heard, discretion should normally be exercised by refusing to allow service. The reason is that this form of jurisdiction is exorbitant, and we would not recognise a foreign judgment based on similar jurisdictional grounds (although Denning LJ once suggested we would, in *Re Dulles Settlement (No 2)* [1951] 2 All ER 69, this has been repudiated and was clearly obiter and wrong). It is only where the plaintiff satisfies the onus of proving that he could not obtain justice in the alternative forum at all, or only at excessive cost, delay or inconvenience that leave should be granted.

None of this had been shown by the plaintiffs. The Kuwait court could perfectly well hear the case, and since the main issues were of fact it might be in a better position to do so than the English court; also, it would, it seemed, apply English law to determine the points of law.

Two suggestions were repudiated. That of counsel that the practice and procedure of 'civil law' courts would make the Kuwait court less able to decide matters of fact was stigmatised as based on a natural prejudice in favour of our own procedure.

The other, by Sir John Donaldson MR (who was the only judge out of the nine who heard the case to wish to give leave) that the English Commercial Court is not just a national but an international commercial court with unrivalled expertise was rightly rejected. Though these characteristics may account for the relative popularity of the Commercial Court as a place to which disputes are voluntarily submitted by foreigners, that is not reason for compelling them to come here against their wishes.

There had been some cases (for example *Coast Lines Ltd v Hudig and Veder Chartering NV* [1972] 1 All ER 451) in which the courts have shown a tendency to stretch matters so as to allow service under RSC Ord 11. Perhaps this decision may act as a corrective to any such departure from principle.

Official Solicitor v Stype Investments (Jersey) Ltd concerned claims of the Inland Revenue on the estate of the late Sir Charles Clore (C). (For proceedings by the Revenue see *IRC v Stype Investments (Jersey) Ltd* [1982] 3 All ER 419.) The plaintiff, as administrator appointed at the behest of the Crown, brought an action against S Ltd, a Jersey company, and sought leave to serve the writ on S Ltd under several paragraphs of Order 11, r 1. Under a declaration of trust between C and S Ltd in 1979 C had conveyed a landed estate in England to S Ltd on trust to hold it as bare trustees for C, to convey it to him or a purchaser from him as he should direct and to account to him for the proceeds of sale and for the rents or profits pending sale. At C's request S Ltd agreed by a contract made here to sell the land to an English company for just over £20m. C later died and the sale was completed after his death. Almost all the purchase money was remitted directly to S Ltd in Jersey. Only about £60,000 to £75,000 was left in England.

Whitford J gave leave under three heads of r 1. Under para (b), since this was a case in which a deed or contract affecting land in England was sought to be enforced. The argument that it was not since the land had been sold was rejected; when the declaration of trust was made it concerned land here; therefore it was a contract which ascertained the obligations of the defendants touching the landed estate. The contrary conclusion would surely have been absurd.

The action fell also under para (e) since it was an action as to property situate within the jurisdiction of the trusts of a written instrument which trusts ought to be executed in accordance with English law. But *what* property situated in England? It would be laughable to say, the £60,000 to £75,000 here, when there was more than £20m in Jersey; the 'property' was not therefore the cash, but the right to an account of it.

Paragraphs (f) and (g) applied since a breach within the jurisdiction was alleged of a contract made here.

Whitford J was critical of Ord 11 in its existing form, mainly because it had not been redrafted to meet modern conditions; he suggested a reconsideration of its terms. This was true not only of the paragraphs with which he had to deal, but of a few others as well, for example, paras (h) (i) and (j). The impending entry into force of the entirety of the Civil Jurisdiction and Judgments Act 1982 and ratification of the Brussels Convention of 1968 made such reconsideration necessary as well as timely. It is worthy of note that what seems a somewhat tortuous and artificial interpretation of the word 'property' in para (c) will be redundant, since under the equivalent new para (j) the trust will not have to be of property in England.

Multinational Gas and Petrochemical Co v Multinational Gas and Petrochemical Services Ltd concerned an application for leave to serve out of the jurisdiction under RSC Ord 11, r 1(i)(h) on the ground that a tort was committed within the jurisdiction and under r 1(j) that the action being properly brought against a person duly served within the jurisdiction a person out of the jurisdiction was a necessary or proper party thereto.

The facts are complex; three oil companies joined in an enterprise (M). They formed a company (S) in the UK which had offices in London and advised M about business and finance. M had no place of business here or elsewhere. The oil companies nominated M's directors, who met outside the UK to make decisions. M later ceased trading and was wound up with assets of £34,000. It appeared that S might have negligently advised M, but S would be unable to satisfy any judgment that might be given against it in M's favour. M's liquidator, having served S now sought to serve the oil companies and M's directors on the ground that the oil companies' decisions were the result of M's directors allowing S in London negligently to prepare inadequate financial estimates.

The Court of Appeal held unanimously with respect to para (h) that, applying the 'substance of the tort' test laid down in *Distillers Co (Biochemicals) Ltd v Thompson* [1971] 1 All ER 694, PC, and applied in such cases as *Castree v GR Squibb & Sons Ltd* [1980] 2 All ER 589, the cause of action substantially arose abroad where M's directors made the relevant decisions and not in England where S acted on them. Under the new para (f) service may be allowed if the tort was committed and the damage sustained here or if it resulted from an act committed within the jurisdiction. The result would not therefore be different.

As regards para (j), the first question was, was the action properly brought against S here? If the defendant could not possibly be liable, it is not so brought: *Witted v Galbraith* [1893] 1 QB 577. That is to say, the action must not have been brought solely to be able to serve the absent defendant and thus get him before the court. Suppose, however, as here, the English defendant might be liable, but there is no chance of his being able to satisfy a judgment against him? There seems to be little practical difference between this and the previous situation. But there may be some point in suing him if only to establish liability. The court thought that if this were so, the action might be said to be 'properly brought'. All then turns on the motives of the plaintiff; if his sole purpose is to be able to serve the absent defendant, and he does not genuinely desire to sue the English one, the action is not properly brought. If, however, the predominant reason is to be able to sue the absent defendants, though there is a genuine desire to serve the English defendant, Lawton LJ thought that was quite enough reason for withholding leave. The majority, May and Dillon LJ, thought that this did not matter. One can, of course, see the distinction between this case and that in *Witted v Galbraith*, but sympathy must lie with Lawton LJ, for the view of the majority, in a doubtful case, is rather technical. It scarcely seems to operate the spirit rather than the letter of Ord 11, and hardly shows a desire to resolve a doubt in favour of the foreigner, which is what it is supposed to be shown.

But the point need not be laboured, for under the forthcoming para (c), the word 'properly' disappears. Also, in future it will be possible to serve absent defendants when the first person to be served was also out of the jurisdiction.

On the second question, were the absent defendants 'necessary and proper parties'? by reason of Dillon LJ switching sides to join Lawton LJ the plaintiff lost. The majority held that by reason of a rule of English company law, the absent defendants had a complete defence to any action against them. May LJ dissented on the point, but this does not concern us here.

For discussion of the company law aspects of the case, see pp 82–85 above.

Stay of actions

In two cases the courts were asked to stay proceedings on the basis of the judgments in *MacShannon v Rockware Glass Ltd* [1978] 1 All ER 625, HL. In neither did they actually do so.

In *Coupland v Arabian Gulf Petroleum Co* which is discussed elsewhere (see p 87 above) Hodgson J was asked to do so, but refused since justice could be done as well here as abroad, in Libya. The point was not raised before the Court of Appeal.

Of more interest and importance is a case of lis alibi pendens. In *The Abidin Daver* [1983] 3 All ER 46 CA the Court of Appeal refused to stay English proceedings brought by owners of a Cuban vessel against those of a Turkish ship arising out of a collision which, in the words of Sir John Donaldson MR was, if the evidence of both sides was accepted, between two anchored and immovable ships which were at least one mile appart on the Bosporus in Turkish waters. The Turks had brought an action against the Cubans in the Turkish court (from whose windows could be seen the locus of the collision). In applying the *MacShannon* test to a case where there were foreign proceedings several factors had to be considered, many of which pointed to Turkey, if that were a place in which justice could be done between the parties at substantially less inconvenience and expense than in England, and if a stay would not deprive the plaintiff of a legitimate personal or juridical advantage. The court held that *The Tillie Lykes* [1977] 1 Lloyd's Rep 124 was good law and that the mere existence of foreign proceedings was not a bar to a claim in this country. Perhaps the strongest reason that was given for the decision was that the plaintiff would by a stay lose the advantage of controlling the action here and not having to counterclaim in Turkey.

The risk remains, therefore of the English and Turkish courts coming to different results.

The learned Master of the Rolls gave as one advantage for the plaintiff the centuries-long experience of the English Admiralty Court, and doubted whether the Turkish courts had that experience 'which was a mater of history and geography'. Why this lack of experience should hinder the Turkish courts from deciding a relatively simple case is not, perhaps, apparent. The House of Lords appears to have been unimpressed by this, since it allowed the Turkish owners' appeal, some members frankly stating that in this field of law it is time to acknowledge that the courts' attitude to lis alibi pendens is indistinguishable from *forum non conveniens*: (*The Abidin Daver* [1984] 1 All ER 470).

Restraining foreign proceedings

The English courts have always been understandably reluctant to enjoin a person subject to their jurisdiction from continuing proceedings in a foreign court, the obvious reason being that this might be construed as an attempt, though an indirect one, to interfere with that court's exercise of its own jurisdiction. The principles to be applied when such an injunction is requested were stated by Lord Scarman in *Castanho v Brown & Root (UK) Ltd* [1981] 1 All ER 143 to be the same as those to be applied when the court is asked to stay proceedings before itself.

The reluctance referred to might be expected to be less marked where the foreign proceedings were instituted in breach of an agreement to submit the dispute to settlement by the English courts or by arbitration here. The situation has hardly ever arisen heretofore, no doubt because this is a popular place to settle disputes, because of the presence here of commodity markets and because commercial men tend to stand by their agreements. In *The Lisboa* [1980] 2 Lloyd's Rep 546, the Court of Appeal refused to restrain foreign proceedings, but they only amounted to arresting a ship to obtain security, and there was some doubt whether what had happened abroad fell within the exclusive English jurisdiction clause.

However, in *Tracomin SA v Sudan Oil Seeds Co Ltd (No 2)* [1983] 3 All ER 140 the Court of Appeal, reversing Leggatt J, restrained the foreign proceedings.

Sudanese sellers under a contract for the sale of peanuts, when sued by the Swiss buyers in the Swiss court, failed to inform the latter of the effect under English law, the proper law of the contract, which the Swiss court was trying to apply, of the effect under English law of an exclusive English arbitration clause in the contract. So the Swiss court assumed that English law was the same as Swiss law, under which the clause was not incorporated in the contract, exercised its jurisdiction and gave judgment for the buyers. This was affirmed on appeal. (As to the non-recognition of this judgment see the discussion at p 96 below.) The sellers instituted arbitration proceedings in England and asked Leggatt J to enjoin any further proceedings in Switzerland or elsewhere. He refused, saying that the Swiss court's decision was a proper one, since the sellers had forfeited their right to rely on the English arbitration clause by their own default in not correctly informing the Swiss court as to English law.

The Court of Appeal, while castigating the sellers for their default, would have none of this. The sellers' behaviour did not cancel out the behaviour of the buyers in acting in deliberate breach of their agreement. The judge had, in refusing a stay, exercised his discretion wrongly. He had not given sufficient weight to the possible inconsistency between the Swiss judgment and any arbitral award. Moreover, since the sellers could still resort to arbitration here, the Swiss judgment not being recognised here (*Tracomin SA v Sudan Oil Seeds Co Ltd (No 1)* [1983] 3 All ER 137, the arbitrators could assume an appellate role over the findings of the Swiss court. The injunction was granted on terms which reflected the sellers' negligent conduct of the Swiss proceedings.

One hopes that the courts will be as astute to hold parties to their promises when they start proceedings here in violation of their agreements to settlement of disputes abroad.

Where no action is brought in England and there is no English jurisdiction or arbitration clause, there is much less reason for the court to restrain foreign proceedings than when either of these factors is present: see *Castanho v Brown & Root (UK) Ltd*, where English proceedings had been started but leave was given to discontinue them. Indeed in the one relevant previous case an injunction to restrain proceedings in France was refused on the ground that the point of law involved could perfectly well be taken there: *Settlement Corporation v Hochschild* [1965] 3 All ER 486.

But in two recent and perhaps unusual cases, one of great political as well as legal importance, such an injunction has been granted. In *Smith Kline & French Laboratories Ltd v Bloch* [1983] 2 All ER 730 an English resident started an action for alleged breach of contract in the United States courts. The contract was made in England between that resident and the English subsidiary of an American company and was governed by English law. He expected to benefit by the contingency fee system and the prospect of higher damages awarded by juries in America. But he could only get his case heard by suing the American company when it was obvious that only the English subsidiary could possibly be liable. The Court of Appeal dismissed the defendant's appeal against the granting of an injunction to both the English and American companies, holding that the English court was the natural forum and that, applying *MacShannon v Rockware Glass Ltd*, the balance to be struck between the parties was in the plaintiff's favour.

One question which has been somewhat confusingly answered in the cases on staying of actions or restraining proceedings abroad since the House of Lords threw open the whole issue in *The Atlantic Star* [1973] 2 All ER 175 has been, what are the 'legitimate personal or juridical advantages' to the plaintiff in proceedings here or abroad as the case may be which should be considered when staying or restraining as requested? One would have thought that the prospect of higher damages is one of these and so Lord Scarman said in *Castanho v Brown and Root (UK) Ltd*. In the present case, Lord Denning MR emphatically denied that this was so. One apparently looks in vain for some real principles in the area of law under discussion. That being said, the *Smith Kline and French* case seems to have been sensibly decided.

The obvious problem which can arise in such a case is that there might well be an unseemly conflict of jurisdiction between our courts and foreign courts, with the parties caught in a cross-fire. This happened in the case just discussed in which the American judge had enjoined the American parent from coming to seek relief from the English courts (Lord Denning wished they could all sit down together and discuss it). The situation has arisen even more dramatically in *British Airways Board v Laker Airways* [1983] 3 All ER 375.

This arose out of the collapse and liquidation of Laker Airways early in 1982. The British liquidator of Laker commenced proceedings in the United States under the Sherman Act (1890) and Clayton Act (1914) anti-trust laws, alleging that British Airways and British Caledonian had conspired with other airlines and manufacturers of aircraft to bring about Laker's demise. If Laker won it would be entitled to treble damages, that is, the sum awarded by way of compensation, trebled. None of this would be enforceable against the British airlines here because of the Protection of Trading Interests Act 1980, s 5, but could be enforced in the United States against their aircraft and other assets. The airlines therefore applied to the court for an injuction to restrain the liquidator from proceeding further in the United States, contending that it would be unjust to them and contrary to public policy as manifested by the attitude of Her Majesty's government to allow the action to proceed.

Parker J at first instance refused to do this, holding, inter alia, that the test which had to be applied was that stated by Lord Salmon in *MacShannon v Rockware Glass Ltd*, that is, whether the defendant could show that to restrain him would produce injustice to him. He could do so, since he could only pursue the anti-trust action in the United States; if enjoined from so doing, he had no remedy anywhere.

The public policy arguments, derived from the Protection of Trading Interests Act 1980 and from government statements, Parker J regarded as irrelevant. He pointed out that the Act was directed at what we regard as invasions of our sovereignty, but that this could not be said of a case in which the United States applied its own anti-trust laws to companies carrying on business in that country, even if the greater part of the business and what was complained of took place outside it.

Next, the Secretary of State promulgated the Protection of Trading Interests (US Anti-Trust Measures) Order 1983. This order and general direction also issued were made under the Protection of Trading Interests Act 1980, ss 1 and 2. (An attempt to have them declared ultra vires and invalid failed.) These had the effect of prohibiting the United Kingdom airlines from complying with any requirement or prohibition imposed on them under the anti-trust laws and with any requirement for the production of documents or commercial information in the United States action.

In the view of the Court of Appeal, this made all the difference. *Castanho v Brown and Root (UK) Ltd* posed the question whether in all the circumstances it was appropriate to grant the relief sought in order to avoid injustice or, put another way, whether grant or refusal would create the lesser injustice. In answering this, the court observed that the British airlines were only two of the ten possible defendants in the United States court, but their disappearance would affect Laker's remedies, especially as regards discovery. What then would the airlines lose if the proceedings were not restrained? Loss of time, expense and disruption of their business. Also, they were entitled to rely indirectly on the treaty with the United States of 1977 (known as the Bermuda 2 Agreement) which regulates international air carriage between the two countries and under which each government is entitled to designate airlines of its own nationality to fly particular routes, in the sense that if the United States were to accept the view of Her Majesty's government as to its applicability, Laker's claim would be rendered wholly unsustainable. Perhaps most important, though, was the fact that the direction made under the 1980 Act prevented the airlines from complying with any US judgment pursuant to the anti-trust laws, so laying them open to the US courts levying execution on their aircraft. Further, they prevented them discovering documents; this would damage Laker's prospects but would damage theirs the more, since Laker could get some discovery from the other defendants, whereas they were disabled from effectively defending the US action. The order and directions, by rendering the issues wholly untriable, were decisive and made it unjust to allow the liquidator to proceed.

Since the House of Lords has granted leave to appeal ([1983] 1 WLR 1293) and the appeal is due to be heard in the first half of 1984 lengthy comment is not required. One has some agreement with the Court of Appeal; a better example of 'forum shopping', that much derided activity, it is difficult to imagine; why one British company should be allowed to sue others in America when it could not do so in Britain and be thus protected by American law is hard to understand. It may be thought that that the exercise of jurisdiction by a US court in such a case is a copy-book example of the exorbitant claims of the United States to regulate business within or without that country, for what real interest of the United States is involved? On the other hand, as Parker J pointed out, all parties carry or carried on business there, which has not always been the case when United States courts and authorities have sought to extend the application of their laws to conduct and to corporations abroad. Moreover, the taking of steps by foreign governments to prevent their companies from complying with United States court orders is exactly what makes those courts complain, leading as it does to the suspicion that those governments and companies are conspiring to protect the companies by persuading the American courts not to exact complince with those orders. The decision of the House of Lords is awaited with interest and anxiety.

Foreign judgments

Tracomin SA v Sudan Oil Seeds Co Ltd (No 1) illustrates the operation of ss 32 and 33 of the Civil Jurisdiction and Judgments Act 1982 on foreign judgments rendered before the entry into force of those provisions on 24 August 1982, when the proceedings for their enforcement had not been concluded by that date.

These sections, which were enacted partly to deal with the difficulties caused by *Henry v Geoprosco International* [1975] 2 All ER 702, provide that, in general, a foreign judgment cannot be recognised or enforced if the bringing of the proceedings was contrary to an agreement under which the dispute in question was to be settled otherwise than by proceedings in the courts of that country (s 32) and that amongst matters which are not to be treated as submission to the foreign jurisdiction are (i) an appearance to contest the jurisdiction, or (ii) to ask the court to dismiss or stay the proceedings on the ground that the dispute in question should be submitted to arbitration or to the determination of the courts of another country or (iii) to protect, or to obtain the release of, property seized or threatened with seizure (s 33).

These provisions could have been tailor-made to cover the facts of the *Tracomin* case in which the parties had agreed to submit disputes to arbitration in England, but the buyers had nevertheless started proceedings in Switzerland. The Swiss court had rejected the sellers' application for the equivalent of a stay of the proceedings on the ground that there was submission to arbitration in England because, it held, the clause was not incorporated in the agreement. The question before Staughton J, when the buyers sought to prevent the English arbitration instituted by the sellers from proceeding, was whether the Swiss judgment should be recognised, rather than enforced. This recognition, clearly, was precluded by both s 32 and s 33.

The Court of Appeal, which upheld Staughton J [1983] 1 All ER 404 was only concerned with whether these particular proceedings were affected; it was argued by the buyers that they were not; the Swiss judgment was given in January 1982 and was affirmed on appeal in April 1982; the proceedings in England were heard in June 1982 but not concluded when ss 32 and 33 came into force. It was contended that the sections did not have retrospective effect on pending actions so as to preclude recognition. Under the transitional and savings provisions of Sch 13 to the 1982 Act, certain judgments were excepted from ss 32 and 33, but only if registration under statute had been effected or proceedings at common law for enforcement finally determined before the date of their entry into force. Since the present proceedings had not been finally determined then, they must fall outside these savings and recognition was clearly barred.

In *The Despina GK* [1983] 1 All ER 1, Sheen J held applying dicta of Sir Robert Phillimore in *The City of Mecca* (1879 5 PD 28 that the Admiralty Court had a duty founded on comity to enforce a decree of a foreign Admiralty court, so that where a Swedish judgment for the plaintiffs ordering them to be paid a certain sum had not been wholly satisfied and the plaintiffs had arrested the ship in order to obtain the balance due, the English court had jurisdiction to issue a warrant for the arrest of the vessel when it entered an English port. The defendants' main argument was that when the ship was arrested in Sweden they had put up security and thus purchased its freedom from further arrest. Sheen J distinguished *The Kalamazoo* (1851) 15 Jur 885 and *The Point Breeze* [1928] P 135 chiefly on the ground that in those cases the writ was set aside since the ship was not in those cases still the property of the judgment debtor when it was arrested in England; in the present case it was.

A curious decision was delivered by the Court of Appeal in *Israel Discount Bank of New York v Hadjipateras* [1983] 3 All ER 129. It is clear law that, provided a foreign judgment is rendered by a court of competent jurisdiction in the view of the English courts, it will be enforced here subject to very limited defences. In particular, the judgment debtor is not allowed to reopen the merits of the case by putting forward a defence which he raised unsuccessfully abroad, or which he could have pleaded but which he did not (*Ellis v McHenry* (1871) LR 6 CP 228). The sole exception to this is the defence of fraud: *Abouloff v Oppenheimer* (1882) 10 QBD 295; *Syal v Heyward* [1948] 2 KB 443, an exception which is widely regarded as illogical, but is, like a plea that the foreign judgment was rendered in breach of natural justice, based on English public policy.

In *Hadjipateras*, the bank applied under RSC Ord 14 for summary judgment to enforce a New York judgment on a guarantee given by the defendant who was under age when the first gave it. He had not defended the New York proceedings; his defence was that he had given the guarantee when acting under the undue influence of his father. The bank had instituted an action in England also, and he preferred to raise the defence in those proceedings. He had been granted leave to defend the present proceedings as having a good arguable case. This was reversed by the Court of Appeal, whose decision is perfectly justifiable on the ground that he should have raised the defence in New York, whose law had not been shown to be different from English law.

Almost certainly the defendant knew this; his defence was in significantly different terms; that it is contrary to public policy to enforce a foreign judgment based on a cause of action which arose from a transaction which would be unenforceable here by reason of English public policy, and that a contract induced by duress or undue influence is such a transaction. The court accepted all this but still said that the defence failed because it was not raised in New York.

This bristles with difficulties. Quite apart from the dubious proposition that such a transaction is unenforceable by reason of public policy (surely it is voidable in Equity on the ground that undue influence vitiates consent), the authorities cited in support of the proposition of public policy forwarded (see at pp 133–4) have little or nothing to do with the point. The exception is *Re Macartney* [1921] 1 ChD 522 to 528, where Astbury J, misreading *Rousillon v Rousillon* (1880) 14 ChD 351, stated that 'foreign judgments founded upon contracts contrary to public policy or rights of that character' are unenforceable and refused to enforce a judgment ordering a putative father to pay perpetual maintenance to his illegitimate daughter.

It may be accepted that the proposition is true, but *Re Macartney* and the present case are hardly good examples of it. But the Court of Appeal's judgment suffers from two flaws: the defence to enforcement was not undue influence but public policy. The court says that the point should have been taken in New York. But how could the defence of English public policy have been taken there? Second, as we have seen, fraud is a defence to enforcement whether or not it was or was not pleaded in the foreign action, but a public policy defence deriving from undue influence can only be raised here if it could not have been pleaded abroad. Why this distinction between fraud and other heads of public policy? (Fraud is subsumed under public policy as regards non-recognition of foreign divorce decrees: Recognition of Divorces and Legal Separations Act 1971, s 8; *Kendall v Kendall* [1977] Fam 208.)

This, it is submitted, is all of a muddle, and perhaps explicable on the basis that the answer to the defendant was so simple that the members of the Court of Appeal did not direct their minds to the matter as closely as they might have done.

Consumer Law

C J MILLER, BA, LLM
Barrister, Professor of Law, University of Warwick

Bargain offers

The complexities of the Price Marking (Bargain Offers) Orders 1979 (SI 1979 364, as amended) formed the background to the case of *West Yorkshire Metropolitan County Council v MFI Furniture Centre Ltd* [1983] 3 All ER 234. The respondents, MFI, had advertised a 'Nicole six drawer chest' as being for sale at £24.95, which they described as a 'bargain price' and 'Britain's lowest price'. They had further adverised Welsh dressers at £69.95, a figure which was variously described as a 'special clearance price' and an 'end of range clearance price'. In both instances the Crown Court at Bradford had allowed MFI's appeal against conviction for offences against the order and the apcllants were now appealing by way of case stated to a Divisional Court of the Queen's Bench Division. The contention was that the Bradford Magistrates' Court had been correct in finding that the above claims contravened arts 2(1)(a) and 3(1)(b) of the order in as much as they (i) indicated that a price for the retail sale of goods was lower than 'the amount of another price for the sale of goods of the same description', and (ii) were not within the range of comparative price comparisons permitted by art 3(2).

So far as the first advertisement was concerned the issue was essentially whether the words 'bargain price etc' invited a comparison between that price and some other (higher) price. The Crown Court had placed itself in the position of an ordinary shopper and found that such a person 'would not necessarily come to the view that "bargain price" meant the price offered was lower than another price for something of the same description; he might feel that he was getting an advantageous price in the sense of good or excellent value for money'. In the judgment of the Divisional Court this was the correct approach to adopt and since the Crown Court's conclusion in favour of MFI was to be viewed as one of fact rather than law it was not appropriate to interfere. In general this seems, with respect, to be right, even though in the context of a consumer protection provision one might quibble at whether the question should be couched in terms of what an ordinary shopper would necessarily (as opposed to might reasonably) assume. No doubt it is likely—although the question remains one of fact—that the same conclusion would be reached if an advertisement states that goods are 'only' or 'just' £x, as opposed to '*now* only' £x. Whether consumers are in reality more vulnerable to suggestions that they are getting a preferential price and not simply excellent value is another matter. (Incidentally, neither 'only' £x nor 'now only' £x falls within the terms of the draft order proposed by the Department of Trade in December 1982. This would require that the higher comparative price be either stated or calculable; so that '50p off: £5.99' would prima facie fall within the draft order—although it might also be within an exception to it—but 'Reduced: now only £5.99' would not.)

In the case of the second advertisement involving Welsh dressers at a 'special clearance price' of £69.95 the issue was somewhat different. Here the respondents, MFI, submitted that the comparison which they had drawn was not with 'the amount of another price for the sale of goods of the same description', but was rather with a previous higher price for the very same goods. Article 3(1)(b) did not, it was argued, apply to such a comparison.˙It is not wholly clear whether, in allowing the prosecution's appeal in this case, the Divisional Court was discounting the argument entirely. In any event Robert Goff LJ said (at 240):

> 'In my judgment, such a submission really flies in the face of reality. Let me take the case of a vendor of goods who has 30 articles of the same description, all of which are sitting in his basement because he has not been able to sell them. He puts them up for sale as a special clearance offer. Clearly he would be indicating that the price of those goods or each of them was lower than the amount of another price for the sale of goods of the same description. That would be an almost classic example of a case where the statute applies. I cannot see how the situation would be any different if there was one article of goods in the basement to which the offending words were applied. The same principle would apply. In other words, the words 'goods of the same description' embrace in this context a particular item of goods which is marked down, so to speak, as against itself.'

On the facts of the case, where presumably many substantially similar if not identical Welsh dressers had been sold by MFI, the conclusion is undoubtedly right. However surely it must also be right that art 3(1)(b) does not apply where the article which is marked down is unique (for example, a second-hand car); nor, it is submitted, where it is clear from the context that the *only* comparison being made is with an earlier price for the self-same goods (for example, a three piece suite in a small upholstery shop). Section 11(1)(b) of the Trade Descriptions Act 1968 covers comparisons with 'the price at which *the goods* or goods of the same description were previously offered..."' (emphasis supplied) and its twenty-eight days and six months rule must be complied with (or disclaimed), but this is not true of art 3(1)(b) of the 1979 order which applies only to comparisons with 'another price for the sale of goods of the same description'. (For an expression of a similar view see the Notes for Guidance issued by the Department of Trade in December 1979). Other cases decided or reported in 1983 and of general interest and import-ance in this area include *Comet Radiovision Services Ltd v Williamson* (1983) 91 Monthly Review 143; [1983] Crim LR 632, and *R v J Sainsbury Ltd* (1983) 91 Monthly Review 45—(the 'Discount 81. Good Food Costs Less at Sains-bury's' case).

Small claims

Unlike certain other jurisdictions the United Kingdom does not have small claims courts as such, nor even a separate small claims division within the county courts. What we have, rather, is a small claims procedure which is an integral part of the county court system and yet designed very much with the benefit of consumers in mind. This attempt to simplify procedure and make the courts accessible to ordinary litigants owes much to the work of the old

Consumer Council and the present National Consumer Council (see especially 'Justice out of Reach: A Case for Small Claims Courts', Consumer Council 1970, and 'Simple Justice', National Consumer Council 1979). Accessibility requires (as a minimum) both a relatively uncomplicated procedure and a measure of protection against the incurring of substantial legal costs where only small amounts of money are involved. It can make no sense to venture £1,000 in an attempt to recover £100. Arbitration before a registrar is meant to provide a simple procedure which is apt to be used by a litigant in person and the 'no costs' rule, the protection against running up a substantial bill for legal costs when claims are unsuccessful. However, as *Newland v Boardwell* and *MacDonald v Platt* [1983] 3 All ER 179 illustrate, there is another side to the coin and insurance companies may use the procedure to their advantage also.

These cases (and it is sufficient to confine ourselves to the facts of the former) both arose out of motor vehicle accidents in which the plaintiffs had limited their claim for damages to a sum not exceeding £500. The effect was to bring the case within the scope of CCR 1936 Ord 19, r 1(4) which provides that: 'Any proceedings in which the sum claimed or amount involved does not exceed £500 shall stand referred for arbitration by the registrar upon the receipt by the court of a defence of the claim . . .' (Such a reference may be rescinded but this is not immediately relevant to the present discussion.) So far as costs are concerned Ord 19, r 1(11) provides that no solicitors' charges shall be allowed as between party and party in respect of any proceedings referred to arbitration except (a) the costs which were stated on the summons, (b) the costs of enforcing the award and (c) 'such costs as are certified by the arbitrator to have been incurred through the unreasonable conduct of the opposite party in relation to the proceedings or the claim therein.'

In *Newland v Boardwell* the costs stated on the summons were the court fee (£28) and solicitors' charges (£21) which, assuming the action to be successful, were recoverable under head (a). The defendant (effectively an insurance company) admitted negligence but nonetheless filed a defence stating that 'the injuries, loss and damage alleged are not admitted'. In reality it could not seriously be contended that *no* damage to the plaintiff had flowed from the admitted negligence and so the usual practice would have been to submit to an interlocutory judgment being entered, whilst leaving the question of damages to be assessed. However, by entering a defence the defendants triggered off the 'no-costs' rule and in the words of Cumming-Bruce LJ (at 184), made no bones about this being no more than a device to take advantage of Ord 19, r 1(4). In the judgment of the Court of Appeal this was a 'misuse of the pleading process' and a course 'designed to exclude the plaintiff in each case from the benefit of the summary procedure of interlocutory judgment for damages to be assessed, while at the same time debarring the plaintiff from seeking the exercise of the court's discretion to award costs in his favour occasioned by a specious defence'. The question was whether the terms of Ord 19, r 1(11)(c) (see above) were apt to deprive the insurance companies of the protection which they were seeking. The arbitrator had issued a certificate based on a finding of 'unreasonable conduct' and the Court of Appeal agreed that this was justified. However this was not the end of the matter since solicitors' charges could be recovered by virtue of r 1(11)(c) only to the extent that they had been 'incurred *through* the unreasonable conduct of the opposite party'. Cumming-Bruce LJ dealt with the point (at 184) as follows:

> '"Through" in this context must, in our opinion, have the meaning "in consequence of". The words 'to have been incurred through the unreasonable conduct of the opposite party" cannot affect any costs incurred before the occurrence of the unreasonable conduct of the defendant. If either plaintiff incurred further solicitors' charges for services rendered between the date of the summons and the filing of the defence, those charges would seem to be made unrecoverable by para (11)'.

It is submitted, with respect, that this must be correct—although presumably in an appropriate case 'unreasonable conduct' may occur before the defence is actually filed.

What then of charges incurred after the occurrence of the unreasonable conduct? Dealing with these his Lordship said:

> 'The plaintiff has expressly restricted his claim to the limit of the small claims procedure. He must be taken to have known that, if a defence were filed, the case would be automatically referred for arbitration, in which event, if he continued to employ a solicitor, he would be prohibited from recovering any solicitors' charges from his opponent except under Ord 19, r 1(11)(c). If he does not protect himself by determining the solicitor's retainer, his liability to pay any solicitors' charges arising thereafter will, in our judgment, have been incurred as a consequence of his own failure to protect himself and not as a consequence of the reference to arbitration or to the filing of a defence which occasioned that reference.'

With respect this seems far less satisfactory, especially in view of the regret expressed by the Court of Appeal in reaching a decision which was far from inevitable. No doubt the failure to determine the solicitor's retainer was *a* cause of the plaintiff's liability to pay further charges but surely it was not the sole cause. However, in view of the decision even consumers with cast-iron cases would be well advised to learn how to undertake 'do-it-yourself' litigation, avoiding solicitor's charges beyond those stated on the summons.

Sunday trading

Absurdities within the law are not apt to promote respect for it, more especially when they occur in areas which are immediately apparent to the general public. Neither is a situation in which the law is widely and openly flouted. Frequently the two go hand in hand, as in the case of the Shops Act 1950 and the laws governing Sunday trading where the anomalies are too well known to need rehearsing at length. (One may sell a bottle of gin and 'girlie' magazines on Sunday but not a bible or a tin of milk for a baby's bottle etc,—unless of course the shop is in Scotland.) The area is one in which the major consumer organisations have been campaigning for years but opposition from such unlikely combinations as sabbatarians, shopworkers (USDAW) and, it must be said, environmentalists, has proved highly effective. As recently as February 1983 Mr Ray Whitney's Shops (Amendment) Bill (apparently the 16th attempt at reform) was soundly defeated by 205 votes to 105, thus failing to obtain a second reading. For their part local authorities are under a statutory duty to enforce the Act (see s 71 of the Shops

Act) although the penalties (£50 for a first and £200 for a second or subsequent offence) are far too low to constitute a serious deterrent to major chain stores intent on Sunday trading in the face of criminal prosecutions.

It was against this background that the Court of Appeal heard the case of *Stoke-on-Trent City Council v B & Q (Retail) Ltd* [1983] 2 All ER 787 where the stores concerned (Home Charm Retail Ltd and B & Q (Retail) Ltd) were all involved in selling 'do-it-yourself' equipment in contravention of the Act. The court's decision countenances the invoking of s 222(1) of the Local Government Act 1972 and allows local authorities following a proper consideration of the issues, to seek injunctions to restrain breaches of the legislation. Such authorities may consider this 'expedient for the promotion or protection of the interests of the inhabitants' of the area in as much as it may promote inter alia fair competition, avoid public money being wasted on useless litigation and (more generally) facilitate the fulfilling of the duty to enforce the Act. No element of public nuisance need be involved; nor need there be evidence of public complaints. Of course the injunction (and its associated sanctions for contempt) is a much more potent remedy than a prosecution and, in any event, even those whose deliberate policy it is to break the criminal law normally regard court orders as standing on a different footing. (Whether this is because courts are considered more deserving of respect than Parliament is unclear.) Obviously the present decision is of considerable importance both to administrative lawyers and, more immediately, to local authorities and their trading standards departments. Whether the decision is desirable as a matter of policy (given that it was common ground that local authorities are not entitled to use the civil courts generally to control criminal conduct) is, no doubt, a matter on which opinions will differ. Since 1972 there have been opportunities for Parliament to increase the penalties of the Shops Act 1950 and on one view this would have been the better way of combatting any widespread flouting of the law. This has not been done. Yet it is possible that the decision may finally stimulate legislation since, as Lawton LJ observed (at 791), 'cases may reveal to Parliament weaknesses and anomalies in the law which call for change.' What is quite clear is that the anomalies of the present law remain as indefensible as ever.

Limitation clauses

Although it is quintessentially a commercial case, the decision of the House of Lords in *George Mitchell Ltd v Finney Lock Seeds Ltd* [1983] 2 All ER 737 may be important also in those consumer transactions where exemption or limitation clauses are not void but are subject rather to the test of reasonableness. This is true of situations where goods are damaged or lost (perhaps in a house removal, dry cleaning or film processing) or where holidays go badly wrong: see generally the Unfair Contract Terms Act 1977, ss 2(2) and 3. Similarly it is by no means unknown for companies to purport to require consumers to indemnify them in respecy of their liabilities to a third party. Such clauses are subject also to a test of reasonableness: see s 4 of the 1977 Act. (Of course if a contract term is void—for example by virtue of s 6(2) or s 7(2) of the 1977 Act—enquiries into questions of construction and reasonableness are not in point.)

Several points in the speech of Lord Bridge (with which the other members of the House of Lords agreed) are of interest in the present context. First there is the reaffirming of the distinction taken in *Ailsa Craig Fishing Co Ltd v Malvern Fishing Co Ltd* [1983] 1 All ER 101 between, on the one hand, exclusion and indemnity clauses, and, on the other, limitation clauses. The latter are not to be judged by the same exacting standards of construction as the former and, one might add, they must in turn be distinguished from provisions for liquidated damages. Whether it is actually helpful to create this third category of clause may be doubted, if only because the maximum damages specified in some limitation clauses are so derisory as to be virtually tantamount to an exclusion clause, thus suggesting that the distinction is one of degree rather than kind (for example one such term of a house removal contract provides as follows: 'The liability (if any) of The Contractors for any loss, failure to produce or damage shall be limited to either (a) the cost of repairing or replacing the damaged or missing article or (b) to Ten Pounds for any article, suite, service or complete case or package or other container and the contents thereof respectively including plate, plated goods and/or other valuables whichever is the smaller sum.'). Second, in applying the statutory test of reasonableness, Lord Bridge placed considerable emphasis on the fact that it was the defendant's practice to attempt to negotiate settlements at a figure which was higher than that provided for by the clause. This was regarded as 'a clear recognition . . . that reliance on the limitation of liability imposed by the relevant condition would not be fair or reasonable' (ibid at 744). Of course the difficulty about this is that it may discourage companies from attempting to reach sensible compromises of deserving claims. The other factors mentioned by Lord Bridge as being relevant, namely the presence of negligence and the availability to the defendants of insurance cover, are potentially applicable also in the context of consumer transactions. Finally the decision is important as emphasising that the area is one in which there may be 'room for a legitimate difference of judicial opinion as to what the answer should be'. This being so, the appeal courts should not interfere with a decision as to whether a clause is 'fair and reasonable' 'unless satisfied that it proceeded on some erroneous principle or was plainly and obviously wrong' (ibid at 743). In fact the bulk of the steady trickle of (largely unreported) cases to date has been decided in favour of the party contesting a clause's effectiveness to exclude or limit liability.

For further discussion of these cases see Professor Furmston's article on Contract, p 112 below.

Weights and measures

Note the decision in *Bellerby v Carle* [1983] 1 All ER 1031 discussed at p 152 below.

Contempt of Court

C J MILLER, BA, LLM
Barrister, Professor of Law, University of Warwick

Introduction

There have been periods in 1983 when contempt of court was constantly in the headlines. However, relatively few of the incidents and cases fall within the scope of the present annual review. The National Graphical Association has attracted widespread publicity for its refusal to obey court orders prohibiting unlawful secondary action in relation to the Messenger Newspaper Group. Fines and sequestration of assets followed as a normal consequence of this civil contempt—as indeed was the case in the early 1970s with the containerisation disputes at Chobham Farm and elsewhere. At one stage there were fears that the TUC might find that its own assets were at risk and the *Socialist Worker* called hopefully for a general strike. However wiser counsels prevailed. In another incident the *Guardian* newspaper was ordered (s 10 of the Contempt of Court Act 1981 notwithstanding) to return a photostatic copy of a memorandum from the Secretary of State for Defence entitled 'Deliveries of Cruise Missiles to RAF Greenham Common—Parliamentary and Public Statements'. The copy of the document had been provided by an anonymous source (see *Secretary of State for Defence v Guardian Newspapers Ltd, The Times,* 17 December 1983, CA) and a young lady has since been charged with an offence under the Official Secrets Act. Again, some of the Greenham Common women have been imprisoned for contempt, having disrupted the proceedings of the Newbury Magistrates' Court (see *The Times,* 19 August, 3 and 15 November 1983). Without in any way condoning disruptive conduct, some magistrates seem, at least on the basis of newspaper reports, to have used the newly acquired powers of s 12 of the Contempt of Court Act 1981 in relatively trivial cases. Like students who chatter in libraries, people who have conversations in the public gallery of magistrates' courts are normally best escorted from the premises and not dealt with for contempt. Only slightly more serious was a case in which a man was reported as having been arrested and fined £100 for contempt after lighting a cigarette in the public gallery at West London Magistrates' Court (see *The Times,* 29 December 1983).

Of the cases within the scope of this review, one is concerned with the reporting of committal proceedings and the others with matters of civil contempt. None of the decisions seems to be especially controversial.

Reporting committal proceedings

The general background to the restrictions on reporting committal proceedings was noted briefly in last year's review (All ER Rev 1982, p 61) where reference was made to the problems which arise where there are two or more co-accused and no unanimity as to whether restrictions should be lifted. The

matter is now governed by the Magistrates' Courts Act 1980, s 8(2A), and in
R v Leeds Justices, ex p Sykes [1983] 1 All ER 460 the Divisional Court had an
early opportunity to discuss this important provision. Section 8(2A)
provides as follows:

> 'Where in the case of two or more accused one of them objects to the making of
> an order under sub-s (2) above [that is to say, an order that reporting of the
> committal proceedings be permitted], the court shall make the order if, and
> only if, it is satisfied, after hearing the representations of the accused, that it is in
> the interests of justice to do so.'

Sykes and several co-accused including Priestley had been charged with
conspiracy to rob. Priestley wanted reporting restrictions lifted, principally,
it seems, so as to enable him to make a public protest about allegedly unfair
police conduct. The magistrates agreed that they should be lifted and made an
order to this effect, having corrected an earlier error in which they had
purported to lift the restrictions in respect of Priestley alone. (There is no
power to lift restrictions 'piecemeal'. It must be done in respect of all the
defendants or not at all.) Sykes then applied successfully to have the order
quashed, the Divisional Court holding that the magistrates had not made a
proper inquiry into the matter nor held the balance fairly between the
accused. In reaching this decision Griffiths LJ stressed (at 462) that the prima
facie rule is against the reporting of committal proceedings and that an order
lifting restrictions should be made against the wishes of an accused only when
'a powerful case is made out'. This is especially so where the ground of the
objection is 'that there is a risk that if the proceedings are widely reported, the
reports may colour the views of the jury which ultimately has to try the case'.
This seems, with respect, to be clearly right. No doubt the balancing exercise
will be more difficult where a co-accused feels strongly that publicity will
cause witnesses to come forward on his behalf.

Postponing reporting and anonymity for witnesses

In a related area Lord Lane CJ has issued a Practice Note [1983] 1 All ER 64
concerning orders made under s 4(2) (postponement of reporting of proceedings) and s 11 (conferring of anonymity) of the Contempt of Court Act 1981.
The Note requires that such orders be committed to writing and kept as a
permanent record. Moreover an order must state '(a) its precise scope, (b) the
time at which it shall cease to have effect, if appropriate, and (c) the specific
purpose of making the order.' Generally the area is one of considerable
complexity and controversy (see Borrie and Lowe *Law of Contempt* (2nd edn,
1983) ch 7), and even if ss 4(2) and 11 are founded on the common law and
defensible in principle there is little doubt that the very existence of the Act
has greatly increased the extent to which the powers have been used in
practice. Orders which were once, it seems, wholly exceptional are now
much more commonplace. Indeed in one trial for rape Judge Miskin is
reported (see *The Observer*, 16 October 1983) as having ordered that the press
refrain from naming a prominent MP whom the defendant had accused of
gross sexual improprieties. The MP who later issued a statement denying the
accusations was not a witness and had in any event been named in open court.
Accordingly the basis of the order is at best obscure.

For a further interesting case involving magistrates hearing a plea of mitigation in camera, see *R v Reigate Justices, ex p Argus Newspapers Ltd, The Times*, 20 May 1983.

Civil contempt

The decision of the Court of Appeal in *Peart v Stewart* [1982] 2 All ER 369 which was discussed in last year's annual review (All ER Rev 1982, pp 67–69) was overruled by the House of Lords ([1983] 1 All ER 859) in a judgment which was itself rapidly reversed by statute. The principal issue in the case was whether, when committing for contempt for breach of injunctions (including injunctions under s 1 of the Domestic Violence and Matrimonial Proceedings Act), county courts were to be treated as superior or as inferior courts for the purposes of s 14(1) of the Contempt of Court Act 1981. Although normally 'inferior' courts, the Court of Appeal had held that by virtue of s 74(1) of the County Courts Act 1959 and s 19 of the 1981 Act such courts were superior courts for this purpose. The powers exercised in granting injunctions were 'equivalent to those of the High Court' and the maximum term of 'one month in the case of committal by an inferior court' (s 14(1) of the 1981 Act) did not apply. The House of Lords was unanimous in its disagreement with this view, holding that the Act envisaged a division of courts into 'two mutually exclusive classes' (see ibid at 862 per Lord Diplock). Accordingly a term of one month's imprisonment was the maximum permissible. In Lord Diplock's opinion, with which the other members of the House of Lords agreed, the expression 'any other court exercising . . . powers equivalent to those of the High Court' referred to such superior courts of records, whether existing or to be created in the future, as were not named in s 19. It did not apply to an inferior court when it was exercising powers normally associated with the High Court.

The decision is said to have 'caused some concern amongst matrimonial practitioners' (see (1983) 133 NLJ 412) and the Court of Appeal's judgment has been effectively restored by the County Courts (Penalties for Contempt) Act 1983. Section 1 of this Act provides that:

> 'In section 14 of the Contempt of Court Act 1981 (penalties for contempt of court), after subsection (4) there shall be inserted—
> "(4A) For the purposes of the preceding provisions of this section a county court shall be treated as a superior court and not as an inferior court".'

The immediate effect of this provision is to raise the maximum penalty for contempt in a county court to two years' imprisonment—unless there is a more specific lower limit, as under s 157 of the County Courts Act 1959 (wilfully interrupting proceedings etc) where the maximum penalty remains one month. Another incidental consequence (see [1983] 1 All ER 859, 863 per Lord Diplock) is the removal of the limit of £500 on the maximum fine which is allowed by s 14(2) of the 1981 Act. There is now no limit to the fine which may be imposed by a county court on the breach of an injunction although it remains open to the contemnor to appeal.

Enfield London Borough Council v Mahoney [1983] 2 All ER 901 is another decision of general interest. The defendant, who seems to have been something of an eccentric, had refused to comply with a High Court order made by Taylor J that he hand over to the plaintiff local authority a lead object called the Glastonbury Cross. The cross, which was of considerable historical interest and intrinsic value, had come into his possession when the authority was dredging a lake. Precisely why he had refused to hand it over to the authority is unclear (conceivably even to the defendant himself) but it seems that the underlying reason was a grievance against an errant solicitor and a conviction that law and order had broken down. According to Watkins LJ (at 904): 'He had asserted as much to the United Nations but that international body seems to have taken little or no interest in him.' In any event his refusal to obey the order led in April 1982 to his being committed by Croom-Johnson J to Her Majesty's Prison at Highpoint. The committal was for two years—the maximum term permissible under s 14(1) of the Contempt of Court Act 1981 and one intended presumably for the worst cases. There he was, a 'model prisoner' who showed 'no marked desire to go home' and who was indeed apparently prepared to stay there 'until Doomsday'. He attracted the attention of the press. Fame and publicity had been achieved. In January 1983 the Official Solicitor, whose duty it is to review and report quarterly on all cases of persons committed to prisons for contempt, caused the contemnor to be brought before Croom-Johnson J and applied for his release. The contemnor remained obdurate and the application was refused, with costs being awarded against the Official Solicitor. It was from this decision that the Official Solicitor was appealing to the Court of Appeal which ordered the contemnor's release. He had been punished sufficiently for his contempt in refusing to obey the order and it was clear that continued imprisonment would not serve a coercive purpose. Indeed it seems that it might have been positively welcomed as a means of obtaining further publicity for the contemnor's grievance. It is submitted with respect that the Court of Appeal's decision was entirely right and that there was nothing to be gained from the defendant's continued imprisonment. Martyrdom is rarely an attractive proposition and, as certain trade unions have discovered, the contempt power can lend itself readily to exploitation.

The Court of Appeal's decision to allow the Official Solicitor's appeal on the question of costs is welcome also since in such cases it must be right to depart from the general rule whereby costs follow the event. The role of the Official Solicitor is of crucial importance in contempt cases and as Watkins LJ observed (at 907), 'it would be a positive disservice . . . to bring any possible form of dissuasion to him from acting in cases of this and other similar kinds.' It would be otherwise if he were to act 'with impropriety or wholly unreasonably' but this possibility seems more hypothetical than real. (For general discussion of the role of the Official Solicitor in contempt cases see *Borrie and Lowe*, pp 446–448; Miller *Contempt of Court* (1976) pp 258–259).

Re British Concrete Pipe Association [1983] 1 All ER 203 touches on the interesting question of the liability of successors in title and others for breach of an undertaking or injunction given by or made against their predecessors. This is not a matter which has attracted much attention in English courts (see *Miller*, pp 252–253) although there are some American cases in point. For example, in one such case an injunction restraining a named person as dean of admissions in a university faculty was regarded as being binding on his successor in office (see *Lucy v Adams*, 224 F Supp 79 (ND Ala, 1963, affd 328 F

2d 892, 1964)). The difficulty about this approach is the in personam nature of injunctive relief. In any event the question of implied transference did not arise in the *British Concrete Pipe Association* case since by virtue of the Steel Companies (Vesting) Order 1970 Stanton and Staveley's 'obligations' vested in British Steel 'without further assurance'. In the judgment of the Court of Appeal these 'obligations' included the burden of an undertaking given to the Restrictive Practices Court by Stanton, and British Steel was in contempt for breaking it. The court left open the difficult question of whether there would have been 'an automatic contempt of court by operation of law' if Stanton's earlier undertaking had happened to cover an activity which the corporation was later found to have been carrying on on vesting day. It is submitted that a contempt should not be regarded as arising 'by operation of statute' in such a case. RSC Ord 45, r 5(1) does not require that the breach be 'wilful' and still less that it be contumacious. However, this does not preclude insistence that it be at least volitional in the sense of being a matter over which the defendant has some control. (Perhaps the matter would be different if the corporation had failed to take an opportunity so to arrange its affairs as to desist from the activity before the vesting day.) Some admittedly indirect support for this view is to be found in the decision of the Court of Appeal in *R v 'K'* (*The Times*, 19 August 1983), holding that duress is a defence to a person allegedly in contempt for refusing to give evidence.

Finally, attention is drawn to a Practice Direction ([1983] 2 All ER 1066) whereby the President of the Family Division has 'directed that on application for the release of a contemnor from prison the contemnor should be present in court to hear the outcome of the application'. An exception is made for certain cases in which the provisions of the Mental Health Act 1959 apply.

Contract

MICHAEL P FURMSTON, TD, BCL, MA, LLM
Barrister, Professor of Law, University of Bristol

1 Formation

Only two cases in 1983 involved problems in formation of the contract and in each case the major difficulty involved a different problem. In *Wettern Electric Ltd v Welsh Development Agency* [1983] 2 All ER 629 there were negotiations between the parties for the grant of a licence of a factory unit by the defendants to the plaintiffs who were a plastic manufacturing company. By a letter dated 21 June 1979, the Agency offered the plaintiffs a 12-month licence of the unit from 25 June 1979 on terms almost entirely in the Agency's favour. The letter stated: 'If you accept this licence on the above terms, will you please complete the acknowledgement and acceptance at the foot of the enclosed copy and return it to us at your earliest convenience'. The plaintiffs did not complete the acknowledgement at that time, but on 25 June went into occupation of the unit. In August defects began to appear in the unit which became progressively worse. By the end of the year the unit had become dangerous and the plaintiffs had had to evacuate it. The plaintiffs did not in fact return the approval form until 19 December while they were moving out to other accommodation, though the defendants had written asking for it both in October and again in mid-December.

The principal question was whether a term was to be implied in the licence as to the condition of the premises (see p 115 below) but Judge Newey QC, sitting as a High Court judge, had first to consider how the contract had been concluded. His view was that the act of the plaintiffs in going into occupation on 25 June was not an acceptance of the Agency's offer of a licence since that offer prescribed that acceptance was to be made in another manner. His view rather was that the plaintiff's going into occupation was a counter offer to enter into a contractual licence on the terms set out in the defendant's letter which was accepted by the defendant's permitting the plaintiffs' to occupy the premises. This view seems a little elaborate since the plaintiffs' counter offer was on exactly the terms of the defendant's original offer. It is only necessary to create this complication if it is assumed that the defendant's suggested mode of acceptance was mandatory. There seems no need to make this assumption which indeed is liable to cause considerable inconvenience. Offerors often suggest ways in which their offers should be accepted, but there is no reason to assume that as a rule alternative ways of acceptance will not be equally satisfactory. Obviously there might be acts manifesting the plaintiff's agreement which were not acceptable to the defendants as a form of acceptance, but since the plaintiffs could only go into occupation of the factory unit with the consent of the defendants, this can hardly be considered such an act. The judge was alternatively prepared to hold that the 'acceptance' of 19 December, was retrospectively effective. It was perhaps fortunate that nothing termed on this distinction as to the way in which the contract came into existence. Although there is no doubt at all that a contract can be entered into retrospectively after performance has started, it is hardly possible that the parties contemplated that the plaintiffs' occupation of the factory unit was free of legal consequences until the licence terms were the subject of a formal acceptance.

In *Damon Cia Naviera v Hapag-Lloyd International* [1983] 3 All ER 510, the parties were negotiating for the sale and purchase of three ships through brokers. On 4 July 1977 the broker for the buyers sent an official firm offer for all three vessels at a price of US $2,250,000. The offer was made on behalf of Messrs Raftopoulos of Athens and/or for company or companies to be nominated by them. (The arbitrator found that the Raftopoulos brothers did not in fact intend to buy the ships personally but to nominate one or more companies controlled by them as the buyer). Over the next few days further telex messages were exchanged so that by 8 July 1977 there was a concluded contract for US $2,365,000, the only matter outstanding being the name of the purchasing company or companies. On that day the broker for the sellers sent to the broker for the buyers a telex message which reconfirmed the arrangement and said that he was drawing up a memorandum of agreement. The arbitrator found as a fact that at this stage both brokers considered that there was a concluded contract. The memorandum of agreement was to be in Norwegian Shipbrokers' Association's Sale Form which contained a provision 'as a security for the correct fulfilment of this contract, the buyers shall pay a deposit of 10% . . . of the purchase money on signing this contract.'

Both the arbitrator and Leggatt J thought that on these facts, although no memorandum of agreement had ever been signed, there was a binding contract made by the exchange of telexes but on the terms of the memorandum of agreement. The main argument to the contrary by the buyers was that there was no contract until the deposit was paid as payment of the deposit was a condition precedent to the coming into existence of an enforceable contract. There would have appeared to be no merit at all in this argument were it not that it was accepted by Goulding J in *Myton Limited v Schwab-Morris* [1974] 1 All ER 326. Such reasoning illustrates an elementary confusion between a condition precedent to the coming into existence of the contract and a condition precedent to some of the obligations of one of the parties being enforceable. It may well be that where a deposit is payable by the buyer, some of the seller's obligations are dependent on the buyer having paid the deposit; it is a very different matter to suggest that the buyer could postpone the coming into existence of the contract by not paying the deposit. It is true there has been some discussion as to whether contracts for the sale of land are in a special category in this area but where the question is simply when the contract comes into existence the law of contract should be the same for sales of land and for sales of ships. See the decision of Warner J in *Millichamp v Jones* [1983] 1 All ER 267 at 274 that—

> 'the weight of authority is in favour of the view that a requirement in a contract for the sale of land that a deposit should be paid by the purchaser does not constitute a condition precedent, failure to fulfil which prevents the contract coming into existence, but is in general to be taken as a fundamental term of the contract, breach of which entitles the vendor, if he so elects, to treat the contract as at an end and to sue for damages including the amount of the unpaid deposit.'

Another complication in the *Damon* case was that after the telex message of 8 July which was treated as completing the contract, there were delays owing to the uncertainty as to which company would be nominated as the purchaser by the Raftopoulos brothers. The buyers' broker several times confirmed that there was a contract and on 1 August 1977 sent a telex stating 'Buyers hereby nominate as purchasing company Messrs Damon Companiera Naviera SA Panama'. It appears that the Raftopoulos brothers did not acquire effective control of Damon until a few hours after the sending of this telex on 1 August 1977. It was argued that this timetable made it impossible for the contract to have been made on behalf of Damon. Leggatt J rejected this contention. The telex of 1 August purported to be a novation of the original contract. There is no doubt that the original contract contemplated such a novation and permitted the original named buyers, Raftopoulos brothers, to name other buyers. The only difficulty was as to the authority of the brokers to act on behalf of Damon. At the time of the broker's telex Damon existed but was not controlled by the brothers nor were they then officers of Damon. However, it was held that on such facts very little was needed to show that the agreement had been adopted and ratified by Damon and since Mr Menelaos Raftopoulos had been appointed as chairman of Damon he had actual, or at least apparent, authority to ratify on Damon's behalf and had done so. (Other problems which arose in this case about the recovery of the deposit are discussed in section 6, p 123 below).

2 Exemption clauses

The House of Lords delivered two important judgments on exemption clauses. By a curious coincidence the first, the appeal from Scotland in *Ailsa Craig Fishing Co Ltd v Malvern Fishing Co Ltd* [1983] 1 All ER 101 involved the Securicor conditions of contract which were the subject of the leading English decision in *Photo Production Ltd v Securicor Transport Ltd* [1980] 1 All ER 556, although in this case the question was whether the conditions effectively limited liability rather than excluding it altogether. The relevant provision (condition 2(f) of the Special Conditions of Contract) provided that—

> 'If, pursuant to the provisions set out herein, any liability on the part of the company shall arise (whether under the express or implied terms of this contract, or at common law, or in any other way) to the customer for any loss or damage of whatever nature arising out of or connected with the provision of, or purported provision of, or failure in provision of the services covered by this contract, such liability shall be limited to the payment by the company by way of damages of a sum [limited in various ways].'

The House of Lords held that this condition was effective to limit liability. In doing so very important observations were made about the correct approach to the construction of limitation clauses. Lord Wilberforce said that a limitation clause must be clear and unambiguous and must be construed contra proferentem but that it was not proper to attempt to creat ambiguities by strained construction since limitation clauses were not to be treated with the same hostility as exclusion clauses. As Lord Fraser explained there are good reasons for treating exemption clauses and limitation clauses to some extent differently. It is significantly less likely that a contracting party would willingly agree to exempt the other party from liability altogether than that he would agree that the other party's liability was to be limited in amount. Economically the appropriate limits for liability will depend on the risk that is being undertaken and the charge that is being made for it.

George Mitchell (Chesterhall) Ltd v Finney Lock Seeds Ltd [1983] 2 All ER 737 is the first decision to reach the House of Lords involving the question of reasonableness in relation to the Unfair Contract Terms Act 1977. The appellants, a firm of seed merchants, contracted to sell to the respondents, farmers in East Lothian, 30lb of Dutch Winter White Cabbage Seeds, at a price of £201.60. The respondents planted some 63 acres of their land with the seeds. The resultant crop was worthless. There were two reasons for this. The first was that the seed delivered was not in fact winter seed but a variety of autumn seed. The second was that even as autumn seed it was of inferior quality. This was an undoubted breach of contract and the only effective question was whether liability had been successfully limited by a provision in the appellants' standard conditions that their liability was limited to replacing the defective seeds or refunding the payment made for them.

In the Court of Appeal [1983] 1 All ER 108, although all three judges had held for the buyers, there had been differences of opinion. Kerr LJ and Oliver LJ had held the limitation clause ineffective by applying common law techniques of hostile construction. Lord Denning MR, in his last judgment, held that the clause as a matter of construction covered the events which had taken place, but that it was unreasonable within the statutory test laid down by the Supply of Goods (Implied Terms) Act 1973 and the Unfair Contract Terms Act 1977.

It is pleasing to record that on this occasion at least the House of Lords was entirely in agreement with Lord Denning MR. As in the *Ailsa Craig* case, the House of Lords deprecated the use of excessively hostile techniques of construction, since the passing of statutory controls on exemption clauses 'had removed from judges the temptation to resort to the device of ascribing to the words appearing in exemption clauses a tortured meaning so as to avoid giving effect' to them ([1983] 2 All ER 737 at 739 per Lord Diplock).

The central question in the appeal was therefore whether the seller's limitation clause was to be treated as reasonable. Perhaps the most important feature of the leading speech by Lord Bridge was the observation at 743 that since the question of reasonableness presented room for legitimate differences of judicial opinion, 'the appellate court should treat the original decision with the utmost respect and refrain from interference with it unless satisfied that it proceeded on some erroneous principle or was plainly and obviously wrong'.

In considering the question of substance a number of the relevant factors were equivocal. The evidence was that similar limitations were used in all seed contracts and had been for many years; these limitations had never been the subject of negotiation between representatives of farmers and seed merchants but on the other hand they had never been objected to by the National Farmers Union. A most important factor in favour of the finding that the limitation was unreasonable emerged in fact from evidence led by the seller to the effect that in practice it had always made payments in excess of the contractual limit where it regarded the complaints as 'genuine' and 'justified'. This was treated by the House of Lords as clear evidence that the sellers themselves did not regard their terms as reasonable. This argument is perhaps not wholly convincing as businessmen often find it convenient and commercially sensible not to insist on their strict rights. A desire to retain the goodwill of customers can be at least as important a factor in this respect as feelings about the reasonableness of one's own behaviour. In addition one may suspect that the payments in fact made have not in the past been anything like as large as the amount of damages (over £61,000) awarded in this case. In any case if this is a decisive factor it can be met easily by the draftsman simply raising the limit of liability from the contractual price to some relatively modest figure, like five times the price, combined with a policy of meanness in the settlement of disputes in the future. Two other factors to which rather less weight was attached in this case are more likely to occur in the future. They are, first, that the delivery of the wrong seed involved serious negligence and secondly, that the evidence showed that sellers could insure against delivering the wrong seeds at a premium which would not significantly increase the price. It is suggested that this last factor is in fact very important since it must usually be reasonable to encourage contractual arrangements which place the loss on the person who can most readily insure and it will often therefore be unreasonable to shift the loss in the opposite direction.

See also the article on Consumer Law, p 103 above.

3 Implied terms

The long and interesting judgment of Hirst J in *Fraser v Thames Television Ltd* [1983] 2 All ER 101, turns largely on disputed questions of fact and on the working out of problems in the law of confidence, but it also involved a question on the implication of contractual terms. Much simplified, the facts were that Mr Fraser and the three other plaintiffs, established actresses, conceived the idea that the three actresses might form a rock group and that the four plaintiffs together might develop an idea for a television series, part fact and part fiction, to be based on such a group. The plaintiffs had exploratory discussions with Thames Television. As a result, for £500, Thames Television were given an option over a series based on this idea and agreed to give the three female plaintiffs first refusal of the three parts in the series. In due course Thames Television failed to give the plaintiffs first refusal of the parts on the ground that one of the plaintiffs would not be available, since she was committed to a major part in a theatrical production. This was held not to be a good reason since that engagement had been entered into, in part, because of the failure of Thames Television to give prompt notice of their production schedule. Furthermore, insufficient time had been left to see whether the difficulties caused by these conflicting commitments could be overcome. Having failed to honour the undertaking to give the plaintiffs first refusal, Thames Television produced a highly successful series known as 'Rock Follies' based on the idea and using three other actresses. Hirst J held that the option contract expressly covered both the use of the idea and the engagement of the three actresses for the three major parts. The contract also expressly provided that if the three actresses declined the parts, it should be permissable for Thames to go ahead with the idea using three other actresses. The judge therefore concluded that it was an implied term that if the girls were willing to perform the series, Thames would not go ahead without using their services as actresses.

In *Wettern Electric Ltd v Welsh Development Agency* (the facts of which have been given on p 110 above) the main issue was whether the licence which had been granted to the plaintiffs included an implied term that the unit was of sound construction and reasonably suitable for the purposes required by the plaintiffs. The defendant's argument was that such terms were not implied into contracts to sell the freehold or into leases and that it would be anomalous therefore to imply such a term into the licence. The judge held that there was no principle that terms as to condition could not be implied into a licence. The defendant's argument seems very difficult to maintain in view of the willingness of the House of Lords to contemplate implication into the council tenancy in *Liverpool City Council v Irwin* [1976] 2 All ER 39. The judge concluded that whereas there was no principle that obligations were to be implied as a matter of course in licences of land, there was no reason why such terms could not be implied under the *Moorcock* principle where it was necessary in order to give business efficacy to the contract. He further held that in the circumstances of the case it was so necessary and that such a term should be implied.

4 Mistake and misrepresentation

The cases under this heading are remarkable mainly for the fact that by chance, the facts of *Bell v Lever Bros* [1932] AC 161 and *Leaf v International Galleries* [1950] 1 All ER 693 are very nearly reproduced though the legal issues presented by the facts turn out in 1983 to be very different. In *Sybron Corpn v Rochem Ltd* [1983] 2 All ER 707, [1983] BCLC 43 (see p 66 above and p 176 below), the respondent company employed the appellant as a manager to oversee its European operations. He was a member of a pension scheme under which he opted for early retirement on 30 September 1973. Under the scheme an employee taking early retirement was entitled to be repaid his own cash contributions, but the disposition of the balance of benefits was to be at the company's discretion. The company chose to pay the defendant a lump sum of some £13,000 and to buy life insurance policies for the benefit of the defendant and his wife. Later it was discovered that the employee together with a number of other employees had been engaged in dishonest conduct in that, while employed by Sybron they set up a competing company and funnelled business to it. The plaintiff brought an action against the employees and in particular claimed repayment of the lump sum of £13,000 and an assignment of the insurance policies from the defendant. The plaintiffs did not seek to argue the question of contractual mistake, not only because that was in a sense foreclosed by *Bell v Lever Bros* but also because as regards discretionary treatment of the company's own contributions there was no contract. Instead the company argued that they were entitled to repayment as the money had been paid under a mistake of Act.

The relevance of *Bell v Lever Bros* lies not in the area of common mistake but in that of fraud and non-disclosure. The Court of Appeal in *Bell v Lever Bros* held that Bell and Snelling were under a duty to disclose to their employers their breaches of duty and that failure so to do invalidated the compensation arrangements. However, the House of Lords by a majority took the opposite view and counsel for the employee here, not unexpectedly, argued that his position was not distinguishable. One obvious distinction is that in *Bell v Lever Bros* Bell and Snelling had forgotten about their misconduct at the time when the compensation agreement was made so that their conduct was innocent; in the present case there was no doubt that the employee was well aware at all relevant times that he was committing major breaches of his contract of employment. Furthermore these breaches were continuing and not spent as they had been in *Bell v Lever Bros* and were part of a general conspiracy involving numerous other employees. The Court of Appeal concluded that although *Bell v Lever Bros* was authority against any general duty in a servant to disclose his own misconduct and did not support a general duty in a servant to report the misconduct of fellow servants, an employee in a managerial position must be under a duty to report to his superiors on malpractices of fellow servants of which he knows.

In *Peco Arts Inc v Hazlitt Gallery Ltd* [1983] 3 All ER 193 the plaintiff in 1970 bought from the defendants, a well-known reputable art gallery, a drawing which both parties thought to be by J A D Ingres. In fact 11½ years later the plaintiff discovered that it was undoubtedly a reproduction. These facts of course remind one of the facts of *Leaf v International Galleries,* but the legal issue presented to Webster J was quite different. Clearly the plaintiff's causes of action were barred by limitation, unless she could bring herself within s 32(1)(c) of the Limitation Act 1980 which provides: '[where] the action is for relief from the consequences of a mistake, the period of limitation shall not begin to run until the plaintiff has discovered the . . . mistake . . . or could with reasonable diligence have discovered it.' There was no dispute that the plaintiff had not discovered the mistake until 1981. The only effective issue in the case was therefore whether the plaintiff could with reasonable diligence have discovered that the drawing was a reproduction. Webster J concluded that reasonable diligence 'means the doing of that which an ordinarily prudent buyer and possessor of a valuable work of art would do having regard to all the circumstances, including the circumstances of the purchase.' He further held that the plaintiff was not lacking in reasonable diligence being entitled initially to rely on the reputation of the defendant and having in any case in 1976 had the drawing revalued for insurance purposes by an expert who cast no doubt on its authenticity.

In *Resolute Maritime v Nippon Kaiji Kyokai, The Skopas* [1983] 2 All ER 1, Mustill J had to decide a short point on a preliminary issue of law concerning the effect of s 2(1) of the Mispresentation Act 1967 which provides for liability 'where a person has entered into a contract after a mispresentation has been made to him by *another party thereto* . . .' Mustill J held that the words 'another party thereto' can only refer to another party to the contract and cannot cover agents or persons employed by agents.

5 Economic duress/Restraint of trade

In *Alex Lobb (Garages) Limited v Total Oil GB Ltd* [1983] 1 All ER 944 the plaintiffs were a company and a mother and son who were the shareholders and directors of that company. The mother and son wished to develop a piece of land on which the freehold was held by the company as a garage and filling station and in 1964 they borrowed £15,000 from the defendants on the security of the premises. The charge contained a covenant tying the plaintiffs to the defendants' petrol during the currency of the loan which was repayable over 18 years. Further advances on similar terms were made in 1965 and 1968.

By the end of 1968 the company, although making a trading profit, was not generating sufficient profit to service the debt. The plaintiffs approached the defendants and discussions took place about possible refinancing arrangements at all of which the plaintiffs were separately represented and advised. The result of these negotiations was that the plaintiffs granted the defendants a 51-year lease of the premises in return for a premium of £35,000 and the defendants immediately leased back the premises to the plaintiffs for 21 years at a rent of £2,250 a year. This leaseback was on the defendants' standard terms which included a 21-year petrol tie, provisions for mutual break in the underlease at the end of 7 and 14 years and an absolute prohibition on assignment. This transaction was completed by July 1969. The payment of the premium enabled the defendants to pay off their existing debts but left effectively no working capital. Since the rent on the lease was greater than the cost of servicing the previous debt at 1968 rates of interest the transaction made no great contribution to remedying the plaintiffs' financial problems and in particular left them, as they had been throughout, undercapitalised. During the early 1970s the plaintiffs sought to renegotiate the agreement and in 1977 obtained the consent of the defendants to the addition of the son's adult children as tenants. By June 1976 however, the plaintiffs were indicating that they might challenge the validity of the transaction and in June 1979 they issued a writ claiming to have the transaction set aside on the grounds that it was procured by economic duress; was a harsh and unconscionable bargain; resulted from abuse of a fiduciary and confidential relationship; or was a transaction between mortgagor and mortgagee improperly entered into. Alternatively the plaintiffs contended that the petrol tie was an unreasonable restraint of trade. This combination of old and new grounds for attacking the transaction was clearly not lacking in width and much of Peter Millett QC's careful judgment turns on an elaborate investigation of the facts.

The plaintiff's claim of economic duress failed. It was true that the plaintiff company and the individual shareholders were in great financial difficulties but these were primarily of their own making. The pressure which was being exerted on them by creditors was coming from their bank and a finance house and not from the defendants. It was true that the defendants imposed tough terms but this was largely because they were unenthusiastic about entering into the transaction which in view of the plaintiffs' inability to resolve their financial difficulties did not appear particularly attractive to them. It could not be shown either that the plaintiffs entered into the transaction unwillingly or that it was a product of improper pressure by the defendants. Furthermore, the plaintiffs had failed to take prompt steps to have the transaction set aside once the pressure was removed.

Similarly it was not shown that the transaction was an unconscionable bargain. Although the terms insisted on by the defendants were not generous to the plaintiffs, there was no ground for criticising their conduct. The plaintiffs had throughout been separately advised and the defendants put no pressure on the plaintiffs to accept the proposed arrangements. There was no evidence that they thought they were acquiring the site at an undervalue; indeed they had had the lease valued and had been advised that they had paid a fair price. The argument based on a fiduciary relationship was more easily disposed of. The judge did not think that the parties were in a fiduciary relationship nor, if they were, did he think that the defendants had abused it.

The arguments on restraint of trade also presented very considerable difficulties. These arose largely from the reasoning canvassed in *Esso Petroleum Co Ltd v Harper's Garage (Stourport) Limited* [1967] 1 All ER 699 that 'restraint of trade appears . . . to imply that a man contracts to give up some freedom which he otherwise would have had' (per Lord Reid). It follows that a tie covenant imposed by a lessor on a lessee would normally not be in restraint of trade since the lessee would never have had freedom to sell free from the tie. However the judge held, surely correctly, that the lease and leaseback must be regarded as a single transaction and that the practical effect of the agreement was that the plaintiffs were very significantly extending the length of the tie to which the filling station was previously subject. Another difficulty was that the freehold was in the company so that it was the company which leased the premises to the defendants but the defendants had leased back the site to the son in his personal capacity. Although in a sense the son had never been subject to a tie, public policy is concerned with substance and not with form and the connection between the son and the company was so close that the practical effect of the transaction if upheld would be greatly to extend the tie. The effect of this was that the tie was invalid though the lease and leaseback themselves were upheld as valid.

6 Remedies

1983 has seen no fewer than seven reported cases involving problems on the law of remedies in contract including two major decisions of the House of Lords. In *Export Credits Guarantee Dept v Universal Oil Products Company* [1983] 2 All ER 205, the House of Lords was asked to consider whether the penalty rules were capable of being applied where the sum alleged to be a penalty was not payable on an event which is a breach of contract as between the plaintiff and defendant. It answered this question in the negative. The facts of the case were complex and involved a multiparty multicontract arrangement for the construction of an oil refinery in Newfoundland. Much simplified the relevant facts were that under one of the contracts the defendants agreed to construct the refinery for a Newfoundland company. The contract was to be financed by a banking consortium which had agreed to provide funds in return for a series of promissory notes issued by the Newfoundland company. The payment of these promissory notes was in turn guaranteed by the plaintiffs Export Credits Guarantee Department in consideration of a premium of over £1m paid by the defendants to the plaintiffs as part of a further agreement by which the defendants undertook that if the guarantees were called up while they (the defendants) were in breach of the construction contract they would reimburse the plaintiffs in full. In fact many of the promissory notes were in due course dishonoured by the Newfoundland company and the banking consortium claimed some £39m from the plaintiffs who in turn claimed under the guarantee against the defendants. The House of Lords held on a preliminary issue affirming the lower courts, that it was not open for the defendants to argue that the £39m was a penalty since it was not payable on an event which was a breach of contract as between the plaintiffs and defendants (although it did depend on a breach of contract between the defendants and the Newfoundland company). It is clear, also, that on the facts of the case, it would have been very difficult to argue that the sum was truly a penalty, that is, a sum which was not a reasonable pre-estimate of the plaintiffs' loss, since the sum was in fact the exact amount of the plaintiffs' loss. What the defendants had done was to undertake 'on demand [to] pay to the guarantors a sum equal to that paid by the guarantors to Kleinworts as aforesaid'. It seems clear that the defendants' undertaking was coterminous with the plaintiffs' loss as would normally be the case in a contract of guarantee. It is true that the defendants' liability may have been very large in amount in proportion to the breaches of their contract with the Newfoundland company, which triggered off their liability under the guarantee. But it is often the case that a small breach can cause a large loss.

Of course there may be other cases in which A agrees to pay to B a sum of money on an event which is not a breach of contract between A and B and in which the sum of money is not related to the loss caused to B by the event. In some of these cases there might well be a better argument on the merits that the penalty rules should be applicable since sometimes whether the rules are applicable or not appears to be a question of drafting of the agreement. A classic example of this is the case of *Alder v Moore* [1961] 1 All ER 1 where the result turned on whether the agreement between the parties was one in which the defendant agreed to pay a sum of money to the plaintiffs if he played professional football again or one in which he made two promises, the first not to play professional football again and the second to pay money if he broke the first. It appears that the penalty rules while clearly applicable to the second contract are not applicable to the first. This might be thought to make too much turn on questions of drafting but the whole thrust of the reasoning in all three courts in this case is that this is the law. This is confirmed by the explicit approval given by Lord Roskill delivering the only reasoned speech in the House of Lords to the unreported decision of the Court of Appeal in *Philip Bernstein v Lydiate Textiles* [1962] CA Transcript 238.

In *Scandanavian Trading Tanker Co v Flota Petrolera Ecuatoriana, The Scaptrade* [1983] 2 All ER 763 the House of Lords considered the scope of the equitable doctrine of relief against forfeiture. The case was in effect a sequel to the series of decisions of the House of Lords starting with *Mardorf Peach & Co v Attica Sea Carriers of Liberia, The Laconia* [1977] 1 All ER 545 and culminating with *A/S Awilco v Fulvia The Chikuma* [1981] 1 All ER 652. In these cases the House of Lords held, in each case reversing decisions of the Court of Appeal, that a withdrawal clause in a time charterparty dependent on failure promptly to pay the time hire could be exercised even in respect of a very short period of delay in payment and even where the failure to pay promptly was not the personal fault of the charterer but arose from some malfunction in the banking system. In *The Laconia* Lord Simon of Glaisdale had suggested that it might be open to the court to mitigate the effect of such a clause by invoking equitable relief against forfeiture. Although there were dicta on this question in later cases the present case is the first one in which the matter has been properly argued in an appellate court. Both the Court of Appeal and the House of Lords agreed that there was no jurisdiction to give relief against forfeiture.

The principal doctrinal reason given by Lord Diplock delivering the leading speech for rejecting the jurisdiction was that to give relief would be tantamount to ordering specific performance of the contract. Equitable relief against forfeiture should therefore be limited to cases where the court would have jurisdiction to grant specific performance, that is, of course, principally cases involving land. A time charter is essentially a contract for the provision of services, which is the very paradigm of a contract not specifically enforceable. This argument is reinforced by an indepedent argument that the effect of withdrawal is not to divert the charterer's money into the owners hands since 'moneys paid by the charterer prior to the withdrawal notice that puts an end to the contract for services represent the agreed rate of hire for services already rendered' (per Lord Diplock).

These arguments are supported by practical considerations. The freight market is notoriously volatile and speculative and it is doubtful if the courts should interfere to adjust the contractually agreed risks of delays in payment, however venial. Furthermore, prompt decisions on questions of this kind are very desirable. If the court were held to have jurisdiction to grant relief, this would inevitably require an investigation of the merits which would take considerable time. This would not only delay the decision of the court but make that decision difficult to predict.

The judgment of Mustill J in *Paula Lee Ltd v Robert Zehil & Co Ltd* [1983] 2 All ER 390 contains a very interesting discussion of the handling of claims to damages where the defendant has alternative methods of performance. As Mustill J pointed out, there are statements in the cases that in such cases damages should be calculated by reference to a presumed mode of performance which is that least profitable for the plaintiff; least burdensome to the defendant; or that the defendant is not liable in damages for not doing that which is he not obliged to do. Although these three formulations undoubtedly overlap, they are not identical. In certain circumstances a defendant might be advantaged by a mode of performance less than the minimum because this enabled him to avoid other losses elsewhere.

In the present case the plaintiffs, who were dress manufacturers, had appointed the defendants to act as their sole distributors in certain middle eastern countries. Under the agreement the defendants undertook to buy not less than 16,000 garments per season and the agreement made no provision as to the sizes or styles of the garments comprising the minimum obligation. The defendants repudiated the agreement and argued that the plaintiff's claim for damages should be calculated on the basis that they would be entitled to choose in any one year 16,000 of the plaintiff's cheapest dresses. This argument was rejected and Mustill J drew an instructive distinction as to the correct analysis of the agreement. As to the quantity of dresses to be bought, the defendants had contracted to buy a minimum of 16,000 but were entitled to buy many more. The defendants therefore had a clear choice as to the number of dresses they would buy and damages needed to be calculated on the basis that the defendants could elect to buy the minimum quantity. As to the range and quality of the dresses, however, Mustill J held that the defendants' choice was not unfettered and that the agreement must be read subject to an implied term that the garments must be selected in a reasonable manner since for the defendants to chose 16,000 garments of the same size, style and colour and no others at all 'would alienate their wholesalers, deprive the plaintiffs of anything but a ludicrous presence in the territory and kill the market not only for the current season but for those which were to follow.' Of course even if the defendants were obliged to make a reasonable selection, there were no doubt a variety of selections which could be classified as not unreasonable. Within this variety the damages again were no doubt to be calculated on the basis that the defendants would make the cheapest reasonable selection.

In *C & P Haulage v Middleton* [1983] 3 All ER 94 the Court of Appeal had to consider the problems arising in the assessment of damages where the contract which has been broken turns out to have been a bad bargain for the plaintiff. The appellant, a self-employed engineer, had been granted a contractual licence to occupy the premises for renewable periods of six months. It was a term of the licence that any fixtures put in by him were not to be removed at the expiry of the licence. Despite this term he spent considerable sums of money in making the premises suitable for the automobile engineering which he planned to carry out thereon. Ten weeks before the end of the second term the licence was wrongfully terminated by the respondents. The appellant was allowed by the local authority to transfer his business to the garage at his own home where he carried it on well beyond the end of the second six month term. The appellant claimed that he was entitled to recover by way of damages the money which he had spent on improving the licenced premises.

Although this terminology is not used by the court, it is clear that the plaintiff here is seeking to calculate damages on a reliance basis rather than on an expectation basis. There is no doubt that the plaintiff can in appropriate cases seek to quantify his damages in terms of wasted expenditure which he has incurred in reliance on the contract rather than of the profits he would have made if the contract had been carried out. A classic example is *Anglia Television Ltd v Reed* [1971] 3 All ER 690 where the plaintiffs recovered some £3,000 of wasted expenditure on preparations for a film which were rendered nugatory by the defendant's repudiation of the contract. (In that case the plaintiffs probably proceeded on the basis that establishing the profits that would be made by a film that had never been filmed, would be too speculative a basis of claim but the parties and the court probably proceeded on the implicit assumption that the film, if made, would at least have generated sufficient income to cover the plaintiffs' expenditure). The difficulty in *C & P Haulage* was that although the appellant had incurred substantial expenditure after the contract, this expenditure was wasted not because of the defendants' breach but because the contract was in any case an unwise one for him to have made since the defendants could certainly have elected to terminate the contract at the end of the second six months and retained the fixtures. Since the appellant was able to carry on his business at his own home free of charge and was relieved of having to pay rent to the respondents, he was in financial terms at least as well off, possibly better off, than he would have been if the contract had run its course for another ten weeks. In coming to the conclusion that the appellant was not entitled to more than nominal damages the Court of Appeal found assistance in the Canadian case of *Bowlay Logging Ltd v Domtar* [1978] 4 WWR 105, which in turn relied on the judgment of Learned Hand CJ in *L Albert & Son v Armstrong Rubber Co* 178 F 2d 182 (1949).

The application of the rules of mitigation of damage gave rise to an instructive difference of opinion in *London and South of England Building Society v Stone* [1983] 3 All ER 105. In this case the plaintiffs had advanced money on a mortgage to the purchaser of a house. Before the advance they had instructed the defendants to carry out a valuation. The valuation was carried out negligently and failed to disclose that the dwelling-house suffered from serious subsidence which rendered it valueless. This was clearly a breach of contract and it was accepted that if the plaintiffs had known of the condition of the house they would not have advanced money on it as security.

The subsidence later became apparent and the plaintiffs spent some £29,00 on having the premises repaired. The plaintiffs did not seek to enforce against the borrower the contractual provision in the mortgage that the borrowers were to keep the buildings in good and tenantable repair.

It was not seriously suggested that the plaintiffs could recover the cost of the repairs since these were clearly excessive in relation to the value of the house which only fetched £26,500 when sold some two years later. The plaintiffs' effective claim was that they had advanced £11,800 towards the purchase of the house on security which was worthless and that they had therefore lost the whole of the advance that they had made. The trial judge, while accepting that as a starting point, had held that account should be taken of the plaintiffs' right to sue the borrower on the personal covenant to repay. Although he thought the whole of the debt could not be recovered from the borrowers, who were financially hard pressed, he put the value of the personal covenant at £3,000 and deducted that from the amount of the advance. This reasoning was rejected by O'Connor LJ and Stephenson LJ. Their reasoning, however, was not quite identical. Stephenson LJ was clear that if the borrower had in fact repaid the mortgage from his personal resources the plaintiffs would have suffered no loss. O'Connor LJ, on the other hand, thought that if the borrowers had contributed to the cost of the repairs (which would in effect be a form of repayment of the sum advanced) this should not be taken into account. The critical question, however, was whether the plaintiffs ought in order to mitigate their loss to have sued the borrowers. The majority thought not on the grounds that a plaintiff need only take reasonable steps to mitigate his loss and that in the circumstances it was reasonable for the plaintiffs not to sue on the personal covenant. Sir Denys Buckley took a different view. He did not consider that the matter involved the operation of the doctrine of mitigation but that calculation of damages should proceed 'on the basis that the covenantor is likely fully and punctually to discharge his obligations without any act on the part of the plaintiff.' If it should appear that the covenantor's personal financial position was such that this was not likely then there should be a discount to take into account that possibility. This was precisely what the judge had done and his judgment should be affirmed.

Although the opinion of Sir Denys Buckley has much logic to commend it, it is thought that the majority opinion is more convenient, since it places liability on the one party in the case who is clearly at fault. Furthermore, if the decision in *Yianni v Edwin Evans* [1981] 3 All ER 592 is correct, the borrower could have recovered against the defendant. Therefore it follows that by bearing the cost of the repair itself the plaintiff had simply taken onto its own shoulders initially a burden which if borne by the borrower could have been transfered to the defendant. It does not seem rational that the allocation of the losses between the three parties should depend on whether the mortgagor or mortgagee bears the initial cost of the repairs.

The decision in *Damon v Hapag-Lloyd* [1983] 3 All ER 510 (the facts of which have been given above, p 111) illustrates the advantage to a seller of agreeing for the payment of a deposit by the buyer. In that case the contract was to sell the three ships at US $2,365,000. After the buyers repudiation the sellers sold the ships for US $2,295,000 so that their actual loss was US $70,000. The contract, however, required that the buyers pay a deposit of 10% that is US $236,500. It was held that the seller was entitled to sue for the unpaid deposit although it was much greater than his actual loss. It is instructive that if the contract had instead provided for payment by way of damages of a sum equal to 10% of the purchase price, it would have been open to the buyer to argue that this was not a reasonable pre-estimate of the seller's loss and therefore penalty. It is not clear that the rules about penalties and deposits fit together very harmoniously in this respect.

In the 1982 Review we noted the decision of the Court of Appeal in *Astro Exito Navegacion SA v Southland Enterprise Co Ltd* [1982] 3 All ER 335 (All ER Rev 1982, p 82). This decision has now been affirmed by the House of Lords [1983] 2 All ER 725 but for reasons that did not involve examining the correctness of the Court of Appeal decision on the availability of interim mandatory injunctions.

See also the article on Damages, pp 168 and 170, below.

7 Discharge

Despite the presence of several other important House of Lords decisions during the year the decision in *Paal Wilson & Co v Partenreederei Hannah Blumenthal* [1983] 1 All ER 34 has strong claims to be regarded as the most interesting contract case of the year. The decision is a sequel to the decision of the House of Lords in *Bremer Vulkan Schiffbau Und Maschinenfabrik v South India Shipping Corpn* [1981] 1 All ER 289. It will be remembered that in that case the House of Lords held that an arbitrator did not have an inherent jurisdiction to dismiss an arbitration for want of prosecution in the way in which a judge has been held to since *Allen v Alfred McAlpine* [1968] 1 All ER 543. The majority of the House of Lords held that an agreement to arbitrate was a contract in which both parties undertook mutual obligations to press forward with the arbitration, and discharge of the contract depended on application of general principles of contract law. As far as discharge by breach is concerned, a party to an arbitration will not usually be able to rely on this doctrine in respect of a long delay by the other party since he will himself be guilty of a similar breach, the obligation to proceed being mutual and not unilateral.

In the present case the dispute arose out of a 1969 contract for sale of a ship and the arbitration started in 1972 when both parties appointed an arbitrator (but a third arbitrator was never appointed). In 1974 the buyers delivered their points of claim and some four months later the sellers delivered their defence. Between 1974 and 1980 there was intermittent exchange of letters between the two sides. When the buyers in July 1980 suggested that a date be fixed for the arbitration the sellers issued a writ claiming that the agreement had been discharged either by the buyers' repudiation or by frustration or by mutual agreement.

The agreement based on repudiation was really hopeless unless the House of Lords were prepared to reconsider the *Bremer Vulkan* case. Although the decision had been criticised in a number of first instance and Court of Appeal decisions, the House of Lords were clear that it was not appropriate to reconsider it. Although the House of Lords in *Bremer Vulkan* had chosen between two eminently arguable positions, there was nothing in later developments to indicate that the matter should be reopened so soon.

The House of Lords did recognise that a contract to arbitrate might be terminated by frustration but they were agreed that the present contract was not so frustrated because—

> 'there are two essential factors which must be present in order to frustrate a contract. The first essential factor is that there must be some outside event or extraneous change of situation, not foreseen or provided for by the parties at the time of contracting, which either makes it impossible for the contract to be performed at all, or at least renders its performance something radically different from what the parties contemplated when they entered into it. The second essential factor is that the outside event or extraneous change of situation concerned, and the consequences of either in relation to the performance of the contract, must have occurred without either the fault or the default of either party to the contract' (per Lord Brandon [1983] 1 All ER at 44).

Neither requirement was met in the present case. The contract had not been subject to an extraneous event but simply to the delay of the parties and that delay was a breach by each party of its obligations. This reasoning seems absolutely conclusive though it does leave open the question of what kind of extraneous event would be treated as frustating a contract to arbitrate. Would it be sufficient if a major witness died or important documentary evidence was destroyed? On one view this would satisfy the test, but it is clear that litigation would not be brought to an end by such events and it would seem odd that an agreement to arbitrate should cease to be effective in circumstances where the parties were still entitled to have recourse to the courts.

Perhaps the most interesting and important part of the judgment is the discussion of implied abandonment of the contract. It was sufficient on the facts of the case to say that there were sufficient intermittent acts over the period between 1974 to 1980 to negative an argument based on implied abandonment but the House of Lords did in fact devote considerable care to explaining the underlying principles. Lord Brandon (at p 47) pointed out that a contract might be implicitly abandoned in two ways:

> 'The first way is by showing that the conduct of each party, as evinced to the other party and acted on by him, leads necessarily to the inference of an implied agreement between them to abandon the contract.'

This method clearly involves the making of a binding contract to abandon the contract to arbitrate.

> 'The second method is by showing that the conduct of B, as evinced towards A, has been such as to lead A reasonably to believe that B has abandoned the contract, even though it had not in fact been B's intention to do so, and that A has significantly altered his position in reliance on that belief.'

This second method clearly involves a species of estoppel. One should perhaps note that there is a further question which has to be considered in relation to abandonment of contracts to arbitrate which is whether the claimant is simply abandoning his right to proceed by arbitration or whether he is abandoning his substantive claim. In all the cases so far it appears to have been assumed that successful arguments based on long delay under whatever conceptual label would lead to the end of the proceedings. Clearly, however, it is logically possible that the parties might implicitly agree not to resolve their differences by arbitration without having agreed that the differences were not to be litigated.

In this respect the decision in *Allied Marine Transport v Vale Do Rio Doce Navegacao SA, The Leonidas D* [1983] 3 All ER 737 provides a very useful supplement to the *Hannah Blumenthal*, since in this case Mustill J held that the arbitration agreement had indeed been abandoned by the parties. He also considered whether the abandonment was of the reference to arbitration or of the claim. On the facts he had no difficulty in concluding that if there was abandonment it would be of the reference and of the claim and not merely of the reference. Where the argument on implicit abandonment is essentially based on inaction, it will usually be very difficult to spell out an implicit agreement to abandon the reference but to maintain the claim.

As Mustill J points out the making of an agreement to abandon a claim does present some problems both in relation to consideration and in relation to offer and acceptance. As far as consideration is concerned it is treating the respondent's abandonment of his rights under the reference as sufficient consideration for the claimant's abandonment of his substantive rights under the claim. At first sight the respondent does not seem to have given up much but as Mustill J observes if the reference disappears so does the respondents right to obtain an award in his favour on liability or as to costs. Similarly one cannot usually spell out offer and acceptance merely from inactivity and silence but that is clearly regarded as possible in the present context. In the present case Mustill J was able to infer an agreement to abandon since the claimants had begun the arbitration very quickly and then totally stopped. Further there were acts by an apparent intermediary of theirs which suggested that they were not serious about the arbitration. He held that this conduct amounted to tacit representation by the claimants that they did not intend to pursue the reference. He concluded that the respondents could accept this tacit offer by doing nothing at all and that they had so accepted. Alternatively the respondents could show that the claimants were estopped from pursuing the claim because they (the respondents) had taken none of the steps which they should have done to prepare the defence of the claim.

In last year's Annual Review (All ER Rev 1982, p 80), we considered the decision of the Court of Appeal in *Afovos Shipping Co SA v Pagnan* [1982] 3 All ER 18. This decision has now been affirmed by the House of Lords [1983] 1 All ER 449. It will be remembered that the case concerned the so-called 'anti-technicality' clause under which an owner with a right to terminate a time charter for failure promptly to pay hire agrees to give 48 hours' notice of his intention to withdraw after failure to make due payments. In this case an instalment was due on 14 June and did not arrive at the owners' bank at that day because of an error in the banking system. (The owners' bank had continued to list a telex number which was no longer in use by them but had been transferred to a completely different company. By mischance the charterers' bank sent a telex to that number having failed to get through to the telex numbers which were still in use. The company which received the telex transmission did not point out the mistake so that the charterers' bank had no reason to think that the money had not safely been transferred.) At 1640 hours on 14 June the owners agents sent a telex to the charterers, 'Owners have instructed us that in case we do not receive the hire which is due today, to give charterers notice as per-clause 31 of the charter party for withdrawal of the vessel from their service'. Then at 1920 hours on 18 June a telex was sent terminating the charter (two of the days between 14 and 18 June not counting as being Saturday and Sunday). The House of Lords affirmed the decision of the Court of Appeal that the owners' notice was premature since there had been no failure to pay until midnight on 14 June. The decision on this point seems, if one may say so, very clear and straightforward. Perhaps the most interesting part of the speeches concerns therefore a somewhat desperate attempt by the owners to invoke the doctrine of anticipatory breach. This provoked Lord Diplock to the important observation ([1983] 1 All ER at 455) that—

'The doctrine of anticipatory breach is but a species of the genus repudiation and applies only to fundamental breach. If one party to a contract states expressly or by implication to the other party in advance that he will not be able to perform a particular primary obligation on his part under the contract when the time for performance arrives, the question whether the other party may elect to treat the statement as a repudiation depends on whether the threatened non-performance would have the effect of depriving the other party of substantially the whole benefit which it was the intention of the parties that he should obtain from the primary obligations of the parties under the contract then remaining unperformed. If it would not have that effect there is no repudiation.'

Although one had believed that this was probably the law it was not easy to find such a clear, unequivocal and authoritative statement of it elsewhere in the cases.

Although the decision of the Court of Appeal in *Antaios Cia Naviera SA v Salen Rederierna AB, The Antaios* [1983] 3 All ER 777 is primarily concerned with questions of leave to appeal both from an arbitrator to the High Court and from the High Court to the Court of Appeal on the question on leave to appeal from the arbitrator, it also involves discussion of some interesting problems of termination.

For this purpose the facts may perhaps be stated as follows. Under a time charterparty the owners were entitled to withdraw the vessel in certain circumstances and on 7 May 1980 discovered that the charterers had committed acts which they considered entitled them to withdraw. They told the charterers that they considered them to be in breach and that they reserved the right to withdraw the vessel without prejudice to any delay in doing so. On 20 May 1980 the owners in fact purported to withdraw the vessel. There can be little doubt that as a rule notice of withdrawal must be given within a reasonable time after the default and what is a reasonable time is essentially a matter for the arbitrator. However this rule has been explained on two quite different grounds. One is that it is an implied term of contract, the other is that delay in exercising the right to withdraw will amount to waiver or found an estoppel. It can be plausibly argued that a statement by the owners that they are reserving their rights would be inconsistent with a waiver or estoppel but would be ineffective on the implied term approach. In effect the arbitrators took the implied term approach and the question before the Court of Appeal was whether the possibility that the waiver approach might be correct should have constituted a ground for the judge giving leave to appeal from the arbitrator. The Court of Appeal thought not since the question for the judge would be not whether the arbitrators had proceeded on the wrong view of the law, but whether they had got to the wrong conclusion. The majority of the Court of Appeal at least thought that the arbitrators would have got to the same conclusion on these facts whichever juridical basis the rule had. Sir John Donaldson MR and Fox LJ thought that an owner could not unilaterally extend the time for making up his mind by stating that he was reserving his rights, though there might well be facts known only to the owner which would be relevant to the question of what would be a reasonable time. If he made these known to the charterer that might well justify an extension of what would be a reasonable time.

The trapping of ships in the Shatt Al-Arab by the outbreak of the Iran/Iraq war has given rise to many arbitrations concerned with whether charterparties have thereby been frustrated. This was the factual background to the decision in *Kodros Shipping Corpn v Empresa Cubana de Fletes* [1982] 3 All ER 350 noted in last year's review (All ER Rev 1982, p 77), but that case effectively turned on the charterers' obligations as to 'a safe port'. The frustration question was squarely raised in *Finelvet AG v Vinava Shipping Co Ltd, The Chrysalis* [1983] 2 All ER 658. In this case the time chartered ship docked at Basrah on 14 September 1980. Eight days later on 22 September war broke out between Iraq and Iran. The vessel continued to discharge her cargo and by 1 October was ready to proceed to Muscat where she was due to be redelivered to the shipowners. The vessel was prevented from leaving Basrah by the Iraqi port authorities. On 14 November the charterers purported to cancel the charterparty and the evidence was that by 24 November it was the view of most informed people in shipping circles that the obstacles to navigation, including sunken ships in the Shatt Al-Arab, were such that vessels trapped there were unlikely to be able to leave safely for at least several months and probably for much longer. The dispute between the parties was as to the date on which the contract was frustrated. The charterers contended that the contract was frustrated on 22 September when war was declared. The shipowners contended that the charterparty was not frustrated until 24 November. The practical effect of this difference was, of course, that if the ship owners were correct the charterers would be under a continuing obligation to pay hire until 24 November. The arbitrator held that the contract was not frustrated until 24 November.

The charterers' major argument was that the contract was frustrated automatically by the outbreak of war. If this argument was correct then the charterers would inevitably succeed since the arbitrator would then have made a mistake on a question of law. After a careful examination of the authorities, however, Mustill J rejected so broad a proposition. In some cases the outbreak of war would bring the doctrine of supervening illegality into play because it would convert the contract into one to trade with the enemy. In other cases, however, the outbreak of war would not itself prevent the performance of the contract. Performance would be prevented if at all rather by the events which took place in furtherance of the war. These effects would depend on all the circumstances and in many cases would have to await events since one could not presume that the war was to be of indefinite duration or extent.

The charterers' alternative argument was that the arbitrator had got the date of frustration wrong. A number of different arbitrators have held that apparently similar contracts have been frustrated over quite a wide range of dates between September and December 1980. Mustill J held, however, that the arbitrator had correctly directed himself on the question of law and that the date he had chosen was well within the range of dates which a reasonable arbitrator having correctly instructed himself could choose. It follows that the arbitrator had made no mistake of law.

See also the article on Arbitration, pp 20 and 22 above.

8 Money paid under a mistake

The decision in *Avon County Council v Howlett* [1983] 1 All ER 1073 raised an interesting question on estoppel as a bar to repayment of money paid under a mistak of fact but unfortunately the question was presented to the court in a very odd form which makes the decision less helpful than it might otherwise have been. The plaintiffs alleged that owing to a mistake in their computerised wages system they had overpaid the defendant over a period of two years some £1,007. After some dispute the mistake was held to be a mistake of fact and the money was therefore prima facie repayable.

The judge held that the defendant was unaware of the mistake, reasonably believed that the sum he received was his and had expended it all. Despite this, the defendant pleaded that he had only expended part of the money that he had received. The defendant's counsel refused to amend this pleading, apparently because both the council and the relevant trade union wished to use this case as a test case, since there have been many similar over payments in local government. The question thus artificially posed for the court was whether the defendant who had relied on the payer's representation that the money was due and spent part of it could resist repayment of the whole. This question was artificial in another sense, since of course there had never been a single payment of £1,007 but a whole series of small payments over a long period. The Court of Appeal were strongly inclined to the view that as a rule if the payer were estopped from claiming that money had been paid under a mistake of fact this would leave him with no cause of action and therefore partial expenditure by the payee in the faith that the payment was due would usually suffice. This statement was, however, not unnaturally, qualified by observations that there might well be circumstances in which it would be unconscionable to allow the defendant to retain the balance in his hands.

Criminal Law and Sentencing

G J BENNETT, MA
Barrister, Lecturer in Law, University of Leeds
BRIAN HOGAN, LLB
Barrister, Professor of Law, University of Leeds

General principles

1 Mens rea

The decisions of the House of Lords in *R v Caldwell* [1981] 1 All ER 961 and in *R v Lawrence* [1981] 1 All ER 974 called into question—some might say, threw into confusion—what was thought to be the settled meaning of recklessness in relation to the mens rea of crime. The concept of recklessness has had a chequered history but after *R v Cunningham* [1957] 2 All ER 412, CCA it seemed to be settled that recklessness always postulated that the defendant consciously realised that his conduct involved a risk of causing a harm proscribed by the criminal law, but nevertheless unreasonably took the risk of causing that harm. *Caldwell* decided that, at least in the context of criminal damage, a person might be accounted reckless not only where he foresaw the risk of destroying or damaging the property of another but also where his conduct was such as to create an obvious risk that property would be destroyed or damaged and he gave no thought to there being any such risk.

A question arguably left open by *Caldwell* and *Lawrence* was whether the risk created should be one that would have been obvious to the reasonable man, or one which would have been obvious to the defendant. A particular defendant might have physical or mental limitations which made the risk not obvious to him when it would have been to the reasonable man not having those limitations. In *Elliott v C (a minor)* [1983] 2 All ER 1005 the Court of Appeal held that this question had not been left open and that the court had no option but to declare that the test was entirely objective. This led to the astonishing conclusion that a 14-year old girl who was attending the remedial class at school and who had passed a night wandering sleeplessly away from home, could be convicted of arson when at about 5 in the morning she set fire to some white spirit in a garden shed which led to its destruction. The magistrates found that while the girl had some idea that white spirit was inflammable, she had no idea of the conflagration that might be caused and that this risk would not have been obvious to her had she given thought to the matter. The magistrates were held to be wrong in directing their minds to what might have been obvious to an inexperienced, backward and exhausted 14-year old; the test was whether the risk would have been obvious to the reasonable man.

Though he felt constrained to agree with the result, Robert Goff LJ said that he would be lacking in candour if he were to conceal his unhappiness about the conclusion to which *Caldwell* and *Lawrence* impelled the court. But there was no way in which the authorities could be distinguished and while the court certified the point as to whether a person was reckless even though the risk, had he thought about it, would not have been obvious to him, it refused leave to appeal. The House of Lords subsequently dismissed the defendant's petition for leave to appeal.

While the definition of recklessness given by the House of Lords in *Caldwell* was strictly in the context of criminal damage, Lord Diplock made it clear that the definition was applicable whenever recklessness (or reckless, or recklessly) appeared in a modern statute. The definition was promptly extended to reckless driving in *Lawrence* and has been extended to recklessness as to consent in rape (*R v Pigg* [1982] 2 All ER 591). But it was accepted in *Caldwell* that this definition of recklessness did not apply to the interpretation of 'maliciously' for there, as was authoritatively established by *Cunningham*, what was required was an intention to bring about the proscribed harm, or recklessness in the sense of actual foresight of a perceived risk which it was unjustifiable in the circumstances to take.

It might have been concluded from this that the *Caldwell* definition of recklessness applied *only* where the term 'reckless' (or its variants) appeared in a modern statute and that where it was established in the context of other crimes where the *concept* of recklessness was employed that foresight of consequences was postulated, the subjective test would continue to govern. Take assault, for example. It is established by *R v Venna* [1975] 3 All ER 788, CA that an assault may be committed intentionally or recklessly and in the context of that case it seems clear that recklessness was assumed to be subjective. The trial judge had directed the jury that the defendant could be convicted of an assault if, during his arrest by the police, he kicked out 'knowing that there are officers about him and knowing that by lashing out he would probably or is likely to kick somebody' (at 792) and the Court of Appeal entirely approved of this direction.

But the assumption that recklessness in the context of assault (and in the context of other crimes for that matter) always requires foresight is called into question by the decision and by dicta in *R v Seymour* ([1983] 2 All ER 1058). This decision is considered in detail below (p 138), but two points need to be noted here. The first concerns the decision. Manslaughter, which is a common law offence of long standing if ever there was one, may be committed where D causes death being reckless as to any personal injury. *Seymour* establishes that recklessness in this context is satisfied by *Caldwell* recklessness, that is, subjective awareness of risk, though it will of course, suffice, is not a requirement where the risk is obvious and the defendant gives no thought to the possibility of there being any such risk.

It can be argued that what is sauce for recklessness in the context of manslaughter is sauce for recklessness in the context of assault. The second point is that this view receives considerable support from the following remarkable dictum of Lord Roskill, delivering the judgment of the House ([1983] 2 All ER at 1064)—

> 'My Lords, I would accept the submission of [counsel] for the Crown that once it is shown that the two offences [*Sc* manslaughter and causing death by reckless driving] co-exist it would be quite wrong to give the adjective "reckless" or the adverb "recklessly" a different meaning according to whether the statutory or the common law offence is charged. "Reckless" should today be given the same meaning in relation to all offences which involve "recklessness" as one of the

elements *unless Parliament has otherwise ordained* [emphasis added]. . . . That simple and single meaning should be the ordinary meaning of those words as stated in this House in *R v Caldwell* and *R v Lawrence.*'

If the *Caldwell* definition of recklessness stands excluded only when Parliament 'otherwise ordains' it looks as though the *Caldwell* definition is poised to make almost a clean sweep. Presumably it could not apply where the legislation uses expressions such as 'knowingly' or 'knowing or believing' since a man who gives no thought even to the most obvious risk cannot be said to 'know' or 'know or believe' that risk exists. Presumably, too, the use of the word 'maliciously' must be considered a case where Parliament 'otherwise ordains' since it was accepted in *Caldwell* itself that recklessness there postulated an awareness by the defendant of the risk. But many offences in which the concept of recklessness is employed (and assault provides an example) are defined by the common law so there is no question of Parliament ordaining a meaning other than the *Caldwell* meaning. *Caldwell* recklessness is rapidly gaining ground and such defences as the commentators threw against it are being rapidly overrun.

And all this within a few years of *DPP v Morgan* [1975] 2 All ER 347 which was regarded as the time as a great victory by those who favoured the subjective view of criminal liability. That case held that a man was entitled to be acquitted of rape if he honestly believed that the woman was consenting, however crass his error might have been. *Caldwell* can be seen as turning, even outflanking, the decision in *Morgan*. So in *R v Pigg* it was held that a man may be convicted of rape where there is an obvious risk that the woman is not consenting and he gives no thought to there being no such risk. After *Morgan* and before *Caldwell* it seemed to be clear law that a man who honestly believed in the woman's consent did not have the requisite intention or recklessness whether he adverted to the issue and decided that she was consenting, or whether it never occurred to him that she was not consenting. Either way he does not consciously take the risk that she may not be consenting. But the effect of *Caldwell* and *Pigg* is that the defendant may be convicted of rape in the latter situation if the risk of her not consenting would have been obvious to the reasonable man. Thus liability for rape may turn on the finest and most puzzling of distinctions.

But though the decision in *Morgan* may have been turned it has not been overrun, and it was applied in *R v Kimber* [1983] 3 All ER 316. The defendant, while visiting a mental hospital, did acts to a woman he knew to be a patient there which would have amounted to a sexual assault if she had not consented to them. The defendant claimed that he had inferred from her conduct that she was consenting but added that he was 'not really interested in [the victim's] feelings at all'. The recorder directed the jury that the issue was whether the victim had in fact consented and whether the defendant thought or believed she was consenting was irrelevant.

While the defendant's conviction was upheld, the Court of Appeal held that this was a misdirection. The court, rejecting an observation made in *R v Phekoo* [1981] 3 All ER 84 that *Morgan* applied only in cases of rape and declining to speculate as to which other crimes it might apply, held that *Morgan* did apply to indecent assault. What had to be proved by the prosecution was that the defendant intentionally or recklessly applied force to the victim without her consent. If he did not so intend because he believed she was consenting the prosecution fails to prove the charge. Furthermore, 'It is the defendant's belief, not the grounds on which it is based, which goes to negative the intent' ([1983] 3 All ER at 319).

The court here concluded that had the jury been properly directed they would inevitably have found that the defendant was reckless. The court appears clearly to have had *Cunningham* recklessness in mind; the defendant's state of mind could be described as 'couldn't care less'. But it would seem that the defendant could also be accounted reckless if he had given no thought whatever to the risk that she was not consenting, if that risk would have been obvious to the reasonable man. The logic of *Caldwell* and *Pigg* (such as it is) must apply to recklessness in the context of indecent assault as it does to rape. The one point of distinction is that the Sexual Offences (Amendment) Act 1976 uses the expression 'reckless' and thus attracts the *Caldwell* definition because it appears in a modern statute. The Sexual Offences Act 1956, s 14(1) contains no definition of sexual assault which is therefore a matter of common law, thus attracting the *Cunningham* definition of recklessness. But this line of escape from *Caldwell* has been jeopardized by Lord Roskill in *R v Seymour* in the passage ([1983] 2 All ER at 1064) cited on p 130, above.

R v Miller [1983] 1 All ER 978 also bears on the vexed issue of recklessness. Since the Court of Appeal's decision was dealt with last year (All ER Rev 1982, p 85) and since the House of Lords decision in this year was taken in as a matter of convenience, there is no need to rehearse it again. It is, though, worth a reminder that where the defendant inadvertently sets in train events which continue to cause harm and subsequently becomes aware of that harm, it is his responsibility to take steps reasonably available to prevent or minimise further harm. That responsibility arises, however, *only* where he becomes consciously aware of the danger he has created (that is, *Cunningham* recklessness applies at this stage), but once he becomes aware of the danger he may be liable if he either consciously takes the risk of further harm, or he gives no thought to there being any such risk where the risk would be obvious to the reasonable man (that is, *Caldwell* recklessness applies at this stage).

It is a relief to turn to a case on mens rea where *Caldwell* does not get a mention. In *R v Taaffe* [1983] 2 All ER 625 the defendant was charged with being 'knowingly' concerned in the fraudulent evasion of the prohibition on the importation of cannabis contrary to the Customs and Excise Management Act 1979, s 170(2), and the Misuse of Drugs Act 1971, s 3(1). Customs officers had found the defendant in possession of certain packages which in fact contained cannabis. The defendant claimed that he picked up the packages from a third party in Holland, that he believed the packages contained money and that he further believed (mistakenly as it turned out) that currency was subject to a prohibition against importation.

The trial judge ruled that even if the defendant's version was accepted the jury would have to be directed to convict, so the defendant changed his plea to guilty and was sentenced. Allowing his appeal, it was held that to substantiate the charge it had to be proved that the defendant should know, 'in the ordinary sense of the word "know"', that the goods were subject to a prohibition. Knowledge would be satisfied if he knew the goods to be subject to a prohibition even though 'he may not know the precise nature of the goods'. Presumably the defendant could have been convicted had he thought the packages to contain any goods which the legislation defines as 'prohibited goods'.

But where, as here, the goods he supposed himself to be carrying did not fall within the category of prohibited goods, there could be no offence. He has to be judged on the facts as he believed them to be and on that assumption no offence was committed.

Might the defendant have been convicted of an attempt? On his own admission he was trying to bring into the country goods (money) which he believed to be prohibited and he failed in that endeavour. It is submitted that he could not be convicted of an attempt. If he believes that he is importing what are in law prohibited goods he may be convicted of an attempt, as where he believes he is importing cocaine when the substance is flour. But where he believes that he is importing goods which belong to the prohibited class when they do not so belong, it is thought that he cannot be convicted of an attempt. Though the Criminal Attempt Act 1981 has substantially modified the position relating to impossibility in attempts, it surely does not make it an offence to attempt to commit an offence not known to the law. The intent must be an intent to commit an offence to which s 1(1) of the Act applies and that must entail a reference to offences under English law. There is, of course, an offence of importing prohibited goods but the 'goods' are not defined to include money, hence the defendant could not be convicted of attempting to commit that which was not an offence under the law.

2 Automatism and insanity

'[I]t is not every frantic and idle humour of a man, that will exempt him from justice, and the punishment of the law,' said Tracy J in the course of the trial of Edward Arnold for the shooting of Lord Onslow ((1724) 16 St Tr 695). What does, fell to be considered in *R v Sullivan* [1983] 1 All ER 577, [1983] 2 All ER 673 and *R v Bailey* [1983] 2 All ER 503.

In *R v Sullivan* the defendant was charged with two counts under ss 18 and 20 respectively of the Offences Against the Person Act 1861. It was undisputed that Sullivan had attacked an elderly man in the flat of one of his neighbours. His defence, which was supported by cogent medical testimony, was that he had done so while in the final stage of an epileptic seizure. The trial judge ruled that this amounted to a defence of insanity rather than automatism. Not surprisingly, the defendant changed his plea to guilty of the s 20 charge in order to avoid the consequences of a successful defence. Both the trial judge and the prosecution agreed to the case being disposed of in this way. In contrast to the mandatory committal which would have been the result of a finding of insanity, the sentence handed down by the court was probation under medical supervision. His appeal that the trial court's finding had deprived him of the chance of an acquittal on the basis of automatism was rejected by both the Court of Appeal and the House of Lords, although the reasoning in each case was somewhat different.

In *R v Quick* [1973] 3 All ER 347 at 356a Lawton LJ had remarked:

> 'In our judgment no help can be obtained by speculating (because that is what we would have to do) as to what judges who answered the House of Lords

question in 1843 meant by disease of the mind, still less what Sir Mathew Hale meant in the second half of the 17th century. A quick backward look at the state of medicine in 1843 will suffice to show how unreal it would be to apply the concepts of that age to the present time.'

It is therefore a little surprising to find that Lawton LJ in *R v Sullivan* rested the judgment on the common law of insanity upon which the M'Naghten rules were regarded as a humane gloss relating chiefly to the problem of insane delusions. The court drew a distinction between those cases where the accused was wholly deprived of his understanding and memory and those where he suffered from delusions which took control of his faculties. The present case was more appropriately classified as an example of the former, and therefore could have been regarded as a 'visitation of God' and insanity within the pre-1843 common law. For this reason the judge had been correct in regarding epilepsy as legal insanity.

It is, of course, quite true that the M'Naghten rules were not given in the course of any judicial proceedings. Nevertheless, for 140 years they have been regarded as the legal test of insanity and it is difficult to see what purpose Lawton LJ's brief descent into the realms of mediaeval derangement was likely to serve. If an accused is to be regarded as insane when, as a result of a disease of the mind, he does not know the nature and quality of his act or that it was wrong, it is surely implicit in the M'Naghten rules that he is to be regarded as insane in the even more extreme case when he does not know what he is doing at all.

In any event, the House of Lords rejected this approach entirely. The M'Naghten rules had long been treated and were to be regarded as a comprehensive definition of legal insanity. The answers to the second and third questions put to the House were 'perfectly general' in their terms. Further, this was the approach taken in *Bratty v A-G for Northern Ireland* [1961] 3 All ER 523. Lord Diplock pointed out the close similarity between the present case and *Bratty*, the crucial difference being the absence in *Bratty* of any adequate medical evidence on which a jury might have found that the defendant had indeed been suffering from psychomotor epilepsy.

The decision by the House of Lords to classify epilepsy as legal insanity is in keeping with their earlier decision in *Bratty* and the observations of Lord Devlin in *R v Kemp* [1956] 3 All ER 249 at 253 which together also make clear that medical and legal notions of insanity are not identical. Nevertheless, there are obvious advantages in trying to ensure that legal medical and public notions of insanity in the context of a criminal trial do not lose all contact with each other. Epilepsy is not an uncommon medical condition. Is there any proper justification for attaching the stigma of a verdict of insanity to a condition that neither doctors nor most jurors would have regarded as appropriately labelled in this way? It seems that the humane solution adopted to this dilemma by the courts is to allow the defendant to plead to the charge and so enable the judge to pass a sentence appropriate to the defendant's condition. If legal principle has to be circumvented by such unseemly charades, what justification can these be for retaining the present rule?

Lord Diplock, giving a decision with which all members of the House concurred, frankly admitted his misgivings about attaching the legal label of insanity to one suffering from psychomotor epilepsy but considered that only Parliament could institute reform. Paradoxically, the decision in *Sullivan* makes the position of the defendant even more precarious. If epilepsy is an issue in the case, it now seems impossible for a court to overlook the fact that such a finding would amount to a plea of insanity.

Merely to introduce an updated statutory definition of insanity is unlikely to be a sufficient reform. An examination of the efforts of American courts to recast the traditional M'Naghten test of insanity, culminating in the formulation contained in section 4.01 of the Model Penal Code, suggests that there is a limit to what can be done even if some improvement is clearly possible.

What makes the present situation, as illustrated by *Sullivan*, particularly unsatisfactory is the inflexibility of the law's response to a defendant suffering from mental illness. Both the Court of Appeal and the House of Lords drew attention to the policy of the M'Naghten rules as being to protect society from future dangerous conduct by the accused, but it hardly follows that the draconian measure of mandatory committal is an appropriate way to deal with the problem. One obvious reform would be simply to abolish the mandatory committal as an inevitable consequence of a finding of insanity and so relieve the defendant from the pressure to plead guilty to an offence for which he has, in reality, no criminal responsibility. Others have suggested that when a defendant successfully pleads automatism a court should have the power to make discharge conditional on receiving treatment to prevent a recurrence of the unconsciousness. By reducing the gulf between sane and non-insane automatism, courts might be less tempted to classify as 'insane' persons believed to present a danger to society but hardly regarded as insane in any medical or popular sense of the word. Unless, however, such a reform was combined with an alteration in the legal definition of insanity, this would not help those already so classified. Since the decision in *Sullivan* this is already arguably too broad a category.

The shortcomings of the present law relating to insanity received detailed treatment by the Butler Committee in its 1975 Report of the Committee on Mentally Abnormal Offenders (Cmnd 6244). One of its recommendations was an expanded defence of 'not guilty on evidence of mental disorder' (para 18.18). Such a finding would enable the court to make any order it considered appropriate. This could range from discharge without any order to in-patient treatment with a restriction order (paras 18.42–18.45). Reform of some kind is clearly long overdue.

In *R v Bailey* [1983] 2 All ER 503 the issue that arose was the relationship of automatism to diabetes. The defendant was again charged with assault under ss 18 and 20 of the Offences Against the Person Act 1861. His defence was automatism based on the fact that the attack had taken place while he was unconscious as the result of hypoglycaemia brought about by his failure to take sufficient food after a dose of insulin. The recorder directed the jury that the defence of automatism did not apply to a self-induced capacity, and 'self-induced' in this context included the defendant's failure to take sufficient food. Following this direction the defendant was convicted and appealed on the basis that the summing up was inaccurate both in respect to the s 18 and s 20 offences.

Insofar as the recorder suggested that self-induced incapacity is not a defence to a crime which requires a specific intent, such as s 18 wounding, the direction was quite clearly wrong and contrary to the decision of the House of Lords in *DPP v Majewski* [1976] 2 All ER 142. The interest of the case lies rather in the holding by the Court of Appeal that self-induced automatism may be a defence to a basic intent crime such as unlawful wounding under s 20.

In *R v Quick* [1973] 3 All ER 347, a case which also raised the issue of diabetes in the context of a basic intent wounding, Lawton LJ said at 356:

> 'A self-induced incapacity will not excuse (See *R v Lipman* [1969] 3 All ER 410) nor will one which could have been reasonably foreseen as a result of either doing, or omitting to do something, as, for example, taking alcohol against medical advice after using certain prescribed drugs, or failing to have regular meals whilst taking insulin.'

The Court of Appeal in *Bailey* regarded this passage as being obiter. Whilst a voluntary consumption of alcohol or drugs would not negative the mens rea of a crime of basic intent, this case was to be distinguished from that where a person failed to take sufficient food after insulin so as to avert hypoglycaemia. In the case of drugs or alcohol it was stated to be common knowledge that those who took excessive amounts of these substances may cause harm to others. The mens rea element of a basic intent crime was supplied by their recklessness in deliberately undertaking a course of conduct generally known to lead to dangerous or aggressive behaviour. Drugs and alcohol apparently raise a conclusive presumption of such recklessness. It was said not to be common knowledge, even amongst diabetics, that a failure to take adequate sustenance 'may lead to aggressive, unpredictable and uncontrollable conduct'. Consequently self-induced automatism may in certain circumstances amount to a defence and the passage quoted from Lawton LJ's judgment required some qualification.

The whole doctrine of intoxication and the division between specific and basic intent owes more to judicial policy-making than logic. In particular, the notion of basic intent is anomalous in that, even as explained by the Court of Appeal, it appears somewhat at odds with the normal requirement of a concurrence of actus reus and mens rea. To have extended liability to a diabetic who innocently fails to take the required amount of food after insulin would have been difficult to justify.

The court's decision leaves open the possibility that the defence would not be available if the prosecution could establish that the defendant made a conscious decision not to take appropriate sustenance with knowledge that this was likely to result in 'aggressive, unpredictable or uncontrolled behaviour'. In such a case the Crown would have established the requisite degree of recklessness to justify conviction for an assault in that, conscious of a risk to others, the accused had chosen to run that risk. Although the Court of Appeal was specifically concerned with assualt, the reasoning presumably extends to all crimes of basic intent.

The decision in *Bailey* leaves untouched the view implicit in *R v Quick* that if a defendant's condition arises simply from diabetes this amounts to a plea of insanity. If it has arisen from taking insulin, this is automatism since this is regarded as an external factor and not a disease of the mind within the M'Naghten rules. The affront to common sense involved in labelling a diabetic as insane was noted in *Quick* itself and reinforces the need for reform noted in the discussion of *Sullivan*.

What if one who suffered from psychomotor epilepsy failed to take a drug which had been prescribed for him and normally was completely effective in controlling his condition? Would a subsequent assault committed in the course of an epileptic seizure be attributable to legal insanity or to the external factor of failure to take the drug? Even if the policy behind the defence of insanity is as Lord Diplock stated in *Sullivan* ([1983] 2 All ER at 678), 'to protect society against recurrence of the dangerous conduct', it is difficult to envisage that this situation is what the House of Lords had in mind. Such a condition is neither uncontrollable nor prone to recur if the defendant takes the appropriate medication and can hardly justify mandatory committal. For this reason it would seem preferable to treat such a case as closer to *Quick* in regarding the drug as the causative element and making available a defence of automatism. If the defendant was conscious of his failure to take the drug and aware that this would in all likelihood lead to violent, aggressive or unpredictable behaviour, it is difficult to see why he should not be subject to the reasoning in *Bailey*. If knowledge of the recklessness of his conduct is now the critical element in assessing a defendant's liability for self-induced automatism there seems no obvious reason for distinguishing diabetes from epilepsy in this regard.

3 *Inchoate offences*

Impossibility in the context of incitement provided the bone of contention in *R v Fitzmaurice* [1983] 1 All ER 189. The defendant's father concocted a scheme to defraud a security firm by informing the police that there was a plan to rob a security van so that he, the father, would receive a reward. To lend an air of verisimilitude, he asked the defendant to find someone to carry out a robbery on a woman carrying wages between a bank and a factory. Clearly the father placed more faith in the adage that there is no honour among thieves than on the shibboleth that blood is thicker than water, for he disclosed none of his fraud to his son who in good faith (if good faith is possible in such matters) secured the services of B who in turn recruited C and D. Tipped off by the father, police arrested B, C and D before the 'robbery' took place but B's conviction for conspiracy to rob was quashed on its appearing that he had been the victim of a trick and that there was no woman carrying money to be robbed. The defendant now appealed against his conviction for inciting to rob, arguing that he could not be convicted of inciting B to commit a crime that was impossible.

Incitement is still governed by the common law rules ralating to impossibility which were laid down by the House of Lords in *Haughton v Smith* [1973] 3 All ER 1109 for attempts and in *R v Nock* [1978] 2 All ER 654 for conspiracy. These cases, it will be recalled, decided, respectively, that a person could not be convicted of attempting, nor of conspiring, to commit a crime where the achievement of the objective was physically impossible. In their application to attempt and conspiracy both decisions have been reversed by statute but the question is whether they still apply to incitement.

The Court of Appeal in *Fitzmaurice* accepted that the principles of *Haughton v Smith* and *Nock* continued to apply to incitement but that did not end the matter. The crucial question is the course of conduct which the alleged incitor is encouraging. Thus if the incitement is in general terms (for example to kill an unspecified victim or effect a burglary at unspecified premises) the incitor may be properly convicted though there is a subsequent agreement to kill X who is already dead or a subsequent agreement to enter premises that have been burned down. Consistently with this the defendant's conviction could be upheld. At the time he recruited B he believed 'he was recruiting for a robbery not for a charade'. That it later became a charade did not mean that at the time of the recruitment the defendant did not incite B to rob.

The distinction may, however, be a fine one and a more satisfactory solution would be a statutory amendment bringing incitement into line with conspiracy and attempt.

Board of Trade v Owen [1957] 1 All ER 411, HL decided that it was not an offence to conspire in England to commit an offence abroad and this principle is now given statutory effect by s 1(4) of the Criminal Law Act 1977. In *A-G's Reference (No 1 of 1982)* [1983] 2 All ER 721 the Court of Appeal declined to modify the principle so as to make indictable in England a conspiracy to defraud persons abroad although the conspiracy might incidentally cause economic loss to persons in England. To create such an exception, said Lord Lane CJ, would mean adopting an immensely wide test; whenever a conspiracy to be carried out abroad sent ripples back to England to wash over some economic interest it would mean that an indictment would lie in England.

Offences against the person

1 *Manslaughter and causing death by reckless driving*

R v Seymour [1983] 2 All ER 1058 is a case which has relevance not only to the relationship between manslaughter and causing death by reckless driving but also has implications (see p 130 above) for the meaning of recklessness generally in the criminal law.

Seymour had been living with Mrs Burrows and one day he left the house in high dudgeon following a quarrel with her. It does not appear what they quarrelled about but, from the tragic consequences, tempers must have run, and stayed, high. A little later Seymour bumped into Mrs Burrows. Quite literally, for he at the time was driving an 11 ton lorry and she a Vauxhall car. So the contest, for a contest there was, strongly favoured Seymour from the start. Mrs Burrows backed the Vauxhall, got out of it on the off-side, approached the lorry and began addressing remarks to Seymour. Seymour then drove his lorry forward intending, as he claimed, to push the Vauxhall out of the way. He did this so violently that he knocked the Vauxhall some 10 or 20 feet, wrenching off one of its tyres. In so doing Mrs Burrows was crushed between the two vehicles and so severly injured that, as an ambulanceman said, had she been picked up in the normal way she would have broken in two. She died a week later.

Seymour was charged with manslaughter. He offered to plead guilty to causing death by dangerous driving but the prosecution declined to accept his offer and the trial for manslaughter went ahead.

It is perhaps a little unfortunate that we have fashioned an expression 'motor manslaughter', which suggests that in some way it stands apart from other forms of manslaughter. It does not and if the point needs to be made, it was made years ago by Lord Atkin in *Andrews v DPP* [1937] 2 All ER 552. The weapon does not matter; it may be a motor car or a machete.

But if there is no *legal* difference between motor cars and machetes, there has long been a *social* one. Juries have down the years shown a toleration for the dangerous handlers of motor vehicles that they have not shown for the dangerous wielders of machetes; hence the creation in 1956 of the offences of causing death by dangerous or by reckless driving. After 1956 motorists, it seems, were rarely, if ever, charged with manslaughter; a charge of manslaughter was likely to be brought against a motorist only in the exceptional case when the vehicle had been used as a weapon, where there had been an element of deliberation.

Not only that, but charges of causing death by *reckless* driving were rarely if ever brought and year after year the Criminal Statistics record only prosecutions for causing death by *dangerous* driving. No doubt this was because prosecutors, bent as they always are on an easy ride for themselves, realised that whatever had to be proved to support the dangerous driving charge (and though the courts were never all that helpful in telling them what this was), it was much less than had to be proved on the reckless driving charge.

Indeed, no less an authority than Lord Atkin had presciently issued a warning nearly 20 years before the creation of the offence of causing death by reckless driving that to charge this offence would involve the prosecutor in proving what he would have to prove on a charge of manslaughter. 'It is difficult to visualise', he had said ([1937] 2 All ER at 556), 'a case of death caused by "reckless" driving, in the connotation of that term in ordinary speech, which would not justify a conviction for manslaughter...'

This prescience of Lord Atkin was borne out in *Jennings v US Government* [1982] 3 All ER 104 and by the House of Lords. The state of California had sought Miss Jennings' extradition on a charge of manslaughter arising from a motor accident in El Segundo when she knocked down and killed a cyclist. It was argued on behalf of the defendant that she could not be convicted of manslaughter here but only of causing death by reckless driving which was not an extradition crime under the Treaty. That argument was rejected, Lord Roskill, speaking on behalf of the House, stating unequivocally that causing death by reckless driving was manslaughter by the law of England.

In between times, that is in between 1956 when causing death by dangerous or reckless driving were introduced and 1983 when *Seymour* was decided, two things had happened. One was that dangerous driving and causing death by dangerous driving were abolished by the Criminal Law Act 1977. The second was that following *R v Caldwell* [1981] 1 All ER 961 the House in *R v Lawrence* [1981] 1 All ER 974 gave to reckless driving a definition that went at least some of the way to mopping up the area left vacant by the abolition of dangerous driving. On a charge of reckless driving, said Lord Diplock ([1981] 1 All ER at 982), the jury should be satisfied of two things—

> '[F]irst, that the defendant was in fact driving the vehicle in such a manner as to create an obvious and serious risk of causing physical injury to some other person who might happen to be using the road or doing substantial injury to property; and second, that in driving in that manner the defendant did so without having given any thought to the possibility of there being any such risk or, having recognised that there was some risk involved, had none the less gone on to take it.'

Logically, if reckless driving is defined in a certain way, then causing death by reckless driving is driving in that way and causing death. So if Seymour, as he evidently did, created an obvious and serious risk of doing substantial damage to property and thereby caused death, he should be guilty of causing death by reckless driving whether he had given thought to the risk or not. Two plus two should equal four. But our law of manslaughter, draconic as it undoubtedly is, does not make a man guilty of manslaughter merely because he inadvertently causes death when intentionally or recklessly damaging property.

The trial judge (Bush J) evidently grasped this point because he indicated to counsel that while he would use the '*Lawrence* direction' on recklessness, he would do so without reference to damage to property and he subsequently learned from Lord Roskill that he was 'entirely right' to do so.

No doubt counsel for Seymour was grateful for this concession but so far as he was concerned it was only half the loaf. *Lawrence* recklessness could of course be met by objective (*Caldwell*) recklessness requiring no actual foresight by Seymour of any risk to Mrs Burrows. Counsel argued that if causing death by reckless driving amounted to manslaughter (and only 14 months ago the House of Lords had unequivocally confirmed that it did), then what had to be proved was that Seymour actually foresaw some risk of harm to Mrs Burrows.

It is respectfully submitted that counsel's argument was entirely right, that where a charge of manslaughter is based on recklessness as to personal injury this requires that the defendant is actually aware that he is creating a risk of harm to the person. But his argument was rejected by the trial judge who proceeded to give the *Lawrence* direction (stripped of the reference to damage to property) and for this he received a second accolade from Lord Roskill.

So far so bad but it gets worse. So far, and consistently with *Jennings*, the House has held that causing death by reckless driving amounts to manslaughter but for this purpose has given to recklessness an objective (*Caldwell*) meaning which it did not formerly bear in the context of manslaughter. But now Lord Roskill goes on to recognise that there is a difference between causing death by reckless driving and manslaughter after all. 'Parliament', he said ([1983] 2 All ER at 1064, 1065)—

> 'must however be taken to have intended that "motor manslaughter" should be a more grave offence than the statutory offence. While the former still carries . . . life, Parliament has thought fit to limit the maximum penalty for the statutory offence to five years' imprisonment . . . This difference recognises that there are degrees in turpitude which will vary according to the gravity of the risk created by the manner of a defendant's driving . . . in the future it will only be very rarely that it will be appropriate to charge "motor manslaughter": that is where . . . the risk of death from a defendant's driving was very high.'

Thus there is no difference but there is a difference. There is no difference because causing death by reckless driving always amounts to manslaughter. From the fact that there is no difference it follows that the prosecution cannot charge the defendant in the alternative with manslaughter and with causing death by reckless driving. One good reason for not allowing that is that it is allowed in Scotland. But another reason, almost as compelling, was that since *Jennings* it was 'clear law that these offences co-existed and their ingredients were identical in point of law' ([1983] 2 All ER at 1065).

They are, however, different in that 'motor manslaughter' requires a greater degree of turpitude which the OED states means vileness, depravity, wickedness. It is thus for the prosecutor to decide whether a particular piece of driving which causes death is so bad that it can be described as vile, depraved or wicked. If in his view it can, then he may chance his arm on a charge of manslaughter. If not, he would do better to stick to the statutory offence because if the jury rejects manslaughter there can be no alternative conviction of, nor any subsequent prosecution for, the statutory offence.

It is, perhaps, possible to have some sympathy for Lord Roskill though it might not be enough to bring tears to your eyes. What he may be doing is to remind us that the *social* difference between 'motor manslaughter' and causing death by reckless driving is still with us. There is no reason to suppose that juries would be any less reluctant to convict motorists of manslaughter now than they were in the past; in other words juries will convict of manslaughter only in very bad cases. They are, however, prepared to convict for the statutory offence because, even though the House of Lords has said that the commission of the statutory offence is manslaughter in all but name, the *name* is important to the jury. That name, causing death by reckless driving, does not carry with your ordinary juryman the same stigma as manslaughter and, however irrational in point of law this may be, he is in fact prepared to convict of the statutory offence where he would not convict for the offence at common law. If this is what Lord Roskill was getting at then we can probably live with this idiosyncrasy in the law relating to motor manslaughter and causing death by reckless driving.

But that is not quite where the matter rests because *Seymour* has general implications for the law. It is part of the ratio of *Seymour* that where on a charge of manslaughter the prosecution relies on recklessness as to personal injury the correct direction would be based on the *Caldwell/Lawrence* definition. Thus the need to rely on gross negligence as to death or serious bodily harm virtually disappears; all that needs to be shown is that the defendant failed to appreciate that there was an obvious risk of some personal injury.

Furthermore, as has been pointed out in the general discussion of mens rea (p 130, above), there are dicta in *Seymour* which suggests that the *Caldwell* test for recklessness is more pervasive than some at first thought and that it applies whenever recklessness is employed 'unless Parliament has otherwise ordained'.

2 Murder, manslaughter and the 'aimed at' doctrine

In *R v Mitchell* [1983] 2 All ER 427, CA the defendant did something which, in the eyes of the common man, is far more provocative of disorder than piracy, blasphemy and wife-beating; it is called queue-jumping. So when the defendant sought to outflank the huddled masses in the Tottenham Post Office an altercation predictably broke out as 72-year old Mr Edward Smith remonstrated with him. Just as predictably again the defendant sought to win the argument not by an appeal to reason (for who can reason in favour of queue-jumping?), but by striking Mr Smith a blow in the mouth. A second blow or push followed which caused Mr Smith to fall against 89-year old Mrs Crafts and both crashed to the ground. Mrs Crafts sustained a fractured femur which brought on a pulmonary embolism causing her death.

On the face of it a simple enough problem, calling only for a line or three on transferred malice, and a line or three more on constructive manslaughter. But Staughton J, delivering the judgment of the Court of Appeal, devoted six pages to the matter, the complicating factor being the so-called 'aimed at' (or 'directed at') doctrine.

The 'aimed at' doctrine made its debut in the black comedy which was staged in 1960 called *DPP v Smith* [1960] 3 All ER 161. Delivering a monologue on behalf of himself and the other Law Lords, Viscount Kilmuir said this (at 167)—

> 'The jury must of course in such a case as the present make up their minds on the evidence whether the accused was unlawfully and voluntarily doing something to someone. The unlawful and voluntary act must clearly be aimed at someone in order to eliminate cases of negligence or of careless or dangerous driving.'

Perhaps this passage, along with the remainder of Viscount Kilmuir's speech, would have slipped quietly beneath the waves had not Lord Hailsham in *Hyam v DPP* [1974] 2 All ER 41, bent on salvaging something from the shipwreck of *DPP v Smith*, found in the aimed-at doctrine something that was worthy of preservation. By dint of much underwater exploration in the silt that had accumulated around the rotting hull, he found two passages of 'permanent value' ([1974] 2 All ER at 50). One was the definition of 'grievous bodily harm' and the other was—

> '... the earlier passage where Viscount Kilmuir LC says: "The unlawful and voluntary act must clearly be aimed at someone to eliminate cases of negligence or of careless [or dangerous] driving."'

Lord Hailsham went a little further because he thought that the reckless driver, though he might be guilty of manslaughter, would not ordinarily be guilty of murder 'because he is not at least ordinarily aiming his actions at anyone in the sense explained in *DPP v Smith*'. But Lord Hailsham immediately added that if he were (*sc* aiming at someone) then he could be convicted of murder and cited *DPP v Smith* as just such a case ([1974] 2 All ER at 55).

All very curious. The reckless motorist is ordinarily not guilty of murder because he neither intends, nor foresees as (highly) probably, the death of or grievous bodily harm to any other road user. If, however, he does, then he is as guilty as if he had used a bomb, a gun or a knife. Nor can it make a scrap of difference that the identity of his victim is not known to him. If he realises that his driving creates a (high) probability of death but carries on regardless, it cannot matter that the person killed turns out to be his local tax inspector whose death he had always dearly wished, or his favourite son whose death he would never wish.

Indeed Lord Hailsham conceded that the aimed-at requirement did not require that the defendant should in fact kill the victim he aimed at. If Mrs Hyam 'aimed at' anyone it was Mrs Booth, but the deaths she in fact caused (and it is safe to assume that she bore them no malice) were those of Mrs Booth's two daughters. 'It does not matter', said Lord Hailsham ([1974] 2 All ER at 56), '... that the act and the intention were aimed at a potential victim other than the one who succumbed'. Rather surprisingly this last point was overlooked in *Mitchell* for it surely disposed of the point at issue in that case. Whatever the status of the aimed-at doctrine, it cast no doubt or limitation on the doctrine of transferred malice.

Between *Hyam* and *Mitchell* was the case of *R v Dalby* [1982] 1 All ER 916, CA which might be regarded as the high-water mark of the aimed-at doctrine. Dalby and his pal, O'Such, were drug addicts. Dalby had lawfully obtained on prescription 32 tablets of diconal, a Class A controlled drug. He handed some of these to O'Such who used them to inject himself intravenously at about 8 pm. Later that evening O'Such had another friend help him to a second intravenous injection though it was not established whether this was with the diconal supplied by Dalby or with some other substance. But no matter because the jury was evidently satisfied that O'Such's subsequent death was owing at least in part to the administration of diconal.

So far as manslaughter by unlawful act was concerned there was one unlawful act involved namely, the supply by Dalby of a prescribed drug. The jury was then asked whether that supply was a substantial (ie not merely trivial) cause of death and the jury concluded that it was.

Dalby's counsel argued that unlawful act manslaughter required that the unlawful act be 'directed at' the victim and that the supply was not such a direct act. The argument was accepted by the court ([1982] 1 All ER at 919)—

> 'In the judgment of this court, where the charge of manslaughter is based on an unlawful and dangerous act, it must be directed at the victim and likely to cause immediate injury, however slight.'

Suppose, though, that a member of the jury that had convicted Dalby, and out of the boundless interest in English criminal law that affects intelligent jurymen, had read this. He might be puzzled. If the act was not directed at O'Such, who on earth was it directed at? This was hardly a case where it might be supposed that Dalby had given the diconal tablets to O'Such thinking that O'Such would pass them on to other unspecified and unidentified third parties. He knew that O'Such was going to inject himself and was present when he did so.

So it might seem an unsatisfactory explanation to the juryman to say that the act was not aimed at O'Such. The true explanation why Dalby was not guilty of *manslaughter by unlawful act* is that far-reaching, ramshackle and barbarous as is the doctrine of manslaughter by unlawful act, it is at least limited by the requirement that the unlawful act be the cause of the death. Here the unlawful act, *the supply*, did not cause the death; death was caused by *taking* the drug which is not an unlawful act. In fact Waller LJ realised this—

> 'The difficulty in the present case is that the act of supplying a controlled drug was not the act which caused direct harm. It was an act which made it possible, or even likely, that harm would occur subsequently, particularly if the drug was supplied to somebody who was on drugs. In all the reported cases, the physical act has been one which inevitably would subject the other person to the risk of some harm from the act itself. In this case, the supply of drugs would itself have caused no harm unless the deceased had subsequently used the drugs in a form and quantity which was dangerous' ([1982] 1 All ER at 919).

It is submitted that this passage contains the true ratio of *Dalby*, and that it would have been better if Waller LJ had stopped there and not have obfuscated the issue by the bogus requirement, for that is what it is, that the act should be directed or aimed at the victim.

It is important to appreciate that Dalby may have been convicted of manslaughter on other grounds. Waller LJ pointed out that there might be circumstances like the present which might justify a finding of manslaughter by gross negligence but the court was not concerned with that issue since it was not raised. Probably Dalby could not have been convicted under this head because there was no gross negligence as to death or serious injury but he might have been convicted under the third head of recklessness as to any personal injury. Neither of these heads would have involved *causation* problems. If a defendant supplies cocaine *to be taken* by his friend, being grossly negligent of the risk of death or serious bodily harm this creates, or being reckless whether this will cause him any bodily harm, he may be convicted of manslaughter if death results. What he may not be convicted of is manslaughter *by unlawful act* since that doctrine requires that the unlawful act be the cause of death, not some further act which is triggered, or made possible, by the anterior unlawful act, or is made foreseeable by it.

Essentially Staughton J in *R v Mitchell* came to this conclusion. He saw that the issue was one of causation and added that if the court in *Dalby* had been saying that the unlawful act must be aimed at the very person who was killed, he would respectfully hold that it was not part of the ratio of that case. Moreover, said Staughton J, no one had thought to question the convictions in *DPP v Newbury* [1976] 2 All ER 365 where the defendants dropped a stone on the passing train not knowing whether or whom it might kill, and in *R v Pagett* (1983) 76 Cr App R 279 where the armed defendant used a girl as a shield against possible retaliation by police officers, because the person in fact killed had not been aimed-at by the defendants.

The conclusion offered, therefore, is that the aimed-at doctrine has no place in the criminal law. Sired by *DPP v Smith* it was born from stock of the poorest pedigree and ever since has led a sickly life. The hope must be that it is not going to have a protracted terminal illness and that at the next opportunity the courts will unceremoniously consign it to the knacker's yard.

3 Wounding

Delivering the judgment of the Divisional Court in *JJC (a minor) v Eisenhower* [1983] 3 All ER 230 Robert Goff LJ pointed out that the meaning of 'wound' for the purposes of ss 18 and 20 of the Offences Against the Person Act 1861 had not apparently come before the courts in over a hundred years. A series of cases between 1830 and 1850 had settled that a wound was constituted by a break in the whole skin (the dermis or inner skin as well as the epidermis or outer skin) though it was also accepted that a break in the whole skin of an inner cavity, such as the mouth, would suffice.

The defendant was engaged in an incident in which the victim was hit in the area of his left eye causing a bruise. Obviously a bruise (or black-eye) would not constitute a wound but the justices felt constrained to hold that there was a wound in this case because fluid filling the front part of his eye abnormally contained red blood cells which indicated a rupture of an internal blood vessel. It was held that the justices were wrong so to conclude. An internal rupture may cause bleeding but it is impossible to conclude from this that there has been a rupture of the whole skin which a wound requires.

4 *Offensive weapons*

An offensive weapon is defined by s 1(4) of the Prevention of Crime Act 1953 to mean—

> 'Any article made or adopted for causing injury to the person or intended by the person having it with him for such use by him.'

The definition envisages three types of weapons: (a) those made for causing injury (for example, a bayonet, knuckle-duster or a grenade); (b) those adapted for causing injury (for example, a bottle broken so that the jagged edge can be thrust into a victim's face); and (c) any article possessed for the purpose of causing injury.

In *R v Simpson* [1983] 3 All ER 789, CA it was held, following *Gibson v Wales* [1983] 1 All ER 869, DC that a flick-knife fell within (a) and that juries should be directed accordingly. Flick-knives are designed to be brought into use with the minimum of delay to the assailant and the minimum of warning to the victim. 'By their very design in this way they betray the purposes for which they are made' ([1983] 3 All ER at 794).

Where an offensive weapon, in whatever category, is carried in a public place its possession can be justified by the defendant establishing 'lawful authority or reasonable excuse'. But the significance of holding that a weapon falls within (a) is that the circumstances would have to be highly exceptional to establish a reasonable excuse. A possible case would be that of a sailor who kept such a knife where it might be a matter of life or death to cut a rope instantly. But the studied parsimony of the courts in construing 'reasonable excuse' indicates that mere absence of a purpose to use the knife to injure, or to possess it as a curio or plaything, would not constitute a reasonable excuse.

Sexual offences

1 *Meaning of 'brothel'*

The world of the 'massage parlour' received a judicial visitation in the case of *Kelly v Purvis* [1983] 1 All ER 525. The defendant assisted in the management of a licensed massage parlour which did indeed provide massage and sauna services. Further, clients could obtain extra services, involving masturbation by the masseuses, for an additional fee. This fee was usually paid directly to the individual masseuse rather than being treated as part of the business takings. The defendant was aware of the situation and acted on occasions as a masseuse herself. The novel feature of this case was that one service not apparently on general offer was 'full sexual intercourse'. The stipendiary magistrate dismissed the information under s 33 of the Sexual Offences Act 1956 for the offence of assisting in the management of a brothel on the basis that, although the women concerned were common prostitutes, the absence of evidence of intercourse was fatal to the contention that this was a brothel.

The Divisional Court held that evidence of intercourse was not necessary to bring a charge under s 33 of the 1956 Act, although the reasoning required to reach this result was somewhat indirect. The 1956 Act does not define 'brothel' and the meaning must therefore be derived from the common law. In *Gorman v Standen, Palace-Clark v Standen* [1963] 3 All ER 627 Lord Parker stated that, at common law, a brothel was the same thing as a 'bawdy house'. This meant a place 'resorted to by persons of both sexes for the purpose of *prostitution*'. The question to be answered by the court therefore became, did the women's conduct amount to prostitution? In the somewhat similar case of *R v Webb* [1963] 3 All ER 177 it had been held that 'prostitution' was not confined to cases where the woman offered her body for sexual intercourse but, quoting Darling J in *R v de Munck* [1918–19] All ER Rep 499, 'is proved when it is shown that a woman offers her body for purposes amounting to common lewdness in return for payment'. Consequently, the provision of services such as masturbation under the circumstances set out in the case was capable of leading to a finding that there was a 'brothel' within the meaning of the 1956 Act. It remains true, of course, that there must be more than one woman involved.

The court went on to make the point that a brothel may still be found to exist even where there is no finding that the women charged for sexual intercourse. The authority from which this could be derived was *Winter v Woolfe* [1931] All ER Rep 623. Undergraduates from Cambridge were resorting to a house and dance room in Fen Ditton where there was evidence that illicit intercourse took place. It is perhaps a reflection of a different age that the setting for this case was premises where a 'thé dansant' was apparently held every Sunday afternoon. There was no evidence that the women had charged; as for the occupier of the premises, 'there was no evidence that the respondent made any profits out of the conduct of the premises other than that arising out of the sale of teas and similar refreshments'. Avory J held that this was still an arrangement capable of being classified as a 'brothel', and the present court clearly approved this analysis. The case also makes clear that similar conduct involving homosexual practices could lead to a finding that there was a brothel as a consequence of s 6 of the Sexual Offences Act 1967.

2 Disorderly houses and living off immoral earnings

If the term 'brothel' covers a general diversity of situations, it seems that the term 'disorderly house' is even wider. This is only one of the surprising aspects of the case of *R v Tan* [1983] 2 All ER 12.

The defendants were convicted on counts charging the keeping of a disorderly house and living on the earnings of prostitution contrary to s 30 of the Sexual Offences Act 1956. What was provided at the respective premises was indicated by one of the advetisements placed in a 'contact magazine' which was publicly available. One of them read:

> 'Humiliation enthusiast, my favourite pastime is humiliating and disciplining mature male submissives, in strict bondage. Lovely tan coloured mistress invites humble applicants, TV, CB, B, D and rubber wear, 12 pm to 7 pm Mon to Fri 89 Basement Flat, Warwick Way, Victoria, SW1.'

As Parker J put it, 'The services provided at both premises were of a particularly revolting and perverted kind. Straightforward sexual intercourse was not provided at all'. Unfortunately, neither did the Court of Appeal provide a key to the abbreviations whose decipherment will undoubtedly lead to the consumption of many otherwise profitable student library hours.

The essence of the defendants' appeals on the disorderly house counts was that the operations of a single prostitute providing sexual services, in private, to one client at a time, and with no other parties present, was incapable of amounting to a 'disorderly house'. Notwithstanding the court's concession that, 'the trend is for the criminal law to withdraw from concern with what takes place between consenting adults in private' the defendants' convictions were affirmed. It seems that the trenchant comments of Professor Seaborne Davies on the decision in *Shaw v DPP* (6 JSPTL (NS) 104) and the approach to law reflected in the implementation of the Wolfenden Report have made only a modest impact on the Court of Appeal's analysis of this novel prosecution.

The offence of keeping a disorderly house is still largely derived from the common law and could well have benefitted in the past from either statutory clarification or abolition. The court's perusal of the authorities indicate its hopeless vagueness. For example, the court took the case of *R v Berg, Britt, Carré and Lummies* ((1927) 20 Cr App R 38) as authority for the view that:

> '(a) there must be some element of keeping open house, albeit the premises need not be open to the public at large, (b) the house must not be regulated by the restraints of morality, or must be unchaste or of bad repute, and (c) it must be so conducted as to violate law and good order' ([1983] 2 All ER at 17).

One may wonder whether placing advertisements in contact magazines only purchased by those wishing to gain access to such services really butresses the finding that the defendants were issuing 'a public invitation to resort to the premises for the purpose of indulging in perverted and revolting practices'. A neon sign, to take an example used by the court, placed over the doorway might well be said to constitute a public invitation, but a newspaper advertisement of this kind seems hardly in the same category. If the public are offended by such signs the indecent advertisement legislation provides a more suitable remedy. As for (b), what is meant by the constraints of morality? In matters of social custom and sexual mores it is notoriously the case that today's perversion is tomorrow's orthodoxy. Requirement (c) does not require that there be any element of public nuisance. In fact, it is hardly a requirement at all. It is superfluous to both (a) and (b) and is an example of a conclusion being confused with a premise.

The Court of Appeal's formulation of the test, namely that the services, 'are of such a character and are conducted in such a manner (whether by advertisement or otherwise) that their provision amounts to an outrage of public decency or is otherwise calculated to injure the public interest to such an extent as to call for condemnation and punishment' is both vague and in large part circular. The court's final warning that the judgment and sentences, 'will, we hope, serve as a warning to others that to invite the public to resort to premises and there indulge in conduct going beyond the limits which a jury regards as tolerable is criminal conduct', notwithstanding that the premises are private and the conduct not otherwise criminal, is a reminder that legal moralism is still alive, if not well.

The second novel issue raised by the appeal was the criminal law's approach to the phenomenon of a sex change operation. The charge under s 30 of the 1956 Act makes it an offence for a man to live off the earnings of a prostitute. Gloria Greaves, having undergone such a sex change operation, claimed that he should not be treated as a man for the purposes of the Act. The court rejected this approach. The well-known civil case involving April Ashley, *Corbett v Corbett* [1970] 2 All ER 33, had held that one born a man and who remained biologically a man was indeed a man for the purpose of marriage. The court chose to adopt this approach.

The view of the Court of Appeal on this issue could hardly be regarded as entirely unreasonable. Nevertheless, the complexities of the issue might have warranted closer investigation. This is an area where views both medical and popular may have changed somewhat in the years since the decision in *Corbett*. For example, the New Jersey Superior Court in *MT v JT* (1976) 355 A 2d 204 considered the case of *Corbett* and took the position that the law should recognise a change of sexual identity.

Offences against property

1 *Theft and appropriation*

If David Morris and James Burnside have a sense of humour, it must tickle them near to death that when at their local supermarkets they attached to goods price labels removed from goods bearing a lower price they would make their way to the Court of Appeal ([1983] 2 All ER 448) to the House of Lords ([1983] 3 All ER 288) and be on their way to becoming household names to generations of law students.

On the face of it what they did was preparatory to committing a fraud; namely, obtaining those goods from the store by a deception as to the true price. Morris did in fact perpetrate his fraud and was arrested after he had passed the check-out; Burnside was arrested before he had reached the check-out. Both were convicted of stealing the goods. Since Morris had passed the check-out he might have been convicted of obtaining by deception (he was in fact charged with this but no verdict was taken) and the House of Lords thought it 'preferable' to prosecute for deception in such cases. But Burnside was arrested at the check-out before he paid for the goods; presumably he was standing in the queue and unless his conduct could be regarded as 'more than merely preparatory' (Criminal Attempt Act 1981, s 1(1)), he was not guilty of an attempt to obtain, and in his case it was theft or nothing.

The House of Lords concluded that both had rightly been convicted of theft for both had dishonestly appropriated the goods when they switched the labels. The argument that Morris and Burnside had not appropriated the goods because they still acknowledged the store to be the owner of them (they were yet to buy them) and had thus not assumed *all* the rights of the owner was met by the answer that appropriation as defined in s 3(1) required only an assumption of *any* of the rights of the owner. To swap the owner's price labels was an assumption of one of the owner's rights.

In a significant respect the judgment of the House of Lords differs from that of the Court of Appeal. The Court of Appeal had suggested that a removal of goods from shelves in a supermarket with dishonest intent would constitute theft. The House of Lords disagreed and approved *Eddy v Niman* (1981) 73 Cr App Rep 237, DC where it was held that there was no appropriation of goods removed from the shelves to a trolley though there was evidence that the taker intended to steal. The House appears to lean to the view that for an appropriation there must be some overt unauthorised dealing, and the judgment does not necessarily call into question the view of appropriation expressed in *R v Skipp* [1975] Crim LR 114 and *R v Meech* [1973] 3 All ER 939 that appropriation requires some unauthorised dealing in the property.

The practical effect of *Morris* may thus be only minor, particularly when the House is suggesting that the label-switcher should be allowed to progress through the check-out and be charged with deception. The general notion that appropriation connotes an unauthorised dealing remains and it is not an appropriation to deal with goods in an authorised way with intent to steal those goods.

2 *Deception and post-dated cheques*

When a cheque is drawn it will normally bear the date of making and may then be presented for payment. The nature of the representations involved in tendering a cheque have been canvased in a number of cases, not least by the House of Lords in *Metropolitan Police Comr v Charles* [1976] 3 All ER 112 but the essence of the matter has probably never been better put than by Pollock CB in *R v Hazelton* (1874) LR 2 CCR 134 at 140—

> 'I think the real representation made is that the cheque will be paid. It may be said that that is a representation as to a future event. But that is not really so, it means that the existing state of facts is such that in the ordinary course the cheque will be met'.

Accordingly, a drawer is guilty of deception if he knows his cheque will not be met or if he is reckless whether it is or not. Does it make any difference that the cheque is post-dated? Not according to the Court of Appeal in *R v Gilmartin* [1983] 1 All ER 829. Such a cheque does not imply that there are funds in the bank (though neither does a cheque dated as issued) and indeed constitutes a request to the payee to defer presentation because the drawer cannot, or does not wish to meet it before the deferred date. But the drawer nonetheless represents that the *existing* state of facts is such that it will be met on presentation and if the drawer *then* knows that the cheque will not be met, or is reckless whether it will be met or not, he has made a deception.

3 *Handling and recent possession*

The so-called doctrine of recent possession allows the prosecution on a charge of theft or receiving to tender the evidence that the defendant was found in possession of the goods after the theft. The weight to be attached to that evidence will of course turn on how close to the time of the theft the possession is proved to have been and other circumstances indicating that the possession was not innocent. The Court of Appeal held, and with respect inevitably so held in *R v Ball* [1983] 2 All ER 1089 that such evidence may be tended not only where the handling takes the form of receiving but where it takes any of the other forms of handling (such as assisting, or removing) specified in s 22(1) of the Theft Act 1968.

4 Taking conveyances without consent

The expression 'without the consent of the owner' (or substantially similar expressions) appear in many statutory contexts both criminal and civil, but in whatever context it appears the effect of fraud upon the consent raises difficult issues. In the civil law the courts usually face the problem as to which of two innocent parties should bear the loss of the fraud of a third and hence they will generally hold that fraud vitiates consent only where it induces a fundamental mistake. Consent is not ordinarily considered as vitiated because the deceived party would have done otherwise had he known the true facts. In the criminal context, where the fraudulent party's criminal liability is at issue, there is perhaps no compelling reason why the courts should not say that a victim has not given consent when he has been deceived into giving that consent; where, but for the defendant's lies, he would have declined to give his assent.

But in *Whittaker v Campbell* [1983] 3 All ER 582 which involved a charge of taking a conveyance without the consent of the owner contrary to s 12(1) of the Theft Act 1968, the Divisional Court held that the owner (the director of a hiring firm) had consented to the taking of a van under hire though he would not have done so had the defendants not falsely asserted that one of them held a valid driving licence. To substantiate their fraud the defendants had with them a valid licence in the name of a third party and one of them signed the hiring agreement in the third party's name.

On facts like these even a first year law student would begin to salivate. All the classic cases from *Cundy v Lindsay* (1873) 3 App Cas 459, HL, down to *Lewis v Averay* [1971] 3 All ER 907, CA bear on the point at issue. This sort of problem is the very staple of the intermediate examination in contract.

In the light of the authorities (that is, the authorities on the crime of taking conveyances) it is submitted that the court's conclusion was right. Those authorities appear to establish, though there is room for a difference of opinion about this, that if the owner does not consent to the *use* to which the defendant puts the vehicle (for example, he agrees to its use for a day and the defendant uses it for a week, or he agrees to its use for a journey from London to Leeds and it is used to drive to Edinburgh) then the defendant may commit the offence. But if the owner agrees to the use then no offence is committed, though the owner would not have consented had he not been misled into thinking that the defendant was licensed or insured for that use. Such a case was *Whittaker v Campbell* where the owner was not misled in any respect as to the use to which the van was to be put but was misled into agreeing to that use by the representation that there was a licenced driver for the van.

There is much to be said for reconsidering *Whittaker v Campbell*. If the taker knows perfectly well that the owner of the vehicle would not part with its possession but for false representations made by the taker, why should the taker be able to say, as against the owner, that the owner has consented?

Miscellaneous offences

1 Dangerous drugs

Conflicting Crown Court decisions on the meaning of 'cocaine' in para 1 of Part 1 of Sch 2 to the Misuse of Drugs Act 1971 were resolved by the Court of

Appeal in *R v Greensmith* [1983] 3 All ER 444. The court took the view that 'cocaine' was a generic word which may embrace the direct extracts of the coca leaf as well as the 'substances or products' which may result from a chemical transformation. Cocaine may have a number of forms but it is still 'cocaine' for the purposes of the 1971 Act.

A practical consequence of the decision is that when charging an offence contrary to s 5(3) of the 1971 Act, it is only necessary for the Crown to allege or prove that the defendant was in possession of 'cocaine'. It is unnecessary to establish whether it is cocaine in its natural form or a product resulting from the application of a chemical process to the natural form.

2 Corruption

The cases of *R v Braithwaite, R v Girdham* [1983] 2 All ER 87 concerned the proper interpretation of 'consideration' within the meaning of the Prevention of Corruption Acts 1906 and 1916. Both defendants admitted that they had received goods or services respectively from persons who were contractors to their employer, the British Steel Corporation. By virtue of s 2 of the 1916 Act, once it has been shown that 'any money, gift or other consideration has been paid or given to or received' by a person, the burden of proof is on that person to prove that the benefits were not corruptly received. The defendants claimed that they had paid or always intended to pay for the goods or services. The trial judges both took the view that, on their own admission, having received such goods or services, the defendants satisfied the conditions of s 2 of the 1916 Act. The appeal was based on the assertion that, under these circumstances, they had not received 'consideration' within the meaning of the 1906 and 1916 Acts. The prosecution had not proved their failure to pay, and so had not crossed the threshold which obliged the defendants to discharge any burden of proof.

Not surprisingly, the Court of Appeal rejected this contention. In practice, it is likely to be difficult or impossible for the prosecution to establish that benefits had not been paid for. That, the court noted, was undoubtedly the rationale behind s 2 of the 1916 Act. 'Consideration' was to be given its legal meaning, the classic definition of which was to be found in *Currie v Misa* (1875) LR 10 Exch 153. It connoted, 'the existence of something in the shape of a contract or bargain between the parties'. Accordingly, once it was established that the contractor had furnished what could be regarded as 'consideration' in the sense in which that term was used in the law of contract, the accused could be called on for an explanation. Of course, a good explanation would have been that full value had been paid for the benefit.

The interpretation given by the Court of Appeal to 'consideration' emphasises the heavy burden placed on those acting within the public services to show that they are acting properly. It remains true, however, that the prosecution must establish the receipt of a benefit beyond reasonable doubt before a defendant is obliged to discharge his burden on a balance of probabilities.

3 Weights and measures

In *Bellerby v Carle* [1983] 1 All ER 1031 the defendants were charged under s 16(1) of the Weights and Measures Act 1963 with possession of an unjust measuring instrument following on an inspection by a consumer protection officer. Although the defendants were joint licensees of the premises, the relevant measuring equipment was supplied and maintained by a brewery. The defendants were expressly forbidden to interfere with or adjust the equipment and had no reason to believe it was faulty. The House of Lords decided that even though the defendants or their agents were the only persons authorised to use the equipment, this in itself did not mean that they were in possession of the equipment for the purposes of the Act. Since the instruments were supplied and maintained by others, they were not guilty of the offence charged. Their degree of control over the equipment was not under the circumstances sufficient. The case makes clear that the possession offence under s 16(1) is one of strict liability. Nevertheless, the element of 'possession' must be established in the first place.

Sentencing

Penalty points and disqualification

In *R v Kent* [1983] 3 All ER 1 the defendant was committed to the Crown Court for sentence following a number of convictions by a magistrates' court. The judge, inter alia, disqualified the defendant for 12 months and ordered that his licence be endorsed both with particulars of the offences and with a total of 8 penalty points pursuant to s 19(1) of and Sch 7 to the Transport Act 1981. The Court of Appeal was sympathetic to the difficulties experienced by courts in the operation of such complex provisions and offered general guidance on some common errors. The error in this case was to impose both disqualification and penalty points, which was contrary to the terms of s 19(1) of the 1981 Act and s 101(1) of the Road Traffic Act 1972. Either a judge can disqualify the defendant and order that his licence be endorsed with particulars of the offence, or he could order the endorsement of the particulars and combine this with endorsement of the penalty points.

It might also be noted that the effect of even a short disqualification is that existing penalty points are removed so that a driver begins with a clean licence after his disqualification has ended (s 19(3), Transport Act 1981).

2 Disqualification and mitigation

It has become an accepted part of sentencing policy that persons who are imprisoned after repeated convictions of driving while disqualified, and who seem to be 'incapable of leaving motor vehicles alone', should not be punished by a period of disqualification extending for a substantial period after their release. The reasoning behind the policy is that it is simply an invitation to the offender to commit further offences, is counter productive, and so contrary to the public interest. The difficulty that arose in *R v Thomas* [1983] 3 All ER 765 was, could this policy be reconciled with the restrictive wording of the Transport Act 1981? The Court of Appeal held that it could still be used as a reason to mitigate the length of disqualification in a case involving obligatory disqualification under s 19(2) of the 1981 Act. The difficulty arose because s 19(6) listed a number of factors which were not to be taken into account in deciding 'that there are grounds for mitigating the normal consequences of the conviction' under s 19(2). One of these is in s 19(6)(B), 'hardship, other than exceptional hardship'. This case did not involve, on the facts, exceptional hardship, but the Court of Appeal decided that it was not taking into account 'hardship' to the defendant in mitigating the punishment. Rather, it was implementing the public interest reflected in the sentencing policy. This was not a reason that was excluded by s 19(6).

One obvious anomaly created by this decision is that a driver with a very bad driving record may suffer a shorter period of disqualification than one with a less damaging record because the latter may be someone to whom this special policy does not apply. The court considered this point and took the view that the apparent distinction in treatment could be explained by the fact that the less serious offender would only probably suffer a fine in addition to his disqualification, not the more drastic penalty of imprisonment.

Criminal Procedure

GRAHAM ZELLICK JP, MA, PHD
Professor of Public Law, Queen Mary College, University of London

The charge

Grievous and actual bodily harm: alternative verdicts

The House of Lords, reversing the Court of Appeal ([1983] 1 All ER 993), has held that a count alleging grievous bodily harm includes an allegation of assault occasioning actual bodily harm, so that it was open to a jury to return a not guilty verdict on the charge but instead to find the defendant guilty of occasioning actual bodily harm: *R v Wilson* [1983] 3 All ER 448.

The Court of Appeal, following its own decision in *R v Springfield* (1969) 53 Cr App R 608, had concluded that the offence of *inflicting* grievous bodily harm did not necessarily include the offence of *assault* occasioning actual bodily harm.

An alternative verdict may be returned if the allegation in the indictment expressly amounts to an allegation of another offence; if it impliedly amounts to such an allegation; if it expressly includes such an allegation; or if it impliedly includes such an allegation. The words 'amounts to' and 'includes' were not synonymous. These were the possibilities derived by Lord Roskill, with whom all their Lordships agreed, from s 6(3) of the Criminal Law Act 1967. It was not a question of 'necessary steps' or of 'major' or 'lesser' offences. The issue was not whether the allegations in the charge *amounted* to an allegation of the other offence, but whether they expressly or impliedly *included* the other offence (cf *Archbold, Criminal Pleading, Evidence and Practice* (41st edn, 1982) para 4–459 et seq). What, then, is expressly or impliedly included in a charge of inflicting grievous bodily harm?

It must, said Lord Roskill, include the infliction of actual bodily harm because infliction of the more serious injuries must include infliction of the less serious injuries. But does 'inflicting' include 'assault'? Lord Roskill accepted that grievous bodily harm could be inflicted without there necessarily being an assault; but inflicting also could include inflicting by assault, in which case the allegations in the charge impliedly *included* 'inflicting by assault'.

This appears to broaden the concept of what has sometimes been called 'the lesser included offence'. Lord Roskill was alive to its dangers. It was for the trial judge, before leaving the possibility of conviction of another offence to the jury, to ensure that the defendant was not exposed to the risk of conviction on a charge which had not been fully explored during the trial. The defendant must have had the opportunity of meeting the alternative in the course of his defence. It should also be added that the prosecution must have led evidence capable of sustaining such a conviction. The better course in practice is for the alternative count to be expressly charged in the indictment. This decision of the House of Lords is a remedy for sloppy prosecutors and it is difficult to welcome it with any enthusiasm.

Duplicity

The House of Lords, in *Chiltern District Council v Hodgetts* [1983] 1 All ER 1057, overruled *Parry v Forest of Dean DC* (1976) 34 P & CR 209, DC, and held that an information which alleged initial failure to comply with an enforcement notice under s 89(5) of the Town and Country Planning Act 1971 'on and since a certain date' was not bad for duplicity. Non-compliance with a 'desist notice' is a single offence and not a series of separate offences committed each day. Only after conviction is a separate offence committed each day that the non-compliance persists. Lord Roskill, with whom all the others agreed, saw no objection to the practice of charging the offence 'on and since' a specified date, though he thought it might be preferable if the offence were charged between two specified dates.

Costs of the prosecution

Following the appellants' convictions for murder and conspiracy to import and supply heroin, the trial judge ordered the appellants to pay the prosecution costs: one was ordered to pay £1m, the second £20,000, another £10,000, and the last £5,000. It emerged at the trial that vast sums of money were involved in the trafficking in heroin and also that it had been excessively costly to bring the appellants to justice. The Crown estimated the costs of the prosecution to be at least £1,320,000.

The appellants challenged the orders for costs and it fell to the Court of Appeal in *R v Maher* [1983] 2 All ER 417 to elucidate the meaning of the words 'the costs incurred in or about the prosecution and conviction' in s 4(1) of the Costs in Criminal Cases Act 1973.

The prosecution's estimate included items of £32,000 for jury expenses; overtime payments and travelling expenses of the investigating officers amounting to £300,000; and a similar sum for security at the courthouse and the judge's lodgings. Although 'incurred in or about the prosecution and conviction', were they part of the 'costs'?

'Costs', said the court, did not mean 'the cost of' the whole prosecution irrespective of who paid them. 'Incurred' meant incurred by the prosecutor (see also s 3(3) of the 1973 Act). Jury expenses were not attributable to the prosecution; and the other items listed were even more remote. None could be charged to the Director of Public Prosecutions, who handled the prosecution, and could not therefore be included in any bill of costs.

Counsel's fees, the Director's costs and witnesses' expenses amounted to £188,000 and the court therefore reduced the trial judge's orders to £175,000, £2,000 and £1,000 respectively, making a total of £180,000.

Orders for costs should not be made which are beyond the means of the accused. A plea of guilty is merely a factor to be taken into account in determining whether or not to make an order and, if so, in what sum. The instant cases were sufficiently unusual to justify the making of orders even though the accused were sentenced to long terms of imprisonment.

The court urged prosecutors to be in a position to supply the trial judge in appropriate cases with a realistic estimate of their costs.

Costs of the defence

In *R v Miller* [1983] 3 All ER 186, Lloyd J (sitting with two assessors) had to confront the problem from the other side. Did an order under s 3 of the Costs in Criminal Cases Act 1973 that 'the costs of the defence' being 'the expenses properly incurred by him in carrying on the proceedings' be paid out of central funds cover costs which the defendant's employer had otherwise intended to pay on his behalf? The taxing authority at the Central Criminal Court, and on appeal the Master, disallowed such costs. Lloyd J reversed the decision.

The issue goes wider than costs to be borne by an employer: it would appear to apply equally to a trade union or an insurance company, for example.

It was argued by counsel for the Lord Chancellor's Department that the words 'incurred by him' in s 3(3)(*a*) meant 'paid by him', drawing a distinction between this formula and the words 'incurred in or about the defence' found in s 4(1)(*b*).

In corresponding civil cases, *Adams v London Improved Motor Coach Builders Ltd* [1921] 1 KB 495, CA, *Davies v Taylor (No 2)* [1973] 1 All ER 959, HL, and *Lewis v Averay (No 2)* [1973] 2 All ER 299, CA, the same argument had been rejected. What mattered was whether the solicitors were acting for the party. If so, he became liable for their costs, even if some other body or person had undertaken to pay them. There would have to be a clear agreement, either between that other body or person and the solicitors or between the party and the solicitors, that the party was not to be liable for the costs before the situation changed. Lloyd J rejected the contention that there was any distinction in this context between criminal and civil cases. Only if there were evidence establishing a clear agreement, express or implied, that the solicitors would in no circumstances seek to obtain payment from their client, could the taxing officer decline to pay the costs out of central funds.

The decision is clearly right. Indeed, one might even question the rule that the defence costs were not payable out of central funds where such a binding agreement did exist. Why should the third party be denied reimbursement simply because he has bound himself to indemnify the defendant? If the court has thought it proper to order the defence costs to be paid out of central funds, the fact that some other person or body has agreed otherwise to bear those costs would seem to be wholly immaterial. Some change in the wording of the statute is called for.

Magistrates

Reporting of committal proceedings

Until 1967, there were no restrictions on the reporting of committal proceedings. It was the publicity arising from the committal proceedings against the late Dr Bodkin Adams, who died during the year under review—subsequently acquitted at his trial for murder—that led to the enactment of a provision barring the reporting of anything but the formal details unless the defendant himself or a co-defendant requested that the restriction be lifted. Following the committal proceedings against Mr Jeremy Thorpe and others, which attracted enormous press attention, in which one co-defendant applied for the restriction to be lifted, thus forcing all the others to forgo their right to the restriction, contrary to their wishes, the law was modified so as to give the magistrates a discretion in a case where one of two or more accused objects to the lifting of the restriction sought by the other. Section 8(2A) of the Magistrates' Courts Act 1980 provides that on such an application where one of the co-accused objects, the court shall make the order if satisfied that it is in the interests of justice to do so. An order if made applies to the proceedings as a whole and extends to evidence against all the defendants. Thee is no discretion if a single accused applies or, where there is more than one accused, none of the others objects.

R v Leeds Justices, ex p Sykes [1983] 1 All ER 460, DC, is the first case to deal with this new provision. The court declined to venture any definition of the phrase 'in the interests of justice', though it adopted the observation of Shaw LJ in R v Horsham Justices, ex p Farquharson [1982] 2 All ER 269, 289, CA, that in this context it referred only to the interests of justice as affecting the particular defendants.

The starting point is that prima facie committal proceedings should not be reported. A powerful case for lifting the restriction over the objections of one of the accused had to be made out. In the present case, the principal reason for the accused's application was his desire to secure publicity to the behaviour of the police about which he proposed to protest. Publicity was not desired, for example, to bring the case to the attention of potential witnesses. Another accused objected, but the magistrates nonetheless lifted the restriction. The Divisional Court could see no benefit to the ultimate fairness of the accused's trial in allowing the proceedings to be reported and it could not stand against the fear of a co-accused that any publicity might prejudice his trial. Certiorari thus went to quash the order of the magistrates to lift the reporting restrictions. In considering whether to allow reporting, magistrates must weigh the advantages claimed by the applicant to his trial against the prejudice to that trial feared by an objecting co-accused.

Failure to prove service: trial a nullity and rehearing possible

Where service of an adjournment notice has not been proved, the trial and conviction of the defendant in his absence are a nullity and the magistrates, not being functi officio, can relist the case for hearing, even though more than 28 days have elapsed. The power under s 142 of the Magistrates' Courts Act 1980 to set aside the conviction and direct a rehearing within 28 days has no application where the proceedings in question are a nullity. If, however, the notice has been properly served, the trial would not be a nullity and the justices would be functi officio after the 28-day period allowed by s 142(4). These conclusions were reached by the Divisional Court in R v Seisdon Justices, ex p Dougan [1983] 1 All ER 6.

Hearing informations together

In Clayton v Chief Constable of Norfolk [1983] 1 All ER 984, the House of Lords dealt with 'an important question of practice and procedure in magistrates' courts' (p 965 h): must the defendant consent before two or more informations may be tried together; must two or more defendants consent for the trial together of those defendants charged on separate informations? In the result, unnecessary technicality has been swept away and common sense leading to a sensible procedure has triumphed.

Lord Roskill, with whose speech all other members of the committee agreed, had no doubt that a magistrates' court did have jurisdiction to try more than one information at the same time. Several Divisional Court judgments to the contrary were therefore untenable. Unless restricted by statute, magistrates' courts, observed Lord Roskill, guided where necessary by higher courts, were entitled to develop their own practice and procedure and to adapt it to contemporary needs. Practice and procedure must not be allowed to become inflexible: they were the servants not the masters of the judicial process. The 19th century authorities disclosed no consistent practice and were not helpful in resolving the problem. Rules of practice and procedure had, however, evolved this century making it irregular for a magistrates' court to try more than one information at the same time without the defendant's consent and to try several defendants charged on informations in the absence of their consent, even where the facts were all closely related.

But such rules, said Lord Roskill, though designed to avoid injustice, were becoming an obstacle to the simple and sensible administration of justice. It was of particular importance that the administration of justice in magistrates' courts should be simple and sensible and any rule of practice or procedure which made their task more difficult or demanded subservience to technicalities was to be deprecated and the House should therefore encourage the adoption of rules which conduced to the better attainment of justice.

Lord Roskill could not see why, when indictments could contain several counts and charge more than one person, magistrates' courts should be compelled to try each information or offender separately unless the accused consented. No statute enjoined such a result, and common sense dictated that magistrates should in the interests of justice have a discretion as to how they dealt with these problems. It would be better if the practice enunciated in *R v Assim* [1966] 2 All ER 881, 887–888, CCA, in relation to trials on indictment, applied to magistrates' courts. A defendant charged on several informations where the facts were connected should, if the justices thought fit, be heard together; likewise, if two or more defendants were charged on separate informations with connected facts, they too, if the court thought fit, should be heard together.

Justices should inquire both of the defence and the prosecution if there was any objection and, in the event of any disagreement, should rule as they think right in the overall interests of justice. Consideration should also be given to the matter if the defendant was not present. Absence of the defendant's consent should not be regarded as a complete and automatic bar. Before allowing a joint trial, justices should ask whether it would be fair and just to the defendants. It was not the object of the change to invite magistrates to embark on long and complicated trials with many charges or offenders being tried at the same time. They were to adopt whatever was the fairest course to everyone concerned in the circumstances.

Trial of summons and cross-summons together

Distinguishing *Clayton v Chief Constable of Norfolk* (supra), the Divisional Court, in *R v Epsom Justices, ex p Gibbons* [1983] 3 All ER 523, has held that a summons and a cross-summons can in no circumstances be tried together, even if the parties agree. A not uncommon procedure in the magistrates' court has thus been prohibited.

A number of difficulties in allowing such trials was identified by the court. The defendant's rights not to cross-examine, to make a submission of no case to answer, and to decline to give evidence were all compromised when that person was both prosecutor and defendant. There could be problems about the order in which witnesses would be called, who would go first and who would make the final address. The court, therefore, entirely rejected the possibility of hearing such cases together, though some consideration might usefully have been given to the problems of hearing them separately. The court's conclusion may well be right, but the arguments are perhaps more evenly balanced than the judgment admits.

Dismissing charge without hearing evidence

Without any consideration of the authorities, the relevant law or the reasons—indeed, without the citation of a single case—the Divisional Court in *R v Birmingham Justices, ex p Lamb* [1983] 3 All ER 23 has held that justices cannot dismiss a case on grounds of supposed injustice without hearing the evidence. All they can do is reflect any sense of injustice at the end of the prosecution case by finding no case to answer, or after the defence has been presented, by acquitting, or even after conviction, by imposing a nominal penalty; it should be added that it can also be reflected in the matter of costs. But there is no power to dismiss a summons simply because it would be unjust or prejudicial to allow it to proceed.

The point is, however, more complicated and is bound up with the question of whether or not to allow an adjournment. This is recognised by Woolf J in agreeing with the principal judgment given by McNeill J. Woolf J accepts that magistrates have a discretion whether or not to adjourn cases and rightly observes that that discretion must be exercised judicially, in which event they must be just to the prosecution as well as the defendant, and they must not therefore refuse an adjournment to give a semblance of justification for a decision to dismiss.

But while it is clear that it is not for the court to prejudge the evidence and dismiss cases improperly, the power to refuse an adjournment in an appropriate case, because, for example, of the unfairness to the defendant of further delay for which the prosecution is responsible, though the inevitable result is dismissal of the prosecution, is a much-needed power to control and regulate proceedings in the magistrates' courts. If this case simply holds that refusing an adjournment and the consequential dismissal must not be used to dispose of cases which the justices feel should not be prosecuted further, then it is unexceptionable and plainly correct; and it is submitted that it says no more than this. But if it purports to say that the prosecution must always be allowed to present its case and adjournments must be allowed so that it can do so, whatever the circumstances or the history of the case, then it goes much too far, would rob the court of a much-needed power to remain master of its procedures and would be quite untenable. It is submitted that the case is in fact authority only for the narrower view. On so important a matter, a somewhat more carefully formulated and considered judgment—reserving it if necessary—is required.

Ex p Lamb was relied on by the Divisional Court in *R v Dorking Justices, ex p Harrington* [1983] 3 All ER 29, where the magistrates, not wishing to fix an alternative date, dismissed charges without asking the prosecution whether they were in a position to proceed forthwith, which was a breach of the rules of natural justice and quite improper. See further p 163, below.

Test of bias: computerised registers

In *R v Liverpool City Justices, ex p Topping* [1983] 1 All ER 490, the Divisional Court quashed by certiorari a conviction because the magistrates had failed to give proper consideration to the question of whether they should continue to hear a case when they were aware that there were a number of other charges outstanding against the defendant.

The test which magistrates are to apply is whether there is the appearance of bias, not whether there is actual bias. As to whether there must appear to be a real likelihood of bias or only a reasonable suspicion of bias, the court thought there was little difference between the two formulations. The question to ask is: would a reasonable and fair-minded person sitting in court and knowing all the relevant facts have a reasonable suspicion that a fair trial was not possible?

The court also expressed its view on computerised register sheets, which list all outstanding charges against a defendant and any convictions awaiting sentence. It was 'most undesirable', for four reasons, to put such a document before the magistrates: defendants in person will not know what information has come to the attention of the court and will therefore be deprived of any opportunity to challenge the court; even those who are represented may not know what material has been put before the court; a defendant might be averse to seeking an adjournment for the case to be heard by a different bench, with its attendant expense and delay, thus obliging him to run the risk of prejudice; and the occasions on which it may be necessary to apply for the trial to take place before another bench should be as few as possible. The practice was giving administrative convenience priority over the requirements of justice. Moreover, it was wrong in law, since the court register should contain only entries in respect of matters on which the court is to adjudicate, and a declaration to that effect was granted.

See for further discussion, the article on Evidence, p 202 below.

Forfeiting a recognisance

Civil or criminal?

According to the Divisional Court in *R v Marlow Justices, ex p O'Sullivan* [1983] 3 All ER 578, an application to forfeit or estreat the recognisance of a person who has been bound over to keep the peace and be of good behaviour is both substantively and procedurally a civil proceeding and thus falls to be determined by the civil standard of proof.

The court distinguished those cases holding that a breach of a recognisance which required the court to sentence on the original matters leading to the recognisance must be proved beyond reasonable doubt; but this was not so where the only issue was forfeiture of the recognisance, for two reasons. First, because proceedings for the forfeiture or estreatment of a recognisance are civil, as the Court of Appeal held in *R v Southampton Justices, ex p Green* [1975] 2 All ER 1073: it was not a 'criminal cause or matter' and appeal lay from the Divisional Court, not direct to the House of Lords, but to the Court of Appeal, Civil Division. That, however, was in relation to a surety's recognisance for an appearance in court, not a recognisance to be of good behaviour or to keep the peace, but the court saw no material difference between the two.

Secondly, the proceedings were civil because of their form. Section 120(2) of the Magistrates' Courts Act 1980 provides that a recognisance may be forfeited only by order made on 'complaint', which in the court's view is the term used chiefly in respect of civil proceedings, 'information' being used otherwise (see also s 50 of the Act).

It is surprising that this point has not arisen before. The court's conclusion is defensible on the authorities but is perhaps undesirable. There is certainly a difference between estreating a recognisance for non-appearance, which fact at least will necessarily have been proved beyond question, and some conduct complained of by a third party which is said to be in breach of the obligation to keep the peace or be of good behaviour. Although a bind over is not a criminal conviction, it is a power residing with a criminal court and proceedings for forfeiture may involve a substantial sum of money—it was £1,000 in the instant case—possibly greatly in excess of the likely fine in comparable circumstances, and revolves around allegations of conduct similar to normal criminal proceedings and typically associated with ill-feeling and long-standing disputes between the parties. The protection of the criminal standard of proof would not be unreasonable and the attention of the Law Commission to this matter in their general review of binding over is necessary.

Relevance of means

The means of a surety under a bail recognisance are relevant in determining whether to estreat all or part of the recognisance. Judicial review was therefore granted of a decision by magistrates to exclude any evidence of the surety's means when determining the amount of the recognisance to be forfeited since there had been no change in circumstances, but to take them into consideration only in relation to the method of payment: *R v Uxbridge Justices, ex p Heward-Mills* [1983] 1 All ER 530. The case was accordingly sent back to be considered afresh by a different bench.

The magistrates' error is understandable, since the surety's means are examined before the surety is accepted. If he has not the full sum readily available, he should not stand surety in that sum; he is warned that he stands to lose all of it if the defendant fails to appear and the risk is carefully emphasised. Only the surety's efforts and diligence in ensuring the accused's appearance and perhaps any factors relating to the accused would thus seem to bear on the question of forfeiture (see *R v Southampton Justices, ex p Green* [1975] 2 All ER 1073 at 1077–78, per Lord Denning MR).

In *R v Southampton Justices, ex p Corker* (1976) 120 SJ 214 (the judge here relying on the full transcript of the judgment), the Divisional Court, while adverting to the danger of undermining the system if a surety could escape his obligation subsequently by claiming he was impecunious, since he must have regard to it before entering into the recognisance, nevertheless accepted that it was of relevance when any question of forfeiture arose. The relevance of means was also referred to by the same court in *R v Horseferry Road Magistrates' Court, ex p Pearson* [1976] 2 All ER 264 at 266–267, by Woolf J in *R v Waltham Forest Justices, ex p Parfrey* [1980] Crim LR 571, DC (the judge again quoting from the transcript), in *R v Crown Court at Ipswich, ex p Reddington* [1981] Crim LR 618, DC and in an unreported decision of the judge in the instant case, McCullough J (*R v Crown Court at Oxford, ex p Jones and Jacobs*, 29 June 1982).

The principles derived from the authorities by McCullough J were that the full recognisance should be forfeited unless it appeared fair and just that a lesser sum or even nothing at all should be forfeited, the burden of satisfying the court to remit all or part of it falling on the surety.

In determining whether to forfeit all or part of a recognisance, a court will doubtless be slow to respond to a surety's claim that he lacks the resources, particularly where this contradicts, as it invariably must, whatever statements he made originally as to his means. A change in financial circumstances since that time is, of course, another matter. All this decision says is that the court must hear any evidence or representations on the surety's means and consider it appropriately: it does not assimilate the principles as to means in the case of fines with those in relation to forfeiting a surety's recognisance. The two situations remain quite different.

Appeal

Home Secretary's reference to the Court of Appeal: scope of the appeal

Under s 17(1)(*a*) of the Criminal Appeal Act 1968, the Home Secretary may refer the whole of the case of a person convicted on indictment to the Court of Appeal, Criminal Division. That case is then 'treated *for all purposes* as an appeal to the court by that person' (emphasis added). It is also open to the Home Secretary under para (*b*) to refer 'any point arising in the case'. In *R v Chard* [1983] 3 All ER 637, the House of Lords has held that a person whose case has been referred under para (*a*) is to be treated as if he were a person on whom a general right of appeal to the court had been conferred by s 1 of the Act on any ground, whether of law or fact, without the need to obtain the court's leave. The appellant is thus not confined to any point or points mentioned in the Home Secretary's letter of reference. It is the 'whole case' that is referred, which includes all questions of fact and law involved in it. This was the plain, unequivocal meaning of the statutory language, notwithstanding the fact that Parliament had re-enacted that language in the light of Court of Appeal decisions taking a narrower view. Those Court of Appeal decisions are accordingly overruled.

Where on a reference the appellant argues grounds which are unconnected with the reasons leading to the reference and they were unsuccessfully argued in the original appeal, the court will give weight to the previous judgment on the point or points, from which it will be slow to differ.

The House was unanimous in rejecting the proposition that where certain words in a statute had received a judicial construction and Parliament subsequently repeated them without alteration, Parliament must be taken to have used them with that meaning attaching to them. There was no such inflexible rule of statutory interpretation.

Power of the Divisional Court on judicial review—R v Dorking Justices, ex p Harrington [1983] 3 All ER 29

On an appeal by the prosecutor by way of case stated from the magistrates' court to the Divisional Court, an acquittal can be turned into a conviction, pursuant to ss 111 and 112 of the Magistrates' Courts Act 1980; but some defects in the magistrates' court—notably, failure to comply with the rules of natural justice—must be challenged, not by case stated, but by judicial review (*R v Wandsworth Justices, ex p Read* [1942] 1 All ER 56), and it is not open to the court to quash by certiorari an acquittal where the defendant has been in jeopardy (*R v Middlesex Justices, ex p DPP* [1952] 2 All ER 312). It is otherwise if there has been such a mistrial as to render the proceedings a nullity, since the defendant was not in truth in jeopardy.

The court recorded its disquiet at this anomaly but felt constrained by the authorities to reach such a conclusion. Whether there was scope to distinguish the *Middlesex Justices* case, which concerned a verdict of a jury at quarter sessions, and whether the breach of natural justice-nullity distinction could have been more fully considered and might have afforded a basis for intervention, are open questions, but it seems clear that the 'anomaly' is untenable and could and should be abandoned by the House of Lords. Eventually, the simplest solution would be for statute to provide for all reviews by the Divisional Court of magistrates' decisions to be brought by way of case stated whatever the nature of the alleged defect or irregularity.

Damages

J R SPENCER, MA, LLB
Fellow of Selwyn College, Cambridge

Personal injuries cases

During 1983, as in 1982, the courts continued to wrestle with damages for wages during the 'lost years', which are recoverable as a result of *Pickett v British Rail Engineering Ltd* [1979] 1 All ER 774. This laid down that a person who is injured so as to be unable to work, and whose expectation of life is reduced, may claim not only for lost pay during his shortened period of life, but also for what he would have earned during the period of his life which is now lost. Many practical problems arise when calculating these extra damages. In three first instance cases discussed in 1982 All ER Annual Review at p 102 it was held that where the plaintiff was a married man who spent most of his income on maintaining his family, his damages for the 'lost years' were what he would have earned during those years, less his 'living expenses'; and that his 'living expenses' did *not* include what he spent on maintaining his family. Consequently, the sum awarded for wages in the 'lost years' was the greater part of his expected pay in that period. Of these cases, *Harris v Empress Motors Ltd* has now been to the Court of Appeal: [1983] 3 All ER 561. After a thorough review of the existing case law, the general approach at first instance was approved. O'Connor LJ said (at 575):

'In my judgment three principles emerge.
(1) The ingredients that go to make up "living expenses" are the same whether the victim be young or old, single or married, with or without dependants.
(2) The sum to be deducted as living expenses is the proportion of the victim's net earnings that he spends to maintain himself at the standard of life appropriate to his case.
(3) Any sums expended to maintain or benefit others do not form part of the victim's living expenses and are not to be deducted from the net earnings.'

Whilst accepting them in principle, however, the Court of Appeal disagreed with the first instance cases on one significant detail. Hitherto it had been said that a family man's own living expenses should be assessed in round figures as a proportion of the total household expenses—as is done when working out his family's dependency in a Fatal Accidents Act claim—but the Court of Appeal now said this was wrong in a 'lost years' case. Instead, they said a judge should divide the plaintiff's expenditure into three groups: (a) what he would have spent exclusively on himself; (b) what he would have spent exclusively on maintaining his family; and (c) expenditure for the shared benefit of all the family: 'the cost of housing, that is to say rent or mortgage interest, rates, heating, electricity and gas, the cost of running a motor car, the telephone and . . . the television licence'. A family man's living expenses consist of (a) plus a proportion of (c) related to how large a part of the family he himself was; and heading (b) should be disregarded. This formula, the Court of Appeal explained, will tend to give slightly greater 'living expenses' than the usual Fatal Accidents Act calculation produces, and consequently a smaller award of damages in the end.

Is this sensible? Damages for wages during the 'lost years' were invented to protect the dependants of a living plaintiff with a reduced expectation of life from being left without support at his forthcoming death, when the fact that he had sued during his lifetime would deprive them of a claim under the Fatal Accidents Act. For no good reason, the new claim was then extended to the case where the injured person had been killed, and the claim was brought on behalf of his estate—when the dependants would indeed have a Fatal Accidents Act claim, and the 'lost years' damages to the estate served no useful social purpose. Where the plaintiff has died—which was what had happened in *Harris v Empress Motors Ltd*— there is therefore every reason to minimise the 'lost years' award. But the Administration of Justice Act 1982 precludes a 'lost years' claim by the estate of any plaintiff who dies after 1 January 1983, and soon the only 'lost years' claims will be brought by living plaintiffs, whose dependants will have no Fatal Accidents Act claim. As a result of *Harris*, those dependants will end up rather worse off than if they did have such a claim (although better off, of course, than if there were no 'lost years' claim at all). In such a case, however, they are likely to reap the benefit of the injured plaintiff's substantial award for non-pecuniary losses, which will not come their way in many or most cases where the Fatal Accidents Act avails them, so perhaps we need not shed too many tears over them.

The Court of Appeal also took the opportunity to issue guidance on calculating a 'lost years' award where P is a single man without dependants. Approving what Webster J has said in *White v London Transport Executive* [1982] 1 All ER 410, it adopted what has been called the 'surplus funds' approach. The judge should work out what P would have spent each year to maintain life: housing, food, clothes etc. He should add to this what a single person in P's station would normally spend each year on his social life, holidays, and car (if any). The total should be deducted from P's net annual income, and if anything is left, it is the 'multiplicand' for wages in the 'lost years'. This formula obviously gives a much smaller award than in the case of a person with dependants, and rightly so, it is submitted. There is some point in giving a living plaintiff damages for 'lost years' where he has dependants who will lose his support on his death, but there is precious little where the plaintiff is a single man with no dependants. Damages for lost earnings are awarded to see that the plaintiff who cannot work has something to live on. There is no reason why a defendant should have to pay P what he no longer needs to live on after P is dead—or, come to that, sums over and above what P would have needed and used to survive on. Since P receives compensation for pain, suffering and loss of amenity over and above his lost earnings, awarding a dependant-free plaintiff damages for wages during the 'lost years' is giving him a pure windfall. Still less is there any reason for giving them when P is already dead and the claim is brought by the estate—as it still may be where he died before 1 January 1983—because the person who gets the windfall then is often someone for whom there is no reason at all to feel sorry.

Single young men tend to marry. Should a 'lost years' award to a young single man take account of this? In *White v London Transport Executive*

Webster J thought not (the commentary in 1982 All ER Rev is unfortunately incorrect on this). A dictum in *Harris v Empress Motors Ltd* (at 577b) nevertheless doubts whether a single plaintiff is to be seen as 'an eternally single man'. And in *Adsett v West* [1983] 2 All ER 985, another case involving a claim by a deceased single plaintiff's estate, McCullough J thought that such a plaintiff should generally be treated as permanently single, unless (as there) clear evidence existed that he would shortly marry, in which case a more generous 'lost years' award could be given. *Adsett v West* is also interesting in that the judge refused to award anything at all for lost investment income during the 'lost years', but did allow a claim for an inheritance which would probably have come the plaintiff's way if he had lived a little longer. It is respectfully submitted that it would be better if a 'lost years' claim by a single person without dependants were never increased to take account of the possibility of marriage. If P is alive, then to put it crudely, any spouse he or she later marries will know what they are taking on. It is surely going too far to give P an award of damages specifically to enable him or her to endow with a pension any marriage partner brave enough to take him or her on. To do so would restore P's necessarily dented marriageability, no doubt. But loss of marriage prospects are already supposed to be covered in the award for loss of amenity. And where the single dependant-free P is dead and the claim is brought by the estate, such an award is even more ridiculous (in *Adsett v West*, for example, the person who ultimately benefited seems not to have been the girl-friend P was likely to marry, but P's father—who also collected the damages his son's estate was awarded for the son's losing the legacy which his father could not now leave him!).

Three other personal injury cases reported in 1983 are of interest.

The Privy Council judgment in *Selvanayagam v University of the West Indies* [1983] 1 All ER 824 is notable for a remark that where an injured plaintiff refuses to undergo an operation which might have made him better, the burden is on him to show that his refusal was reasonable. As Kemp points out (see (1983) 99 LQR 497), this is contrary to the generally accepted rule governing the burden of proof on mitigation of damage, and is also contrary to two Workmen's Compensation Act cases in the House of Lords, *Steele v Robert George & Co (1937) Ltd* [1942] 1 All ER 447 and *Richardson v Redpath Brown & Co Ltd* [1944] 1 All ER 110, where it was said to be for the defendant to show the refusal to undergo the operation was unreasonable. On this point, *Selvanayagam v University of the West Indies* is therefore an authority to be treated with caution.

Jones v Jones [1983] 1 All ER 1037 raised a slightly unusual question of remoteness. D negligently inflicted severe head injuries upon P, as a result of which his wife found him impossible to live with, left him taking the children, and divorced him. P, unable to work, was clearly entitled to a large award for loss of earnings and medical expenses. Could he also claim the additional financial loss he was likely to suffer if and when his wife successfully brought claims for secured maintenance and a lump sum in proceedings ancillary to the divorce? Stocker J thought that given the accident really led to the divorce, and provided it could be proved that it would really cost P more to maintain his family separately from himself than under the same roof, damages for this loss could be awarded; but as P had produced no figures to substantiate this, this part of the claim failed. In principle it seems quite fair to make a defendant pay for the full cost of maintaining the plaintiff's family as well as the plaintiff himself, even where this is greater because they now have to live in separate houses. But everything would surely be much simpler if this could be done by giving the dependants a claim in their own name.

In *Wright v British Railways Board* [1983] 2 All ER 698 a plaintiff challenged in the House of Lords the Court of Appeal ruling in *Birkett v Hayes* [1982] 2 All ER 710 that an award of damages for non-pecuniary losses in a personal injury case carries interest at no more than 2% (see 1982 All ER Review, p 104). The House of Lords said that 2% was right. After an erudite analysis, Lord Diplock calculated that if the injured plaintiff had received his damages for pain and suffering etc immediately after the accident at the tariff then prevailing, and had then prudently invested them, he would have ended up with approximately the award he got on the tariff prevailing at the date of trial, plus 2%. Thus the apparently mean rate of interest which the Court of Appeal—reluctant to award any interest on non-pecuniary losses at all—had decreed, was fair.

In *Graham v Dodds* [1983] 2 All ER 953 the House of Lords cleared up an important doubt about the calculation of damages under the Fatal Accidents Act. As everyone knows, in principle this is done by estimating the annual value of the dependency, which is called the 'multiplicand', and multiplying this by a figure related to how long the dependency would have lasted, which is called the 'multiplier'. It is also settled law that for various reasons the multiplier must not usually be greater than 16, however many years the dependency would really have gone on. In a case of a dependency of, say, 25 years, when the multiplier will be no more than 16, it is clearly important to know whether the notional 16 years runs from the death or the trial. If there was a gap of six years between the death and the trial, and the 16 years runs from the trial, P will recover the first six years loss of dependency as special damages, plus 16 times the multiplicand for future loss. If, on the other hand, the 16 years runs from the death, then the award of special damages wipes out the first six years of the multiplier, and P gets only ten times the multiplicand for the future. In *Graham v Dodds* the House of Lords concurred in a single speech by Lord Bridge which ruled that the 16 years runs from the death. This must be so, their Lordships said, because otherwise 'the longer the trial of the dependants' claims could be delayed the more they would eventually recover'.

One would expect the position to be the same where it is not a Fatal Accidents Act case, but a claim by a living plaintiff who has suffered personal injury and is seeking damages for future loss of earnings. Surprisingly, however, Lord Bridge hinted that here it might be different, quoting with approval a passage from Lord Fraser's speech in *Cookson v Knowles* [1978] 2 All ER 604, 614–615:

> 'In a personal injury case, if the injured person has survived until the date of trial, that is a known fact and the multiplier appropriate to the length of his future working life has to be ascertained as at the date of trial. But in a fatal accident case the multiplier must be selected once and for all as at the date of death, because everything that might have happened to the deceased after that date remains uncertain.'

Be that as it may, it is as true in a personal injuries case as in a Fatal Accidents Act case that to run the multiplier from the date of trial is to encourage the plaintiff to delay bringing his claim to trial. Perhaps this consideration will induce the courts to apply the rule in *Graham v Dodds* to personal injury cases when the time comes.

Negligence: surveyors and valuers

When a house is bought, this usually involves a building society, and also a surveyor, who is paid to value the property either by the building society, or by the purchaser, or both. Occasionally he negligently overvalues the property. Of recent years, the courts have considered the building society's surveyor's liability to the buyer (*Yianni v Edwin Evans & Sons* [1981] 3 All ER 592) and the buyer's surveyor's to the buyer (*Perry v Sidney Phillips & Son* [1982] 3 All ER 705, see also All ER Rev 1982, p 105). Now in *London and South of England Building Society v Stone* [1983] 3 All ER 105 the Court of Appeal has considered the building society's surveyor's liability to the building society.

At the building society's request, D surveyed the house which the Robinsons wished to buy, and proclaimed it worth the £11,880 which the building society proposed to lend upon it. The Robinsons bought it, borrowing most of the price from the building society, to which they mortgaged it. As usual, they also personally covenanted to repay, and made themselves liable to pay for vital repairs. Then it was discovered that the house was completely worthless because it had inadequate foundations and was literally about to fall down; whereupon the building society agreed to pay for underpinning, which in the end cost twice what it had lent on the property. Later, when the Robinsons sold the now underpinned house, they repaid the £11,880 advance, but this cheered the building society only a little, because in a sense it was being repaid in its own money. It therefore sued D, whom Russell J held to have been negligent. The building society appealed to the Court of Appeal against Russell J's assessment of damages.

The Court of Appeal accepted that prima facie the measure of damages must be the difference between what the building society lent on the negligent valuation, and what it would have lent on a careful one. As it would have lent nothing on a careful valuation, this calculation yielded the full £11,880 advanced. To what extent, however, would particular factors in a given case justify departing from this measure? In *Baxter v Gapp & Co Ltd* [1939] 2 All ER 752 the Court of Appeal seemed to have accepted that the mortgagee's entire loss flowing from the negligent advice could be recovered if this was greater. There, the mortgagor had completely defaulted, the mortgagee sold the property at a loss incurring a number of expenses in the process, and was awarded these expenses as well as the portion of the loan the sale of the house failed to cover. In the present case, P did not seriously try to recover the full cost of the underpinning, apparently accepting that although it had good commercial reasons for spending more on the property than had been advanced on it, these were not reasons which would justify making D pay more than P would have lost if it had simply cut its losses and written off the loan. Thus P was content to ask for no more than £11,880. However, at this point D argued that *Baxter v Gapp* worked in reverse, and if P had really lost less than the difference between what he lent and what he should have lent, P could claim no more than the actual loss. If a mortgagee managed to recover part of the advance from the mortgagor before he defaulted, it could only sue the surveyor for the balance, and likewise if it had made him pay part of the cost of the repairs. If it could have done so, but neglected to do so, it must credit the surveyor for what it could have recovered from the mortgagor if it had tried. The Robinsons were not well off, but if the building society had determinedly squeezed them it might have made them pay £3,000. Thus, said D, P must knock £3,000 off the £11,880 it would have been able to claim if the Robinsons had not been worth powder and shot.

This argument was accepted by Russell J at first instance, and by Sir Denys Buckley on appeal. The majority of the Court of Appeal, however, rejected it. O'Connor LJ viewed relations between the building society and the Robinsons as nothing to do with the surveyor. Stephenson LJ said the question was whether the building society has unreasonably failed to mitigate its loss—which it had not, as a plaintiff is not bound in mitigation to embark on a risky lawsuit, or to damage its commercial reputation, and squeezing the Robinsons into near-insolvency would have involved doing both.

It is respectfully submitted that the majority of the Court of Appeal is right. *Yianni v Edwin Evans & Son* suggests that if the society had made the Robinsons pay for the repairs, the Robinsons could have recouped this in tort from the surveyor. Thus it hardly lay in the surveyor's mouth to complain that by not doing so, the building society was making him pay more than his fair share.

What would have happened if the building society had in fact induced the Robinsons to contribute towards the cost of underpinning is doubtful. O'Connor LJ said that this would have been irrelevant. Stephenson LJ said that an actual contribution, as against the possibility of enforcing one, should be taken into account. And as we have seen, Sir Denys Buckley would have reduced the building society's damages to take account of even the possibility.

Defamation

In *Blackshaw v Lord* [1983] 2 All ER 311 the defendants appealed against a jury award of £45,000 damages for libel, which they complained was excessive. The Court of Appeal entirely agreed: Fox LJ said it was 'too much', Dunn LJ said it was 'much too high', and Stephenson LJ described it as 'over the top'. Nevertheless, following the usual flaccid custom, the Court of Appeal refused to quash it. The question was whether £45,000 was an award which no reasonable jury could have made, and although the Court of Appeal judges themselves strongly disagreed with it, that did not mean that no reasonable jury could have thought it was correct.

So when is a jury award of libel damages so large that no reasonable jury could have given it? The jury is asked what compensates P for a harm which is not his loss in cash terms, but the mere fact that his reputation has been dented. They are also to understand that P is entitled to substantial compensation for this even though no one believed a word D said, and logic suggests that there is therefore no dent in it. In abstract, no sum awarded according to such nebulous rules is demonstrably too high or too low, so it is hardly surprising that the Court of Appeal can rarely say that no reasonable jury would have awarded it. Such an award can only be too high or too low by differing from the accepted tariff; but there is no accepted tariff, because juries are not told what other juries have awarded, and according to this case, other jury awards are to be disregarded by the Court of Appeal as well.

Dunn LJ regretted all this, and wished that Parliament had enacted the recommendations of the Faulks Committee—one of which was that the judge should assess damages in defamation cases. Surely, however, the remedy is to some extent in the hands of the courts themselves. If the Court of Appeal in *Ward v James* [1965] 1 All ER 563 could find it had the power to reverse jury awards in personal injury cases merely because it disagreed with them, it could presumably do the same in libel cases too. And if they really wanted to, surely the courts could also allow juries to be told of awards in comparable cases.

Contract

Where P sues D for breach of contract, he usually claims damages for loss of the bargain, asking the court to put him in the position he would have been in if the contract had been performed. Sometimes, however, he claims the money he has thrown away instead: his 'reliance loss'. In *Anglia TV v Reed* [1971] 3 All ER 690 the Court of Appeal through the mouth of Lord Denning MR said that a plaintiff may choose for himself which loss he sues for. There, however, the wasted expenditure was clear, but it was very uncertain what the loss of profits would have been. Can a plaintiff elect to sue for wasted expenditure where it can be shown that his loss of profits would have been less? In *C & P Haulage v Middleton* [1983] 3 All ER 94 the Court of Appeal (Ackner and Fox LJJ) answered this question with a resounding 'no'. P, a self-employed motor-mechanic, was granted a licence by D to carry on his business in a part of D's yard, and spent £1,761.51 in fitting out. D then threw him out in breach of contract, but by a stroke of good luck, P was able to remove his business to another site where he did not have to pay any rent for a year, and so saved rent payable to D which was more than his wasted £1,761.51. P could therefore expect only nominal damages for loss of the bargain, and tried to claim his wasted expenditure instead. The Court of Appeal distinguished *Anglia TV v Reed* on the ground that there the loss of profits could not be assessed, and held that here P could not elect to sue for wasted expenditure. If in the end P is actually better off by reason of D's breach of promise, there is no reason to make D pay him damages for breaking it, and P is therefore entitled to nominal damages only.

It is a well-known rule that where the defendant could have performed the contract in several different ways, damages for loss of P's bargain are assessed on the assumption that the defendant would have chosen the method least beneficial to the plaintiff. Thus, for example, in *Laverack v Woods of Colchester Ltd* [1966] 3 All ER 683 the Court of Appeal ruled that damages for wrongful dismissal must be calculated with reference only to P's wages, bonus payments being disregarded if the employer was not legally obliged to pay them. In that case, however, Diplock LJ added that the court would also assume that D would not cut off his nose to spite his face by selecting the method of performance least favourable to P should this also be disastrous for himself. This line of thought prevailed with Mustill J in *Paula Lee Ltd v Robert Zehil & Co Ltd* [1983] 2 All ER 390. P, a dress manufacturer, engaged D as his sole agent in Kuwait and Saudi Arabia, D undertaking to handle at least 16,000 dresses per annum. When P sued D for repudiating the contract, D argued that damages should be assessed on the basis that D would have ordered only 16,000 of P's cheapest dress, all in the smallest size—on which basis P's damages would be small. Mustill J rejected this. Although on a narrow reading of the contract it was arguable that D could have fulfilled his obligation to P by doing this, the arrangement was really a joint marketing venture which would have collapsed with loss to both sides had D so behaved. Damages should therefore be calculated on the assumption that D would have ordered the cheapest selection of different garments which he would have had a chance of selling.

Other cases

Calabar Properties Ltd v Stitcher [1983] 3 All ER 759, CA, is discussed in the section on Landlord and Tenant (see p 242 below). Two cases raising the question of damages for conversion, *Chubb Cash Ltd v Crille & Son* [1983] 2 All ER 294 and *Hillesden Securities v Ryjak Ltd* [1983] 2 All ER 184, are considered in the chapter on Commercial Law (see pp 41–45 above).

Employment Law

PATRICK ELIAS, LLB, MA, PHD
Barrister, Fellow of Pembroke College, Cambridge

Introduction

In the All England Reports for 1983 there are four House of Lords and six Court of Appeal decisions relating to aspects of labour law, as well as a few important cases decided by lower courts. Although most of these decisions are concerned with points of statutory construction arising out of the ever-increasing volume of legislation in this area, the courts are also actively involved in developing common law principles in new and potentially important ways.

Employee or independent contractor—A question of law or fact?

One of the most elusive and difficult tasks facing the labour lawyer is to distinguish between the self-employed worker, employed under a contract for services, and the employees working under a contract of service. Yet the distinction is fundamental since a whole array of rights are given to the latter but not the former, including the right to claim for redundancy pay and unfair dismissal. The problem of categorisation arises at two levels. First, it has been notoriously difficult for the courts to agree upon how the test for distinguishing these categories should be formulated. At various times preference has been shown for different tests, but as May LJ commented in *President of the Methodist Conference v Parfitt* [1983] 3 All ER 747 at 755—

> 'The tasks which people carry out and the contexts in which they do so daily became so much more numerous, more diverse and more sophisticated that no one test or set of tests is apt to separate contracts of service and contracts for services in all cases'.

Secondly, even where there is a consensus about the appropriate test to be applied in any particular case, difficulties arise in applying the test to the facts of a particular employment relationship. Reasonable people, even applying the same test, may reach different conclusions.

The question that had to be decided by the Court of Appeal in the case of *O'Kelly v Trusthouse Forte plc* [1983] 3 All ER 456 was this: where an appeal is limited to points of law only, in what circumstances can the appellate court interfere with the classification of the employment relationship adopted by the lower court? To put the same question in a more formal legal way, to what extent is the classification a question of law, and to what extent a question of fact? As the Employment Appeal Tribunal had pointed out in this case, there has been a pronounced difference of judicial view on the answer. The Tribunal added that it was highly desirable that the Court of Appeal should settle the matter one way or another.

The particular issue in the *Trusthouse Forte* case was whether certain banqueting staff employed by Trusthouse Forte from time to time for particular banquets were employees of the company and eligible to present complaints for unfair dismissal. The industrial tribunal had concluded that they were not. It put particular emphasis on the fact that the workers were not contractually obliged to accept work for any particular banquet, nor were the employers obliged to offer it. This was so despite the fact that in reality workers refusing to accept work when offered jeopardised the likelihood of their being offered such work in future. On appeal, the Employment Appeal Tribunal refused to interfere with the tribunal's finding that there was no continuing contract of employment between the parties. However, the EAT held that the workers were employed under a contract of employment each time they entered into an engagement for a particular banquet, so that the relationship consisted of a series of successive employment contracts with no contract subsisting between banquets. The EAT took the view that this possibility had not been considered in the judgment of the industrial tribunal. The employers appealed contending that the question of how to categorise the employment relationship was purely one of fact, that the findings of the industrial tribunal were inconsistent with the notion that there was a series of separate contracts of employment, and that consequently the EAT was not empowered to substitute its own view for that of the tribunal. Alternatively, they argued that if the industrial tribunal had not considered what might be termed the 'separate contracts' issue, the EAT should have remitted the case to the industrial tribunal to consider this question.

The Court of Appeal upheld the appeal, although it rejected the appellant's contention that the issue of classification posed a pure question of fact. However, it failed to provide the unequivocal guidance sought by the EAT. The majority (Sir John Donaldson MR and Fox LJ) held that the process of clarifying the employment relationship involved both questions of fact and law. The Master of Rolls described the position as follows:

> 'The test to be applied in identifying whether a contract is one of employment or for services is a pure question of law and so is its application to the facts. But it is for the tribunal of fact not only to find those facts but to assess them qualitatively and within limits, which are indefinable in the abstract, those findings and that assessment will dictate the correct legal answer. In the familiar phrase, it is all a question of fact and degree.
>
> It is only if the weight given to a particular factor shows a self-misdirection in law that an appellate court with a limited jurisdiction can interfere.'

On this basis that the only ground for intervention in the absence of a clear misdirection is on the classic *Edwards v Bairstow* test ([1955] 3 All ER 48), namely that no reasonable tribunal, properly directing itself as to the material facts, could have reached the particular conclusion of that tribunal. Fox LJ adopted a similar approach saying that although in a general sense the question of classification was one of law, it resolved itself into a question of fact in individual cases. Both their Lordships held that the industrial tribunal in this case must have considered and rejected the contention that there was a series of separate employment contracts relating to each banquet, and that this conclusion could not be faulted in law.

But Ackner LJ dissented. After an extensive review of the authorities he concluded that the question of classification was essentially one of law so that the EAT could properly reach its own conclusion as to the legal nature of the employment relationship in the light of the facts as found by the industrial tribunal. His Lordship explicitly followed the view expressly adopted by Stephenson LJ in the Court of Appeal in *Young and Woods Ltd v West* [1980] IRLR 201. He accepted that certain questions should properly be treated as matters of fact and degree, such as the meaning of reasonableness (*UCATT v Brain* [1981] ICR 542) or whether a breach of contract amounts to a repudiatory breach (*Woods v WM Car Services (Peterborough) Ltd* [1982] ICR 693.) But he rejected the view that the determination of the true legal nature of the employment relationship fell into that category. However, on the facts he thought that the industrial tribunal had not considered the 'separate contracts' issue and that the case should accordingly be remitted to it to determine that question.

Another decision of the Court of Appeal was faced with the classification of an unusual employment relationship in *Methodist Conference (President) v Parfitt* [1983] 3 All ER 747. The respondent was a Methodist minister who had been dismissed by the governing body of the Methodist church for alleged misconduct. He sought to claim for unfair dismissal but the church contended as a preliminary point that the respondent was not employed under any contract at all, and particularly not a contract of employment. An interesting feature of the case was that although both the industrial tribunal and the EAT found that there was a contract of employment, in each case the legal chairman (Waterhouse J in the EAT) dissented. The Court of Appeal vindicated their dissent and upheld the church's appeal. Dillon LJ, delivering the leading judgment, held that the spiritual position and functions of the minister precluded any contractual relationship at all. His Lordship accepted that this was not necessarily the position and that in an appropriate case a contractual relationship could exist. But it was inapt to treat the relationship as governed by a contract of service unless there were clear indications to the contrary. May LJ reached a similar conclusion but by a slightly different route. For whereas Dillon LJ appears to have treated the spiritual nature of the minister's position as essentially inappropriate for analysis in contractual terms, May LJ emphasised the fact that there was no intention to create legal relations. For good measure he held that even if there was a contract, it was not a contract of service.

Remedies for breach of contract

A potentially revolutionary case in the field of wrongful dismissal is the decision of Woolf J in *R v BBC, ex p Lavelle* [1983] 1 All ER 241. The applicant was employed by the BBC under a contract of employment which expressly included the BBC's staff regulations. These contained, inter alia, a disciplinary procedure to be follwed where misconduct was alleged against an employee. The applicant claimed that she had been dismissed in breach of these procedures and applied under RSC Ord 53 for judicial review of the decision to dimiss her, seeking certiorari to quash the decision coupled with an injunction to prevent the director from hearing her appeal until certain criminal proceedings, arising out of the same alleged act of misconduct, had been heard.

Notwithstanding the statutory basis of the BBC itself, Woolf J held that Order 53 was inappropriate on the grounds that 'the application for judicial review is confined to reviewing activities of a public nature as opposed to those of a partly private or domestic character'. He held that the disciplinary procedure was a purely domestic or private character since it was dependent solely on the contract of employment. (And see *Law v National Greyhound Racing Club* [1983] 3 All ER 300, CA, where a similar conclusion was reached. Sed quare whether the same principle would apply if the relevant procedures had a statutory flavour, eg where they are given approval by a ministerial order: see the decision of Hodgson J in *R v East Berkshire Health Authority, ex p Walsh* (1983) Times 15 November.) However, this did not terminate the proceedings for under Ord 53, r 9(5) the court has power in circumstances where a declaration or injunction or damages is sought, to treat the action as if it had been commenced by writ. This the court proceeded to do. The vital question then arising was this: would the court grant an injunction to restrain the dismissal of an employee which was effected in breach of contractually agreed procedures? Or did any remedy sound merely in damages? The traditional view, and the weight of the authorities, favoured a remedy in damages only. There is extensive support for the granting of a declaration or injunction in circumstances where the employee holds an office or a post which is to some extent regulated by statute. But traditionally these relationships have been distinguished from what is frequently termed the 'pure master and servant' case. There the orthodox view has been that no such remedies will be granted, at least not unless the case is a wholly exceptional one where trust and confidence in the employment relationship remains despite the dismissal: see *Hill v CA Parsons & Co Ltd* [1971] 3 All ER 1345. Woolf J rejected this orthodox approach. There had been signs that the courts might do so in previous cases, notably *McClelland v Nothern Ireland General Hospital Board* [1957] 1 WLR 594, *Stevenson v United Road Transport Union* [1977] 2 All ER 941 and *Jones v Lee* [1980] ICR 310. But arguably these cases were equivocal since they might have been explained on the traditional office holder or statutory basis (though the judges in those cases did not expressly justify their decisions on the traditional view). In contrast, *Lavelle* is quite unambiguous. Woolf J was well aware that he was departing from orthodoxy, and he justified his decision on the following grounds (p 252 b to d):

> 'When one has regard to the framework of this employment, one finds that the BBC has engrafted on to the ordinary principles of master and servant an elaborate framework of appeals. This framework restricts the power of the BBC as an employer to terminate the employee's employment. It clearly presupposes that the employee should have more than one opportunity of being heard. It may be right, as was submitted, that the reason this is done is to avoid any question of the dismissal being regarded as being unfair. However, here I would adopt the argument advanced by counsel for the applicant that the employment protection legislation has substantially changed the position at common law so far as dismissal is concerned. In appropriate circumstances the statute now provides that an industrial tribunal can order the reinstatement of an employee. It is true that the order cannot be specifically enforced. However, the existence of that power does indicate that even the ordinary contract of master and servant now has many of the attributes of an office, and the distinction which previously existed between pure cases of master and servant and cases where a person holds an office are not longer clear.'

This case therefore supports the proposition that courts will treat a dismissal as invalid either if it is in breach of some substantial contractual limitation on the power to dismiss, or if it is in breach of some fundamental procedural requirements incorporated into the contract. The impact of statutory developments on the common law is plain to see. And in circumstances where the unfair dismissal remedies are limited in scope and efficacy, the practical significance of strengthening common law protections should not be underestimated.

The employee's duty of good faith

In a classic case on the law of mistake in contract, the House of Lords in *Bell v Lever Bros* [1931] All ER Rep 1 held that an employee is under no duty to disclose to his employer his own previous misconduct and any payment made to the employer by the employer in ignorance of that misconduct cannot be recovered on the grounds of mistake. However, in a decision reached some four years later in the Court of Appeal, *Swain v West (Butchers) Ltd* [1936] 3 All ER 261, it was held that in certain circumstances an employee is under a positive duty to disclose the misdeeds of his fellow servants. The case of *Sybron Corpn v Rochem Ltd* [1983] 2 All ER 707, [1983] BCLC 43 neatly raised the question of which of these principles should triumph when they are in conflict. To put it colloquially: although you need not sneak on yourself, you must at least in some circumstances sneak on your fellow employees. But must you do so when by so doing you will be sneaking on yourself too? The Court of Appeal unanimously held that you must.

The facts were that the respondent company employed the appellant as a manager to oversee its European operations. In 1973 the appellant had applied for early retirement and was paid various sums under a discretionary bonus scheme. Subsequently it was discovered that he was a party to a grand commercial fraud whereby he, in company with certain of his subordinates, had in breach of his duty to the company deprived it of substantial sums. The company not unnaturally sought to recover the pension payments and contended that they had been paid under a mistake of fact, namely their ignorance of the fraudulent conspiracy, which ignorance had been maintained by the appellant's failure, in breach of contract, to disclose the fraud of his fellows. So the question was: did this obligation exist even though the appellant would thereby inevitably incriminate himself? Whilst all their Lordships were in no doubt that it did, they had some difficulty in distinguishing *Bell v Lever Bros*. For in that case two employees each committed misconduct to the knowledge of the other and yet no one seems to have thought that in the absence of a duty to disclose their own peccadilloes, they might have been under a duty to disclose those of the other. Stephenson LJ confessed to finding this puzzling but nevertheless held that there was such a duty. He also adopted a distinction drawn by Walton J at first instance who had held that *Bell* was concerned with a case where the two employees were of equal status so that the duty of disclosure did not lie. However, this does not seem to be an accurate description of the facts in *Bell*. Nor is it clear why there might be a duty to disclose the misdeeds of a superior or inferior but not an equal. Fox LJ provided an equally unconvincing distinction, saying that *Bell* was concerned with past completed breaches rather than continuing ones, though why the duty to disclose should cease when the evil deed is done is not easy to fathom. Kerr LJ simply limited *Bell* to its facts and held that it did not preclude the existence of a duty to disclose the wrongdoings of others.

However, their Lordships all emphasised that there is no universal obligation to disclose the misconduct of fellow employees. As Stephenson LJ commented, 'whether there is such a duty depends on the contract and on the terms of employment of the particular servant'. But all their Lordships were in no doubt that a senior executive like the appellant was by virtue of his position under a duty to disclose serious misconduct calculated to harm the company.

This decision significantly restricts *Bell*. Furthermore, Kerr LJ thought that *Bell* probably did not apply in any event to fraudulent acts by the employee. (And see the decision of Glidewell J in *Horcal v Gatland* [1983] BCLC 60 which represents a further attempt to restrict the scope of the *Bell v Lever Bros* principle.)

For further discussion, see pp 66–68 and 115 above.

Unfair dismissal: eligibility and age limits

Section 64 (1)(b) of the Employment Protection (Consolidation) Act 1978 sets an upper age limit for those eligible to claim for unfair dismissal. It provides that the unfair dismissal provisions do not apply to the dismissal of an employee who has 'attained the age which, in the undertaking in which he was employed, was the normal retiring age for an employee holding the position which he held, or, if a man, attained the age of sixty-five, or, if a woman, attained the age of sixty.'

The interpretation of this provision has proved to be highly controversial. It took a majority decision of the House of Lords in *Nothman v London Borough of Barnet* [1979] 1 All ER 142 to establish that the subsection establishes only one barrier and not two: if there is a normal retiring age then whatever age that is, anyone over that age is ineligible to claim, and it is only in circumstances where there is no normal retiring age that recourse is had to pensionable age. But difficulties remained with the term 'normal retiring age'. It spawned much litigation, being the subject of four Court of Appeal decisions (*Nothman v London Borough of Barnet* [1978] 1 All ER 1243; *Howard v Department of National Savings* [1981] IRCR 40; *Post Office v Wallser* [1981] IRLR 37; and *Waite v Government Communications Headquarters* [1983] 1 CR 359. These were not wholly consistent, but the dominant view was that the term 'normal retiring age' meant the age when a person could be required to retire under his contract. However, the House of Lords decision in the *Waite* case [1983] 2 All ER 1013, has departed from this approach and construed the phrase in what is submitted is a far more satisfactory way. For as Lord Fraser pointed out in judgment concurred in by the rest of their Lordships (Lords Keith, Scarman, Bridge and Templeman), to treat the concept in purely contractual terms gave a wholly artificial meaning to the word 'normal'. That word suggests that the relevant age should be that at which employees actually retire rather than the age when the employer is contractually entitled to require their retirement. His Lordship accepted that the contractual retiring age was relevant insofar as there is a presumption that the normal retiring age is the contractual age. But that presumption can be rebutted by evidence that employees in fact normally retire later, or perhaps at different ages, so that there is no normal retiring age. He commented:

'Having regard to the social policy which seems to underlie the Act, namely the policy of securing fair treatment, as regards compulsory retirement, as between different employees holding the same position, the expression 'normal retiring age' conveys the idea of an age at which employees in the group can reasonably expect to be compelled to retire, unless there is some special reason in a particular case for a different age to apply.'

But he added that 'normal' is not a synonym for 'usual'. The proper test is 'what would be the reasonable expectation or understanding of the employees holding that position at that relevant time'.

The *Waite* case also demonstrates that it will not be easy to rebut the presumption that the contractual retiring age is the normal retiring age. On the facts, just over one quarter of the relevant group had retired after the specified contractual retiring age but that was held to fall 'far short of showing that the contractual retiring age had been abandoned or departed from'.

Continuity of employment

Establishing the appropriate period of continuity of employment is often a condition precedent to the enforcement of statutory rights. Yet although the theory behind continuity is simple enough, the detailed provisions found in Sch 13 to the 1978 Act are highly complex. One of the most difficult provisions to construe is para 9(1)(b) of the Schedule which specifies that continuity continues even when an employee is 'absent from work on account of a temporary cessation of work'. *Ford v Warwickshire CC* [1983] 1 All ER 753 is the second House of Lords' decision on the construction of these few words, the first being *Fitzgerald v Hall, Russell & Co Ltd* [1969] 3 All ER 1140.

The appellant was employed as a part-time lecturer at one of the respondent's colleges of further education. She had been employed on a series of eight fixed-term contracts which began with the commencement of the academic year and ended automatically on its termination. For the duration of the summer vacation, therefore, the appellant did not work for, and was under no subsisting contract of employment with, the respondents. The appellant was not re-engaged for the academic year 1979 and complained of unfair dismissal. But it was clear that unless she could somehow show that the vacations did not destroy continuity, she could not have sufficient continuous employment to be eligible to claim. She contended that the vacations did not breach continuity but were saved by para 9(1)(b). She failed before the industrial tribunal, the EAT and the Court of Appeal, all of whose decisions were unanimous, but succeeded where it mattered most, before the House of Lords.

As Lord Brightman indicated in his judgment, their Lordships felt difficulty with two facets of the phrase. First, could it be said that the appellant was 'absent from work' in circumstances where she was under no contractual obligation to attend work? His Lordship observed that one would not usually refer to a person as absent from work where employment had ceased due to the termination of a fixed-term contract. But para 9 was not envisaging the usual use of the word. Indeed, their Lordships accepted that the provision operated only where there was no existing contract of employment, an interpretation which is reinforced by the cross-heading to para 9 but which had not been adopted in some other cases which must now, therefore, be considered overruled: see especially *Lloyds Bank Ltd v Secretary of State for Employment* [1979] 2 All ER 573. It followed that the paragraph could apply only where there had been a termination of the contract. Furthermore, in *Fitzgerald's* case it had been applied to a case where an employee's contract had been terminated and he had been re-employed and as Lord Brightman recognised, no logical distinction could be drawn between that case and one where a person's employment had ceased on the termination of a fixed-term contract.

The second difficulty was one of causation. Granted an absence from work, could it be said to be 'on account of a temporary cessation of work' or was it more accurately described as on account of the expiry of a fixed-term contract? Initially their Lordships found difficulty with this point but finally were unanimous in holding that the former was the proper cause. Again it is submitted that *Fitzgerald's* case had really decided the issue. If an employee could be said to be absent an account of a temporary cessation of work rather than on account of his dismissal when he is dismissed, why does the same analysis not apply when his dismissal results from the termination of a fixed-term contract? As both Lords Diplock and Brightman commented, the fact that the unavailability of work had been foreseen and anticipated in the contract itself did not present the absence from being on account of the cessation of work. Both thought that this conclusion was fortified by the statutory definition of dismissal which treats both the non-renewal of a fixed term contract and the termination on notice of an indefinite contract as a dismissal. An additional justification is that the Court of Appeal had reached a similar conclusion in an analogous situation in *Nottinghamshire CC v Lee* [1980] ICR 635. There it was held that a dismissal could be for redundancy, ie on account of a cessation of work, notwithstanding that it was foreseen that the cessation could arise when the contract was entered into. The Court of Appeal rejected the view that the dismissal was on account of the termination of the fixed-term contract rather than the cessation of work. Happily, although their Lordships in *Ford* did not refer to that decision, their conclusion is consistent with it.

In this case it was accepted that the interval between the fixed-term contracts was temporary. But as Lord Diplock noted, this is entirely a question of fact and degree for the industrial tribunal. He added that continuity will be preserved for seasonable employment only if the interval between two successive seasonal contracts is so short in comparison with the length of the season during which the employee is employed as properly to be regarded as a temporary cessation.

Dismissal for union activities

Section 58 of the 1978 Act makes it automatically unfair for an employer to dismiss an employee if the reason is that *the employee* is, inter alia, a member of a trade union or has taken part in the activities of the union at the appropriate time. Basically the s 58 protection is granted to enable employees collectively to join unions and take part in their activities. Together with s 23 of the Act, which protects against action short of dismissal, it provides the statutory safeguard for freedom of association. But this essentially collective right is, in typically English fashion, couched in individualistic terms. The disadvantage of framing the right in this way is amply demonstrated by the Court of Appeal decision in *Carrington v Therm-A-Stor Ltd* [1983] 1 All ER 796. The appellant company was unsympathetic, and indeed hostile, to trade unions. Nevertheless a majority of workers joined a union and the union made a request for recognition. In response, the company decided to dismiss 20 employees but left it to the charge hands to make the selection. The industrial tribunal found as a fact that the selection was not made on the basis of union membership, although in fact all the dismissed employees were union members.

The four respondents in this case were all dismissed workers alleging that they had been unfairly dismissed. They had insufficient continuity of employment to bring a claim for unfair dismissal in the normal way. However, if it could be established that their dismissals were for a s 58 reason, they would be automatically unfair and the lack of continuity would not be a bar. However, the industrial tribunal held that on the wording of the section no individual could show that he had been dismissed because of his union membership or activity so that the appellants were unable to present their claims. The EAT upheld the employees' appeals, but the Court of Appeal reinstated the industrial tribunal's decision.

Before the Court of Appeal the employers ran two arguments. First, they alleged that the dismissal could not be for a s 58 reason since the charge hands were not motivated by trade union considerations. The court had no difficulty in rejecting this contention: it confused the reason for the dismissal with the basis of selection. Furthermore, s 59 of the Act, which establishes that in certain circumstances a dismissal for redundancy which would otherwise be fair may be rendered unfair by the method of selection, clearly indicates that they are different things.

Secondly, the employers argued that the dismissal was not carried into effect because of the particular individual's participation in union activities. It was because of the union's plea for recognition. Counsel for the employees sought to argue that s 58 should be construed so as to recognise its essentially collective dimension. He contended that if action is taken against the union because of its activities, that action must be treated as having been taken because of the activities of each and every member. Sir John Donaldson rejected this argument in the following way:

> 'I regard this as a valiant attempt at purposive construction of the statute, but in my judgment it goes beyond permissible limits. As I read the section it is concerned solely with the dismissal of *an* employee and provides that it shall be regarded as unfair if the reason was that *the* (ie *that*) employee had done or proposed to do one or more specified things. The reason why each of the four employees was dismissed had nothing to do with anything which the employee concerned had personally done or proposed to do. The section therefore has no application.'

Consequently, the employees were left without protection despite May LJ's acceptance that the section was 'clearly aimed at a mischief very similar to that which befell the employees'. Furthermore, not only does the decision take outside the protection of s 58 a dismissal of individuals taken because of the activities of the union itself; it also means that if, say, a shop steward's brother is dismissed because of the steward's activities, he will not be protected by the section either. No doubt he could normally establish an unfair dismissal in the usual way, but only, of course, if he has sufficient continuity of employment.

Industrial action

Although s 15 of the Trade Union and Labour Relations Act 1974, as amended, gives specific statutory protection for picketing in certain defined circumstances, successive cases have construed this right so as to give immunity only against wrongs inevitably committed by the protected act of picketing itself, eg *Hunt v Broome* [1974] 1 All ER 314, *Kavanagh v Hiscock* [1974] 2 All ER 177. This restrictive approach was again adopted by the Divisional Court in *British Airports Authority v Ashton* [1983] 3 All ER 6. Some employees in the course of a trade dispute picketed at a control post which, although it was used to control the entry of vehicles into the airport, was actually situated within the precincts of the airport itself. The employees were arrested and charged with contravening two bye-laws which regulated the use of the airport. The magistrates dismissed the information, one of their reasons being that since the pickets were acting within s 15, their actions could not be rendered unlawful by any bye-laws. The appeal of the Airports Authority was successful against this part of the decision. Mann J commented that s 15 did not in terms confer a right to attend on land against the will of the owner and 'it could be astonishing if Parliament intended that such a right should be implied'. Although there was no English authority directly on the point, the court treated the Irish decision in *Larkin v Belfast Harbour Commissioners* [1908] 2 IR 214 as persuasive authority. In that case O'Brien LCJ had said that s 2 of the Trade Disputes Act 1906, a statutory predecessor of s 15, was 'never intended to authorise as a matter of right an invasion into a man's house, or entry against the will of the owner into a place of business'. However, the court accepted that the appellants were not in quite the same position as a private landowner, for as the Court of Appeal decision in *Cinnamond v British Airports Authority* [1980] 2 All ER 368 demonstrated, the public has a right of access to the airport for the purpose of taking advantage of the services provided by the airport. But this did not affect the substance of the matter since picketing did not fall within the range of activities for which a right of access was granted. On the facts, however, the court held that the picketing was not necessarily unlawful at all. It did not contravene one of the bye-laws which rendered unlawful certain public demonstrations, since it was held that picketing did not fall into that category. And the court held that the case should be remitted to the magistrates to make further findings before it could be said that the picketing contravened the other bye-law.

The case of *Merkur Island Shipping Corp v Laughton* [1983] 2 All ER 189 gave the House of Lords its first opportunity to consider the meaning of s 17 of the Employment Act 1980, which has sought to restrict the range of secondary action which can lawfully be taken in furtherance of a primary dispute. As in a number of other recent industrial action cases to reach the courts, the dispute arose from the activities of the International Transport

Workers Federation and their campaign to eradicate the low pay and poor working conditions found on many vessels sailing under flags of convenience.

The detailed facts of the case are important. Essentially they were as follows. The respondents in the appeal were shipowners who had chartered their ship to charterers on a time charter, and the charterers in turn had sub-chartered to sub-charterers. Both the charter and sub-charter provided that all relevant port charges should be paid by the charterers. In pursuance of this clause the sub-charterers had entered into a contract with the tugowners at Liverpool for the provision of tugs when necessary to assist their vessels. However, in order to put pressure on the shipowners for allegedly paying rates below those stipulated by the ITWF, union officials persuaded the tugmen employed by the tugowners, in breach of their respective contracts of employment, to black the vessel and refuse to assist it out of the port. The shipowners sought an interlocutory injunction claiming that the union officials had unlawfully interfered with the performance of the charter and had interfered with the business of the shipowners using unlawful means. They succeeded before Porter J, the Court of Appeal and the House of Lords.

Lord Diplock, in whose judgment the rest of their Lordships concurred, adopted the three-stage approach for determining liability in the case of secondary action first suggested by Brightman LJ in *Marine Shipping Ltd v Laughton* [1982] 1 All ER 481 at 489. The first stage is to establish common law liability, the second to determine whether s 13 of the Trade Union and Labour Relations Act 1974 gives immunity, and the third to determine whether s 17 of the 1980 Act restores liability.

His Lordship had no doubt that the tort of interfering with the performance of a contract by unlawful means was clearly established at common law. Any doubts had been removed by Lord Denning's judgment in *Torquay Hotel Co Ltd v Cousins* [1969] 1 All ER 522. The elements of the tort, said his Lordship, were the same as those required to establish liability for indirectly inducing a breach of contract, effectively with the substitution of interference with performance for breach. Lord Diplock approved the judgment of Jenkins LJ in the leading case of *D C Thomson & Co Ltd v Deakin* [1952] 2 All ER 361 at 379–380, where the following four elements were set out:

> '... first, that the person charged with actionable interference knew of the existence of the contract and intended to procure its breach; secondly, that the person so charged did definitely and unequivocally persuade, induce or procure the employees concerned to break their contracts of employment with the intent I have mentioned; thirdly, that the employees so persuaded, induced or procured did in fact break their contracts of employment; and, fourthly, that breach of the contract forming the alleged subject of interference ensued as a necessary consequence of the breaches by the employees concerned of their contracts of employment.'

Subsequent cases, however, have shown that knowledge of the contract does not mean such knowledge of the detailed terms that the inducers must have inevitably known that they were inducing breach. It suffices that they are reckless, not caring if there is a breach or not: *Emerald Construction v Lowthian* [1966] 1 All ER 1013. Lord Diplock took this a stage further in *Merkur Island*, taking his lead from Sir John Donaldson's judgment in the

Court of Appeal ([1983] 1 All ER 334). He held that it is not actually necessary to know that there is a contract in existence at all: it suffices if the inducers know that there almost certainly are commercial contracts in force and that their actions will almost certainly bring about a breach of interference with the performance of such contracts. Query whether a mere probability that such contracts exist will be enough to found liability.

Consequently stage one established liability. But stage two undisputably provided immunity. So the crucial question was whether liability was restored under stage three by s 17. If the shipowners were parties to the contracts with the tugowners there is no doubt that this would have been protected secondary action. This is because s 17 permits secondary action where the action is designed to induce or interfere with the performance of a commercial contract between the primary employer with whom the union is in dispute and a customer or supplier with whom he has direct contractual relations. But the existence of the two charter contracts put the shipowners at two removes from the shipowners. By their action the union was hitting at the target shipowners through the charterers and sub-charterers. Furthermore, Lord Diplock expressly rejected an argument by the union that only the intermediate parties could complain of unlawful secondary action and take advantage of s 17. He held that there was no justification for assuming that Parliament intended to deny the employer who was the primary party to the dispute from reaping a benefit from the restricted immunities.

On a traditional approach to statutory interpretation it is difficult to see how the decision could have been otherwise. But the case indicates how the existence of a chain of commercial contracts may render it impossible for a union lawfully to impose pressure on an employer directly through those commercial contracts where the union cannot act through the immediate customer or supplier. The legality of industrial action is made to depend on the vagaries of how the employer decides to run his business.

Industrial action and dismissal

When Parliament introduced a law of unfair dismissal it had to decide how to treat dismissals arising out of taking part in industrial action. Should they be considered automatically fair, or unfair, or should it depend on all the circumstances of the case? Parliament's answer in s 62 of the 1978 Act was complicated and ostensibly adopted a position of neutrality: provided the employer dismisses all those participating in the action and does not selectively re-engage, no tribunal has jurisdiction to hear their complaints of unfair dismissal. So the principle is that no discrimination should be shown as between participants in the industrial action (a principle which has been retained, though in a modified form which strengthens the employer's hand, following amendments to s 62 effected by s 10 of the Employment Act 1982). A crucial question, therefore, is what constitutes industrial action? The issue arose in *Power Packing Casemakers v Faust* [1983] 2 All ER 166. Three employees were dismissed for refusing to participate in an overtime ban. They were not contractually required to work overtime. Could their action constitute 'industrial action' within the meaning of s 62 notwithstanding that they were acting in accordance with their contracts? The Court of Appeal held that it could. Neither the wording nor the legislative history of the provision required establishing that the action should involve a breach of contract. According to Stephenson LJ, industrial action covered any refusal to work used as a bargaining counter, whether in breach of contract or not. He added that 'an industrial tribunal and the lay members of the Appeal Tribunal may be trusted to recognise industrial action when they see it.'

Trade union expulsions and the Bridlington Agreement

The House of Lords decision in *Cheall v Association of Professional, Executive, Clerical and Computer Staff* [1983] 1 All ER 1130 is of vital concern to all TUC affiliated unions. It involved the question of whether an expulsion of a union member carried out in order to implement a decision made under the Bridlington Agreement is lawful. The Bridlington Agreement is an agreement between unions affiliated to the TUC. It is designed, inter alia, to prevent one union poaching members from another. Where this occurs the original union can complain to a disputes committee set up under the auspices of the TUC and if the committee finds a breach of the Bridlington rules it may require the poaching union to expel the newly-received member and to recommend that he should return to his original union. In *Spring v National Amalgamated Stevedores and Dockers Society* [1956] 2 All ER 221 it was held that any such expulsion would be unlawful unless a union had an express rule permitting it to expel to implement a Bridlington award. Following that decision the TUC recommended a 'model rule' which has been adopted, sometimes with minor variations, by the vast majority of affiliated unions. The APEX rule is as follows:

'Notwithstanding anything in these rules its executive council may, by giving six weeks' notice in writing, terminate the membership of any member, if necessary, in order to comply with a decision of the Disputes Committee of the Trades Union Congress'.

In this case the appellant union expelled Cheall in accordance with that rule. The Court of Appeal held that the expulsion was unlawful (see the discussion in last year's Annual Review, All ER Rev 1982, pp 114–115), though Sir John Donaldson delivered a powerful dissenting judgment. That dissent was vindicated on appeal to the House of Lords.

The respondent alleged that the expulsion was unlawful for four reasons. First, he contended that although the rule could be relied on where a person was inadvertently recruited in breach of Bridlington, it could not be invoked where the breach was conscious and deliberate. He sought to justify this distinction on the basis of the House of Lords decision in *New Zealand Shipping Co Ltd v Société des Ateliers et Chantiers de France* [1919] AC 1 where their Lordships had expressed the well-known principle of construction that a party to a contract cannot rely on his own contractual breach to justify invoking a clause enabling him to terminate the contract. But there were two difficulties with applying this principle in this case. First, any breach of duty committed by recruiting in breach of Bridlington did not constitute the breach of any duty owed to Cheall; it merely involved the breach of duty owed to the union from which Cheall was recruited. Secondly, if any breach of duty to the original union prevented the model rule being relied on, it would mean that the rule could never be used to justify an expulsion at all. It would be wholly ineffective. It was to avoid this absurd conclusion that counsel for the respondent sought to distinguish inadvertent breaches from deliberate ones. But Lord Diplock, who delivered the only judgment in the House of Lords, held that there was no warrant for this distinction and that the principle in the *New Zealand* case could not be relied on in these circumstances.

The second and third arguments were both based on natural justice. Cheall argued that he should have been given the right to make representation both to the disputes committee and subsequently to the executive committe of APEX before they resolved to expel him in accordance with Bridlington. Both arguments failed. As to the former, Lord Diplock pointed out that the only parties to the dispute before the disputes committee were the unions themselves and that in these circumstances natural justice did not extend to giving rights to the individual. As to the latter, natural justice was not required because it would have been pointless. There was only one decision which the union could have taken, and representations could have made no difference. Indeed as Bingham J had said at first instance, it would have been 'a cruel deception' to give a hearing when any representations would have been irrelevant.

Finally, it was optimistically argued that the Bridlington principles themselves were contrary to public policy on the grounds that they restricted the right of the individual to join a union of his choice. Reliance was placed on art 2 of the European Convention on Human Rights and Fundamental Freedoms which protects the right to freedom of association. Lord Denning had been attracted by this argument in the Court of Appeal, but it was given short shrift by Lord Diplock. It was, he said, impossible to contend that arrangements which promise orderly industrial relations and increase the union's bargaining strength are contrary to public policy. He did accept, however, that different considerations might apply where the operation of the principles put a person's job in jeopardy. This suggests that they might not withstand an attack based on the right to work doctrine first formulated by Lord Denning in *Nagle v Feilden* [1966] 1 All ER 689. However, since that doctrine is infringed only where the union acts arbitrarily or capriciously, it is difficult to see how it could apply to a decision to expel taken to implement a Bridlington award.

Miscellaneous

The case of *Oliver v J P Malnick & Co (a firm)* [1983] 3 All ER 795 raised an interesting question of who is the employer of an articled clerk in a solicitor's office. The appellant was a woman who alleged that her former employers, a firm of solicitors, had infringed the Sex Discrimination Act 1975 by offering her lower remuneration than that paid to a male articled clerk. But the firm contended that the employer was the particular partner to whom she had been articled and not the firm, so that there was no discrimination by the firm. This contention succeeded before the industrial tribunal but failed before the EAT who were able to consider fresh evidence not available before the industrial tribunal. On the facts the EAT held that she was employed by the firm. A significant factor was that the evidence indicated that the Law Society envisaged that the normal arrangement for articled clerks would be a dual system of employment by the firm, and articles with a particular partner.

Finally the House of Lords' decision in *Mandla v Dowell Lee* [1983] 1 All ER 1062 also has significant implications for employment law, though the case was not directly concerned with employment. Their Lordships held that discrimination against Sikhs constituted discrimination because of ethnic origins, and was therefore unlawful under the terms of the Race Relations Act 1976. Effectively this is saying that 'ethnic origins' includes 'ethnicity'—a desirable conclusion if the purpose of the Act is to be promoted, but one which sits uneasily with an earlier decision of the House in *Ealing London Borough v Race Relations Board* [1972] 1 All ER 105 where the House held that the concept 'national origins' did not embrace 'nationality'. Lord Fraser and Lord Templeman, whose judgments were concurred in by the rest of their Lordships (Lords Edmund Davies, Roskill and Brandon) also held that discrimination is not justifiable within the meaning of s 1(1)(b)(ii) of the Act merely because the discriminator genuinely believes it to be justifiable. On the other hand Lord Fraser denied that to be justifiable the discriminator must show that the discrimination was necessary. It will suffice if he can show that it is justifiable irrespective of race, colour, nationality or ethnic or national origins. The Court of Appeal decision in *Panesar v Nestlé Co Ltd* [1980] ICR 144 where discrimination was justified on hygienic grounds, was cited as a good example of justification providing an acceptable defence.

European Community Law

C J GREENWOOD, MA, LLB
Fellow of Magdalene College, Cambridge

Introduction

The All England Law Reports for 1983 contain only a few decisions on European Community law, none of which rival the constitutional significance of *Garland v British Rail Engineering Ltd* [1982] 2 All ER 402 (Elias, All ER Rev 1982, pp 115–6) on the relationship between Community law and English law. Nevertheless, the procedural aspects of that relationship are explored in a number of decisions, while the two most important cases—the judgment of the Court of Justice of the European Communities in Case 155/79 *A M & S Europe Ltd v Commission of the European Communities* [1983] 1 All ER 705 and the decision of the House of Lords in *Garden Cottage Foods Ltd v Milk Marketing Board* [1983] 2 All ER 770—are of considerable significance for the enforcement of Community competition law.

The A M & S case

A M & S Europe Ltd v Commission of the European Communities raised the question of how, if at all, Community law gives effect to a concept known in English law as legal professional privilege. The question arose in the context of an investigation by the Commission under EC Council Regulation 17 into alleged violations of the rules on competition law contained in arts 85 and 86 of the EEC Treaty. Article 14 of Regulation 17 empowers the Commission "to examine the books and other business records" of an undertaking which is the subject of an investigation. In the course of an investigation into the activities of A M & S Europe Ltd (the applicants), the Commission inspectors demanded production of certain documents in the applicants' possession, which the applicants maintained were protected by legal professional privilege. The documents fell into three categories (see at 726):
  (i) requests for legal advice;
  (ii) documents containing legal advice; and
  (iii) documents summarising legal advice.
Some of the lawyers involved in giving and summarising the legal advice were in private practice. Others were 'in house' lawyers employed by the applicants or by another company in the same group. The applicants brought proceedings under art 173 of the EEC Treaty, challenging the validity of a Commission decision ordering disclosure of the documents.

Initially, the case proceeded on the basis that the only issue between the parties related to the procedure for establishing whether particular documents were privileged, for the Commission had conceded the principle that certain types of document giving or seeking legal advice should not be used as evidence in its investigations. However, it gradually became clear that considerable differences existed about the legal basis for withholding such documents and about the scope and extent of legal professional privilege in

Commission proceedings. In addition, important questions of principle were raised by the interveners in the case, the French Republic, denying that Community law recognised any concept of legal professional privilege, while the Consultative Committee of the Bars and Law Societies of Europe (CCBE) maintained that the right to confidential communication between lawyer and client was a fundamental human right which the Community was obliged to respect (on the protection of human rights in Community law, see M H Mendelson 'The European Court of Justice and Human Rights' (1981) 1 Yearbook of European Law 125) and the United Kingdom strongly supported the applicants' arguments. In the end the Court decided that the questions of principle had to be fully argued and they were discussed by the parties, the interveners and two advocates-general (Warner and Slynn). There were, therefore, three issues before the Court:

(i) did Community law recognise a principle of legal confidentiality; and if it did

(ii) what was the scope of that principle; and

(iii) how should a dispute about its application in a particular case be resolved? (at 728).

On the first question, since no express provision on legal confidentiality appeared in the EEC Treaty or Community legislation, if such a principle existed in Community law, it had to be because it was one of the general principles of law recognised by the laws of the member states. While some recognition of the principle of legal confidentiality existed in the laws of all the member states (see A-G Slynn, at 729–33), there was considerable divergence over the legal basis for this principle (eg whether it was a right of the client or a duty of the lawyer) and the means by which effect was given to it. This led France to argue that there was too much disparity amongst the national laws for any general principle to be derived from them. The Court, however, accepted A-G Slynn's submission that these differences of detail did not prevent the general principle that communications between lawyer and client should be protected from forming part of Community law, and held that Regulation 17 had to be interpreted as respecting that principle (at 742, paras 18–22). The Court also accepted A-G Slynn's submission that the basis of the principle was the right of the individual to turn to his lawyer for advice (para 23, p 742), rather than any right of the lawyer. The judgment thus rejected the idea that there was a distinction between documents found in the hands of the lawyer and those found in the hands of the client.

Nevertheless, when it came to determine the scope of the principle of legal confidentiality in Community law, the Court adopted a more restrictive approach than that suggested by the two advocates-general. It noted that protection of legal confidentiality was common ground amongst national laws only insofar as it was subject to two restrictions. First, the communication had to be for the purposes of the client's 'right of defence', that is to say, in the context of actual or prospective litigation. The privilege against production under Regulation 17 was therefore confined to communications between lawyer and client after proceedings under Regulation 17 had been commenced and to earlier communications related to the subject matter of the investigation. However, the Court's application of this test to the facts of the case before it demonstrated that this first requirement is not unduly restrictive. Most of the documents whose disclosure was in issue had been drawn up in 1972 or early 1973 when the applicants had taken legal advice about the likely effects of the United Kingdom's entry into the EEC and the consequent application of Community competition law in the United Kingdom on certain aspects of their operations. The advice had been sought because the applicants thought they might be subjected to a Commission investigation, but that investigation did not, in fact, take place until 1978. Nevertheless, the Court held that the first requirement was satisfied (at 744, paras 33–4).

The second requirement, however, has proved more controversial. The Court held that the principle of legal confidentiality protected only communications with independent lawyers, ie 'lawyers who are not bound to the client by a relationship of employment' (at 742, paras 21 and 24). The exclusion of communications with 'in house' lawyers from the scope of legal confidentiality is particularly surprising since both the Commission and A–G Slynn had accepted that no distinction should be drawn between employed and independent lawyers so long as they were subject to the same rules of professional conduct and the same degree of professional supervision. The only justification advanced by the Court was a brief statement that the protection of legal confidentiality was based on a conception of the lawyer's role as that of an independent advisor whose duty was to the administration of justice as well as to his client and whose conduct was subject to professional ethics and discipline (at 742, para 24). While communications with an employed lawyer who is not subject to any professional code clearly ought to be outside the scope of privilege, this passage in the judgment is scarcely a sufficient response to the advocate-general's submissions in respect of employed lawyers who are subject to proper professional supervision. Nevertheless, the Commission has refused to mitigate the effect of the judgment on in house lawyers either by an administrative concession or by legislation (Commission Practice Note, Bull EC 6–1983, point 2.1.60; noted, Faull (1983) 8 EL Rev 411). One of the reasons advanced by the Commission, which may help to explain the Court's decision, is that the degree to which employed lawyers are subject to professional codes varies considerably from state to state. If communications with in house lawyers were to be privileged in some states but not in others, the conduct of competition investigations would be no longer the same throughout the Community.

The Court also added a further restriction peculiar to Community law. While it held that the nationality and place of residence of a lawyer within the Community was irrelevant for the purposes of application of the doctrine of confidentiality, the doctrine would not apply unless the lawyer was entitled to practise his profession in one of the member states. Communications with non-EEC lawyers were not protected from the Commission's right of investigation (at 743–4, paras 25–6). In its Practice Note (see above) the Commission has attempted to alleviate the concern aroused, especially in the United States, by this aspect of the decision by stating an intention of negotiating agreements with non-Community states for protection of legal communications on a basis of reciprocity.

On the question of the procedure by which disputes over claims to legal professional privilege were to be resolved, the Court was faced with a dilemma attributable in part to the inquisitorial procedure of the Commission. The Commission had argued that the decision whether or not a particular document was privileged had to be taken by the Commission inspector and that, in the last resort, this entailed a right to examine the entire document. The applicants, not surprisingly, contended that such disputes should be resolved by reference to a third party and suggested the use of an independent expert or arbitrator, while A-G Warner suggested that the matter should be determined by the appropriate national court. The Court was clear that the proposals put forward by A-G Warner and the applicants were unacceptable. Decisions in disputes of this kind would have a major effect on the enforcement by the Community of a vital area of Community law and had therefore to be resolved at a Community, rather than a national level (para 30, p 743). The Court's solution was to find that the power to adjudicate on claims of privilege belonged to the Commission but that an aggrieved party could challenge a decision ordering production of documents by bringing proceedings before the Court of Justice. Although such proceedings would not automatically suspend the Commission decision, the Court has power to grant interim measures of protection in an appropriate case. The Court's reference to this power was clearly an attempt to answer the Commission's arguments about the delay inherent in such a procedure while also reassuring the applicants. While it is difficult to see that the Court could have decided the point differently, this aspect of the decision is likely to prove fertile ground for future litigation.

For further discussion of the A M & S decision, see Ghandhi (1982) 7 EL Rev 308; Boyd, ibid, p 493; Faull (1983) 8 EL Rev 15; Duffy (1982) 132 NLJ 580 and Forrester (1983) 20 CMLR 75. On general principles of law in Community law, see Hartley *Foundations of European Community Law* (1980), Ch 5 and Akehurst (1981) 52 BYIL 29.

Relationship between Community law and English law

1 *Garden Cottage Foods Ltd v Milk Marketing Board [1983] 2 All ER 770, HL*

Although this case only came before the House of Lords on an interlocutory appeal, their lordships' decision has been hailed as a 'milestone in the integration of the United Kingdom into the legal system of the European Communities' (editorial, (1983) 8 EL Rev 219). The importance of the decision is that it goes a long way to establishing that there is a remedy in damages in the English courts for breach of art 86 of the EEC Treaty (which prohibits the abuse of a dominant position within the Common Market or a substantial part thereof). The Court of Justice of the European Communities decided some time ago that art 86 has direct effect and confers upon individuals rights which the national courts must enforce (Case 127/73 *Belgische Radio en Televisie v S V SABAM* [1974] ECR 51). The choice of procedure and remedies remains however, a matter for the national courts. Yet until the *Garden Cottage Foods* case, there was very little indication of what remedies might be available to the victim of art 86, apart from a dictum of Lord Denning MR in *Application des Gaz SA v Falks Veritas Ltd* [1974] 3 All ER 51 at 58 to the effect that arts 85 and 86 created new torts for which the English courts would use 'the remedies which we have available', a proposition which had been doubted, also obiter, by Roskill LJ in *Valor International Ltd v Application des Gaz SA* [1978] 3 CMLR 87. The decision of the House of

Lords is therefore likely to be of considerable importance.

The action arose out of a decision by the Milk Marketing Board to confine its sales of 'bulk butter' to four independent distributors. Prior to this decision, the plaintiff had purchased large quantities of bulk butter from the Board, most of which it had then resold to a Dutch customer. The plaintiff alleged that the effect of the Board's decision was to make it impossible for the plaintiff to continue with its business. 90% of its bulk butter had been purchased from the Board, which was much the largest supplier in the country, and the plaintiff maintained that it could not purchase bulk butter from any of the distributors now supplied by the Board at a price which allowed it to resell at a profit. The plaintiff brought an action against the Board alleging that the Board's refusal to continue supplying it with butter violated art 86 of the EEC Treaty and seeking an injunction, restraining the Board from withholding supplies from the plaintiff, and damages. The plaintiff also sought an interlocutory injunction. Parker J was prepared to accept that the plaintiff had made out an arguable case that the Board was in breach of art 86 but, following *American Cynamid Co v Ethicon* [1975] 1 All ER 504, he refused to grant an interlocutory injunction on the ground, inter alia, that damages would be an adequate remedy. This decision was reversed by the Court of Appeal ([1982] 3 All ER 292), largely because of doubts about whether a remedy in damages was necessarily available for a breach of art 86. Although Lord Denning MR and May LJ both expressed the view that damages ought to be available, the Court of Appeal considered it possible that the court would eventually decide that the only available remedy was a permanent injunction and were thus unwilling to refuse the plaintiff an interlocutory injunction in case damages turned out to be unavailable in this kind of action. The Court of Appeal also disagreed with some of the other grounds for Parker J's decision.

The decision of the Court of Appeal was in turn reversed by the House of Lords. Lord Diplock (with whom three other members of the House agreed), reiterating what he had said in *Hadmor Productions Ltd v Hamilton* [1982] 1 All ER 1042 (Elias All ER Rev 1982, pp 118–20), held that the Court of Appeal would only have been entitled to interfere with the judge's exercise of his discretion if it considered that his decision had been based on a misunderstanding of the law. Since the only question of law on which the Court of Appeal appeared to differ from Parker J was whether he had been right to assume that a remedy in damages existed for violation of art 86, that issue was central to the case. As art 86 has direct effect, the rights which it creates are 'enforceable Community rights' to which s 2(1) of the European Communities Act 1972 requires the English courts to give effect. Lord Diplock was not prepared categorically to state that a remedy in damages was therefore available for a breach of art 86 which inflicted loss on its victim but he did say that it would be difficult to argue that such a breach did not give rise to a cause of action of the nature of an action for breach of statutory duty. He also considered the proposition that such a breach might give rise to a cause of action for which an injunction would be the only remedy to be 'quite unarguable' (at 777 h–j). Such a cause of action would be entirely new to English law. Since Parker J had not therefore misunderstood the law, his original order had to be reinstated.

Two aspects of this case require further comment. First, there is a sense in which the decision of the House of Lords is indeed a milestone and a very welcome one. For far too long there has been a tendency to regard European Community law as somehow being in the English legal world but not of it, a set of rules of which the English courts were required to take notice but which were quite distinct from the familiar world of torts, contracts, commercial law and the like. Although the House of Lords did not finally determine that breach of art 86 of the EEC Treaty can give rise to an action for breach of statutory duty, it is now unlikely that the courts will decide otherwise. Community law is thus at last becoming properly incorporated into the mainstream of English law. The decision is, of course, of considerable significance for the future enforcement of arts 85 and 86 of the Treaty and, as such, will probably be welcomed by the Commission whose resources are constantly under strain as a result of the increasing volume of complaints of violation of Community competition law. It also, however, raises questions about the enforcement of other provisions of the Treaty which impose obligations on individuals as well as on member states. Will a remedy in damages now be held to exist in respect of a breach of eg art 119 (equal pay) or the provisions on free movement of workers?

Secondly, however, it should be noted that the decision is not an unmixed blessing. As Professor Jacobs has pointed out ((1983) 8 EL Rev 353), the United States experience in awarding damages for breaches of competition laws is not altogether a happy one. Moreover, the availability of a remedy in damages for breaches of art 86 has its disadvantages for the enforcement of Community competition law. As Lord Wilberforce said in his dissenting opinion in *Garden Cottage Foods*, the only remedies provided by Community law itself are orders restraining future violations and fines, which are not paid to the injured party. The existence of a different and, in some cases, more attractive, national remedy, the availability of which will vary between member states may, lead to less uniform enforcement of the competition provisions throughout the Community. Ironically, the remedy which national courts are far better equipped than the Community institutions to provide, and the practical absence of which is a weakness in the existing structure for the enforcement of competition law, is interlocutory relief (see the statement by the Commission quoted by Lord Denning MR [1982] 3 All ER 292 at 298).

2 *R v Goldstein [1983] 1 All ER 434, HL*

The defendant had been convicted of importing into the United Kingdom 'citizens' band' radio sets, the manufacture and importation of which was forbidden by statutory instrument. The only issue at the trial had been whether the ban on imports of the sets was contrary to art 30 of the EEC Treaty (which prohibits quantitative restrictions on imports and measures having equivalent effect) and thus of no effect insofar as it applied to imports from other member states. Since the ban clearly fell within the terms of art 30, the case turned on whether the ban could be justified under art 36 on grounds of public policy, public security or the protection of health and life of humans. The burden of establishing that the measure was justified rested on the prosecution, which was required to show not only that the ban was intended to achieve one or more of the objectives listed in art 36 but also (1) that those objectives could not have been achieved by less restrictive means, and (ii) that the measures adopted were not disproportionate to the ends they were designed to achieve. The judge treated all these issues as issues of law and heard evidence in the absence of the jury about the dangerous effect which the radio sets would produce (eg interference with aircraft landing systems, communications etc). He then ruled that the ban was justified under art 36 and the defendant was convicted. He appealed, contending that the judge should have directed the jury as to the correct interpretation of arts 30 and 36 and left it to the jury to determine on the evidence whether the ban was reasonably necessary in order to achieve the art 36 objectives.

The Court of Appeal [1982] 3 All ER 53 (Bennett, All ER Rev 1982, p 99) and the House of Lords dismissed the appeal. The question whether a particular ban on imports was reasonably necessary under art 36 was a question on the 'meaning or effect' of a provision of the EEC Treaty and was thus to be treated as a question of law under s 3(1) of the European Communities Act 1972. It made no difference that it was necessary to call evidence to establish whether the ban was proportionate to the objective and whether that objective could have been achieved by other means. Nor did it make any difference that the issue had only arisen on a submission of no case to answer made at the close of the prosecution's case. The question whether the ban was justified under art 36 was decisive of whether an offence of importing these radio sets from another member state still existed. It was therefore pre-eminently a question of law.

References to the Court of Justice of the European Communities

The guidelines laid down by Lord Denning MR in *HP Bulmer Ltd v J Bollinger SA* [1974] 2 All ER 1226 concerning the circumstances in which it will be appropriate for an English court to refer questions to the Court of Justice under art 177(2) of the EEC Treaty have received further attention in *Customs & Excise Commissioners v ApS Samex* [1983] 1 All ER 1042 (Bingham J). The case concerned the conditions imposed in a licence for the import of yarn from Sourth Korea granted by the United Kingdom authorities under powers contained in EC Council Regulation 3059/78. The defendant sought a reference to the Court of Justice to determine the proper intepretation of the regulation and the scope of the powers which it left to the member states. Bingham J applied the criteria set out by Lord Denning MR in deciding (a) whether a decision on a question of Community law was necessary to enable him to give a judgment, and (b) whether he should exercise his discretion to order that a reference be made. He answered both questions in the affirmative. The interest of the case lies in Bingham J's application of two of the *Bulmer v Bollinger* guidelines relating to the judge's exercise of his discretion.

In *Bulmer v Bollinger* Lord Denning MR had said that, in deciding whether or not to order a reference, the court should consider the difficulty of the question of Community law raised; unless the point was 'really difficult and important it would seem better for the English judge to decide it himself' ([1974] 2 All ER 1226 at 1236). In applying this test Bingham J was clearly of the view that the Court of Justice was better equipped to decide questions of Community law, since it had procedural advantages, a panoramic view of the Community and the different legal traditions of member states and greater familiarity with the application of Community law. In particular, he held that "the choice between alternative submissions may turn not on purely legal considerations but on a broader view of what the orderly development of the Community requires" ([1983] 1 All ER 1042 at 1056) which the Court of Justice was far better placed to determine. It is submitted that this approach is clearly correct and that English courts should be very wary of holding that it would be better for them to decide a point of Community law for themselves.

Lord Denning MR also required the courts to balance the delay and expense of a reference against the wishes of the parties. While Bingham J accepted that a reference should not be made simply because one party intended to appeal against a refusal to refer questions to the Court of Justice, he emphasised that if a case went to the Court of Appeal and a reference was then ordered, the expense would be far greater than if the reference had been made by the trial court. Provided that the facts had been established or agreed, there was much to be said for the trial court ordering a reference if it considered it necessary, even though one of the parties objected. Although Bingham J was sensitive to the dangers of overloading the Court of Justice, his decision is a welcome indication of a greater willingness on the part of the English courts to make use of art 177(2).

Evidence

ADRIAN A S ZUCKERMAN, LLM, MA
Fellow of University College, Oxford

Expert evidence

The opinion rule, it is generally assumed, forbids witnesses to testify to their opinions; they must confine themselves to statements of fact. As an exception to this rule, when the determination of an issue of fact calls for special skill or knowledge, an expert on such matters may give his opinion so as to assist the court to adjudicate on the issue. The rule and its exception presuppose, therefore, that a distinction between a statement of fact and a statement of opinion is a feasible one. Two cases this year draw attention to the artificiality of this assumption.

In *R v Abadom* [1983] 1 All ER 364, on a charge of robbery, the issue was the identity of tiny glass fragments found on the accused's shoes. According to the prosecution they came from a pane of glass which the robbers broke during the robbery. Expert A gave evidence to the effect that he had carried out an experiment on the fragments of glass found on the accused and on the control sample which came from the scene of the crime and found them both to have an identical refracture index. Expert B then testified that he had studied the statistics of the refractive index of broken glass collated by the Home Office from reported experiments made by forensic laboratories. From these, expert B concluded that the particular refractive index of the glass in question occurred in only 4% of all the samples analysed. The defence objected to the reliance on these statistics on the grounds that they constituted hearsay (for discussion of hearsay see p 204 below).

Counsel for the defendant argued that an expert should not be entitled to rely for his conclusions on reports of fact about which he had no personal knowledge. The Court of Appeal rejected this argument for the common-sense reason that—as Kerr LJ put it—

> '. . . to exclude reliance on such information on the ground that it is inadmissible under the hearsay rule might inevitably lead to the distortion or unreliability of the opinion which the expert presents for the evaluation by a judge or jury' ([1983] 1 All ER at 367).

The court therefore concluded that—

> 'In the context of evidence given by experts it is no more than a statement of the obvious that, in reaching their conclusion, they must be entitled to draw on material produced by others in the field in which their expertise lies' (at 367).

It is, however, to be noted that there is no magical difference between the fact of the refractive index of the glass in question—which had to be proved by admissible evidence—and the refractive index of the glass examined in the reported experiments that gave rise to the statistics, and on which the expert was allowed to rely without the need of proof by admissible evidence. Facts from which statistics are derived are not any the less facts because the expert

draws a general conclusion from them; they cannot be said to be opinion—
they are the foundation for opinion. The reason why the facts in this last
category need not be proved in the ordinary way is this. Their importance
does not lie in the accuracy of each individual fact reported but in the general
pattern that emerges from the accumulation and totality of such facts. This
totality is not likely to be distorted by a mistake here and there. The
generality that the expert derives from statistical data is not really different
from the generalisations we form about ordinary affairs, such as those
concerning recent possession of stolen goods, or silence in the face of a direct
accusation. By contrast, the refractive index of the glass in question is crucial
in the litigation, and a mistake about it may make all the difference between
acquittal and conviction. It is right, therefore, that we should insist here on
admissible evidence. Kerr LJ put it as follows:

> '. . . where the expert relies on the existence or non-existence of some fact which
> is basic to the question on which he is asked to express his opinion that fact must
> be proved by admissible evidence . . .' ([1983] 1 All ER at 368).

A similar distinction arises from *H v Schering Chemicals Ltd* [1983] 1 All ER
849. The plaintiffs sued for damages for personal injuries allegedly caused by
the negligence of the defendants in the marketing and manufacturing of a
drug. The plaintiff proposed to adduce as evidence summaries of research
done in various institutions, articles in medical journals, letters from practitioners published in journals and the like. Brightman J held that such documents were inadmissible as being hearsay. At the same time he indicated that
these materials could be referred to by experts 'as part of the general corpus of
medical knowledge falling within the expertise of an expert in this field' (at
853). His Lordship then explained that even though the facts reported in the
articles were not strictly proved they were none the less of probative value as
forming part of the experts' general knowledge.

(For a discussion of the function of expert psychiatric evidence concerning
the accused's veracity see *R v Mackenney and Pinford* (1983) 76 Cr App R 271).

The burden of proof

i *Proof of handwriting*

The golden thread of the English criminal law—that the accused's guilt must
be proved beyond reasonable doubt—has been reinforced by the decision in
R v Ewing [1983] 2 All ER 645. The issue in this case was the interpretation of
s 8 of the Criminal Procedure Act 1865 which provides:

> 'Comparison of the disputed writing with any writing proved to the satisfac-
> tion of the judge to be genuine shall be permitted to be made by the witness, and
> such writings, and the evidence of witnesses respecting the same, may be
> submitted to the court and jury as evidence of the genuineness or otherwise of
> the writing in dispute.'

It had been held by Court of Appeal in *R v Angeli* [1978] 3 All ER 950 that
when a writing is adduced for the purpose of comparison, under s 8, its
genuineness need only be established on the balance of probabilities. This
ruling, as O'Connor LJ pointed out in *Ewing* (at 653), could have resulted in
an accused being convicted when his guilt had not been proved beyond

reasonable doubt. This might happen as follows. The prosecution alleges that the disputed writing is in the accused's hand. The prosecution then proceeds to establish the identity of the handwriting by comparison with a sample, the genuineness of which is proved merely on the balance of probability. It could not then be said that the accused's guilt has been made out beyond reasonable doubt. In *Ewing* the court felt free to depart from the decision in *Angeli* since it considered it to have been decided per incuriam. In *Angeli* the court proceeded on the assumption that the words, 'writing proved to the satisfaction of the judge to be genuine' in s 8 of the 1865 Act, were intended by the legislature to indicate the standard of proof required on the issue. Since s 8 applied equally to civil cases as well as to criminal ones, and since the words of the statute cannot bear different meanings in different contexts, the court in *Angeli* concluded that the standard indicated by s 8 was the balance of probabilities. But the above assumption was contrary, as O'Connor LJ explained in *Ewing* (at 651–2), to the House of Lords' decision in *Blyth v Blyth* [1966] 1 All ER 524 where it had been held, in a different context, that a section requiring a party to 'satisfy' a judge merely indicates that that party bears the burden of proof, and does not suggest any particular standard. Applying this authority, O'Connor LJ said—

> 'the words in s 8 of the 1865 Act, "any writing proved to the satisfaction of the judge to be genuine", do not say anything about the standard of proof to be used, but direct that it is the judge, and not the jury, who is to decide, and the standard of proof is governed by the common law . . .' (at 653).

His Lordship then concluded that in criminal cases the standard was always the ordinary criminal standard of proof beyond reasonable doubt, though when s 8 applied in civil cases the standard will be the civil standard.

ii *Presumption of recent possession*

The scope of the presumption of recent possession was considered in *R v Ball* [1983] 2 All ER 1089, which is discussed in the article on Criminal Law (p 149, above).

iii *Habeas corpus and the nature of proof beyond reasonable doubt*

The principle that guilt must be proved beyond reasonable doubt if it is to warrant a conviction, can be weakened not only by the creation of exceptions but also, and perhaps more insidiously, by blurring the distinction between proof beyond reasonable doubt and proof on the balance of probabilities. Yet this is exactly the outcome of certain dicta by Lord Scarman in *Khawaja v Secretary of State for the Home Office* [1983] 1 All ER 765. One of the issues before the House of Lords concerned the standard of proof borne by the executive in habeas corpus proceedings when it is called upon to make out the legality of the detention of an individual. There had been some authority both for the view that the legality was to be established beyond reasonable doubt and for the view that it needed only to be shown on the balance of probabilities. Lord Scarman, it would appear, considers the difference to be of little importance, for he said (at 783)—

'My Lords, I have come to the conclusion that the choice between the two standards is not one of any great moment. It is largely a matter of words.'

He drew on the Court of Appeal's decision in *Bates v Bates* [1950] 2 All ER 458 in order to pose the rhetorical question: 'If a court has to be satisfied, how can it at the same time entertain a reasonable doubt?' (at 783). But the view implied in this dictum (ie that satisfaction is not a matter of degree) is inconsistent with another view adopted by Lord Scarman from *Bates v Bates* (at 459) to the effect that there are varying degrees of probability within the standard of preponderance of probability, and that the degree of probability required in any given case depends on the gravity of the matter. If the degree of probability can vary, so can the degree of satisfaction. His Lordship himself seemed to be accepting this when he went on to conclude (at 784):

'. . . where the burden lies on the executive to justify the exercise of a power of detention, the facts relied on as justification must be proved to the satisfaction of the court. A preponderance of probability suffices; but the degree of probability must be such that the court is satisfied. The strictness of the criminal formula is unnecessary to enable justice to be done; and its lack of flexibility in a jurisdiction where the technicalities of the law of evidence must not be allowed to become the master of the court could be a positive disadvantage inhibiting the efficacy of the developing safeguard of judicial review in the field of public law.'

This is a most ominous pronouncement. It seems to relegate the golden thread, the requirement that guilt be proved beyond reasonable doubt, to a mere inflexible technicality of the law of evidence. In fact there is nothing technical about this requirement. It is designed to be understood by ordinary laymen. It requires the jury to apply a method of reasoning with which they are familiar from ordinary affairs of life. The standard implies that guilt is proved if, and only if, all explanations of the facts that are consistent with innocence have been rejected by them. An hypothesis of innocence must not be rejected as long as there is some real, appreciable, possibility—however small—that the hypothesis is right. Where no reasonable (ie really appreciable) doubt can be entertained about innocence, guilt has been established beyond reasonable doubt. Why this method of reasoning, exercised daily by juries, should be too complicated for judges to apply in habeas corpus cases, it is difficult to comprehend. Unless, of course, the House of Lords wishes to impose a lighter burden of justification on the executive. But if this is—as it seems to be—the case, should we not be told, openly and directly, that the executive may restrain the freedom of the individual even where the facts justifying the restriction are not conclusively established?

This case is also discussed in the article on Administrative Law, pp 15 and 17 above.

Character of the accused

(i) *Section 1(f)(ii) of the Criminal Evidence Act 1898*

One of the worst features of English criminal justice is s 1(f)(ii) of the Criminal Evidence Act 1898. It lays down that an accused giving evidence in his own defence may be cross-examined on his criminal record if

'the nature or conduct of the defence is such as to involve imputations on the character of the prosecutor or the witnesses for the prosecution . . . '

An accused who denies the incriminating evidence given by the witness for the prosecution may lay himself open to cross-examination on his record. This, in turn, may prejudice him to such an extent as to render a conviction inevitable. Why, one may ask, should a denial of the offence which, if true, would suggest that the witnesses for the prosecution have committed perjury, justify bringing the accused's record into the open? The answer seems to be: tit-for-tat, or as Lawton LJ explained in *R v Britzman* [1983] 1 All ER 369—

> 'When allegations of the fabrication of evidence are made against prosecution witnesses, as they are these days, juries are entitled to know about the characters of those making them' (at 372, cf *R v Paraskey* (1983) 76 Cr App R 162).

Applied to confessions, this doctrine has serious consequences. If the accused denies having confessed to the police, the implication necessarily being that the police officers are lying, the prosecution may thereupon cross-examine the accused on his previous convictions. If our sense of justice is usually outraged by the suggestion that previous convictions should be laid on the scales on a charge for an offence wholly unconnected with previous offences, should the same not occur where such convictions are introduced when the accused argues that he did not make the confession alleged by the prosecution? Even in this last case there is no good reason for exempting the prosecution from its normal duty of establishing its case without appeal to prejudice. Moreover, the revelation of a criminal record in these circumstances makes it easier for the unscrupulous policeman (though rare, not an unknown phenomenon) to fabricate evidence against persons with previous convictions. Sadly, however, since *Selvey v DPP* [1968] 2 All ER 497 the courts have found it difficult to ameliorate the injustice of s 1(f)(ii) of the 1898 Act. The absence of any change of heart in this respect may be observed in *Britzman*. Britzman was charged with burglary. The evidence against him consisted of two incriminating statements alleged by the police to have been made by him; one during interrogation, the other while conducting a shouted conversation with his co-accused who was being detained in a separate cell. Britzman's defence was simply to deny that the alleged interrogation took place or that he had shouted the alleged words. The trial judge thought that notwithstanding the delicacy shown by the accused and his counsel in denying the police officers' evidence, imputations against their character were made and the proof of previous convictions under s 1(f)(ii) was allowed. On appeal Britzman's counsel conceded that s 1(f)(ii) sanctioned such course, but argued that the judge had wrongly exercised his discretion in allowing the accused's record to be adduced. He referred to the practice of some judges in exercising their discretion against admissibility where the defence refrained from making specific allegations of misconduct; a practice with which Lawton LJ was familiar (at 372).

The Court of Appeal has now put paid to this practice. It held that where the defence's case is that the confession was not made, it amounts to an allegation that the policemen made up the confession, and that, in turn, involves an imputation on the characters of the officers. Lawton LJ then went on to explain—

'If in any case that is the reality of the position and would be seen by the jury to be so, there is no room for drawing a distinction between a defence which is so conducted as to make specific allegations of fabrication and one in which the allegation arises by way of necessary and reasonable implication' (at 372–3).

In so holding the court preferred the forthright approach adopted in *R v Tanner* (1977) 66 Cr App R 56 and in *McGee v Cassidy* (1979) 70 Cr App R 247 to the more tortuous, but also more liberal, reasoning in *R v Nelson* (1978) 68 Cr App R 12. In the latter case the Court of Appeal was prepared to hold that a denial of the making of a confession amounted—in the words of Lord Dilhorne in *Selvey v DPP* [1968] 2 All ER 497, 508—'to no more than a denial of the charge . . . in emphatic language', and was not to be considered as an imputation on the police. It cannot, of course, be denied that logically there is little, if any, difference between a direct allegation that the police officers have concocted the confession and are perjuring themselves in adducing it at the trial, and a denial by the defence that the confession has never been made. The latter entails the former in most circumstances. But such distinction— however tenuous—has the advantage of reducing the injustice of s 1(f)(ii).

A little bit of illogicality is perhaps preferable to a great deal of injustice; especially as some illogicality is inevitable in the interpretation of s 1(f)(ii), if one is not to give way completely to the potential harshness and arbitrariness of the section. Indeed, Lawton LJ himself could not acquit himself completely of drawing artificial distinctions. While holding that no distinction can be drawn between an allegation that the policemen committed perjury and one that they conspired to commit perjury he found it necessary to allow that—

'when an allegation is one of perjury only, discretion may have to be exercised in favour of the defendant more readily than with a conspiracy allegation, having regard to what was said by Viscount Dilhorne in *Selvey*' (at 373).

Nor are the other guidelines set out by the Court of Appeal for the exercise of discretion free from illogicality. Lawton LJ said that where the accused denies making only a brief incriminating statement, such as: 'Who grassed on me this time?', his denial would not amount to an imputation. But, according to his Lordship, the position would be different if the denial is of a long and detailed interrogation (at 373–4). Since in both instances the accused implies perjury by the police, it is not easy to see why the fabrication of a short statement is less perjurous than a long one. Another guideline suggests that permission to introduce previous convictions pursuant to s 1(f)(ii) should not be given where the evidence against the defendant is overwhelming (at 374). It seems paradoxical that the courts should be prepared to show sensitivity to the demands of justice only when a conviction is otherwise secure.

Section 1(f)(ii), it may be suggested, brings our criminal justice into disrepute and it is regrettable that the Court of Appeal found it necessary to treat it with greater respect than it deserves.

Yet not all is bad in this respect. We also have a clear indication from another panel of the Court of Appeal, that the judiciary is beginning to appreciate the mischief caused by the rule that denial of a confession can result in licence to resort to the accused's criminal record. In *R v Watts* [1983] 3 All ER 101 the accused was charged with indecent assault on a woman. He was not identified by the complainant, but as the complainant's description fitted him generally and as he had a record for sexual assaults, he was interviewed by the police. The prosecution adduced incriminating statements allegedly made by the accused at this interview. In evidence the accused denied the attack and denied making the statement attributed to him. Whereupon the prosecution was given leave under s 1(f)(ii) of the 1898 Act to cross-examine him on his record. It then transpired that the accused had committed a number of offences of indecent assaults on very young girls. A conviction by the jury then followed.

It is well established that previous convictions are admissible under s 1(f)(ii) only as going to the credit of the accused and not as evidence that he committed the offence charged. The rationale of s 1(f)(ii) is, as we have seen, that if the accused makes derogatory imputations about the character of the prosecution's witnesses, then the jury should be told of the accused's own character so as to be able to deal fairly with his allegations against the witnesses. I argued in All ER Rev 1982, pp 128–131, that the distinction between relevance to the issue and relevance to credibility is misconceived and that any rule of law based on it is bound to do mischief. *Watts* seems to bear out this suggestion, for—as Lord Lane CJ pointed out—asking the jury not to infer guilt from previous convictions 'requires the jury to perform difficult feats of intellectual acrobatics' ([1983] 3 All ER at 104). This is so because the jury is bidden to ignore common sense, to side-step rational inference. The Lord Chief Justice made this point when he said:

> 'The jury in the present case was charged with deciding the guilt or innocence of a man against whom an allegation of indecent assault on a woman was made. They were told that he had previous convictions for indecent assaults of a more serious kind on young girls. They were warned that such evidence was not to be taken as making it more likely that he was guilty of the offence charged, which it seems it plainly did, but only as affecting his credibility, which it almost certainly did not' (at 104).

This dictum (it is submitted) is of considerable importance and potential, for it suggests a readiness on the part of the court to look at the real effect of the evidence and call a spade a spade. Once the court does this, and the pretence that the evidence is not really relevant to guilt is cast away, the court is in a position to give its attention to the crucial question: Did the evidence contribute to the correctness of the conviction, or did it create a risk of wrong conviction? In the case under consideration the court felt no hestitation in pronouncing that—

> 'The prejudice which the appellant must have suffered in the eyes of the jury when it was disclosed that he had previous convictions for offences against young children could hardly have been greater' (at 104).

The Lord Chief Justice indicated, however, that the result might have been different had the previous convictions involved dishonesty or had they involved such similarity as to be admissible as similar fact evidence. As evidence in this last category would have been admissible in chief, the question of applying s 1(f)(ii) does not arise. Where previous convictions involved dishonesty, however, the argument is somewhat more problematic. The argument presumably is that offences involving dishonesty would be relevant to the question of whether the accused should be believed on his oath. But even in this case admissibility would not be automatic, for the paramount test is the real effect of such evidence, as was suggested in *Maxwell v DPP* [1935] AC 309 at 321—

> '... the question whether a man has been convicted ... ought not to be admitted ... if there is any risk of the jury being misled into thinking that it goes not to credibility but to the probability of his having committed the offence of which he is charged.'

Once it is accepted, though, that previous offences should not be allowed to contribute to the probability that the accused committed the offence charged, very serious consideration should be given to whether they have any further legitimate function in the ascertainment of guilt and whether they should be admitted at all.

ii *Bias in trial judge or magistrate from knowledge of other misconduct by accused*

As we have seen, knowledge by the trier of fact of an accused's previous misconduct can seriously prejudice the accused. The rules concerning similar fact evidence are designed to reduce the danger of such prejudice. This rule is not concerned with situations where the trier of fact had heard of such misconduct before the commencement of the trial. That the law protects accused persons from such bias too may be seen from *R v Liverpool City Justices, ex p Topping* [1983] 1 All ER 490. The accused appeared before magistrates on a charge of criminal damage. The magistrates had been provided with computerised court sheets concerning the accused from which it appeared that charges of seven other, and wholly unconnected, offences were pending against the accused. Ackner LJ, in the Divisional Court, held that it was 'most undesirable that such a document should be put before the magistrates' (495). The court also decided that where, as here, allegations of bias have been made, the proper test to be applied was not a subjective one, the test was not directed to ascertaining whether the justices were actually prejudiced. The correct test according to Ackner LJ, is 'whether there is the appearance of bias, rather then whether there is actual bias' (at 494). Reliance was placed on *Allinson v General Council of Medical Education and Registration* [1894] 1 QB 750 and on *Metropolitan Properties Co v Lannon* [1968] 3 All ER 307, 310 where Lord Denning MR said:

> 'The court will not enquire whether he [the magistrate] did, in fact, favour one side unfairly. Suffice it that reasonable people might think he did. The reason is plain enough. Justice must be rooted in confidence and confidence is destroyed when right minded people go away thinking "the judge was biased".'

Ackner LJ concluded, therefore, that the crucial question was: 'would a reasonable and fair minded person sitting in the court and knowing all the relevant facts have a reasonable suspicion that a fair trial for the applicant was not possible?' (at 494). As the answer to this was in the affirmative the Divisional Court granted a declaration quashing the conviction.

A little later this decision came to be considered by the Court of Appeal in *R v Ewing* [1983] 2 All ER 645 where it was somewhat restricted in scope. Ewing was on trial for a large number of offences of theft and fraud. At the opening of the trial, the judge held a trial-within-a-trial to determine the admissibility of the accused's statements to the police. For some reason the judge was provided with a medical report containing hearsay statements suggesting that the accused had feigned mental illness in the past. When, during the voir dire, it appeared that the accused was behaving oddly in the witness box, the judge indicated that he was going to bear in mind the medical report. As the medical report had not formally been given in evidence and as it was in any event inadmissible, the accused argued the judge's reliance on it caused him to be biased. He relied in this respect on *R v Liverpool City Justices*, above. But the Court of Appeal distinguished this case on the ground that 'the position of the judge working with a jury on a trial on indictment in the Crown Court is different from that of justices trying a case as judges of fact' (per O'Connor LJ at 649).

While a difference exists in relation to issues of fact that are within the province of the jury, no such difference is present, it is suggested, in respect of issues of fact which are to be decided by the judge himself. O'Connor LJ observed that in the course of a jury trial many occasions arise where the judge hears facts that are discreditable to the accused, and yet it has never been held that this taints the judge with bias and disqualifies him from trying the defendant. Such occasions arise, his Lordship pointed out, when the judge determines questions of admissibility or when a co-accused has pleaded guilty and his statement blames the accused. Besides, he continued, it is desirable that the judge should know the accused's antecedents in order to be able to safeguard him against him accidentally throwing away his shield against cross-examination on past misconduct. All this is, of course, true but not quite comparable to the situation in hand. A distinction should be drawn between facts that are prejudicial because they suggest the accused's guilt generally, and facts which prejudice or bias the judge in respect of the very issue of fact which he has to decide himself. Facts which suggest guilt generally do not, by and large, disqualify a judge because it is not for him but for the jury to pronounce on guilt or innocence. However, it is quite another matter when the judge, as here, has to decide, in the voir dire, whether the accused is telling the truth, and he happens to have in front of him a report suggesting that the accused is a liar. Moreover, given the serious consequences to the accused from the judge's decision to admit a confession, it is particularly important that the process of the voir dire should be free from any suggestion of bias. It could therefore be argued that the limitation placed by the Court of Appeal in *Ewing* on the decision in *R v Liverpool City Justices* is not justified. Fortunately, however, the ratio of *Ewing* is somewhat weakened by the fact that the trial judge had already been informed by other, admissible, evidence of the accused's proclivity. Besides, the Court of Appeal expressed the view that it would have been better if the judge had not seen the report suggesting that the accused was a liar ([1983] 2 All ER at 649–650).

Hearsay

(i) *Narrowing scope of Myers v DPP*

In *Myers v DPP* [1964] 2 All ER 881 the House of Lords refused to make any concession to common sense in the application of the rule against hearsay. It preferred to leave its reform to the legislature. According to its traditional formulation the rule lays down that 'a statement other than one made by a person while giving oral evidence in the proceeding is inadmissible as evidence of any fact stated' (*Cross on Evidence* (5th edn, 1979) 462). In *Myers* the House of Lords decided that the rule must be strictly applied except where the situation comes under one of the recognised exceptions. As hopes for legislative reform faded, the decision became a serious obstacle to rational reasoning and the courts have begun contriving ways of circumventing it.

R v Shone (1983) 76 Cr App R 72 is such a case. The accused was charged with handling three car springs that were allegedly stolen from a spare-part firm. The prosecution called a clerk of the firm to produce the stock record, explain how it was kept and show that it contained no entry to the effect that the springs, which had admittedly been received by the firm, had been sold. From that the jury was to infer that the springs must have been stolen. The defence, relying on *Myers*, argued that the firm's records were hearsay. This argument was rejected by the Court of Appeal, drawing support from its decision in *R v Patel* [1981] 3 All ER 94. In this last case the issue was whether the accused was an intelligent entrant. The court decided that if the Home Office record of legal entrants is produced and if it does not include the accused's name, the inference may be drawn that the accused is an illegal entrant; provided that the record is produced by the person responsible for its compilation. Applying this reasoning in *Shore* the court held that the record produced by the firm's clerk—

> '. . . was not hearsay, but direct evidence from which the jury were entitled to draw the inference . . . that all three springs were stolen. If there had been only one spring found in the appellant's possession, which was traceable to Longs [the firm], the absence of a record of sale or legitimate disposal would have been evidently relatively insignificant . . . the absence of such a record in respect of all three of the springs which featured in this case was overwhelming' ((1983) 76 Cr App R at 76).

Fortunately, both *Patel* and *Shone* show little respect for *Myers v DPP*. Neither in *Patel* nor in *Shore* did the compilers of the record have, presumably, personal knowledge of the facts recorded in the entries. If the compiler of the Home Office record of legal entrants makes an entry of name A, this is because it was reported to him that A had lawfully entered, he himself never sees A nor personally checks his credentials. According to *Myers* an entry in the record of A's name cannot be given as evidence that A was a legal entrant. By the same token, it could be argued, absence of an entry in respect of an event which is normally recorded would also be inadmissible for the purposes of showing that the event did not take place.

This argument was ignored in a further case this year.

In *R v Abadom* [1983] 1 All ER 364, mentioned earlier in relation to expert evidence, the Court of Appeal reiterated its support for *Shone* and *Patel* saying that—

'. . . the bounds of that decision [*Myers v DPP*] appear to be still unsettled in cases of systematically compiled records where evidence about the conclusions to be drawn from such records is adduced from witnesses who were themselves concerned in their compilation in the ordinary course of their duties' (at 367–8).

If *Myers* is unsettled it is because the Court of Appeal sees now the necessity of limiting the scope of this decision. The necessity is indeed pressing and the Court of Appeal's recent rulings are therefore welcome. The courts seem willing now to concentrate on the circumstantial significance and reliability of the evidence rather than strictly and fruitlessly apply a technical rule from which the House of Lords refused to depart in *Myers*.

(ii) *Computer hearsay*

A great deal of information is nowadays stored in and dispensed by computers. The effect of the hearsay rule on the admissibility of such information is considered in *R v Ewing* [1983] 2 All ER 645 where the accused was charged with forgery and one of the issues was whether he had drawn a certain sum of money from his bank account. For proving this the prosecution adduced a computer print-out showing the state of the accused's bank account. It was decided that the print-out was admissible by virtue of s 1 of the Criminal Evidence Act 1965, because it was a document which was 'or formed part of a record relating to any trade or business', because it was a 'document' within s 1(4), because it was compiled from information supplied by persons who had personal knowledge within s 1(1)(a) and because such persons could not be reasonably expected to have any recollection of the matter within s 1(a)(b). *R v Pettigrew* (1980) 71 Cr App R 31 was distinguished on the ground that there nobody had any personal knowledge of the matters stored in the computer. Section 1 of the Criminal Evidence Act was also considered in *R v Wood* (1983) 76 Cr App R 23. (For admissibility of bankers' records under the Bankers' Books Evidence Act 1879 see *R v Dadson* (1983) 77 Cr App R 91.)

Public interest immunity

The House of Lords has again turned its attention to the principles involved in adjudicating on a claim of immunity from discovery of documents on the ground that disclosure would contraray to the public interest. The case in question is *Air Canada v Secretary of State for Trade* [1983] 1 All ER 910. It arose from a substantial increase of landing charges at Heathrow airport by the British Airports Authority (BAA). The BAA is a statutory body that owns and manages the airport, and is by statute subject to the financial supervision of the Secretary of State for Trade. A number of airlines (the plaintiffs) objected to the increase in charges. They brought an action against the Secretary of State, claiming that he had directed the BAA to increase landing charges for a purpose which was foreign to the proper exercise of his supervisory powers, namely, to reduce the public sector borrowing, and that in doing so the Secretary of State acted unlawfully and ultra vires. At the discovery stage the Secretary of State produced the documents passing between his department and BAA regarding the increase in charges, but he claimed public interest immunity for documents containing communications between government ministers and briefs, minutes and memoranda prepared for the use of ministers, all of which related to the formulation of government policy. This policy was concerned with BAA, with the limitation of the public sector borrowing and with the exercise by the Secretary of State of his power to control the BAA's borrowing.

The matter came before Bingham J who decided that as the documents were clearly relevant he would inspect them and would order their production if he came to the conclusion that they could assist the court to determine the true state of affairs. He thought that if the documents were found useful for that purpose, their production should be ordered even if they could only help the minister's case and not that of the plaintiffs. His decision was reversed by the Court of Appeal, with which the House of Lords was in broad agreement.

The starting point for the discussion must be, as the House acknowledged, *Conway v Rimmer* [1968] 1 All ER 874. It laid down that no documents were absolutely privileged or immune from discovery. It was for the court to decide, whenever a claim was made, whether the public interest demanded that documents should remain undisclosed. In determining this the court had to balance the public interest in non-disclosure against the cumulative weight of two factors; one general and one specific, the general factor being the public interest in the proper administration of justice and the specific factor being the harm that the individual litigant was likely to suffer from being unable to have recourse to the information in question.

There was no dispute concerning the public interest in non-disclosure. The documents in question in *Air Canada v Secretary of State for Trade* were concerned with the working of the Cabinet, and as Lord Fraser put it— '. . . while Cabinet documents do not have complete immunity, they are entitled to a high degree of protection against disclosure' ([1983] 1 All ER at 915). Similarly, Lord Wilberforce stated that the documents—

> '. . . relate directly to the making of decisions as to government policy in a sensitive area, viz the economic and financial policy of the government . . . and familiar contentions are put forward as to the need to protect them against disclosure in the interests of the confidentiality of the inner working of government and of the free and candid expression of views' (at 919).

That being the case, attention had then to be given to the other side of the equation—the public interest in the administration of justice and the potential harm to the litigant from non-disclosure. The documents were necessarily relevant, otherwise they would not have been listed by the Secretary of State in the list of documents. Moreover, Lord Fraser was prepared to assume that the documents were, in the words of RSC Ord 24, r 13, 'necessary . . . for disposing fairly of the cause', by the standard applicable where no public interest was involved (at 915). But this was not the end of the matter, for what was in dispute here was whether the interests of the litigant in obtaining access to the documents outweighed the public interest in secrecy.

How is the court to assess the likely effect of the production or non-production of a document on the outcome of the litigation? In some cases this may be obvious from the nature of the document. For example, the document may be merely a record of information which is otherwise publicly known. In many cases, however, it may not be evident that the documents are of little probative significance. In such cases the court could not possibly decide the significance of the document to the litigation without knowledge of its contents. It was for this reason that Bingham J proposed to inspect the documents for which immunity was claimed.

The House of Lords, however, took a different view. It held that before the court could inspect a document the party seeking production must surmount a hurdle; or as Lord Fraser explained—

> '. . . in order to persuade the court even to inspect documents for which public interest immunity is claimed, the party seeking disclosure ought at least to satisfy the court that the documents are very likely to contain material which would give substantial support to his contention on an issue which arises in the case, and that without them he might be "deprived of the means of . . . proper prosecution" of his case . . .' (at 917).

The rest of the House seems to have been in agreement on this point. But even this unanimity in the highest authority of the land cannot stifle the obvious question: How is a litigant to prove that a certain document is very likely to help his case when he has never seen it, when it is kept hidden in the drawer of his opponent's desk? To require a litigant to prove that which is known to his opponent but not to himself is not only to impose on him an unfair burden but also to undermine the balancing process and the whole edifice erected by *Conway v Rimmer*. Indeed, there are many passages in the speeches which confirm this impression and which suggest that the House is inclined to retreat from the liberal approach heralded by the *Conway* case.

While their lordships were in agreement that, before inspection by the judge, the party seeking discovery must establish that the documents were likely to affect the outcome of the case, there was a disagreement as to what it was that the party had to establish. As we have seen, Bingham J thought that it had to be established that the documents in question could help the court to determine the issue in dispute; that documents would have to be disclosed even where they could only help the case of the party resisting disclosure. The Court of Appeal disagreed and so did a majority of the House of Lords. Lords Wilberforce, Edmund-Davies and Fraser held that a party seeking discovery must prove that the documents were likely to advance his own case, that it was not enough that the document might help his opponent's case. Lord Wilberforce explained this as follows:

> 'In a contest purely between one litigant and another, such as the present, the task of the court is to do and be seen to be doing justice between the parties, a duty reflected by the word "fairly" in the rule [RSC Ord 24, r 13]. There is no higher or additional duty to ascertain some independent truth. It often happens, from the imperfection of evidence, or the withholding of it, sometimes by the party in whose favour it would tell, that an adjudication has to be made which is not, and is known not to be, the whole truth of the matter; yet, if the decision has been in accordance with the available evidence and with the law, justice will have been fairly done' (at 919).

The views expressed here give rise to important questions about justice in adjudication that are beyond the scope of the present review. It might, nevertheless, be observed that it is by no means clear that a court's judgment which fails to take into account material evidence can command public respect and confidence, especially where the existence of such evidence is generally known.

Lords Scarman and Templeman disagreed with the majority on this point.
They considered that a duty of discovery arises even though a document is
wholly favourable to the party resisting discovery. Lord Scarman explained
that discovery—

> '. . . assists parties and the court to discover the truth. By so doing, it not only
> helps towards a just determination: it also saves costs. A party who discovers
> timeously a document fatal to his case is assisted as effectively, although less to
> his liking, as one who discovers the winning card; for he can save himself and
> others the heavy costs of litigation' (at 925).

Quite apart from the theoretical difference between the approach of the
majority and the minority on this point, this difference of opinion is of
considerable practical importance. For under the majority's view the burden
falling on the party seeking discovery is much greater than it would be under
the minority approach. Given that the party seeking discovery does not
know what is in the document, he is likely to find it easier to show that the
document is likely to affect the case of one or the other of the parties than to
show that the unseen document is likely positively to advance his own case.
The combined effect of the majority's decision, that the party seeking discovery must prove the significance of the documents and that such significance
must be favourable to his own case, amounts to a reversal of the principle that
a party seeking to withhold documents from discovery bears the burden of
showing that the public interest so requires. This principle was pronounced
by Lord Edmund-Davies himself in *D v NSPCC* [1977] 1 All ER 589 where
he said:

> 'The disclosure of all evidence relevant to the trial of an issue being at all times a
> matter of considerable public interest, the question to be determined is whether
> it is clearly demonstrated that in the particular case the public interest would
> nevertheless be better served by excluding the evidence despite its relevance. If,
> on balance the matter is left in doubt, disclosure should be ordered.'

Now it seems if the matter is left in doubt the court must decide for the party
opposing disclosure and not for the one who seeks it.

The above passage from *D v NSPCC* also demonstrates a concern that is
wholly absent in the present case. This is the public interest in seeing that all
relevant evidence is available to the courts, sometimes referred to as the
public interest in the administration of justice. Indeed, the passage from Lord
Wilberforce's speech (quoted on p 207 above) seems to negate this concern
altogether, for it suggests that the public interest in the administration of
justice is satisfied as long as a judgment is based on the evidence produced,
however incomplete it might be. One would have thought that respect for
the administration of justice is as much influenced by the degree to which a
judicial outcome accords with reality; the more judgments deviate from what
are known to be the facts, the more they are likely to fall into disrespect. This
is why equity attached such great importance to discovery, and this is why
the emergence of new evidence sometimes justifies the re-opening of a
judicially settled dispute.

Perhaps it is understandable that the courts should recoil somewhat from
the liberalism and the evenhandedness implicit in the *Conway v Rimmer*
approach, especially in the face of conduct such as gave rise to *Home Office v
Harman* [1982] 1 All ER 532 (see All ER Rev 1982 p 222). But it is to be feared

that the present case might have undesirable consequences on discovery law generally, quite apart from public interest immunity. This is due to an inclination to justify restrictions on discovery in public interest immunity cases by reinterpretation of discovery law generally. Consider the following dictum from Lord Fraser's speech—

> 'In an adversarial system such as exists in the United Kingdom a party is free to withhold information that would help his case if he wishes perhaps for reasons of delicacy or personal privacy. He cannot be compelled to disclose it against his will' ([1983] 1 All ER at 916).

There seems to be a confusion here between the adduction of a document or testimony as evidence at the trial and its disclosure to the opponent. Our adversarial system leaves it to the parties to pursue their causes and prosecute them as they wish. The parties are free to adduce or refrain from adducing any evidence they like (subject to admissibility rules). It does not, however, follow from this freedom of adducing evidence that there is a comparable freedom in regard to the disclosure or non-disclosure of evidence to the opponent. Equity developed discovery so that justice may be done despite the adversarial pandering to self-interest. Left to their own devices parties would suppress unfavourable evidence and take advantage of all lawful means to impede their adversaries. Discovery curbs this freedom by ordaining that all relevant documents must be put on the table. If a party has in his possession a document that is wholly favourable to his own case and which, for reason of delicacy, he does not wish to make public, he can certainly refrain from putting it in evidence in open court. But he must disclose it to his opponent and the law ensures the party's privacy by imposing on the opponent a duty of secrecy with respect to information obtained in discovery proceedings.

The principal rules concerning discovery appear in the Rules of the Supreme Court. Order 24, rr 1, 2, envisage discovery of documents 'relating to any matter in question between the parties'. As the Supreme Court Practice 1982, p 447, explains, these words—

> '. . . are not limited to documents which would be admissible in evidence (*Compagnie Financière v Peruvian Guano Co* (1882) 11 QBD, per Esher MR at 62, 63; *O'Rourke v Darbishire* [1920] AC 581 at 630), nor to those which would prove or disprove any matter in question: any document which, it is reasonable to suppose, "contains information which may enable the party (applying for discovery) either to advance his own case or damage that of his adversary, if it is a document which may fairly lead him to a train of inquiry which may have either of these two consequences" must be disclosed (*Compagnie Financière, etc, supra* at 63).'

In *Air Canada* Lord Edmund-Davies referred to these matters, cited *Glasgow Corpn v Central Land Board* 1956 SC (HL) 1 at 18, 20 where Lord Radcliffe spoke of the need that 'a litigant who has a case to maintain should not be deprived of the means of its proper presentation by anything less than a weighty public reason', and then concluded ([1983] 1 All ER at 921):

> 'It follows that, at every stage of interlocutory proceedings for discovery, the test to be applied is: will the material sought be such as is likely to advance the seeker's case, either affirmatively or indirectly by weakening the case of his opponent?'

His Lordship then added—

> 'It is accordingly insufficient for a litigant to urge that the documents he seeks to inspect are *relevant* to the proceedings. For although relevant, they may be of merely vestigial importance, or they may be of importance (great or small) only to his opponent's case. And to urge that, on principle, justice is more likely to be done if free access is had to all relevant documents is pointless, for it carries no weight in our adversarial system of law'.

To remove any doubt his Lordship then observed that he had 'been speaking of legal practice and procedure in general' (at 922). These obiter dicta represent a fundamental departure from present principles. Order 24, rr 1, 2 and 3, where the words 'document . . . relating to any matter in question between the parties' appear, deal with the duty of disclosing the existence of documents in the list documents. Once the existence of documents has been revealed, the parties may then inspect each other's documents; see Ord 24, r 9. Indeed, under the present rules, subject to claims of privilege, the obligation to give discovery and to give inspection are co-extensive: *Supreme Court Practice* 1982, 446–447. A claim to privilege is a claim to immunity from inspection not from disclosure. To quote the White Book again (p 451):

> 'Some classes of documents, although they must be disclosed in the affidavit of documents as "relating to matters in question in the action", are nevertheless privileged from production and inspection'.

However, Lord Edmund-Davies' dictum seems to cut down the duty of disclosing the existence of a document as well as the duty to produce it for inspection. It seems to give licence to a party to say: 'This document, although relevant, can only help my own case, so I need not disclose its existence.' Once a party has suppressed the existence of a document, it is very difficult for the opponent to challenge his judgment on the value of the document. Lord Edmund-Davies requires the seeker of the document to prove that it might help his case; but now can he do so without knowing about its existence, let alone its contents? Furthermore, a party can hardly ever be sure that a document in his possession is only helpful to his own case and not that of his opponent, for he can never fully appreciate to what use his opponent might put the document. It may lead the opponent to an unexpected train of inquiry, it may have quite an unforeseen significance when put side by side with other documents or information in the hands of the opponent. At the time of providing a list of documents, the party making the list would not usually know what is in his opponent's possession.

For our adversarial system to be free of abuse, it is essential that the parties should be obliged to make frank and full discovery of all relevant materials in their hands. To impose restrictions on this principle of fairness and equality before the law is to undermine the fairness and perhaps even the efficiency of our system of the civil process of adjudication. It is hoped, therefore, that the opinions in *Air Canada* will remain confined in their effect to the area of public interest immunity. Even within those confines it would be useful to remember that many a dictum in that case goes far beyond what was necessary in order to determine the issue. Their Lordships proceeded on the assumption that the documents in question offered no assistance to the plaintiffs' case and, therefore, there was little to place on the scales to counteract the public interest of secrecy.

Legal professional privilege

An interesting question regarding the scope of legal professional privilege was considered in *R v King* [1983] 1 All ER 929. The accused was charged with conspiracy to defraud. Before the trial the defence sent a number of documents to a handwriting expert in order to obtain his view on the authenticity of handwriting. At the trial the prosecution called the expert to produce the documents submitted to him by the defence and to recount his opinion on their genuineness. The defence objected, contending that these matters were covered by legal professional privilege; a contention rejected by both the trial judge and the Court of Appeal. Dunn LJ, speaking for the latter, explained why acceptance of the defence's contention could give rise to unacceptable consequences:

> 'It would be strange if a forger could hide behind a claim of legal professional privilege by the simple device of sending all the incriminating documents in his possession to his solicitors to be examined by the expert' (at 931).

It was therefore decided that all that was privileged was the communication between the solicitor and the expert, as made for the preparation of the case for trial. Documents sent to the expert which would not otherwise have been privileged had they been retained by the accused, continued to be un-privileged, whether placed in the possession of the accused's solicitor or sent to an expert. It was further held that while the communications between the accused's solicitors and the expert were privileged, the expert's opinion was not privileged and he was correctly asked to state it in evidence at the trial. This last point is perhaps not as straightforward as it may seem. By holding the expert's opinion to be free from privilege, the court removed much of the efficacy of the privilege which it accorded to the communications between the accused's solicitors and the expert. These communications were made for the sole purpose of obtaining the expert's opinion, and if the latter is un-privileged then the confidentiality of the solicitor-expert communications is obviously undermined. The court's approach is, however, supportable on the ground that, to use Dunn LJ's words, 'the court is entitled, in order to ascertain the truth, to have the actual facts which the expert has observed adduced before it in considering his opinion' (at 931).

See also *A M & S Europe Ltd v Commission of the European Communities* [1983] 1 All ER 705 (in the article on European Community Law, p 187, above).

Right against self-incrimination

Section 72 of the Supreme Court Act 1981 was discussed in relation to Anton Piller orders in *Universal City Studios v Hubbard* [1983] 2 All ER 596. See the article on Practice and Procedure, p 268 below.

Family Law

RUTH L DEECH, MA
Barrister, Fellow of St Anne's College, Oxford

1 Cohabitation

Fewer cases were reported this year and it may be that the principles already established in cases concerning allocation of assets on the break-up of a union are providing sufficient guidelines to avoid the need to resort to litigation. The one point that was determined this year was the approach to be taken to the date of valuation of a share in a jointly-owned house. Now that it is relatively straightforward to establish a share in property for the benefit of the unmarried partner, the date of valuation may be crucial on the assumption that property prices will continue to rise. In *Gordon v Douce* [1983] 2 All ER 228, CA, the plaintiff's 25% share in the home, originally purchased in the defendant's name, was admitted and there was no appeal against the holding of the trial judge that the property should be transferred into joint names on trust for sale, nor was it doubted that the principles applying to the married and the unmarried should be the same. The plaintiff's appeal was against the decision that the valuation of her share should be made as of 1980, the date of separation. In this case the court departed from the holding in *Bernard v Josephs* [1982] 3 All ER 162, CA (All ER Rev 1982, p 150) that the valuation of the share should be at the date of appeal. In the view of Fox LJ there was no rigid rule that a mistress's share should be valued at separation. The important factor was the time when the purposes of the trust came to an end, which might or might not coincide with the date of separation. In this case the woman remained in the house with young children of the relationship and the purpose of the trust would remain in being until sale; then, and only then, should valuation take place.

2 Occupation of the matrimonial home

Ouster injunctions, as they have come to be called, have become increasingly popular in recent years, due in part to the augmented statutory provisions for them and perhaps also to the stronger tactical position in relation to ultimate settlements of property and custody questions that is secured by a spouse who remains in sole occupation of the home from very soon after the breakdown of the marriage. In 1982 concern had been expressed in some quarters that such injunctions, with their apparent long-term benefits, were too readily granted and, moreover, there emerged a clash of judicial opinion in the Court of Appeal (All ER Rev 1982, pp 151–52) concerning the proper principles to be applied in determining whether or not a husband should be required to vacate the matrimonial home. One approach taken was that the welfare of the children and their need for a suitable home with their mother should prevail; the other, that there should be an objective consideration of the merits of the behaviour of the parties involved and that one should be ousted only when it was reasonable to do so in his case. Strong arguments could be made for either approach and a House of Lords' decision on the matter was awaited more for the finality that it would bring than in support of one point of view. Reversing the Court of Appeal decision, [1983] 1 All ER 1017, the House of Lords in *Richards v Richards* [1983] 2 All ER 807, preferred the latter approach (Lord Scarman dissenting) but did so for wholly unexpected reasons and with equally unlooked for results for the procedures to be followed in such cases. The decision dominated all family law developments in the year under review.

Mr and Mrs Richards had married in 1974 and had two young children. In 1982 the wife petitioned for divorce, citing the husband's behaviour, but he denied her allegations and the trial judge, the Court of Appeal and the wife's own counsel, rather surprisingly on examination of the evidence, regarded the grounds of her petition as 'flimsy'. The wife could not secure satisfactory alternative accommodation for herself and the children and so she sought an ouster injunction by interlocutory application in the divorce suit on the grounds that she would not live with the husband and could find no shelter other than the matrimonial home. The case was atypical in that the parents had continued to share the day-by-day care of the children and by the time the case reached the House of Lords the children were remaining in the home while the parents took turns in caring for them, the mother in occupation on weekdays, the father at weekends. The trial judge and the Court of Appeal regarded the possibility of the husband's eviction as unjust to him but felt constrained to hold that the children's needs were of paramount consideration, as in *Samson v Samson* [1982] 1 All ER 780, CA (All ER Rev 1982, p 151), and that if their welfare demanded the presence of their mother in the home, this should weigh more heavily than the court's disbelief in the mother's claim that she could not live under the same roof as her husband. This scepticism as to her claim, the ready dismissal of her severe reaction to the husband's behaviour and the apparent pre-judging of the success of her divorce petition, do not altogether square with the emphasis on breakdown and individual degrees of tolerance enshrined in current divorce law. Their Lordships all agreed that on the facts the wife had never made out a case for excluding the husband from the home and so the husband's appeal was allowed unanimously.

Rather than resolving the clash between the jurisprudence of *Samson v Samson*, that the children's welfare was paramount in housing and of *Myers v Myers* [1982] 1 All ER 776, CA, that there must be reasonable grounds for a wife to refuse to live in the home with her husband, the House of Lords returned to statutory guidelines, the long-neglected s 1 of the Matrimonial Homes Act 1967 (now Matrimonial Homes Act 1983). The law was to be put back on its statutory tracks:

> 'it was with growing astonishment, as the citation of the relevant authorities by counsel for the appellant husband proceeded, that your Lordships found that they contained for the most part no reference whatever either to the statutory powers which enable courts to make ouster orders at all, or to the statutory principles' (per Lord Brandon at 826 j).

According to Lord Hailsham, the Matrimonial Homes Act 1967 was intended to codify and to spell out the jurisdiction of the High Court and county courts in ouster injunctions, the criteria to be applied to decisions were listed exhaustively in s 1(3) of that Act (now s 1(3) of the 1983 Act), and the intention of Parliament thus to govern injunctions law should not be by-passed by resort to earlier Acts and the development of a separate body of case law.

The governing criteria set out in s 1(3) of the Act are (a) the conduct of the spouses; (b) their respective needs and financial resources; (c) the needs of any children; and (d) all the circumstances of the case, and no one criterion is expressed to be superior to another. This means that, as in *Richards*, the applicant's own conduct is relevant and also that of either party towards their children. Needs may be governed by the situation relating to custody of children, for the custodian will probably have the greater need for the available accommodation: so, if Mrs Richards had been regarded as genuinely unable to return to the matrimonial home, her application might have been successful for, unlike her husband, she had not been able to find any alternative lodging. Apart from those considerations, the welfare of the children did not prevail (Lord Scarman dissenting) and the older cases of *Elsworth v Elsworth* (1979) 1 FLR 245, CA, *Myers v Myers, Samson v Samson, Bassett v Bassett* [1975] 1 All ER 513, CA, and *Walker v Walker* [1978] 3 All ER 141, CA, were all wrong in so far as they subordinated the needs of the children to the conduct of the spouses or vice versa or treated injunctions as a matter of housing. In considering the needs of the children, it was not necessarily in their interests that 'either parent should be allowed to get away with capricious, arbitrary, autocratic, or merely eccentric behaviour' (per Lord Hailsham LC at 817 c).

In response to the argument that s 1 of the Guardianship of Minors Act 1971 made children's welfare paramount in any decision in any court touching on their custody or upbringing, it was determined by the majority that this welfare principle applied only in proceedings in which children's custody or upbringing were directly in issue, and not where these were incidental to ouster proceedings between parents. Indeed, according to Lord Brandon, s 1(3) of the Act was meant to exclude the paramountcy of welfare that might otherwise have prevailed by virtue of the pre-existing s 1 of the Guardianship of Infants Act 1925. Lord Scarman, on the other hand, relied on *J v C* [1969] 1 All ER 788, HL, as establishing the universality of the welfare principle, pointing out that this would avoid a possible clash between orders affecting the personal rights of the parents and, inevitably, their children and orders relating solely to legal custody. Although on the facts of *Richards* it was neither reasonable nor necessary to exclude the father from the home, generally, in Lord Scarman's opinion, the most important occasion to present itself for promoting the welfare of the children is precisely during divorce proceedings (at 822b).

Their Lordships' conclusions apply equally to the Domestic Violence and Matrimonial Proceedings Act 1976, which extends ouster injunction jurisdiction to the unmarried yet is also without specific guidelines of the sort set out in the Matrimonial Homes Act and in the Domestic Proceedings and Magistrates' Courts Act 1978, s 16(2). There will, no doubt, be difficulties in applying the criteria of the Matrimonial Homes Act, referring to spousal conduct, to applications by the unmarried for ouster injunctions. A further limitation on the extent of the Domestic Violence and Matrimonial Proceedings Act was the suggestion by Lord Brandon (at 828d) that it was limited to cases of violence, contrary to the opinions of their Lordships in *Davis v Johnson* [1978] 1 All ER 1132 and despite the express limitation of s 2 of the 1976 Act to violence in the provisions relating to attachment of the power of arrest, in contrast to the absence of such limitation in s 1.

How much difference will be made by this newly-restored substantive law, as opposed to the procedural limitations, considered below? Many of the old cases, excepting *Samson* and *Richards* itself in the Court of Appeal, were approved on their facts, the decisions to oust being justifiable by s 1(3) of the Matrimonial Homes Act. It may well be that injunctions will be granted no less frequently in future, subject only to a more stringent examination of the wife's case for excluding her husband. Possession of the children need no longer be manipulated, if it ever was, in order to guarantee sole occupancy of the home. When the Matrimonial Homes Act was first enacted, the court had no power, as it now has by virtue of s 24 of the Matrimonial Causes Act 1973, to transfer a home to an ex-wife on divorce or to maintain her indefinite occupation, and these major considerations of the present would have played no part in what were seen as the short-term remedies provided by the 1967 Act. *Richards* is a timely reminder of the danger, of which their Lordships were plainly aware, of tactical use of injunctions to put a wife in an unassailable position in relation to later property and custody claims in divorce. In the case of council housing, ouster proceedings had sometimes been brought mainly because the local authority would not accept the wife as officially homeless until she had done so, and if wives in future find it harder to obtain injunctions and fail to do so as a result of *Richards*, they may be regarded by the local authority as intentionally homeless and ineligible for aid under the Housing (Homeless Persons) Act 1977.

Further complications are evident in considering the instructions of the House of Lords in relation to the proper procedure to be followed in applications for injunctions.

Before the judgment in *Richards*, the Matrimonial Homes Act procedure as such had been little used, although of course the registration of Class F charges has become commonplace. The Matrimonial Homes Act power to exclude had been regarded as defective because of the ruling in *Tarr v Tarr* [1972] 2 All ER 295, HL, that the wording of s 1 was insufficient to achieve total exclusion of the owner of the home. This was reversed by s 3 of the Domestic Violence and Matrimonial Proceedings Act 1976, s 4 of which removed the other limitation of the Matrimonial Homes Act, namely, that it could not be used to control the rights of married joint tenants. Nevertheless, resort to s 1 of the Matrimonial Homes Act continued to be rare, because injunctions were by then readily available in a broad range of situations under the 1976 Act and because it was convenient to seek ouster as part of a divorce or judicial separation suit. The system appeared to work well and was sufficient to encompass bans on molestation and on entering the neighbourhood of the matrimonial home. The Domestic Violence Act was seen as extending the jurisdiction to cover three additional situations of pressing need—the unmarried, the attachment of a power of arrest to injunctions, and applications in county courts without the need to commence divorce proceedings, which might have been precipitate in some circumstances. From 1976 the effective choice for applicants was between applications ancillary to divorce proceedings, s 1 of the Domestic Violence Act and s 16 of the

Domestic Proceedings and Magistrates' Courts Act 1978, extending to magistrates' courts.

Nevertheless, the paramountcy of the criteria of the Matrimonial Homes Act in *Richards* also led their Lordships to confine the procedure and jurisdiction of courts in injunction proceedings to the demands of that Act alone. According to Lord Brandon (at 831), if the proper practice and procedure had been followed in the past, it would have been unlikely that the substantive demands of s 1(3) of the Matrimonial Homes Act would have been overlooked for so long. The practice had grown up of issuing a summons in the suit when application was made for an ouster order during the pendency of the suit. The correct procedure now is that laid down in r 107(1) of the Matrimonial Causes Rules 1977 (SI 1977/344) applying r 104 relating to s 17 of the Married Women's Property Act 1882. Whether a suit is pending or not, applications for injunctions to the High Court should be made by originating summons in Form 23 and likewise in the county court by virtue of the County Court Rules 1981, Ord 47, rr 2 and 4. Following *Richards*, it is a fact that the courts were misguided for more than a decade in dealing with ouster injunctions as applications ancillary to divorce and part of the inherent power, instead of separately under the Matrimonial Homes Act or the Domestic Violence Act. The details of the correct procedure were given by Lord Brandon, in whose view the jurisdiction of the Supreme Court was based solely on statutory powers, first s 45 of the Supreme Court of Judicature (Consolidation) Act 1925, then s 37 of the Supreme Court Act 1981, and predominantly s 1 of the Matrimonial Homes Act, which had removed the jurisdictional requirement that injunctions had to be in support of a legal right. As in substance, so in procedure: the Matrimonial Homes Act was intended to govern and absorb inherent or common law powers.

Whether or not there is still an inherent power in the court to grant injunctions ancillary to the main suit depends on a reading of the legislative history. In Lord Brandon's estimate, the Matrimonial Homes Act was an exhaustive statement of the jurisdictional power, leaving nothing beyond it. According to Lord Scarman, however, the Matrimonial Homes Act was not a substitute for the court's inherent power to protect parties, but additional, and the changes directed by Lord Brandon would be neither necessary nor convenient.

Lord Scarman's view might have prevailed had the court had the benefit of the citation before it of *National Provincial Bank v Ainsworth* [1965] 2 All ER 472, HL, the case that led to the passage of the Matrimonial Homes Act. The problem in the mid-1960s appeared to be that injunctions could only be granted in support of proprietary rights (and, possibly, the wife's common law right: *Silverstone v Silverstone* [1953] 1 All ER 556, PDA) and it was often the case that the wife had none; more important, she was held to have no common law or equitable right of occupation as a wife sufficient to bind third parties if her husband sold or charged the home to strangers. The main purpose of the Matrimonial Homes Act was to crystallise and express in property terms that right of occupation of the wife which had been so vulnerable, and the rights granted to her in s 1 were a prelude to the registration innovation of s 2. The language and concept of the court's inherent power to grant injunctions only in support of proprietary rights was used as a stepping stone to extension of that power in a new direction, not in replacement or even consolidation. So much did the court's inherent powers to grant ancillary injunctions remain in use after 1967 that it was considered necessary by Parliament to enact in the Domestic Violence and Matrimonial Proceedings Act 1976 that injunctions could be sought without the need to start proceedings for divorce—surely a superfluous provision if this course had then been the only correct one. No doubt the House of Lords was denied the legislative history of injunctions in argument in *Richards* because it would not originally have appeared necessary to defend the practice of seeking injunctions in divorce suits. In future, however, applications separate from divorce proceedings will have to be commenced if ouster relief is sought, whether under the provisions of the Domestic Violence Act or the Matrimonial Homes Act, the latter having the advantage of express provisions for orders ancillary to exclusion itself, and the correct form of order, if the application is successful, should follow as closely as possible the wording of s 1 of the Matrimonial Homes Act (per Lord Brandon at 832) and should not follow the pre-*Richards* formula of requiring the husband to vacate the matrimonial home and not return to it. The judgment was implemented by a Practice Direction [1983] 2 All ER 1088 which in addition drew attention to the need to transfer a cause to the High Court in cases where a divorce suit is proceeding in the county court and a party applies in the Principal Registry for ouster.

A number of questions concerning the appropriate jurisdiction remain open. Where there exist areas not specifically covered by the provisions of the Matrimonial Homes Act then, presumably, the still existing general statutory powers of the courts to grant injunctions may be relied on, that is, s 37 of the Supreme Court Act 1981 and s 74 of the County Courts Act 1959: for example to protect children after their parents' divorce has removed them from the scope of the Matrimonial Homes Act, as in *Phillips v Phillips* [1973] 2 All ER 423, CA, and *Stewart v Stewart* [1973] 1 All ER 31, Fam D. This much was suggested by Lord Hailsham at 814 and 817. Presumably in wardship proceedings, which are largely unfettered by detailed statutory provisions and where the child's welfare is undoubtedly paramount, a parent might be excluded from the home. The position in custody proceedings is similar. In *Re W (a minor)* [1981] 3 All ER 401, CA, Brandon LJ (as he then was), approved the ability of the High Court and county courts to support a custody order by interlocutory injunction; this case was not overruled in *Richards* and may be upheld on the ground that the welfare principle of the Guardianship of Minors Act 1971 undoubtedly prevails where the custody of the child is directly in issue, and that custody cases are not covered by the Matrimonial Homes Act so as to confine practice within its framework.

Other situations that do not come within the four corners of the Matrimonial Homes Act and thus may be governed by the inherent power of the court are: eviction from non-matrimonial premises, the subject of litigation; eviction of third parties, as in *Jones v Jones* [1971] 2 All ER 737, CA; preservation of the home pending decisions about it in ancillary proceedings, as in *Stewart v Stewart;* and, as from the start, to protect a proprietary interest of one party in the home. Non-molestation orders may presumably still be granted ancillary to petition, being a type of order not covered by the Matrimonial Homes Act, although expressly provided for by the Domestic Violence Act. It is not clear how to invoke the court's power to ban a husband from the vicinity of the home, another situation not expressly covered by the

Matrimonial Homes Act. Nor is it certain that the power of arrest, first provided for by s 2 of the Domestic Violence Act, will attach to orders made under s 1 of the Matrimonial Homes Act.

The procedural innovations of *Richards* may cause more problems than the merits of the case. Clearly two separate sets of proceedings must be maintained in the average case of divorce petition followed by application for ouster relief. In relation to the latter, the county court only has jurisdiction in the district of the applicant or the respondent or their home, and since not all county courts are divorce courts, the two proceedings may be in different courts, although one of the parties could apply for transfer. This has the possibility of confusion and the certainty of giving rise to further costs, and the legally aided divorce petitioner will have to obtain a new legal aid certificate to cover her ouster application. There is less chance of recovery of these extra costs by the Fund for if those relating to ouster applications are distinct from those relating to the matrimonial suit, they may not, as has hitherto been the practice, be aggregated and charged, where appropriate, on the matrimonial home. In future the legal aid costs of the ouster application cannot be secured in isolation on any property or money recovered in the principal suit. All these matters are under review and merely to outline them is to support Lord Scarman in his plea for reform:

> 'The statutory provision is a hotchpotch of enactments of limited scope passed into law to meet specific situations or to strengthen the powers of specified courts. The sooner the range, scope, and effect of these powers are rationalised into a coherent and comprehensive body of statute law, the better' (at 818 c).

In the meantime, greater use will have to be made of the Matrimonial Homes Act. It had sunk into disuse before *Richards,* s 1 applications representing only a tiny fraction of the many thousands of ouster injunctions sought annually, the great majority of which were made as interlocutory applications in divorce.

Once a decree absolute has dissolved a marriage, the courts have been reluctant to intervene with ouster injunctions. The post-*Richards* confinement of the jurisdiction to the Matrimonial Homes Act and the Domestic Violence and Matrimonial Proceedings Act makes this all the more likely. Clearly the courts' powers are directed towards husbands and wives and persons living with each other, save in exceptional circumstances. This is confirmed by *White v White* [1983] 2 All ER 51, CA, a case in which a non-molestation order had been granted in favour of an ex-wife who, after decree absolute, sought to attach a power of arrest to that order under the provisions of s 2 of the Domestic Violence and Matrimonial Proceedings Act. The question was whether such jurisdiction existed, as s 2 refers to 'parties to a marriage' and, in support of her case the ex-wife argued for a liberal interpretation of that phrase analogous to that of *McLean v Nugent* (1979) 1 FLR 26, CA, relating to the cohabitation requirement in s 1(2). It was held by Cumming-Bruce LJ, however, that ss 1 and 2 provided only for parties to a subsisting marriage and that there was no jurisdiction to attach a power of arrest to an existing injunction after decree absolute unless the former spouses were still living together. The appropriate remedies for the divorced couple were to be found in the Matrimonial Causes Act 1973. Reeve J suggested (at 58e) that the power to grant injunctions might exist even after decree absolute if necessary for the protection of children.

3 Magistrates' domestic jurisdiction

This year has seen important elucidation of the provisions of the Domestic Proceedings and Magistrates' Courts Act 1978 and may herald an upturn in the rate of use of the summary jurisdiction. *Bergin v Bergin* [1983] 1 All ER 905, Fam D, concerned an appeal by a wife against the dismissal by the magistrates of her application for an order against her husband based on acts of violence by him such that she could not reasonably be expected to live with him. The magistrates found that the wife had not been in fear and that her account of the husband's behaviour was exaggerated. Her appeal was allowed and the finding of the magistrates described as 'perverse'. Heilbron J held that the approach of magistrates to ss 1 and 2 of the 1978 Act should be brought in line with that of the High Court to s 1(2)(*b*) of the Matrimonial Causes Act (the 'behaviour' ground) and, accordingly, the proper test to be applied to the allegations was that laid down by Dunn J in *Livingstone-Stallard v Livingstone-Stallard* [1974] 2 All ER 766, Fam D, at 771 and confirmed by Roskill LJ in *O'Neill v O'Neill* [1975] 3 All ER 289, CA, at 295d:

> 'would any right thinking person come to the conclusion that this husband has behaved in such a way that this wife cannot reasonably be expected to live with him, taking into account the whole of the circumstances and the characters and personalities of the parties?'

While it is convenient to have the one test in all courts, it may be that the test is at so low a level that it accords ill with the retention of desertion as a ground in the magistrates' court (s 1(*d*) of the 1978 Act) and in the divorce court (s 1(2)(*c*) of the 1973 Act) for, so long as desertion remains as a legal concept, then it is negated by the establishment of a 'just cause' for departure (eg per Simon P in *Young v Young* [1962] 3 All ER 120 at 124). If the new behaviour ground is easier to establish than 'just cause', then it would be possible for a wife to succeed in establishing a case of behaviour by the husband when she herself could be said to be in desertion, there being no just cause provided by him to justify her departure. Moreover, it has been held repeatedly that desertion and behaviour are not to be equated or confused as grounds for divorce (*Morgan v Morgan* (1973) 117 SJ 223, Fam D; *Pheasant v Pheasant* [1972] 1 All ER 587, Fam D and *Stringfellow v Stringfellow* [1976] 2 All ER 539, CA). Equally it may be true that such niceties are out of date if the main object of the magistrates' courts is now the relief of need without regard to fault.

The other doubtful point concerning *Bergin* is whether grounds of complaint in the magistrates' court should in fact be interpreted in the same fashion as grounds for divorce. The grounds in s 1(2) of the 1973 Act are in truth indicators of irretrievable breakdown. If the same tests are applied in the magistrates' courts then they too are dealing with irretrievable breakdown of a marriage in finding the complaint established. Yet the function of the magistrates' courts has been said to be 'to provide first aid in a marital casualty clearing station' (Matrimonial Proceedings in Magistrates' Courts (1973) Law Com no 53, para 24; cf Report of the Committee on One-Parent Families (1974), Cmnd 5629, para 4.67).

Similar disagreements over the precise nature of the task of the magistrates' courts appertain to *Robinson v Robinson* [1983] 1 All ER 391, CA. A homesick wife left her soldier husband and refused to join him overseas. The magistrates decided that her desertion was 'gross and obvious misconduct' that should be taken into account under s 3(1)(g) of the 1978 Act so that her application for financial provision, although successful, resulted in a far smaller order in her favour than would otherwise have been the case. The wife's appeal was dismissed. The Court of Appeal had no doubt that s 3(1)(g) of the 1978 Act, although differently worded, was of the same effect as the proviso to s 25(1) of the Matrimonial Causes Act and permitted a complainant's own conduct to be taken into account in assessment. The guidelines developed in *Wachtel v Wachtel* [1973] 1 All ER 829, CA, and subsequent cases on divorce should apply so that in exceptional cases, such as the present one where the husband was regarded as totally blameless, the wife's conduct was to affect the matter because it would offend a reasonable man's sense of justice to leave it out of account in deciding financial provision, applying *Kokosinski v Kokosinski* [1980] 1 All ER 1106 at 1117, Fam D; *Evans v Evans* (1981) 2 FLR 33 at 36, Fam D and *S v S* (1982) 12 Fam Law 183, Fam D. This latter formulation of the relevant test is now preferred to the 'obvious and gross' phrase and foreshadows the new provision concerning conduct and maintenance to be found in the 1983 Matrimonal and Family Proceedings Bill, cl 3. The court also expressed the view that it should not interfere with the justices' finding unless clearly satisfied that they were wrong.

Despite the failure of the wife's appeal, it is still remarkable that she should have been granted a maintenance order at all, for her desertion would have barred her completely before the 1978 change in the law and it is, moreover, difficult to discern the ground of her complaint against her husband. If her desertion nevertheless renders him guilty of failure to provide reasonable maintenance, there can be no circumstances, even adultery, relieving him of that obligation in marriage. On that basis, the function of the magistrates is the relief of need, regardless of the circumstances and of marital obligations. As suggested in relation to *Bergin v Bergin*, the appropriateness of the injection of concepts developed in divorce law into the magistrates' law depends on the view taken of the latter's task and, in the event, a small order against the husband may be of little benefit to the wife.

The difficulties of enforcing such orders was apparent in *R v Dover Magistrates' Court, ex p Kidner* [1983] 1 All ER 475, QBD. The magistrates had purported to remit certain arrears of child maintenance payable by the husband but, because the wife lived in a different area from the husband, the court had overlooked its duty, under r 44 of the Magistrates' Courts Rules 1981, to notify the wife of its intention to remit and to give her the opportunity to make representations. There is no appeal against a magistrates' order to remit arrears due to be enforced under s 13(3) of the Guardianship of Minors Act 1971 or s 29 of the Domestic Proceedings and Magistrates' Courts Act, so the wife sought to quash the remission order by application to the Queen's Bench Division for judicial review of the decision and she succeeded in obtaining certiorari. Woolf J pointed out that it was desirable for an applicant in such circumstances to include a request on her application that the matter should be dealt with by a judge of the Family Division rather than of the Queen's Bench Division. This expedient would, in his opinion, result in a speedier disposal of the matter and in a decision in line with those of the Family Division in relation to appeals from magistrates' courts. The matter was remitted to the magistrates for reconsideration after the applicant had been given the opportunity to make her representations. The whole episode highlights the need to rationalise family court jurisdiction.

4 Divorce

Questions of procedure were again uppermost in 1983. A counterpart to the complexities of *Richards v Richards* is *Mitchell v Mitchell* [1983] 3 All ER 621, CA, an interlocutory appeal arising because the respondent husband, having defended in person an application for an ouster injunction had thought that by so doing he was also defending the wife's petition for divorce and failed to acknowledge service or file an answer within the prescribed time limits. When he realised that decree nisi was about to be pronounced against him, he applied for it to be postponed and for leave to file an answer to the petition out of time. Cumming-Bruce LJ, granting leave, divided the cases into three categories. One, those where the applicant had been deceived, with the result that the proceedings took place behind her back: a rehearing would be granted almost automatically. Two, where the applicant chose not to defend originally but had changed her mind: the court would have to be convinced that it was probable that the decree was obtained contrary to the justice of the case. Three, where the applicant had been anxious to defend but through ignorance or lack of full advice had been unaware of the need to take the proper procedural steps: the applicant would have to satisfy the court that she had a case which, if accepted, might well lead to a different result (applying *Nash v Nash* [1967] 1 All ER 535, PDA). *Mitchell* fell in this third category, having arisen from a mistake made by the husband's solicitor.

> 'The interest which lies at the root of the jurisdiction to set aside a decree nisi on the ground that the respondent through ignorance or his solicitor's failure failed to file an answer in time is the public interest. That interest is to ensure that decrees of dissolution of marriage shall not be allowed to stand if a respondent has a case which may well succeed and, if heard and successful, will have a result different from the result obtained in undefended proceedings' (at 635–36).

A more technical defect occurred in *Batchelor v Batchelor* [1983] 3 All ER 618, Fam D, that is, failure to serve a summons on the petitioner prior to the making absolute of a decree by the respondent, a requirement to be found in r 66(2) of the Matrimonial Causes Rules 1977, SI 1977/344. The husband, who had been respondent to the divorce petition, had had the decree made absolute without service of the summons, acting on registry advice. The wife's application to have the decree absolute set aside was refused on the ground that the defect was not a fundamental mistake in the proceedings and thus rendered the decree not void but merely voidable. The discretion to avoid was not exercised because the husband had remarried and the wife had accepted proper and generous financial provision. It may be that procedural reforms directed in particular to simplification of the rules concerning decree absolute (if the nisi/absolute distinction is not to be abolished) could eliminate the complexities evident in this case.

Far worse deception was revealed in *Ebrahim v Ali (orse Ebrahim) (Queen's Proctor intervening)* [1983] 3 All ER 615, Fam D. The husband and wife parted on the day of their marriage (probably undertaken for immigration purposes) and four years later the husband filed a divorce petition containing allegations of behaviour which must have been false. It was not served on the wife nor was any order made dispensing with service. This failure rendered the ensuing decree absolute a nullity. Since no valid disposal had ever been made of the case, the proceedings were pending, thus justifying the Queen's Proctor in intervening under s 8(1)(b) of the Matrimonial Causes Act on the basis of information given to him. Clearly, the Queen's Proctor still has a valuable rôle as watchdog over Special Procedure.

5 Financial relief

A few details of the law were clarified. In *Jones v Jones* [1983] 1 All ER 1037, QBD, the plaintiff claimed damages from the defendant in respect of personal injuries and included in his claim additional damages in respect of the secured maintenance and lump sum that his wife was claiming from him in divorce proceedings, the marriage having broken down as a result of the injuries. The plaintiff had already been awarded a sum which included the amount he would have expended on his family if the marriage had subsisted but claimed extra sums because, as he put it, it was well known that it cost a husband more to maintain his family after a divorce than it did to maintain them in his own house in a subsisting marriage, so that the support element in the award was insufficient. Stocker J suspected that the husband's contention was correct but unproven and, in any case, the judge considered it unlikely, as being a breach of comity, that in the wife's maintenance claim the Family Division would regard as available resources a sum specifically awarded to the husband by the Queen's Bench Division for his own future maintenance and held for him by the Court of Protection.

The confidence of the judge may have been misplaced for, in fact, there is a conflict of judicial opinion in the Family Division regarding the taking into account of damages for injuries in calculating the assets of a husband. In *Armstrong v Armstrong* (1974) 4 Fam Law 156, the Court of Appeal treated as personal to him damages that the husband had received for minor injuries. In *Jones v Jones* [1975] 2 All ER 12, CA, the sum awarded to the wife by the Criminal Injuries Compensation Board was regarded as relevant only insofar as any part of it related to loss of future earnings and not if it related to pain and suffering, the crux of the case being that it was the husband who had attacked and disabled the wife. In *Claxton v Claxton* (1981) 12 Fam Law 62, Fam D, the court refused to take into account the invalidity benefits received by the husband and his disabled second wife in calculating the income of the husband available to meet the first wife's claims. However, in *Daubney v Daubney* [1976] 2 All ER 453, CA, the Court of Appeal found no decision to bind them to leave out of account resources acquired through damages; indeed, it would be contrary to s 25(1)(a) of the 1973 Act to disregard them. In *Cawkwell v Cawkwell* (1978) 9 Fam Law 25, CA, a former matrimonial home, purchased with the aid of the husband's industrial injuries compensation, became the object of a *Mesher* order, ultimately to be divided as to two-thirds to the wife, the remainder to the husband. The conclusion to be drawn may be that damages will be taken into account on the initial assessment but that their origin and purpose, whether for pain and suffering or otherwise, and the way in which they have been spent, especially if on accommodation (as in *Daubney*) will all be highly relevant factors in determining the size of the order to be made. Reverting to *Jones* [1983] it can only be hoped that the size of the order in favour of the wife would not go beyond the family maintenance element in the husband's damages, there being no guarantee against encroachment on the amount earmarked for his own upkeep.

By way of contrast, the husband in *Walker v Walker* [1983] 2 All ER 909, CA, enjoyed a surprisingly protected position. The wife, petitioner in divorce proceedings, applied under s 37 of the Matrimonial Causes Act 1973 for an order preserving for her benefit the resettlement grant that the husband had received on his recent discharge from the army. The registrar ordered the Paymaster General to pay the sum into court until such time as the financial relief issues were settled. The Ministry of Defence objected, successfully, because the wording of s 203(1) and (2) of the Army Act 1955 forbade any assignment of, charge on or diversion of military pay. This provision may be traced back for at least a century and its original purpose is comprehensible. Nevertheless, it must be an unintended result that an army wife involved in matrimonial proceedings today should be prevented from relying on divorce provisions giving necessary protection to petitioners in general. Pay or allowances payable to the debtor, member of HM Forces, are equally exempt from the operation of the Attachment of Earnings Act 1971, s 24(2)(*b*), although other means exist for enforcing awards against military personnel.

6 Divorce and the matrimonial home

The disadvantages of the so-called *Mesher* method of allocation of the home under s 24 of the Matrimonial Causes Act 1973 were alluded to last year (All ER Rev 1982, pp 158–59) and further examples and criticism of the effects of such orders appear in 1983. Unfortunately, by the time that the Court of Appeal had voiced its disapproval, many thousands of such orders had come into existence and no doubt as the time comes for the property to be sold under the terms of the order they will have to be unscrambled in the pages of future law reports. Although the preferred order now is to permit indefinite postponement of sale in favour of the wife, often subject to a ban on cohabitation or to payment of an occupational rent to the ousted spouse (*Harvey v Harvey* [1982] 1 All ER 693, CA; *Brown v Brown* (1981) 3 FLR 161, CA), the *Mesher* order is still regarded as a well-established technique in some quarters (*Tinsdale v Tinsdale* (1983) 4 FLR 641, CA, per Dunn LJ at 645).

Carson v Carson [1983] 1 All ER 478, CA, decided as long ago as 1981, should change that appoach permanently. In 1975 the court made in favour of the wife a typical *Mesher* order, concluding it with the words 'or until further order of the court'. After a few years the wife's economic position had worsened and the husband was failing to comply with orders to make periodical payments. The wife, fearing the difficulties that would come about when the house had to be sold, applied to Ewbank J for a second property transfer order, giving her the house absolutely. For jurisdiction, she relied on the words 'or at any time thereafter' in s 24(1) and on the open-ended phrase at the end of her original property transfer order. Failing that, she sought leave to appeal out of time against the order of 1975. The Court of Appeal unanimously refused to reopen matters, although sympathetic to her plight. Ormrod LJ described the case a 'a very good example of the chickens coming home to roost with the *Mesher v Mesher* type of order which became so fashionable in and around 1975 and afterwards. It was not for some little time that the dangers of the . . . order came to be appreciated' (at 482–83). All the wife's methods of attack on the original s 24 order failed, for Parliament had expressly excluded such variations from s 31 of the 1973 Act and it was too late to give leave to appeal when the order had been acted on. Although this may not at first appear to be an obstacle, for the husband's arrears of maintenance might have been offset against a further deprivation of property, it was suggested that to reopen matters might not result in a better deal for the wife for, on the other side, the husband had acquired new liabilities by remarriage that could equally be taken into account.

Norman v Norman [1983] 1 All ER 486, Fam D, presented another facet of the same problem. A *Mesher* order in favour of the wife had been made in 1979 and sale still appeared to lie some time off in the future. The husband's pre-existing mental illness had worsened and he needed his share of the capital represented by the home to house himself, there being no other resource open to him. He applied under s 24A of the Matrimonial Causes Act 1973 for immediate sale. In 1981 the Matrimonial Homes and Property Act, s 7, inserted in the 1973 Act s 24A, which enabled the court to make orders for the sale of property. Wood J held that power to order sale of the house that had been settled under the order of 1979 was not affected by s 24A. Section 31(2)(*f*), also inserted by the 1981 Act, allowed variation of orders made under s 24A(1) but not of orders made under s 24(1)(*b*) which remained final. It is therefore very important that property adjustment orders should clearly separate those made under s 24, which are final, and those made under s 24A. Wood J suggested that, had the words 'until further order' been attached to the original order of 1979, as in *Carson*, supra, the court might have had the power to bring forward, though not to postpone, the time for sale of the house. The summons was adjourned to give the husband the opportunity to argue that these words should be read into the 1979 order and to issue a summons under s 30 of the Law of Property Act 1925, the appropriate section for dealing with disagreements between trustees for sale, as were these spouses. It must remain open to question, however, whether the Chancery Division could properly use that section to undermine a trust for sale established by the Family Division under another statute and intended to be final. If so, then logically s 24 should be amended to provide for variation, at the very least of orders made before the clear condemnation of *Mesher*. The plight of Mr Norman also shows how the proviso to s 25(1) has been improperly interpreted in some property allocation cases: had the marriage continued to exist, the housing situation could have been adapted to the exigencies of the husband's illness and he would not have been reduced to possibly inappropriate council accommodation while the wife was in employment and four of the five children were financially self-supporting (cf *Martin (BH) v Martin (D)* [1977] 3 All ER 762, CA and *Harvey v Harvey* [1982] 1 All ER 693, CA). The courts have yet to find the proper principles on which to exercise the discretion of s 24 of the Matrimonial Causes Act in middle-range housing and, moreover, extra litigation of the type described above must serve only to further diminish the ultimate proceeds of sale if the parties are legally aided.

A prayer in a petition for relief and property transfer was held not to be such notice as would effect severance of a joint tenancy in *Harris v Goddard* [1983] 3 All ER 242, CA. The prayer was a mere request to the court to consider whether at some future time to exercise its jurisdiction under s 24. This finding enabled the widow to claim the whole of the home on the death of the husband whom she was about to divorce.

Although the court purported to approve the finding of severance in *Re Draper's Conveyance, Nihan v Porter* [1967] 3 All ER 853, ChD, the true distinction is hard to perceive except that *Re Draper* concerned severance by issuance of a summons under s 17 of the Married Women's Property Act 1882.

7 Child care

The perennial problems of the relationship between the courts and the local authority acting under child care legislation presented themselves again: it cannot be long before a fresh statutory rationalisation of all the powers is demanded.

In *Re R (a minor) (child in care: access)* [1983] 2 All ER 929, CA, as a result of custody proceedings between divorced parents, a judge, acting pursuant to s 43 of the Matrimonial Causes Act, had committed the child into the care of the local authority. Section 43(7) of the same Act gives the court power to vary or discharge provisions made under the section. The local authority refused access to the father, who applied to a judge for a direction that he should be granted access under s 43(5). Despite the express statutory provision enabling the grant (added by the Child Care Act 1980, Sch 5, para 34(*b*)) the judge held that he was limited to an administrative-style review of the exercise of the local authority's discretion in respect of a child committed to care under s 43: such committals take effect as receptions into care under s 2 of the Child Care Act 1980 and the trend of recent decisions concerning intervention has undoubtedly been one of restraint on the part of the judiciary. The father's appeal to the Court of Appeal failed on the facts of the case but the court held that there did exist the jurisdiction to order access to a child received into care under s 43 had the court been so minded. The cases of *A v Liverpool City Council* [1981] 2 All ER 385, HL and *Re Y (a minor) (child in care: access)* [1975] 3 All ER 348, CA, were distinct, concerning, as they did, judicial intervention in the exercise of local authority powers over children received into care under s 1 of the Children and Young Persons Act 1969 and s 7(2) of the Family Law Reform Act 1969 respectively. The enabling language of s 43 was far stronger than that of other sections and was an original jurisdiction, not merely a review jurisdiction. In practice, however, the court will be slow to contradict a properly-made decision of the local authority.

The final case, *Re C (a minor) (wardship: care order)* [1983] 1 All ER 219, Fam D, concerned a child who had been made a ward of court and in whose respect subsequently a care order had been made under s 7(7) of the Children and Young Persons Act 1969, in favour of Norfolk. The issue was whether the wardship court now had the power, notwithstanding the existence of the earlier care order, to make a new, more convenient, care order in favour of Leeds. Relying on the dictum of Lord Roskill in *A v Liverpool City Council*, supra, that 'the wardship jurisdiction of the court could properly be invoked in addition to the statutory jurisdiction of the local authority because it was only in this way that the result which was best in the paramount interest of the child could be achieved, the local authority and juvenile court being unable within the limits of their powers to achieve that result' (at 393).

Balcombe J decided that the existence of the first care order did not preclude the wardship court making another one, as required by the welfare of the child. The result was that the earlier care order was superseded, although technically undischarged, and attention was drawn to the desirability of taking steps to secure the discharge of that juvenile court order. There is an analogous problem when a High Court custody order supersedes an earlier inconsistent order made in the magistrates' court.

Land Law

P J CLARKE, BCL, MA
Barrister, Fellow of Jesus College, Oxford

1 Conveyancing: deposits

Millichamp v Jones [1983] 1 All ER 267 (D Hayton [1983] CLJ 197, Anon (1983) 99 LQR 162, J W Carter (1983) 99 LQR 503) is of considerable interest to conveyancers. The plaintiff had sold land, part of a farm, to the defendant; there was also an agreement under seal granting the plaintiff an option to purchase land from the defendant, provided that there should be a notice of intention to purchase and payment of deposit within a prescribed time. The plaintiff gave notice timeously, but did not pay the deposit. The defendant had agreed to help financially with the purchase of a farm, and the plaintiff was to have an option to buy certain land not earlier than ten years and not later than ten years and six months from the granting of the option. The comment may be made that this arrangement looks suspiciously like a mortgage (equity looking to the substance not to the form), but this point does not seem to have been considered.

The first issue was whether the payment of a deposit was a condition precedent (non-payment thus preventing a contract from coming into existence), a condition subsequent (failure to pay the deposit thus bringing about the automatic discharge of the contract) or a breach of a fundamental term of the contract (the contract then being specifically enforceable or a remedy in damages being available). The last view was adopted, not following Goulding J in *Myton v Schwab-Morris* [1974] 1 All ER 326; the authority of the latter had been undermined by *Pollway Ltd v Abdullah* [1974] 2 All ER 381 and *Johnson v Agnew* [1979] 1 All ER 883.

However, although the defendant's case looked strong, Warner J went on to consider whether (i) the contract had been breached, and, if so (ii) there had been a breach of a term. The judge found that the clause requiring payment of the deposit was a fundamental term, entitling the defendant to treat the contract as discharged, but held that the plaintiff's conduct was 'a mere oversight', and this was insufficient to entitle the defendant to treat the contract as discharged. It is at this point that the learned judge's reasoning becomes difficult to follow. He stated that there were some cases where a mere failure to pay on time a sum due under the contract was insufficient to entitle the potential payee to treat the contract as repudiated, presumably because the breach of the term was insufficiently serious. He does not indicate, however, where the line is to be drawn—perhaps there is to be an element of discretion: in cases such as the one before him the judge held that the defendant should tell the plaintiffs that he intended to treat their breach as repudiatory, and give them an opportunity of complying with their obligation. Only if they made it clear that they could or would not comply with it, would there be a sufficiently clear breach of contract. From the option-holder's point of view, such an attitude is benevolent: he does not have to remember to pay on time, and if he forgets, he must be reminded. The owner/vendor, however, will never know with certainty whether a contract has 'gone off', and must remind the other party of his opportunity to comply before declaring him in breach. Presumably the problem can be solved by the owner/vendor making the deposit payment clause one where 'time is of the essence'. Stating that an option is to be exercised within a relatively short period, and requiring payment of the deposit to be *upon* such exercise is, apparently, not enough.

From the point of view of the conveyancer, the case, although indicating a need to be ultra-careful, is tolerable. But as far as contractual doctrine is concerned, the case is difficult to follow. Warner J found that there was a breach of a term; on ordinary contractual principles, if there is a breach of a condition or of a fundamental term, that is sufficient for the contract to be repudiated. The gravity of the breach is irrelevant. Unless conveyancing contracts are in some way different from ordinary commercial contracts, Warner J's analysis seems in conflict with current contractual thinking. One final point, however, which the judge did not consider, was that in another area of land law, rent review clauses in leases, time is not normally 'of the essence' unless expressly stated (see eg *United Scientific Holdings Ltd v Burnley BC* [1977] 2 All ER 62), and it may be that the law relating to contracts affecting land is developing along different lines from that affecting mercantile contracts.

2 Joint tenancy: severance

Harris v Goddard [1983] 3 All ER 242 states, simply, that a wife's petition for divorce, seeking 'such order . . . by way of transfer of property and/or settlement of property and/or variation of settlement in respect of the [property]', the property being held on a joint tenancy in equity, does not sever such tenancy; the husband had died before the divorce petition could be heard. The Court of Appeal held that the fact that the joint tenants were husband and wife had no bearing on their ability to sever; the remarks of Lord Denning MR in *Bedson v Bedson* [1965] 3 All ER 307 at 311 to the contrary were not followed. A notice in writing, if it was to be effective under the Law of Property Act 1925 s 36(2), had to take immediate effect; a notice that expressed a desire that the severance should occur in the future was not effective. On the facts of *Harris v Goddard*, there was clearly not a severance, but the comparison with *Re Draper's Conveyance* [1967] 3 All ER 853 is more difficult to accept. *Re Draper's Conveyance* was a case under the Married Women's Property Act 1882; under that Act the court had power to declare—but not to alter—the rights of husband and wife (*Pettitt v Pettitt* [1969] 2 All ER 385). In *Draper*, the wife had asked for the property to be sold; either this was effective as a severance or it had no effect at all: the court could not vary the property rights of the parties. This, perhaps, is the explanation: on an application under the Married Women's Property Act 1882, the court could not themselves sever the joint tenancy, and so found that the joint tenancy had been severed by the wife's act. However, that argument begs the question: there was an intention to sever but this did not mean that severance had in fact occurred. Certainly, as Dillon LJ points out ([1983] 3 All ER at 247 d) Mrs Harris's divorce petition was less precise than Mrs Draper's request, and Mrs Harris' wishes could have been satisfied by means other than severance, but Mrs Draper had asked for the sale of the property and a distribution of the proceeds 'equally'. Unless that last word is taken as a notice of severance, her claim could be regarded as an indication that the proceeds of sale, but not the property itself, should be held on a tenancy in common.

3 Land charges

A short, but important, point was decided by Kilner Brown J in *Stockler v Fourways Estates Ltd* [1983] 3 All ER 501. Was a Mareva injunction a 'writ or order affecting land . . . for the purpose of enforcing a judgment'? It is established that the Mareva injunction is interlocutory in nature, and may lead to no final judgment in the plaintiff's favour. As a result, there is no judgment to enforce, and the Land Charges Act cannot apply. The effect, presumably, is that the land in question could be sold and the purchaser would take free of any claim, the vendor being in breach of the injunction. One sympathises with the plaintiff in his desire to freeze, against any third party, any of the defendant's land within the jurisdiction, but the Land Charges Act was surely not intended to be applied so widely.

4 Leases

From time to time, a case about taxation throws light on basic principles of property law. *Cottage Holiday Associates Ltd v Customs & Excise Comrs* [1983] STC 278, [1983] QB 835, is such a case, discussing as it does, the fundamentals of leases. Cottage Holidays owned land upon which they were building holiday cottages for letting on a time-sharing basis. Each tenant was given a lease; under this, the lessee was entitled to occupy a cottage for a period in a year (usually one week) for a period of 80 years, on payment of a lump sum, a peppercorn rent, and a management fee. Value added tax was charged on the grant of such lease; the taxpayer contended that the grant of the lease was zero-rated, as it was a grant of a 'major interest'; this, according to the VAT legislation, meant, in relation to land, 'the fee simple or a tenancy for a term certain exceeding twenty-one years'. The taxpayer contended it granted an 80-*year* lease; the commissioners argued that the lease was for 80 *weeks*.

There has never been any difficulty in the concept of a lease being granted for a discontinuous term: thus, in *Smallwood v Sheppards* [1895] 2 QB 627, a lease for three successive Bank Holidays was regarded as one letting (even though the period of occupation was not continuous (at 629). Woolf J, in *Cottage Holiday Associates*, relied on this passage: the term, he said was not continuous. But, with respect, Wright J had said in *Smallwood v Sheppards* that there was a single letting, not that the period of the letting was discontinuous; it was 'one agreement for the possession and use of the ground on three occasions'. However, in *Cottage Holiday Associates* the learned judge used other arguments, including one based on the precise construction of the deed: the habendum of this read 'to hold unto the lessee for the holiday period in each year'. This point, however, is also not without difficulty. Counsel for the commissioners had taken the view for the purpose of the case that the lease was for a single discontinuous term (though had reserved the right to argue otherwise in a higher court). The habendum of the lease is difficult to reconcile with this approach; it appears as if there is intended to be a series of annual leases (some of which, as the judge hinted, would be caught by LPA 1925, s 149(3), which provides that leases to take effect more than 21 years in the future are void). However, the judge accepted the basis of counsel's reasoning but, having accepted it, did not give the reasoning its full force; if there was a single 'term' (the word used in the VAT legislation), then it began on the date of first occupation, and ended on the last day of the last occupation, such a period, of course, being in excess of 21 years.

There is no doubt that the judge was influenced by the general framework of the VAT legislation—a 'holiday let' for one week a year does not look like a long lease! But, as has been pointed out above, there are difficulties with what was, without doubt, a commonsense approach. Common sense, however, is not necessarily decisive where property principles are concerned, and the effect in other branches of the land law may not be inconsiderable. Woolf J mentioned the effect of the Housing Act 1961, ss 32 and 33; although the facts of the case do not appear to raise the issue, the scope of some of the sections dealing with the formalities in the property legislation may fall to be considered: LPA 1925, s 54(2) and LRA, ss 8 and 70(1)(k), in particular, may cause some difficulties. Certainly there are strong arguments for requiring a lease which extends over 80 years to be formally created or substantively registered, but such a view seems to fly in the face of Woolf J's decision. The issues await fuller analysis and clarification.

5 Licences

It has long been established that a lease of land contains no implied term as to fitness for purpose: see eg *Bottomley v Bannister* [1932] 1 KB 458 at 468. In *Wettern Electric Ltd v Welsh Development Agency* [1983] 2 All ER 629 Judge Newey QC, sitting as a judge of the High Court, had to consider whether a licence of land could imply such a term. Cases such as *Bottomley v Bannister* are something of an anomaly; as long ago as 1843, the Court of Exchequer in *Smith v Marrable* (1843) 11 M & W 5 held that a term should be implied that a furnished house should be fit for habitation, ie not infested by bugs. Judge Newey explained that licences did not convey estates in the land, nor did they give the licensee legal possession. Too much emphasis can be placed on both these statements; a license cannot create a legal estate in the land, but a contractual licence may, it seems, create an equitable interest in the land capable of binding third parties: *Midland Bank v Farmpride Hatcheries* (1980) 260 EG 493, similarly, an estoppel licence may be protected by an order creating a fee simple, which, ex hypothesi, is good against the world: *Pascoe v Turner* [1979] 2 All ER 945. As far as the second point is concerned, licensees may obtain, in fact, legal possession, and may even be entitled to it as of right. The judge's further comment, however, that statutory protection is afforded to leases, not licences, is fundamental and correct, though the effect of the Housing Act 1980, s 48 should not be forgotten. The net effect, however, was that there were sufficient differences between leases and licences to permit an implication of a term as to fitness for purpose: the process of implication and the content of the term are considered in the chapter on Contract (p 110 above).

In *Gloucestershire CC v Farrow* [1983] 3 All ER 1031 (see also p 236), Goulding J briefly referred to an argument on equitable estoppel: he cited, without comment, that counsel had relied on the five probanda in *Wilmott v Barber* (1880) 15 Ch D 96 at 105–106, and assumed that there was need for the plaintiff to have incurred expenditure or otherwise altered its position for the worse on the faith of the mistaken belief. Although this was not a case on licenses, it is somewhat surprising that the broader test of Oliver J in *Taylor Fashion Ltd v Liverpool Victoria Trustees Co Ltd* [1981] 1 All ER 897 at 918 g, whether it was '. . . unconscionable for the defendants to seek to take advantage of the mistake which . . . everybody shared' was not considered (see also *Amalgamated Investment and Property Co Ltd v Texas Commerce International Bank Ltd* [1981] 3 All ER 577, affirming [1981] 1 All ER 923). On the facts of the case, it is unlikely that the broader test would have made a difference to the success of counsel's submission, but it reflects the current uncertainty on virtually any aspects of the law relating to estoppel and to licences.

6 Covenants

Since the decision of the Court of Appeal in *Federated Homes Ltd v Mill Lodge Properties Ltd* [1980] 1 All ER 371, the law relating to the passing of the benefit of a restrictive covenant in equity has been in a state of uncertainty. In *Federated Homes*, LPA 1925, s 78 was used as a method of automatically annexing the benefit of a restrictive covenant to land, and this caused consternation both in Lincoln's Inn and in the academic world (see eg (1981) 97 LQR 32, (1982) 98 LQR 205). In *Roake v Chadha* [1983] 3 All ER 503, Judge Paul Baker QC, sitting as an additional judge of the High Court, considered the impact of *Federated Homes* on s 78 of the 1925 Act. The facts of *Roake v Chadha* are simple: land in Wembley was conveyed by W to L. L made various covenants, including one not to build more than one house on any plot of land sold. The wording of the covenant was clearly intended to bind L's land, and the covenant was made with W, 'but so this covenant shall not enure for the benefit of any owner or subsequent purchaser of [W's] [retained land] unless the benefit of this covenant shall be expressly assigned . . .' The plaintiff, Roake, was W's successor in title, and wished to sue Chadha, L's successor in title, who wished to build a second house on his plot; the benefit of the covenant had not been assigned. The action arose in a rather unsatisfactory form under RSC Ord 14, but this did not prevent Judge Baker QC from dealing with the substantive issues of law clearly and concisely. It was clear that there was no scheme of development or express annexation of the covenant to the land, so if the benefit were to pass, it had to be by virtue of LPA, s 78:

> 'a covenant relating to any land of the covenantee shall be deemed to be made with the covenantee and his successors in title and the persons deriving title under him or them, and shall have effect as if such successors and other persons were expressed.'

Judge Baker QC found that the relevant parts of the judgment of the Court of Appeal in *Federated Homes* were not obiter. The remedy in *Federated Homes*—an injunction against the defendant—could have been granted without reliance on s 78, but the decision of the court, affecting as it did two areas of land (the 'red' land and the 'green' land) could not have been reached without reliance on that section. In other words, the Court of Appeal *need* not have relied on s 78, but did so. (A point that does not seem to have been raised in *Roake v Chadha* was that in *Federated Homes* the defendant was the original covenantor, and therefore the passing of the benefit in equity, as distinct from law, need not have been considered.)

Counsel in *Roake v Chadha* argued that *Federated Homes* was wrongly decided, citing, in particular, G H Newsom QC's article in (1981) 97 LQR 32 (though not, it seems, the supplementary note in (1982) 98 LQR 205). Judge Baker would have none of this: as a first instance judge, he was bound to follow a decision of the Court of Appeal. (One wonders what the learned judge, in his capacity as editor of the Law Quarterly Review, really thought!) The 'correctness' or otherwise of *Federated Homes* was thus not considered; in view of the poor press the decision has received, it is worth noting, however, (i) that all *Federated Homes* does is to give LPA, s 78 its natural meaning: to quote Lord Wilberforce in a slightly different context: 'these words are ordinary words of plain English, and should, in my opinion, be interpreted as such' (*Williams & Glyn's Bank Ltd v Boland* [1980] 2 All ER 403 at 412g, on LRA 1925, s 70(1)(g)); (ii) that the case achieved a much-needed simplicity in the passing of the benefit of covenants relating to the land—*if* the covenant relates to the land of the covenantee, the benefit will pass; (iii) it is only necessary to consider the rules relating to the passing of the benefit of the covenant in equity if the burden has also passed: if the burden has passed then the covenantor's successor will be arguing that, although he has taken subject to the covenant's burden, the plaintiff does not have the right to enforce. To many, such an argument is unmeritorious.

Counsel argued that s 78 had to apply automatically because, unlike s 79, it was not subject to a contrary intention. Commentators on the Conveyancing Act 1881, s 58 (the predecessor of s 78) thought it odd that no such contrary intention existed, but the draftsman of the 1922, 1924 and 1925 legislation made no change. Counsel could see no reason of policy why s 78 had to apply, notwithstanding any stipulation to the contrary (cf LPA 1925, s 146) and Judge Baker was 'far from satisfied' (at 508 c) that the section had mandatory effect. It is difficult to see, however, without in some way writing in the requirement of a contrary intention, how the section can be avoided where it would otherwise apply.

Judge Baker then stated that even if s 78 were mandatory, on the proper construction of the document, it might not apply. This point can be accepted readily enough: if A owns a house and garden and sells the garden to B with a covenant that, during A's occupancy of the house, B will not build in the garden, that covenant can be seen as personal to A rather than relating to A's land and thus s 78 would not apply to it. Such a covenant can surely be registered: it affects the covenantor's land. However the covenant in *Roake v Chadha* is somewhat different: the covenant appears to relate to the land of the covenantee rather than to be a personal covenant, but can pass only by assignment. It is at this point that the judge's reasoning becomes difficult to follow. He cites a passage from Brightman LJ's judgment in *Federated Homes* (at 381), where the learned judge, speaking of the problem of deciding whether a covenant is annexed to the whole or to each and every part of a piece of land, states, '... if the benefit of a covenant is, on a proper construction of a document, annexed to the land', then it is normally annexed to every part. Judge Baker relies on this for the proposition that 'despite s 78 the benefit may be retained and not pass or be annexed to and run with the land' (at 508e). With respect, the passage seems to refer to the decided cases on express annexation, rather than to s 78 itself. Moreover it is difficult to see how, unless contrary intention is being allowed by implication, Brightman LJ's words can apply to s 78, unless he is considering a covenant *annexed* to land, as distinct from a covenant *relating* to it. Certainly, construing the document was precisely how a contrary intention was found in cases on s 79: see *Re Royal Victoria Pavilion, Ramsgate* [1961] 3 All ER 83, and *Sefton v Tophams* [1966] 1 All ER 1039. The argument may be that as the benefit of the covenant can only pass by assignment it is a personal covenant, but this does not seem to be the way the judge's reasoning proceeds. In short, Judge Baker seems to accept that there may be covenants which relate to the covenantee's land but to which s 78 does not apply, despite the lack of a possibility of contrary intention being considered, but without any real indication as to the type of covenant that may fall outwith the scope of s 78.

The most tantalising part of *Roake v Chadha* is the judge's consideration of the argument that LPA 1925, s 62 may operate to pass the benefit of a covenant. The idea that s 62, or its predecessor, the Conveyancing Act 1881, s 6, may operate to pass the benefit of covenants as 'rights and advantages . . . appertaining or reputed to appertain to the land' at the time of conveyance is not new: the question was argued, but not decided, in *Rogers v Hosegood* [1900] 2 Ch 388; the arguments for using s 62 in this way are succinctly stated by D J Hayton (1971) 87 LQR at 570–573. At first instance in *Federated Homes*, Mr John Mills QC, sitting as a deputy judge of the Chancery Division, appears to have relied on s 62 as the basis for his decision in favour of the plaintiffs, though his reasoning is nowhere stated ([1980] 1 All ER at 376f). On the facts of *Roake v Chadha*, Judge Baker considered the covenant was not a 'right appertaining or reputed to appertain to the land within s 62', as the covenant in terms precluded the passing of the benefit save by assignment. This, with respect, is not necessarily clear: the word 'appertaining' is defined in the Oxford English Dictionary as meaning 'pertaining, belonging, proper, appropriate'; these are wide definitions, and surely mean that the covenant must relate to the land, as distinct from pass automatically with it. However, Judge Baker expressed doubt as to whether s 62 could ever operate in the way proposed: counsel had suggested that s 62 operated only to pass legal rights rather than equitable rights. Although Judge Baker thought there 'might be something in this' (at 509 f) it is difficult to see why s 62 should be so limited: the Conveyancing Act 1881, on which it was based, was, after all, passed after the Judicature Acts 1873–1875!

7 Easements

Bradburn v Lindsay [1983] 2 All ER 408 is primarily a case on tort (see p 341) but merits a brief mention because of the discussion of the easement of support. One half of a pair of semi-detached properties had been pulled down, and the case involved the responsibility of the owner of the land, on which the house had previously stood, to maintain a party wall which had divided the two properties and which was now the outer wall of the surviving semi-detached property. The action was complicated by the fact that the party wall did not extend into the roof space, this being open. Judge Blackett-Ord V-C, sitting as an additional judge of the High Court, distinguished *Phipps v Pear* [1964] 2 All ER 35, as a party wall was not involved, the two properties in *Phipps* being, technically speaking, detached, and found for the plaintiff: LPA 1925 Sch I, Pt V, para 1 was decisive, as the property the subject of the action was a 'party wall or other party structure... held in individual shares', and a right of support was thus implied.

8 Mortgages

The feature of this year's cases on the subject of mortgages is that most of them are not dealt with in a traditional manner based on long-established principles of equity particularly relevant to mortgages. One case, though with wide implications, turns on the precise construction of the Building Societies Act, while two decisions are really matters of contract, or based on general principles of equity.

In *Nationwide Building Society v Registry of Friendly Societies* [1983] 3 All ER 296, the plaintiffs sought a declaration that they were entitled to make loans secured by a legal charge where the principal to be paid was index-linked, provided always that the principal repaid could never, in cash terms, be lower than the amount lent. On construing the Building Societies Act 1962, the judge found that such loans were permissible. However he was not asked to, and could not, decide whether such a charge, if created, could be attacked on the grounds of unconscionability or otherwise. However, as the judge noted, index-linking of mortgage repayments of principal and payments of interest had already been permitted in *Multiservice Bookbinding Ltd v Marden* [1978] 2 All ER 489. This, however, was a case of a loan by a private individual to a company, secured on the company's business premises and it does not inevitably follow that the reasoning would apply to cases where an institution is lending to a private individual on the security of the latter's home. However, there seems no reason why such loans should not be permitted: if a house owner/purchaser is given a choice of an 'ordinary' mortgage or one that is index-linked, and he is given the opportunity of taking independent advice, there seems no reason to rewrite the mortgage bargain on the grounds of unconscionability (cf *Cityland & Property (Holdings) Ltd v Dabrah* [1967] 2 All ER 639), provided always that the other terms of the mortgage are themselves unexceptionable. The emphasis in *Multiservice* was on the way in which the terms were imposed (ie were they imposed in a morally reprehensible manner, see at 502 a). Certainly any arguments based on economic duress or inequality of bargaining power would seem doomed to failure.

These issues, however, were to the fore in *Alec Lobb (Garages) Ltd v Total Oil GB Ltd* [1983] 1 All ER 944 (see also P Jackson [1983] Conv 465). The case is considered in the chapter on Contract (p 116 above), but there are aspects of the case of great interest to land lawyers. First, the case illustrates that the division between the law of contract and the law of mortgages is now virtually non-existent. The plaintiff claimed that the transaction was procured by economic duress, or resulted from the defendant's abuse of a fiduciary or confidential relationship in a common enterprise (both matters traditionally regarded as being contractual) or that the bargain was harsh and unconscionable, or was a transaction between mortgagor and mortgagee improperly entered into (both traditionally part of the law of mortgages). (The last claim, in fact, was based on 'restraint of trade'—an area of the law of contract: see *Esso Petroleum Co Ltd v Harper's Garage (Stourport) Ltd* [1967] 1 All ER 699.) The facts relied on to support these four claims obviously overlapped, and the learned judge treated the claims as part of one general question. Second, the case contains an exposition of the law on 'harshness and unconscionability', which attempts to state the elements that 'have almost invariably been present' (at 961 e). One party must have been at a serious disadvantage to the other, so that circumstances existed of which unfair advantage could be taken; second, the weakness of one party must have been exploited by the other party in a morally culpable manner; third, the resulting transaction must have been, not merely 'hard or improvident, but overreaching and oppressive'. In short, there had to be an impropriety which 'shocks the conscience of the court'. These requirements inevitably descend, in any particular case, to matters of fact, degree, and opinion: the language used by the judge is similar to, but not identical with, that of Browne-Wilkinson J in *Multiservice Bookbinding Ltd v Marden* [1978] 2 All ER 489. Once again, judges are forced to draw lines as matters of impression and discretion; such decisions are inevitable, but do nothing to help the litigant to predict the result of his case. Have we really advanced, in analytical terms, far beyond Lord Henley's remark in *Vernon v Bethell* (1762) 2 Eden 110 at 113, that 'necessitous men are not, truly speaking, free men'?

A second issue of interest is that the judge held that a lease by the plaintiff and a lease-back by the defendant to him was subject to the doctrine of restraint of trade. This seems contrary to the basis on which the Court of Appeal decided *Cleveland Petroleum Co Ltd v Dartstone Petroleum* [1969] 1 All ER 201, but seems in accord with the result (and, perhaps, the unarticulated reasoning) of the House of Lords in *Esso Petroleum Co Ltd v Harper's Garage (Stourport) Ltd*.

National Westminster Bank plc v Morgan [1983] 3 All ER 85, turns entirely on the presumption of undue influence. A husband and wife mortgaged their house to the plaintiff bank; there was no allegation of express influence, but the Court of Appeal found that there was a relationship of confidentiality (though this did not always exist between a banker and customer), and that the plaintiff bank had not ensured 'that the person liable to be influenced ha[d] formed an independent and informed judgment after full, free and informed thought' (at 93 d per Slade LJ). On the facts, the wife had been misled as to the scope of her liabilities; an independent adviser would have presented her with the true facts. The mortgage was thus set aside. The significant point is that, as far as one can tell from the report of the case, there was nothing in the terms of the mortgage themselves which would have been sufficient to merit the intervention of equity; what mattered was the relationship of the parties, and their conduct—even if only the conduct by omission, of not ensuring that independent advice was available, or taken. In so far as a trend is emerging in cases where the courts are asked to set aside mortgage transactions, it may be that the conduct of the parties in the negotiations leading to the transaction are at least as important as the transaction itself. The practical consequences are fundamental: even though a standard-form mortgage has received judicial approval in one case, it may run foul of the presumption of undue influence in another: in short, total uncertainty may prevail. Moreover, problems may arise if, as is not impossible, building societies (and perhaps banks) set up their own conveyancing departments. If the implications of the *Morgan* case are as wide as they seem, any such institution with its own conveyancing department runs the risk of any of its mortgages being upset, primarily because the mortgagor has received no independent advice!

The fourth case on mortgages this year was *Tse Kwong Lam v Wong Chit Sen* [1983] 3 All ER 54. The facts were complicated, but the issue before the Privy Council, on appeal from Hong Kong, was simple: could a company, effectively controlled by the mortgagee, buy the mortgaged property when the mortgagee sold under its power of sale. The judgment of the Board, delivered by Lord Templeman, confirmed that a mortgagee was not trustee of his power of sale, but that he was under a duty 'to take reasonable precautions to obtain the true market value of the mortgaged property at the date on which he decides to sell it' (Salmon LJ in *Cuckmere Brick Co Ltd v Mutual Finance Ltd* [1971] 2 All ER 633 at 646). As the mortgagee was not a trustee the mortgagor could take no action based on a trustee's conflict of duty and interest; all depended on whether the mortgagee had taken reasonable precautions. Notwithstanding that the mortgagee in *Tse Kwong Lam* had advertised and sold the property by auction, and that the company controlled by the mortgagee had been successful at that auction, the facts that no professional advice had been taken as to the most effective way to market the property and that the terms on which the property was sold would have been hard to comply with save for someone well acquainted with the property, prevented the mortgagees from satisfying Salmon LJ's test.

9 Manorial rights: highways

Any laws relating to manorial rights have an antique ring about them, notwithstanding that manors or reputed manors may be purchased and the alleged appurtenant rights used for commercial purposes. However, the Highways Act 1980, s 31(1) (re-enacting the Highways Act 1959, s 34) provides that 20 years user of a right of way over land enjoyed by the public as of right without interruption will be sufficient for the way to be dedicated as a highway, unless there is evidence that there was no intention to dedicate it. In *Gloucestershire CC v Farrow* [1983] 2 All ER 1031, Goulding J had to consider the operation of this section in connection with a dispute involving the market square at Stow-on-the-Wold. Goulding J took a broad view of the section, taking the view that s 31 was intended to prevent 'lengthy and expensive antiquarian investigation when highway rights are called in question' (at 1038 c). This seems in accord with common sense; no market had been held this century, and to allow a commercial enterprise (the third defendants) to operate a weekly market obstructing the long-assumed rights of way seems anachronistic. What does not appear to be explained is that the twice-yearly fair, held in the Market Place by virtue of manorial rights that had been leased, may have interrupted the alleged right of way. Goulding J accepted that the rights to hold the fair and to hold the market were the subject of separate grants, but did not relate them to the question of interruption.

10 Miscellaneous

The following may be briefly noted: *TRH Sampson Associates Ltd v British Rlys Board* [1983] 1 All ER 257 (consideration of the term 'accommodation work' within s 68 of the Railway Clauses Consolidation Act 1845: a mere change of user by adjoining landowners does not necessarily relieve the Railways Board of liability).

Landlord and Tenant

PHILIP H PETTIT, MA
Barrister, Professor of Equity at the University of Buckingham

Common law

The first three cases are each concerned with different aspects of rent review clauses. In the first, *Torminster Properties Ltd v Green* [1983] 2 All ER 457 the Court of Appeal had to decide a novel point, namely the effect of a surrender of a lease on a claim for increased rent fixed after the surrender. The decision at first instance, which was affirmed on appeal, was discussed in All ER Rev 1982, pp 183, 184. It will be remembered that under the rent review clause in this case it was provided that if the review rent had not been determined by the review date, the lessee continued to be liable to pay the original rent, and on the quarter day following the date on which the review was ultimately determined there became due as a debt payable by the lessee to the lessor the difference, duly apportioned, between the original rent and the review rent. In the Court of Appeal Stephenson LJ, with whom Kerr LJ agreed, accepted that the basic obligation of the lessee was to pay the review rent once the review date had passed. The basic obligation is unaffected by the fact that at the review date it may not be known what the review rent will be. The obligation is an obligation to pay the increased rent when it is determined and is analogous to a contractual obligation to pay for goods at a price to be fixed by a third party. The debt is due at the review date, though it waits to be payable until the expiration of the delay period and the determination of its amount. It is owed from the review date until surrender, after which it becomes payable retrospectively. Though there may not be a debt until the review rent has been fixed, there is a liability. Even if the debt does not exist until quantified, from the review date until surrender there is a contractual obligation to pay it when quantified. This obligation is not destroyed or discharged by a surrender. However, until the review rent is determined the lessor has no right to sue for the as yet undetermined rent, though he can sue for a declaration that the lessee is liable to pay it when determined. There is no breach of an obligation prior to the determination of the review rent, but there is an antecedent obligation accruing before the surrender puts an end to the lease. The lessee is under a contractual duty to pay the original rent so long as he holds the lease and to pay the difference between that and the review rent on the quarter day following the determination of the review rent: and the duty is unaffected by a surrender of the lease.

   Amherst v James Walker Goldsmith & Silversmith Ltd [1983] 2 All ER 1067 raised a different point on a rent review clause for the Court of Appeal. The tenants were the lessees under a 28-year lease from 24 June 1961. The original rent was £2,500 for the first 14 years, and thereafter a rent of £2,500 or such higher sum as should be ascertained under the provisions of the rent review clause. As is commonly the case, the rent review was to be initiated by the landlords submitting an assessment of the open market rent to the tenants by a specified date, in this case 25 December 1974. There were further provisions, as to which time was expressed to be of the essence of the contract, and as to what was to happen if the assessment was not agreed. The landlords allowed 25 December 1974 to pass without issuing a triggering assessment, and on 25 January 1975 sought an extension of time, which was refused. As the law was then understood the landlords had lost their opportunity to obtain an increased rent, but the position was changed by the House of Lords' decision in *United Scientific Holdings Ltd v Burnley BC* [1977] 2 All ER 62. As anyone who knows anything about rent review clauses is well aware, their Lordships decided in that case that the presumption is that time limits prescribed by a rent review clause are not of the essence of the contract. Following that decision there were proceedings in which it was held that in the *Amherst* lease there was nothing in the terms of the rent review clause to rebut this presumption. It was not, however, until the hearing of those earlier proceedings that the landlords realised that they had never issued a triggering assessment. This they did on 10 May 1979 and the question in the present proceedings was whether the delay in issuing the notice was unreasonable and itself invalidated the notice.

The Court of Appeal, affirming the decision at first instance, held that where on the true construction of the lease time is not of the essence in serving a landlord's notice for a rent review, mere delay by the landlord in serving his notice, however lengthy and even if coupled with hardship to the tenant, does not destroy his contractual right to serve the notice. The landlord's right to serve the notice continues unless the tenant can show either that the contract, or that part of it, has been abrogated or that the landlord has precluded himself from exercising it. The tenant may do this by showing that the contract has been repudiated, for instance where he has served a notice calling on the landlord to exercise his right within a reasonable time or not at all, and such notice is ignored, or where some event has happened which estops the landlord from relying on his right. But mere delay, even if coupled with hardship to the tenant, will have no effect unless the combination amounts to an estoppel. The most that can be said where there has been long delay is that, as a matter of inference from the circumstances in which the delay occurred, the landlord has made a representation that he does not intend to claim a higher rent. This could lay the foundation of an estoppel, but even so the landlord will not be estopped unless the tenant has acted on the representation to his prejudice. Some earlier rent review cases had referred to the 'abandonment' by the landlord of his contractual rights. Oliver LJ and Lawton LJ are surely right, however, in saying that the unilateral signification of an intention not to exercise his contractual right cannot bind the landlord save as a promise (promissory estoppel) or as a representation followed by reliance (equitable estoppel) or as a consensual variation of the agreement or as a repudiation accepted by the other party.

Oliver LJ, who gave the leading judgment, discussed the relevant cases, in some of which are to be found dicta suggesting that unreasonable delay, at least where it caused hardship to the tenant, would defeat the landlord's rights. These dicta were not followed, and the only actual decision on the point, that of Foster J in *Telegraph Properties (Securities) Ltd v Courtaulds Ltd* (1980) 257 EG 1153, was overruled insofar as it rests on simple delay or abandonment. Oliver LJ preferred the views of Slade LJ in *London & Manchester Assurance Co Ltd v G A Dunn & Co* (1982) 265 EG 39 at 135 denying mere delay as a factor nullifying the landlord's rights.

At first sight this decision may appear to be hard on tenants. As the court pointed out, however, this is not really so. First, if the landlord does not act within a reasonable time after the specified date, the tenant can serve a notice on the landlord calling on him to exercise his right within a reasonable time or not at all. And, secondly, since in practice reviews are always upwards, delay by the landlords will operate to the tenants' advantage, because although an increase in rent, when ultimately made, will operate retrospectively, the tenant will have had the use of the money in the meantime.

(There appears to be a misprint on p 1069, line g2: "handy" should read "hardy".)

In *Lear v Blizzard* [1983] 3 All ER 662 there was an option to renew a lease for a further term of 21 years 'at a rent to be agreed between the parties hereto or in default of agreement at a rent to be determined by a single arbitrator'. Improvements had been made to the demised premises by a predecessor in title of the tenant, to which the landlord gave his consent after the event. The parties failed to agree a rent and the first question for the determination of which the arbitrator applied to the court was whether he should apply an objective test, ie determine what would be a reasonable rent for the demised premises, together with the improvements, on the open market; or a subjective test, ie what would be a fair rent for these particular landlords and this particular tenant.

The landlords relied strongly on the House of Lords decision in *Ponsford v HMS Aerosols Ltd* [1978] 2 All ER 837 where the majority applied an objective test to a rent review clause expressing the rent to be £9,000 pa 'or such sum whichever shall be higher as shall be assessed as a reasonable rent for the demised premises for the appropriate period'. There seems much to be said for the views of the dissenting minority in that case, Lords Wilberforce and Salmon, who did not think that a rent increased because of improvements paid for by the tenant could sensibly be regarded as a 'reasonable rent' within the ordinary and natural meaning of those words. However, the majority view must be followed where there is no material difference in the language.

The Court of Appeal held in *Thomas Bates & Son Ltd v Wyndham's (Lingerie) Ltd* [1981] 1 All ER 1077 that the language of the rent review clause before them was materially different from that in *Ponsfords v HMS Aerosols Ltd*. In the later case there was to be paid on review 'such rents as shall have been agreed between the lessor and lessee'. The lease was first rectified by inserting an arbitration clause, and then as a matter of construction it was held that the rent should be such as it would have been reasonable for the particular landlord and the particular tenant to have agreed. There should be taken into account all considerations which would affect the mind of either party in connection with the negotiation of such a rent, including past expenditure by the tenant on improvements.

In *Lear v Blizzard* Tudor Evans J was surely right in holding that the language before him was, with immaterial differences, indistinguishable from the language of the clause in *Thomas Bates & Son Ltd v Wyndham's*

(Lingerie) Ltd and was to be construed in a subjective sense. Having so held, Tudor Evans J had to determine to what extent the expenditure on improvements was to be taken into account. On the one hand he dismissed the landlord's argument that no account should be taken of such expenditure when the tenant did not himself carry out the improvements but took the premises by assignment; on the other hand he did not accept the tenant's argument that the improvements must necessarily be wholly disregarded. In his view, a tenant by assignment steps into the shoes of the previous tenant and is entitled to say, if it be the fact, that he paid for the improvements then and to claim that the improvements be wholly or partly disregarded according as he shows that he paid wholly for, or contributed partly towards, the improvements.

The third question Tudor Evans J had to decide related to inflation, in view of the fact that the new lease was for 21 years. The landlord argued that there should be a premium or percentage uplift to take account of the fact that in the new lease there was no provision for a rent review. Tudor Evans J referred to *National Westminster Bank Ltd v B S C Footwear Ltd* (1980) 42 P & CR 90, where the Court of Appeal held that an arbitrator's power to determine the rent did not include a power to direct that the rent should be periodically reviewed: there was no power to introduce any variations between the orginal and the renewed lease. Templeman LJ's answer to the argument that if the arbitrator fixed the rent at the beginning of 21 years for the whole period, the landlord is in danger of not getting the fruits of inflation which he might otherwise get if there were rent review clauses, was that 'what the landlords' predecessors in title gave away the landlords cannot now take back'. Tudor Evans J held that Templeman LJ's observation was equally applicable to the landlord's attempt to protect himself against inflation by adding a premium or percentage uplift; an attempt which if it were to be carried through, would involve a high degree of speculation. He accordingly held that no premium should be added.

With respect, Templeman LJ's judgment is not entirely satisfactory. In this sort of case the landlord is not seeking any 'fruits of inflation'; he is merely wishing to maintain his return in real terms. He is not so much seeking a profit as seeking to avoid a loss. It may well be a hardship to a landlord where the original lease may have been granted at a time when short rent review periods were far from being the norm. One question that was not raised was whether the same objection would be taken to fixing an index-linked rent: it will be recalled that judicial approval has recently been given to the grant of an index-linked mortgage by a building society: *Nationwide Building Society v Registry of Friendly Societies* [1983] 3 All ER 296. It is arguable that this should be permissible—it would not involve a variation of the original lease and the arbitrator would be doing no more than determine the rent—but in the light of the approach of Templeman LJ and Tudor Evans J one cannot be at all confident that the courts would recognise a distinction.

National Westminster Bank Ltd v Hart [1983] 2 All ER 177, CA, is an interesting and unusual case. The books are full of cases where the substantial question is which of two innocent parties is to suffer: the substantial question in this case was which of two parties was to receive an undeserved benefit. The facts were simple. A house built in 1867 was let on a 99-year lease expiring 25 March 1967. In 1921 the residue of the term was acquired by CP & CW Cowles (who were a partnership) who sub-let in 1947 to the defendants. The sub-lease expired in 1965, but the defendants remained in possession and continued to pay rent to the sub-lessors. After the death of the survivor of the Cowles in 1978, leaving the plaintiffs as executors, the defendants said that they would not pay any further rent until they were satisfied that the plaintiffs had good title. The plaintiffs did not provide any further information and in due course started proceedings for arrears of rent. There was no doubt but that the Cowles' title as lessees expired on 25 March 1967. Furthermore no heir or assignee of the original freeholders could be discovered.

Both at first instance and on appeal there were two pairs of cases considered—*Carlton v Bowcock* (1885) 51 LT 659 and *Hindle v Hick Bros Manufacturing Co Ltd* [1947] 2 All ER 825 which favoured the landlord, and *Fenner v Duplock* (1824) 2 Bing 10 and *Serjeant v Nash Field & Co* [1903] 2 KB 304 which favoured the tenant. The judge below took the view that the reasoning in the two pairs of cases was inconsistent and, preferring the reasoning in the first pair, decided in favour of the landlord. On appeal the cases preferred at first instance were distinguished on the ground that they were concerned with claims by the assignee of the reversion whereas in the other pair of cases, like the one before the court, the landlords' title had determined.

The Court of Appeal thus had good authority for the proposition that 'a tenant, though he cannot dispute the right of his landlord to demise, may show that his title has expired' (*England d Syburn v Slade* (1792) 4 Term Rep 682 as cited by Best CJ in *Fenner v Duplock, supra*). It seems, however, inconsistent with the law as stated in *Industrial Properties (Barton Hill) Ltd v A E I Ltd* [1977] 2 All ER 293 where Lord Denning MR said:

> 'If a landlord lets a tenant into possession under a lease, then, so long as the tenant remains in possession *undisturbed by any adverse claim*—then the tenant cannot dispute the landlords' title.'

If the present case is to stand as an exception to this general principle, it produces the anomaly that a landlord who has never had a legal title is in a stronger position than one who has had one which has now come to an end.

In conclusion it may be added that Sir David Cairns alluded to another unsatisfactory feature of the case in his penultimate paragraph when he observed that the plaintiffs might have been able to contend that they had acquired a possessory title, but this argument was not open to them on the pleadings.

The decision in *Calabar Properties Ltd v Stitcher* [1983] 3 All ER 759 is to be welcomed as clarifying the application of fundamental principles as to the measure of damages to breach by the landlord of a repairing covenant. All that need be said of the facts is that as a result of the landlord's breach, rainwater penetrated into the flat making it damp and damaging the decorations. The tenant and her husband lived in these unsatisfactory conditions for five years after making complaint to the landlord before the flat eventually became uninhabitable and the tenant took alternative rented accommodation. She lived in this accommodation for a further two years before the action was heard. On the appeal to the Court of Appeal, there was no appeal by the landlord on the issue of liability, and there was neither cross-appeal nor appeal in relation to the two items of damages awarded at first instance, viz (i) £4,604.44 for the diminution in the value of the flat to the tenant from the date of the first complaint to the hearing, the damages being based, in the absence of other evidence, on the cost to the tenant of making good and redecorating the flat less one-third for the element of betterment and (ii) £3,000 for the disappointment, discomfort, loss of enjoyment and ill-health suffered during the five years the tenant and her husband occupied the flat.

At first instance the judge refused to make any award (a) for the running costs, eg rent, rates and service charges, of the flat during the two years when it was uninhabitable and (b) for diminution in the market value of the flat during the two-year period prior to the hearing based on the capital value of the flat or its rack rental value. The tenant appealed against the disallowance of these heads of damage; the landlords sought to uphold the judge's decision and argued, inter alia, that the appeal should be dismissed because neither of these two heads had been pleaded.

On the first head, running costs, the county court judge had rejected the claim because he considered it comparable to expenses incurred in taking another house, which he regarded as irrecoverable on the authority of *Green v Eales* (1841) 2 QB 225. It is not entirely clear whether that case so decides, but the Court of Appeal agreed that, if it did, it was wrongly decided. The tenant in the instant case could have claimed the expenses of alternative accommodation. The case in fact took a surprising time to reach the court (four years, eight months) and when the counterclaim was settled no such claim could have been made because the tenant was still living in the flat: but the counterclaim should presumably have been amended when the flat became uninhabitable and the tenant took alternative accommodation.

On the second head, the tenant's appeal failed for two reasons: first the technical one that it involved using an undisclosed expert's report as a basis for assessing damages without giving the landlords the opportunity of calling expert advice on valuation. Secondly, because to submit that what the tenant had lost by the landlord's breach was the consequent diminution in the value of the flat as a marketable asset was to ask the court to take a wholly unreal view of the facts—nor is *Hewitt v Rowlands* [1924] All ER Rep 344 an authority for the proposition that it is in every case necessary to obtain valuation evidence.

Even if those two heads of damages had been in principle recoverable, the tenant would still have failed because neither had been pleaded, and this was essential in fairness to the landlord. Nor could the tenant be allowed to amend and present a new or additional case at this stage—apart from possible injustice to the landlord, it is in the public interest that there should be an end to litigation.

The Court of Appeal, as already indicated, took the opportunity of stating what principles should be applied, and also sought to dispel the notion that when damages are claimed by a tenant for breach of a landlord's repairing covenant they must always be assessed by reference to the diminution in the open market value of the premises and that they can never include the cost of alternative accommodation while the repairs are being carried out.

The fundamental principle is that damages should, so far as possible, place the tenant in the position he would have been in if there had been no breach. But, as Griffiths LJ observed: 'This object will not be achieved by applying one set of rules to all cases regardless of the particular circumstances of each case'. One must look at the particular facts of each individual case to see what damage the tenant has suffered and what would be fair compensation therefor. For instance, if the tenant had bought the lease as a speculation intending to assign it, to the knowledge of the landlords, the diminution in rental (or capital) value might be the true measure of damage. In a case like the present where the premises have become uninhabitable by reason of the breach of covenant and it is clear that the landlord has no intention of doing the repairs unless ordered to do so by the court, the tenant has two reasonable options. One is to sell and move elsewhere permanently: if this option is chosen the measure of damage would be the difference between the price obtained and what would have been the open market value if the covenant has been duly performed. The other option is to move into temporary accommodation and sue the landlords to force them to carry out the repairs and then return to the premises after the repairs have been done. The tenant in that event is entitled to the cost of redecoration caused by the breach of covenant, the cost of the alternative accommodation and general damages for the unpleasantness of living in the premises as they deteriorated until it became uninhabitable.

General statutory provisions

In *Land Securities plc v Receiver for the Metropolitan Police District* [1983] 2 All ER 254 Megarry VC had to determine what was the standard of proof required when a landlord sought the leave of the court under s 1 of the Leasehold Property (Repairs) Act 1938 to bring an action for forfeiture of the lease and for damages in respect of the tenant's breach of a repairing covenant. It will be remembered that s 1(5) provides that leave is not to be given unless the landlord 'proves' that the requirements of one of the five paragraphs in sub-s 5 are satisfied.

In order to succeed in his application a landlord, it was said, has to leap three hurdles. The first is that there is a breach of a repairing covenant; the second that s 1(5) is satisfied; and the third, assuming that the first two have been surmounted, is whether the court ought to exercise its discretion in favour of granting leave. The first two very much go together, for there is no separate requirement of establishing a breach of covenant, though the existance of a breach is clearly assumed under each head in s 1(5) except the last. Megarry V-C took as an illustration para (a) where what the landlord is required to 'prove is that "the immediate remedying of the breach in question is requisite for preventing substantial diminution in the value of his reversion" and so on.' In his view the word 'proves' governs a compound requirement which includes the immediate remedying of the breach, and this being requisite to prevent substantial diminution in the value of the reversion. The existence of the breach cannot be segregated out of this compound requirement and given a different standard of proof from the rest of it. Megarry VC added that even under para (e), which does not expressly refer to a breach of covenant, the landlord must show that he has a prima facie, or arguable, case for there being a breach in order to establish that there are special circumstances making it just and equitable for leave to be given.

As to what the standard of proof should be, Megarry V-C was bound to follow the Court of Appeal decision in *Sidnell v Wilson* [1966] 1 All ER 681 but there was considerable argument as to what that case decided. In the earlier case Lord Denning MR and Harman LJ said that the landlord must show a 'prima facie case'. Diplock LJ, however, preferred to use the expression 'arguable case' on the ground that the other phrase invites an enquiry at the hearing of the application into evidence contradicting what in the first instance is a prima facie case and therefore might lead to a complete trial of the action on the application, which all the members of the court were agreed should not happen. For this reason Megarry V-C said that if the term 'prima facie case' is used it is to be understood in the sense of a case made out by the landlord without the need to go into any rebutting evidence put forward by the tenant.

On these facts, which involved the unsatisfactory condition of the cladding on New Scotland Yard—a curious feature of the case was that the landlord was objecting to the tenant paying £5m on repairs and wanted only £½m to be spent—Megarry V-C had little difficulty in deciding that the landlord 'on the lowly standards of proof that apply' had established that the case fell within paras (a) and (d) of s 1(5). He therefore had to consider the third hurdle, that of the discretion of the court. He cited the judgment of Ungoed-Thomas J in *Re Metropolitan Film Studios Ltd v Twickenham Film Studies Ltd (Intended Action)* [1962] 3 All ER 508 where that judge observed (at 517) that the discretion under the 1938 Act is

> 'of an interlocutory nature, not to be exercised to exclude the lessor from his rights subject to the wide discretion given to the court under s 146 [that is, of the Law of Property Act 1925], unless the court is clearly convinced that, despite compliance with the requirements specified in the paragraphs of sub-s (5), the application should be refused'.

Megarry V-C, however, thought that the discretion of the court was much less fettered than is suggested by subjecting it to the words 'clearly convinced', though on the facts he was 'clearly convinced' that leave should be refused. All the matters which the landlord wanted resolved could be resolved more conveniently and in less time and at less cost in other proceedings that had already been initiated between the parties. It was therefore unnecessary for the landlord to sue for forfeiture and damages under the 1938 Act.

Business tenancies

The crucial issue in *Lloyds Bank Ltd v City of London Corpn* [1983] 1 All ER 92 related to the exercise of the court's discretion under RSC Ord 21, r 3(1). The case concerned a lease due to expire on 18 December 1980. The tenants took the first step by serving a notice under s 26 on 8 February 1980 requesting the grant of a new tenancy to begin on 25 December 1980 for a term of 14 years at an annual rent of £20,000. On 31 March 1980 the landlords served a counter-notice under s 26(6) intimating that they would oppose the grant of a new tenancy on the ground set out in s 30(1)(f), namely that they intended to demolish or reconstruct the premises and could not do so without obtaining possession. In accordance with the statutory procedure the tenants applied to the court for a new tenancy on 5 June 1980, but in July 1980 the landlords informed the tenants that they would abandon their opposition to the grant of a new tenancy.

From January 1980 onwards, and particularly after the landlord's counter-notice, the tenants were uncertain whether they would be able to continue in the premises. Alternatives were investigated and at the end of July or the beginning of August the tenants decided that they would close their branch on the premises in question and accordingly would not want a new tenancy. The decision was initially regarded as confidential and was not communicated to the landlords until 20 October 1980. The communication included a claim by the tenants for statutory compensation under s 37, which, as amended by the Law of Property Act 1969, expressly gives the tenant a right to compensation where an application is withdrawn and the only grounds specified in the landlords' notice under ss 25 or 26(6) are one or more of those contained in paras (e), (f) and (g) of s 30(1). The landlords were not prepared to consent to a subsequent application by the tenants to discontinue the proceedings for a new tenancy, except on the basis that the tenants undertook not to seek compensation. Accordingly the tenants issued a motion for leave to discontinue their proceedings for a new tenancy. Under RSC Ord 21, r 3 discontinuance of High Court proceedings requires the leave of the court which may order the proceedings to be discontinued 'on such terms as to costs, the bringing of a subsequent action or otherwise as it thinks just'. The landlords argued that the tenant should be put on terms not to claim compensation, but the judge at first instance gave the tenants unconditional leave to discontinue and this was affirmed by the Court of Appeal.

The point had previously come before Whitford J in *Young, Austin & Young Ltd v British Medical Association* [1977] 2 All ER 834 where the judge on granting leave to discontinue, did impose a term that the tenants should not pursue any claim for compensation. He took the view that otherwise injustice would be done to the landlords for, if the matter were to proceed in the circumstances that the tenants were no longer seeking the fresh tenancies which they had originally sought, their action would be dismissed and their right to compensation would go. He was, however, somewhat concerned by the fact that if the same point arose in the county court, the tenants would have a right to discontinue without leave and would have a right to compensation under s 37. The Court of Appeal, however, in this instant case disapproved this decision and the result would now be the same in the High Court and the county court.

Since the court was concerned with the exercise of a discretion, it was entirely proper that it should look to the policy of the legislation and the principles on which it is based. The approach of the court is indicated by the observation of Templeman LJ that a landlord who serves a counter-notice under s 30(1)(e), (f) or (g) is to be regarded as 'asserting a right to inflict loss or damage on the tenant by requiring the tenant to quit the premises'. The counter-notice, it was said, creates difficulties for the tenant who cannot know whether the landlord will succeed in his opposition or not. A prudent tenant will therefore cast around for alternative courses of action and involve himself in enquiries and investigations that he would not otherwise have made. Nor do the tenant's difficulties disappear if the landlord withdraws his opposition—the landlord may still, for instance, argue that the new tenancy granted should be of short duration. A landlord who serves a counter-notice under s 30(1)(e), (f) or (g) brings pressure to bear on the tenant to consider the advisability of quitting the premises. Accordingly, it was held, he is to be regarded as presenting the tenant with a choice between the doubtful possibility of a new tenancy and the certainty of compensation under s 37. Once such a counter-notice is served, the landlord has no right both to recover the premises and to avoid the payment of compensation. Accordingly the court will always, in its discretion, allow the tenant to withdraw unconditionally unless the landlord has been prejudiced, and the fact that the landlord will be obliged to pay compensation is not in itself evidence of prejudice because the Act provides for compensation to be paid if the landlord has served a counter-notice. The moral for the landlord is to think even more carefully before serving a counter-notice under s 30(1)(e), (f) or (g) because once this has been done he will normally have to pay compensation, except of course where the tenant continues with his application and obtains a new tenancy notwithstanding the landlord's opposition. It may be added that if the court makes an order for the grant of a new tenancy, the tenant has a right to have the order revoked within 14 days. If the tenant exercises this right, he will not be entitled to compensation.

Agricultural holdings

Epsom & Ewell Borough Council v C Bell (Tadworth) Ltd [1983] 2 All ER 59 raised a short point on s 2(1) of the Agricultural Holdings Act 1948. The facts were that the company had held land from the council under tenancy agreements which did not confer any security of tenure. The last of these was granted on 1 February 1977 for a period of 364 days, expiring in due course by effluxion of time on 30 January 1978. Negotiations took place for a further like term of 364 days on the expiry of the then existing term, but no new tenancy agreement was ever executed. The company, however, remained in possession and tendered two quarter's rent which was accepted by the council, though subsequent tenders were rejected. It was agreed by the parties that the effect of the company holding over, and the acceptance of rent by the Council, was by implication to create a new term of 364 days.

The effect of s 2 of the 1948 Act was that this agreement by implication would give the company security of tenure 'unless the letting or grant was approved by the Minister before the agreement was entered into'. Well before the original term had expired the Minister had executed an approval, and the question before the court was whether it was valid and affective. The relevant parts of the approval related to 'the letting by an agreement to be entered into after the date hereof of the land . . . for use as agricultural land for the period of 364 days commencing on 31 January 1978.'

The first argument by the company was that the Minister did not have power to approve the grant of a tenancy by implication of the land which arose in the events which occurred. This is a question of construction of the section. In the only previous case on this part of the section, *Finbow v Air Ministry* [1963] 2 All ER 647, McNair J did not think that the section required that the approval must be given ad hoc and suggested that the Minister might

approve lettings or grants of particular types without considering the proposed letting or grant. Judge Rubin took a somewhat different view. In his
opinion the section had to be construed as if it read, 'unless the letting or grant
of the land which was ultimately let was approved by the Minister before the
agreement was entered into . . .' On this construction the duty of the Minister
is to apply his mind to the letting or grant of a particular piece of land, though
he is not concerned with the particular terms of the agreement to be entered
into which, ex hypothesi, have not then been entered into and, indeed, may
not by then have been finally settled. He accordingly had power to grant the
approval he did grant. If it failed on the first point, the company had a second
argument, namely that the approval did not apply to the particular tenancy
which in fact came into being by the implication arising from the holding
over and the payment of rent. Although one's first reaction on reading the
section may perhaps be to assume that the agreement referred to means an
agreement in writing, it was held that it is well settled on general principles
that a tenancy of agricultural land for 364 days may be created not only by an
agreement in writing but also by an agreement under seal, an oral agreement,
or by implication arising from a holding over and payment of rent. However
it arises there is none the less an agreement and there is no reason why it
should not be covered by an appropriately worded approval. On the facts of
this case it was held to be clear that it was covered by the Minister's approval
and the tenant therefore did not have security of tenure.

Rent Act cases

In *Hill v Rochard* [1983] 2 All ER 21 the appellants were statutory tenants of
The Grange, a period country house with a large number of rooms, a staff
flat, outbuildings, stable, a large garden and a field across the road, the total
amount of land being some one and a half acres. They enjoyed their life-style
in the isolated dwelling with its unimpeded views and space for pets. They
wanted the flat for living-in help and ample accommodation to enable them
to keep open house for their friends and relatives. The trustee landlords
thought the rent of £2,100 was an unreasonably low return on an asset valued
at £90,000–£100,000 and wished to sell it with vacant posession and reinvest
the proceeds of the sale. Various offers of alternative accommodation were
refused by the tenants, and ultimately the landlords bought a house for
£52,500 specifically for the purpose of rehousing the tenants. This was a
modern detached house with four bedrooms, two living rooms, a double
garage and a garden of about ⅜ acre in a pleasant estate on the outskirts of a
village about three and a half miles from The Grange. The offer of this
property as suitable alternative accommodation having likewise been refused
by the tenants, the landlords sought possession under s 98(1)(a) and Part IV of
Sch 15 to the Rent Act 1977. The county court judge made the order and the
only effective ground of appeal was that the judge had misdirected herself in
respect of the test to be applied in determining whether or not the accommodation offered by the landlords constituted suitable alternative accommodation. The most relevant statutory provision is contained in para 5(1)(b)
of Part IV. This imposes the condition that the alternative accommodation
offered must be 'reasonably suitable to the means of the tenant and to the

needs of the tenant and his family as regards extent and character . . .' Both Dunn and Eveleigh LJJ stated clearly that 'needs' means 'needs for housing' and that the question is whether the accommodation offered is reasonably suitable for the tenant's housing needs as regards extent and character. As to extent, a four bedroomed house with two living rooms was held to be clearly extensive enough for an elderly couple living alone. As to character it was said that you consider the actual tenant and his standard of living, but from the point of view of accommodation needs. *Redspring Ltd v Francis* [1973] 1 All ER 640 establishes that the environment can be taken into account—on the facts of the present case the tenants would still be able to enjoy the amenities of country life in the alternative accommodation offered. In relation to the character of the house it is the tenants' *needs* that have to be considered, not their peculiar wishes and desires and their own particular taste for amenities. This echoes *Wilson v Cunningham* (1929) 45 Sh Ct Rep 353, not cited, where 'needs' was said to mean reasonable needs, not luxuries, and not to be synonymous with the tenant's wishes. On the facts, the amenities such as the paddock and outbuildings which enabled them to keep their animals were not the sort of advantages the Rent Acts were intended to protect. The appeal was accordingly dismissed.

Dunn LJ set out the arguments of counsel for the appellants, who relied particularly on *MacDonnell v Daly* [1969] 3 All ER 851 (explained on a point not relevant here is *Mykolyshyn v Noah* [1971] 1 All ER 48) and *Redspring Ltd v Francis*, supra, and argued that the court is concerned with the needs of the actual tenant in question, and that those needs include the ability of the particular tenant, in his new accommodation, to follow the life-style which he had enjoyed in the old accommodation. It is disappointing that Dunn LJ says nothing about the decision of the Court of Appeal in *MacDonnell v Daly*, that where a tenant is protected for combined dwelling and professional purposes, the alternative accommodation must be suitable for his needs which include not only his living, cooking and sleeping but also his professional needs—in that case an artist's studio. Of course at the time that case was decided a mixed business and residential tenancy could be within the Acts, but no reference was made to professional or business needs in the predecessor to para 5(1)(b). It is doubtless right to go first to the relevant statutory provisions, but decisions on such provisions should not be ignored.

Eveleigh LJ, agreeing with Dunn LJ, relied on *Briddon v George* [1968] 1 All ER 609 and *Middlesex County Council v Hall* [1929] All ER Rep 398 to support his view that 'needs' is restricted to needs for the purpose of habitation. However, in *MacDonnell v Daly*, which was cited to the court and indeed referred to by Dunn LJ, Lord Denning MR said, 'but those cases were in the Divisional Court and cannot survive the subsequent decision of the Court of Appeal in *McIntyre v Hardcastle* [1948] 2 KB 82'. In the same case Edmund Davies LJ, doubted whether *Briddon v George* was rightly decided, and said he was wholly in agreement with the views expressed by Lord Denning MR. Megaw LJ agreed with both Lord Denning MR and Edmund Davies LJ.

Though the result in *Hill v Rochard* may well be right, the failure to deal adequately with the earlier decisions leaves the law less clear than it might otherwise be and makes it a matter for regret that leave to appeal to the House of Lords was refused. Apart from precedent, the interpretation given to para 5(1)(b) is a reasonable one and one suspects it is likely to be followed, *MacDonnell v Daly* perhaps being distinguished as no longer appropriate since business tenancies have been taken outside the Acts. It may be added that previously, in a very different sort of case, the Court of Appeal, while fully accepting the decision in *Redspring Ltd v Francis*, refused to extend it in *Siddiqui v Rashid* [1980] 3 All ER 1984. In that case the tenant had friends in London and attended a mosque there, but worked in Luton, where he was offered alternative accommodation. It was held that the character of the property did not include the matters on which the tenant relied, namely friends in London and the mosque.

Trustees of Henry Smith's Charity v Willson [1983] 1 All ER 73 raised the interesting question as to whether a statutory tenant can validly sublet the whole of the dwelling-house, but no binding answer was given as the case was decided on other grounds. The essential facts were that a lease for eight years from 29 September 1971, containing a covenant not to assign without the consent of the landlords, had been granted by the plaintiff landlords to a Mr Neale. Mr Neale assigned the lease to Mrs Willson who in turn assigned the residue of the term to her husband, the first defendant, a few days before the expiry of the term. The validity of these assignments was not in dispute. On 29 September 1979 Mr Willson became a statutory tenant, and on 6 June 1980 he entered into a transaction with Mrs Blakeney, the substantial defendant. According to the only documentary evidence, a letter from Mr Willson to Mrs Blakeney, the transaction was a monthly tenancy at a rent of £75 per calendar month plus rates etc, but this was far from being the whole transaction. Mrs Blakeney in fact paid Mr Willson the sum of £13,450 as consideration for the transaction, and was told by Mr Willson that he had no intention to return to the flat and was giving up his occupation forever.

The plaintiff's agents became aware of the occupation of the flat by Mrs Blakeney, and on 18 September 1980 acquired knowledge sufficient to support a waiver of any unlawfulness involved in the occupation, if their subsequent acts sufficed to constitute a waiver. The agents forthwith decided not to demand or accept any further rent, but owing to an administrative error in their office a further demand was sent to Mrs Willson. There was no evidence that the demand in fact reached Mr Willson, and no further rent was actually accepted. On these facts the landlords sought prossession against both Mr Willson and Mrs Blakeney. The county court judge made an immediate order for possession against Mr Willson, on the grounds that he no longer occupied the flat as his residence, and further or alternatively under Case 6 on the grounds that he had sublet the whole flat without the landlords' consent and that in all the circumstances it was reasonable to do so. There was no appeal by Mr Willson, but the landlords appealed against the refusal of the judge to make an order against Mrs Blakeney.

A statutory tenancy cannot, of course, be assigned, and it was clear that the facts did not fall within para 13 of Sch 1—change of statutory tenant by agreement—as this requires that the landlords be a party thereto; moreover it is an offence for any person to require the payment of any pecuniary consideration for entering into such an agreement. Accordingly the only hope for Mrs Blakeney was to establish that she was a lawful sub-tenant and protected by s 137. Slade LJ was in fact very doubtful whether the transaction in question could properly be said to constitute a 'subletting' at all, but left the point open as he held that Mrs Blakeney could not succeed even if it did. In order to suceed she had to establish that the premises had been 'lawfully sublet' to her within s 137. It is well established that a subletting in breach of a covenant in the tenancy is unlawful. The subletting here, without the land-lords' consent, was therefore unlawful unless it could be brought within a proviso in the lease that no consent was required for a furnished subletting for a term not exceeding six calendar months in any one year. It was contended that Mrs Blakeney had a monthly periodic tenancy and that this fell within the proviso, but it was held that in this context the proviso covered only a *fixed* term not exceeding six months and the subletting, such it was, accord-ingly fell outside it.

It is also well established that it is possible for the unlawfulness of a subletting to be waived so as to render the subletting a lawful one, and it was contended that the sending of the demand for rent was such a waiver. The court had no hesitation in affirming earlier decisions which decide that the strict common law on waiver is modified in relation to statutory tenancies. It is accepted that in the case of a contractual tenancy not only the acceptance of rent due after knowledge of the breach, but also the despatch by the landlord and the receipt by the tenant of an unambiguous and unqualified demand for future rent will ordinarily constitute an affirmation of its continuance, even though the demand is due to some mistake in the office of the landlord or his agent and there was no intention on the part of the person who actually sent the demand to waive a breach. However, it is a different matter in the case of a statutory tenancy. Here the landlord has no right of forfeiture and no choice. The statutory tenancy continues until it is determined by notice by the tenant or by order of the court. The landlord is entitled to demand the rent so long as the statutory tenancy continues. A mere demand for rent, therefore, is not an act consistent only with an election to treat the subletting as lawful. At most in this context it is equivocal. On the facts it was clear that there had been no waiver.

A further ground on the facts for allowing the landlords' appeal was that the demand for rent which was alleged to constitute a waiver had been sent not to the tenant Mr Willson, but to his wife. In the absence of any evidence that it ever reached Mr Willson it could not possibly support a waiver. It is the actual communication, rather that the preparation, of the rent demand, which would have to be relied on for this purpose.

Both Slade and Ormrod LJJ discussed the fundamental question whether a statutory tenant has the capacity to grant an effective subtenancy of the whole of the demised premises. Slade LJ pointed out that though there is substantial support for the view of textbook writers that he has no such capacity, the cases are not direct authorities on the point. He referred to the conceptual difficulties involved in treating a person as deriving a valid title as subtenant from a statutory tenant, where the tenant is giving up possession of the whole of the premises, for it is an essential feature of a statutory tenancy that it continues only if and so long as the tenant occupies the dwelling-house as his residence. Slade LJ referred to some of the statutory provisions but did not choose to commit himself to an opinion. Ormrod LJ however, was prepared to say that the statutory provisions do enable a statutory tenant to sublet, pointing out that it is a mistake to try to impress common law concepts on to the legal relationships created by the Rent Act. He relied on s 137 which clearly contemplates that a statutory tenant can validly sublet the whole of a dwelling-house and create the legal relationship of statutory tenancy between the landlord and the subtenant; s 98 with Sch 15, Case 6 which makes subletting without consent of the whole of the dwelling-house a ground for possession; and s 3(3) which provides in effect that the statutory tenancy continues unless the tenant gives a notice of appropriate length to determine it, even when he is not occupying, and not intending to reoccupy the premises. It may be added that a tenant who is only temporarily absent and who retains the necessary animus possidendi and corpus possessionis does not lose his Rent Act protection by subletting.

As Ormrod LJ said, the result was a disaster for Mrs Blakeney, but legally it was inevitable that the case should have gone the way it did. One can only share Ormrod LJ's hope that she will be able to obtain redress in other proceedings.

The extraordinary thing about *Western Heritable Investment Co Ltd v Husband* [1983] 3 All ER 65 is that it was necessary to take it to the House of Lords. The appeal from the Extra Division of the Court of Session concerned the construction of s 42(2) of the Rent (Scotland) Act 1971 which is in identical terms to s 70(2) of the Rent Act 1977: this is the subsection relating to scarcity value in determining a fair rent. In the Court of Session Lord Avonside, with whom Lord Kincraig concurred, said that the suggestion that the Act was designed to favour tenants was insupportable, and held that the provision that "it should be assumed that the number of persons seeking to become tenants . . . is not substantially greater than the number of . . . dwelling-houses", created an irrebuttable presumption of fact that there is no scarcity, whatever the true facts may be. In the House of Lords their Lordships had no doubt that in fact the 1971 Act *was* designed to favour tenants by protecting them from any increase of rent which would otherwise have been caused by demand exceeding supply. The effect of s 42(2) (s 70(2)) is to direct that the fair rent is to be determined on the hypothetical assumption that there is no scarcity of accommodation to let. Accordingly, if there is such scarcity in fact, some allowance or deduction may have to be made for it when actual rents (or the return on actual capital values) are used for determining fair rents. Whether any allowance or deduction should be made, and if so, how much it should be, are questions of fact to be determined on the evidence, mainly of experts in valuation.

Lord Keith and Lord Brightman confirmed that the best guide to a fair rent is comparables which do not reflect, or are discounted so as not to reflect, scarcity value. A fair return on capital value, leaving aside the precise definition of 'capital' and what is a 'fair' return, was said to be a notoriously unreliable method of valuation, normally only used as a last resort. Certainly there is no duty on an assessment committee to take into consideration a fair return on capital as one of the circumstances in s 42(1) (s 70(1)). If capital value is used, it may well be that a shortage of houses for letting may have the effect of inflating the price paid for vacant possession. It would, however, be bad valuation practice to proceed on a rigid rule of thumb basis of applying an assumed fair rate of return to vacant possession capital value. There are many factors which a valuer should keep in mind in order to arrive at a reasonable result, and these include the statutory hypothesis postulated by s 42(2) (s 70(2)).

Leasehold enfranchisement

Eton College v Bard [1983] 2 All ER 961 raised a short point on the definition of a 'long tenancy' in the Leasehold Reform Act 1967. The lease in question had been granted by the Eton Housing Association from 17 November 1969 until 24 June 2063 'or until this Lease shall cease (otherwise than by death or bankruptcy) to be vested in a Member of the Association (whichever shall be the earlier)'. The relevant part of the definition of 'long tenancy' in s 3(1) of the 1967 Act provides that it means 'a tenancy granted for a term of years certain exceeding twenty-one years, whether or not the tenancy is (or may become) terminable before the end of that term by notice given by or to the tenant or by re-entry, forfeiture or otherwise . . .'

It was argued, first, that the lease fell outside the Act because it did not fall within the first part of the definition as being held for a 'term of years certain exceeding twenty-one years'. It was not 'certain' because it was liable to be brought to an end if it ceased to be vested in a member of the association. The defendant, it was argued, failed at the first hurdle and it was unnecessary to consider the remaining words of the subsection. Slade LJ was clearly right in saying that the two parts of the subsection must be read together as meaning that a term which would *otherwise* qualify as a 'term of years certain exceeding twenty-one years' shall not fail to qualify *merely* because the tenancy is or may become terminable before the end of that term in the manner mentioned. It was further argued that 'terminable' was limited to meaning 'capable of being terminated by the act of one or more parties to the lease'; and that the phrase 'or otherwise' in the subsection must be construed eiusdem generis with re-entry and forfeiture and was not apt to include the mere happening of an event, such as ceasing to be a member of the association (as opposed to the act of an interested party), on which the lease is limited to determine before the expiration of the maximum stated duration of the term. The court held, however, that 'terminable' is to be construed as covering both a liability to be determined by the act of one or other party to the lease, and a liability to come to an end on the happening of an event on which the lease is limited to determine; and that the words 'or otherwise' are apt to include, and do include, the latter situation. In holding that the case fell within the definition both Slade and Oliver LJJ referred to the test suggested by Russell LJ in *Roberts v Church Commissioners for England* [1971] 3 All ER 703, though Oliver LJ did not think it very helpful. According to Russell LJ '. . . to fulfil the definition a tenant must at some point of time be, or have been, in a position to say that subject to options to determine, rights of re-entry and so forth, he is entitled to remain tenant for the next 21 years . . .' The tenant in the present case was in a position to say that, subject to a premature termination of the term occurring through his ceasing to be a member of the association or purporting to assign it to a person who was not a member or through other events entitling the lessors to forfeit the lease, he was entitled to remain tenant for more than the next 21 years. The tenancy was accordingly within s 3(1).

Housing Act 1980

In *Governors of the Peabody Donation Fund v Higgins* [1983] 3 All ER 122 there was no dispute as to the facts and the question was whether a technical legal device was effective to achieve the desired end. The facts were that the landlords had granted the father a weekly tenancy in 1971 which included an absolute prohibition against assignment, and this tenancy became a secure tenancy by virtue of s 28 of the 1980 Act. The daughter had occupied the premises as her only or principal home for a long period of time, and would have been entitled under s 30 to succeed the father under the secure tenancy if he had died. The father, however, was still alive; what he wanted to do was to vacate the premises himself, but leave his daughter in possession as a secure tenant. It will be remembered that under s 37 if a secure tenancy is assigned it ceases to be a secure tenancy unless, inter alia, the assignment is to a person in whom the tenancy would or might have vested by virtue of s 30 had the tenant died immediately before the assignment. The daughter was clearly a competent assignee within the section, but the difficulty was that the tenancy contained, as we have seen, an absolute prohibition against assignment. Nothing deterred, the father purported to assign the tenancy to his daughter and the question was whether this purported assignment was effective, notwithstanding that it was a clear breach of the prohibition of the tenancy. If it was effective, the daughter would be entitled to claim a secure tenancy under s 37.

The landlords argued, however, and the county court judge accepted, that s 37 only applied to a lawful assignment, ie an assignment which was not in breach of any condition of the lease but an assignment in exercise of the lawful rights of a tenant. It was further submitted and the judge held, that the effect of the absolute prohibition against assignment was that the purported assignment had no effect in law. On this basis, the father having vacated the premises and the daughter having no right to be there, being a trespasser, the landlord, without complying with the requirements of s 33 sought an order for possession against each of them, and the orders were granted by the judge.

On appeal the decision was reversed. First, it was held, following the Court of Appeal decision in *Old Grovebury Manor Farm Ltd v W Seymour Plant Sales & Hire Ltd (No 2)* [1979] 3 All ER 504, that the assignment was effective to pass the father's interest to the daughter, notwithstanding that it was in breach of the prohibition in the tenancy. Secondly, it was held that s 37 was not restricted to assignments which can be said to be lawful in the sense that they are not in breach of the terms of the particular tenancy. Both Cumming-Bruce and May LJJ were influenced by the fact that in the Rent Act 1977, in provisions dealing with sublettings, the draftsman used the expression 'lawfully sublet', and they had no doubt that the draftsman of the 1980 Act was well aware of this. There was no ambiguity and no reason to impose quite a drastic limitation on the clear words used. Accordingly the daughter was a secure tenant by virtue of s 37 and the landlords were not entitled to an order for possession against her as a trespasser. The landlords could, however, claim possession on ground 1 of Sch 4, namely that an obligation of the tenancy had been broken, to wit assignment in breach of the prohibition against assignment, but they could not do this in the present proceedings because they had not complied with the procedure laid down in s 33, without which the court has no jurisdiction to make the order. Of course, if a claim were to be made based on ground 1, the court under s 30 could not make an order unless it considered it reasonable to do so. There would seem to be much to be said for the view that prima facie it would be reasonable to make an order against an assignee who knowingly acquired an interest by reason of the very breach on which the claim for possession is based. But the decision on that must wait for another day.

State immunity—covenants in leases

In *Intpro Properties (UK) Ltd v Samuel* [1983] 2 All ER 495, a London house had been let to the French government in 1979 (not in 1971 as misprinted in the head-note) for four years. The lease included a covenant not to use the premises for any other purpose than that of a private dwelling-house for a named diplomat. It also contained the usual covenant by the tenant to permit the landlord to enter the premises to inspect them and carry out any necessary repairs.

The diplomat occupied the premises as a house and for use in carrying out his social obligations as a diplomat. Dry rot was discovered in 1982, but the plaintiff landlords were refused access. The question before the court of Appeal was whether the English courts had jurisdiction to hear a claim for damages for breach of covenant or whether the French government was entitled to immunity under the State Immunity Act 1978. Under the Act effect has to be given to the immunity even though, as was the case here, the State does not appear. It was accepted that no order for an injunction or specific performance could be made by virtue of s 13(2) (see also art 31(3) in sch 1 to the Diplomatic Privileges Act 1964).

The general immunity conferred by s 1 is, by s 6(1), excluded as respects proceedings relating to immovable property in the UK or '(b) any obligation of the State arising out of its interest in, or its possession or use of, any such property...' Prima facie this would have covered the facts of the case. Section 16(1)(b) however provides in effect that s 6(1) does not apply to proceedings which satisfy two conditions:

(i) they concern a State's title to or its possession of property; and

(ii) that property is used for the purposes of a diplomatic mission.

It was held that neither of these conditions was satisfied and the French government was therefore not entitled to immunity.

As to the first there is a significant difference between s 6(1)(b) and s 16(1)(b) in that the former, but not the latter, refers to the 'use of property'. In the light of this it was held that s 16(1)(b) is limited to proceedings in which a state's title to or right to possession of property in the strict sense is in question. This is consistent with the opinions of commentators, with which the court agreed, on the construction and effect of art 31 in Sch 1 to the Diplomatic Privileges Act 1964 which gives a corresponding immunity to diplomats themselves as contrasted with the sovereign states which those diplomats represent.

As to the second condition, it was held that to be within it the premises must be used for the professional diplomatic purposes of the mission. The incidental performance of social obligations is not enough. This construction is again consistent with the provisions of the 1964 Act.

A final point was whether the validity of the claim for damages was affected by the fact that, by virtue of art 30 in Sch 1 to the 1964 Act, the private residence of a diplomatic agent enjoys the same inviolability and protection as the premises of the mission itself. No order could be made to compel the French Government or its diplomat living there to permit entry to the plaintiffs or their agents. It was held that immunity is a matter of procedure, not of substance, and that the statutory provisions giving full effect to the physical inviolability of diplomatic premises should not be allowed to operate as a bar to proceedings otherwise permitted by the statutes where the relief sought is merely damages for breach of covenant.

Police

GRAHAM ZELLICK, JP, MA, PHD
Professor of Public Law, Queen Mary College, University of London

The law governing the police and their activities continues to arouse much interest, particularly in relation to the government's Police and Criminal Evidence Bill. The courts, too, have been active. They have caused the Police Complaints Board to rely on their own judgment as to whether disciplinary action is called for against a police officer even when the Director of Public Prosecutions has decided that he should not be prosecuted; they have clarified the mental element required in the offence of obstructing a police officer; they have held that, as with arrest, the search of a person is lawful only if the reason for it is first communicated; and they have come to a surprising and indeed dubious conclusion that an arrest is lawful only if it is exercised for a valid purpose. In all these decisions, the courts have approached the balance between individual rights and police powers with care and sensitivity.

Police complaints and double jeopardy

Part of the bargain struck between the government and the police in connection with the introduction in 1976 of the new arrangements for dealing with complaints against the police was the acceptance of the double jeopardy principle: a police officer convicted or acquitted of a criminal offence may not be charged with a disciplinary offence which is in substance the same as the offence for which he has been tried (Police Act 1976, s 11(1); to be re-enacted by the Police and Criminal Evidence Bill, cl 94(1))—as in the *Waldorf* case ((1983) *Times*, 23 December, p 1)—although he may, if convicted, be dealt with for the specific disciplinary offence of having been found guilty of a criminal offence (ibid, s 11(2)). Under the 1976 Act, the Police Complaints Board receives a copy of the report of the investigation of every complaint (s 2(1)) and may direct the bringing of disciplinary charges (s 3(2)). In discharging this function, the board is required to 'have regard to' any guidance given by the Home Secretary (s 3(8)). In a circular, the Home Secretary has said that there should not normally be disciplinary proceedings where the Director of Public Prosecutions has already decided that criminal proceedings should not be taken if the evidence required to substantiate a disciplinary charge is the same as that required to substantiate the criminal charge. The double jeopardy principle contained in s 11 is thus much extended. (All investigations of complaints indicating that a criminal offence has been committed by the officer must be referred to the DPP: Police Act 1964, s 49(3). This is to be changed by the Police and Criminal Evidence Bill, cl 82, which will allow less serious matters to be dealt with without reference to the DPP: see Home Office, Police Complaints and Discipline Procedures, (Cmnd 9072, October 1983) paras 36–38.)

The board, though not uncritical of the result, took the view that disciplinary proceedings were generally precluded if the DPP had decided against criminal proceedings (see The Triennial Report of the Police Complaints Board (Cmnd 7966, 1980) paras 98–104). Criticism of this situation has also emanated from Lord Scarman (The Brixton Disorders (Cmnd 8427, 1981) para 7.26) and from the House of Commons Select Committee on Home Affairs (HC 98, 1981–82). (See generally Greaves 'Double Jeopardy and Police Disciplinary Proceedings' [1983] Crim LR 211.) But the board's understanding of the position and its practice were not beyond challenge in the courts.

In *R v Police Complaints Board, ex p Madden* and *ex p Rhone* [1983] 2 All ER 353 (McNeill J), judicial review of two decisions by the board not to give further consideration to complaints against police officers because the DPP had decided against prosecution—and because the board regarded itself as bound by the Home Secretary's guidance not to question this decision—was successfully sought.

McNeill J accepted that the standard of proof in police disciplinary proceedings was the same as in the criminal courts. Nevertheless, the question was not one of fairness to police officers but whether the board had discharged its statutory obligation to consider complaints. It was not open to the board to limit its statutory role. The requirement to 'have regard to' the Home Secretary's guidance meant only that it could not be ignored: it did not mean, as the board supposed, that the board was obliged to follow it. Equally, it was not open to the board to fetter its discretion—curiously, McNeill J described this as an aspect of natural justice—by accepting as binding the decisions of the DPP. Accordingly, certiorari issued to quash the board's two decisions.

The board decided against an appeal and modified its policy, though it would not re-open any earlier cases. It does not, of course, mean that the board must come to a conclusion different from the Director's. So long as it considers the case fully, it is entitled to conclude that disciplinary proceedings are not called for.

Obstructing the police—mental element and motive

The offence of obstructing the police again came before the courts (see All ER Rev 1982, pp 203–205, which includes a reference to one of this year's cases, *Moore v Greene* [1983] 1 All ER 663, which is not therefore discussed here). In *Hills v Ellis* [1983] 1 All ER 667, DC, the appellant saw two men fighting after a football match, one of whom he believed to be the innocent party. On seeing a police officer arrest this person, the appellant sought to inform the police officer that he was arresting the wrong man. As he could not be heard above the noise, he grabbed the officer's elbow. Another officer informed the appellant that he might be arrested for obstruction if he did not desist. He persisted, and was arrested and charged, and convicted by the magistrates, though absolutely discharged.

It was never suggested that the officer's arrest was anything but lawful: he was therefore acting 'in the execution of his duty' (Police Act 1964, s 51(3)). It was submitted that the appellant's conduct was not 'wilful', as required by s 51(3), which Lord Parker CJ has defined as meaning both intentional and without lawful excuse (*Rice v Connolly* [1966] 2 All ER 694, 652, DC). The appellant's conduct here was not without lawful excuse, it was maintained, because he had a moral duty to draw the officer's attention to the fact that he was arresting the wrong man. The court rejected the contention, Griffiths LJ believing it would be intolerable if citizens could lay hands on the police and obstruct them because they thought some other person should be arrested. A private citizen had no lawful excuse to interfere with a lawful arrest. Presumably, the proper course of action is to inform some other police officer at the scene or attend at the police station and give a statement.

It was further argued that the appellant's conduct was not wilful because it lacked the hostility to the police and the intention of obstructing the police said in *Willmott v Atack* [1976] 3 All ER 794, 800 per Croom-Johnson J, to be required. The defendant in *Willmott* had apparently intervened in an arrest to help the police but did so ineptly and the man being arrested escaped. Croom-Johnson J held that the obstruction, since it evinced no hostility to the police and was not intended to obstruct, was not wilful. Similarly, it was argued that the appellant's conduct here was not characterised by any hostility towards the police. Griffiths LJ, however, held that the expression 'hostility towards the police' meant 'aimed at the police', which the appellant's actions clearly were.

McCullough J was not entirely happy with Croom-Johnson J's phrase, since motive and emotion are irrelevant in the criminal law. In his view, 'wilfully obstructs' means doing deliberate acts with the intention of bringing about a state of affairs which, objectively regarded, amounted to an obstruction, and that accurately described the appellant's conduct here.

The court certified that the question—whether the mens rea for this offence was merely the intent to do a deliberate act with the intent of bringing about a state of affairs which viewed objectively amounted to an obstruction of the police—was a point of law of general public importance, but refused leave to appeal.

Search of the person: reason to be given

It has long been the case that an arrest without warrant is lawful only if the person being arrested is told the reason for it, unless it is impractical in the circumstances (*Christie v Leachinsky* [1947] 1 All ER 567, HL). As Viscount Simon put it, a person 'is only required to submit to restraints on his freedom if he knows in substance the reason why it is claimed that this restraint should be imposed' (ibid at p 573). This principle has now been applied to searches of the person, whether at common law (following an arrest) or under statute (eg the Misuse of Drugs Act 1971, s 23(2)).

In *Brazil v Chief Constable of Surrey* [1983] 3 All ER 537, DC, convictions for assaulting police officers in the execution of their duty were quashed because the appellant had not been told the reason why she was required to undergo a search in the police station following her arrest and her assault on the officers who forcibly searched her was therefore lawful resistance to the officers who were not acting in the execution of their duty.

As with an arrest, the circumstances may be such that reasons need not be given, as where it is perfectly obvious or where it is practically impossible because the person is, for example, causing a commotion or is drunk. The court was understandably anxious to avoid laying down an exhaustive list of such circumstances.

The court also applied *Lindley v Rutter* [1981] QB 128, DC, where it had been held that there was no general power to search all arrested persons at the police station, but it was permissible only on certain grounds. In the present case, the police officer told the appellant that everyone brought into the police station had to be searched for his own safety, whereupon the appellant struck the officer across the face with her handbag. The approach of the officer was plainly in conflict with the decision in *Lindley v Rutter*, since the officer failed to address her mind to the question of whether in these circumstances a personal search of the appellant was justified. The court therefore concluded that the officer was not acting in the execution of her duty and the conviction could not be sustained.

The court accepted that the appellant's conduct constituted a common assault. It is also clear that on the facts the proposed search of the appellant would, in the light of *Lindley v Rutter*, have been unlawful; but it is not clear that such a statement of intended action without more takes a police officer out of the scope of his lawful duty. The appellant's violent response was premature. Had she intimated her refusal, the officer might have had second thoughts, or called a superior. If the officer had persisted, her conduct would have been unlawful and violent resistance by the appellant would have been justified, but on these particular facts, the court's conclusion that the appellant was not guilty of the offence is difficult to accept. Its general conclusion, however, about the giving of reasons is to be warmly welcomed.

Arrest: proper purpose

Mohammed-Holgate v Duke [1983] 3 All ER 526 is one of those cases in which the result is beyond question but the reasoning is open to criticism. (See Zellick 'The Purpose Behind An Arrest' [1984] Crim LR 94.) The county court judge had awarded the plaintiff £1,000 damages for wrongful arrest. The arrest was wrongful, notwithstanding the officers' reasonable suspicion that the plaintiff had committed an arrestable offence, because the object of the arrest had been to induce a confession, whereas she could have been questioned without being arrested. The two-judge Court of Appeal—neither of them normal members of the court—disagreed and held that interrogation with a view to securing a confession was a legitimate purpose of an arrest and the arrest in question was therefore lawful. It is certainly settled law and common practice that interrogation may follow an arrest and the conclusion cannot therefore be criticised. But the court accepted (in an unreserved judgment) that for an arrest to be valid the power had to be exercised for a legitimate purpose and if the officer's reason for the arrest fell outside such a purpose, the restraint was unlawful.

This is a wholly novel notion. It was not argued before the court but 'disposed of by assertion and acceptance' (p 531). The error seems to have arisen from a misunderstanding of a passage in the Report of the Royal Commission on Criminal Procedure (Vol 1, Cmnd 8092, 1981, para 3.66, p 41)—in any event an unusual source of authority—which does no more than explain the various reasons why an arrest may be carried out—for example, to prevent the suspect destroying evidence, interfering with witnesses, warning accomplices or repeating the offence, or to dispel or confirm the reasonable suspicion. It follows from the last of these that the suspect may be questioned before he is either charged or released. It is not suggested, however, that these factors have any bearing on the legality of the original arrest. Improper treatment after arrest may be tortious but the original arrest, if otherwise valid, is unaffected. What was in the officer's mind at the time of the arrest, provided he acted on reasonable grounds and satisfied the various procedural requirements, is irrelevant. The reader of the cited passage in the Royal Commission's Report is referred by the Report to the accompanying discussion in the companion volume (The Investigation and Prosecution of Criminal Offences in England and Wales: The Law and Procedure, Cmnd 8092–1). The reference is to a section on questioning by the police and the right to silence in the chapter on police powers and procedures at the police station (ch 3, para 68, p 24 et seq): arrest is covered in the preceding chapter where the court's view is not supported.

The court also relied on a dictum in a Privy Council opinion (*Hussien v Chong Fook Kam* [1960] AC 942, 948, per Lord Devlin), but this merely indicates that a police officer, though he has grounds to arrest, may choose in the exercise of his discretion not to do so, which is obvious enough. A *duty* to arrest is rare: see, however, All ER Rev 1982, p 201.

A change of this magnitude would require full argument before the court and would need to be fully reasoned in the judgment. Reference to relevant authorities is also to be expected. Whether or not this may be regarded as a mere obiter dictum or perhaps a decision per incuriam, it is to be hoped that other courts will treat it with caution. There is nothing necessarily wrong with judges making new law, but they ought at least to be aware that they are doing so.

The Appeal Committee has granted leave to appeal: [1984] 1 WLR 34.

Negligence

For discussion of a police officer's duty of care when driving a motor vehicle see the article on Tort, p 336 below.

Practice and Procedure

ADRIAN A S ZUCKERMAN, LLM, MA
Fellow of University College, Oxford

Mareva injunctions

The zest for Mareva injunctions has continued unabated: in 1983 the number of applications for Mareva injunctions was double that of 1979, as Lloyd J observed in *PCW Ltd v Dixon* [1983] 2 All ER 158, 160. However, due to the great interest taken in this subject by the Court of Appeal in the preceding year, the scope for great battles of principle has diminished somewhat. Nevertheless, three decisions in the Commercial Court add some fine and interesting touches to the existing principles.

The first of these, *Oceanica Castelana v Mineralimportexport* [1983] 2 All ER 65 constitutes an intriguing sequel to *Galaxia Maritime SA v Mineralimportexport* [1982] 1 All ER 796, discussed at All ER Rev 1982, p 215. The first plaintiffs obtained injunctions restraining ships loaded with coal belonging to the defendant, a Romanian trading organisation, from leaving the jurisdiction. While appeals against these orders were pending and in an attempt to release their cargo, the defendant agreed to provide the plaintiffs with a guarantee by Barclays Bank International. For that purpose the defendant caused the Romanian Bank of Foreign Trade to make a cash deposit with Barclays to secure the guarantees. However, before the guarantees were actually issued the Court of Appeal discharged, in *Galaxia*, the injunction against the ships, which duly sailed out of the jurisdiction. As this decision left unaffected the injunction so far as other assets within the jurisdiction were concerned, the plaintiffs notified Barclays Bank that the Mareva injunctions applied to the funds deposited to secure the guarantees. On advice from their clients, Barclays Bank wrote to the original plaintiffs saying that the fund did not belong to the defendant but to the Romanian bank which deposited it. The plaintiffs refused to accept this and Barclays was compelled to apply to the court to have the injunction discharged.

Lloyd J found that the fund indeed belonged to the Romanian bank and discharged the injunction. He was critical of the original plaintiffs for not accepting, as soon as they were notified by the bank of the position, that the injunctions did not apply to the deposit, observing that—

> 'Banks and other third parties are sufficiently harassed by applications for Mareva injunctions as it is. It is important that they should be able to look to the plaintiffs for greater co-operation than they have received in this case' (at 69).

This was not the end of the matter, nor the reason for which the case deserves notice. Before Barclays Bank applied to court, the solicitors for the first plaintiffs were approached by a new plaintiff who had a claim against the Romanian bank. An injunction restraining the bank from removing its assets out of the jurisdiction was obtained. This order undoubtedly applied to the fund, discussed above, in the hands of Barclays Bank. As it happened the Romanian bank had taken substantial term loans from Barclays Bank and the question arose whether Barclays should be allowed to set off against the frozen fund interest which had become due to it before the injunction and also interest which was going to fall due in future. An ordinary defendant who is subject to a Mareva injunction can apply to court to vary the injunction so as to enable him to pay his ordinary debts. A bank, Lloyd J held, should not be in a position worse than that of an ordinary creditor. Indeed, the bank would now have an advantage. Before a defendant is allowed to meet his liabilities from frozen funds he has to show that he has no other assets, free from the injunction, from which to satisfy his liabilities: *A v C (No 2)* [1981] 2 All ER 126. By contrast, the bank, according to Lloyd J (at 70), does not have to disclose the state of its client's account nor give any other information about him; it can assert its right against its client without more. In so holding, Lloyd J was giving effect to the Court of Appeal warning in *Galaxia* that Mareva orders must not be allowed to interfere 'with the performance of a contract between the third party and the defendant which relates specifically to the assets in question . . .' ([1982] 1 All ER 796 at 800, per Kerr LJ).

While Lloyd J's decision on this point is certainly just, since the plaintiff cannot expect to obtain by means of a Mareva injunction priority over other creditors, his decision on the next issue is less obviously so. This was concerned with the question of how much money should be frozen for the protection of the new plaintiff, whose claim against the Romanian bank amounted to about £2m. The plaintiff argued that the amount caught by the injunction should be £2m *plus* the sum needed to satisfy Barclays' set-off rights in respect of future instalments and the repayment of the principal: if only £2m were frozen, the sum would progressively melt away in satisfaction of Barclays' set-off rights against the Romanian bank. Suppose the future indebtedness of the Romanian bank to Barclays to be £3m, the injunction, according to the plaintiff, should be in respect of £5m. Lloyd J rejected this argument, saying—

> 'I can see no ground on which the bank could . . . refuse to repay . . . [the £3m in the example] to its customer, in respect of which, ex hypothesi, it would have no existing right of set-off. It is true that the £2m subject to the Mareva injunction would then gradually be reduced as the bank exercised its right of set-off in the future. But this is an inevitable consequence of a defendant who is subject to a "maximum sum" Mareva injunction . . . and who has no other free assets, being allowed to pay his debts as they fall due' (at 71).

He also expressed the hope that in future Mareva injunctions would be so drafted as to allow banks to exercise set-off rights against frozen accounts without the need of applying to the court for variation of the order.

While it is understandable that the court should not incautiously extend a Mareva order to cover sums which might become liable to be set-off against the frozen account in future, this decision opens the way to abuse. For a person could now make his bank deposit immune to Mareva jurisdiction by a simple device: if he deposits, say, £1m and immediately takes out a £1m (or somewhat less) loan secured on the deposit, the loan fund can then be taken out of the jurisdiction or disposed of in some other way. Should a Mareva injunction be issued against the deposit account, all the depositor will have to do in order to avoid its consequences is refrain from repaying his loan to the bank, and allow the latter to look to the deposit for repayment by way of set-off. Moreover, if in future injunctions will be so drafted as to allow set-off automatically, the draining of the frozen account could happen without the plaintiff, who had obtained the injunction, even hearing about it. Not only would such a result defeat the purpose of the order but it might also have another highly undesirable consequence. The plaintiff might proceed to trial assuming that there are in existence funds which justify the expense of litigation, only to find out, on receiving a favourable judgment, that the funds subject to the order had completely been paid out to the bank.

For these reasons, it is suggested that Lloyd J's decision is to be regretted. To deny the bank the right of set-off might not be as unjust as it appears at first sight. The bank had no present set-off right. Moreover, Barclays did not, presumably, even have a right to prevent the Romanian bank from drawing out all its money there and then, so as to forestall any future set-off right. But since Barclays had no right to look upon this particular account as security for the loans it had advanced to the Romanian bank, it would not have caused Barclays great injustice to be told that it could not exercise its set-off against the £2m subject to the injunction—especially as it was likely that Barclays had obtained adequate security for the loan. There is, therefore, no overwhelming need in cases such as this to allow the bank to set off interest payments owed to it by the defendant against a deposit frozen at the request of the plaintiff. In any event, a bank should not be allowed to do so except on proof that it has no other reasonable way of protecting its interests. Above all, it would be very unwise to allow banks to deplete frozen accounts without reference to the courts or, at the very least, without notice to the plaintiff who obtained the injunction.

Another case involving the rights of third parties is *Project Development v KMK Securities* [1983] 1 All ER 465, where innocent third parties affected by a Mareva injunction successfully applied to the court for variation of the order. The decision is, however, only reported on the issue of costs. Parker J considered the criterion by which costs should be awarded to a third party who has obtained a variation. He held that they should be taxed on the solicitor and own client basis, though subject to the special direction that, notwithstanding RSC Ord 62, r 29, the burden of establishing the reasonableness of incurring the costs and of their amount should be on the third party to whom the costs were awarded. In so deciding, Parker J rejected the plaintiff's argument that the costs should be taxed on a party and party basis, since this might result in reasonable costs being disallowed as not being strictly necessary. He observed—

'. . . a plaintiff who resorts to the draconian remedy of a Mareva injunction should expect to pay such costs' (at 466–7).

Finally, mention must be made of *PCW Ltd v Dixon* [1983] 2 All ER 158, [1983] BCLC 105. The case is discussed fully in the article on Company Law p 78, above.

Anton Piller orders

The Anton Piller jurisdiction has continued to present the courts with tricky problems. It is convenient to start by considering the contribution made by the Court of Appeal in *WEA Records Ltd v Visions Channel 4 Ltd* [1983] 2 All

ER 589 where it clarified the law on three points of practical importance. The first concerns the correct course to be taken for challenging an ex parte Anton Piller order. The court decided that although it had jurisdiction under s 16(1) of the Supreme Court Act 1981 'to hear and determine appeals from any judgment or order of the High Court', such appeals should be wholly discouraged. The preferred procedure is to apply to the High Court itself to discharge the order: being ex parte, the court stressed, an Anton Piller order is provisional in nature and can be discharged or modified by the court which made it (RSC Ord 32, r 6). Indeed, the order itself would commonly notify the party to whom it is directed (as it did in the case under consideration) that he is at liberty to move to vary or discharge the order. Consequently, Sir John Donaldson MR stated that—

> '. . . it is difficult, if not impossible, to think of circumstances in which it would be proper to appeal to this court against an ex parte order without first giving the judge who made it or, if he was not available, another High Court judge an opportunity of reviewing it in the light of argument from the defendant and reaching a decision' (at 593).

The right of seeking to discharge an Anton Piller order is, however, more theoretical than practical. The party against whom an order is made (we shall refer to him as the defendant) first hears of it when it is served on him. But at that moment he also becomes bound to comply with it and to allow the plaintiff's solicitors to inspect his property and remove evidence found there. Of course, the defendant may refuse immediate compliance and make an urgent application to the court to set aside the order. But as the Master of the Rolls pointed out—

> '. . . defendants who take this line do so very much at their peril. If they succeed in getting the order discharged, all well and good. But if they fail, they will render themselves liable to penalties for contempt of court' (at 592).

In the case with which the Court of Appeal was dealing, the defendant, upon receipt of the order, promptly complied with it and only subsequently applied to have it discharged on the ground that the material available before the court at the time was insufficient to justify the making of the order. The defendant further sought the return of the material seized in pursuance of the order and a declaration that admissions made in compliance with it should be declared inadmissible. An argument was put that in deciding whether or not the Anton Piller order was rightly made the court should confine itself to the material which was before it at the ex parte stage, taking no cognizance of the evidence discovered as a result of the compliance with the order. This was flatly rejected by the court. The Master of the Rolls said—

> 'I regard this as wholly absurd. The courts are concerned with the administration of justice, not with playing a game of snakes and ladders' (at 594).

If the defendants suffered damage as a result of the order they should seek to recover from the plaintiff under the latter's counter undertakings as to damages. Indeed his Lordship considered the appeal an abuse of process. Moreover, the court emphasised that whenever the propriety of an order was in question, the court should consider all the relevant evidence, including that which was obtained in consequence of the execution of the order. As Dunn LJ put it—

'If consequent on the grant of the Anton Piller order the evidence showed that the order was in fact justified, then the fact that the evidence before the judge was not as strong as it ultimately became does not... provide a ground for challenging the order itself' (at 595).

It follows, therefore, that once an ex parte Anton Piller order has been granted its course is almost unstoppable: it can hardly be arrested before execution and once executed it cannot, to all practical purposes, be undone. In view of the urgency which is involved in situations justifying such orders, the above consequences are almost inevitable. But this makes it all the more important to issue such orders with the greatest circumspection.

Lastly, mention must be made of a rather curious feature of the *WEA Records Ltd* case. At the ex parte hearing the plaintiffs revealed to the judge certain information which they considered to be so sensitive and confidential that they asked that it should not be imparted to the defendant at a later stage. The Court of Appeal strongly condemned this practice. The Master of the Rolls could not 'visualise any circumstances in which it would be right to give a judge information on an ex parte application which cannot at a later stage be revealed to the party affected by the result of the application' (at 591). If the identity of an informant required protection, then it should not be revealed to the judge either, the court held. Moreover, if the situation has arisen, as in the preent case, that information was withheld from a party then there was no justification for withholding it from the party's solicitors. They were, the court observed, just as much officers of the court and just as much to be trusted as counsel, and were similarly liable for breach of the court's trust.

Solicitors' obligations concerning material disclosed as a result of Anton Piller orders were directly considered by Falconer J in *Customs & Excise Commissioners v AE Hamlin & Co* [1983] 3 All ER 654. The case is discussed in the article on Solicitors, p 296 below.

Falconer J's attention to the Anton Piller jurisdiction was called upon in yet another case: *Universal City Studios v Hubbord* [1983] 2 All ER 596. The plaintiffs' solicitors, in execution of an Anton Piller order, took from the defendant's premises documents and other goods which were connected with alleged infringements by the defendant of the defendant's copyright in certain films. Subsequently the defendant applied for the Anton Piller order to be set aside and for all materials to be returned to him with an undertaking that they would never be disclosed or used for any purpose, including a pending application by the plaintiffs for interlocutory relief. The defendant's ground for the application was that the materials obtained, and questions which he would have to answer respecting them, could incriminate him in criminal offences of distributing pornographic films. The case turned on interpretation of s 72 of the Supreme Court Act 1981.

Section 72 withdraws the privilege against self-incrimination in certain proceedings and with respect to certain offences. The proceedings in which the privilege is removed are defined by sub-s(2) as being—

'(a) proceedings for infringement of rights pertaining to any intellectual property or passing off;
(b) proceedings brought to obtain disclosure of information relating to any
infringement of such rights or to any passing off; and

(c) proceedings brought to prevent any apprehended infringement of such
rights or any apprehended passing off.'

The offences in respect of which only the privilege is removed, referred to as
'related offences', are defined in s 72(5) as follows—

'(a) in the case of proceedings within subsection 2(a) or (b)—
  (i) any offence committed by or in the course of the infringement or
      passing off to which those proceedings relate; or
  (ii) any offence not within sub-paragraph (i) committed in connection
      with that infringement or passing off, being an offence involving fraud
      or dishonesty;
(b) in the case of proceedings within subsection 2(c), any offence revealed by
    the facts on which the plaintiff relies in those proceedings . . .'

The proceedings in the present case were brought by the plaintiffs for
interlocutory injunctions restraining the defendant from infringing their
copyright and so fell within s 72(2)(c) of the 1981 Act. The plaintiffs therefore
argued that the privilege against self-incrimination was removed in respect of
'any offence revealed by the facts on which the plaintiff relied', according to
s 72(5), para (b) of the definition of related offence. The defendant submitted
that the words 'any offence' should be narrowly interpreted to include only
offences of the kind mentioned in para (a)(i) and (ii) of the definition. Falconer
J rejected this submission, holding that he saw no reason to limit the language
of the statute and saying that—

'The definition in para (b) is in striking contrast to the definition of the offence
under sub-paras (i) and (ii); and I see no reason whatsoever for limiting the
offence in para (b) of the definition . . .' (at 608).

This decision, it should be noted, produces a paradoxical result. If the
plaintiff brings proceedings for an actual infringement of his rights
(s 72(2)(a)) or for disclosure of information concerning such infringement
(s 72(2)(b)) then the removal of the right of self-incrimination is limited to
offences which arose from or were connected with the actual infringement
(s 72(5), para (a) of the definition). But if no infringement has yet taken place
and the defendant has not as yet committed any tort, and the plaintiff brings
an action for injunction against possible future infringements, then the
defendant loses his right against self-incrimination concerning 'any offence'
revealed by the facts on which the plaintiff happens to rely (according to para
(b) of the definition in s 72(5)). Thus a defendant who has not as yet committed any tort is in a worse position than a defendant who has perpetrated
tortious actions. Furthermore, the restrictions in para (a) of the definition
could always be side-stepped by bringing proceedings for interlocutory
remedies as well as proceedings for substantive relief. In most circumstances,
where there has been a past infringement of copyright, there would also exist
good reasons for apprehending future infringement. Indeed, this was the
situation in the case under consideration. It would therefore appear that
there was much more in the defendant's argument than was allowed for by
Falconer J.

The difference between paras (a) and (b) of the definition is explicable not
so much by a desire on the part of the legislature to allow less scope for the
privilege under the latter para than under the former, as by the difference
between paras (a) and (b) of s 72(2) and para (c) of the same. Namely, since

s 72(2)(a) and (b) deals with infringements that have already taken place, the definition of the offences in para (a) of 'related offences' in s 72(5) can be made to refer to such actual infringements. However, proceedings under s 72(2)(c) are concerned with only potential infringements; it is therefore considerably difficult and awkward to find a definition which connects past offences (in respect of which the privilege against self-incrimination is removed) with future infringements not yet perpetrated. This does not mean that there is no good reason why such nexus should not be required when it comes to the interpretation of s 72(5), para (b) of 'related offences'. The need to avoid the above-mentioned paradox, and the scope which a wide construction of 'any offence' offers for side-stepping the restrictions in paras (a) and (b) of s 72(5), provide good enough justification for a narrow interpretation of those words.

Before leaving this case mention must be made of another aspect of Falconer J's judgment. He also considered what would be the defendant's rights if his privilege against self-incrimination had remained unaffected by s 72 of the Supreme Court Act 1981. In *Helliwell v Piggott-Sims* [1980] FSR 356 the Court of Appeal decided that where evidence in respect of which the defendant had a perfectly good privilege against self-incrimination had in fact come into the plaintiff's possession as a result of executing an Anton Piller order, then it was admissible for the plaintiffs in future proceedings and there was no discretion to exclude it. Falconer J distinguished the case on the ground that in *Helliwell* no application had been made to set aside the Anton Piller order. In view of *WEA Records Ltd v Visions Channel 4 Ltd* discussed above, Falconer J's distinction can no longer be supported.

Discovery and interrogatories

Three cases deserve some notice. In *Kirkup v British Rail Engineering Ltd* [1983] 3 All ER 147 the plaintiff sued his employer for personal injuries, ie deafness, which allegedly resulted from prolonged exposure to excessive noise over many years of employment in British Rail workshops. On a summons for directions, the master ordered that the plaintiff was to disclose his non-medical expert's report first and that the defendant was to disclose its report 42 days thereafter. The plaintiff appealed, contending that the order should have been one of mutual and simultaneous disclosure. His argument was rejected both by the High Court and the Court of Appeal. The latter held that where the plaintiff's allegations covered a long time and referred to several aspects and locations of the defendant's industrial operations, it was right to expect the plaintiff to first indicate the conditions which he claims lead to his injuries: for until the defendants knew what the plaintiff's experts said, they were not in a position to direct their minds to the precautions that they might have taken or to ascertain the noise level at any particular place and time. The master was therefore held to have exercised correctly his discretion under Ord 38, r 37. Sequential exchange of expert reports seems to have been adopted in this case as a measure of providing the defendant with fuller information about the allegations against him. As such the order was doubtless more efficient and less costly than an application for further and better particulars.

The other cases concerned with discovery are discussed elsewhere: *Buckley v Law Society* [1983] 2 All ER 1039, in the article on Solicitors and *Air Canada* v Secretary of State for Trade (No 2) [1983] 1 All ER 910 in the article on Evidence.

An elucidating judgment on the duty of a company in answering inter-rogatories is to be found in *Stanfield Properties v National Westminster Bank* [1983] 2 All ER 249. Megarry V-C held that a company answering inter-rogatories must provide information known to it as a company and not confine itself merely to information known to the officers compiling the answers. For that purpose the company 'must procure the making of proper inquiries from the company's officers, servants and agents . . .' (at 250). Such enquiries must be addressed to all persons who might possess information and must, therefore, not be confined to persons who owe a duty to the company to impart their knowledge to it. The test is one of reasonableness, and it may be reasonable for a company to make enquiries amongst its former employees for the purpose of answering interrogatories. Consequently, the person answering the interrogatories on behalf of the company must state that he had discharged his duty of making diligent enquiries of all officers, servants and agents of the company who might reasonably be expected to possess some relevant knowledge. In the absence of such a statement the party administering the interrogatories would be justified in questioning whether the company had properly complied with its duty. Where the company's former officers had some relevant knowledge, such knowledge must be imputed to the company. But if, as was the situation in this case, they have disappeared, the company must state its answers why it could not obtain the information sought.

Service out of jurisdiction

This topic has received attention at every level of the judicial hierarchy. It should be noted that the rules concerning service out of jurisdiction are to undergo considerable transformation by the Civil Jurisdiction and Judgment Act 1982 which incorporates the EEC Convention on Civil Jurisdiction and Enforcement of Judgments. This will result in a new Order 11, which has already been formulated. The amendments are to come into operation by statutory instrument and this is expected to happen in 1984. For exposition of the new arrangements see *Supreme Court Practice 1982* (6th Supp, 1983) and 52 Halsbury's Statutes (3rd edn) 381. The cases are discussed in the article on Conflict of Laws, p 89, above.

Amendment correcting name of party

The Court of Appeal had opportunity to consider the extent of Ord 20, r 5(3) which states—

> 'An amendment to correct the name of a party may be allowed . . . notwith-standing that it is alleged that the effect of the amendment will be to substi-tute a new party . . .'

In *Evans Construction Co v Charrington & Co Ltd* [1983] 1 All ER 310 two constructions of the rule competed for recognition. The first, the narrow one, was that the rule was confined to mistakes as to name so that amendment would not be allowed where its result would be to substitute one party by another. The second, the broad one, was that the rule went further and allowed a plaintiff, who had intended to sue one person but mistakenly named another, to amend so as to name the intended defendant. This broad construction was adopted by a majority of the court: Donaldson LJ (as he then was) and Griffith LJ. Waller LJ, dissenting, preferred the narrow construction, believing that the rule was intended only as a cure for mistakes as to name and not for mistakes as to identity. This nebulous distinction has been, one would have thought, sufficiently discredited in another branch of the law so as to leave little to commend it. We should, therefore, be grateful to the majority for eschewing it.

Although the court adopted a liberal construction, it should be borne in mind that it too has limitations. A plaintiff would be allowed to substitute defendant A for B, if he has all along intended to sue A and not B, whom he mistakenly named as a party. But if B was named because he was believed to be the person responsible for the matters complained of, the plaintiff's action falls outside Ord 20, r 5(3) (at 317 per Donaldson LJ). To make a good case for amendment the plaintiff would have to satisfy the court of the conditions set out in r 5(3). That is, first, that the mistake was a genuine one. Secondly, that it was not misleading or such as to cause any reasonable doubt as to the identity of the person intending to sue or intended to be sued. Thirdly, and this is not expressly mentioned in r 5(3), that it would be just to make the amendment.

A plaintiff who has succeeded to obtain leave to correct the name of a party so as to add a different party may find himself out of time for service on the new party. Here the Court of Appeal was very helpful too. Donaldson LJ held that:

> 'Ord 20, r 5(3) is itself hedged with every sort of protection for the intended defendant... Those protections will of themselves make a successful application under RSC Ord 20, r 5(3), something of a rarity, and in my judgment if leave to amend or correct would otherwise be given under that rule, the court should not hesitate to make any necessary extension of time...' (at 319).

Dismissal of action for want of prosecution

Two cases touch upon one of the less satisfactory aspects of this topic. The principles upon which an action is to be dismissed for failure to comply timeously with the important steps for bringing an action to trial were gathered by Lord Diplock in *Birkett v Jones* [1977] 2 All ER 801 at 804–5 and set out as follows:

> 'The power should be exercised only where the court is satisfied either
> (1) That the default has been intentional and contumelious, eg disobedience of a peremptory order of the court or conduct amounting to an abuse of the process of the court; or
> (2) (a) that there has been inordinate and inexcusable delay on the part of the plaintiff or his lawyers, and (b) that such delay will give rise to a substantial risk that it is not possible to have fair trial of the issues in the action or is such as is likely to cause or to have cause serious prejudice to the defendants either as between themselves and the plaintiff or between each other or between them and a third party.'

It has for some time been assumed that there is a sharp distinction between dismissal on ground (1) and dismissal on ground (2) above. This has now been reiterated by the Court of Appeal in *Bailey v Bailey* [1983] 3 All ER 495 and by Goulding J in *Greek City Co Ltd v Demetriou* [1983] 2 All ER 921. It amounts to this: if the action is dismissed under (1), namely, for disobedience of a peremptory order or contumelious conduct, then a second action by the plaintiff based on the same cause of action could be dismissed as abuse of process; by contrast, if the dismissal of the first action is for reasons mentioned in (2), namely, for inordinate and inexcusable delay, a second action by the same plaintiff against the same defendant could not, usually, amount to abuse of process and would not, therefore, be dismissed for this reason. Consequently where the limitation period has not yet passed, there would be little point in dismissing an action under (2), however flagrant and inexcusable the delay, because the plaintiff would be free to bring a fresh action.

Indeed, Lord Diplock himself acknowledged this in *Birket v James* (at 801, 808) when he said:

> '. . . I am of the opinion that the fact that the limitation period has not yet expired must always be a matter of great weight in determining whether to exercise the discretion to dismiss an action for want of prosecution where no question of contumelious default on the part of the plaintiff is involved; and in cases where it is likely that if the action were dismissed the plaintiff would avail himself of his legal right to issue a fresh writ, the expiry of the limitation period is generally a conclusive reason for not dismissing that action that is already pending.'

Goulding J felt constrained to follow this and refrained from dismissing the action in the *Greek City Co* case, despite the fact that the plaintiff's conduct had been such as to cause prejudice to the defendant. There, in order to avert interlocutory injunctions, the defendant had given certain undertakings which restricted his trade, so that while the plaintiff was procrastinating, the defendant was incurring losses. Goulding J felt that it would have been proper in the circumstances to dismiss the action but for the fact that the limitation period has not expired and the plaintiff could bring a fresh action. Two cases were cited in support of dismissal. The first, *Hytrac Conveyors v Conveyors International Ltd* [1982] 3 All ER 415 was distinguished on the ground that it was concerned with an Anton Piller order, and that there the dismissal of the action was justified by the plaintiff's misuse of the Anton Piller order 'as a means of finding out what charges to make' (at 418 per Lawton LJ; see All ER Rev 1982, pp 221–2). The second case, *Janos v Morris* [1981] 3 All ER 780 was distinguished on the ground that there the first action was dismissed only after a peremptory order.

The Court of Appeal in *Bailey v Bailey* also agreed that the *Janos* case was confined to dismissal after a peremptory order (at 497–8 per Dunn LJ). However, one may ask, as did counsel for the defendant in *Bailey v Bailey*: why should there be a difference between a plaintiff who deliberately disregards an order of the court, and a plaintiff who deliberately disregards the rules of the court? In either case, it seems, it would be unfortunate and harmful, to respect for the court and its rules, if a plaintiff whose first action was dismissed were allowed to bring further actions in place of that which was struck out. Rejecting the above argument, Dunn LJ said—

> '. . . it seems to me that there is a distinction in principle between a situation in which an action has been struck out for disobedience of the order of the court

and where the action has been dismissed for want of prosecution because the plaintiff, although he may have failed to obey the rules of court, has issued his second writ quite lawfully within the limitation period and in circumstances in which, . . . it is difficult, if not impossible, to say that this action constitutes an abuse of the process of the court' (at 499, relying on *Tolley v Morris* [1979] 2 All ER 561, 563 and *Birkett*).

With respect, this dictum merely reiterates the view that a distinction of principle exists rather than giving reasons for its existence. It fails to respond to the crucial question: why should we adopt or support such a distinction?

It could be argued in favour of the present position that a plaintiff who delays prosecuting an action begun well before the expiry of the limitation period should not be in a worse position than one who delays bringing his action until almost the end of the limitation period. There are, however, two answers to this argument. First, the prejudice from delay in bringing an action primarily involves the risk of loss of evidence or deterioration of it, but there is an additional and special prejudice in holding up proceedings already begun, namely, the prejudice to the defendant of having an action hanging over his head (see *Biss v Lambeth etc Area Health Authority* [1978] 2 All ER 125 per Lord Denning MR). Secondly, the argument proves too much, for if the plaintiff has a right to delay the proceedings as much as he likes during the limitation period, then no peremptory order preventing him from doing so should be made; and if made and disobeyed, the order should not prevent him from bringing a fresh action within the limitation period. But under the present law the judge does have powers to prescribe strict time limits for the conduct of the action, and to dismiss it for failure to comply with the order (see *Pryer v Smith* [1977] 1 All ER 218). And, as we have seen, when an action has been dismissed on this ground the plaintiff cannot bring a fresh one in its place even within the limitation period.

There does not seem to be, it is submitted, any good reason for distinguishing between disobedience of a peremptory order and disobedience of the rules of court. Where there has been a failure to comply with a peremptory order and the defendant applies to have the action struck out, in view of the finality of the decision the court will dismiss the action only if there are compelling grounds for doing so. Why should not a judge considering a similar application, though in the absence of a peremptory order, have the same power to bring the matters to an end in appropriate cases—especially when the delay has been inordinant, inexcusable and such to prevent the possibility of a fair trial? By insisting on a peremptory order before dismissal for want of prosecution, one only adds to the complexity of litigation. There seems little justification to impose this burden on the defendant, particularly as defendants are not always in a position to know in advance the consequences of the plaintiff's delay or, indeed, his reasons. Besides, defendants would always be inhibited by the risk of augmenting costs. Furthermore, the hearing of an application by the defendant for a peremptory order gives the plaintiff no advantage or protection which he would not have at the hearing of an application to strike out the action. For, even where there has been disobedience of a peremptory order, the court still has to be satisfied that the plaintiff's delay was such as to justify dismissal.

It would, it is suggested, make a considerable contribution to the expedition of actions and to efficiency to abandon the present distinction and to hold that whenever an action has been dismissed for want of prosecution, the bringing of a fresh one in its place could amount to abuse of process. This would not mean that a second action would automatically amount to abuse, the courts always having discretion in this matter. But it will always be for the plaintiff bringing a second action to persuade the court that there are sufficiently strong reasons to allow him to proceed with a second action. He would be in a position similar to that of a plaintiff wishing to bring an action outside the limitation period under s 33 of the Limitation Act 1980.

Finally, even if the courts are not prepared to abandon completely the present distinction, some progress could still be made in the direction suggested here under the present state of authority. Dismissal under the first head of Lord Diplock's dictum can be ordered, as we have seen, whenever the default has been 'intentional and contumelious'. Disobedience of a peremptory order is only mentioned as an example and is, therefore, not exhaustive. It follows that intentional delays which are, on account of their length or their consequences, such as to create great prejudice or prevent fair trial, could be considered as falling into the first head. In extreme instances, therefore, it is possible under the present law to obtain a final dismissal for want of prosecution even in the absence of a peremptory order.

Costs

i *In small claims procedure*

In *Newland v Boardwell* [1983] 3 All ER 179 the Court of Appeal considered an important point of costs which arose from two separate appeals involving an identical issue. The plaintiff in each case brought a claim in negligence for injuries and damage arising from road accidents. Insurance companies were the effective defendants. It was obvious, on the facts, that the negligence caused some loss to the plaintiffs. Since the claims were to unliquidated damages the simplest way for a defendant to proceed would have been to allow judgment to be entered against him, leaving the damages to be assessed at a separate hearing, where he could put the plaintiff to proof of the measure of damages claimed. While this course would have given the defendant ample opportunity to dispute the quantum of damage, it also had a drawback in that the registrar would be possessed of the normal discretion of awarding costs against the defendant. To avert the risk of costs each defendant adopted an ingenious course. They admitted negligence but denied liability to loss (ie denied that the loss resulted from the negligence). This brought CCR 1936, Ord 19, r 1(4) into operation according to which, upon receipt of the defence—the claim not exceeding £500—the case is automatically 'referred for arbitration by the registrar'. In such proceedings, r 1(11) of the same order decrees—

> 'No solicitor's charge shall be allowed as between party and party in respect of any proceedings referred to arbitration under Order 19, r 1(4), except for . . . (c) such costs as are certified by the arbitrator to have been incurred through the unreasonable conduct of the opposite party in relation to the proceedings or the claim therein.'

Having entered a defence denying liability, the defendants made a payment into court. It was accepted by the plaintiffs and the only remaining question was one of costs. There was no dispute that the plaintiffs were entitled, in the usual way, to the plaint fee and to solicitor's charge for preparing the claim. The issue was whether the plaintiffs were entitled to solicitor's costs incurred after the filing by the defendants of their defences. It was common ground that the defences were filed for the sole purpose of bringing the case under the no-costs provision. The registrar awarded the plaintiffs' costs holding that they were 'incurred through the unreasonable conduct' of the defendants, within r 1(11)(c). The Court of Appeal too felt that the device employed by the defendants amounted to 'a misuse of the pleading process'—as Cumming-Bruce LJ put it (at 184)—and that the conduct of the defence was unreasonable. Nonetheless the Court of Appeal found in favour of the defendants, holding that the plaintiffs' expenses were not incurred 'through' the filing of the defences, as para (c) specifies. The plaintiffs knew, or should have known, that solicitors' costs were not recoverable once the case was referred to arbitration. Once the reference was made it was open to the plaintiffs to terminate their solicitors' retainers. Consequently, the Court of Appeal held, the plaintiffs' costs were incurred by their own failure to dismiss their solicitors and not by the plaintiffs' conduct.

This seems a harsh result, and it is hardly alleviated by the court's regret at arriving at it or by the suggestion that plaintiffs might in future try to get the defence struck out, or attempt to have the reference to arbitration rescinded under Ord 19, r 1(5). The court's judgment concluded with the following words—

> 'We think there is room for doubt whether this result really accords with what the rule-making authority intended to be the proper consequence of CCR 1936, Ord 19, r 1(11)(c)' (at 185).

If so, it is difficult to see why the doubt should not have been resolved the other way.

ii Costs after withdrawal of payment into court

A hitherto undecided point of costs was considered by the Court of Appeal in *Garner v Cleggs* [1983] 2 All ER 403: the defendant pays into court a sum of money in satisfaction of the claim (under RSC Ord 22, r 1(11)); the plaintiff fails to exercise his right to accept the payment (Ord 22, r 3(1)); the defendant then applies for permission to withdraw the notice of payment into court (under Ord 22, r 1(3)), succeeds and withdraws the money; the plaintiff then obtains judgment against the defendant for a sum lower than the one paid into court; is the plaintiff entitled to the costs of the litigation? The Court of Appeal's answer is clearly, 'Yes'. It was held that it was not fatal to the plaintiff's position that he had not accepted payment during the 21 days, during which he was entitled to take out the money as of right. As Robert Goff LJ put it, 'he was entitled to wait and consider his position after the expiry of the 21-day period, though on risk as to costs incurred meanwhile' (at 407). Once a notice of payment into court has been withdrawn, the plaintiff loses the option of accepting the money. By withdrawing payment, Lawton LJ explained, the defendant put it completely beyond the power of the plaintiff to do anything about the money in court, '. . . he has to fight the action or abandon it' (at 405). Once this has happened the plaintiff no longer has the option of avoiding the costs of litigation. Hence, the court held, the plaintiff was entitled to costs except in respect of the period between the payment into court and the time at which the notice of payment was withdrawn.

There is one aspect of this eminently sensible decision that might give rise to difficulty. Once the 21-day period has passed the plaintiff cannot take out the money except by order of the court: Ord 22, r 5. The court will make such order only if there has not been a change of circumstances which renders it unfair to the defendant to make such order. Thus no order will be made if, for instance, the defendant's chances of success have substantially increased in the meantime. In the instant case the defendant served notice of payment into court on 11 August 1981. On 13 October the defendant became aware of evidence which was thought to be highly unfavourable to the plaintiff's case. The notice of payment into court was withdrawn on 26 February 1982. According to Lawton LJ, if the plaintiff had applied for an order to take out the money after 13 October, he would not have been granted leave because of the emergence of the new evidence. Consequently, his lordship thought that the plaintiff was not liable to costs from that date onwards, rather than from the withdrawal of the notice of payment several months later. It is submitted that it is better to regard the actual withdrawal of the notice as the cut-off point. Otherwise considerable scope for dispute will open up and courts will find themselves having to consider hypothetical questions as to what the court would have ordered had the plaintiff made an application (which in fact he never did). For as long as the plaintiff did not apply to take out the funds in court, he should be regarded as taking the risk as to costs.

iii *Calderbank order*

As we have seen, a defendant against whom a money judgment is sought may avert the costs of litigation by making a payment into court. If the claim is for some other relief, such as injunction, can the defendant take a comparable course? Such a course was suggested in *Calderbank v Calderbank* [1975] 3 All ER 33, where it was said that a defendant may offer to settle the action and submit to whatever injunctions or relief is appropriate. He may, at the same time, state that the offer is without prejudice but subject to him (the defendant) retaining the right to bring the matter up on the issue of costs. In *Computer Machinery Co v Drescher* [1983] 3 All ER 153, Sir Robert Megarry V-C expressed the view, obiter, that this procedure was not confined to proceedings in the Family Division to which *Calderbank* applied, but could be adopted in all proceedings. The Court of Appeal has since come to the same conclusion: *Cutts v Head* [1984] 1 All ER 597.

Another aspect of *Computer Machinery* which may be noted here is the decision that evidence may be tendered as to costs and that evidence on this issue is not necessarily confined to previously adduced evidence.

Appeal

i *Against decision to give leave to defend in proceedings for summary judgment*

On two occasions the Court of Appeal has commented on the newly re-instated right of appeal (by leave) against a judge's decision to give leave to defend in an application for summary judgment under RSC Ord 14. Section 18(1) of the Supreme Court Act 1981 fails to re-enact the prohibition

of such an appeal which was contained in s 31(1)(c) of the Supreme Court
of Judicature (Consolidation) Act 1925, which has been repealed.

In *European Asian Bank v Punjab and Sind Bank* [1983] 2 All ER 508 the court
decided that an appeal against leave to defend was by way of rehearing and
was not limited to a mere review of the judge's exercise of discretion. The
reason for this, it was held, is that Ord 14, r 3(1) lays down conditions upon
the fulfilment of which the judge has to give judgment for the plaintiff. These
conditions are: (1) that the court has not dismissed the plaintiff's application
for some procedural flaw and (2) the defendant has not satisfied the court
either (a) that there is an issue or question in dispute which ought to be tried
or (b) that there ought for some reason to be a trial. 'Once these three
possibilities are eliminated, it is very difficult indeed to conceive of circumstances where the court should not give judgment for the plaintiff . . .' it was
decided (at 515). The court indicated that the use of the word 'may' in r 3(1)
does not change the position that once those conditions have been fulfilled the
judge is left with only 'a discretion of the most residual kind' (ibid). Robert
Goff LJ contrasted r 3(1) of Ord 14 with r 4(3) of the same order, which
confers on the court a discretion to impose conditions on leave to defend. In
the latter case, he observed, appeal is by way of review of the judge's exercise
of discretion. All the same, the Court of Appeal was at pains to emphasise the
distinction between cases where leave to defend is given because the judge
decides that there is a triable issue of fact and cases where he decides that there
is a triable issue of law. In an appeal against a decision of the former kind the
Court of Appeal would be highly unlikely to reverse the judge's decision
([1982] 2 All ER at 516).

This last point was also stressed by Sir John Donaldson MR in *Lloyds Bank
plc v Ellis-Fewster* [1983] 2 All ER 424, 426 where he said—

> 'I cannot believe that it was ever intended that the Court of Appeal should move
> into a new era in which it regularly questions decisions of judges to grant leave
> to defend on the basis that there is a triable issue of fact.'

If, however, leave to defend was given on the ground that there was a
triable issue of law—as was the position in the *European Asian Bank* case—
then the appeal assumes a different character. Here the Court of Appeal
would consider the matter afresh. Indeed, in the last-mentioned case the
Court of Appeal undertook to determine there and then the issue of law
around which the dispute revolved, so as to make redundant a trial on the
issue. Robert Goff LJ's pronouncement on this point seems to indicate the
court's future approach—

> 'It may offend against the whole purpose of Ord 14 not to decide a case which
> raises a clear-cut issue, when full argument has been addressed to the court, and
> the only result of not deciding it will be that the case will go for trial and the
> argument will be rehearsed all over again before a judge, with the possibility of
> yet another appeal . . .' ([1983] 2 All ER at 516).

This attitude undercuts, therefore, much of the force of the main argument
against appeals from decisions giving leave to defend.

ii *Appeal from registrar of Court of Appeal to single judge*

Section 58(1) of the Supreme Court Act 1981 and the new Ord 59, r 14(11) have been helpfully commented upon by Griffith LJ in *C M Van Stillevoldt BV v E L Carrier Inc* [1983] 1 All ER 699. He held that on appeal to a single judge of the Court of Appeal from the refusal of the Court's registrar to extend time for setting down an appeal, the single judge was to consider the matter afresh and exercise his own discretion. Thus the appeal is not confined to review of the exercise of discretion by the registrar.

Note should also be taken of what Griffiths LJ said about applications to change the dates of hearings of appeals—

> '... I take this opportunity now to warn the profession that the attitude of the court to the previous lax practices is hardening in order to ensure for the benefit of all litigants that the business of the Court of Appeal is conducted in an expeditious and orderly manner' (at 703).

iii *Appeal to the House of Lords*

In *Re Poh* [1983] 1 All ER 287, HL it was decided that the House had no jurisdiction to entertain a petition for leave to appeal against refusal of the Court of Appeal to grant leave to apply for judicial review under RSC Ord 53.

iv *Citation of unreported cases in the House of Lords*

The practice of citing unreported cases has received short shrift in the House of Lords. Indeed, the House went as far as to lay down a restrictive procedure to be followed when counsel proposes to rely on unreported cases. This procedure was formulated by Lord Diplock and unanimously subscribed to by the rest of their Lordships in *Roberts Petroleum Ltd v Bernard Kenny Ltd* [1983] 1 All ER 564, [1983] BCLC 28. Lord Diplock said—

> 'My Lords, in my opinion, the time has now come when your Lordships should adopt the practice of declining to allow transcripts of unreported judgments of the Civil Division of the Court of Appeal to be cited on the hearing of appeals to this House unless leave is given to do so, and that such leave should only be granted on counsel's giving an assurance that the transcript contains a statement of some principle of law, relevant to an issue in the appeal to this House, that it is binding on the Court of Appeal and of which the substance, as distinct from the mere choice, of phraseology, is not to be found in any judgment of that court that has appeared in one of the generalised or specialised series of reports' (at 568).

The restrictive practice was born of the belief that unreported cases are on the whole of little general importance, ie that they remain unreported due to their unoriginal or limited content. Statistically this assumption is probably correct, for it is very unlikely that an important case would escape the searching gaze of all the editors of the numerous law reports which nowadays compete for subscribers. Nevertheless, the fact remains, and should not be forgotten, that the choice of whether a case is reported is not made by the judges giving judgment but by the editors of the law reports.

The reasons given by Lord Diplock for instituting this new practice appear in the following dictum—

> 'In a judgment, particularly one that has not been reduced into writing before delivery, a judge, whether at first instance or on appeal, has his mind concen-

trated on the particular facts of the case before him and the course which the oral argument has taken. This may have involved agreement or concessions, tacit or explicit, as to the applicable law, made by counsel for the litigating parties in what they conceived to be the interests of their respective clients in obtaining favourable outcome of the particular case' (at 567).

His Lordship went on to observe that since the primary duty of the Court of Appeal was to dispose of the dispute before it—

'. . . propositions of law may well be stated in terms either more general or more specific than would have been used if he who gave the judgment had in mind somewhat different facts, or had heard a legal argument more expansive than had been necessary in order to determine the particular appeal' (ibid).

It may be argued (see Bartholomew (1983) 133 NLJ 781) that these reasons cut across both reported and unreported cases, that in all cases in composing his judgment a judge concentrates on the issues before him and on the course which counsel's argument has taken. However, it would be pusillanimous to deny that judges never deliver judgment with an eye to the future. It is not uncommon for not only the House of Lords but also the Court of Appeal to approach a case with consciousness of the law-making potential. When labouring under the awareness of such responsibility, judges do take great care in definition and phraseology, in general statements and qualifications (as Lord Diplock himself testified, at 567). Unfortunately, judges do not, usually, stamp decisions of principle with a distinguishing mark. The law reports contain important and unimportant, helpful and unhelpful, original and wholly derivative cases. Our troubles do not stem from a failure to distinguish between reported and unreported cases, but from a failure to exercise greater discrimination between important and unimportant decisions, between decisions which define and sharpen a principle and decisions which merely apply it to a particular set of circumstances. It is the proclivity towards reliance on as many cases as possible that is the cause of the ills. It is this proclivity that feeds the demand for the numerous so called 'specialised' law reports, and which drives practitioners still further—to the stores of the Supreme Court Library and to the infinitely capacious memory of LEXIS— in search for yet more judicial pronouncements.

The facility of the legal profession of distinguishing the wood from the trees seems to have weakened somewhat. It seems to have become acceptable to cite all the decisions dealing with the same issue, or with similar issues, irrespective of their importance. In this respect the judiciary bears equal responsibility for the excessive respect it shows and the unwarranted attention it pays to cases merely on account of their being reported. And even less discrimination is practised with respect to the form in which a decision has been reported. Not infrequently judges, from the lowest to the highest instance, are to be found citing cases reported (if they can be so described) in the *Criminal Law Review*, the *Solicitor's Journal* or merely in *The Times*. In these, and other similar publications, judgments are not fully reported verbatim, they are merely summarised and, at times, commented on. But such summaries, although useful for some purposes, can hardly be regarded as reliable sources of the law of the land. We have a recent illustration of the risk involved in relying on summaries in *Computer Machinery v Drescher* [1983] 3 All ER 153 at 157. Unreported but fully reproduced judgments have at least the advantage of completeness and there is, therefore, little justification for treating them differently from reported summaries.

It is probably lack of confidence that leads to the citation of every single decision connected with the issue, and to the ransacking of the stores of unreported cases for this purpose. It is a pity that in trying to eradicate this timorousness the House of Lords has chosen to draw a formal line between reported and unreported decisions rather than insist on the substantial, though intellectually more exacting, distinction between the important and the unimportant.

Note should also be taken of another practice recommended for expediting counsel's argument in the House of Lords. It was felt in *R v Goldstein* [1983] 1 All ER 434 at 438 that where counsel relies on a series of propositions of law, he should include them in his printed case or, in default of that, hand them in as a typed statement at the hearing. The purpose of this is to spare their Lordships the irksome and time-consuming task of taking down such propositions in long-hand when they could readily be provided by counsel.

Execution

i *Charging orders*

It is not a common occurrence that the House of Lords entertains an appeal involving charging orders, nor that in a sequence of litigation, begun before the registrar, each successive step should result in a reversal of the judgment of the preceding instance. We have just such a case in *Roberts Petroleum Ltd v Bernard Kenny Ltd* [1983] 1 All ER 564, [1983] BCLC 28 (see also p 61 above). The issue that reached the House of Lords arose in this way. The plaintiff obtained against the defendant company judgment and a charging order nisi; the defendant company then went into liquidation; the question, therefore, was: should the charging order be made absolute? If the answer is, 'Yes', the judgment creditor becomes a secured creditor and obtains priority over the assets charged. If the answer is, 'No', the judgment creditor has to take his place amongst all other unsecured creditors. Two competing principles support these propositions. The first holds that a judgment creditor is generally entitled to enforce the judgment in his favour by all the means of execution afforded by the law. The second holds that when a judgment debtor has become insolvent, all the unsecured creditors should be treated equally, each receiving a pari passu share of the inadequate fund available. These two principles leave, as far as the present question goes, no scope for compromise. A choice has to be made adopting the one or the other. As it happened the question fell to be resolved under s 35 of the Administration of Justice Act 1956 and the then in force RSC Ord 50. These have now given way to s 6 of the Charging Orders Act 1979 and the new Ord 50, though according to Lord Brightman, speaking for the House, the position on the question discussed here would be the same under the new provisions.

The House of Lords found no difficulty in preferring the principle of equality between creditors. Under company law, once the appropriate decision for winding up has been taken (either compulsorily or voluntarily) a statutory scheme for dealing with the assets of the company comes into operation. Consequently, Lord Brightman held—

> 'Neither the precarious existence of the charge nor the precarious possession of the receiver [under the order nisi] seems to me to afford a convincing reason for

consolidating the position of the judgment creditor vis-à-vis the general body of unsecured creditors and thereby defeat quoad that asset the statutory scheme which was already in full force and effect.' (at 573)

The House of Lords concluded that in the circumstances described above the charging order should not have been made absolute.

This solution seems preferable to the awkward compromise between the two competing principles that the Court of Appeal had adopted. According to this view an order nisi should be made absolute unless the creditors have agreed on a scheme of arrangement which had a reasonable prospect of success. Such a rule would have not only produced uncertainty but would also have offered an inducement to judgment creditors to strive to defeat any scheme of arrangement. In this respect the House of Lords' solution has the advantage of helping, as Lord Brightman put it, 'to avert an unseemly scramble by creditors to achieve priority at the last moment.' (at 576)

ii   *Sale by sheriff in execution of judgment*

Two cases deal with the protection given to a sheriff who, acting innocently under a writ of fieri facias seizes, on the judgment debtor's premises, goods belonging to a third party (the claimant) and sells them in execution of the writ.

When a dispute has arisen whether the goods belonged to the judgment debtor or to the claimant the sheriff will apply to the master by way of an interpleader summons under RSC Ord 17, r 2. The master can then make a protective order under Ord 17, r 2(4) that no action be brought by the claimant against the sheriff. Such an order in effect protects the sheriff from any action in conversion (for, generally speaking, a sheriff may be sued in tort as any other citizen). Order 17, r 8 confers a wide discretion on the court in dealing with the sheriff's application for protection. It empowers it to 'make such order as to costs or any other matter as it thinks just'. The court will make a protective order, according to Glidewell J in *Observer Ltd v Gordon* [1983] 2 All ER 945, unless the claimant can show that it was fairly arguable that his claim against the sheriff overrode the sheriff's possible defences. Two such defences may be available to the sheriff. The first is statutory: s 15 of the Bankruptcy and Deeds of Arrangement Act 1913 reads—

> 'Where any goods in the possession of an execution debtor at the time of the seizure by the sheriff. . . are sold by such sheriff. . . without any claim having been made to the same . . . no person shall be entitled to recover against the sheriff . . . for any sale of such goods . . . unless it is proved that [he] had notice, or might by making reasonable enquiry have ascertained that the goods were not the property of the execution debtor . . .'

As the sheriff in this case had no actual notice, had no reasonable grounds for instituting an inquiry and, furthermore, was unlikely to discover the true ownership even if he had made inquiries, the judge decided to afford the sheriff the requested protection.

The second protection which a sheriff may seek is under the common law and this is more fully considered by the Court of Appeal in *Newman v Bakeaway Ltd* [1983] 2 All ER 935. Here, as in the previous case, the goods seized on the judgment debtor's premises in fact belonged to the claimant, who proceeded against the sheriff because the goods had been sold at gross undervalue. It seems settled that the sheriff would be awarded a protection order only 'if no substantial grievance' had been suffered by the claimant: *London, Chatham & Dover Ry Co v Cable* (1899) 80 LT 119; *Cave v Copel* [1954] 1 All ER 428. The question in *Newman* was whether the fact that the goods had been sold at gross undervalue could be considered a 'substantial grievance'. This is an important question since the sheriff is duty bound to sell by auction the goods seized in execution, and auctions are not always calculated to secure the best price. Geoffrey Lane LJ was prepared to hold that, on the authorities, 'where there is great difference between the value of the goods and the price realised that may on some occasions be a ground for not granting protection on the sheriff' (at 940). Unfortunately, Sir John Pennycuick and Megaw LJ did not find the authorities all that clear and preferred to reserve their judgment on this point. Since the former thought that in view of the uncertainty in authority 'it would not be right to preclude the claimant from bringing an action for conversion against the sheriff...' (at 943), gross undervalue must now be considered a ground for 'substantial grievance', until the Court of Appeal decides to the contrary. But note that their Lordships were at one in deciding that even if sale at gross undervalue was 'substantial grievance', that was not conclusive: the judge still retained discretion in the matter.

iii *Miscellaneous*

Finally, two decisions deserve mentioned on account of their practical significance, if not their theoretical importance. First, in *Brooks Associates Inc v Basu* [1983] 1 All ER 508, judgment creditors wished to attach monies standing to the judgment debtor's credit with the National Savings Bank. Since the bank is part of the Crown, they applied to the High Court under RSC Ord 77, r 16(2) for an order under s 27(1) of the Crown Proceedings Act 1947, as amended by s 139(1) of the Supreme Court Act 1981. The bank contended that since its head office was in Glasgow it was out of the jurisdiction of the English courts; under RSC Ord 49, r (1) the court could only attach a debt payable to a judgment debtor by a person 'within the jurisdiction'. This argument was rejected by Woolf J. He held that in respect of its banking activities the Crown, by virtue of the United Kingdom, was always within the jurisdiction of the English courts. The attachment order was accordingly made.

The second case to be mentioned is *Hart v Emelkrik Ltd* [1983] 3 All ER 15. The plaintiffs had long leases of flats in a building. The freeholder had failed to exercise his right to collect rents and to perform his landlord's covenants to manage the property and maintain it in good repair. At the instigation of the tenants Goulding J decided to exercise his discretion under s 37 of the Supreme Court Act 1981 empowering the High Court to 'appoint a receiver in all cases in which it appears to the court just and convenient to do so...' The main object of the appointment was to enable the receiver to take all necessary steps for the preservation of the property and the protection of the leaseholders' interests. The receiver was, therefore, empowered to receive and give good receipt for rents, profits and all other monies payable under the leases and to manage the property in accordance with the rights and obligations of the reversioner.

Shipping

ROBERT P GRIME, BA, BCL
Senior Lecturer in Law, University of Southampton

1 Insurance

The decision of the House of Lords in *The Salem* [1983] 1 All ER 745, briefly mentioned as a 'postscript' to the article on Shipping in the All England Law Reports Review for 1982 (All ER Rev 1982 p 251), was undoubtedly the most important case of marine insurance in the year, but will not be further reviewed here.

Athens Maritime Enterprises Corpn v Hellenic Mutual War Risks Association (Bermuda) Ltd, The Andreas Lemos [1983] 1 All ER 590 concerns the short point of some practical importance but no great legal difficulty. However, the case may well be remembered as much for its facts and for the colourful language of its judgment as for anything. The Andreas Lemos, while anchored in the Chittagong roads, had four of her mooring lines stolen and a fifth damaged, as well as suffering other relatively minor losses (in all amounting to $US 5,754.40) on account of the incursion by night of a gang of moderately courageous men armed with knives. When challenged, the gang had at first offered resistance to cover their retreat but when the crew advanced on them, the master carrying the ship's pistol, the second officer firing distress rockets, they broke and leapt into the sea. The question before Staughton J was whether such a loss was covered by the vessel's insurance.

The system of cover afforded for war and certain analogous risks in the London marine market can be described as a 'layer' or 'onion-skin' system. In this regard, the picture has changed with the introduction of the new Institute forms of marine policy, a process which began in 1982 and seems likely to be complete by the middle of 1984. The events in question occurred in 1977, and the vessel's insurance was based upon the now deceased Lloyd's SG policy. This policy, in its archaic language, covers several of the risks of war, and other violent activity:

> 'men of war, fire, enemies, pirates, rovers, thieves, jettisons, letters of mart and countermart, surprisals, takings at sea, arrests, restraints and detainments of all kings, princes and people, of what nation, condition or quality soever.'

Many of these words have acquired specialised meanings: some have lost all significance. Much is covered. Some seems not to be. Whatever cover may exist, it has to be considered in the light of the Free of Capture and Seizure Clause (FC & S Clause) which, at least from 1898, was invariably inserted into all marine policies. This clause excludes from all cover in respect of capture, seizure, warlike operations 'civil war, revolution, rebellion, insurrection or civil strife arising therefrom, or piracy'. If war risk cover is to be bought, and the market for that is separate from the marine risk market, then the FC & S Clause is deleted, the cover it would exclude thereby reinstated, and certain additional war risks inserted. But this does not include whatever remains in the marine policy with the FC & S Clause attached.

A further, and different, cover might be obtained under the Strikes, Riots and Civil Commotions Clause, against 'strikers, locked-out workmen, or persons taking part in labour disturbances, riots or civil commotions' and 'persons acting maliciously'. The whole pattern, which has been much improved by the new regime, was described by Mocatta J in *Panamanian Oriental SS Corpn v Wright* [1970] 2 Ll Rep 365 as 'tortuous and complex in the extreme'.

The owners of the Andreas Lemos had covered both her war and 'riot' risks by entering her in a mutual assurance association, the defendant to the action. The rules of the association offered cover for piracy, riots and persons acting maliciously, in so far as they were not covered by the ordinary marine hull policy, with the FC & S Clause attached. All three were offered as grounds for holding the defendant association liable, although the third was raised only to be reserved in case the matter went to higher authority. 'Persons acting maliciously' was thought by Lord Denning in *The Mandarin Star* [1969] 2 All ER 776 to be confined to the acts of those motivated by spite or ill will: but *The Mandarin Star* had not been followed by the Court of Appeal in *The Salem* [1982] 1 All ER 1057 when *The Andreas Lemos* fell to be argued, and since that case was in train for the House of Lords, it would seem wise for counsel to reserve it. As it turned out, this was not one of the issues settled by the House when the speeches were delivered in *The Salem* some eight months after Staughton J decided *The Andreas Lemos*.

It was argued that the knife-wielding gang that came aboard the Andreas Lemos, however piratical in a Hollywood sense, could not be pirates in law because at the time of the attack the vessel was in Bangladeshi territorial waters and not upon the high seas. Although there was room for argument, it would seem that piracy in Public International Law might only occur on the high seas. However, as regards domestic law, and in particular the construction of a marine insurance policy, there was direct authority. In *Republic of Bolivia v Indemnity Mutual Marine Insurance Co* [1909] 1 KB 785, the Court of Appeal had been prepared to hold that an act of piracy might occur on a river, a tributary of the Amazon, many miles inland. The authority of the case was somewhat weakened, however, by the fact that the court also held that the acts in question were not piratical at all. However, the dicta were clever, and Staughton J followed them. Nevertheless, he was unable to hold that the events constituted piracy. Piracy required force: it was 'forcible robbery'. The only force used here was force in self-protection while escaping. Applying ordinary principles of criminal law, force used in getting away after a theft could not make that theft 'robbery', still less 'forcible robbery'.

> 'It is not necessary,' concluded his Lordship, 'that the thieves must raise the pirate flag and fire a shot across the victim's bows before they can be called pirates. But piracy is not committed by stealth. This case is very near the borderline: but it must not on that account be allowed to make bad law' ([1983] 1 All ER at 600).

Was it then a riot? 'If one takes the word in its current and popular meaning, nobody but a Sloane Ranger would say of this casualty, "It was a riot".' Although invited by counsel to adopt a specific meaning for this word, Staughton J returned again to English domestic law. Relying upon the well-known authority of *Field v Receiver of Metropolitan Police* [1904–7] All ER Rep 435, he held that there could be no riot unless the thieves achieved their purpose by putting someone in fear. They did not. So, just as they could not be accounted pirates, they were not rioters either.

The decision may not be of high importance, but it has some significance. Commercial reality, as Staughton J pointed out, would distinguish between clandestine theft, secret pilferage and the like, and violent, overt action. That accords with the accepted interpretation of the word 'thieves' which, in the words of Rule 9 of the statutory Rules for the Construction of the Policy in Schedule 1 of the Marine Insurance Act 1906, 'does not cover clandestine theft'. On the other hand, the theft in *The Andreas Lemos* was overt, even violent, although the human victims were never fearful. The case is, in truth, on the borderline: it may not be easy to reconcile with, for example, a case such as *La Fabrique de Produits Chimique SA v Large* (1922) 13 Ll L Rep 269, in which Bailhache J held that the breaking down of two doors with crowbars was enough to make the theft 'non-clandestine' or violent, notwithstanding the fact that no violence had been offered to any person.

2 Bills of lading under charterparties

In the All ER Rev 1982 we noted the decision of Staughton J in *Astro Valiente Compania Naviera SA v Pakistan Ministry of Food and Agriculture (No 2), The Emmanuel Colocotronis (No 2)* [1982] 1 All ER 823, in which he held that a clause in a bill of lading issued under a charterparty incorporating the 'conditions' of the charterparty was sufficient to incorporate into the bill a London arbitration clause from that charterparty. In *Skips A/S Nordheim v Syrian Petroleum Co Ltd, The Varenna* [1983] 2 All ER 375, 3 All ER 645, that decision was not followed by Hobhouse J and disapproved by the Court of Appeal.

The issue is a simple one which, perhaps because it has been the subject of so much litigation, has become complicated. But it is also a simple issue in which the policy considerations are nicely balanced: such issues are of their nature likely to be much fought over. If the holder of a bill of lading is to be bound by the terms of a charterparty, he is to be bound by the terms of a document which he may not have an opportunity (not even the legal right) to inspect before the bill is issued. On the other hand, the shipowner who charters his ship in circumstances where it is envisaged that bills will be issued by the charterer to the consignors of goods, to be assigned to the consignees, is incurring liabilities in terms of those bills; for the bills constitute the terms of the contract of carriage between himself, as shipowner, and the holder of the bill, as cargo-owner. The shipowner has no more control of the contents of the bills than the consignor has of the contents of the charterparty.

The solution adopted by the parties both in the *Emmanuel Colocotronis (No 2)* and in the *Varenna* was for the charterparty specifically to require that the most important terms of the charterparty (including in both cases the arbitration clause) should appear in the bills of lading. In the *Varenna* there was in addition a clause whereby the charterers undertook to indemnify the shipowners in respect of losses caused by any failure to issue bills in accordance with the charter. It is not clear from the report whether the charter in *Emmanuel Colocotronis (No 2)* contained such a provision. In either case, failure to issue proper bills was in the contemplation of the parties to the charterparty. This point was specifically made by Hobhouse J in the *Varenna*

([1983] 2 All ER at 377 g), while Staughton J in *Emmanuel Colocotronis (No 2)* made the same point obliquely when he pointed out that to comply with the requirements of the charterparty in the matter of expressly including terms in the bills of lading would mean that the bills would 'contain a considerable volume of writing' and that it would be 'unlikely that there could be printed forms prepared in advance' ([1982] 1 All ER at 826 g). What actually happened in both cases could not therefore have been unexpected: the bills of lading briefly declared that the holders were to be bound by the conditions of the charterparty but did not expressly include the relevant clauses.

The older case law, clustering around *T W Thomas and Co Ltd v Portsea Steamship Co Ltd* [1912] AC 1, supported the proposition that the use of the word 'condition' in a clause in a bill of lading designed to incorporate some of the provisions of the charterparty ought to be restricted to conditions which might fall to be complied with by the holder of the bill in the completion of the carriage—conditions are to delivery, for example. Conditions which were not necessary for the operation of the bill of lading as a bill in the hands of the receiver were not to be incorporated merely by the use of such a term. In *Emmanuel Coloctronis (No 2)* however, Staughton J obtained support from the line of authority ending in *The Rena K* [1979] 1 All ER 397, for the proposition that the word 'condition' in the bill was only insufficient to incorporate an arbitration clause which, in its terms, did not apply to disputes arising out of the bills; but that it was apt to incorporate an arbitration clause of general application. Then he pushed the development a little further by holding that in that case, although the arbitration clause was in its terms of the first sort, yet since the charterparty directed that same arbitration clause to be incorporated into the bills, on this occasion it might be incorporated since the charterparty clearly intended arbitration to apply to bills. A not inaccurate way of describing this conclusion would be to say that, once the bill of lading holder had been directed by the 'conditions' clause into the charterparty, he was fixed by knowledge of and bound by all those terms of the charterparty which *the charterparty* had intended to be part of the bill of lading.

In those terms, that conclusion could be criticised: it is unrealistic in that, in fact, the bill of lading holder will not have had a sight of the charter and it is not consonant with the apparent expectations of the owner and charterer. If the owner imposes upon the charterer the duty of incorporating the arbitration clause into the bills which he issues, and takes an indemnity clause in case he does not, is it reasonable, if he does not, to assign the risk to the bill of lading holder?

In the *Varenna*, counsel for the holders of the bill of lading felt unable to base himself on the broadest interpretation of the decision of Staughton J in *Emmanuel Colocotronis (No 2)*. With this, Hobhouse J clearly agreed. The function of the court was to interpret the bill of lading. The charterparty had contractual force only as between the parties to it—owner and charterer. To give effect to the intention declared therein to incorporate an arbitration clause into the bills of lading gave to it a wider contractual significance. Further, it was proper to give to the word 'conditions' a confined meaning. The word was a part of a technical phrase in a standard form contract, its meaning hallowed by many judicial decisions and years of usage. Such a meaning ought not lightly to be altered. *Emmanuel Coloctronis (No 2)* was emphatically not followed.

The Court of Appeal was able to go further. The case was not only followed, it was disapproved. Of the three members of the Court of Appeal, two (Sir John Donaldson MR and Oliver LJ) gave substantial judgments. Both saw the matter as a decision as to which of the two puisne judges, Staughton J or Hobhouse J was right. As the Master of Rolls expressed it: 'The second pair of parties to this appeal appear to be Staughton and Hobhouse JJ'. All expressed sympathy with Staughton J:

> 'In principle I have considerable sympathy with this view, but this is a corner of the law where the commercial customers, shipowners, shippers and receivers, attach supreme importance to certainty, and where particular phrases have established meanings and effects it is not the policy of the law to seek to change them even if, in the absence of precedent, there would be a case for so doing' (per Sir John Donaldson MR [1983] 3 All ER at 648 f)

> 'I would have considerable sympathy with Staughton J's approach . . . were the matter res integra, although even then I am impressed by the argument of counsel for the plaintiffs with regard to the importance of clarity in seeking to incorporate an arbitration clause. But the matter is not res integra . . . ' (per Oliver LJ [1983] 3 All ER at 652 a)

> 'Alas! with no enthusiasm I am obliged to say that I have reached the conclusion that the weight of authority is opposed to that view.' (per Watkins LJ [1983] 3 All ER 653 j)

The court unanimously supported the approach adopted by Hobhouse J. The matter was to be understood in terms of the bill of lading not the charterparty and the word 'condition' was to be given its old, restricted meaning—that is to say 'conditions that are appropriate to the carriage and delivery of goods' and certainly not arbitration clauses or other 'collateral' matters.

Is this, then, to be understood as a victory for ancient conservatism over modern liberalism, for crabbed technicality over flexible rationality? Hardly. In policy terms it may perhaps better be seen as the recognition that it is the responsibility of the shipowner to exercise proper supervision over the activities of the charterer, or to take the consequences. Maybe we should say no more than that the *Verenna* puts beyond argument what the word 'condition' in an incorporation clause in a bill of lading means. Beyond that, the only legal significance of the case lies in the refusal to follow Staughton J in sanctioning licences to prospect for contractual terms from one contract to another. As Oliver LJ put it ([1983] 3 All ER at 650):

> 'It clearly cannot be sufficient to assert that the bill of lading refers generally to the charterparty and that that reference therefore, as it were, incorporates all the provisions of the charterparty because the holder of the bill of lading has notice (either actual or constructive) of the charterparty'.

The last time we were warned of the dangers of confusing imputed knowledge with contractual acceptance was by Lord Devlin in *McCutcheon v David MacBrayne* [1964] 1 All ER 430.

3 Negligent navigation and carriage of goods by sea

For almost as long as carriers by sea have used contractual stipulations to reduce the strict liabilities placed upon them by the common law as common

carriers, they have sought to exclude liability for the disasters and catas-
trophes of navigation. These include not only irresistible natural events like
storms and hurricanes, but also that more common class of sinkings and
strandings which are attributable to faults or errors in the navigation of the
ship. So exemptions for errors in navigation, or fault in navigation or
management, have been a regular feature of contracts for the carriage of
goods by sea or the use of ships.

Article IV(2)(a) of the Hague Rules exempts carriers from liability for 'loss
or damage arising or resulting from . . . act neglect or default of the Master,
mariner, pilot or the servants of the owner in the navigation or management
of the vessel'. That clause was enacted as s 4(2) of the United States Carriage
of Goods by Sea Act 1936, as well as directly by the United Kingdom
Carriage of Goods by Sea Acts 1924 and 1971. In *Seven Seas Transportation Ltd
v Pacifico Unico Corpn, The Oceanic Amity* [1983] 1 All ER 672, that provision
was incorporated into a time charterparty whereby the Oceanic Amity was
chartered for 20 to 40 days by Seven Seas to carry out a lightening operation
of their own vessel, Satya Kailash, inward bound but overladen with a cargo
of grain for Tuticorin in India. During the operation the Oceanic Amity was
negligently navigated, collided with the Satya Kailash and damaged her. The
question for Staughton J in the Commercial Court was whether the article
was effective to cover this sort of loss or damage.

The Hague Rules were designed to regulate the carriage of goods by sea
under bills of lading. The claims primarily envisaged were ordinary cargo
claims—claims by cargo-owners for damage or loss of their cargo in the
course of transportation. At first sight, claims between shipowners arising
out of a collision between their two vessels do not seem to be within that
intention. But before Staughton J could proceed to decide whether the
wording was apt to cover the claim, the same general issue had to be faced as a
matter of incorporation. The Hague Rules apply to carriage under bills of
lading. They would not, therefore, of their own force apply to this arrangement: no bills of lading were issued and, although the charterparty could be
regarded as a contract for the carriage of goods from outside the port of
Tuticorin to a wharf within the port, in was in a business sense a contract
whereby one carrier obtained the assistance of another to complete a contract
for the carriage of the cargo-owner's goods. The parties had, indeed, sought
to incorporate the Hague Rules expressly, although they had done this via the
incorporation of the US Carriage of Goods by Sea Act 1936. Clause 24 of the
charterparty made the charter 'subject to' a 'clause paramount' which began:
'This Bill of Lading shall have effect subject to the provisions of the Carriage
of Goods by Sea Act of the United States . . .' However clumsy and aesthet-
ically unsatisfying a device this was, the intention of the parties was plain—to
introduce into the charterparty such parts of the statute as were appropriate.
Staughton J had little difficulty in holding it to be effective, the more so since
the way to that conclusion had already been marked by the House of Lords in
Adamastos Shipping v Anglo-Saxon Petroleum Co [1958] 1 All ER 725.

The major question was whether 'loss or damage' in the exemption could
be extended beyond loss or damage to goods. In the *Adamastos* case, the
House of Lords, by a majority, had been prepared to extend the phrase
beyond the physical damage to or loss of goods to economic loss suffered by
the charterer. In that case the vessel was chartered on a consecutive voyage

charterparty and, due to the negligence of the owners' servants, the vessel suffered several delays, whereby the charterer was unable to complete the expected number of voyages. But that extension has been made with some wariness. In particular, great emphasis has been placed upon Article II of the Rules (s 2 of the US Carriage of Goods by Sea Act) which applied the responsibilities, liabilities, rights and immunities established by the Rules to the carrier 'in relation to the loading, handling, stowage, carriage, custody care and discharge' of the goods that were carried. Staughton J accepting that approach, held 'loss or damage' to be wide enough to cover damage to the charterer's own vessel, provided that such damage occurred in relation to the handling of the goods. In this, he reached a decision consonant with the only cited authority of substantial relevance. In *Australia Oil Refining Pty Ltd v R W Miller and Co Pty Ltd* [1968] 1 Ll Rep 448, the High Court of Australia had to decide whether damage done by the chartered ship to the charterer's wharf was subject to the immunity conferred by Article IV(2)(a). The decision is not easy to interpret, since the court appeared to decide that, although the 'immunities' of the Hague Rules had been incorporated, Article IV(2)(a) was not sufficient to cover the claim in that regard, since the Rules were to be understood as dealing only with cargo claims. However, the charterparty also contained a clause specifically incorporating, in terms, the substance of Article IV(2)(a). The majority of the court held that that clause, as understood in the particular context of the contract and its expected performance, sufficed to cover the claim. Even so, concern had been expressed that 'loss or damage', though not restricted to physical injuries to the cargo, ought to be restricted to losses caused in connection with the handling of cargo. It should not, for example, cover uncovenanted collisions on the high seas between the carrying vessel and another which happened to belong to the charterers.

In truth, contracts like those used in *Oceanic Amity* and the *Australia Oil* case are only in the most theoretical sense contracts for the carriage of goods by sea. The difficulties flow from the adoption by the businessmen concerned of a form designed for such carriage to achieve the aim of exception from liability for careless management of a ship. In the present case, Staughton J in the highest traditions of the Commercial Court, gave a practical business answer.

However, the fate of a more open attempt to avoid liability might not be so happy. In the *Oceanic Amity*, Staughton J went on to consider, clearly and consciously obiter, the significance of the common form 'errors in navigation' exception, which was also included in the charterparty. Clause 16 provided:

> 'The Act of God, enemies, fire, restraint of Princes, Rulers and People and all dangers and accidents of the Seas, Rivers, Machinery, Boiler and Steam Navigation and errors of Navigation throughout this Charter Party always mutually excepted.'

Did 'error in navigation' include negligent navigation? Staughton J held that it did not. He reached that conclusion by a well-known path that winds through a well-charted field named '*contra proferentem*'. It is way-marked by cases such as *Re Polemis and Furness Withy and Co Ltd* [1921] 3 KB 560, *Alderslade v Hendon Laundry* [1945] 1 All ER 244, *Canada Steamship Lines Ltd v R* [1952] 1 All ER 305, *Smith v South Wales Switchgear* [1978] 1 All ER 18, *Photo Production Ltd v Securicor* [1980] 1 All ER 556 and *Lamport* and *Holt Lines Ltd v Coubro and Scrutton M and I Ltd, The Raphael* [1982] 2 Ll Rep 42. The principle, in simplified form, seems to be that general exemptions will not cover liability for negligence in the absence of express reference or utterly unavoidable implication.

While Staughton J declared his decision on the 'errors in navigation' exception to be unnecessary to the decision, Bingham J also in the Commercial Court some five months later, was faced in *Industrie Chimiche Italia Centrale SpA v Nea Ninemia Shipping Co SA, The Emmanuel C* [1983] 1 All ER 686, with that as the sole issue for decision. The Emmanuel C had been chartered under New York Produce Exchange form for one round transatlantic trip, had grounded in the St Lawrence through negligent navigation and had become a total loss. Bingham J held that clause 16 of this charter, in terms exactly similar to those used by clause 16 of the Oceanic Amity's charter, was not apt to afford a defence to the owners. He decided thus, agreeing with Staughton J (after much more extensive argument on the point) on deceptively simple grounds. Neither 'negligence' nor any synonym therefor had been used. It could not be assumed, given the tradition of such exclusion, that if the parties had intended exclusion of their own negligence, they would not have used such language. Such nice squeamishness was not to be expected.

Exclusion of liability for the consequences of negligent navigation, therefore, requires express words. That must be a good result: it will make for greater clarity, even honesty. But these two cases, with *The Raphael*, at least arguably constitute a distinct change. And given the slow rate at which commercial documentation changes, we may see many more charters with common-form 'errors in navigation' exception which does not cover negligent navigation, though the parties expect it to.

4 Collisions

Since the middle of the nineteenth century there have been regulations designed to prevent collisions at sea. However, the measures adopted in successive Acts of Parliament for ensuring that such regulations are observed have never been simple. Apart from enforcement through the medium of the public law, by the imposition of criminal sanctions, there has always been a consequence in the civil law. For many years, until the passing of the Maritime Conventions Act 1911, breach of appropriate regulations had an impact upon civil claims which was specifically described and regulated by statute. This reached its final form in the so-called 'statutory presumption of fault', which was abolished by the Maritime Conventions Act.

The interaction between the civil and criminal dimensions of the regulations still exists, although it is rare to find cases on the criminal side. One such rarity is *Bradshaw v Ewart-James* [1983] 1 All ER 12, a decision of the Divisional Court on a case stated by the Ramsgate magistrates who had dismissed a prosecution of the master of a passenger ship for breach of s 419(2) of the Merchant Shipping Act 1894, in that the ship had failed to cross a traffic separation lane in the English Channel 'as nearly as practicable at right angles' as required by r 10(c) of the current collision regulations. Section 419(2) imposes a penalty upon the master 'if an infringement of the collision regulations is caused by' his 'wilful default'. At the time of the alleged infringement in this case, the ship was in the charge of the chief officer and the master was not on the bridge. How then could it be said that the infringement has been caused by his wilful default?

The argument in support of this somewhat startling proposition runs thus: although s 419(2) creates the criminal offence, the duty of the master, upon which it is based, is imposed by s 419(1), which is intended to create a general legal obligation to obey, significant in civil as well as criminal contexts and it is accepted that that duty is 'non-delegable'. It can also be argued that it was Parliament's intention to make the master strictly responsible for the observance of the regulations and that the only on-board criminal liability is placed upon the master. However, the argument does require that the word 'wilful' be accorded no greater meaning than 'conscious'.

The matter was free from authority and Lord Lane CJ, who gave the judgment of the court, had little difficulty in refusing to allow the development of another crime of strict liability, relying upon the decision of the House of Lords in *Vane v Yiannopoullos* [1964] 3 All ER 820. The duty imposed under s 419(1) might be non-delegable, but Captain Ewart-James' absence from the bridge gave him a good defence under s 419(2). The decision was followed, and somewhat extended, by a different Divisional Court in *Taylor v O'Keefe, The Nordic Clansman* [1984] 1 Ll Rep 31, where a defence of honest belief in the inapplicability of the rule in question was allowed. For conviction under s 419(2) proof of intention or recklessness on the part of the master was required.

A legal issue of a more familiar, if more complex, kind was decided in *Polish Steam Ship Co v Atlantic Maritime Co and Others, The Garden City* [1983] 2 All ER 532, another piece of litigation arising from the collision in March 1969 between the Zaglebie Dabrowski and the Garden City. After two separate actions which established the division of loss and the extent of liability, proceedings were started by the owners of Zaglebie Dabrowski to limit liability under s 503 of the Merchant Shipping Act 1894, as amended, and they paid into court a sum representing the limitation figure together with interest from the date of collision. Some four years later, judgment was given in the limitation proceedings and orders were made for the distribution of the sum paid into court. The present proceedings concerned further sums earned by way of interest on the money paid into court since 1978, such money having been placed on short-term investment account throughout the four years between payment and judgment. The owners of Zaglebie Dabrowski contended that the owners of Garden City were entitled only to simple interest on that part of the sum which represented the limitation figure over the four years from payment to judgment and interest upon that sum plus its interest between judgment and payment. Interest upon that part of the sum paid into court in 1978 which represented notional interest since the date of collision should be returned to the plaintiffs, being interest upon interest.

Parker J was not convinced. The practice of paying money into court benefited the plaintiff to limitation proceedings, for thus they could avoid possible currency fluctuations and the like. Further, by paying the money in, the owners of Zaglebie Dabrowski had consolidated into one fund both principal and interest. The whole should be paid out in satisfaction of the claims of the Garden City.

5 Actions in rem

There have been two cases reported in 1983 which would extend the limits of the right to proceed in rem. The Admiralty Court's jurisdiction in rem is set out in s 20 of the Supreme Court Act 1981, replacing, with amendment, s 1 of the Administration of Justice Act 1956. In *The Despina GK* [1983] 1 All ER 1, Sheen J was asked to exercise a jurisdiction not specified in the enumerated heads of jurisdiction in s 20(2). A successful cargo claim had been made in rem in the Swedish Admiralty Court. However, only part of the award damages were paid and, when the vessel entered an English port, the cargo owners commenced proceedings in rem for its arrest.

The rights of a plaintiff to arrest a ship in Admiralty cannot be stated simply. The position will vary depending upon whether there is a maritime lien or a statutory lien, whether or not the vessel has been released on bail. However, two propositions might be made: first, that there is no rearrest after bail (*The Kalamazoo* (1851) 15 Jur 885 which authority was followed in *The Point Breeze* [1928] P 135); second, that there can be no rearrest after judgment since the right of arrest deriving from the cause of action is merged in the judgment (*The Alletta* [1974] 1 Ll Rep 40). The Despina GK had been arrested in Sweden and released after the owners put up security and, further, the plaintiff cargo owners had recovered judgment against her in Sweden. However, in *The City of Mecca* (1879) 5 PD 28, Sir Robert Phillimore had asserted that the Admiralty Court had an ancient, pre-statutory, jurisdiction, founded on international comity to enforce the decrees of foreign admiralty courts. The decision of Sir Robert Phillimore had, however, been reversed on appeal.

Sheen J accepted the jurisdiction and allowed the arrest. He pointed out that Sir Robert Phillimore had been reversed on the facts, in that the jurisdiction asserted by the foreign court in that case was different from that which the English Admiralty Court would have had in the matter. That was not so in the present case. Sheen J however, was not prepared to go as far as Mr D R Thomas, the learned author of the British Shipping Laws volume on *Maritime Liens* (1980) Stevens, for whom the right of a foreign judgment creditor was equivalent to that of the holder of a maritime lien. Whereas the latter could, on the ancient and reliable authority of *The Bold Buccleugh* (1852) 7 Moo PCC 267, follow the res into whomsoever's hands it might pass, the right to proceed in rem to enforce a foreign judgment debt was, Sheen J held, available only when the ship belonged to the judgment debtor when arrested.

The St Anna [1983] 2 All ER 691 concerned not a judgment creditor but a party in whose favour an arbitration award had been made. The plaintiffs were charterers, the defendants owners, of the St Anna. As such, they might undoubtedly have proceeded in rem in pursuit of their claim. Instead they went to arbitration in virtue of a clause in the charterparty and, after publication of the award, the ship was appraised and sold in in rem proceedings in the English Admiralty Court at the suit of the mortgagees. The arbitration award was not satisfied and plaintiffs obtained leave to enforce it as a judgment, under s 26 of the Arbitration Act 1950. The plaintiffs now sought to proceed in rem against the proceeds of the sale (which were sufficient to satisfy both them and the mortgagees) now lying in the Admiralty Court. They contended that their claim was a 'claim arising out of an agreement relating to the carriage of goods in a ship' within s 20(2)(h) of the Supreme Court Act 1981.

Sheen J found for the plaintiffs. In *Bremer Oeltransport GmbH v Drewry* [1933] All ER Rep 851 the Court of Appeal had treated the enforcement of an arbitration award in respect of a charterparty as an action for the enforcement of a contract (the charterparty) for the purposes of service out of the jurisdiction. Despite the doubt that seemed to have been cast upon that by the Court of Appeal in *The Beldis* [1936] P 51, Sheen J was prepared to base his decision on it, fortified by the encouragement given by Lord Diplock and others in *The Jade, The Eschersheim* [1976] 1 All ER 920, to give to the words of what is now s 20(2)(h) 'their ordinary, wide meaning'. The arbitration award was based upon the charterparty which was clearly an agreement relating to the carriage of goods in a ship.

6 General average

General average may well be the most ancient part of maritime law. It is the subject of the Les Rhodia de jactu, which was known to Justinian. It now includes any 'extraordinary sacrifice or expenditure' incurred for the preservation of the voyage. The costs of general average are distributed rateably among those benefiting—the participants in the marine adventure, ship, cargo and freight. Whereas, no doubt, general average began by being concerned with spreading among the other cargo owners and the shipowner the cost to a cargo owner of goods jettisoned during a storm, the typical general average act today is rather the hiring of a tug by the shipowner. Modern general average claims are essentially claims by shipowners against cargo.

A general average claim carries a lien. The practice is, therefore, that in order to release cargo at the termination of the voyage 'average bonds' are signed and are supported by letters of guarantee from the cargo insurers. The actual adjustment of the average contributions may take several years.

In *Castle Insurance Co Ltd v Hong Kong Islands Shipping Co Ltd, The Potoi Chau* [1983] 3 All ER 706, the Privy Council had to decide when time began to run in general average. The Potoi Chau ran aground during a voyage from the Far East to Jeddah, Hodeidah, Aden and Bombay. She was salvaged by professional salvors and eventually reached Aden and Bombay, where her remaining cargo was discharged, subject to the usual bonds and guarantees. The writ was issued in good time, that is to say, within six years of the first of the general average acts, but is was issued by the ship managers rather than the shipowners. At a later date, the owners were joined. That was more than six years after the bonds had been signed and the guarantees issued. The joining did, however, occur within six years of the preparation of the average adjustment and statement.

Lord Diplock, giving the judgment of the Board, approved and followed a decision of Megaw J in *Chandris v Argo Insurance Co Ltd* [1963] 2 Ll Rep 65 to the effect that the date of the accrual of a cause of action in general average was the date of the general average sacrifice or expenditure giving rise to the claim. That undoubtedly was the usually accepted view, but until this case it might have been thought that an argument might be based upon the incorporation of the York-Antwerp Rules. The York-Antwerp Rules are the result of a series of international conferences designed to regulate the practice of general average. They are invariably incorporated into bills of lading. One of the functions of the Rules is to transfer to the consignee liability to meet general average contributions. Any claim, therefore, against the consignee must be based upon that contract which also requires an average adjustment. In Lord Diplock's judgment, however, this did not affect the matter. The cause of action had accrued at the time of the general average act and the person primarily liable was whoever happened at that moment to be cargo owner. The effect of the incorporation of the Rules into the bill of lading was simply to transfer that existing liability to the transferee of the bill. But time still began to run with the act. Lord Diplock was firm that the adjustment had no significance. It was not binding: it could be, and frequently was, challenged.

But did such reasoning apply to the signing of average bonds coupled with the issue of insurers' guarantees? In *Schothorst and Schuitema v Franz Dauter GmbH, The Nimrod* [1973] 2 Ll Rep 91 Kerr J had applied Megaw J's reasoning and had decided that the issue of average bonds had no postponing effect. With that conclusion Lord Diplock disagreed. Unlike the incorporation of the York–Antwerp Rules, the signing of an average bond constituted a new contract whereby, in consideration for the release of the shipowner's possessory lien, the consignee accepted personal liability. In the case of an insurer's guarantee, the insurer also undertook a primary liability. In both cases, the liability was to pay a sum of money on the happening of a future event, that is, the adjustment and the preparation of the statement. In the terms of that contract, the obligation could not arise until that event occurred, which meant, in the instant case, that the shipowner was not time-barred against the consignees and the insurers.

This is a technical matter and apparently a small point. But it may have substantial consequences. In this case it has the effect of extending the limitation period by four years. In shipping, where short limitation is the rule, that is a significant change.

Solicitors

BRIAN HARVEY, MA, LLM
Solicitor, Dean of the Faculty of Law, University of Birmingham

Introduction

1983 has been a year when the Law Society and the way in which it has undertaken some of its duties has been much in the news. The bifurcated status of that body was examined last year in *Swain v The Law Society* [1982] 2 All ER 827, All ER Rev 1982, p 262. At the end of 1983 the Lay Observer published a report stating that the Law Society had been seriously at fault on five occasions in connection with the complaints laid against a solicitor, Mr Glanville Davies, who was struck off the role of solicitors by a High Court Judge in October 1983. The complaints primarily concerned a bill of costs for £198,000 in respect of which the Lay Observer said that the client in question had a valid ground for complaint about the 'gross overcharging', and the Law Society had failed to deal properly with his complaint. The Law Society accepted the Lay Observer's criticisms. This unhappy affair conceals, of course, the huge amount of work which that body does perform on behalf of the profession and the public and it is worth noting that members of the Council and the Law Society's Committees act in that capacity purely voluntarily and without fee. One of the more onerous duties which the Council of the Law Society undertakes, pursuant to Sch 1 to the Solicitors Act 1974, is to intervene in the conduct of a solicitor's practice. It was matters arising out of such an intervention that form the background to the first case considered.

Buckley v The Law Society [1983] 2 All ER 1039

The background to this case rests in s 35 of and Sch 1 to the Solicitors Act 1974 under which the Council of the Law Society are given important powers of intervention in the conduct of a solicitor's practice. Schedule 1 both sets out the circumstances in which the Council may intervene (Part I) and the powers which the Council may exercise (Part II). Since this was an interlocutory matter, the full facts giving rise to the Law Society's action were not fully disclosed. However, such action was precipitated by a resolution of the Professional Purposes Committee of the Council of the Law Society made on 29 July 1982. It is interesting to observe that Sir Robert Megarry V-C stated, with regard to this, that 'no question now arises on the power to delegate'.

The grounds on which the Council exercise their powers were set out in para I(1) of the Schedule, namely that the Council had reason to suspect dishonesty on the part of a solicitor, and were satisfied that a solicitor had failed to comply with rules made under the Act, namely the Solicitors' Accounts Rules 1975.

It appears that the solicitor's defence may depend on what the learned judge stated to be 'considerable evidence to the effect that his financial difficulties are at least in part due to certain acts by a partner of his (who is now dead) in relation to the deposit in a conveyancing transaction'.

In order to dispute an intervention by the Law Society under the statutory powers, and particularly the vesting in the Society of all monies held by the solicitor or his firm in connection with his practice, the solicitor must issue an originating summons after being served with notice of the Law Society's resolution. This procedure is laid down in para 6 of Sch 1 to the 1974 Act. The solicitor in question duly issued his originating summons in the Chancery Division applying for an order directing the Society to withdraw the notice and for consequential relief. By a further notice of motion (under RSC Ord 24, r 7(1)), the solicitor sought an order for discovery. The real point at issue was the extent of the documents to which such an order could relate. The motion asked that the Law Society should be ordered to make discovery of a wide range of documents relating to the Council's resolution, including reports, inter-departmental memoranda, minutes and draft minutes, statements of witnesses, working papers, correspondence and so on.

Counsel for the Law Society took a number of objections to the proceedings as a whole. The argument that the exercise of its public function of intervening in a solicitor's practice could only be questioned in an application for judicial review, and not in an ordinary action, was not accepted by the learned judge. In this particular case the applicant had no option but to proceed by way of originating summons in the Chancery Division in accordance with para 6, r 6(1) of the Solicitors Act 1974.

The real issue, however, was whether the Law Society ought to be exempted from the process of discovery in respect of documents other than those which provide factual evidence, as distinct from mere expressions of opinion, relating to the solicitor's honesty. In particular, counsel argued, the court ought not to force the Law Society to disclose documents which showed the internal thinking of the Law Society. Megarry V-C held that the Law Society should not in these matters be exempt from the process of discovery. The duty under which they acted was distinct from the discharge of the public functions exercised by, eg a bench of magistrates or a coroner. But in ordinary litigation even the Home Office is subject to the process of discovery—see, eg, *Williams v Home Office* [1981] 1 All ER 1151. The objections of counsel for the Law Society were held not to outweigh the public interest in making disclosure in the interests of justice.

To what documents should this order for discovery apply? This question was not specifically decided since the learned judge gave liberty to reapply if the parties were unable to agree the documents. However, he gave the following guidance:

> 'It seems to me that the Society should make discovery of all documents which tend to show any grounds for suspecting the solicitor's dishonesty in connection with his practice or any Trust of which he was a Trustee or any grounds which indicate that he was not dishonest'.

He went on, furthermore, specifically not to exempt documents merely because they were internal documents or even, with some hesitation, draft minutes. The learned judge stated the test to be that of Brett LJ in *Compagnie Financière et Commerciale du Pacifique v Peruvian Guano Co* (1882) 11 QBD 55 at 63, that these might not 'fairly lead' the solicitors 'to a train of enquiry' which may advance his case or damage that of the Society. However, any order for discovery is, it was emphasised, subject to all claims that a particular document is privileged or exempt from discovery on some other ground.

The implications of this decision for the workings of the Professional Purposes Committee could be important. If it is now clear that internal memoranda, including inter-departmental memoranda, may in due course be subjected to publicity, they should be drafted (if at all) in the light of this possibility. Committees of anybody directed to exercise functions judicially will expect their preliminary observations to be kept confidential. A free exchange of views is not otherwise possible. It must now be borne in mind that the minutes of such meetings, and the working papers on which they are based, may have to be disclosed to the person whose affairs the committee is discussing, subject to any claims as to privilege etc. Whether this is really in the public interest is at least debatable. Any person in the position of the solicitor in question should, of course, be entitled to all documents containing facts, witnesses' statements etc which could affect his defence. Statements by way of preliminary opinion by members of the adjudicating committee could very reasonably be argued to be in an entirely different category. The free exchange of views on such occasion is surely very much in the public interest. It is now debatable whether the judgment in this case will unduly inhibit any such discussion which must be recorded.

A rather different angle on the duty to disclose material in a solicitor's possession to third parties arose in *Customs & Excise Commissioners v A E Hamlin & Co* [1983] 3 All ER 654. Although the core of the case concerns the extent of a solicitor's undertaking when obtaining an Anton Piller order, the remarks of Falconer J are of general interest and merit a short comment.

Briefly, solicitors had obtained Anton Piller orders against two defendants in connection with the alleged infringement of copyright in certain films and video cassettes. As a condition of obtaining the order, the plaintiff's solicitors (H & Co) gave the usual express undertakings, firstly to inform the defendants of their right to seek and obtain legal advice before complying with the order and, secondly, 'that all records, tapes, equipment, documents or other articles obtained as a result of this order will be retained in their safe custody or to their order until further order'.

A complexity was introduced when the Commissioners of Customs & Excise, who had been investigating the defendants' business, formed the view that there might have been fraudulent evasion of value added tax. Accordingly they wished to inspect and copy the documents or articles which were now in the solicitors' custody pursuant to the Anton Piller orders. The question was whether H & Co were within their rights in refusing access to these documents to the commissioners without a court order (although one of the defendants had expressly authorised them to allow such access), despite the existence of a statutory duty under s 35 of the Finance Act 1972 of any relevant person to furnish to the commissioners information relating to the goods in question. The Commissioners now argued that it was not necessary for them to obtain a court order to allow them to inspect and take copies of the relevant documents.

The learned judge pointed out that the purpose of giving H & Co, as solicitors for the plaintiffs in the action in which the Anton Piller orders were made, physical custody of the material was, of course, to ensure preservation of the documents and goods from destruction or defacement. The order had been made against the solicitors' express undertaking that the material obtained as a result of the order 'will be retained in their safe custody or to their order until further order'. The 'further order' refers to a further order of the court.

The learned judge recalled part of the speech of Lord Diplock in *Home Office v Harman* [1982] 1 All ER 532 at 538, when he stated:

> 'This is why an order for production of documents to a solicitor on behalf of a party to civil litigation is made on the implied undertaking given by the solicitor personally to the court (of which he is an officer) that he himself will not use or allow the documents or copies of them to be used for any collateral or ulterior purpose of his own, his client or anyone else; and any breach of that implied undertaking is a contempt of court by the solicitor himself. Save as respects the gravity of the contempt, no distinction is to be drawn between those documents which have and those which have not been admitted in evidence; to make use for some collateral or ulterior purpose of the special advantage obtained by having possession of copies of any of an adverse party's documents obtained on discovery is, in my view, a contempt of court'.

In the circumstances it was held that it was indeed necessary for the commissioners to obtain an order of the court to exercise their right to inspect and copy the documents in question, and it was appropriate that the Commissioners should have that Order.

Status of an articled clerk

The precise contractual relationship between a solicitor, the firm in which he is a partner and the solicitor's articled clerk came before the court by a side wind in *Oliver v JP Malnick & Co* [1983] 3 All ER 795. What occurred was that Miss O was interviewed by a partner of a firm (Mr M) when she had answered an advertisement. She was subsequently offered a post on the firm's headed notepaper, though the letter was written by Mr M and included the phrase, 'I shall be glad to offer you the position as Articled Clerk . . .' Before the Deed of Articles could be executed Miss O found that a male articled clerk, articled to another partner in the firm, had a salary of £500 pa greater than hers. She made a claim for equality of salary, but this was refused. She therefore complained to an industrial tribunal alleging unlawful discrimination. She named the firm, but not Mr M, as the respondent. Section 6(3) of the Sex Discrimination Act 1975 exempts from the duty not to discriminate employers employing less than six employees.

At the hearing before the industrial tribunal, counsel for the solicitor's firm submitted successfully that articles of clerkship were a personal contract between the clerk and the individual partner and therefore Mr M was excepted from liability under s 6(3) of the 1975 Act. The industrial tribunal made a 'very full and closely reasoned decision' which included recognition of the points that the salary of the articled clerk was paid by the firm, the articled clerk's time was spent for the benefit of the firm as a whole and the common custom of articled clerks is to state that they are articled to a particular firm (rather than an individual partner). Nevertheless the industrial tribunal, influenced by the Law Society 'model' articles which are expressed to be between the clerk and the individual partner, decided that the clerk was articled to that partner. In coming to this conclusion the industrial tribunal also considered that a contract of apprenticeship is customarily a contract of employment between the named parties and is strictly personal to those parties.

Miss O appealed to the Employment Appeal Tribunal. At the hearing Miss O was given leave to bring in further evidence in the form of an affidavit from the Secretary of the Education & Training Committee of the Law Society. The Secretary gave evidence that there was a Working Party set up to consider the position of articled clerks in 1977. Their report included the following passage: 'Most Articled Clerks, though articled to a partner in a firm, do not necessarily spend their time working for their principal, but in effect have a dual capacity in being articled to a Partner and employed by a firm.'

It was this concept of a 'dual system', ie that the clerk should be articled to the individual solicitor but *employed* by the firm, which was crucial. In the Law Society's specimen deed of articles and notes thereto, the articles are expressed to be entered into between an individual solicitor and the articled clerk, and the notice appended thereto sets out model terms and conditions of employment. These notes make it clear that the contract of employment is with 'the firm'. The Secretary also gave evidence that in the view of the Education & Training Committee of the Council of the Law Society, an articled clerk will normally be employed by the firm.

In the light of this new evidence the Employment Appeal Tribunal was able to regard the case in quite a different light. All the evidence pointed to Miss O having been engaged as an articled clerk under the dual system. This involved being articled to Mr M personally but being employed by the firm. She was paid by the firm, was in the firm's tax records as an employee of it and her work was done for the firm generally. The offer of articles written in the first person was unsurprising 'since it was dealing with the undoubted personal obligation of articles'. Since Miss O had left before a deed of articles could be executed, there was no higher source of evidence at which to look. The Law Society's model deed was the best evidence of what the parties intended to do. Therefore the Employment Appeal Tribunal decided that Miss O, whilst articled to Mr M, was employed by the firm. The case would therefore be remitted to the industrial tribunal to consider the claim on its merits.

Negligence

Although *Ashcroft v Mersey Regional Health Authority* [1983] 2 All ER 245 was not a claim for breach of the duty of care by a solicitor to a client, nevertheless there was some elucidation from Kilner Brown J as to the degree of care required of a professional person and when this is broken.

The action concerned a disastrous operation on the plaintiff's left ear by a surgeon of long experience, great skill and high reputation. The operation resulted in paralysis caused by damage to the facial nerve. Although the operation had clearly gone wrong, the question was whether the surgeon was negligent.

The surgeon in question admitted that there must have been an accident but expert opinion differed on whether the surgeon had done anything which could be categorised as negligent. The learned judge posed the question as follows:

> 'The question for consideration is whether, on a balance of probabilities, it has been established that a professional man has failed to exercise the care required of a man in possession and professing special skill in circumstances which require the exercise of that special skill'.

He went on to say 'that the more skilled a person is the more the care that is expected of him'.

In the event, and after some agonising, the learned judge accepted the surgeon's evidence that he had used the forceps as he always did, without excessive force, and the injury was an unforeseeable accident.

The judgment in this case cuts through the complex medical evidence impressively. However, it perhaps makes too great a difficulty of the law relating to professional negligence, tortuous though that can be. It would surely have been simpler to start from the premise that a routine operation of this sort should not go wrong. If it does there is a prima facie ground for supposing the presence of negligence on the res ipsa loquitur principle. It would then need evidence rather stronger than on the balance of probabilities that the result was an unforeseeable accident. Evidence from one other leading practitioner as to how the accident occurred and that it could have been foreseen should prima facie have been sufficient. The learned judge himself admits that another judge might have come to a different conclusion, so too much should not hang on the difficult assessment of complex medical issues in this case. However, the lesson for solicitors is reasonably plain. If something goes wrong with professional legal services there must be an implication in the first instance of the lack of application of the requisite skill—spondes peritiam artis. In the case of non-contentious work in the legal profession, the absence of the requisite care is usually less debatable on the facts. An example, as it happens, occurred in *McNamara v Martin Mears & Co* (1983) 127 SJ 69. The learned judge in that case stated in the context of divorce that it was the duty of a solicitor to make proper enquiries as to the assets and circumstances of the parties to a divorce before advising on a settlement. Failure to do this resulted in an inadequate settlement. The result was that the solicitor's firm in question was held liable to the plaintiff client for $8,000 damages plus interest.

Costs

A number of cases on costs are discussed in the articles on Criminal Procedure, p 156 and Practice and Procedure, pp 273–275 above.

Brief reference was made last year to the decision in *Bartletts de Raya v Byrne*, a case probably too straightforward to merit reporting in the All

England Law Reports but which is briefly reported at (1983) 127 SJ 69. On appeal from the county court the Court of Appeal held that although s 69(2) of the Solicitors Act 1974 required a solicitor to sign the bill in his own name or in the name of the firm, the section did not require the full name to be written. As an abbreviation here used was an obvious contraction of the firm's name, the signature could be regarded as a signature in the name of the firm. However, the Court of Appeal added the salutory warning that signatures on solicitors' bills of costs had given trouble down the years and it would be a sensible course for them to put matters beyond question by using the full name of the firm.

Legal professional privilege

See the discussion of *R v King* [1983] 1 All ER 929 in the article on Evidence, p 211 above an *A M & S Europe Ltd v Commission of the European Communities* [1983] 1 All ER 705 at pp 187–190 above (European Community Law).

In retrospect, 1983 was scarcely an exciting year insofar as the All England Law Reports reflect activity in the junior branch of the profession. However, 1984 promises to be more exciting in other and perhaps less pleasant ways, with further reforms of conveyancing and conveyancers heading the list of possible changes which affect the ever more complex and onerous job which most solicitors try to do.

Succession

C H SHERRIN, LLM, PHD
Barrister, Senior Lecturer in Law, University of Bristol

Introduction

There are three cases relevant to the law of succession reported in 1983 which although concerned with diverse and relatively minor points, are interesting and well worth noting. A case on the law of wills concerns the scope of the privilege relating to seamen's wills; whilst the law of intestate succession and actions under the Fatal Accidents Acts are considered respectively in the other two cases.

Privileged wills

The time-honoured privilege of soldiers and seamen to make nuncupative wills (Wills Act 1837, s 11) is often regarded as an unnecessary relic in these more literate days of instant communications. However, the Law Reform Committee (1980, Cmnd 7902) somewhat lamely, perhaps, did not recommend either its abolition or modification and it survives as part of the law of succession. The reported case of *Re Jones (decd)* [1981] 1 All ER 1 emphasised the continuing relevance of privileged wills with reference to a soldier on actual military service in Northern Ireland. Further it must be remembered that the privilege extends not only to soldiers in actual military service but also to a 'mariner or seaman being at sea' (Wills Act 1837, s 11) and in these cases there is no requirement of military service. It was this provision, potentially very wide, that was invoked, ultimately unsuccessfully, in *Re Rapley's Estate* [1983] 3 All ER 248. The deceased was an underage apprentice seaman with a steamship company when he drew up a written will signed, but not attested. He died many years later without having made any further will and the earlier document was propounded by his mother as a privileged will. The deceased was at the time he made the will undoubtedly a mariner or seaman by calling; the question was whether he was 'at sea' when he made the will. The will was drawn up whilst he was at home on leave between voyages and before he had received orders to join his next ship. There is, in fact, considerable authority indicating that the privilege is not literally confined to wills made whilst 'at sea' but can cover wills made ashore in particular circumstances.

Judge Finlay QC reviewed the relevant authorities which he thought established the following propositions. First, it has to be shown that the testator was serving either in the Royal Navy or the Merchant Navy. Secondly, it matters not whether the testator be a man or a woman, nor in what capacity he or she served or was employed, provided that the nature of the service was sea service. Thirdly, the evidence must justify a finding that the testator was 'on maritime service' in the sense that the testator either (a) was already in post as a ship's officer, or (b) was already a member of a particular ship's company serving in that ship, or (c) was being employed by owners of a fleet of ships and having been discharged from one such ship was already under orders to join another ship in that fleet.

In the present case the judge regarded as crucial the fact that when the deceased signed the document, he was on leave and had not yet received orders to join a ship. The judge declined to accept that the mere contemplation of being appointed to another ship was sufficient. On this narrow ground the judge distinguished cases such as Re Hale's Goods [1915] 2 IR 362; Re Newland's Estate [1952] 1 All ER 841; and Re Wilson's Estate [1952] 1 All ER 852 (in all of which the privilege had been succesfully invoked but in all of which orders to join a ship had been received), and declined to hold the document to be a valid testamentary disposition. Whilst one might sympathise with that result in practical terms, since there is little theoretical justification for affording the privilege to persons ashore in the circumstances of these cases, it must be said that the grounds of distinction between the facts of the present case and those of the three cases mentioned above, are narrow and technical. However, in the interests of confining the privilege within reasonable limits the decision is to be welcomed.

Exclusion from intestate benefit

The law of intestate succession is contained in statutory provisions which dictate, in cases to which they apply, the distribution of the property according to the particular circumstances of the case. Since the beneficiaries take by force of statutory provision there was, at one time, a view that intestate benefits could not be disclaimed. The contrary was assumed by Walton J in Re Scott [1975] 2 All ER 1033 and although this assumption was challenged (see Goodhart 40 Conveyancer 292), the feasibility of disclaiming benefits under an intestacy has been generally recognised, not least by s 68 of the Finance Act 1978. An analogous point arising out of the mandatory character of the statutory provisions is the extent to which a deceased can, by inter vivos or testamentary direction, seek to exclude all or some of his next of kin from their prima facie intestate benefit. Where the exclusion relates to all, then it is nugatory as Stuart V–C stated in Lett v Randall (1855) 3 SM & G 83.

'... supposing the testator annexed a clause of exclusion from any further part of his estate to the legacy he gave to each of the next of kin, would that have excluded everyone to whom the Statute of Distribution gave the property in case of intestacy? The answer must be certainly not if the clause of exclusion extends to all the next of kin. . . .' (at 89)

However, in the same case it was also stated that '... the exclusion by declaration of one or some only of the next of kin, if it be valid, must enure to the benefit of the rest, and has the same effect as a gift by implication to them of the share of those who are excluded'. It was this latter situation which arose in the recent case of Re Wynn (decd) [1983] 3 All ER 310, where a testatrix made a will which simply read: 'I, Olga Wynn, revoke all previous wills today 9th Jan 1981. I hereby wish that all I possess is not given to my husband Anthony Wynn'. It was accepted on all sides that this wording meant 'I hereby wish that nothing I possess is given to my husband Anthony Wynn'.

Warner J decided in favour of the validity of the direction, applying the rule stated in *Jarman on Wills* (8th edn, 1951) vol 2, p 684, that a declaration excluding one or some only of the next of kin if made in clear and appropriate language is valid, and operates as a gift by implication to the rest of the share of those who are excluded. The judge thought that the gift to the other persons entitled on intestacy could be implied in such cases unless the contrary intention was expressed. This conclusion is interesting because it could previously have been argued on the cases with some justification that such an exclusion was void unless there was some positive indication in the will of an intention to benefit the others.

In some cases (see, eg, *Re Holmes* (1890) 62 LT 383) the direction will be so worded as to preclude the named next of kin from taking under the will of the testator but not from taking on his intestacy, and in such cases the direction is, of course, perfectly valid. The judge rejected the argument that the facts before him created such a situation since the express revocation in the will of all previous wills without making any fresh disposition of property inevitably resulted in an intestacy and the words could thus only have been meant as an exclusion of the husband from taking on intestacy. This exclusion resulted, as noted above, to the benefit of the other persons entitled as next of kin.

Actions under the Fatal Accidents Acts

In *Austin v Hart* [1983] 2 All ER 341, the Privy Council was concerned with an interesting point concerning locus standi to bring an action for damages under the Fatal Accidents Acts. The case was on appeal from Trinidad and Tobago and concerned the construction of a local ordinance which was in similar terms to the English Act of 1846. This provision is no longer applicable in England, having been replaced by s 2 of the 1976 Act, which in turn has been substituted, without material change, by the Administration of Justice Act 1982. However, the prevalent English law in this respect has remained largely unchanged over the years and thus it is thought that the Privy Council decision has some relevance to the position in England. The primary rule governing the commencement of actions under the Fatal Accident Acts is that the action should be brought by and in the name of the executor or administrator of the deceased. However, if there is no executor or administrator or if no action has been brought within six months of the death by the executor or administrator, then the action may be brought by and in the name of all or any of the persons for whose benefit an executor or administrator could have brought it (see s 3 of the 1982 Act, substituting new provisions for ss 1 to 4 of the Fatal Accidents Act 1976, with effect from 1 January 1983).

The situation in *Austin v Hart* was that relatives had commenced proceedings under the Fatal Accident legislation within six months of the death and notwithstanding that an executor had been appointed. The defendants took the technical point that the relatives had no locus standi. The Privy Council was able to reject that contention holding that since the executor had not, within the six months period, applied for probate, or commenced any action himself, the irregularity was one which in effect was cured without amendment by the mere lapse of time. In view of the fact that it caused no possible prejudice or injustice to the defendant the court thought that it should not be regarded as nullifying and invalidating the whole proceedings. The court (per Lord Templeman at p 344) commented that it would be unfortunate if the existence of an executor, known or unknown to the dependants, invalidated an action which at all times belonged in equity to the dependants merely because the dependants did not sue in point of form in the name of the executor but sued in their own names. The position would be different if the executor had himself brought proceedings within the six months of the death, in which case the action by the dependants could have been stayed or dismissed. Cases such as *Ingall v Moran* [1944] 1 All ER 97, and *Finnegan v Cementation Co Ltd* [1953] 1 All ER 1130 where the action was brought in a representative capacity which the plaintiff did not possess and where the proceedings were thus a nullity, were distinguished.

Taxation

JOHN TILEY, MA, BCL
Barrister, Fellow of Queens' College, Cambridge

1 Introduction

1983 has been a disturbing year for reported tax cases. Familiar questions have been answered in unfamiliar ways and new concepts have been created sometimes to lie alongside and sometimes to overlay existing and well-tried ideas. The result is an increasing untidiness in the law. In part this untidiness may stem from the accidents of the litigation system, by which is meant not only the rather curious form of appeal that lies in tax cases but also the almost unpredictable willingness or unwillingness of the courts to allow argument on points not raised below. However, the untidiness derives also from an unresolved and fundamental question—what sort of law is tax law? Students are familiar with the division between prospective law—ie law which should be certain because people will plan their legal activities in the light of those rules, eg contract or land law—and retrospective law—where the law is concerned with the aftermath of events, eg tort. This dichotomy leaves the judges with a difficult job of classification since while, on one view, tax is clearly within the first category, particularly where matters such as estate planning are involved, our subject may also be seen to have to fit into the second category since other areas of tax law call for the application of broad concepts to a wide variety of factual circumstance, for example the area of the definition of emolument and the calculation of earnings for trade. The issue is confused by the unease which some judges feel when presented with schemes which are designed to take advantage of an apparent certainty in the law. For some judges tax law is not just a matter of private right for there is also an element of social engineering and a fairness between different taxpayers. These shades of view are reflected in general public attitudes towards the tax system. This is not the place to analyse the question of whether one view is more sound than another—it is enough to record the fact that these different views are held and that the judicial reaction is a faithful reflection of the general public view.

In this connection one should remember that the judges are not usually tax specialists. This can lead to a tension between the specialists (by which one means not only the lawyers and accountants but also the Inland Revenue) and the generalists, amongst whom the judges are to be placed. This division is not meant to suggest that the specialist is always right. Indeed it should be a cause for concern to the specialist when the courts reach a conclusion that the specialist finds startling. There is, however, a general problem of public administration when the Inland Revenue come to take one view of the law and to find cases decided by the courts which are inconsistent with that view.

Some of these points can be illustrated by the decision of Stephen Brown J in *R v Inland Revenue Comrs, ex p Harrow London Borough Council* [1983] STC 246. By the Development Land Tax Act 1976, a charge to development land tax will arise if a project of material development is begun. However by s 18 of the Act an exemption is given for projects begun within three years of the acquisition of the land. In this case a company bought land in July 1976. Shortly after that purchase the council made a compulsory purchase order on the land. On 9 July 1979 the council served the owners with a notice to treat and a notice of entry and took possession of the land later that month. Meanwhile, however, the owners had acquired planning permission for the land and, in accordance with s 18, they delivered a notice to the Inland Revenue stating that on 5 July 1979 they had begun a project of material development. The case proceeded on the basis that while the owners intended to begin the works involved, there was no intention to carry the works out to completion. At that time the council was entitled to the benefit of any development land tax payable by the owners but no such tax would be due if the project of material development had been started on 5 July 1979. The Board of Inland Revenue agreed with the taxpayer that the project had been begun. The court upheld the claim of the council that the project had not been begun. In reaching this conclusion the judge placed weight on the fact that the evidence showed that the works alleged to be specified operations were in reality 'colourable operations undertaken solely for the purposes of attempting to avoid the incidents of development land tax'. The judge then ruled that the decision reached by the Board of Inland Revenue not to assess the company to tax was unreasonable, and that the Board had misdirected itself in law and based its decision on extraneous considerations; the judge also observed that the board had been mistaken in its belief that it had complete and unfettered discretion in the matter.

This case is of interest not just because of the observation on the nature of the discretion afforded—or not afforded—to the Inland Revenue by the legislation but also because of the approach of the judge which was, if one may say so, a very common law approach. There must be many landowners who began projects of material development before the introduction of development land tax in August 1976 in the expectation that the mere digging of a trench would suffice to ensure that the development began before the date the tax became operational. This was a practice in which the Board of Inland Revenue seems to have concurred. The present case shows that the Board were probably wrong in this save where there was a definite intention to carry the project through to completion.

2 Coming to terms with Ramsay

Probably the most important question worrying tax practitioners at the moment is how far the courts are going to allow the Revenue to invoke the principle laid down by the House of Lords and the decision in *Ramsay v IRC* [1982] STC 174. The 1983 cases shed light on or raise three issues. It is clear that final resolution of the relative weight of the *Ramsay* principle and that laid down by the House of Lords nearly 50 years ago in *IRC v Duke of Westminster* [1936] AC 1 must await the 1984 cases if not later still.

The first question is whether it is open to the taxpayer to invoke the *Ramsay* principle. This was suggested by Sir John Donaldson MR in *Pattison v Marine Midland Ltd* [1983] STC 269 at 276 where he described the *Ramsay* case as introducing a new and refreshing philosophy which brought both taxpayers and tax gatherers back into the real world, and added that he thought that counsel for the company had exercised extraordinary restraint in not accusing the Crown of 'doing an inverted *Ramsay*' on the taxpayer—by inventing an artificial accountancy scheme which served no commercial purpose and was designed solely to create a liability to tax. However, 1983 also saw a case in which the taxpayer raised the *Ramsay* issue directly. The case is *Ewart v Taylor* [1983] STC 721. Unfortunately, Vinelott J held that it was not necessary for him to decide whether it was open to the taxpayer to invoke the *Ramsay* principle. Counsel for the Crown had conceded that if the Crown claimed that a series of transactions constituted an arrangement within the statutory definition of a settlement, in this case FA 1965, s 42, or an integrated scheme within the *Ramsay* principle, it was open to the taxpayer to claim and adduce evidence to show that the transactions comprised in the arrangement or scheme were wider than those relied on by the Crown. Vinelott J, however, made two points on this concession. The first was that if what was in issue was an arrangement within the definition of a settlement, then it was open to the taxpayer to rely on the existence of that arrangement whether or not the Crown sought to do so. However, the second was that he would not necessarily agree that, because the Crown relied on a series of transactions as constituting a single composite scheme within the *Ramsay* principle, it was necessarily open to the taxpayer to claim that the scheme included other transactions than those relied on by the Revenue. In any event it was not necessary for the issue to be decided since the burden of proof in such case lay with the taxpayer and that burden had not been discharged.

The issue concerned a series of transactions in three stages. Although the Commissioners had described the various transactions as 'closely interlocked' and, according to Vinelott J, not only closely interlocked 'but for all practical purposes inseparable', nonetheless they could not be treated as one composite scheme by the taxpayer. The reason was that on the facts found by the Commissioners there was at least a possibility that while stages one and two might have been carried through, stage three might not have been carried through. As Vinelott J explained it, in all the cases in which the Crown succeeded in establishing that a series of transactions should be regarded as steps in a single composite scheme, the scheme has been conceived as a single integrated scheme in the sense that the parties entered into it on the understanding that the scheme would be carried through as a whole or not at all, and that if as a result of some unforeseeable event (adopting Lord Wilberforce's analogy) the machinery had become jammed or (adopting Lord Russell's analogy), the stylus had stuck in a groove before the record had been fully played, each of the parties would have been obliged (though without being contractually bound) to assist in restoring everyone to his original position, at least so far as that could be done without exposing any party to any fiscal or other penalty. Although it was possible and even probable that stage three would have been carried, the facts as found by the Commissioners did not rule out the possibility that stage three might have been left unimplemented. One is left to speculate, on what higher courts might do with this analysis if it were advanced by a taxpayer seeking to defeat a Revenue plea based on *Ramsay*.

The second issue on the *Ramsay* principle is what the Appeal Courts were going to do with the decision of Vinelott J in *Furniss v Dawson* [1982] STC 267. In that case Vinelott J declined to apply the *Ramsay* principle where to do so would be to override transactions which were intended to have 'an enduring legal effect regulating the position of the parties'. The facts were set out last year (see All ER Rev 1982, pp 187–290). The case has now been to the House of Lords and is reported in [1984] 1 All ER 530. Discussion of it must wait until next year.

The third matter which has arisen in the year arises, unfortunately, only as a matter of inference. This issue is as to the effect of a direction by the Revenue or the courts that a transaction is to be regarded as 'fiscally a nullity'. In *Cairns v MacDiarmid* [1983] STC 178, the Court of Appeal agreed with Nourse J that a scheme involving the apparent payment of a sum by way of interest did not enable the payer to claim relief for interest under the terms of FA 1972, s 75. This matter was reviewed in last year's Annual Review (see All ER Rev 1982, p 284) and is not investigated again. In rejecting the claim to relief Sir John Donaldson MR first held that the interest was not annual interest therefore did not qualify for relief but then went on to provide an alternative approach which stemmed from *Ramsay*. As the Master of the Rolls put it, although the transaction was no sham, it lacked all reality. Kerr LJ also agreed that the decision of the House of Lords in *Ramsay* made the appeal hopeless. What this judgment leaves unresolved is this. If the effect of the *Ramsay* decision was that no deduction could be claimed for the payment, did it *necessarily* follow that the payment was not an interest receipt of the person to whom it was made; thus the issue is whether the payment is taxable in the hands of the recipient. This matter was unresolved.

3 Deductions

The decision of the Court of Appeal in *Nabi v Heaton* [1983] STC 344 is a welcome reversal of the decision of Vinelott J at first instance. In this case a taxpayer had separated from his first wife to whom he had been married in England but had later married a second wife under a Muslim ceremony in the country of his domicile. The second marriage being valid under the law of the country of his domicile, the question for the court was whether the taxpayer was entitled to the higher personal allowance available to a married man living with his wife. The case is of great interest in the general law relating to personal reliefs but of even greater interest for the manner in which the Court of Appeal reversed the first instance decision. In upholding the taxpayer's claim the court simply accepted a submission from counsel for the Crown that this was a case where, on reconsideration, the Revenue did not feel able to support its own victory in the court below!

The second case calling for mention under this heading is *Cairns v MacDiarmid* [1983] STC 178 in which the court held that no interest relief could be claimed under FA 1972 s 75. This case has been mentioned above. It is of note in the present context in view of the comments of the Court of Appeal, reversing the first instance judge, and holding that the payments were indeed payments of interest although, since they were not annual interests, they did not qualify for relief under FA 1972 s 75. The question whether the effect of the *Ramsay* decision was to deprive the payment of the character of interest in the hands of the recipient has been mentioned above.

The third case concerns loss relief. This was *Butt v Haxby* [1983] STC 239. The short point at stake was whether the taxpayer was entitled to take a part of his loss as being entitled to relief under TA 1970, s 168 and the balance of that loss under FA 1978, s 30. The court held that the taxpayer had to choose and that he was not allowed to apportion the loss between these two heads of relief.

Another case on loss relief is mentioned under 'Corporation tax' p 318 below.

4 Schedule E—employment income

There are three cases of interest and importance this year. The first, *Wicks and Johnson v Firth* [1983] 1 All ER 151 was commented upon in last year's Annual Review at some length in the light of the decision of the Court of Appeal (see All ER Rev 1982, pp 281–282). The decision of the House of Lords, which was referred to in that earlier Review, illuminates with great clarity the division between the two views that can be held. The issue, it will be recalled, was whether benefits consisting of a scholarship awarded to the child of a higher-paid employee, could be treated as a benefit of that higher-paid employee by reason of the provisions of FA 1976, s 61 or whether the exemption of scholarship income in TA 1970, s 375 applied not only to exempt the scholar himself but also his parent, the higher-paid employee. By four votes to one the House of Lords upheld the taxpayer's argument and allowed the appeal. The House was unanimous in holding that the benefits were provided at the cost of the employers within the meaning of s 61(3) and therefore the benefit was deemed to be provided by reason of the relevant taxpayer's employment thanks to s 72(3).

Enough was said last year as to why it is that most tax lawyers find this decision exceedingly difficult to understand. As indicated in the opening passage to this year's Review, it must be stressed that that comment is not necessarily meant to indicate that the House of Lords was wrong!

Since the House of Lords' decision, Parliament has intervened to reverse the decision but only on the narrowest basis and with extensive transitional relief. From this it follows that the case remains of general importance and that s 61 is prevented from applying not only in the circumstances listed in s 62 but also when some general provision or general doctrine excludes the recipient from liability to income tax. Presumably this gloss applies only where the sum would in other circumstances be income of the receipt but this remains to be explored. One imagines that the circumstances left for exploration are not particularly great.

Two matters perhaps deserve comment before leaving the case. The first is that nothing was said in the course of the judgments in the House of Lords as to whether the payment would have fallen within s 61 if it had not been for the deeming provision in s 72(3). There is therefore no comment on suggestions of the Master of the Rolls as to the test of causation to be applied in these cases. The other matter is the rather curious reasoning of Lord Bridge as to the effect of an Inland Revenue press release. When these scholarships first received attention from the Revenue, the Revenue indicated a thoroughly reasonable line that would be taken with regard to scholarships pending the decision of the courts. Some of those cases which the Revenue indicated they would not pursue would, if the decision of the House of Lords had been the same as that of the Court of Appeal, have now fallen into charged tax. Lord Bridge thought this weakened the Revenue's position. It is rather unfortunate that this press release should be treated in this way since it must operate to inhibit the Revenue from offering similar and welcome guidance in any similar disputed area.

The second and relatively brief case is a decision on the availability of capital allowances under Schedule E. Under FA 1971, s 47(1) capital allowances can be claimed for machinery or plant which is necessarily provided for use in the performance in the duties of the employment. *White v Higginbottom* [1983] STC 143 is a neat decision fully in line with the interpretation of this phrase in TA 1970, s 189. A clergyman had acquired a slide projector for use in parish work. The expense was clearly capital but the court held that it was not necessarily provided for use in the performance of the duties of his office since he could have managed perfectly well without a slide projector. If the General Synod now pronounces that all vicars should acquire slide projectors, we shall presumably be due for another round of this litigation.

The third and perhaps the most interesting case is *Glantre Engineering Ltd v Goodhand* [1983] 1 All ER 542, [1983] STC 1. This case operates as a necessary restriction on the scope of the decision in *Pritchard v Arundale* (1971) 47 TC 680. In the present case a company required a financial director and made an offer to X, a chartered accountant working for an international firm of accountants based in the city of London. X was a valuable employee of the accounting firm since he had the skill of programming computers. The company offered X the sum of £10,000 as an inducement to him to leave the firm of accountants. The Revenue now brought an action against the company arguing that they had wrongfully failed to deduct tax under the PAYE regulations, an argument which naturally turned on whether the payment was within Schedule E or not. After reviewing various cases, such as *Jarrold v Boustead* [1964] 41 TC 701, and concluding that the purpose behind the payment was not so much compensation for giving up irrevocably the status of a chartered accountant in private practice as compensation for the loss of security that X would suffer on leaving employment of the accountants, Warner J came to the question whether *Pritchard v Arundale* was distinguishable. The learned judge held that the earlier decision was distinguishable in three ways. It is possible to quarrel with each of these three, a fact which may simply show that these are matters of fact and impression and that it is very difficult to lay down rules of much practical guidance other than at a very abstract level. The first point of distinction taken by Warner J was that in *Pritchard v Arundale* the transfer was not made by the future employer but rather by a third party. This seems a rather formal point since in the earlier case the transfer was in fact made by the controlling shareholder in the employing company, the controlling shareholder holding all but 4 of 51,000 shares in that company, and the transfer was made as part of the service contract. The second point of distinction was that in the earlier case Mr Arundale was not 'merely changing one employment for another; he was giving up the status of senior partner'. This point is not finished off by Warner J and so one is left to wonder whether his Lordship is drawing a sharp distinction between the status of a partner and the status of an employee or whether the question is simply one of fact. If it is the latter one should note that in the new case the employee was giving up the prospects of partnership with his present employer and, just as significantly, the security that went with that employment. The third point taken was that Mr Arundale was to receive his shares forthwith even though the employment did not begin until later. By contrast in the recent case there was no such term and the payment was actually made in his first month of service as an employee. There seems to be some substance in this point but Warner J went on to point out that if Mr Arundale had died before his service began he would have been entitled to retain the shares, whereas if the employee in the present case had taken the money and then gone to work for a different firm instead, there would have been a breach of the agreement. This seems a rather curious point to make. Surely it would have been equally true that if X had died immediately he had received the £10,000, no action would have lain against the estate for recovery of the money. Equally there seems little doubt that if Mr Arundale had received the shares in his new employing company but, before entering into work with them, had gone off to work for another company instead and so never taken up his employment, the shares would have gone back to the controlling shareholder. All in all, the Revenue must be pleased to have a decision which they can use in reply to taxpayers who invoke *Pritchard v Arundale* (and the later decision in *Vaughan-Neil v IRC* [1979] STC 644) but must also be left with the feeling that further litigation is inevitable. Meanwhile one notes the Revenue's favourite tactic of attacking the employing company rather than the individual concerned, a tactic that they have used to great effect in expanding the scope of the PAYE system to a whole range of workers who may well not fall strictly within Schedule E. This, however, is to anticipate later litigation.

5a Business income—scope

There is a short case on the scope of Schedule D, Case I. In *Griffiths v Jackson* [1983] STC 184 properties had been acquired for letting rooms to students, the taxpayers supplying laundry and cleaning services. Vinelott J, reversing the decision of the Commissioners, held that this did not amount to a trading operation but rather income falling under Schedule D, Case VI. This decision is in line with a number of other recent decisions, eg *Gittos v Barclay* [1982] STC 390. The decision is therfore to be welcomed.

5b Business income—receipts

There are two cases to note here. The first is the decision of the Court of Appeal in *Pattison v Marine Midland Ltd* [1983] STC 269. This was a rather delayed appeal from the decision of Vinelott J reported at [1981] STC 540. The facts can be briefly stated. The taxpayer company, the United Kingdom subsiduary of an American bank, issued subordinated unsecured loan stock to the value of US $15m; the stock was issued to two subsidiaries of its parent company resident in the United States. The money thus raised was used in making dollar deposits. The company did not speculate in foreign exchange transactions but tried whenever possible to match any loan in a foreign currency so as to avoid any exchange risk. Some years later the company paid off the loan stock. By that time sterling had declined against the dollar so that the sterling cost of the repayment was much greater. At first instance Vinelott J, reversing the Commissioners, held that a taxable profit was realised on repayment of the loan stock since the funds were withdrawn from the pool of assets used in the banking business and the shift in the value of the dollar simply meant that there was a profit in sterling terms. Vinelott J also held that the loss accruing to the company on the repayment of the loan stock was on capital account and therefore not allowable in computing the profits of the business. Moreover, as was not decided but was agreed by all concerned, the loss was not in respect of an asset and therefore there could be no allowable capital gains loss arising. Before the Court of Appeal the case had a much narrower compass. The Court of Appeal held that while there was an obligation on any company to pay its tax in sterling, there was no obligation on it to keep its books in sterling. Moreover, translating the value of dollars into sterling at the end of each accounting period did not of itself create any profit when the business itself in that accounting period was expressed in terms of a foreign currency and no profit arose in those terms. It followed that there was no taxable profit arising when the loan was repaid even though this meant a withdrawal of funds from the pool of dollars. The case may best be understood in terms of simple analogies. If I have an asset, say an apple, which I lend out, my profits are derived from the hiring fees derived rather than from any change in the value of the apple itself. By contrast, if I run a business in which I buy and sell apples, profits arise if I sell the apples for more than I have to pay for them. What the bank had done was somewhere between the two. It had not bought and sold the foreign currency since it did not speculate in foreign exchange transactions. However, it was not quite like the loan of the apple since the asset used in the business was not a single asset but rather a fungible commodity, ie money. The Court of Appeal chose to equate a fungible commodity with a particular asset and thus hold that no profit arose.

The case can thus be seen as a very neat illustration of the point that no profit arises simply because of a change in the value of some of the assets used in the business where those assets are not trading stock. It also shows how narrow the compass of the decision is. Thus there is nothing to throw any doubt on the earlier decision in *Bentley v Pike* [1981] STC 360 that in capital gains tax, it is necessary to calculate the gain arising on the disposal of an asset by taking the sterling value of the proceeds of sale and deducting from them the allowable costs expressed in sterling terms and translated into sterling terms at the times that those costs were incurred.

The second case on receipts is a very nice case on timing. In *Symons v Weeks* [1983] STC 195 a firm of architects had a long-term building contract and received progress payments under that contract. On advice the accounts included not the whole sums received but instead an estimated value of work in progress. It seems to have been agreed that these accounts were drawn up in accordance with the prevailing accountancy practice since the Crown were reduced to arguing that the prevailing accountancy practice was not correct. The case is authority for two short propositions. The first is that the prevailing accountancy practice was entirely justifiable—with the result that the figures here used by accountants in computing the architect's profits for the year were much lower than the actual receipts. The second proposition is that where the accounts show figures which are correct in the sense just described, it is not open to the Revenue to re-open them in later years when the aggregate profit for the entire contract was determined. On this second point it is good to find clear authority reasserting the decision of the House of Lords in *British Mexican Petroleum Co Ltd v Jackson* (1932) 16 TC 570. The modern fashion for encouraging the use of hindsight in order to achieve more accurate accounts, a fashion largely based on the much narrower decision in *Simpson v Jones* (1968) 44 TC 599, is thus put in proper perspective. As Warner J said in *Simon v Weeks, Simpson v Jones* cannot apply to a case where accounts have been correctly drawn up. The case is also of interest in that it shows that it may be possible to reverse the usual doctrine of relating back so as to enable a particular payment to be related forward to a later period; all, however turns on the accountancy evidence in such cases.

5c Business income—expenditure

This area is, of course, dominated by the decision of the House of Lords in *Mallalieu v Drummond* [1983] 2 All ER 1095, [1983] STC 665. This case can fairly lay claim to be one of the most disappointing decisions of our supreme tribunal in recent years and it comes as all the more surprising when one discovers that the leading judgment was given by Lord Brightman, a member of the judiciary who has contributed most valuably to tax jurisprudence. The disappointments stem less from the decision itself, than from the way in which the decision is formulated and from all the uncertainties that arise. Ascertaining the ratio of the case is not made any easier by a considerable range of concessions made by counsel on either side, a series that makes it much easier to discover what the case is not about rather than what it is about.

The facts of the case can be briefly stated. The taxpayer was a barrister who was obliged, by the rules of her profession, to wear black clothes when in court. It was also necessary for her to wear a wig and gown but no argument was raised in the case on these items. The short question was whether she was entitled, in computing the profits of her profession, to deduct sums she had spent on the replacement, laundering and cleaning of the clothes worn in court. This in turn depended on whether such expenditure was incurred 'wholly and exclusively for the purposes of [her] profession' within TA 1970, s 130(a). The Commissioners found that when the taxpayer spent the money in this way she had a professional objective in mind, viz to enable her to be properly clothed during the time she was on her way to chambers or to court and while she was thereafter engaged in her professional activity. It seems to have been accepted on all sides that she would not have purchased these clothes for her own private use. Indeed, the Commissioners expressly found that the preservation of warmth and decency was not a consideration which crossed her mind when she bought the disputed items.

Despite this clear finding of primary fact, the Commissioners held that there was a secondary purpose in the purchase in that they were needed to keep her warm and clad during that part of the day when she was pursuing her career; it followed that the expenditure had a dual purpose and that therefore no deduction could be claimed. Lord Brightman pointed out that the General Commissioners involved had themselves been in practice at the Bar but one wonders what conceivable relevance this point can have had. If the expenditure was indeed deductible by this particular taxpayer the fact that the General Commissioners had in their own day not claimed a similar deduction was just as much evidence of their own reluctance to claim an allowable deduction as it was evidence that a deduction was not due.

Slade J at first instance, and the Court of Appeal, agreed in reversing the Commissioners. In view of the findings of primary fact the Commissioners were not justified, in their view, in inferring the duality of expenditure. Thus the matter came to the House of Lords.

Consideration of the judgment of the House of Lords, after noting that Lord Elwyn-Jones dissented while the other members agreed with Lord Brightman, must begin with the concessions that were made. The first concession was made by the Crown in that no point was taken by the Crown in relation to the odd occasions on which the taxpayer might have found it convenient to remain in her working clothes after her work was done and perhaps that the clothes were worn when travelling to and from work. This concession may have had a Machiavellian ring to it.

Counsel for the taxpayer seems to have been equally anxious to establish his reasonableness by stating that he disclaimed any reliance on the fact that his client disliked dark clothing, never purchased it for private use and therefore was not in a position to resort to her private wardrobe to answer the requirements of her profession. For Lord Brightman this disclaimer was rightly made; it would be absurd to suppose that there existed one law for the blonde barrister who lacks a wardrobe of dark clothes and another law for the brunette barrister whose wardrobe of everyday clothes contains many dresses suitable for court appearances. And yet one wonders whether this is not a little too easy. If, which turned out to be the key to the whole case, the issue was whether a subjective intention was conclusive determination of the right to deduct the expenditure, then it ought also to follow that one should consider simply the intention of the particular taxpayer involved in the case. The fact that other members of the Bar had an interest in the outcome of the litigation should not have prevented the House from reaching the right decision in the particular case before it. To make this matter a little sharper one may note that the level of expenditure by business people may vary substantially by reason of their personal characteristics. Thus a businessman with a more efficient metabolism than his neighbour may incur a different amount by way of expenditure on a meal. Similarly, one whose base of operations is close to Heathrow airport may incur less by way of transport costs than one who lives at a much greater distance.

Whatever the rights and wrongs of these concessions they enabled the House of Lords to turn what ought to have been a very simple question in relation to a particular taxpayer into a much broader issue. That broader issue was described by Lord Brightman ([1983] 2 All ER at 1102, [1983] STC at 672) as

'a far wider and more fundamental point, namely the right of any self-employed person to maintain, at the expense of his gross income and therefore partly at the expense of the general body of taxpayers, a wardrobe of everyday clothes which are reserved for work.'

Exception may be taken to this formulation. Thus there is the question whether the far wider and more fundamental point need be solved at all. Secondly, there is the invocation of the general body of taxpayers, an invocation which is a mere rhetorical flourish. Thirdly, there is the crucial word 'everyday', a word which may beg the very issue at stake if it is indeed the case that as far as this particular taxpayer was concerned these particular clothes would certainly not be worn as 'everyday' clothes.

Thus the broad question, whether or not emotively and misleadingly formulated, had to be decided. The decision reached by Lord Brightman was that the original decision of the Commissioners should be upheld because, while the taxpayer may well only have had the professional purpose in her conscious mind, it was inescapable that another object, though not a conscious motive, was the provision of the clothing that she needed as a human being—ie the need to wear clothes to travel to work and wear while at work. He rejected the notion that the object of the taxpayer was limited to the particular conscious motive in mind at the moment of expenditure. He added that he would have found it impossible to reach any other conclusion.

Criticism of the decision of the House of Lords must centre on three main points. First there are the doubts, much expressed already, whether the House actually addressed its mind to the right question. It may be that the issue was not the far wider and more fundamental point that Lord Brightman isolated but rather the question why did this taxpayer incur this expenditure. Enough has been said on this point already. The second criticism of the decision is that it represents a sharp departure from the law as previously understood. All the earlier cases in this area have turned on the particular subjective intention of the individual taxpayer. Lord Brightman now raises a new but rather curious subconscious motive test. Novelty alone is not a ground for criticism but that brings us to the third criticism. The third criticism is that Lord Brightman does not sufficiently relate his new tests to the old law. The old law was clear in that it imposed a subjective test of consciousness; it also provided that the court could ignore an incidental benefit accruing from the expenditure. Thus if the particular intention behind the expenditure was to procure benefit A, which was a purely business one, the fact that there was an incidental benefit of a personal nature, benefit B, did not disqualify the expenditure from being deductible. However, had both A and B been present in the taxpayer's mind when incurring the expenditure, the duality rule would have applied. Lord Brightman's speech tangles this particular skein in two ways. First there is the problem of how a subconscious motive can be put alongside a conscious one. It seems to follow that if there is a conscious business motive A and a subconscious personal motive B, then the expenditure is not deductible. It seems to follow also in the converse case that if the conscious purpose is personal and the subconscious motive is business again the expenditure is not deductible. Thus the taxpayer seems to lose either way. This is not made any easier by the fact that Lord Brightman goes on to distinguish from a subconscious or conscious motive something which he described as the 'effect' of the expenditure. It is not clear how the 'effect' of the expenditure test is to be related to the old 'incidental benefit' test. It may be that the two are intended to be the same but this is not clear from the speech of Lord Brightman. In any event there are going to be very substantial difficulties over the distinction between an effect and a subconscious motive.

Having explained why the decision of the House of Lords comes as something of a disappointment, it may strike the reader as something of a volte-face, if the writer then admits that there is a certain basic sense in what the House of Lords has done. The truth of the matter is that there is something right in Lord Brightman's view that it would be absurd to suppose that there exists one law for the blonde barrister and another for the brunette depending on their various wardrobes. What may be wrong is an attempt to achieve a result by means of the present judicial decision. The fact is that the border area between personal and private expenditure is one of much greater complexity than our present case law seems to allow.

Two other cases deserve mention under the heading of deductions. The first is the decision in *Bolton v International Drilling Co* [1983] STC 70. This is one of the few cases since the decision at the House of Lords in *Tucker v Granada Motorway Services* [1979] STC 393 in which the courts have tried to apply the new test of what is capital expenditure. The case is a short but neat illustration of the new principle. The taxpayer had a drilling rig. Another taxpayer had an option to buy that drilling rig. The taxpayer company made a payment for the cancellation of the option. The court held that the payment was a capital item. Although the taxpayer argued that the money was spent simply to preserve an asset that would otherwise have been lost, that was a false argument since it rested on an inadequate description of the asset itself. The asset was not just the rig but rather the rig subject to the existing option. It followed that when a sum was spent to remove the option a significant improvement in the asset was achieved and therefore the expenditure was capital.

In *Whitehead v Tubbs (Elastics) Ltd* [1983] STC 165 the question was whether a sum paid to secure the modification of the terms of a capital liability was a capital expenditure. Holding that it was capital expenditure, Vinelott J concluded one paragraph with the significant sentence, 'enduring advantage to the borrowers is to be found in the alteration in the terms affecting the loan capital'. Thus attempts to bury the enduring advantage test seem to be doomed!

6 Capital allowances

Three cases call for comment here. The first two cases concern the requirement, initially in CAA 1968, s 18 and later in FA 1971, s 41 that, in consequence of the taxpayer's incurring the expenditure, the machinery or plant must belong to him at some time during the chargeable period. In *Bolton v International Drilling Co Ltd* [1983] STC 70, a case noted under 'Expenditure' above, the court, having held that the payment in respect of the removal of the other company's option to purchase was a capital expense, then had to decide whether the rig belonged to the taxpayer 'in consequence of' that payment. The court upheld the decision of the commissioners and held that it did. This conclusion was related to the fact that, but for the agreement reached, the other company would certainly have exercised its option to purchase.

In *Stokes v Costain Property Investments* [1983] 2 All ER 681, [1983] STC 405, the taxpayer failed to establish his claim to the allowance. The taxpayer was a company which installed lifts in buildings which it was erecting. The company held a 99-year lease on the land but, as was agreed in the case, the effect of installing the lifts in the building was that they became the landlord's fixtures. Harman J held that, as a result, they belonged not to the tenant (notwithstanding his 99-year lease) but to the landlord. This, if one may say so, seems a rather straightforward interpretation of the legislation. The result is a very curious set of significantly differing tax results from slightly different legal situations. One hopes that remedial legislation will be forthcoming.

The third case is another good case, this time on the determination of cost where an asset is acquired in return for foreign currency. In *Van Arkadie v Sterling Coated Materials Ltd* [1983] STC 95, the price was to be paid in Swiss francs in instalments. The question was whether the cost of the asset should be determined by translating the price into sterling as each instalment was paid or whether one should simply use the exchange rate prevailing at the time the contract was made. Very correctly, if one may say so, Vinelott J held that the former contention was correct.

7 Other income

Apart from *Cairns v MacDiarmid,* p 308 above, there is one other case of relevance to the scope of Schedule D, Case III. This is *Ditchfield v Sharp* [1983] 3 All ER 681, [1983] STC 590. This is an unusual case in that it concerns the application of Case III to discounts. Schedule D, Case III taxes the annual profits or gains arising or accruing from discounts. Taxpayers were trustees of a settlement and had acquired promissory notes issued by a company. The notes were originally issued by a company as consideration for purchase of shares and carried no right to interest. The trustees bought them at a figure substantially less than face value; the payment was made in full three years later. The Revenue argued that the difference between the price paid by the trustees and the sum they eventually received was a profit arising from a discount. The court had little difficulty in holding that the purchase had been a discounting transaction, notwithstanding that the purchase was not made directly from the issuing company but, one year later, from a merchant bank and that the sum received by the taxpayers when the note matured was a profit arising from a discount. The only real debate in the case was whether the receipt had to be treated as one of an income nature or whether it was open to the taxpayers to argue that it was of a capital nature. The Commissioners had held that the profit was of a capital nature. At first it seems to have been accepted in the Court of Appeal that this was a question of law rather than a fact. The court held that even if it were a question of fact there was no evidence to support the conclusion reached by the Commissioners. The absence of any interest payable in respect of the notes before maturity was obviously a key factor.

One other point was raised in *Ditchfield v Sharp*. This was whether if a part of the sum received fell to be treated as interest, as distinct from a profit arising on a discount, it was then open to the Revenue to treat the whole sum as a discount. This submission was not accepted by the court however it raises a very difficult question since while both interest and discounts fall within Case III, other rules apply only to interest (eg TA 1970, ss 54 and 248).

The year also saw a case on Schedule B. This was *Russell v Hird* [1983] STC 590 and involved the question whether the taxpayer was in occupation of the woodlands. As a result of this case it is clear that the court has to have regard not only to the question of legal rights but also to the question of how those rights are actually exercised. Where the landowner allowed the taxpayer to exercise his contractual right to enter the land and cut down the trees, the taxpayer had established sufficient occupation to be taxed under Schedule B. One interesting consequence of this is that landowners may do well to refrain from interfering with the exercise of these contractual rights, since the damages recoverable for breach of contract will presumably have to compensate the taxpayer for any extra tax liability that may result from his being assessed under Schedule D, Case I rather than Schedule B!

Finally under this head one should note the decision of Vinelott J in the case of *Carver v Duncan* [1983] STC 310. This case concerns FA 1973, s 16(2)(d). In computing the income of the trust which is subject to additional rate income tax under FA 1973, s 16, it is open to the trustees to deduct those expenses which are properly chargeable to income (or would be so chargeable but for any express provisions of the trust). Vinelott J held that this allowed the deduction of expenses which were (a) authorised expenditure, whether that authorisation stemmed from the general law or under the express provisions of the trust and (b) which could be properly charged to income; the test of what is proper for (b) is whether it is chargeable to income either under the general law or under the express provisions of the trust. Under the terms of the trust the trustees were authorised to take out and maintain life insurance policies and to charge these to income. The effect of the decision is that the premiums payable in respect of those policies were deductible expenses under s 16(2)(d). Vinelott J also said that the word accumulation in FA 1973 did not extend to include income applied in the maintainance of a life or endowment policy. This decision clearly opens the way to some avoidance of the policy behind the legislation and it will be interesting to see whether Parliament intervenes.

8 Corporation tax

Three cases call for mention under this head. The first is *Willis v Peeters Picture Frames Ltd* [1983] STC 453, a rare case on TA 1970, s 483. Following a change in control of the taxpayer company, sales which the company had previously made directly to former customers were now channelled through distribution companies in the same group as the taxpayer company. The inspector of taxes refused the taxpayer company's claim to carry forward its loss under TA 1970, s 177 contending that there had been 'a major change in the customers' outlets or markets for the goods' and so a major change in the nature of conduct of the trade within TA 1970, s 483. The Special Commissioners had allowed the taxpayer company's appeal form the decision of the Inspector and the Crown's further appeal to the Court of Appeal in Northern Ireland was rejected. The question whether a change in the trade was 'major' was a question of fact. It remains to be seen whether this is going to be the first of a number of cases in which the Revenue try to invoke s 483 and which taxpayers take successfully to the courts.

The second case concerns the difficult expression 'expenses of management'; such expenses are deductible from the profits of an investment company under TA 1970, s 304. In *Hoechst Finance Ltd v Gumbrell* [1983] STC 150 the Court of Appeal reversed the decision of Nourse J and held that the particular expenses did not qualify for this relief. The case concerns sums paid by an investment company to a parent company in return for the parent company having guaranteed loan stock which had been placed by the taxpayer company on the Stock Exchange. Dillon LJ, giving the leading judgment in the Court of Appeal, thought that Nourse J had interpreted the word management as meaning something equivalent to running the company's business in too wide a sense; it was not every expense incurred to enable the company to carry on business which amounted to an expense of management. It followed that, to the Court of Appeal, the commission paid under the guarentee was simply part of the cost of acquisition of the funds and therefore not within the relief.

The third case involves a close company. Under what is now TA 1970, s 286, where a close company makes a loan to a participater, the company must make a special payment to the Inland Revenue; the special payment is a sum equal to the ACT that would have been due to the Revenue if the payment had been by way of distribution rather than by way of a loan. The interesting question in *Stephens v T Pittas Ltd* [1983] STC 576 was as to the meaning of the expression loan or advance to a participater. It appeared that money had been misappropriated by the controlling shareholder. The Revenue's claim that this should be treated as a loan or advance was dismissed since there was no element of agreement between the controlling shareholder and the company. The question what is a loan is one relevant in a wide variety of tax contexts, eg FA 1976, s 66 and there is no reason why the principle applied in this case should not be applied in those other contexts as well.

9 Capital gains tax

One of the reasons why tax law is so difficult—and one of the reasons for its occasional uncertainty in direction—is that it is only when sometimes subtle facts have been determined, that it can begin to operate. This has been particularly true of what is now CGTA 1979, s 20, entitled 'Capital Sums Derived From Assets'. Section 20(1) begins by stating that a disposal of assets arises where any capital sum is derived from assets notwithstanding that no asset is acquired by the person paying the capital sum, and then goes on to list four particular situations. In *Davis v Powell* [1977] STC 32 Templeman J (as he then was) held that compensation paid to an agricultural tenant under the Agricultural Holdings Act 1948, by way of compensation for disturbance on his quitting the holding, was not subject to tax under this provision. He stated that the compensation receivable under the legislation was not a capital sum received in return for the surrender of rights but rather was a sum paid where a tenant was faced with a notice to quit and must get out; the tenant was allowed by Parliament to have a sum by way of compensation for irretrievable loss. The reasoning in that decision was applied by Walton J in *Drummond v Austin Brown* [1983] STC 506. Here the taxpayer had been the tenant of business premises. He received notice to quit under part II of the Landlord and Tenant Act 1954 and received some £31,000 from the landlord in respect of his right to compensation for disturbance under that 1954 Act. The Revenue attempted to assess the taxpayer in respect of the sum received on the ground that it fell within what is now s 20. Walton J was content to take as his first ratio that of Templeman J in *Davis v Powell*. Just as the payment to the agricultural tenant in that case was a compensation for disturbance so here too the payment was clearly designed to compensate for otherwise irrecoverable loss. However, Walton J went on to point out that there is a clear distinction between the tenant who hangs on until the end of his tenancy and receives a sum by way of compensation on the one hand and on the other a tenant who having a fag-end to his lease, surrenders that fag-end to his landlord in return for payment. There is thus a clear tax planning advantage in bringing the matter within the scope of the statutory provisions.

Walton J went on to consider what would happen if the statutory right to compensation was to be treated as an asset in its own right which was therefore now being realised in return for money. Even if it had been possible to bring the payment within the scope of CGT in this way, Walton J pointed out that there would be further difficulties. Thus it might be said that the asset was acquired 'not by way of a bargain made at arm's length' and therefore was acquired at market value; quite how the market value of such a right would be determined would be a matter of great difficulty but it might well lead to no net gain at the end of the day. Even if the right to compensation as an asset were held in some mysterious way to be apart of the lease itself and thus to have been acquired at arm's length, there would be problems of valuation.

The interest in *Drummond v Austin Brown* is heightened by the fact that only a few days earlier Nourse J had decided *Davenport v Chilver* [1983] STC 426. The case concerned property in Latvia which was expropriated by the USSR in 1940. The property falls into two groups. The first group consisted of property owned by the taxpayer or by her father who had bequeathed the property to her. In relation to this property the court held that compensation eventually received fell within s 20(1)(a) as compensation for loss of an asset.

The main claim concerned the other group of property. This was property which was in 1940 owned by the taxpayer's mother. The taxpayer's mother died in 1966 leaving the taxpayer a half share in any compensation which might be paid. The compensation followed an agreement between the government of the USSR and the UK in 1967 which led to a treaty in 1968 and a statutory instrument in 1969. The taxpayer therefore argued that, on the strength of *Davis v Powell*, a statutory right to compensation for irretrievable loss could not give rise to capital gains tax. More fully, the taxpayer argued that the statutory right could not be an asset for capital gains tax purposes. Nourse J proceeded to distinguish *Davis v Powell*. First, said Nourse J, *Davis v Powell* was discussed solely in terms in what is now s 20 and therefore did not have to consider the question whether the right to compensation could be an asset in its own right. The other two grounds are more substantial. The second ground involved an investigation of the nature of the right involved. In *Davis v Powell*—as in *Drummond v Austin Brown* which was still to come—the right was compensation 'against the pocket of the landlord for expense which the tenant's pocket is deemed already to have met. It was a mere right to reimbursement'. This point is fully in line with the later decision in *Drummond v Austin Brown*. By contrast the taxpayer in the present case was given a right to a share in a designated fund under the terms of the statutory instrument.

It is the third and last ground of distinction which is perhaps the most curious. It is that the taxpayer did not suffer an irretrievable loss in respect of her mother's property; it was her mother who suffered that loss. From this it followed that the 1969 statutory instrument for the first time conferred an asset on the taxpayer. Before that time she had owned nothing. From this it followed that what she acquired in 1969 was an asset and therefore potentially subject to CGT. The position thus appears to be (1) that the mother suffered a loss in 1940 when her assets were taken away; (2) that she bequeathed the consequent hope of compensation to her daughter and that (3) the daughter only acquired an asset—as distinct from a spes—with the passing of the statutory instrument. If the taxpayer's mother had survived until the statutory instrument came into force it would appear that any sum subsequently paid would have been taxable first as a capital sum received for the loss of her asset but it would seem also to follow that she had another right, viz the right to compensation granted by the statutory instrument itself. Quite how she could have two such rights at the same time is not quite clear and there is certainly no suggestion that the second right superseded the first. Next, suppose that the taxpayer's mother had sold her potential right to compensation. The sum received from such a purchase would presumably not be by way of compensation for the loss of the asset within s 20(1)(a), nor would it be a sum received in return for the forfeiture or surrender of rights within s 20(1)(c). This raises the question of the position of the purchaser which appears to be the same as that of the taxpayer in *Davenport v Chilver*. It appears that what was acquired was a mere spes and that this was not an asset. The first time an asset arose was in 1969 when the statutory instrument was passed.

Apart from these speculations one is left with the fact that Nourse J had distinguished *Davis v Powell* and therefore the taxpayer had an asset. However, whatever joy the Revenue might have derived from this was promptly undone by the judge's decision that the taxpayer acquired her right under the 1969 order and acquired it otherwise by way of bargain at arm's length—as was later suggested in *Drummond v Austin Brown*. It followed that the base cost of the right was not nil but rather the value of the right to compensation in 1969. The matter was therefore referred back to the commissioners for calculating the market value in 1969 and so the base cost and so the chargeable gain.

It cannot be pretended that the situation is as clear and logical as it might be and one expects that much greater play of a rather subtle nature is going to be made when considering the nature of assets in an area such as this.

It is something of a relief to turn to the other cases on CGT for the year. First there is a line of cases which tidy up the law. In *Strange v Openshaw* [1983] STC 416 Peter Gibson J held that where there are rules designed to deal with a specific situation, those rules exclude more general principles. The case concerned the grant of an option. The judge held that the consequence was that the special rules relating to options applied and that there was no room for the application of the part disposal rules even though, on one analysis, the grant of an option created a right in the property subject to the option and therefore came within the definition of a part disposal.

Similar pleasure may be expressed at the decision of Vinelott J in *Williams v Bullevant* [1983] STC 107. Here the issue was the precise time at which CGT liability could be said to arise where assets had become of negligible value. The taxpayer claimed that the assets had become of negligible value in 1974 but did not make the claim until 1978. The notional sale directed by FA 1965, s 23(4) was held to take place not earlier than the date of the claim by the owner and thus to rule out any possibility of its having taken place in 1974. This, if one may say so, seems entirely sensible although the learned judge left open the possibility that the sale might take place when the inspector was satisfied that the value had become negligible rather than the date of the claim; this issue did not arise in the case.

Mashiter v Pearmain [1983] STC 658 is another case involving a problem of statutory construction in which an entirely sensible conclusion was reached. The issue concerned assets held on 6 April 1965 and in particular land reflecting development value. The land had been acquired by the taxpayer's wife in 1950 by way of gift and was disposed of by her in August 1976. If 'expenditure allowable as a deduction' had been incurred before 6 April 1965 the starting point would have been the value on 6 April 1965; if no such expenditure had been incurred a simple time apportionment would have applied. The court held that although the taxpayer's wife was deemed to have acquired the land in 1950 for its then market value, that deemed consideration was not 'expenditure allowable as a deduction' and therefore the time apportionment rule applied. The case is a marvellous example of the complexity of statutory construction.

Lastly, one should note *Gubay v Kington* [1983] 2 All ER 967, [1983] STC 443, the Court of Appeal dismissed the taxpayer's appeal from the decision of Vinelott J commented on in last year's Review. One may however note that Sir Denys Buckley dissented, a fact which may show that to some at least the case is not as straightforward as it appears to be. Meanwhile there is the curious fact that while CGTA 1979, s 155(2) brings TA 1970, s 42 into the capital gains tax area, that income tax provision is expressly made not to impose any greater liability than would arise if it had not been passed.

The year has also seen further application by the courts of the rule laid down by the House of Lords in *Roome v Edwards* [1981] STC 96 as to when property passing from trustees becomes the subject of a separate settlement and when it remains in the principle settlement. The cases are complex on their facts and are *Bond v Pickford* [1983] STC 517 and *Ewart v Taylor* [1983] STC 721.

Finally, there are two cases to note on the international provisions. The first is *Van-Arkadie v Plunket* [1983] STC 54. This concerned a charge arising under what is now CGTA 1979, s 15 where a gain had accrued to a non-resident company which would have been a close company if it had been resident in the UK and which causes a charge on persons resident in the UK with interests in the company. The taxpayer claimed that since he could not compel the company to distribute the gain owing to his minority share-holders status, he should be treated as falling within what is now CGTA 1979, s 13 and entitled to relief for the delayed remittance. This argument, which would have set a completely different objective behind the original legislation, was rejected by Vinelott J. The other case is *Bayley v Garrod* [1983] STC 287 which is a straight-forward application of the rule laid down by the House of Lords in *Leedale v Lewis* [1982] STC 285; the case is an example of what is a just and reasonable apportionment within FA 1965, s 41, later CGTA 1979, s 17 but now replaced by provisions in FA 1981.

10 Anti-avoidance provisions

The year has seen several decisions under this head. The first is *R v IRC ex p Preston* [1983] 2 All ER 300, [1983] STC 257, a case of major importance in the administration of TA 1970, s 460. After much negotiation and the provision of information by the taxpayer, the taxpayer and the Revenue reached agreement with regard to the taxpayer's liability for various years, an agreement which included a payment of capital gains tax in respect of the sale of certain shares. Four years later the Revenue sought to reopen the question of the taxation of those shares so as to contend that there might be a liability under s 460. Woolf J, deciding the taxpayer's application for judicial review, granted a declaration to the effect that the Revenue were not entitled to reopen the matter since they were exercising a discretion unreasonably; this was so even though the Revenue had not contemplated proceedings under s 460 when making the original agreement.

The second case is *IRC v Schroder* [1983] STC 480, a decision on TA 1970, s 478. The issue was whether the taxpayer had power to enjoy the income of a foreign trust, the Revenue's claim being based on s 478 5(e)—'the individual is able in any manner whatsoever, and whether directly or indirectly, to control the application of the income'. While there were trustees of the settlement, there was also a committee of protectors; this committee had the power to remove and appoint trustees and their consent was also required to the exercise of the discretions over the capital and income. The taxpayer had the power to appoint additional members and fill any vacancies occurring in the committee. The taxpayer caused a company to be incorporated in Bermuda, and, owing to the resignation of the other trustees, that company became the sole trustee of the settlement. The court held that although the taxpayer had power over the appointment of trustees, whether directly or through the appointment of committee members, that power was fiduciary and therefore could not properly be used to ensure that he had a majority which would follow his directions. It followed that in the absence of evidence as to the actual activities of the company which was now the trustee, it was not permissible simply to infer that the taxpayer was able to control the exercise by the company of its trustee powers. The court also held that although the commissioners had found that the trustees could be expected to act in accordance with the taxpayer's wishes, it did not follow that he had the power to control the application of income. There was a difference between being able to influence the exercise of their fiduciary powers and controlling the application of the income. To come within the latter situation, the Revenue had to show that the settlor could ensure that the trustees would act in accordance with his wishes and would, in deference to those wishes, disregared their own fiduciary duties. This the Revenue had failed to establish. Since TA 1970, s 478 is framed in terms of significant detail, the sort of detailed approach taken by Vinelott J is perhaps inevitable. Any broad approach to the interpretation of the language of s 478 is going to create a provision of almost unlimited scope. However, this practical problem of evidence which the Revenue must seek to recover from bodies outside their jurisdiction and from areas not renowned for their co-operation with the Revenue makes one wonder how long it will be before the price has to be paid.

The year also saw two cases on TA 1970, s 488. The shorter of these is *Yuill v Fletcher* [1983] STC 598. This is a tailpiece to the earlier decision of the House of Lords in *Yuill v Wilson* [1980] STC 460. In that case it has been held that where the balance of the purchase price was to be released to the vendor only in instalments as certain contingencies occurred, it was not open to the Revenue to charge the taxpayer before those contingencies had occurred. In the present case the contingencies had occurred and, as Walton J held, the Revenue therefore had the power to tax the sums which were being effectively enjoyed.

The other case shows the Revenue successfuly arguing a strict construction of the section so as to cause the taxpayer to come within it. *Page v Lowther* [1983] STC 799 is a decision of the Court of Appeal upholding the decision of Warner J earlier in the year ([1983] STC 61). The land was owned by trustees. The trustees granted a lease to a development company for 99 years. In return for the lease the trustees were to receive not only a rent but also a premium. After much negotiation it was decided that the premium should not be paid when the lease was granted but was to be a set portion of the price obtained by the development company when that company granted underleases of the houses and flats erected by the company. The payments were made directly to the trustees and not via the development company. In this way the trustees received some £1½m. The Commissioners held that the trustees and the development company were not connected persons. It followed that if the trustees were going to fall within s 488 it had to be on the basis that land had been developed with the sole or main object of realising a gain from disposing of the land when developed and a gain of a capital nature had been obtained from the disposal of the land where any arrangement or scheme had been effected as respects the land which enabled a gain to be realised. The trustees argued first that the expression 'arrangement or scheme' had to be construed in the light of s 488(1) which announced that the section was enacted to prevent the avoidance of tax and that the 'avoidance of tax' denoted schemes or arrangments of an artificial nature which were designed to avoid tax under some head of tax other than s 488; it followed that this did not apply to the lease since the trustees had not avoided any tax by simply granting the lease. They further contended that the section required that a gain of a capital nature be obtained from the disposal of the land; the argument was that the relevant disposals if any were the underleases granted by the development company while the gain accrued to the trustees derived from the original disposal when the lease was granted to the building company. These two arguments were rejected both in the Court of Appeal and at first instance. On the first point both courts held that the words of s 488(1) could not be used to limit the operation of the section if the facts otherwise fell within it. On the second point that they held that the first occasion on which the trustees became entitled to payment was when the underleases were granted and therefore the payments received by the trustees were received from the underleases so the sums constituted gains of a capital nature obtained by them. The court also rejected any attempt to limit the scope of s 488 by reference to the side note to the section 'artificial transactions in land'. In reaching this conclusion the court confirmed the general opinion of tax practitioners that this section instead of being headed 'artificial transactions in land' should be entitled 'artificial taxation of entirely natural transactions in land'.

11 Capital transfer tax

The cases on capital transfer tax represents a very mixed bag—and a largely historical one at that. In *Finch v IRC* [1983] STC 157, Vinelott J held that business property relief was not available on the death of a life tenant under a strict settlement who had carried on a farming business on the settled land. In reaching this conclusion his Lordship held that the words 'assets used in the business' meant 'assets of the business which are used in the business'. One cannot help contrasting this with the extremely literal approach of the Court of Appeal in *Page v Lowther*. The matter is of historical interest only in view of the amendment of FA 1976, Sch 10, para 3(1) by FA 1981; for transfers of value after 9 March 1981 the relief would now be available.

A similar change in legislation makes the decision in *Egerton v IRC* [1983] STC 531 also of less interest than it might otherwise be. FA 1975, Sch 5, para 18 contained rules dealing with protective trusts, the effect of which was that when the interest of the principle beneficiary ended and the discretionary trust for the remainder of his lifetime arose, there would be a charge to tax. This was amended by FA 1978 which came into force on 31 July 1978. However the amendment also had the purpose of counteracting certain tax avoidance schemes. For the latter reason the amendments were deemed to have come into force on 11 April 1978. The case of *Egerton* concerned an appointment made on 19 July 1978. The court, upholding the decision of Nourse J at first instance, held that the section was retrospective for all purposes.

The third case is yet again of historic interest only. This the decison of the Court of Appeal in *IRC v Trustees of Sir John Aird's Settlement* [1983] 3 All ER 481, [1983] STC 700 where the so-called 'Franco' scheme was held to fail. FA 1975, Sch 5, para 6(7) as originally enacted provided an exemption in the case of a person who, on surviving another person for a specified period, becomes entitled to an interest in possession as from the other person's death. However the Court of Appeal held that in order to come within this provision beneficiaries had to show that it was the surviving of the other person by the specified period which caused the vesting of their interests. Since the person who was designated was described in the deeds of appointment as 'the person whose death shall occur on Saturday the 29th of November 1975 and who shall be the first (in alphabetical order) of the persons dying on that date to be named in the "deaths" column on the back page of the earliest edition of the newspaper called 'The Times' published in London on Monday 1st of December 1975 . . .', it followed that it was not just their surviving the person there reported as having died but also the publication of the newspaper on that date which caused the interest to vest. The case is an example of the risk of making assurance doubly sure.

The final case is, fortunately, not of merely historic interest. This is *Inglewood v IRC* [1983] STC 133 and concerns the scope of accumulation and maintenance settlements which enjoy favoured treatment under FA 1975, Sch 5, para 15 and, now, FA 1982, s 114. In each of these provisions the first condition is that one or more persons 'will, on or before attaining a specified age not exceeding 25, become entitled to, or to an interest in possession in, the settled property . . .' The court held that where the trust contained a power of revocation and reappointment under which the interests of the beneficiaries could be destroyed and the property be reappointed to another person at the absolute discretion of the trustees, the word 'will' in this rule was not satisfied. That word requires a degree of inevitability which was not available in this case.

12 International

Various international cases have been dealt with under their appropriate headings above. However, one case remains to be commented on. This is the decision of the House of Lords in *Clarke v Oceanic Contractors Inc* [1983] STC 35. This case is of the very greatest importance and rests on a bare majority decision by the House of Lords. It concerned a non-resident overseas company engaged in pipe-laying operations in the North Sea which employed some 400 workers on its barges and other vessels which were based in Antwerp. Some of its operations were carried on in the UK sector of the North Sea and were 'designated areas' under the Continental Shelf Act 1964. The case concerned an attempt by the Inland Revenue to require the company to withhold tax under the PAYE system. At first instance the judge had held that the Revenue were entitled to require this whenever duties of an office of employment were carried out within the UK and that the effect of FA 1973, s 38(6) was to deem emoluments in respect of duties performed in designated areas of the North Sea to come within the UK. This was rejected by the Court of Appeal which said that Parliament could not have intended a foreign entity, not resident in the UK, to be required to deduct tax under the PAYE system and that mere presence, which would enable process to be served in the UK, was not enough to as to give rise to PAYE liability. The House of Lords accepted an argument which appears not to have been put in the lower courts. This argument was that a PAYE liability on an employer arises whenever it can be made effective. To this purpose a trading prescence of the of the corporation in the UK is sufficient. The result is the creation of a brand new category of connecting factor for tax purposes. The category is of uncertain scope. Once again one has the feeling that appropriate legislation passed as soon as the problem arose would have been a much better way of dealing with the problem and that there is much to be said for the dissenting speeches. Meanwhile onc is left wondering what the function of the House is. If it really is to act as a final court of appeal giving considered judgment on points which have been thoroughly rehearsed, it ought not to act as a court of first instance. Thus, this year tax cases leave a mixture of pleasure and unease.

Tort

B A HEPPLE, MA, LLB
Barrister, Professor of English Law in the University of London at University College

Introduction

The reports in 1983 contain several examples of the inadequacies of the law of tort as a system of compensation for personal injuries, in particular in respect of occupiers' liability, wrongful birth, and medical negligence. It was also a year in which opportunities were lost to develop the principles of liability for economic loss: see the discussion of *Tate and Lyle Industries Ltd v Greater London Council* [1983] 1 All ER 1159 under Public Nuisance p 339 below, and cp the decision of Walton J in *Balsamo v Medici* (1983) Times 31 October (to be reported in 1984 All ER), where the judge apparently declined to apply the decision in *Junior Books Ltd v Veitchi* [1982] 3 All ER 201, discussed in All ER Rev 1982, pp 301–305, to an action in tort against a sub-agent. However, some clarification was offered in respect of the concept of 'reliance' on information or advice causing economic loss.

Perhaps the most significant decisions were those relating to the negligent exercise of statutory powers by local authorities in respect of defective premises, and the limitation period for causes of action arising from latent damage to property. There is also an interesting case on the duty to control the conduct of others.

Negligence

Reliance on information or advice

The concept of 'reliance' is increasingly important as a source of liability in tort, yet little attention has been paid to its meaning. The confused senses in which the concept can be used were illustrated by the paradox in Woolf J's reasoning in *JEB Fasteners Ltd v Marks, Bloom & Co (a firm)* [1981] 3 All ER 289. He held that the plaintiffs had relied on audited accounts, negligently prepared by the defendant accountants, in deciding whether to take over a manufacturing company, yet he dismissed their claim for damages on the ground that the accounts had not, to any material degree, affected their judgment in deciding to take over the company. On appeal, it was argued that the judge could not, as a matter of law and logic, find that the plaintiffs relied on the accounts and yet dismiss their claim on the ground that the defendant's negligence was not a cause of their loss. The Court of Appeal upheld the judgment for the plaintiffs on the ground that there was ample evidence to support a finding that there was no 'true reliance': [1983] 1 All ER 583 at 589 h.

But they were critical of the judge for falling into 'a metaphysical trap of his own' when he separated the issues of reliance and causation (at 585 j–586 a). Donaldson LJ (at 588 c) pointed out that there is a narrow and precise sense in which 'reliance' means 'induced' or 'wholly dependent on', and a wider meaning of 'being encouraged or supported in' taking a decision by subsidiary matters which if untrue would not affect the taking of a decision. The judge had used the concept in the latter sense, and then gone on to find that, although encouraged by the accounts, the plaintiffs would not have acted differently if they had known the true position. This kind of ambiguity may be avoided in future if judges heed Stephenson LJ's clear statement of principle (at 589 b):

> '. . . As long as a misrepresentation plays a real and substantial part, though not by itself a decisive part, in inducing a plaintiff to act, it is a cause of his loss and he relies on it, no matter how strong or how many are the other matters which play their part in inducing him to act'.

For further comment see Digby C Jess (1983) 80 LS Gaz 1906.

Negligent exercise of statutory powers

The practical and theoretical implications of the seminal decision of the House of Lords in *Anns v Merton London Borough* [1977] 2 All ER 492, continue to dominate this branch of the law. In *Fellowes v Rother District Council* [1983] 1 All ER 513, the plaintiff claimed that part of his coastal property had been washed away by the sea as a result of the negligence of the coastal protection authority in lowering the height of a groyne on a beach adjoining his property. The question whether the authority could be held responsible for the damage if the alleged facts were proved was tried as a preliminary issue of law by Robert Goff J. This led him to an impeccable formulation of the principles which emerge from *Anns* and other authorities (at 522 b–d) and also to a re-examination of the troublesome earlier decision of the House of Lords in *East Suffolk Rivers Catchment Board v Kent* [1940] 4 All ER 527. In that case the landowner's claim for damages for the prolonged flooding of his land due to the inadequate manpower and resources allocated by the catchment board failed. Lord Wilberforce (in *Anns* [1977] 2 All ER at 501) interpreted this as being a good example of a case where 'operational activity, at the breach in the wall, was still well within a discretionary area, so that the plaintiff's task in contending for a duty of care was a difficult one.' Robert Goff J ([1983] 1 All ER at 522 c) emphasised that the test is not whether the defendant caused the plaintiff fresh or additional damage, but rather whether or not the method chosen to close the breach in the river wall was within the limits of a discretion bona fide exercised. He read Lord Wilberforce to imply that once the public authority have intervened then they may be liable for prolonged or renewed damage consequent upon simply bad workmanship or a workman negligently carrying out instructions, since such a choice of method would not be within the bona fide exercise of the discretionary power (at 522 f). (At the subsequent trial of the action, Michael Davies J dismissed the action and ordered judgment for the defendants.)

Defective premises

The most important practical applications of the *Anns* principles have been in connection with the duty of care of local authorities in the exercise of their statutory powers relating to building construction. Two important decisions have dealt with the nature and extent of the duty owed to building owners. There is an interesting contrast between these decisions by differently constituted benches of the Court of Appeal.

In *Acrecrest Ltd v W S Hattrell & Partners (a firm)* [1983] 1 All ER 17, the developer's architects (who were independent contractors) negligently and in breach of contract designed foundations to be built to a depth of 3 ft 6 in, instead of the required 5 ft. They admitted liability to the developers (the building owners) but claimed an indemnity from the local authority. The authority's building inspector had given instructions, which were not in accordance with the Building Regulations, that on part of the site the foundations be dug to 5 ft but that elsewhere they need only be to the inadequate depth of between 3 ft 6 in and 4 ft. The building was completed in accordance with these instructions as a result of which cracks appeared in the building. In order to recover a contribution the architects had to establish that the local authority, if sued, would have been liable in tort to the developers in respect of the same damage for which the architects were liable, that is the cost of repairs and the sum the building owners had to pay the tenants. The judge held that the architects were entitled to a 25% contribution from the local authority, the architects being 75% responsible for the owner's damage. The Court of Appeal (Stephenson, Donaldson LJJ and Sir David Cairns) dismissed an appeal, holding that the local authority owed a duty of care to an owner who employed builders to construct a building, provided the owner's negligence was not the source of his own loss.

The most significant feature of the judgments is the unanimous view that the local authority owes a duty to take reasonable care in the inspection and approval of building works to a building owner who has contracted the building work to an independent contractor and has not himself been negligent. In the *Anns* case the plaintiffs were occupiers of flats under long leases from the owners who had built them. Lord Wilberforce stated that the local authority's duty is owed to 'owners or occupiers' 'not of course the negligent building owner, the source of his own loss' ([1977] 2 All ER at 504). Implicit in this formulation was that the duty could be owed to the original owners or occupiers as well as to their successors. At the same time the *Anns* case makes it clear that the owner who builds on his own land cannot look to the local authority to insure him against his own negligence. The Court of Appeal in the *Acrecrest* case has decided that Lord Wilberforce meant to include building owners as a class among those to whom the local authority's duty of care is owed, but to exclude the building owner who is negligent on the ground that he is the cause of his own loss. So by the expedient of employing independent contractors to do the work he can in effect place responsibility on the local authority to ensure that the work is done in accordance with the building regulations.

How 'negligent' does the building owner have to be in order to be regarded as the 'source of his own loss'? In the *Acrecrest* case it was assumed, without deciding, that the building owners who were not themselves builders were under a statutory duty to comply with the regulations. But it was held that this did not exclude them from the category of persons to whom the duty of care is owed (at 21 j–22 a, 30 j–31 a, 33 b–c). The owner can safely leave it to others to see that the regulations are complied with. 'The fact that he has opportunities of inspection and control denied to his tenants and assignees does not ... make him "volens" or his cause of action "turpis"', said Stephenson LJ (at 25 g); and Donaldson LJ regarded the building owner as analogous to the employee who committed an offence under the Factories Acts but could still recover from his negligent employer (at 31 a). Only those who deliberately set out to deceive the building inspector, or who deliberately exercise their own judgment disregarding the inspector's requirements (at 30 f–g), or who are actually conscious that the work is being done illegally (at 33 c) would be denied recovery either because of the inability to prove a causal connection between the owner's loss and the inspector's negligence, or because of the action of the principle volenti non fit injuria, or because of the application of the principle ex turpi causa non oritur actio, or for all three of those reasons.

This sympathetic approach to the building owner in breach of statutory duties may be compared with the rejection of the claim against a local authority by a building owner who had acted contrary to the statutory requirements, in the later decision, by a differently constituted court (Lawton, Fox and Slade LJJ) in *Governors of the Peabody Donation Fund v Sir Lindsay Parkinson & Co Ltd* [1983] 3 All ER 417. An inner London borough had approved the design of a drainage system for a building development. One of its inspectors, whom it had appointed to inspect the construction of that system, had failed to notice that the developer's architect (acting as an independent contractor), without official approval, had altered the design and instructed the developer's contractor to build a system which, before the completion of the development, was found to be unsatisfactory. As a result the drainage system had to be reconstructed and the development was delayed for about three years, causing substantial loss (estimated at £1m) to the developers. The developers (the building owners) claimed damages against the contractors, the architects and the London borough. The judge found that the cause of the failure of the drains was the architect's unsuitable design (and not the contractor's workmanship), but he made no finding of negligence against the architects because, before judgment, the developer's claim against them was settled. But he held that the local authority inspector's inaction, in allowing the contractors to go on constructing a drainage system in a way which was doomed to failure, after becoming aware that they were installing a system which did not conform to the approved plans, amounted to a breach of the duty of care he owed to the building owner. He assessed the authority's proportion of liability at 15%. The Court of Appeal allowed an appeal by the local authority, holding that the local authority had discharged its duty by requiring the building owners to deposit plans which provided for a satisfactory drainage system and by properly considering those plans. Although the local authority had power to require the defective drainage system to be remedied, it owed no duty of care to the building owners to exercise that power of enforcement and to prevent the owners from acting unlawfully to their own detriment.

A feature of the *Peabody* case is that the issue was decided on the basis of 'no duty' rather than 'no causal link'. The relevant legislation empowers local authorities to control drainage works with the object of safeguarding the health of occupiers of the premises. All three members of the court recognised that this could give rise to a duty of care to an occupier of a house by a local authority inspector who, through inaction, has failed to require the builder to comply with approved building plans (at 422 fg, 423 j and 426 ef). However, a duty to comply with the statutory requirements, once the plans had been approved, rested on the developers. The developers could not claim that the local authority owed them a duty 'to do that which they ought to have done anyway' (at 422 f, 424 ab, 426 hj). Applying the two-stage approach of Lord Wilberforce in the *Anns* case ([1977] 2 All ER at 498), Fox and Slade LJJ said that although there was a sufficient relationship of proximity between the developers and the local authority, there were considerations of policy to negative that duty. It would be placing 'an unreasonable burden on a local authority' which has approved a proper drainage system, to impose a duty on it to prevent the owner from acting unlawfully and contrary to that approval, merely because notice of the owner's actions had come to the notice of an official of the authority (at 424 g, 426 h).

The *Acrecrest* case was distinguished (at 424 j, 427 bc), primarily on the ground that in that case the foundations were laid in accordance with the specific directions of the inspector, while in the *Peabody* case the developers were acting in disobedience of the specific and proper requirements of the local authority. A conclusion to be drawn is that a breach of statutory duty to comply with the building regulations will exclude a building owner from the ambit of the local authority's duty of care where that breach is contrary to the valid requirements or directions imposed by the authority in the exercise of its statutory powers. On the other hand, if the building owner acts unlawfully, but in accordance with the invalid directions of the local authority, then, the duty of care to him is not negatived. Put more baldly, the inspector owes no duty to the owner to prevent him from breaking the law, but if he gives negligent advice and the owner breaks the law when he accepts and acts on that advice a duty to the owner may arise.

Ultimately, as Lord Wilberforce emphasised in the *Anns* case ([1977] 2 All ER at 504), the nature of the duty to enforce compliance with the byelaws must be related closely to the purpose for which the relevant powers of inspection were granted. The power to inspect the construction of drainage systems was plainly conferred for the protection of the health of occupiers, and not to protect the owner against damage he might suffer through his own failure to observe the requirements of the authority. That is why inaction by the local authority gave rise to no duty towards the defaulting building owners, but could have resulted in liability to occupiers whose health was endangered.

The decision of the House of Lords in *Pirelli General Cable Works Ltd v Oscar Faber & Partners (a firm)* [1983] 1 All ER 65, that the cause of action in tort for negligence in the design or workmanship of a building accrues at the date when physical damage occurs to the building, eg by the formation of cracks due to a defect, seriously limits the utility of the *Anns* principle for subsequent purchasers of defective premises. The House overruled the decision in *Sparham-Souter v Town and Country Developments (Essex) Ltd* [1976] 2 All ER 65, in which the Court of Appeal had taken the view that a cause of action arises only when the plaintiff discovers the bad work, or ought, with reasonable diligence to have discovered it. The discoverability test recognised the injustice of depriving a subsequent owner or occupier of his remedy against a negligent defendant by the arbitrary imposition of a limitation period which started to run before the damage caused by the defendant could even be detected (see [1976] 2 All ER 65 at 80). If the matter were governed by the common law, that result would have been reached by the House of Lords as well, but they decided instead to apply the principle in *Cartledge v E Jopling & Sons Ltd* [1963] 1 All ER 341, that it is a necessary implication of the Limitation Acts that the cause of action accrues as soon as the damage occurs. The principle, described as 'unreasonable' and 'harsh and absurd' in *Cartledge v Jopling*, where it was applied to personal injury claims (and subsequently altered by statute), has now been applied to property damage. This, said Lord Scarman (at 72) 'is no matter of pride'. Fortunately, the Lord Chancellor has referred the problem of latent damage and date of accrual of cause of action to his Law Reform Committee.

It has been argued by Gerald Robertson in (1983) 99 LQR 559, that the *Pirelli* decision does not deprive a subsequent purchaser of his cause of action where one has already accrued to his predecessor in title. The orthodox view (expressed by Lord Wilberforce in *Anns*) is that a cause of action in relation to defective premises vests only in those having a proprietary interest in the premises at the time the damage occurs. Robertson argues that separate duties of care are owed to the original owner and to his successors in title in respect of the same damage; he suggests the avoidance of double recovery by allowing damages to be recovered only by the person who has actually suffered the loss. The argument is unconvincing. The gist of the tort of negligence, as an action on the case, is damage; without damage there can be no cause of action. This makes it illogical to argue that there is a duty owed to a person who suffers no loss. Lord Fraser's dictum in *Pirelli* that the duty is owed to 'owners of the property as a class, and that if time runs against one owner, it also runs against all his successors in title' (at 71 j) so far from indicating that more than one cause of action can accrue when the property suffers damage, points clearly in the opposite direction.

In *Dove v Banhams Patent Locks Ltd* [1983] 2 All ER 833, Hodgson J applied the *Pirelli* principle to a case in which, it was found, a security gate had been negligently fitted by burglary prevention specialists in 1967. The plaintiff purchased the property in 1976 and in 1979 the property was burgled when the burglar was able to force the gate. It was held that the damage occurred when the gate gave way at that time, and not when the work was completed. Hodgson J (at 840) expressed bewilderment at Lord Fraser's remark that the cause of action may not accrue when the physical damage occurs 'perhaps where the advice of an architect or consulting engineer leads to the erection of a building which is so defective as to be doomed from the start' ([1983] 1 All ER at 72). Whatever Lord Fraser had in mind (and it could not have anything to do with the distinction between latent and patent damage) the defective gate in this case was not 'doomed from the start' but only resulted in damage when forced by a professional burglar.

Duty to control the conduct of others

Does a landowner owe a duty of care to an adjoining occupier to secure his land against the entry of trespassers who may damage his neighbour's property? This question was unanimously answered in the negative by the

Court of Appeal in *P Perl (Exporters) Ltd v Camden London Borough Council*
[1983] 3 All ER 161. The council owned adjoining premises, one being
divided into flats and the other being let to the plaintiff company as a clothing
shop with a basement for storage. Thieves broke into the basement and stole
700 garments by entering an unoccupied basement flat in the council's
adjoining premises and knocking a hole in the common wall. The judge
found that the council had not secured the flats, by omitting to maintain an
effective lock on the front door and internal security barriers, despite complaints that vagrants and intruders had been seen near the entrance and other
flats had been burgled. The judge held that it was reasonably foreseeable that
the failure to provide a secure structure would cause damage to the plaintiff's
property and he awarded damages. The Court of Appeal upheld an appeal.

Two important issues of principle were involved: (1) in what circumstances can a person be liable for the acts of third parties? and (2) can an
occupier of premises ever be liable to a neighbour for an omission to act? The
second question was left unanswered, although Waller LJ (at 166 g) thought it
'doubtful', and Oliver LJ (at 167 b–d) pointed out that the omissions to
provide security measures, 'by themselves caused injury to no one'. They
merely failed to impede the entry of trespassers over whom the owners had
no control. The first question was argued in terms that (a) there is no general
common law duty to control the acts of third parties in the absence of a special
relationship with the third party, and (b) in the absence of such a relationship
any damage arising from the act of the third party is too remote: Oliver LJ (at
167 e) regarded these as 'simply two facets of the same problem', and
implicitly Waller LJ followed the same approach. They answered the problem by adopting a restrictive definition of the proximity test. The 'reasonable
foresight' required to impose liability for the acts of independent third
persons 'requires a very high degree of foreseeability' (per Waller LJ at 166 f),
and the act of the third person must be something 'which was either likely or
very likely to happen' (per Oliver LJ at 168 a). This approach was based on
Lord Reid's well-known dictum in *Home Office v Dorset Yacht Co Ltd* [1970] 2
All ER 294 at 300, with the gloss that Oliver LJ had himself put on that
dictum in *Lamb v Camden London BC* [1981] 2 All ER 408. Robert Goff LJ, on
the other hand (at 171–172) preferred to adopt Lord Wilberforce's two-stage
approach to the duty of care in the *Anns* case ([1977] 2 All ER at 498). While
'there may well be cases in which it can be said that the occupier of property
can reasonably foresee that if he leaves property unprotected, thieves may
enter and thereby gain access to neighbouring property' there are considerations of policy which ought to negative a duty of care. In particular it would
be 'startling' (at 172 f) if occupiers of terraced houses had a duty to neighbours to keep their premises securely locked. Oliver LJ, although adopting a
more conceptualistic approach, was similarly concerned with the 'startling
and far-reaching consequences' (at 171 a) of imposing a duty in these circumstances: the neighbour would be able to determine the extent of the duty by
the use to which he chose to put the premises, the more valuable his property
the greater being the security precautions which the adjoining occupier
would have to take. Lurking behind these considerations, is, of course, the
unstated assumption that householders can generally be expected to insure
against the risk of theft to their own premises.

The distinction between active misconduct and passive inaction in relation to the acts of third parties appears to remain of crucial importance in deciding on the existence of a duty of care. So their Lordships were willing to endorse the decision in *Hosie v Arbroath Football Club Ltd* 1978 SLT 122, where the football club were held liable to an injured spectator after the club had failed to provide gates which were sufficiently strong to withstand pressure by other invitees who were known to be deliberately unruly. They had greater difficulty with *Evans v Glasgow DC* 1978 SLT 17 where the defenders had damaged the locks of the pursuer's premises and replaced them with inadequate locks, while demolishing the adjoining premises, and were held liable for thereby facilitating theft and other damage to the pursuer's premises. The distinction between this and the present case, said Oliver LJ (at 170 c), was that the defenders had actually altered the state of their adjoining premises in a way which rendered the pursuer's premises more vulnerable than they would normally have been; they had done damage to the pursuer's premises which had not been properly repaired. So too, said Robert Goff LJ (at 172 b), the defendant will be liable if he presents the wrongdoer with the means to commit the wrong, eg where he hands over a car to be driven by a person who is drunk or plainly incompetent who then runs over the plaintiff (cp *Ontario Hospital Services Commission v Borsoski* (1974) 54 DLR (3d) 339).

Occupiers' liability

In *Salmon v Seafarer Restaurants Ltd* [1983] 3 All ER 729, Woolf J held that an occupier of premises owes the same duty of care to a fireman attending his premises to extinguish a fire as he does to other visitors under s 2 of the Occupiers' Liability Act 1957. An employee of the occupiers of a fish and chips shop negligently forgot to extinguish a gas flame under a chip fryer when leaving the premises for the night. There was a fire which melted the seals of the gas meter allowing gas to escape. There was an explosion in which a fireman, called to the premises, sustained injuries. It was argued for the occupier that the risk of injury by explosion was an ordinary incident of the job of a fireman. Woolf J considered earlier decisions in which firemen were injured, and reached the conclusion that the special skills of firemen should not change the normal approach to the establishing of liability. 'It is only a factor to take into account . . . in deciding whether the negligent act could foreseeably cause injury to a fireman, it is necessary to take into account the skills that are ordinarily expected to be shown by firemen' (at 735 j–736 a). Accordingly, since the sequence of events that occurred was not unusual, there was liability to the fireman. Surprisingly, there was no express reference to s 2(3)(b) of the 1957 Act, but the result is clearly in accord with that provision in view of the finding that this was not a special risk incident to the fireman's calling against which he should have guarded himself.

The decision of the House of Lords in *Titchener v British Railways Board* [1983] 3 All ER 770, is based on the wording of the Occupiers' Liability (Scotland) Act 1960. The 15-year-old plaintiff was severely injured, and her 16-year-old male companion killed, at 11.00 at night when taking a short-cut across a railway line running through a built-up area of Glasgow. Unfortunately, she suffered from post-traumatic amnesia and had no recollection of the accident or the events immediately before it. It was found as a fact that they had climbed up a slope to an embankment on which the railway ran and had passed through a gap in the boundary fence, the condition of which, said Lord Hailsham (at 772 g) 'left much to be desired'. Trains crossed by at intervals of about 20 minutes. The British Railways Board were aware that people passed through the gaps to walk across the line and at least one child had been killed at the same spot. The plaintiff, who had crossed the line on previous occasions, admitted that she was well aware of the danger of walking across the line, and said that when doing so she normally kept a look-out for trains. She said in cross-examination '. . . it was just a chance I took' and the Lord Ordinary evidently accepted that she understood what she was saying despite her amnesia. The 'crucial fact' said Lord Hailsham (at 772 d) was that no averment was made (there being no eyewitnesses) that the train was being driven otherwise than in a perfectly proper manner. The Lord Ordinary, the Inner House of the Court of Session and the House of Lords all decided that her claim for damages must fail.

The first reason put forward by Lord Fraser of Tullybelton (at 774–775), with whom all their Lordships agreed, was that the Board owed her no duty or had discharged their duty, under s 2(1) of the Act to take 'such care as in all the circumstances of the case is reasonable to see that the person will not suffer injury or damage' by reason of any danger due to the state of the premises or any activity upon them. This was based on the finding that the fences along the line, notwithstanding that they had gaps, gave her warning that she would be on railway premises, and she was aware of the dangers. Assuming that in English law she could be classed as a licensee, this approach is reminiscent of the decision in *London Graving Dock Co Ltd v Horton* [1951] AC 737, criticised by the Law Reform Committee in their Third Report (Cmd 9305, para 78), that an occupier discharged his duty to a visitor by a warning sufficient to convey full knowledge of the nature and extent of the danger. Section 2(4)(a) of the English Act of 1957 abrogated the rule in *Horton's* case and confirms that knowledge of the danger by the visitor does not necessarily prevent his recovery of damages (see eg *Bunker v Charles Brand & Son Ltd* [1969] 2 All ER 59, where full knowledge and appreciation of the dangers was held to be insufficient as the plaintiff had not been specifically warned of the dangers by the occupiers). One is led to conclude that a different conclusion might have been reached on this point had the matter fallen to be decided under English law.

The second reason for the decision was that the failure to fence was not the cause of the accident. This rested on a finding by the Lord Ordinary, who disbelieved the plaintiff's evidence that because she was wearing platform shoes she could not have climbed over a wire fence had there been one, that nothing but an impenetrable barrier would have stopped her and her companion.

The third reason was that it was held that the Board had established a defence of voluntary assumption of risk under s 2(3) of the Act (which corresponds to s 2(5) of the English Act). There was 'no room for an argument that [this defence] is out of date or discredited' (at 776 c), and the case of *Slater v Clay Cross Co Ltd* [1956] 2 All ER 625, was distinguished on the ground that the danger in this case was from a train operated in the 'ordinary and accustomed way.' 'Had there been evidence to show that the train which injured [the plaintiff] was driven negligently, like the train in

Slater's case, the risk which materialised would not have been within the risks that [the plaintiff] had accepted' (at 776 f).

If there had been a breach of a duty to fence, then the plaintiff in 'taking a chance' was hardly exempting the Board from any obligation to her. There may be many circumstances where it is reasonable to run a risk, despite the knowledge of danger. The Board would almost certainly have been liable to younger children straying there, or to passengers in trains had vandals or animals come on to the line and caused obstructions (at 772 h). It seems remarkable that a 15-year-old taking a short-cut to a housing estate or brickworks (assuming that a wire fence would have effectively deterred her) should go entirely uncompensated for her permanent injuries. Had the proposal of the Pearson Commission (Cmnd 7054) vol 1, para 1186, been implemented she might have recovered on the basis of strict liability, subject to the defence of voluntary assumption of risk, and to not being a trespasser.

Wrongful birth

In *Udale v Bloomsbury Area Health Authority* [1983] 2 All ER 522, Jupp J disallowed a claim for damages for the cost of raising an 'unwanted' child. The plaintiff had become pregnant and given birth to a normal healthy child after a sterilisation operation which was unsuccessful due to the admitted negligence of a surgeon for whom the defendant health authority was re-sponsible. It was not disputed that she was entitled to damages for the pain and discomfort including anxiety and distress caused by the unsuccessful operation and the loss of earnings during pregnancy, birth and early rearing of the child. (In *Sciurragia v Powell* (1979) 123 SJ 406, damages were also assessed for impairment of the mother's marriage prospects.) But Jupp J held that she was not entitled to damages for the cost of extending the family home for the baby (there were four other children), nor for the cost of rearing the child until the age of 16. A number of reasons of public policy were put forward (at 531), the most important being that it is impossible to value the child's life so as to set this off against the inconvenience and financial disadvantages. The result is one which accords with the general consensus in American courts where this issue had previously been considered. It is true, as Diana Brahams observes in (1983) 133 NLJ 643 at p 645 that an unplanned pregnancy may be a catastrophe and not a blessing for some mothers (eg the victim of a rape), particularly if the baby is handicapped. But the valuation of life has never been successfully achieved in the common law, and it is better to treat the upbringing of children as one of community responsibility, whatever the cause of their birth.

For further comment see C Lewis in (1983) 80 LS Gaz 1045; and G Robertson in (1983) 23 Med Sci & Law 2; (for the position when the child claims, see All ER Rev 1982, p 301).

No immunity for police officers

The Court of Appeal has corrected the statement by Milmo J in *Marshall v Osmond* [1982] 2 All ER 610 at 614 c (criticised in All ER Rev 1982, p 306) which suggested that a police officer driving a motor vehicle does not owe the same duty of care to a suspect whom he is pursuing as to an innocent user of the highway. In the words of Sir John Donaldson MR (at 227 c) 'the duty owed by a police driver to the suspect is . . . the same duty as that owed to anyone else, namely to exercise such care and skill as is reasonable in all the circumstances'. The decision of Milmo J was, however, affirmed on the facts.

Proof of medical negligence

The Pearson Commission (Cmnd 7054) vol 1, para 1326, found that the proportion of successful claims for medical negligence is much lower than for all tort cases. The reasons include the difficulties in obtaining information about the causes of misfortunes, and the reluctance of the medical profession to give evidence against colleagues accused of professional negligence. Even if an expert is found to testify for the plaintiff, the courts have traditionally been unwilling to choose between conflicting expert testimonies, or have been swayed by the confident belief of the defendant doctor in his own carefulness despite the criticism of his colleagues. An example of the latter kind is *Ashcroft v Mersey Regional Health Authority* [1983] 2 All ER 245. Kilner Brown J (at 247 d) was anxious to stress that the suggestion that a greater burden rests on a plaintiff alleging negligence against a doctor

> 'is plainly open to question . . . If there is an added burden, such a burden does not rest on the person alleging negligence; on the contrary, it could be said that the more skilled a person is the more care that is expected of him.'

However, despite the 'formidable' and 'impressive' (at 248 c) evidence of negligence given by the plaintiff's expert, he decided the 'agonising question' (at 248 f) by favouring the defendant doctor's testimony, while recognising 'that other judges might take a different view' (at 248 f). He was led to make a strong plea for a no-fault compensation scheme: 'if there ever was a case in which some reasonable compromise was called for, which would provide some amount of solace for the injured person and avoid the pillorying of a distinguished surgeon, this was such a case' (at 246 b). Disappointingly, this is a reform which the Pearson Commission rejected (para 1371).

The Pearson Commission (para 1336) also turned down proposals for reversing the burden of proof, within the framework of the tort of negligence, on the ground that the result would almost certainly be an increase in defensive medicine. In what may come to be regarded as an extremely important judicial development, Peter Pain J in *Clark v MacLennan* [1983] 1 All ER 416, has gone some way towards casting the burden of proof on the defendant doctor to show first that he was not in breach of duty and secondly, if he fails to show that he was not in breach of duty, that the damage suffered by the plaintiff did not result from the breach. Soon after the birth of her child the plaintiff began to suffer from stress incontinence. It was normal practice among gynaecologists not to perform an anterior colporrhapy operation to treat this condition until at least three months after birth so as to ensure its success and to prevent the risk of haemorrhage. In this case the operation was carried out only four weeks after birth. It was not successful and, despite further operations, the stress incontinence became a permanent disability. Peter Pain J gave judgment for the plaintiff.

The novel proposition in his reasons, which appears to go beyond *McGhee v National Coal Board* [1972] 3 All ER 1008, HL, is that

> 'where there is a situation in which a general duty of care arises and there is a failure to take a precaution, and that very damage occurs against which the precaution is designed to be a protection, then the burden lies on the defendant to show that he was not in breach of duty as well as to show that the damage did not result from his breach of duty' (at 427 g–h).

(The *McGhee* case had dealt only with causation in this way where, unlike the present case, breach of duty was admitted.) Since the departure from general practice had not been shown by the defendants to be justified, there had been a breach of the duty of care owed to the plaintiff, and the defendants had also failed to show that damage suffered had not flowed from their breach of duty. The judge did not refer to the maxim res ipsa loquitur, and it is to be noted that his reasoning goes beyond the traditional scope of that maxim (see *Salmond and Heuston on Torts* (18th edn, 1981) p 225) because the defendants provided explanations consistent with the absence of negligence. The defendants lost because they failed to show on the balance of probabilities that the departure from general practice was justified or that the injury sustained did not result from that breach of duty. This is an approach consistent with recent tendencies in the House of Lords towards inferences of negligence (eg *Henderson v Henry E Jenkins & Sons* [1969] 3 All ER 756). It is a welcome and legitimate development in cases where the judge is faced with conflicting medical expert evidence.

For further comment see Michael A Jones (1984) 134 NLJ 7; (for an example of the application of res ipsa loquitur to an industrial accident, see *Kealey v Heard* [1983] 1 All ER 973).

Consent to medical treatment

In the first half of May 1983 there were two contemporaneous, but unconnected, actions in the Queen's Bench Division in both of which a key issue was, how much must the doctor tell? In both cases, the result was that the doctors knew best, and the patient had no right to know.

Freeman v Home Office [1983] 3 All ER 589 was an unusual case because the plaintiff was allowed to rely only on an allegation of trespass to the person, his claim based on negligence having been held by the Court of Appeal to be statute-barred. A prison medical officer had administered certain drugs to the plaintiff during his imprisonment. McCowan J found on the facts that, contrary to the plaintiff's assertions, the drugs had been administered for a medical purpose without force and with the plaintiff's consent. He then went on, at counsel's invitation, to deal with an alternative submission that for the plaintiff's consent to be operative in law it had to be 'informed', namely the plaintiff must have been told (a) what he was suffering from, (b) what was the precise nature of the treatment being proposed, and (c) what, if any, were the adverse effects and risks involved in the treatment. McCowan J declined to allow this doctrine of 'informed consent' to be imported into the law of battery, and held that it was part of the law of negligence. This is in accord with the views of Bristow J in *Chatterton v Gerson* [1981] 1 All ER 257 at 265 g. All that need be shown in a case of trespass to the person is that there was 'real' consent, and this is done by explaining the general nature of the treatment. Such consent may be vitiated by fraud or misdescription.

McCowan J held, alternatively, that even if informed consent was required, the burden of proving absence of consent was on the plaintiff ('the action fails not because of volenti but because there is no tort' (at 595 a)), and on the facts the plaintiff had failed to discharge this burden. (A further submission based on the interpretation of the Prison Regulations also failed.)

In *Hills v Potter* [1983] 3 All ER 716, Hirst J also followed Bristow J in stating that assault and battery is an inappropriate form of action for a claim for personal injuries resulting from an alleged failure to provide 'informed consent' (at 728 f). This too, was a statute-barred action but one in which discretion was exercised to allow the claims for damages in negligence and trespass to the person to proceed. The importance of Hirst J's judgment is that he rejected an invitation to transplant the North American version of the 'doctrine of informed consent' into English law. It is clear law in England that the doctor must supply the patient with information to enable him to decide whether or not to undergo the treatment. The distinctive features of the doctrine as laid down in Canadian and United States cases relate to the amount of information required and, more importantly, the standard by which the surgeon's conduct is to be judged. As summarised by counsel for the plaintiff (at 721 c), the patient must be given all material details of the proposed treatment, its prospects and the risks inherent in it; and the criterion by which materiality is to be judged is not the medical standard adopted or approved by responsible practitioners skilled in this field, but what the particular surgeon knows or should know would influence his patient in deciding. Hirst J held that the medical standard applied in England; in giving advice prior to an operation a doctor or surgeon did not have to inform the patient of all details of the proposed treatment or the likely outcome and the risks inherent in it. He merely had to act in accordance with a practice accepted as proper by a responsible body of skilled medical practitioners.

In reaching this conclusion he purported to follow the House of Lords decision in *Maynard v West Midlands Regional Health Authority* (1983) Times 9 May. But that was a case in which the medical standard was applied to diagnosis and treatment. By allowing the decision of the lay patient to be judged simply by reference to a body of responsible medical opinion, Hirst J apparently hoped to avoid 'the very formidable problems and potential liabilities which would undoubtedly confront medical men' if the North American standards were applied here (at 778 b). However, this rejection of a more extensive 'right to know' leaves the English patient with the worst of all worlds: a fault-based compensation system without genuine freedom of choice based on full information of the risks which he is to run. If followed, the decision in *Hills v Potter* will be powerful evidence of the need for a no-fault compensation scheme for medical accidents, financed through the National Health Service.

Public nuisance

In *Tate and Lyle Industries Ltd v Greater London Council* [1983] 1 All ER 1159, HL, the Greater London Council (the GLC), with the approval of the Port of London Authority (the PLA), had constructed new terminals for the Woolwich ferry in the River Thames. The design chosen obstructed the water flow causing siltation which materially reduced the depth of water between the main shipping channel and the north bank where for many years Tate and Lyle had operated a refined sugar jetty, and in 1964 had constructed a raw sugar jetty. As a result of the siltation vessels could not reach the jetties to load and unload and Tate and Lyle carried out additional dredging at their own expense between 1967 and 1974. They claimed damages in respect of the costs of this dredging. The House of Lords unanimously held that claims based on breach of riparian rights or contractual rights or on negligence or private nuisance failed, but a majority of 4–1 (Lord Diplock dissenting) held that Tate and Lyle were entitled to maintain an action in public nuisance. The judge found that had an alternative design been adopted it would have resulted in only one-quarter of the accretion caused by the design selected, and accordingly the GLC had to pay three-quarters of the additional dredging costs. The PLA were held not liable since their approval of the plans did not amount to a continuation or adoption of the nuisance.

On the main issue of public nuisance the reasoning of the majority (per Lord Templeman at 1170–71) was that since the Thames is a navigable river over which the public have the right to pass and re-pass over the whole width and depth of the water and Tate and Lyle had suffered particular damage, they were entitled to sue. The issue which divided their Lordships was whether Tate and Lyle could recover the cost of additional dredging in respect of the raw sugar jetty, since the licences for the construction of this jetty were issued after the PLA had approved the construction of the terminals, and the jetty and the terminals were constructed about the same time. According to the majority (at 1175) the consequences of a public nuisance cannot be escaped merely because it was created before the plaintiff suffered damage.

A defence of statutory authorisation failed (Lord Diplock dubitante) because, although the terminals were erected under the authority of the London County Council (Improvements) Act 1962, the GLC had not paid all reasonable care and had regard to the interests of public navigation. The authorisation to 'execute... works' was held to confer immunity in respect of siltation which was inevitable and not in respect of additional siltation due to the design of the terminals. The statute in question may be compared with that which the House of Lords later had to interpret in *Department of Transport v North West Water Authority* [1983] 3 All ER 273. The Public Utilities Street Works Act 1950 provided that if a nuisance was caused by the discharge of water in a street the statutory undertakers were not exonerated from any action at the suit of the street authority. It was held that since there had been no negligence on the part of the statutory undertakers they were not liable for the damage caused as a result of performance of their statutory duty to supply water.

The claim in private nuisance failed because Tate and Lyle had no private rights in connection with the depth of the river (at 1170–71). The aspect of the decision which calls for comment is the rejection of the claim based on negligence. Was the 'engaging simplicity' (at 1164 g) of Tate and Lyle's argument, that the GLC and PLA owed them a duty of reasonable care not to cause them the reasonably foreseeable loss of incurring additional dredging costs in order to carry on their business, as misplaced as the House of Lords thought it to be? The decision in *Junior Books Ltd v Veitchi Co Ltd* [1982] 3 All ER 201, discussed in All ER Rev 1982, pp 301–305, opened the prospect of recovery of economic loss even where no proprietary or contractual interest of the plaintiff is infringed. The High Court of Australia in *Caltex Oil (Australia) Pty Ltd v Dredge Willemstad* (1976) 136 CLR 529 (a decision not referred to in the speeches in the *Tate and Lyle* case) appears to have recognised a duty of care in respect of business losses in circumstances not altogether different from those in the *Tate and Lyle* case. But Lord Templeman (at 1165 j) said that in 'the cited relevant cases from *Donoghue v Stevenson* to *Junior Books Ltd v Veitchi* the plaintiff suffered personal injury or damage to his property', and went on to reject Tate and Lyle's assertion that they had suffered damage to their property caused by interference with their right to use their jetties on the ground that they had no right to a particular depth of water either as riparian owners or by a contract constituted by their licences granted by the PLA to construct their jetties. The categorisation of *Junior Books*, as relating to physical damage, is remarkable in view of the express disclaimer by the majority in that case of any difference between pure economic loss and economic loss caused by physical damage. It was surely arguable that there was a foreseeable risk of economic loss to Tate and Lyle specifically, and not merely as a general class, and that Tate and Lyle had reasonably relied on the depth of water being maintained when they constructed their jetties. But the issue does not appear to have been argued that way, and an opportunity was lost to clarify some of the issues left open in *Junior Books*.

Private nuisance

Bradburn v Lindsay [1983] 2 All ER 408, Chancery Division at Manchester, provides an example of the application of *Leakey v National Trust for Places of Historic Interest and Beauty* [1980] 1 All ER 17, to the situation in which a house is negligently allowed to fall into disrepair and its demolition by consent by the local authority causes loss to a neighbouring landowner by way of loss of support and exposure to dry rot and decay. Neither the possibility that the neighbour might have a right to enter to abate the nuisance, nor the fact that the demolition had been carried out by the local authority freed the owner of the neglected property from liability.

Defamation

Paragraph 12 of Part II of the Schedule to the Defamation Act 1952 lists among 'statements privileged subject to explanation or contradiction'

> 'A copy or fair and accurate report or summary of any notice or other matter issued for the information of the public by or on behalf of any government department, officer of state, local authority or chief officer of police'.

In *Blackshaw v Lord* [1983] 2 All ER 311, the trial judge had approached these words 'in not a strictly literal sense but in a fairly literal way' to include information 'painfully extracted by journalists like a tooth, from an official of a government department acting in the course of his employment'. The Court of Appeal disapproved of this interpretation. In a decision likely to cause concern among investigative journalists, the statutory privilege was held to be confined to information of a formal nature issued on the initiative of a government department and with its authority. Although not limited to written 'hand-outs' or pictures, a government official's ex parte statement made without authority in reply to a journalist's questioning is outside the privilege. Likewise any assumption, inference or speculation by the journalist on the basis of such a statement does not enjoy privilege.

The same decision places a restrictive interpretation on common law privilege, holding that a plea of fair information on a matter of public interest does not constitute a defence at common law. The public at large must have a legitimate interest in receiving the information, and the publisher must have a corresponding duty to publish the report to the public at large. So that where an article in a newspaper contained a report of incompetence on the part of an unnamed civil servant at a time when that allegation had not been made good, it was held that the public at large had no legitimate interest in receiving what was then a mere rumour that the plaintiff was the civil servant in question.

The aspects of this case relating to damages for libel are considered in the section on Damages, p 169 above.

Town and Country Planning

PAUL B FAIREST, MA, LLB
Professor of Law, University of Hull

In 1983, a number of significant decisions concerning town and country planning legislation were reported. Unusually, no less than four decisions of the House of Lords on matters of planning concern were given during the year. Not surprisingly, three of these decisions were about the consequences of enforcement notices, where a rich case law has already developed.

1 Definition of development

The definition of 'development' in the legislation is of vital importance since, of course, 'development' attracts the need for planning permission and 'unpermitted development' attracts the possibility of sanction in the form of enforcement proceedings. Many cases, seemingly trivial on their facts, have been pursued to the Court of Appeal and beyond since, as McAuslan properly reminds us:

> 'there is a point of principle of great moment at stake in all of them. It is this: local planning authorities and the Department of the Environment have an interest in keeping the ambit of development, which is not development for the purposes of the Act, as narrow as possible, thus ensuring that the scope of the control of development is as wide as possible; developers on the other hand have precisely the reverse interest: the more development they can undertake which does not need permission, the freer they are from the planning system' (McAuslan *Land, Law, and Planning* (1975) pp 510–511).

Few cases can have seemed more trivial on their facts than *Backer v Secretary of State for the Environment* [1983] 2 All ER 1021 (David Widdicombe QC, sitting as a deputy judge of the High Court). Caravans have often featured in planning cases; indeed, they have attracted a statute all their own in the Caravan Sites and Control of Development Act 1960. Never yet, however, had a court found it necessary to consider the definition of a 'caravan' contained in s 29(1) of the 1960 Act, presumably because, like the elephant, it could be expected to be recognised when it was seen. The ingenious Mr Backer contrived to pose a novel problem for the court by living in an unadapted Commer van, which contained 'a bed, Valor stoves, cupboards, a filing cabinet, clothes on hangers, tins of oil etc'. If the Commer van constituted a caravan, despite the fact that no physical alteration of the vehicle had taken place, Mr Backer was appropriately the subject of enforcement proceedings. If it was not a caravan, he was presumably living lawfully but uncomfortably. The learned deputy judge, in deciding whether the vehicle was 'any structure designed or adapted for human habitation' (s 29(1) of the 1960 Act) found little help in Road Traffic Act decisions on the meaning of 'adapted', and held that a motor vehicle was not a caravan unless it was either designed for human habitation (which was clearly not the case here) or had been 'physically altered in some way for that purpose'. The decision is presumably of relevance also for the Town and Country Planning Act 1971 which adopts the definition of 'caravan site' in the 1960 Act (see s 290(1) of the 1971 Act).

2 Appeals to the Minister against refusal of development

A narrow but important point divided the House of Lords in *Griffiths v Secretary of State for the Environment* [1983] 1 All ER 439. The applicant, having sought (unsuccessfully) planning permission for the development of his land by the erection of a farmhouse, exercised his right to appeal to the Minister under section 36 of the Town and Country Planning Act 1971. The Secretary of State dismissed his appeal, and on 8 December 1980 a letter was signed and sent from the Department of the Environment informing the applicant of this. The letter was received by the applicant on 13 December 1980.

On 22 January 1981 the applicant applied to the High Court for an order quashing the Secretary of State's decision. The relevant provision of the Town and Country Planning Act 1971 states that a person aggrieved by such a decision may apply to the High Court 'within six weeks from the date on which the order is confirmed or the action taken' (s 245(1)) for such an order to quash. Was the applicant in time?

The six week period, if calculated from the date on which the letter was signed and posted, expired on 19 January 1981. If time began to run from the date of *receipt* of the letter, the period did not expire until 24 January 1981. The issue was thus the simple one of when was the Secretary of State's action taken. The majority of the House of Lords, affirming the decision of the trial judge and the Court of Appeal, although on slightly different grounds, held that the relevant date was the date on which the letter was signed on behalf of the Secretary of State and date-stamped. In so doing, the House of Lords rejected the opinion of the Court of Appeal that the relevant date was the date of posting, although in the event this would have yielded the same result, as signing, date-stamping and posting all took place on the same day. Lord Scarman, in his dissenting speech, held that the crucial 'action', from which time was to run, included both the decision itself and the giving of notice of that decision to the owner or occupier of the affected land.

Lord Bridge, speaking for the majority of the House of Lords, rejected the appellant's contention that he could hardly be a person aggrieved (and thus in a position to invoke s 245) before he knew of his grievance. The language of the statute, he said, was concerned with 'action' by the Secretary of State, and here 'action', as a matter of language, could only refer to the *making* of a decision, not to its notification to third parties. His Lordship found support for this view in ss 51 and 38 of the Town and Country Planning Act 1971. Both these sections relate to different procedures under the Act; s 51 is concerned with confirmation of orders by a local planning authority to discontinue an existing use or alter or remove a building, and s 38 is concerned with directions by the Secretary of State which have the effect of reducing or extinguishing a liability to pay compensation. In both cases time begins to run from the 'confirmation' or 'direction' by the Secretary of State, notwithstanding the statutory obligation (in ss 51(7) and 39(3) respectively) to notify various interested parties of the 'confirmation' or 'direction'. These sections showed, in Lord Bridge's view, that Parliament had discerned a clear distinction between action and the notification of such action to interested parties, and had intended time to run from the date of the action.

He also drew attention to a problem which might arise (assuming the appellant's contention that the date of receipt was crucial to be correct) where a multiplicity of parties was involved. A planning appeal might involve, for instance, A, a potential developer and applicant for planning permission, B, the present owner, and C, an agricultural tenant of the land in question. A, B, and C are all entitled to make representations and, if they do so, they are expressly entitled to notice of the eventual decision on the appeal. Does time only run when the *last* interested person receives the necessary notice? If, by administrative oversight, the decision was never communicated to C, does it follow that C could later challenge a permission which had been granted on the grounds that time had never started to run against him? As Lord Bridge explained, the difficulties would be increased if in the meantime the land had been conveyed from B to A at a price reflecting the value of the planning permission. Worse still, could B rely on the failure to notify C and thus seek to proceed in the High Court even after his own time limit had expired? The answer might be that B's time limit would be governed by the date of notification to B (and C's problems would be none of B's business) but this was not canvassed by the House of Lords, who took refuge in the simple rule (which avoids all these problems) that the date of 'action' was the date on which the date-stamping and signing of the decision letter took place.

So far, so good; but the disquieting fear raised by Lord Elwyn-Jones must be considered. What if, by reason of postal delay or administrative incompetence, the notification takes five weeks to reach the 'aggrieved'? He now has only a week—out of a period which is already short enough in all conscience—to begin proceedings in the High Court. In the instant case, the applicant had five weeks (including Christmas and New Year, when life comes to a stop). Lord Elwyn-Jones found this 'too fortuitous to be reassuring'.

3 Enforcement

A key decision relating to enforcement procedures is *Davy v Spelthorne BC* [1983] 3 All ER 278. In *O'Reilly v Mackman* [1982] 3 All ER 1124, the House of Lords 'laid it down that there exists a distinction between public and private law which goes to the heart of the civil jurisdiction of English courts' (see All ER Rev 1982, p 1). In *Davy's* case the House of Lords had to decide, in the light of their earlier decision, on which side of the line lay an action against a local planning authority for damage caused by their allegedly negligent advice. The House of Lords decided unanimously that the decision in *O'Reilly v Mackman* did not demand that the plaintiff's common law action in negligence be struck out as an abuse of the process of the court, leaving the plaintiff to proceed as best he could under RSC Ord 53.

The facts which gave rise to this question were as follows. Davy was the owner of a factory, and his activities appear to have attracted the attention of the local planning authority. Applications for planning permission by Davy having been either refused or withdrawn, negotiations with the local planning authority about his activities then commenced. Davy alleged that these

resulted in an agreement between himself and the local planning authority;
part of this agreement consisted in an undertaking by Davy not to appeal
against an enforcement notice which the local planning authority would
shortly serve on him. In return the local planning authority undertook not to
enforce the notice for a period of three years. Davy claimed that he kept his
side of the bargain by not appealing, although he claimed that he had only
entered into the agreement because of incorrect and negligent advice about
his rights under the planning legislation which he had received from the local
planning authority. In the present proceedings he claimed damages, an
injunction to restrain the local authority from seeking to implement the
enforcement notice, and an order that the enforcement notice be set aside. In
truth, he claimed, he could have appealed against the original enforcement
notice, but, by reason of the negligent advice he had received, he had
contracted not to do so, with the result that the time for appeal against the
enforcement notice (see s 88 of the Town and Country Planning Act 1971)
had long expired.

In applying for the striking out of Davy's action as an abuse of the process
of the court, Spelthorne Borough Council contended that the claim
amounted in substance to a challenge to the enforcement notice. A claim in
the form selected by Davy was, they said, barred by s 243 of the Town and
Country Planning Act 1971, which provides, as amended, that

> 'the validity of an enforcement notice shall not, except by way of an appeal
> under Part V of this Act, be questioned in any proceedings whatsoever on any
> of the grounds on which such an appeal may be brought...'

To this contention, Lord Fraser, who delivered the main speech in the
House of Lords, had two replies. First of all, what Davy was doing, he said,
was not really a challenge to the validity of the enforcement notice as such.
Had he not relinquished his right to do so, he might in the first place have
contended that the enforcement notice had been served out of time because of
the provisions of s 87(4) of the Act of 1971, but that was not his argument
now. He now contended that the notice as a notice was perfectly valid, but
that he had, in reliance on negligent advice, allowed time to run so that it
became unappealable. As a second argument, Lord Fraser stressed that in any
event the grounds on which Davy now sought to rely were not grounds
specified in s 88(2) of the Act. Essentially, his claim was now that he had
unwisely acquiesced in the notice because of negligent advice as to his rights,
and this was never an issue which he could have pursued by way of the
statutory appeal procedure laid down in s 88(2).

A rather broader contention by the council had also to be faced. They
invoked the words of Lord Diplock in *O'Reilly v Mackman* when he said (at
1134):

> 'it would in my view be contrary to public policy, and as such an abuse of the
> process of the court, to permit a person seeking to establish that a decision of a
> public authority infringed rights to which he was entitled to protection under
> public law to proceed by way of an ordinary action and by this means to evade
> the provisions of Ord 53 for the protection of such authorities.'

Spelthorne Borough Council is undoubtedly a public body; but that does
not, of itself, make any suit against it a public law claim. If Davy had been

impugning or wishing to overturn the enforcement notice itself, that would, following *Cocks v Thanet DC* [1982] 3 All ER 1135 have been a 'public law' claim, but there Davy's whole case in negligence depended on the fact that he had lost his right to impugn the enforcement notice.

The difficulties standing in the way of Davy's negligence claim are obvious, and the House of Lords, while making no decision on its merits, declined to put a further obstacle in his path by telling him he had used the wrong process. In Lord Wilberforce's words, the 'public law' element to his claim was peripheral, and the claimant would in any event have been unable to proceed by way of judicial review.

In this case, the concurring speech of Lord Wilberforce commands particular attention for its valuable discussion of the concepts of 'private law' and 'public law'. The importation of these terms from countries which have separate systems of private and public law was a process to be regarded with caution for, typically, 'English law fastens not on principles but on remedies' (at 285 j). The limitations of Lord Diplock's formulation in *O'Reilly v Mackman* were stressed; the 'abuse of process' argument would only succeed where the claim in question could have been brought by way of judicial review, and even then, there was no universal rule that the judicial review procedure was exclusive and compulsory. Prima facie, a plaintiff may chose his court and his process, and his choice can only be challenged if the defendant can show that his choice is tantamount to an abuse of the court's procedure.

A rather more narrow point was involved in *Young v Secretary of State for the Environment* [1983] 2 All ER 1105. The issue before the House of Lords was the true construction of s 23(9) of the Town and Country Planning Act 1971, which provides:

> 'where an enforcement notice has been served in respect of any development of land, planning permission is not required for the use of the land for the purpose for which it could lawfully have been used if that development had not been carried out'.

The facts of the case were disarmingly complex. A large building had been used for the following purposes:

Use A 1962–1969 Use as a laundry (lawful);
Use B 1969–1970 Use as a light industrial building for food processing (permitted development within the Use Classes Order 1972, and thus lawful);
Use C 1970–1977 Use as a laundry; unlawful, because the reverse switch from Use B to Use A or Use C was not within the Use clauses Order;
Use D 1977 Use as a store of insulating materials: unlawful, as any change from the preceding use (Use C) which was itself unlawful would require planning permission.

The local planning authority served an enforcement notice in respect of *Use D*. The appellant contended he was entitled to revert to *Use B*, the last *lawful* use. If he was right in that contention, he would be within the 'light industrial' sector of the Use Clauses Order, and could thus continue to use the building for the storage of insulating materials, as this would also be within the 'light industrial' sector. He could thus thumb his nose at the local planning authority, all of whose enforcement process would be seen to be a thing writ in water.

The Secretary of State, however, contended that the only use falling within s 23(9) would be the immediately preceding use (*Use C*) and then *only* if it was lawful, which it was not. Since *Use C* was unlawful, this meant that the building could not be used at all without a grant of planning permission, save for a few impractical suggestions, such as agricultural use, where planning permission would not in any event be required.

As an issue of construction, the House of Lords, in a single speech delivered by Lord Fraser, accepted the Secretary of State's argument. Hard though the decision seems, especially in view of the brief duration of *Use B* which broke the continuity which would otherwise have existed between *Use A* and *Use C*, those who engage in unpermitted development do not deserve sympathy to the extent of allowing them to search the planning history of the unit back to the beginning of time on the off chance of discovering a palatable previous lawful user. In accepting the Secretary of State's argument, the House of Lords approved and rehabilitated an earlier dictum to the same effect of Cairns LJ in *LTSS Print and Supply Services Ltd v Hackney BC* [1976] 1 All ER 311 at p 317. This dictum, although doubted by Glidewell J in *Balco Transport Services Ltd v Secretary of State for the Environment* (1981) 45 P & CR 216, 221, had previously enjoyed a partial revival as a result of Glidewell J's recantation of his doubts in the later unreported case of *Blenkinsopp v Secretary of State for the Environment* (28 January 1983, unreported).

A final, minor point on enforcement proceedings was established by the House of Lords in *Chiltern District Council v Hodgetts* [1983] 1 All ER 1057. It was held that an information was not bad for duplicity when it alleged that each respondent had 'on and since' 27 May 1980 permitted certain land to be used in contravention of an enforcement notice. An earlier Divisional Court decision which had held to the contrary (*Parry v Forest of Dean DC*) (1976) 34 P & CR 209 was held to be wrongly decided. Its removal, in view of the practical difficulties which it caused, can occasion little mourning, as earlier attempts to distinguish it had carried little conviction. An important practical suggestion was that offences might in future be charged as having occurred between two specified dates, the earlier being the date on which compliance with the enforcement notice first became due and the later the date of laying the information, or the date of compliance with the notice if the defendant had managed to comply with the notice before the laying of the information.

4 Stop notices

A stop notice is a drastic weapon in the hands of a local planning authority. Non-compliance with a stop notice is a criminal offence, attracting appreciable penalties; in certain circumstances, the issue of a stop notice may involve the local planning authority in a liability to pay considerable compensation (see s 177 of the Town and Country Planning Act 1971), thus proving that the weapon can backfire. For this reason stop notices are used with caution.

One of the few cases concerned with stop notices to be reported in *R v Jenner* [1983] 2 All ER 47. In this case the Court of Appeal had to decide the issue of whether it was possible for a defendant in a criminal prosecution for non-compliance with a stop notice to raise, as a defence, the invalidity of the stop notice.

The appellant carried on at his premises, to the annoyance of his neighbours, certain anti-social activities, including the parking of lorries, the storage of skips, and the tipping of rubbish, all, of course, without benefit of planning permission. The local planning authority served on him an enforcement notice under s 87 of the Town and Country Planning Act 1971; against this, the appellant, who seems to have known a thing or three about planning, lodged an appeal. The local planning authority, possibly suspecting that this was a ploy to gain time, followed up with service of a stop notice. This seems to have left the defendant unimpressed, as he ignored it. The local authority then commenced criminal proceedings, alleging non-compliance with the stop notice, but the appellant, having obtained leave from Glidewell J to enter an application for judicial review of the decision to issue the stop notice, then lost interest in the matter again and did not pursue his application. Committed for trial to the local Crown Court, he then tried to challenge the stop notice in the criminal proceedings, but found himself foiled by the recorder's ruling that it was not permissible to do so. The recorder informed him that the way to challenge the stop notice was to proceed with his application for judicial review.

Quashing the conviction which had become inevitable in light of the recorder's ruling, the Court of Appeal held that the recorder had erred. It was open to the defendant, if he wished, to raise the issue of the validity of the stop notice. In the event, he had wished to claim that he was protected by the closing words of s 90(2) of the Town and Country Planning Act 1971, in that he had been carrying on his unwelcome activities for at least a twelvemonth before the issue of the stop notice, and was thus immune from proceeding by way of stop notice.

Given the drastic nature of the penalties involved, whether in summary proceedings or on indictment, this seems right. Proceedings by way of judicial review, where evidence is usually on affidavit, and where difficult issues of fact are less easy to resolve, seem less appropriate.

5 Conservation areas

The overriding duty of a local planning authority in respect of a designated conservation area was emphasised in the decision of the Court of Appeal (Lawton, Griffiths and Dillon LJJ) in *Windsor and Maidenhead Royal BC v Brandrose Investments Ltd* [1983] 1 All ER 818.

Brandrose, owners of buildings near Windsor Castle, which were situated in a designated conservation area, had demolished the buildings without the prior consent of the local planning authority. Such action was prima facie contrary to s 277A of the Town and Country Planning Act 1971, as amended. The demolition had taken place not because of any desire to flout the law, but because the developers believed that the demolition was contemplated or authorised by the local planning authority in view of an agreement, made in 1976 between Brandrose and the local planning authority in pursuance of the powers granted to the local planning authority by s 52 of the Act, which had been made so as to enable Brandrose and the local planning authority to develop their sites in the centre of Windsor. In addition, a grant of outline planning permission by the local planning authority to Brandrose in 1976, made in partial implementation of the s 52 agreement, was thought by Brandrose to authorise their action, notwithstanding the designation of the area as a conservation area in 1978.

At first instance, Fox J (as he then was), held that by virtue of s 52 of the Act, the local planning authority could not use the powers granted to them by s 277A to forbid demolition, unless the prohibition on demolition was in accordance with the provisions of a statutorily authorised development plan. No such development plan was in existence for Windsor.

Since the buildings had actually been demolished, the proceedings had something of the air of a custard pie fight. Fox J's decision, however, was regarded with apprehension by those responsible for the administration of the planning legislation, and for that reason an appeal was launched, though little would turn on its actual result in the instant case. Lawton LJ, delivering the judgment of the court, reversed Fox J's decision. There was an overriding public duty, under s 277A, resting on the local authority responsible for the conservation area. It followed that the local authority could not, by virtue of agreements made under s 52, so fetter itself so as not to exercise its powers under s 277A. At the end of the day, though, the court refused the declaration sought, since the litigation 'should never have started'. The lawyers doubt- less gained, and the public lost buildings which 'had no historical or architec- tural interest in themselves, but, [which] whilst standing, . . . formed part of an attractive town vista towards the castle'. Perhaps Mr Backer might care to park his Commer non-caravan in the gap.

Trusts

P J CLARKE, BCL, MA
Barrister, Fellow of Jesus College, Oxford

Discretionary trusts

Since the decision of the House of Lords on *McPhail v Doulton* [1970] 2 All ER
228, both courts and academics have been concerned with the questions of
certainty of objects in various types of trusts and powers, and the duties of
trustees and holders of a power. *Turner v Turner* [1983] 2 All ER 745 does not
deal fully with these controversies, but with the simple question of whether
trustees, who had executed trust documents, had in fact exercised their
discretion at all. The trustees were not professionally qualified, and considered themselves as under the command of the settlor who, in his own
words, still regarded himself as 'captain of the ship'.

The judge found that the purported exercise by the trustees of their
discretion was a nullity. the trustees, found the judge, were possessed of a
fiduciary power, and the duties, as stated by Sir Robert Megarry V-C in *Re
Hay's Settlement Trusts* [1981] 3 All ER 786 at 792, had not been fulfilled: there
had been no consideration by the trustees, no exercise of their discretion. On
the peculiar facts, therefore, the judge declared the appointment was a
nullity. This decision seems eminently sensible, but two comments must be
made. First, the judge does not fully explain the duties of the settlement
trustees, though, since there was a breach of the duty to consider (in whatever
sense that term is used) such consideration was unnecessary. Second, the case
leaves open the position where the trustees have given vestigial consideration, ie where they have considered what the settlor has told them, perhaps
informally, and have started their deliberation with a strong prejudice in
favour of following his advice. There are hints in Mervyn Davies J's judgment that if there is 'rancour or dispute' the court may be less willing to
declare an appointment void. Obviously, the onus of proof must be on those
who allege that an appointment is bad, but is not clear how easily, in the
absence of fraud, such an onus may be discharged.

Resulting trusts: co-ownership

Last year's Review (All ER Rev 1982, pp 169–171) contained a critical
comment on the decision of the Court of Appeal in *Bernard v Josephs* [1982] 3
All ER 162, concerning the ascertainment of shares in property held by a man
and his mistress. This issue has arisen again in *Gordon v Douce* [1983] 2 All ER
229. There was no appeal from the county court judge on the share awarded
to the mistress (25%), but Fox LJ (with whom Bush J concurred) considered
the issue nonetheless. He said this:

'... What the court is concerned with in a case such as this is whether, by reason
of an implied or resulting trust the applicant is entitled to a share in property
vested in the other party. That is dependent on whether the partners have so

conducted themselves that it would be inequitable to permit the party in whom
the property is vested in law to deny that the other party has a beneficial
interest.'

It is difficult to see precisely what this means. If there is a resulting trust, it
must presumably be either an automatic or presumed resulting trust (see
Megarry J in *Re Vandervell's Trust* [1974] 1 All ER 47 at 68–69). A 'presumed
resulting trust' is what Fox LJ must be contemplating and, in such a resulting
trust, property is not stated to be held on any trusts. As part of the purchase
price of the house (which was in the husband's name alone) had come from
savings, 'a pool'—as the trial judge described them—such a trust may well
have existed. However, the basis of a resulting trust is not normally considered to be that 'it would be inequitable . . . to deny . . . a beneficial interest'.
Such reasoning is relevant, if at all, in the context of a constructive trust (cf
Binion v Evans [1972] 2 All ER 70, *Hussey v Palmer,* [1972] 3 All ER 744),
though Lord Denning MR in *Hussey v Palmer* purported to equate the two!
Once again, the court is imposing a solution, rather than providing reasons
for one.

The second point made by Fox LJ was that, in general, the principles to be
used in ascertaining shares should be the same, whatever the relationship—
husband and wife, man and mistress, brother and brother. The court,
however, might be influenced by the relationship in drawing inferences as to
the intentions of the partner. This conflates the views of the individual
members of the Court of Appeal in *Bernard v Josephs*, and provides a reasonably satisfactory resolution of the conflict between the views of Lord
Denning MR on the one hand and Griffiths and Kerr LJJ on the other.

The main issue, however, was the date at which the share was to be valued.
This issue was discussed in last year's Review (All ER Rev 1982, pp 170–1),
where the flexible approach in *Bernard v Josephs* was criticised as contrary to
the principles of resulting trusts and to the Law of Property Act 1925, s 53.
However, the question in *Gordon v Douce* was a simpler one; the mistress was
entitled to 25%, but it was unclear at what date the property was to be valued.
The trial judge had found that it was the date of separation that was material;
counsel for the mistress was arguing for a later, unspecified, date. Fox LJ,
however, emphasised that the house in *Gordon v Douce* had been purchased to
provide the mistress and her children with a home; that purpose had not
come to an end. The courts in earlier authorities (*Cooke v Head* [1972] 2 All
ER 38; *Hall v Hall* (1982) 3 FLR 379; *Bernard v Josephs*, supra) had valued the
shares at different dates; the court was entitled to use its discretion, and there
was no rule that the share had to be valued at the date of separation. As the
purpose doctrine is inherently flexible, such discretion is useful, indeed,
inevitable. The report does not indicate on what date the shares were to be
valued; counsel was to address the court on the point.

Constructive trusts

Perhaps the most important—and certainly the longest—case of the year,
involves complicated questions affecting constructive trusts. *Baden, Delvaux
and Lecuit v Société General &c* [1983] BCLC 325 (to be reported in 1984 All
England Law Reports) raises the issue of a banker's duty.

The facts are complicated, and involve the downfall of Investment Overseas Services (Bernie Cornfeld's 'empire'). The particular point in dispute was whether Société General (SG) had, by transferring moneys (some $4m) from a trust account held by it for the plaintiffs to another bank for another account holder, became a constructive trustee and thus liable to account for the plaintiffs for that sum. Peter Gibson J discussed the relevant law at [1983] BCLC 402–421. He began by citing *Snell's Principles of Equity* (28th edn) pp 194, 195, to the effect that there were two main categories of constructive trustee, where moneys subject to a trust are concerned. The first category, 'knowing receipt or dealing', was not relied on by counsel for the plaintiff ([1983] BCLC at 403c). The second category of liability was described as 'knowing assistance':

> 'A person who does not actually himself receive the trust property may also incur liability to the beneficiaries if he knowingly assists in a fraudulent design on the part of the trustee. But "strangers are not to be made constructive trustees merely because they act as the agents of trustees in transactions within their legal powers, transactions, perhaps of which a Court of Equity may disapprove, unless those agents receive and become chargeable with some part of the trust property, or unless they assist with knowledge in a dishonest and fraudulent design on the part of the trustees."'

However, the quotation in the above passage (from the judgment of Lord Selborne LC in *Barnes v Addy* (1874) 9 Ch App 251) implied, as Peter Gibson J pointed out, that it was directed to strangers who did not receive trust property. However counsel for the defendant did not seek (correctly, in the judge's view) to argue that strangers who receive trust property, and thus are at first sight within the 'knowing receipt or dealing' category, could not be liable under the 'knowing assistance' head. This followed the cases of *Selangor United Rubber Estates Ltd v Cradock (No 3)* [1968] 1 All ER 1073 and *Karak Rubber Co Ltd v Burden (No 2)* [1972] 1 All ER 1210.

Counsel for the plaintiffs stated that there were four requirements for a case to be brought within the category of 'knowing assistance': first, the existence of a trust; second, the existence of a dishonest and fraudulent design on the trustee's part, third, the assistance of the stranger in the design, and fourth, the knowledge of the stranger. The judge seemed to accept these, subject to the caveat that 'taken altogether those elements must leave the court satisfied that the alleged constructive trustee was a party or privy to dishonesty on the part of the trustee' (this presumably gives the court a discretion to consider each case on its merits). The first requirement did not necessarily involve a formal trust; it was sufficient that there should be a fiduciary relationship between the 'trustee' and the relevant property. If the trust property was held by a company as a trustee, there was no reason why, in principle, a claim in equity should not arise if the individuals who controlled the company, rather than the company itself, had the relevant fraudulent design. (No argument was raised, it appears in connection with the lifting of the corporate veil: as Peter Gibson J pointed out, 'ex hypothesi, a company can only act through individuals' [1983] BCLC at 405i).

The second requirement, that the relevant design had to be dishonest and fraudulent, was conceded by counsel to mean 'the taking of a risk to the prejudice of another's rights, which risk is known to be one which there is no right to take' (*R v Sinclair* [1968] 3 All ER 241). The third requirement, that there should be assistance, was a question of fact: the act had to be of more than minimal importance, but did not have to result in the inevitable consequence that a loss would occur.

It was on the fourth point that the main legal argument arose. It was agreed that the trustee must know the three elements mentioned above, though it was sufficient that the trustee knew of the trust, but not its details; likewise, he had to know that there was a fraudulent and dishonest design, but did not need to know all of it, and he had to know that his acts assisted the design. The relevant knowledge had to be of facts, not of claims or allegations: see *Carl-Zeiss-Stiftung v Herbert Smith & Co (a firm) (No 2)* [1968] 2 All ER 1233, which, even though the case involved the 'knowing receipt or dealing' category, was decisive on the point. The main dispute was as to what types of knowledge were relevant. It was agreed on all sides that actual knowledge was clearly sufficient, but not necessary. The judge, after exhaustive consideration of the authorities ([1983] BCLC at 407–415), considered that there was no difference between knowledge in 'knowing receipt or dealing' category, and the 'knowing assistance' category. 'Wilfully shutting one's eyes to the obvious' and 'wilfully and recklessly failing to make such inquiries as an honest and reasonable man would make' were clearly sufficient to affix knowledge on the party concerned; moreover 'knowledge of circumstances which would indicate the facts to an honest and reasonable man' was sufficient. Indeed, as the judge points out, the line between this and the previous category is difficult accurately to delineate. The final alleged type of relevant knowledge, 'knowledge of circumstances which would put an honest and reasonable man on inquiry' was, itself, difficult to distinguish from the previous category, and thus should also be considered sufficient.

Having stated this, however, the judge considered that the courts should not be astute to impute knowledge where no actual knowledge existed; in particular, the final variety of 'knowledge' should only exceptionally be imputed to an agent such as a bank acting honestly on its client's instructions but alleged to have provided knowing assistance to a dishonest and fraudulent design. A banker was not expected 'to play the detective'; there could be no duty to make inquiries which are never likely to give the inquirer knowledge of the facts ([1983] BCLC at 416d); moreover, mere suspicion would not justify a bank in refusing to comply with its instructions. Peter Gibson J summarised the position at [1983] BCLC 420c:

> '. . . a bank when put on inquiry remains under a duty not to comply with its customer's instructions either if it acquires knowledge of the intended misapplication of moneys which it holds or whilst it is pursuing its inquiries. It ceases to be under such duty when it receives information, whether in answer to its inquiries or from another source, that the honest and reasonable banker would accept without further inquiry.'

The final point in dispute related to the knowledge to be imputed to a bank which ought to have made but failed to make inquiries or having made inquiries, failed to wait for the answers. Counsel agreed that the court should ascertain on the balance of probabilities what the answers would have been, and whether those answers would have put the honest and reasonable banker on further inquiry. The judge considered whether there was an irrebuttable presumption of truthfulness against the bank: the judge answered this in the negative—in other words, it was for the plaintiffs to prove that the failure to inquire caused loss, and to presume that the bank would have told the truth would make their task much easier. (The case however did not arise on the facts of *Baden, Delvaux & Lecuit*, as a mass of evidence was available).

On the facts, the judge found that SG did not have knowledge of the trust, or of the fraudulent design, and thus did not become a constructive trustee.

Although, on the facts, the claim failed, the judge was prepared to contemplate that certain types of constructive knowledge were sufficient to affix the defendants with liability. It has always been accepted that 'Nelsonian' knowledge (shutting one's eyes to the obvious) is enough to ground liability, but the cases have spoken with uncertain voice on the position where a constructive trustee is honest but negligent. It is too simple to say that the more recent cases ground liability in negligence as well as in dishonesty but it is true that no case before *Selangor United Rubber Estates v Cradock (No 3)* extended the liability to negligence. Counsel in *Baden, Delvaux and Lecuit* did not question the correctness of the decisions in *Selangor* and in *Karak Rubber Co Ltd v Burden (No 2)*; though by agreeing that the decisions were correct, he surely did not imply that the reasoning in them was faultless.

Current academic opinion seems against the attitude that there should be liability imposed on the honest, but negligent agent; and Peter Gibson J, as explained above, emphasised that knowledge should not be lightly imputed, if it were knowledge which would put an honest and reasonable man on inquiry. However, the point remains that knowledge, according to the learned judge, *can* be imputed. Commercial lawyers have long been suspicious of extending the scope of constructive knowledge, but if it is remembered that if it is on grounds of negligence, that protean concept, that constructive knowledge is being extended, such suspicions may more easily be dispelled. Banks, in particular, may be expected to comply with high standards, and, as the editor of *Underhill's The Law of Trusts and Trustees* (13th edn p 334) points out:

> '. . . banks are in a special position and are under a duty to make inquiries about possible breaches of the Companies Act 1948 s 54, and possible abuses of trust accounts, so that these inquiries ought reasonably to be made for the purpose of fixing banks with notice and making them personally liable to account as constructive trustees.'

This passage is not directly relevant, but it indicates the view that the position of banks may be somewhat special. Much turns on the judicial attitude towards commercial morality: in *Hedley Byrne & Co Ltd v Heller & Partners Ltd* [1963] 2 All ER 575 Lord Pearce commented, in the context of negligence, 'How wide the sphere of duty . . . is to be laid depends ultimately on the courts' assessment of the demands of society for protection from the carelessness of others' (at 615).

Baden, Delvaux and Lecuit, like *Selangor* and *Karak* before it, is a first instance judgment which provides a full statement of the law. The matters raised, however, seem to merit appellate clarification, if only to state how the various conflicting—or apparently conflicting—authorities are to be reconciled. Such consideration is eagerly awaited; and one may be sure that it will have to take full account of the extremely careful and thorough judgment of Peter Gibson J.

Charity

The law of charity is popularly regarded as being based on kindness to others, not on commercial bargain. However, from the days of Samuel Smiles, if not before, self-help has been regarded as a virtue. Is helping people to help themselves charitable? It has long been established that a charity cannot trade at a profit unless its profits are ploughed back into the charitable work: see, eg *IRC v Falkirk Temperance Café Trust* 1927 SC 261. Similarly, many institutions exist to provide facilities which are used by people who have to contribute towards the cost of those facilities: *The Abbey, Malvern Wells Ltd v Minister of Town and Country Planning* [1951] 2 All ER 154 (fee paying schools) and *Le Cras v Perpetual Trustee Co Ltd (Re Resch)* [1967] 3 All ER 915 (private hospital charging fees) are two examples.

It is against this background that *Joseph Rowntree Memorial Trust Housing Association Ltd v A-G* [1983] 1 All ER 288 falls to be considered. The plaintiff, a charity, wished to build small dwellings, more or less self-contained, which would be let, on long leases, to elderly people, in consideration of a premium. There were five proposed schemes. In four of the schemes, the elderly (defined as persons over pensionable age) were to contribute 70% of the cost of the dwelling; the other 30% would come from a housing grant. The schemes varied in detail (these details are set out in full in [1983] 1 All ER at 292–4) and were designed, in most cases, so as to avoid the risk of the tenancies being secure and subject to the Leasehold Reform Act 1967; in some cases assignment to spouse, family or members of the tenant's household was permitted; in some, warden's accommodation and services were provided; in some schemes, the tenant's means had to be modest (defined by a trustee in [1983] 1 All ER at 293f as meaning that, after participation in the scheme, 'the tenant's remaining financial resources may be expected not substantially, if at all, to exceed the amount required for the reasonable needs of himself and any dependant of his'.) In one scheme, the lease was assignable to any person over 65, and the tenant could not surrender the lease, nor the landlord release it, save in the case of forfeiture; there would be no housing association grant, the tenant thus paying the full market value. Apart from the last scheme, if the tenant surrendered his interest, died, became a patient under the Court of Protection, or could no longer manage his affairs, he (or his estate) would recover, as a capital sum, 70% of the value of his property at the date of such event. The Charity Commissioners considered these schemes not to be charitable. Peter Gibson J summarised their objections as follows: (i) the schemes provided for the aged only by way of bargain on a contractual basis rather than by way of bounty; (ii) the benefits provided could not be withdrawn at any time if the beneficiary ceased to qualify; (iii) the schemes were for the benefit of individuals, not a charitable class, and (iv) the schemes were a commercial enterprise capable of providing profit for the beneficiary.

The schemes, if valid, would fall within the phrase 'the relief of aged persons' in the now repealed preamble to the Statute of Elizabeth (the Charitable Uses Act 1601). It is trite law that the phrase 'aged, impotent and poor' is to be read disjunctively: *Re Lewis* [1954] 3 All ER 257. Second, the word 'relief' implied that there was a need attributable to their condition as aged, impotent or poor persons which needed alleviating, and which such persons could not alleviate, or only with difficulty alleviate, from their own resources. The authorities, though not with united voice, indicated that there was a need for the aged, as aged, to be relieved, but that there was no need to be concurrent poverty; moreover, as Danckwerts J pointed out in *Re Glyn's Will Trusts* [1950] 2 All ER 1150n, '[a] trust for the relief of aged persons would be charitable unless it was qualified in some way which would clearly render it not charitable': presumably this would mean that it was restricted, for instance, to the aged rich. The learned judge emphasised the need for 'relief' as distinct from the provision of 'benefit'. Although the approach may be simplistic, it seems that what the judge is suggesting is that those receiving charity may be maintained in a modest status or condition of life to which they are accustomed, or may be brought to that level; but they must not have that status or condition improved. Perhaps there is an analogy with the idea that the relief of poverty involves merely stopping someone 'going short'. The language used by the judge is, at first sight, compatible with the statement of Lindley LJ in *Re Macduff* ([1896] 2 Ch 451 at 464) that 'I doubt very much whether a trust would be declared charitable which excluded the poor.' As will be argued later, however, the result of the judge's decision may well be contrary to what Lindley LJ said.

Peter Gibson J quickly dismissed the objection that a charitable provision could be made only by bounty and not by bargain. Likewise, he dismissed the objection that the benefit could not be withdrawn if the beneficiary ceased to qualify. Authority did not require such benefits to be withdrawn (*Re Monk* [1927] All ER Rep 157); if withdrawal were possible, the aged tenants would be unsettled. In any event, the landlords, in practice, would have as much difficulty in obtaining possession from a weekly tenant as from a lessee under a long lease. The third objection was that individuals, not a class, benefitted. This objection was likewise dismissed: there was a charitable class, the aged, from which individuals were selected. This point seems self evident: many charitable trusts benefit individuals (whether by providing education, relieving poverty, or by conferring other individual advantages) and this is never held to be an objection: what is vital, however, is that there is a class by reference to which the selection of the individuals is made.

The last objection was, perhaps, the most significant. On surrender, or other similar circumstances, the tenant (or his estate) would receive 70% of the value of the property at the date of the termination of his interest. This, in times of inflation, would very likely result in a money profit (though not, perhaps, a real profit), and the provision of this profit was a purpose of the charity. The judge found that this was a profit at the expense of the charity; indeed it might be improper, as the charity had provided no capital, that it should receive a benefit.

It is at this point that the judge's reasoning is difficult to follow. He emphasised the distinction between 'relief' and 'benefit', the former, unlike the latter, being charitable. However, it is difficult to see how either 'inflation-proofing' the capital of the tenant, or providing him with an 'equity' in a specially designed house is not a 'benefit'. The argument that 'inflation-proofing' is not a benefit, but only a preservation of the real value of the asset would ring hollow to someone who did not reap such advantages. There is also the point that it is very unlikely that a 'poor' person could qualify for such a home. The costs of such accommodation are not stated, but it would seem unlikely that anyone who had not a house of his own to sell, or reasonably substantial savings, could afford the premium (even at 70% of the purchase price) that the scheme required. What of the retired grandfather who settles most of his property irrevocably on his grandchildren, retaining only a small house, and then claims that he has only modest means?

Admittedly, Peter Gibson J did find that there was a public benefit in deferring the time when the elderly need the services provided by the welfare state. The argument is, perhaps, that the poor benefit because they suffer less competition for the benefits that the welfare state provides. This is not dissimilar from some of Lord Wilberforce's reasoning in *Le Cras v Perpetual Trustee*, but in that case *some* poor people did use the private hospital. That fact, by itself, takes *Rowntree* beyond what Lord Wilberforce contemplated. Moreover, if to that is added the element of profit, the concept of 'relief' seems considerably weakened.

Richard Nobles' note in (1983) 46 MLR 782 emphasises that the decision rests on certain assumptions, essentially of a political nature. Certainly the case does presume (i) that if private resources are deployed to charitable ends, that the public resources deployed to the same end will not decrease, and (ii) that the sale of benefits to those who are not, in most definitions of the term, poor, is a legitimate charitable aim. However, such an attitude may be unreal. The welfare state does not provide all the services that its citizens appear to need, and one of the purposes of private charity is to deal with gaps where there is little or no state-provided benefit. The schemes, although, in a broad sense, providing 'benefits' in an economic sense to the aged, do 'relieve' them in one extremely vital way: they relieve them of the need to depend on others, and preserve their independence and self respect. At a time when the proportion of the elderly in the community is increasing, and is expected further to increase, the preservation of such virtues is surely of general benefit to the public at large.

Variation of trusts

Most cases of variation of trusts arise under the Variation of Trusts Act 1958; the only reported case on variation this year, however, arises under the Trustee 1925, s 57(1) because, it appears from the report, of difficulties under the Variation of Trusts Act 1958 in connection with the representative parties to the action. The issue in *Mason v Farbrother* [1983] 2 All ER 1079 was whether the court had power to vary the provision of a pension fund trust deed so as to widen the existing investment clauses beyond the provisions of the Trustee Investments Act 1961. Judge Blackett-Ord VC, sitting as a judge of the High Court, stated that he had no inherent jurisdiction to vary the trust because it was thought beneficial so to do: this, of course, followed the decision of the House of Lords in *Chapman v Chapman* [1954] 1 All ER 798. The judge, however, stated that there were disputes between the trustees, the members and the society, and there could thus be room for compromise, within the scope of the 'compromise' jurisdiction, considered in the *Chapman* case. But the judge was unhappy about substituting a completely new investment clause; there were remarks of Evershed MR in *Re Powell-Cotton's Resettlement* [1956] 1 All ER 60 at 62 which suggested that sweeping the old away and substituting the new, although perhaps within the compromise jurisdiction, was not a proper exercise of it.

However, Judge Blackett-Ord VC considered he had jurisdiction under the Trustee Act 1925, s 57. Investment clauses involved the 'management or administration' of trust property, and so were within the section; the fact that most post-1958 applications to vary investment powers had been made under the Variation of Trusts Act did not mean that the jurisdiction under the Trustee Act no longer existed.

The judge was thus able to deal with the substantive point of varying the investment powers. The judges of the Chancery Division, after 1961, had indicated that in the light of the then recently passed Trustee Investments Act, the courts would be reluctant to extend investment powers beyond what Parliament had dictated (see *Re Cooper's Settlement* [1961] 3 All ER 636, *Re Kolb's Will Trusts* [1961] 3 All ER 811). However, the judge considered that there were special circumstances: 'in a word, inflation since 1961' ([1982] 3 All ER at 1086–7); the trust was also unusual in that it was 'a pension fund with perhaps something of a public element in it'. With due respect to the learned judge, the former is an excuse, not reasons. This 'special circumstance' is one that is common to all trusts controlled by the Trustee Investments Act; that Act is 23 years old, and has been criticised by the Law Reform Committee in its 23rd Report (Cmnd 8733); surely it would be more honest to state that the jurisdiction to vary a trust (under whatever head jurisdiction is taken) will be used to vary investment clauses, just as it was used in the years immediately after 1958 to widen investment powers beyond those contained in the 1925 Trustee Act.